The Law of Health and Safety at Work

Norman Selwyn

LLM, Dip Econ (Oxon),
Barrister

 Croner

a Wolters Kluwer business

Wolters Kluwer (UK) Limited
145 London Road
Kingston upon Thames
Surrey KT2 6SR
Tel: 020 8247 1175

Published by
Wolters Kluwer (UK) Limited
145 London Road
Kingston upon Thames
Surrey KT2 6SR
Tel: 020 8247 1175

First published January 1982
First Edition 1982
Second Edition 1993
Third Edition 1994
Fourth Edition 1995
Fifth Edition 1996
Sixth Edition 1997
Seventh Edition 1998
Eighth Edition 1999
Ninth Edition 2000
Tenth Edition 2001
Eleventh Edition 2002
Twelfth Edition 2003
Thirteenth Edition 2004
Fourteenth Edition 2005
Fifteenth Edition 2006
Sixteenth Edition 2007
Seventeenth Edition 2008
Eighteenth Edition 2009

© N M Selwyn

ISBN 978-1-85524-749-9

Printed in the UK by Hobbs the Printers Ltd.

FOREWORD

nebosh

Health and safety is important in everyone's working life. Lives and families can be blighted by accidents and long-term ill health caused by poorly managed work activities. Businesses and organisations that manage health and safety well are likely to be more efficient and financially healthier since accidents and ill health can be a major cost to an organisation.

Obviously it is preferable for organisations to ensure the health and safety of their employees, and others affected by their activities, because they believe that it is fundamentally the right thing to do and hence is embedded within the core values of the organisation. However, the law is also there to provide guidance on the standards expected of organisations and the individuals who work for them. The sanctions available where organisations fall short of these expectations should and do act as a deterrent.

The law on health and safety underpins the work of safety and health practitioners who are often charged with helping their organisation to understand and comply with legal requirements. A grasp of the principles of modern safety legislation is essential. "Goal setting" legislation places the responsibility on the creators of risks to find cost-effective solutions to control them. The competent health and safety practitioner enables organisations to carry out their activities safely, efficiently and within the law.

Health and safety law is obviously a significant element in the syllabus of the NEBOSH National Diploma in Occupational Health and Safety. This qualification, accredited by the Office of the Qualifications and Examinations Regulator (Ofqual) at Level 6 in the National Qualifications Framework, is designed to provide the knowledge underpinning competent performance as a safety professional, and fulfils the academic requirements for admission to the Institution of Occupational Safety and Health.

Norman Selwyn's book is one of the most comprehensive of its kind, not only covering the general law on health and safety but also showing how law in other areas, such as employment and discrimination, can impact on the practical management of safety. It deals with legislation in a comprehensible way, clearly showing the links with non-statutory guidance, best practice in managing safety and health, and explaining the impact of case law on statutory duties.

Selwyn is equally enlightening in the field of civil liability. Clear explanations are provided on employers' and occupiers' liability, and case law is used to illustrate the principles involved.

Further, the chapter on particular health and safety issues gives an up-to-date view on the development of the law in key areas. It is gratifying that occupational health and psychosocial issues, often neglected, are given particular emphasis in this chapter.

I have recommended previous editions of Norman's book to numerous students preparing for professional examinations in health and safety over many years. I have no hesitation in similarly recommending this latest edition. It is one of the few books in this field which is immediately understandable to those new to the subject, and is very readable. Changes in legal precedents and new legislation make it essential to keep up to date. Norman Selwyn's book is therefore an essential reference for the experienced practitioner as well as the student.

Teresa Budworth CFIOSH

Chief Executive
National Examination Board in Occupational Safety and Health

June 2009

PREFACE

Although the subject of health and safety at work is of vital importance to every employer, employee and self-employed person, there is an apparent dearth of books which explain the complex legal requirements in a manner that can be readily understood and appreciated by those who are most affected. The aim of this book is to fill that gap. It should be of interest to employers, company secretaries, managers, trade unionists, safety officers, safety representatives, enforcement officers and lawyers, as well as to students who are seeking to be in employment in the future.

The book is intended to be a guide, not a bible. The aim is to promote knowledge, yet at the same time to give understanding. In other words, I have tried not only to state the law, but also to explain it. If the consequence has been a certain amount of over-simplification, I believe that this is a price well worth paying. However, the reader will appreciate that when legal problems arise in practice, it may be necessary to consult the actual statutory provisions or, where necessary, seek expert legal advice.

Health and safety is a ubiquitous subject and it is not easy to draw boundaries. There is no obvious delineation between health and safety at work and health and safety generally. Road traffic, environmental issues, consumer protection, etc all overlap with health and safety at work. Thus I have included some material on "peripheral" matters, but if the line has been drawn somewhat arbitrarily, it is perhaps better to do so than not to draw one at all.

The *raison d'être* of the law on health and safety at work is not always easy to discover, for there are differing social objectives to be achieved. The law is intended to be partly preventative, partly punitive, and partly compensatory. The rules are an amalgam of contract, tort and criminal law. Statutory provisions are interwoven with judicial decisions and, in recent years, Approved Codes of Practice have assumed a greater importance in giving practical guidance. Each industry has its own peculiar problems. Each firm has its own difficulties. Each incident has its own unique features. These variations make the task of preventing accidents difficult for those involved. But however complex these matters may be, ignorance of the legal requirements is the least excuse.

The law on health and safety at work is constantly changing, particularly with the introduction of new regulations and Codes of Practice. Judicial interpretation of the legislation is becoming more significant, even going so far as to extend the impact of health and safety regulations into the fields of sex, race and disability discrimination. It is essential for all concerned with this subject, be they employers, employees, lawyers, students, trade union officials, etc to keep up to date with all the latest developments and, where appropriate, implement those aspects of the law that are relevant to their own circumstances.

This edition includes the provisions of the Health and Safety (Offences) Act 2008, the Regulatory Enforcement and Sanctions Act 2008 and the relevant provisions of the Employment Act 2008. There is mention of the role of Health and Safety Awareness Officers, and recent amendments to a number of regulations have been noted. Some 30 additional legal decisions have been added to the text, including the important cases of *R v Chargot Ltd, R v Porter, Spencer-Franks v Kellog Brown & Root Ltd, Smith v Northamptonshire County Council*, and so on.

I have tried to state the law in accordance with the sources available to me as at 1 June 2009.

Norman Selwyn
juno@selwynfamily.co.uk

Note

In terms of the Interpretation Act 1978, unless the contrary is intended, a reference to a male includes a reference to a female, and vice versa, and a reference to the singular includes the plural. *The Law of Health and Safety at Work 2009/10* has followed this style for ease of reference.

June 2009

CONTENTS

Table of Statutes

Table of Regulations and Orders

Table of Cases

CHAPTER 1

Law and legal institutions

The background to health and safety law

1.1   Legislative intervention in pursuance of the cause of health and safety dates from the Health and Morals of Apprentices Act 1802. This Act was designed to protect young children working in cotton and woollen mills and other factories where more than 20 persons were employed. At that time it was the custom to put four children in a bed during the day and four more in the same bed at night while the daytime occupants were working. It was this type of abuse at which the Act was aimed. Other pieces of minor legislation were passed in the ensuing years, but the real breakthrough came in 1833 when the Factory Act was passed. It provided that four factory inspectors were to be appointed with powers of investigation and prosecution. From that time on the factory movement gathered momentum, although the motives of some of the protagonists were not always of high altruism. Sometimes the legislation was designed to restrict the hours of work of women and young children (indirectly benefiting adult male labour), while other enactments were concerned with establishing safe working conditions. Perhaps the worst feature was the multiplicity of legislation — in 1876, a Factory Commission reported that the law was in a complete state of chaos, with no less than 19 different enactments to be considered. It was not until the Factory and Workshop Act of 1901 that a comprehensive piece of factory legislation was enacted, when all the previous law was consolidated into one statute. One of the more interesting innovations was to give the power to the Secretary of State to make regulations for particular industries, a power which was used extensively to control a large number of different industrial processes. In 1916, this power was extended to permit Welfare Orders to be made dealing with washing facilities, first aid provisions, and so on. A further major breakthrough came in 1937 when the Factories Act was passed. It swept away the old distinctions between the different types of premises (textile factories, workshops, etc) and made detailed provisions for health, safety and welfare. Minor amendments were made in 1948 and 1959, and the various statutes were consolidated once more by the Factories Act 1961, the bulk of which has now been repealed and replaced by new health and safety regulations and Approved Codes of Practice.

1.2 The mining industry was an obvious subject for protective legislation and, in 1842, a Mines and Collieries Act was passed, which was mainly concerned with regulating hours and working conditions of women and children. Work in quarries was brought within the scope of the law by the Metalliferous Mines Regulations Act 1872, and a further major reform took place in 1911 with the passing of the Coal Mines Act. These provisions were strengthened and brought up to date in the Mines and Quarries Act 1954 which, together with regulations made, lays down a comprehensive protective code of legislation for these industries.

1.3 Health and safety legislation for the non-industrial worker came somewhat later. In 1886, the Shop Hours Regulation Act restricted the hours of work of young persons, and the Seats for Shop Assistants Act 1899 may be regarded as an important welfare statute. After many attempts had been made to give legislative cover to office workers, an Offices Act was passed in 1960, but this (and other legislation) was superseded by the Offices, Shops and Railway Premises Act 1963 (now almost totally repealed). Other statutes that regulated hours of work include the Employment of Women, Young Persons and Children Act 1920, Hours of Employment (Conventions) Act 1936 and Young Persons (Employment) Act 1938.

1.4 The original intention of those who framed the legislation was that health and safety laws would be enforced through the use of criminal sanctions but, for two reasons, this emphasis changed over the years. The first was the gradual realisation that a rigorous policy of enforcement by the factory inspectorate would probably lead to the shutdown of large sections of British industry, already fighting hard to maintain its position against competition from foreign countries, which were not necessarily inhibited by such constraints. The policy would also clutter up the courts and require a massive expansion of the machinery for bringing prosecutions. The second and possibly more significant reason for the change in emphasis was the ability of injured workers to bring civil actions in respect of injuries suffered as a result of their employers' failure to observe the statutory duties. This action for breach of statutory duty was first successful in the case of *Groves v Lord Wimborne* in 1898 and, because of the absolute nature of many of the statutory duties, became a fruitful source of financial solace. But the result was to divert the objects of the law away from prosecution and prevention towards a system of civil compensation. As Goddard LJ stated in *Hutchinson v London and North Eastern Rly Co* in 1942, "The real incentive for the observance by employers of their statutory duties is not their liability to substantial fines, but the possibility of heavy claims for damages." Even this, however, was not entirely correct, for most employers realised the value of taking out insurance policies against such claims (a requirement that was made compulsory in 1969) with the result that both the civil and criminal law ceased to be major deterrents.

1.5 At the same time as these developments were taking place, the common law of the country was also becoming active. In a leading case decided in 1837 (*Priestley v Fowler*) a claim based on an allegation of negligence by an employer towards his employee failed. But a few years later, in 1840, a young girl successfully sued when she was seriously injured in a mill accident and was awarded damages (*Cottrell v Stocks*). From then on, common law claims were bogged down with problems arising from the doctrine of "common employment" (abolished in 1948 by the Law Reform (Personal Injuries) Act), the inability to sue at common law if the injured worker had also claimed under the Workman's Compensation Act (amended by the National Insurance (Industrial Injuries) Act 1946), and the inability to claim if the employee had been contributorily negligent (amended by the Law Reform (Contributory Negligence) Act 1945). By 1970, the law on health and safety was largely concerned with issues of compensation.

1.6 In 1970, a committee on health and safety at work was appointed under the chairmanship of Lord Robens, which reported two years later. In its report, the Robens Committee reached some fundamental conclusions. First, although it was generally recognised that the UK had the finest regulatory system of legal controls anywhere in the world, this did not prevent the annual carnage that took place, evidenced by the numbers who were killed or injured. Second, much of the law was obscure and unintelligible to those whose actions it was intended to influence. There was a haphazard mass of legislation, intricate in detail, difficult to amend and frequently out of date. Third, the various enforcement authorities had overlapping jurisdictions, which caused some confusion.

1.7 But the main conclusion of the Robens Committee was that there was one single cause, above all else, for accidents and ill health at work. This was apathy. Apathy at the top, apathy at the bottom, apathy at all levels in between. True, there were a few dedicated people who worked hard at trying to influence people's attitudes, but these rarely had sufficient power or authority to override considerations of production, and in the main, health and safety had a low priority in almost all workplaces. In an attempt to overcome this attitude, the Robens Committee made a number of far-reaching proposals. The first was to devise a system whereby all employers and all employees became aware that health and safety was the concern of everyone, and not just a matter for the dedicated few. As the report stated, "Our present system encourages too much reliance on state regulation, and rather too little on personal responsibility and voluntary, self-generating effort." Next, it was suggested that there was a need for a single comprehensive framework of legislation that would cover all work activity, supported and supplemented by a series of controls to deal with specific problems, and assisted by voluntary standards and more flexible codes of practice. Finally, a more unified enforcement authority was needed, having overall responsibility for initiating legal proposals and giving assistance and advice, possessing stronger enforcement powers, and with the ability to delegate its enforcement functions when necessary.

1.8   The result was the passing of the Health and Safety at Work, etc Act 1974 (HSWA), an important piece of legislation that adopts a fundamentally different approach to the whole subject. In the first place, the Act applies to all employed persons, wherever they work (except domestic servants in private households). This brought into the protective umbrella an estimated eight million "new entrants" who were not hitherto covered by previous legislation. In addition to laying down duties for employers and employees, the Act imposes certain legal requirements on those who manufacture, import, design or supply articles and substances which are to be used at work. Some of the provisions (eg safety policies, safety representatives) are designed to bring about a greater personal involvement of all concerned. New institutions were created, new enforcement powers were enacted, and new concepts, such as the use of Approved Codes of Practice, were introduced. The "old" law, eg the Factories Act and the Offices, Shops and Railway Premises Act, etc, was intended to remain in force for the time being, although the ultimate objective was to gradually repeal and replace it with new regulations, which would be supplemented by Approved Codes of Practice and guidance literature.

1.9   It must not be assumed that HSWA is the answer to all our problems, or that it is a perfect piece of legislation. On the contrary, despite the criticism levelled by the Robens Committee against the legalistic and unintelligible nature of the then-existing law, the Act is turgid, soporific and in parts about as meaningful as medieval metaphysics. Further, it is basically a criminal statute, with appropriate penalties for breaches, and does not confer on anyone the right to make a claim for compensation. This means that most of the cases will start and finish in the magistrates' courts, with the result that there is very little opportunity for authoritative interpretations of the complex legal language. Since the Act was passed, there have been relatively few legal decisions from higher courts, and thus problems and queries remain.

1.10 On the positive side, the Act has been a catalyst for considerable management activity and a greater awareness of responsibility has brought about increased concern for the health and safety of employees. It is, perhaps, too early to judge the psychological impact of the Act, or to evaluate its success, for although it is possible to note some downward trends in the numbers of accidents, there are many other factors that need to be taken into account, and we can never know how many accidents did not happen as a result of a more safety-conscious approach. Between 1974 and 2007 the number of fatal injuries to employees fell by 73%, and the number of reported non-fatal injuries fell by 70%, although whether this welcome reduction in accident rates has been due to a greater awareness of the legal requirements, to proactive safety policies, to changes in manufacturing processes, or to a reduction in the numbers employed in those industries that were traditionally a major source of accidents and ill health, is always going to be a matter for debate. Meanwhile, if the propaganda surrounding the Act brings about a greater awareness that health and safety is everyone's concern, and not merely a matter for those who have a specialised interest in the problem, nothing but good will be the result.

1.11 Since 1974, the Act has been amended by the Consumer Protection Act 1987 (in particular strengthening s.6), the Criminal Justice Act 1991, the Offshore Safety Act 1992 and the Health and Safety (Offences) Act 2008 which has increased the penalties that may be imposed for various breaches. The progressive repeal of the Factories Act and other primary legislation has continued and, more recently, there has been a spate of new health and safety regulations (supplemented by Approved Codes of Practice and Guidance Notes) consequent on our membership of the European Union (EU). Although amendments to the Act have been considered at various times, its basic principles will remain.

1.12 In 1989, the Council of Ministers of the European Union adopted the health and safety "Framework Directive" (89/391/EEC), which deals with the general principles to be applied throughout the EU on health and safety in all work activities (except domestic service). The primary duty for ensuring health and safety at work was placed upon employers, although self-employed persons and employees were also embraced. Five additional "daughter" directives were subsequently adopted dealing with more specific proposals, ie Workplace Directive (89/654/EEC), Use of Work Equipment Directive (89/655/EEC), Personal Protective Equipment Directive (89/656/EEC), Manual Handling of Loads Directive (90/269/EEC) and Display Screen Equipment Directive (90/270/EEC). Further directives have been adopted on carcinogens, biological agents, temporary workers, asbestos workers' protection, construction sites, safety signs, pregnant workers, noise, chemical agents, vibration, and young persons, etc. A number of other directives with health and safety implications have either been adopted or are currently being discussed with a view to adoption (see Chapter 14).

1.13 The former Health and Safety Commission took the view that while generally HSWA was adequate as a means of achieving the appropriate standards, the directives were more prescriptive and detailed, and thus it was necessary to extend the law in order to meet the new standards required by the directives. It was hoped to achieve the desired results by avoiding any disruption with the basic framework laid down in HSWA, and at the same time to continue with the process of modernising the law and repealing out-of-date legislation. Thus the new regulations, together with the Approved Codes of Practice and Guidance Notes should meet the EU standards, and UK law has been adapted accordingly within the existing framework.

1.14 As a general principle, health and safety regulations may give rise to civil as well as criminal liability. Thus where certain familiar statutory provisions, which have hitherto been a prolific source of civil litigation, have been repealed, civil proceedings may in general be brought under the new regulations in due course. But attention must be paid to the individual regulations in order to determine whether civil claims may be brought. All the regulations impose criminal liabilities.

1.15   However, there is as much danger from having too much law as there is from having too little law. Equally, it is necessary to ensure that legal provisions do not overlap, are not out of date, and do not create administrative burdens that outweigh their usefulness. Following a review of the operation of the Regulatory Reform Act 2001 (now almost totally repealed) and the findings of the Better Regulation Task Force, the Legislative and Regulatory Reform Act 2006 was passed.

1.16   The Legislative and Regulatory Reform Act 2006 sets out a simplified procedure for amending legislative provisions contained in Act of Parliament or regulations passed thereunder. The Act enables a Minister of the Crown to introduce Orders before Parliament for the purpose of removing or reducing any burden which results from legislation. A burden can be a financial cost, an administrative inconvenience, an obstacle to efficiency or productivity or a sanction (criminal or otherwise) which affects the carrying on of any lawful activity. The purpose of the Order may also be to ensure that regulatory functions are carried out in a manner which is transparent, accountable, proportionate and consistent, and targeted only at cases in which action is needed. The Order may not create any new criminal offence, or impose, abolish or vary any tax. Prior to making the Order, the minister shall consult with representative interests, as appropriate.

1.17   This power enables the minister to bypass the normal parliamentary procedure for passing legislation by means of a statutory instrument. A draft Order must be laid before Parliament, together with an explanatory memorandum, and the Order will come into force as a result of it being approved by a negative or affirmative resolution Parliamentary procedure, as appropriate.

1.18   A Better Regulation Commission advises the Government on actions which need to be taken in order to reduce unnecessary burdens. This is an independent group of voluntary experts from the private, public and voluntary sectors which provides independent advice about new regulatory proposals. It will work with business organisations to make proposals for regulatory simplification. There is also a Better Regulation Executive which is part of the Department for Business, Innovation and Skills.

1.19   The powers contained in the Legislative and Regulatory Reform Act have been used to repeal a number of outdated health and safety regulations and, more recently, have been used to unify the Health and Safety Commission and Executive (see paragraph 2.2).

1.20   The present situation, therefore, is that the law on health and safety at work is an amalgam of criminal law, civil law and preventative measures. Breaches of the various statutory provisions (and regulations made thereunder) are capable of being criminal offences, in respect of which the wrongdoer may be fined or (in rare circumstances) imprisoned. Civil claims for compensation may arise in respect of injuries received as a result of a failure by the employer to observe the statutory requirements (other than HSWA and other legislation as specified), or a failure to carry out those duties imposed by the common law of the land. The preventative measures can be found in the enforcement notices which may be issued, the greater involvement of the workforce by the appointment of safety representatives and the creation of safety committees, as well as in the more detailed requirements of the new health and safety regulations, in particular with regard to the requirements for employers to carry out risk assessments, undertake health surveillance, appoint safety advisors and so on. Health and safety is also being used to give remedies to workers and employees in employment tribunals, when the employer fails to carry out his legal responsibilities.

1.21   This mixture of legal objectives is reflected in the decided cases, which explain and expand on the nature of the legal duties. For practical reasons, the majority of these cases stem from civil claims, although in recent years there has been an increasing number of decisions in the employment tribunals, which add to our understanding of the legal rules. Care must always be taken not to elevate all such decisions to absolute principles, for the statute is always paramount, and individual cases can only be decided on their own special facts. Legal interpretation is more of an art than a science.

Sources of law

Legislation

1.22   The prime source of law in the UK consists of Acts of Parliament. With the important exception noted in paragraph 1.62 relating to the Treaty of Rome, an Act of Parliament is the supreme law of the land. Parliament, it is said, can make or unmake any law whatsoever. In strict theory, this could lead to severe problems, but in reality there are clearly political and practical limits on what Parliament in fact will do.

1.23 Statute law commences with the introduction of a Bill into either House of Parliament. This will receive a formal First Reading when it is published. The House will then hold a full debate on the general principles behind the proposed legislation, and a vote may be held on a proposal to give the Bill a Second Reading. If successful, the Bill will then be sent to a committee, where it is considered in detail, and amendments may be made. Next, the Bill is presented to a report stage of the full House, when the amendments are considered, and finally, the Bill will receive its Third Reading. It will then go to the other House, where a similar procedure is adopted. When both Houses have passed the Bill, it is presented to the Queen for the Royal Assent, which, by convention, is never refused.

1.24 However, although the Bill is now an Act, its implementation may be delayed in whole or in part. Modern legislation frequently contains powers that enable the appropriate minister to bring the Act into force in various stages, often with transitional provisions. In those cases the law will not come into force until the date specified in a Commencement Order.

1.25 Legislation passed by the UK Parliament since 1988, including statutory instruments, as well as legislation passed by the Scottish Parliament, the Northern Ireland and Welsh Assemblies can be viewed at *www.opsi.gov.uk/legislation/about legislation.htm.*

Regulations

1.26 An Act may confer upon a minister the power to make new or additional law by means of regulations. Such subordinate legislative power has many advantages, for it enables technical proposals to be passed, it is speedier than the procedure adopted for an Act and it enables the law to be amended by a simpler procedure. Regulations must be laid before Parliament and are considered by the Joint Committee on Statutory Instruments, which has members from both Houses. They are not concerned with the policy or merits of the regulations, only the technical competence of the minister to make them. For example, the committee will ascertain whether the regulations are within the powers conferred by the parent Act, and whether they contain any unusual or unexpected use of that power. Some regulations will only become law after an affirmative vote by both Houses of Parliament, but the majority will become law when they are made. However, they can subsequently be vetoed by a negative vote within 40 days of laying. Regulations that are made under HSWA are of this type (see s.82(3)).

1.27   Regulations have the full force of law until they are revoked or amended in some way. It is possible for them to supersede specific provisions of the parent Act. In *Miller v William Boothman & Sons Ltd*, the plaintiff was injured while working on a circular saw, the fencing of which complied with the Woodworking Machinery Regulations 1922. It was argued on his behalf that the employers were still liable for his injury, as they were in breach of the requirements of s.14 of the Factories Act to fence every dangerous part of any machinery. The argument was rejected. The minister had exercised the power vested in him to exclude the provisions of the Act by regulation, and the latter prevailed.

1.28   As has already been indicated, one of the main objects of HSWA is to replace the existing statutory provisions over a period of time with a more streamlined system in which regulations will play a major part. These will fall generally into different categories. First, there will be those regulations that will apply to most or all employment situations (eg the Reporting of Injuries, Diseases and Dangerous Occurrences Regulations 1995). Second, there will be those regulations that are designed to control a particular hazard (eg Lifting Operations and Lifting Equipment Regulations 1998). Third, there are those that will refer to a particular hazard or risk that may be found in a number of industries or processes (eg the Control of Lead at Work Regulations 2002). Fourth, regulations may be introduced in order to further the streamlining process or because the old provisions were out of date (eg the Health and Safety (First Aid) Regulations 1981). Others may be introduced consequentially upon the discovery of a loophole in the law that may have come to light because of some litigation (the Abrasive Wheels Regulations 1970 (now themselves revoked) were made in order to nullify the decision of *Summers (John) & Sons Ltd v Frost*). As a general rule, regulations are designed to supplement and strengthen the provisions of the various Acts of Parliament, spelling out the requirements in greater detail.

1.29 Health and safety regulations made under s.15 of HSWA may be for any of the following purposes and may:
  (a) repeal or modify any existing statutory provision
  (b) exclude or modify in relation to any specific class of case any of the provisions of ss.2–9 (see Chapter 3) or any existing statutory provision
  (c) make a specific authority responsible for the enforcement of any relevant statutory provision
  (d) impose requirements by reference to the approval of the Commission or other specified body or person
  (e) provide that any reference in a regulation to a specific document shall include a reference to a revised version of that document
  (f) provide for exemptions from any requirement or prohibition
  (g) enable exemptions to be granted by a specified person or authority
  (h) specify the persons or class of persons who may be guilty of an offence
  (i) provide for specified defences either generally or in specified circumstances
  (j) exclude proceedings on indictment in relation to certain offences
  (k) restrict the punishment that may be imposed in respect of certain offences.

1.30 In addition to the above, schedule 3 of HSWA contains detailed provisions about the contents of such regulations, sufficient, it is thought, to completely replace the old law, and wide enough to enable the Secretary of State and the HSE to do almost anything in order to promote "the general purposes" of the Act.

1.31 A breach of a duty imposed by regulations is, of course, punishable as a criminal offence. Additionally, a breach may give rise to civil liability, except insofar as the regulations provide otherwise.

The making of regulations

1.32 Health and safety regulations are made by the Secretary of State as a result of proposals made to him by the Health and Safety Executive (HSE). He may also make them on his own initiative, but before doing so he must consult with the HSE and with any other appropriate bodies. If the HSE makes the proposals, it too must consult with appropriate government departments and other interested bodies (HSWA, s.50). The normal practice is for the HSE to initiate proposals in the form of a Consultative Document, which is given a wide circulation to interested bodies, such as employers' associations, trade unions, trade associations and so on. Comments received are considered, and the proposals may be modified in the light of these. Draft regulations are then publicised, amended if necessary, and the regulations, in their final form, are presented to the Secretary of State to be laid before Parliament.

1.33   The prime responsibility for health and safety matters now rests with the Department for Work and Pensions, although it would not be unusual for certain health and safety regulations to emanate from another government department (eg Defence, Transport, Health, etc).

1.34   Since 2005, domestically initiated regulations come into force on 6 April and 1 October each year, in order to increase employer awareness of, and compliance with, new legislation. However, these dates will not necessarily apply to the transposition of EU directives, which generally have their own implementation dates, nor to legislation which affects a single sector.

Orders in Council

1.35   Historically, Orders were promulgated by the Queen in her Privy Council, exercising the royal prerogative. This procedure was a convenient way of avoiding Parliamentary scrutiny, but since the Statutory Instruments Act 1946 this is no longer so, and Orders are now subject to annulment on a resolution of either House of Parliament (see HSWA, s.84(4)). Modern practice is to confer on the appropriate minister the power to make Orders, which again can only be exercised within the powers conferred. For example, s.84 of HSWA empowers the Queen by Order in Council to extend the provisions of the Act outside Great Britain (see Health and Safety at Work, etc Act 1974 (Application outside Great Britain) Order 2001), whereas s.85 enables the Secretary of State to make Commencement Orders.

1.36   As a rough guide, the distinction between a regulation and an Order in Council is that the former is a means whereby the power to make such substantive law is exercised, whereas the latter gives force to an executive act. However, Regulatory Reform Orders might be viewed as being somewhere between an Act of Parliament and a regulation.

Bye-laws

1.37   Local authorities have the power to pass bye-laws for the administration of their own area. These must be within the powers conferred by the parent Act of Parliament, and must also be reasonable. It is possible to challenge the validity of a bye-law in the courts. Model bye-laws, drawn up by the Secretary of State for Communities and Local Government are frequently adopted by local authorities.

Judicial precedent

1.38   The bulk of British law is contained in the decisions made by the judges in cases that come before them in the courts. When a case is decided, the judge will state his or her reasons for that decision. Frequently, the case will be reported in one of the many series of law reports (official or commercial) that exist. From the report, it may be possible to cull the narrow reason for the decision, ie the *ratio decidendi*. Anything else uttered in the course of the decision is regarded as *obiter dicta*, ie things said by the way. Distilling the *ratio* of a case, and distinguishing it from *obiter dicta*, is a legal art.

1.39   Strictly speaking, it is only the decisions of the higher courts that become binding precedents. Other decisions are said to be "persuasive". Thus a decision of the House of Lords will bind all lower courts, and can only be changed by a further decision of the House of Lords itself (a rare occurrence) or by an Act of Parliament. A decision of the Court of Appeal will also bind lower courts but not, of course, the House of Lords. All other lower courts create only persuasive precedents.

1.40   However, lawyers will attempt to avoid inconvenient precedents (when necessary) by using their legal ingenuity. Thus it may be possible to distinguish a previous decision on the ground that the facts are not identical, or that there are material differences sufficient to warrant not following an earlier decision. Since the *ratio* of a case is uncertain, inconvenient remarks may be brushed aside as being *obiter dicta*, on the ground that they were not essential for the actual decision. A court may be asked to refuse to follow a precedent because it was decided *per incuriam*, ie without a full and proper argument on the point in issue. Frequently, there will be an abundance of precedents, and each side will quote those that support its argument. Occasionally, the point may never have arisen for decision before, and the court must reach its conclusions on first principles, thus creating a precedent. It is because of these points that the vagaries, as well as the richness, of British law emerge, but it will also be seen why litigation is so uncertain.

Approved Codes of Practice

1.41 For the purpose of providing practical guidance, in recent years Parliament has authorised a number of organisations to issue Codes of Practice, which, though not having the force of law, may be taken into consideration by the courts and tribunals in appropriate circumstances. So far as this book is concerned, s.16 of HSWA conferred on the HSE the power to approve and issue Codes of Practice for the purpose of providing practical guidance with respect to any of the general duties laid down in ss.2–7 of the Act, or any health and safety regulations or existing statutory provision. The HSE may also approve other codes drawn up by other persons or organisations (eg British Standards). The HSE cannot approve a code without first obtaining the consent of the Secretary of State, and prior to obtaining this, it must consult with government departments and other appropriate bodies. Codes may be revised from time to time and the HSE may, if necessary, withdraw its approval from a particular code.

1.42 A failure on the part of any person to observe the provisions contained in an Approved Code of Practice does not, of itself, render that person liable to any criminal or civil proceedings. But, in any criminal proceedings, if a person is alleged to have committed an offence concerning a matter in respect of which an Approved Code of Practice is in force, the provisions of that code are admissible in evidence, and a failure to observe it constitutes proof of the breach of duty or contravention of the regulation or statutory provision in question, unless the accused satisfies the court that he complied with the requirement of the law in some other equally efficacious manner. Codes, therefore, are guides to good safety practice. If a person follows the requirements of the codes it is unlikely that he will be successfully prosecuted for an offence. If he fails to follow the code, he may be guilty of an offence unless he can show that he observed the specific legal requirements in some other way (HSWA, s.17).

1.43 The purpose of making increased use of Codes of Practice is to avoid built-in obsolescence in legal requirements, and to give practical guidance for the benefit of those upon whom duties are placed by virtue of a statute or regulation. HSWA contains no guidance on the status of Codes of Practice in civil proceedings, but it is likely that a failure to observe their provisions could constitute *prima facie* evidence of negligence, which would have to be rebutted by evidence to the contrary.

Guidance Notes

1.44   The Health and Safety Executive (HSE) frequently issues Guidance Notes, sometimes alongside codes and sometimes independently. Guidance Notes contain practical advice and sound suggestions, and are frequently more informative than the codes (see for example, the Guidance Notes relating to the Safety Representative and Safety Committee Regulations 1977, which are far more helpful than the actual code). Although the Guidance Notes have no legal standing, it is possible to use them as evidence of the state of knowledge at the time of issue. For example, in *Glyn Owen v Sutcliffe*, an Environmental Health Officer (EHO) issued an improvement notice requiring a self-employed shoe repairer to install ventilation in his shop, following complaints about the strong smell of solvent fumes. At an appeal before an employment tribunal, the EHO referred to an HSE Guidance Note, and also to one issued by the British Adhesive Manufacturers Association, both of which warned of the dangers of inhaling solvent vapour, and suggested suitable ventilation and vapour extraction. The employment tribunal affirmed the improvement notice, for the shoe repairer was in breach of his duty under the Act to himself as well as to others (s.3(2)). In *Burgess v Thorn Consumer Electronics (Newhaven) Ltd*, it was held that if employers do not warn employees of the dangers referred to in the Guidance Notes, they may be liable to employees for negligence, as the Guidance Notes indirectly give rise to a duty of care.

The European Union

1.45   As of 1 January 1973, the UK became a member of the European Union (EU) and, by the European Communities Act 1972 (s.2), all obligations arising out of the various treaties that set up the EU are to be given legal effect in this country without further enactment. European law is of particular importance to the study of domestic law on health and safety at work. First, since the object of the EU is economic harmonisation, it would distort market forces if one country could economise on health and safety matters to the disadvantage of others.

Second, a number of changes have been brought about in our domestic law in order to conform to European standards. Third, the EU has introduced the "social dimension" whereby positive steps are taken to increase protections offered to workers from the risks of accidents and ill health at work, and generally raise standards of employment protection throughout the EU. Thus the impact of European law on domestic law is gathering momentum and cannot be ignored. In order to understand European law, we must examine the treaties, the institutions and the nature of European law.

The Treaty of Rome

1.46   This Treaty was signed in 1957 by the six founding states (France, West Germany, Italy, Belgium, The Netherlands and Luxembourg). The UK, Ireland and Denmark acceded to the Treaty in 1973, Greece in 1981, Spain and Portugal became full members in 1992 and Austria, Finland and Sweden joined in 1995. In 2004, a further ten countries joined the EU, with consequential changes in representation in the European Parliament and the European Commission. The most recent countries to join are Cyprus, the Czech Republic, Estonia, Hungary, Latvia, Lithuania, Malta, Poland, the Slovak Republic, Slovenia, Romania and Bulgaria. Croatia and Macedonia are candidate countries, while the application from Turkey to join is being delayed.

1.47   The original Treaty required unanimity between all the Member States before laws could be passed. So far as is relevant, Article 137 of the Treaty stated that one of the objects of the Community was to harmonise laws relating to "employment, labour law and working conditions, basic and advanced training, social security, protection against occupational accidents and diseases, occupational hygiene, law of trade unions, and collective bargaining between workers and employers".

1.48   In 1986, the Single European Act was signed in The Hague and Luxembourg, making certain amendments to the Treaty of Rome, and further amendments were made by the Treaty of Nice in 2001. A system of "qualified majority voting" has been introduced before approval can be given to certain proposals. Each Member State has been allocated a certain number of votes. Germany, Italy, France and the UK each have 29 votes, with the other Member States having progressively fewer. A qualified majority decision requires the support of 255 votes out of a total of 345, must be backed by a majority of Member States, and the countries supporting the proposal must represent at least 62% of the total EU population. The significance is that qualified majority voting can be used to give approval to proposals relating to health and safety matters in the working environment made under Article 138 of the Treaty (see Chapter 14).

1.49 The numbering of the Articles was altered by the Treaty of Amsterdam in 1999, so that Article 48 (free movement of workers) is now Article 39, Article 118 (promotion of employment and working conditions) is now Article 137, Article 119 (equal pay for equal work) is now Article 141, and so on.

The Maastricht Treaty

1.50 In 1992, the Treaty on European Union (the Maastricht Treaty) was signed, expanding the scope of the Community's existing responsibilities, and introducing new policy areas. The ultimate aim is to create European citizenship, a single currency as part of economic and monetary union, a common foreign policy and a common defence policy. The concept of "subsidiarity" was also introduced so that matters which could more usefully be dealt with at local or national level would not be the subject of Community action unless there was no other way the objectives could be achieved. The UK Government had opted out (by Protocol) of certain provisions of the treaty, including the final stage of monetary union.

The Treaty of Lisbon

1.51 The Lisbon Treaty was signed in December 2007 and amends existing EU treaties. It was due to come into force in January 2009, in time for the European elections later in the year, but its implementation has been delayed because every state must ratify the Treaty, and Eire, having voted in a referendum against it, is now seeking to hold another referendum with the hope of obtaining a favourable result. Among other things, the treaty will make the Charter on Fundamental Human Rights legally binding, give the European Parliament more powers by extending the co-decision procedures, and provide for a permanent president, European foreign minister and a reduced number of commissioners.

EU institutions

Council of Ministers

1.52 This is the supreme policy-making body of the EU. Each meeting of the Council is attended by a minister from each Member State. Usually, this will be the respective foreign secretaries, but sometimes, when specific detailed proposals are being discussed, the respective "portfolio" ministers will attend. One member of the Council will hold the presidency for six months and then the position rotates. The Council is assisted by a Secretariat (comprising a staff of some 2500) and preparatory work for the meetings is undertaken by frequent meetings of senior civil servants from the respective countries, known as the Committee of Permanent Representatives.

The European Commission

1.53 This is sometimes described as being the "bureaucracy" of the EU, but perhaps a more accurate description would be the "engine room". Each of the 27 Member States is entitled to nominate one commissioner. However, although appointed by their respective countries, commissioners are totally independent of them. Each commissioner has certain departmental responsibilities and is assisted by a cabinet and directorate general. Decisions are taken on a collegiate basis.

1.54 The European Commission has the responsibility of initiating and drafting proposals for approval by the Council. It acts as a mediator between states, and as a "watch dog" to ensure that EU rules are being observed. Indeed, if the Commission considers that a Member State is failing to comply with an EU law, it can take enforcement action by referring the alleged breach to the European Court of Justice (ECJ) for a ruling (see paragraph 1.57).

1.55 The European Commission has recently adopted a five-year strategy (2007–2012) for health and safety at work, with the aim of cutting work-related illnesses and accidents by a quarter across the EU.

European Parliament

1.56 This body sits in Strasbourg and Brussels and currently consists of 785 Members of the European Parliament (MEPs) elected directly from each Member State. It can express an opinion to the Council of Ministers on proposals that emanate from the Commission, can submit questions to both institutions, and can, as a final sanction, dismiss the Commission on a vote of censure passed by a two-thirds majority. The Single European Act introduced a co-operation procedure, whereby the views of the Parliament must be established prior to the Council of Ministers reaching a common position on any particular proposal (see Chapter 14).

European Court of Justice

1.57   This court sits in Luxembourg, and currently comprises 27 judges and eight advocate generals. Appointments are made for six years. The court gives rulings on the interpretation of European law, either on a reference from the Commission, at the request of the courts of a Member State or on a claim brought by an individual person or corporation in a Member State. Once it has given its ruling, the matter is then referred back to the courts of the Member State for compliance.

European Agency for Safety and Health at Work

1.58   The EU-wide European Agency for Health and Safety at Work has its headquarters in Bilbao, Spain. Its objectives are to promote improvements in health and safety at work by raising awareness and improving the availability of health and safety information. It provides technical, scientific and economic information to Member States, EU institutions and others involved with health and safety at work, and has set up a network to provide and disseminate relevant information within the EU. An administrative board, consisting of representatives of each Member State, three members of the Commission, six representatives from employers' organisations and six representatives from trade union organisations, meet twice each year, and the agency is headed by a director with appropriate staff.

1.59   The agency will also organise training courses for safety experts, ensure the compatibility of national data on health and safety and identify data in need of harmonisation. An annual report is sent to all Member States, the Council of Ministers, the European Commission, and the European Parliament.

1.60   A great part of its work involves the dissemination of information, particularly via its website *http://osha.europa.eu/en*. In this way, expertise in all EU countries can be made available to anyone needing advice and information. The agency seeks to assist people to find practical solutions to health and safety problems which arise in the workplace, investigate methods of communicating health and safety solutions to smaller organisations and, in particular, address the information needs of fragmented workforces.

1.61 There are a number of other European institutions concerned with health and safety at work, including the Advisory Committee on Safety, Hygiene and Health Protection, which consists of representatives of employers' organisations, trade unions and Member States. This committee is consulted by the European Commission on draft directives at an early stage, prior to consultation with the European Parliament (see paragraph 14.9).

European law

The Treaty of Rome

1.62 The Treaty of Rome is the supreme law of all Member States. If an Article of the Treaty is clear, precise, requires no further implementation and does not give discretion to Member States, then it is directly applicable, and does not require the Member States to pass domestic legislation to give it effect. The main significance of this rule relates to the way Article 141 of the Treaty, which requires that there should be equal pay for equal work, has been invoked by courts when national law has failed to ensure compliance, (eg *Secretary of State for Scotland v Wright*). Also significant is Article 39, which requires the free movement of workers within the EU without discrimination (*Van Duyn v Home Office (No. 2)*).

Regulations

1.63 Once a regulation has been passed by the Council of Ministers, it becomes part of the laws of Member States, and overrides any contrary domestic provision. No implementing legislation is needed. A number of regulations have been passed dealing with the transportation of goods and vehicle movements generally, etc. For example, EU Regulation 3820/85 controls the hours of work of drivers of goods and passenger vehicles throughout the Union (see *Prime v Hosking*). In 1993, the Council of Ministers adopted the Existing Substances Regulations (EEC/793/93) establishing a framework for the notification and assessment of existing chemical substances. This regulation was repealed and replaced by the Registration, Evaluation, Authorisation and Restriction of Chemical Substances Regulations EC/1907/2006 (REACH, see paragraph 7.94).

Directives

1.64   A directive passed by the Council of Ministers is binding on Member States as to the results to be achieved, but generally leaves a choice as to form and method. There are a number of problems relating to the precise legal effect of a directive, but it is generally accepted that in the field of health and safety they are not directly applicable in Member States, and do not, by themselves, give rise to any enforceable EU right. Health and safety generally is a topic for considerable activity by the EU and a number of directives have been passed that are either in force or due to come into force within the near future (see Chapter 14). Indeed, the HSE must keep a very close eye on European directives:

    (a) to ensure that our existing laws comply

    (b) to ensure that future changes do not conflict

    (c) to consider ways in which European standards can be implemented.

Decisions

1.65   A decision may be given by the European Commission on any particular case referred to it, either by a Member State, an individual or a corporate body. The decision is only applicable to that case and has no value as a binding precedent.

Recommendations

1.66   The Council of Ministers may make recommendations, which have no binding effect. However, they may be considered by national courts when dealing with a problem arising out of the interpretation of domestic law. In *Grimaldi v Fonds des Maladies Professionelles*, the ECJ held that national courts should take recommendations into account when determining disputes before them, particularly when they purport to clarify the interpretation of laws passed to implement them, or when they are designed to supplement binding EU measures.

European Charter for Fundamental Social Rights

1.67   Following the amendment to the Treaty by the Single European Act, the Commission produced a Charter for Fundamental Social Rights. Some of these proposals were regarded as being controversial and it was not entirely clear whether they could be passed by the qualified majority voting system or require a unanimous vote. For example, the Working Time Directive (93/104/EEC) (see paragraph 14.25) was challenged by the UK Government, which sought to have it annulled in whole or in part, on the ground that there was no direct and objective link between it and health and safety, and therefore it should have been considered under Article 94, which requires unanimous approval. However, the ECJ upheld the validity of the directive (apart from the "Sunday rest day" provisions), holding that a broad interpretation should be given to the powers contained in Article 139 (see *United Kingdom v Council of the European Union*). Other proposals are generally accepted. Currently, directives are being introduced concerning a number of matters raised by the charter. Less controversial are the health and safety directives, which are discussed in Chapter 14. However, it is clear that the European Union is now the major driving force behind health and safety legislation generally, as well as the impetus behind environmental protection and protection from major hazards.

The judicial system in England and Wales

Criminal courts

Magistrates' courts

1.68   These courts are presided over by Justices of the Peace, who are generally non-lawyers appointed by the Lord Chancellor on the recommendation of a local advisory committee. The aim is to select magistrates from a wide cross-section of the local community, so that the bench is a balanced one. Magistrates are advised on points of law by a (usually) legally qualified clerk, but it is the responsibility of the bench to determine the facts and to make a decision. In certain large cities, full-time district judges (formerly known as stipendiary magistrates) may be found. These are qualified lawyers and are paid a stipend. A district judge will usually sit alone, whereas lay magistrates will normally sit in benches of three.

1.69   A magistrates' court has some civil jurisdiction (mainly concerned with matrimonial disputes) but the bulk of the work is criminal and, indeed, over 94% of all criminal cases start and finish in the magistrates' courts. True, the overwhelming majority of these are motoring offences, but a fair amount of petty crime is also dealt with. The powers of punishment are normally limited to imposing a maximum fine of £20,000 (see Health and Safety (Offences) Act 2008, paragraph 3.185), or to send someone to prison for up to 12 months, although the relevant statute will usually contain the maximum penalties. Sometimes, in respect of continuing offences, a fine may be imposed for each day in which the offence is continued.

1.70   Procedurally, there are three types of offences. First, there is a summary offence, which can only be dealt with before a court of summary jurisdiction, ie the magistrates' court. Second, there is an indictable offence, which results in a formal document, known as an indictment, being drawn up. An accused will be brought before the magistrates for them to determine whether or not there is sufficient evidence (or *a prima facie* case) to commit the accused to the crown court for trial (hence these are known as committal proceedings) where the case will be heard before a judge and jury. Third, there are those cases that are triable either way (ie summarily or on indictment) depending on the option exercised by the accused and the gravity of the case, which may cause the magistrates to decide to send the matter for trial or to hear it themselves.

1.71   So far as health and safety legislation is concerned, some offences under the Health and Safety at Work, etc Act 1974 (HSWA) are summary, others are triable either before the magistrates or at the crown court, depending on the seriousness of the offence.

1.72   The overlap between certain statutory provisions may cause some problems. For example, an obligation imposed by a health and safety regulation may be an absolute one (ie the thing must or must not be done, as the case may be, see paragraph 1.127), whereas under HSWA, an offence may be committed only if the accused failed to take steps which were reasonably practicable. In the former case, a failure to do the thing required is an offence, and the fact that it was difficult, or even impossible, to carry out the obligation is no defence, whereas in the latter case, the accused may be able to show that it was not reasonably practicable to do more than he in fact did.

1.73   If a person wishes to appeal from the decision of the magistrates' court on a point of law, this is done by way of a "case stated" to the Queen's Bench Divisional Court. Either the prosecution or the defence may so appeal. Appeals against conviction and/or sentence may be made by the accused to the crown court, and will take the form of a rehearing before a judge (without a jury).

Crown court

1.74   This court will hear indictable offences and those cases (usually of a more serious nature) that the prosecution or defence have elected to have tried before the crown court. Such cases are heard before a judge and jury. It is the function of the judge to ensure that the trial is conducted fairly, and to sum up for the jury on points of law. The jury returns a verdict depending on the facts. Under HSWA, offences are punishable by an unlimited fine, and almost all offences (see paragraph 3.185) may be additionally punished by a term of imprisonment of up to two years. In recent years, there are signs that the courts are prepared to impose stiff penalties for breaches of health and safety law. There are several instances where custodial or suspended prison sentences have been imposed, for example for failure to comply with a prohibition notice. In one case, a sentence of 12 months' imprisonment (as well as a fine) was imposed on a company director who failed to ensure that protective clothing was supplied to a worker who came into contact with a deadly chemical, and who, in consequence, was killed. Substantial fines have also been imposed, the highest recorded being of £15 million (see paragraph 3.188).

1.75   In *R v FJ Chalcroft Construction Ltd* the Court of Appeal ruled that a crown court judge was well within his rights to impose a fine which wiped out the company's annual profits; see also *R v Balfour Beattie*. Following the passing of the Corporate Manslaughter and Corporate Homicide Act 2007 (see paragraph 1.108) the Sentencing Advisory Panel is due to report in 2009, and it has been suggested that a starting point of 2.5% of annual turnover is an appropriate punishment following a conviction when a fatality is involved, and up to 5% for a conviction involving manslaughter.

1.76   An appeal against conviction and/or sentence will go to the Court of Appeal.

Divisional Court

1.77   The Queen's Bench Divisional Court is presided over by (usually) the Lord Chief Justice, who will normally sit with two other judges. This court will hear appeals by way of "case stated" from the decisions of the magistrates' courts. The Divisional Court also hears appeals from decisions of employment tribunals relating to prohibition and improvement notices. The reason appeals against enforcement notices go to this court (instead, as one might expect, to the Employment Appeal Tribunal) is because a failure to comply with one of these enforcement notices is a criminal offence and the Divisional Court is basically a criminal appeal court, hearing appeals from inferior courts and tribunals.

Civil courts

County court

1.78   This is a civil court, which formerly had limited jurisdiction. However, as a result of recent changes, the county court now has concurrent jurisdiction with the High Court in all matters other than specified exceptions. In particular, personal injury claims that are likely to involve less than £50,000 must be started in the county court. Cases will be heard by a county court judge or a circuit judge. "Small claims" of less than £5000 may be heard by a district judge in a special informal procedure.

High Court of Judicature

1.79   For all practical purposes, this is the major civil court, and is presided over by a High Court Judge, sitting in the Queen's Bench Division (there are other specialised courts at this level that deal with commercial matters, admiralty claims, divorce, probate, etc). Juries have long been abolished in all but the most exceptional civil cases and thus the judge will be the sole arbiter of law and fact. This court is based in the Strand in London, but will also hear cases in various parts of the country. So far as this book is concerned, civil claims for industrial accidents, etc are usually heard in this court.

Other courts, etc

Court of Appeal

1.80　This court acts as the appeal court from the decisions of the Queen's Bench in civil matters, the Queen's Bench Divisional Court in criminal matters, from the crown court and county court and the Employment Appeal Tribunal (EAT). It is presided over by the Master of the Rolls who sits with two other Lord Justices of Appeal. Appeals may only be made on a point of law, and thus cases will consist entirely of legal argument.

Supreme Court

1.81　The Constitutional Reform Act 2005 will abolish the appellate functions of the House of Lords when acting in its legal capacity, and it will be replaced by a new Supreme Court, which will consist of 12 senior judges appointed by Her Majesty. It is expected to start functioning in October 2009. The first members of the Supreme Court will be those Lords of Appeal in Ordinary who previously sat in the House of Lords. The Lord Chancellor will lose his judicial functions altogether, but he will be required to respect the rule of law, uphold the independence of the judiciary, and ensure that there is an efficient and effective support system.

1.82　Legal rulings given by the former House of Lords will, of course, still be effective, and will still be referred to in this book. Its decisions, and those of the new Supreme Court will be binding on all lower courts until a different ruling is given, or until the law is changed by an Act of Parliament. But precedence must always be given to European law as interpreted by the European Court, the former House of Lords, or the new Supreme Court.

1.83　For example, in *Equal Opportunities Commission v Secretary of State for Employment*, the House of Lords held that provisions in the Employment Protection (Consolidation) Act 1978 that restricted the rights of part-time workers to obtain redundancy payments and unfair dismissal rights were incompatible with Article 141 of the Treaty of Rome and the Equal Treatment Directive (75/117/EEC), a ruling that forced Parliament to amend the relevant provisions of the Employment Protection (Consolidation) Act 1978.

1.84   The Constitutional Reform Act 2005 has succeeded in separating the powers and functions of politicians and judges, and has thus created a judicial system which is totally independent in fact as well as in theory.

Employment tribunals

1.85   Formerly known as industrial tribunals (renamed employment tribunals by the Employment Rights (Dispute Resolution) Act 1998), these were created in 1964, and now have a wide jurisdiction relating to problems arising out of modern employment legislation. For the purpose of this book, employment tribunals have three important functions, namely to hear appeals against the decision of an inspector to impose a prohibition or improvement notice, to hear claims for unfair dismissal, sex, race, age and disability discrimination, and to hear other claims arising out of the Employment Rights Act 1996 (ie refusal to give time off work to safety representatives, a failure to pay for such time off work, protection in health and safety cases, and a refusal to pay medical or maternity suspension pay). An employment tribunal consists of a legally qualified chairman, with two "wingmen". Decisions of employment tribunals, though not regarded as precedents, are valued for their reasoning and guidance. Any person may represent a party before an employment tribunal, costs are not normally awarded to the winner, and proceedings are generally more informal than in other courts. An appeal against a decision of an employment tribunal on a point of law relating to cases concerning improvement and prohibition notices will go to the Queen's Bench Divisional Court, but appeals on all other matters will go to the Employment Appeal Tribunal.

Employment Appeal Tribunal

1.86   This is a specialised court whose main function is to hear appeals on points of law from the decisions of employment tribunals. It will consist of a High Court judge and two wingmen chosen from each side of industry. Again, procedure is relatively more informal than in other courts, legal representation is not insisted upon, costs are not normally awarded to the winner, and the procedure is designed to hear cases with a maximum amount of simplicity and a minimum amount of delay. A further appeal may be made to the Court of Appeal.

The judicial system in Scotland

1.87   For historical reasons, Scotland has its own distinctive legal system, with its own procedure and, to some extent, legal rules. Acts of Parliament that apply to Scotland must be specifically stated to be so, and frequently the Scottish Parliament will enact legislation which is parallel to English law.

1.88   The Scotland Act 1998 created the Scottish Parliament with devolved responsibility for a wide range of topics, including health, education, local government, economic development, transport, environmental matters, rural affairs and law and order. Matters concerning foreign policy, defence, pensions, benefits, taxation, health and safety and economic and monetary affairs remain with the UK Parliament (see paragraph 1.153).

District Court

1.89   Minor criminal offences are heard summarily by the District Court, which is presided over by Justices of the Peace or a stipendiary magistrate.

Sheriff Court

1.90   More serious criminal offences are heard in the sheriff's court. Under the summary procedure, the sheriff can impose a fine of up to £5000 and/or a prison sentence of up to three months (for offences under the Health and Safety at Work, etc Act 1974, the maximum punishment can be £20,000 and/or 12 months' imprisonment). Under the solemn procedure (where the sheriff sits with a jury of 15) trial is by way of indictment, and an unlimited fine and/or up to two years' imprisonment may be imposed. Certain civil cases can also be heard.

High Court of Justiciary

1.91   This court only hears trials on indictment and has unlimited powers of punishment.

Court of Criminal Appeal

1.92   Appeals from the district court, sheriff's court and the High Court of Justiciary are heard by the Court of Criminal Appeal, which consists of three judges.

Court of Session

1.93 This is the major civil court in Scotland. The Outer House has originating jurisdiction and the Inner House acts as a court of appeal. A further appeal lies to the Supreme Court (see paragraph 1.81).

1.94 So far as the subject of health and safety at work is concerned, there are no differences in the legal rules applied in England and Wales and Scotland. Insofar as cases from Scotland are cited in this book, certain terminology has been transposed into the English equivalent for the sake of consistency and simplicity. In England and Wales, prosecutions may be instituted in the magistrates' court by a Health and Safety Executive (HSE) or local authority inspector, whereas in Scotland the inspector will send a report to the procurator fiscal, who will decide whether or not to prosecute.

Wales

1.95 The Government of Wales Act 1998 created the National Assembly for Wales. It is a devolved assembly (ie not a full legislature) and has limited powers, and cannot pass primary legislation. It has taken over the functions of the Welsh Office (see paragraph 1.155).

Woolf reforms of civil procedure

1.96 Following a report of a committee set up by Lord Woolf, new civil procedure rules have been introduced. The aim is to replace the old system, which was slow, cumbersome and costly, with a new simplified system intended to be fairer, speedier and cheaper. Judges are able to take a more active role by setting strict timetables, documents have to be disclosed at an early stage, new terminology has been adopted (see *Appendix D*), Latin tags have been abolished, and early settlements are encouraged. A failure to comply with the new rules may result in costs being awarded against a party to the proceedings. The overriding objective is to ensure that personal injury litigation is dealt with justly and speedily. In particular, alternative dispute resolution, and mediation or arbitration, are encouraged.

1.97 Pre-action protocols have been issued, with the aim of bringing about more contact between the parties, better and earlier exchange of information within specific time limits, better investigation by both parties so as to enable them to settle claims fairly and early without resort to litigation, and ultimately to enable proceedings to run efficiently if litigation becomes necessary. The aim is to ensure that each side to the dispute is aware of the other side's case as early as possible, so that the precise issues can be identified. A failure to comply with the protocols could lead to essential evidence being excluded, or an award of costs being made against the party in default. The Personal Injury Pre-action Protocol is the main protocol for any civil claims involving health and safety issues.

1.98 A claimant must send the first letter of claim containing all the essential information, and the defendant (or the insurers) must respond within 21 days, and either admit or deny liability within three months. If there is a denial, it must be accompanied by all the relevant documentation. If expert evidence is required (eg a medical or other report), the parties will be encouraged to agree on a single expert, who will prepare a non-partisan independent report. A defendant corporation must appoint an appropriate person to make a "reasonable search" for documents that will be relevant to the case (see paragraph 12.122) and he must certify that he has understood the duty of disclosure and discharged it to the best of his knowledge. Documents must be disclosed timeously.

1.99 Claims will generally fall into three categories, ie:
  (a) small claims, with a financial value of up to £5000 (or personal injury claims up to £1000)
  (b) fast-track claims, which have a value of between £5001 and £15,000; the court will set a strict timetable for the conduct of such cases, and generally they should not last for more than one day in court
  (c) multi-track claims, where the value of the claim exceeds £15,000. Here, the court will take an active role, and arrange case management conferences so that the progress of the claim can be discussed, and strict timetables laid down.

1.100 Pre-action protocols have already been created for personal injury cases of less than £15,000 in value, and a number of other protocols. The Personal Injury Pre-action Protocol and the Pre-action Protocol for Disease and Illness Claims are the main protocols for any civil claim involving health and safety issues. These set out the timetable within which the various procedural steps should be taken, the lists of documents that should be considered for submission, agreement on an expert's report and so on. The statement of case (ie the claim form and defence) must be in plain English and, in particular, the defendant must state which facts are accepted, which are denied, state the defendant's version of the events, and identify those facts of which the defendant has no knowledge and requires the claimant to prove.

1.101　The new system requires full documentation of incidents by health and safety managers and, as will be seen (paragraph 12.122), should also act as an impetus towards ensuring that assessments, testing, maintenance work, training, etc are all carried out, and results recorded, so that proper disclosure statements can be made.

The divisions of substantive law

1.102　All the laws of Great Britain may be found in the thousands of volumes of statutes and judicial decisions that line the shelves of law libraries. For convenience, we tend to subdivide subjects under different headings, each with their own special rules and application. Thus, if a person dies, interested parties will want to know something about the law of wills, or probate or succession, as the case may be. If someone buys a house, he will get involved with land law or conveyancing and so on. In the field of occupational health, safety and welfare, we are mainly concerned with employment law, which is an amalgam of the law relating to contract, tort and crime. Each of these requires a brief examination.

Contract law

1.103　Most people enter into contracts almost every day of their lives. When they buy a newspaper, go on a train journey, eat a meal in a restaurant, etc they are entering into a contract. The law on this subject is made up largely of judicial decisions, supplemented by certain statutory provisions and can be found in any recognised textbook on the subject. Occupational health and safety is fundamentally based on the existence of a contract of employment, and certain aspects of this will be dealt with in Chapter 13. There is some force in the view that the duties which employers owe to employees to ensure their safety and health at work are based on contract as well as tort (*Matthews v Kuwait Bechtel Corporation*, see paragraph 12.3).

Law of tort

1.104   A tort is a civil wrong, ie a wrongful act by one person that gives a right to the injured party to sue for a legal remedy, which is usually, but not exclusively, an action for damages. Torts are subclassified under a number of well-known headings; thus defamation, trespass, nuisance, negligence, etc are all torts, each with its own special rules and legal requirements. We will be concerned to a large extent with the tort of negligence, which is the breach of a legal duty to take care not to cause damage or injury to another. Thus an employer owes a duty to take care in order to ensure the health and safety of the employees (see Chapter 12), as well as to others who may be adversely affected by the work activities. We shall also consider the tort of breach of duty imposed by a statute, which may arise if an employer fails to observe a statutory rule, with the consequence that someone is injured.

Crime

1.105   A crime is an act which is punishable by the state in the criminal courts. Parliament has taken the view that employers and others who fail to comply with certain minimum health and safety standards shall be punished, in order to deter others from breaking the law. It cannot be pretended that the actual amount of the fines imposed acts as a great deterrent, for these seldom reflect the hazard created, nor the ability of the employer to pay. Nonetheless, the adverse publicity and the tarnishing of reputation is regarded as being undesirable. Modern management will take the view that health and safety is an objective to be pursued for its own sake, not through fear of punishment.

1.106   The main purpose of the criminal law is punishment for wilful misconduct or indifference to the consequences. A subsidiary purpose is prevention and deterrence. The criminal law should always be a weapon of last resort, rather than an instant reaction when offences are discovered. Certainly, this is the philosophy behind the Health and Safety Executive (HSE) inspectorate, for the number of prosecutions undertaken will represent only a small fraction of the number of breaches which may be discovered.

Criminal offences

1.107   As has been noted, a breach of health and safety legislation is generally a criminal offence. However, this does not imply that the only criminal offences are those that are in breach of the relevant statutory provisions, for the general criminal law is also capable of being invoked.

Corporate manslaughter

1.108   The Corporate Manslaughter and Corporate Homicide Act 2007 creates a new offence of corporate manslaughter in England, Wales and Northern Ireland, and corporate homicide in Scotland, which replaces the common law offence of manslaughter as it applied to organisations. The offence is committed when an organisation manages or organises its activities in such a way as to cause a person's death in a manner which amounts to gross breach of duty of care. The breach will be gross if it falls far below what can reasonably be expected of the organisation in the circumstances. The way in which the senior managers (who play a significant role in the making of decisions about the whole or a substantial part of the organisation's activities) manage or organise its activities must be a substantial element in the breach.

1.109   A relevant duty of care is owed:
  (a) by an employer to his employees or other persons working for the organisation
  (b) by an occupier of premises
  (c) in connection with the supply of goods or services, construction or maintenance activities, using or keeping of plant, etc and
  (d) from a future date, to persons in custody (eg at a custodial institution).

1.110   A jury must consider such factors as:
  (a) whether the organisation failed to comply with health and safety legislation
  (b) the seriousness of the breach
  (c) how much risk of death the breach posed.

1.111   In addition the jury may also:
  (a) take into account the extent to which the evidence shows that there were attitudes, policies, systems or accepted practices within the organisation which were likely to have encouraged the failure, or to have produced tolerance of it
  (b) have regard to any health and safety guidance that relates to the breach issued by an authority responsible for enforcing health and safety legislation, and
  (c) have regard to any other relevant matter.

1.112   Although the offence applies to most employers (including the Crown, government departments, police, etc), there are a number of exclusions, such as military activities and responses to emergency services (fire and rescue services, etc).

1.113   An individual cannot be convicted of aiding, abetting, counselling or procuring the commission of an offence of corporate manslaughter or corporate homicide, and the common law offence of manslaughter by gross negligence has been abolished in its application to corporations or other organisations. However, individual employees (including directors, etc) may still be prosecuted for manslaughter in respect of their own wrongful acts. There have been a number of cases where a person has been convicted of manslaughter in circumstances where someone has been killed through gross negligence, dangerous conduct, extreme recklessness or wilful flouting of the law.

1.114   The jury may also return a verdict on health and safety charges (eg under the Health and Safety at Work, etc Act 1974, s.37(1)), even when it is considering a manslaughter charge, if it is in the interests of justice to do so.

1.115   A prosecution under the Corporate Manslaughter and Corporate Homicide Act 2007 can only be undertaken by the Director of Public Prosecutions (in Scotland the Procurator Fiscal). If convicted, the court will impose a fine, and may also issue a remedial order requiring the organisation to take specified steps to remedy any relevant breach or any matter resulting from the breach which caused the death, or any health and safety deficiency in the organisation's policies or practices of which the relevant breach appears to be an indication. The court may also impose a publicity order, requiring the convicted organisation to publicise specific information about its failures. An organisation which fails to comply with the terms of the remedial order or publicity order would be guilty of an offence, and liable to an unlimited fine on indictment.

1.116   In respect of work-related deaths, a protocol for liaison has been agreed between the HSE, the Director of Public Prosecutions, and the Association of Chief Police Officers, recognising their respective functions and ensuring co-operation and co-ordination of activities. Thus, the HSE is responsible for enforcing health and safety legislation, the police authorities will investigate to ascertain if a serious criminal offence has been committed, and the Crown Prosecution Service has to decide whether there is sufficient evidence to warrant prosecution for manslaughter.

1.117 It is expected that early in 2009 the Sentencing Guidelines Secretariat will issue guidelines for use in corporate manslaughter cases.

Other criminal offences

1.118 For the purpose of this book, the overwhelming number of criminal offences that might be committed are those specified in the various statutory provisions. It is quite possible for a single occurrence to give rise to more than one offence. For example, the HSE may decide to prosecute for a breach of the Health and Safety at Work, etc Act 1974 (HSWA) at the same time as for a breach of other legislation. Although most offences are likely to arise out of a breach of a specific regulation, there is nothing to prevent a prosecution being brought in respect of an incident under the Health and Safety at Work, etc Act 1974 and/or a specific regulation (*Regina (Juttan Oy) v Bristol Magistrates' Court*). This enables courts to impose the higher penalties contained in the Act rather than the potentially lower penalties that are provided for in regulations generally (see paragraph 3.185).

Defence of due diligence

1.119 A statutory provision may provide that it is a defence for an accused to show that he or she used due diligence to secure compliance with the law. This is a question of fact, and the standard of proof is that of the balance of probabilities (*R v Carr-Briant*). If the accused is an incorporated association (eg a limited company) the prosecution would need to show that the failure to comply was due to the act or omission of a person who can be identified with the controlling mind and will of the company. The default by a subordinate will not necessarily be that of the company. In *Tesco Supermarkets Ltd v Natrass*, a supermarket advertised a washing powder at a discount rate. A customer sought to purchase the item, but was told the special rate stock had been exhausted. The supermarket was prosecuted under the Trade Descriptions Act. In its defence it was argued that the store manager had been responsible for the breach because his system of daily checks had broken down, and further argued that the company had done all it could to ensure that the offence would not be committed. It was held that the company was entitled to plead the defence of due diligence. The store manager did not act *as* the company, but *for* the company. The *mens rea* (guilty mind) of the company could only be derived from the actions of those officers who represented the company's controlling mind.

The overlap of the law

1.120   Since there are no clear boundaries between legal concepts, an act may frequently have two or more legal implications. Thus an accident at work may result in a prosecution for a criminal offence; the same incident may result in a civil claim being brought for compensation. Indeed, in civil proceedings, the fact that there has been a criminal conviction in respect of the relevant incident is admissible in evidence (Civil Evidence Act 1968, s.11) for the purpose of proving that the defendant committed the offence, although it is not conclusive, and rebutting evidence may be given. The majority of legal decisions on health and safety that explain and interpret the various statutory provisions arise out of civil proceedings, a fact that indicates how the law on occupational health and safety tends to work in practice.

Statutory interpretation

1.121   It is the task of the courts to interpret the words used by Parliament, not to legislate, although there can be little doubt in practice that by doing the former they achieve the latter. In recent years, the courts have taken a broader view in respect of reforming legislation and sought to interpret the words by seeking the intentions of Parliament. Indeed, the House of Lords have held that when construing a statute, reference may be made to Parliamentary material (eg *Hansard*) where the legislation is ambiguous or obscure, or leads to an absurdity (see *Pepper v Hart*). An exploration of this aspect of judicial innovation is beyond the scope of this book.

1.122   All modern Acts of Parliament contain a section that deals with interpretation, and they will also define special terms where necessary. The Health and Safety at Work, etc Act 1974 (HSWA) contains four sections (ss.52, 53, 76, 82) which are concerned with the meaning of words and phrases used in the Act, and this practice is to be found in other relevant statutes and regulations. It is to these that reference should be made in the first instance. Words used in health and safety regulations are generally construed in accordance with the parent Act.

1.123   The Interpretation Act 1978 can be looked to for assistance in some circumstances. By that Act, unless the contrary is intended, a reference to a male includes a reference to a female, and vice versa, and a reference to the singular includes the plural. A "person" includes a body of persons (whether corporate or unincorporate), "month" means calendar month, and so on.

1.124   There are a number of rules for statutory interpretation which are well-known and used in legal circles, sometimes with Latin tags. There is the "literal rule", whereby the courts will look at the ordinary and grammatical sense of the words used. If this leads to absurdity or inconsistency, the "golden rule" may be applied, whereby a construction is given which leads to a sensible interpretation, taking into account the whole statute. The tag *ejusdem generis* (of the same species) may be used on occasions. For example, if a statute referred to "any car, van, bus or other vehicle" it is doubtful if the latter phrase would include a bicycle, as the species is clearly motorised transport.

1.125   Sometimes, the courts may look to the interpretation already given to a particular word or phrase when used in another enactment, particularly when the two statutes are dealing with the same or similar subject matter. Thus words used in the Offices, Shops and Railway Premises Act used to be construed on the same lines as identical words used (and judicially explained) in the Factories Act. This is known as construing *in pari materia* (in similar circumstances). (As has been noted (see paragraph 1.96), Latin tags are no longer to be used, but they are still to be found in older cases.)

1.126   The following are some of the words and phrases that are to be commonly found in the law on health and safety generally.

"Shall"; "Shall not"

1.127   These words impose an absolute obligation to do (or not to do) the act or thing in question, and it is not permissible to argue that it is impracticable, difficult or even impossible to do it (or not to do it). Thus, when the Factories Act, s.14 stated that "Every dangerous part of any machinery shall be securely fenced", it imposed an absolute obligation to securely fence, and a failure to do so may have resulted in criminal proceedings or, if someone was injured because of a failure to securely fence, a civil action for compensation. If it was impossible to use the machine when securely fenced, then the Act implicitly prohibited its use (*Summers (John) & Sons Ltd v Frost*) or the occupier of the factory used it at his peril.

1.128 An absolute obligation may be laid down in regulations made under an Act. In *Stark v Post Office* a postman was injured when a part of the front brake of his delivery bicycle broke. It was held that the Post Office was in breach of regulation 6(1) of the Provision and Use of Work Equipment Regulations 1992 (see paragraph 6.55), which provides that, "Every employer shall ensure that work equipment is maintained in an efficient state, in efficient working order and in good repair". The regulations imposed an absolute obligation on the employer, who was liable for damage for the tort of breach of statutory duty.

"So far as is practicable"; "best practicable means"

1.129 This is a high standard, but not an absolute one because if it is impossible to do something, then clearly it is not practicable to do it (*Jayne v National Coal Board*). If something is practicable, it must be done; if the best practical means are required, then it is up to the person on whom the obligation is placed to find the best practicable means, and to constantly bring his knowledge up to date. However, it is not practicable to take precautions against a danger which is not known to exist, although once the danger is known, it becomes practicable to do something about it (*Cartwright v GKN Sankey Ltd*). The test is one of foresight, not hindsight (*Edwards v National Coal Board*). The standard of practicability is that of current knowledge and invention (*Adsett v K and L Steelfounders and Engineers Ltd*). Once something is found to be practicable, it is feasible and it must be done, no matter how inconvenient or expensive it may be to do it. The burden of proof to show that it was not practicable to do something, or to do more than was in fact done, is on the person upon whom the obligation is placed (in civil proceedings) and upon the defendant or accused in criminal proceedings (HSWA, s.40).

"Reasonably practicable"

1.130 This phrase causes more concern to practitioners than any other, although there is no magic or mystery about it. It should be looked at in the following way.

1.131   First, we start off with the presumption that if something is practicable, the courts will not lightly hold that it is not reasonably practicable (*Marshall v Gotham & Co*).

1.132   Second, it is a somewhat lesser standard than "practicable". It is permissible to take into account on the one hand the danger or hazard or injury which may occur, and balance it, on the other hand, with the cost, inconvenience, time and trouble which would have to be taken to counter it. As Asquith LJ stated in *Edwards v National Coal Board*:

> "[The term] 'reasonably practicable' is a narrower term than 'physically possible' and seems to me to imply that a computation must be made by the owner in which the quantum of risk is placed in one scale and the sacrifice involved in the measures necessary for averting the risk (whether in money, time or trouble) is placed in the other, and that, if it be shown that there is a gross disproportion between them the risk being insignificant in relation to the sacrifice the defendants discharge the onus on them. Moreover, this computation falls to be made by the owner at a point in time anterior to the accident."

1.133   By way of example, we may cite *Marshall v Gotham & Co*, where, although the roof of a mine had been tested in the usual way, it collapsed because of the existence of a rare geological fault. It was held that the employers were not liable for the injuries to the plaintiff that ensued. The court held that, "The danger was a very rare one. The trouble and expense involved in the use of precautions, while not prohibitive, would have been considerable. The precautions would not have afforded anything like complete protection against the danger". In the circumstances, the employers had done all that was reasonable.

1.134   The phrase "so far as is reasonably practicable" is not a defence to criminal proceedings, because regulation 21 of the Management Regulations (see paragraph 4.73) provides that "Nothing in the relevant statutory provisions shall operate so as to afford an employer a defence in any criminal proceedings for a contravention of those provisions by reason of any act or default of an employee of his…" (This was a reaction to the case of *R v Nelson Group Services Maintenance Ltd*, see paragraph 3.80). But "so far as is reasonably practicable" must be seen in the context of what is reasonably foreseeable. Thus, if an employee is injured because he has acted contrary to instructions, or contrary to his training, it will not have been reasonably practicable for the employer to do more than he has done (*R v Hatton Traffic Management*). Thus the phrase is not a defence but a qualification of the underlying duty.

1.135 Third, in criminal proceedings, it shall be for the accused to prove that it was not reasonably practicable to do more than was in fact done to satisfy the duty or requirement (HSWA, s.40). However, this can be established by the defendant by the ordinary burden of proof, ie on the balance of probabilities. In effect, s.40 of the HSWA reverses the normal burden of proof that applies in criminal cases, which, generally speaking, lies upon the prosecution. This provision was challenged in *Davies v Health and Safety Executive* as being incompatible with Article 6 of the European Convention on Human Rights, which provides that "Everyone charged with a criminal offence shall be presumed innocent until proved guilty according to the law". However, the Court of Appeal ruled that the imposition of the reversed burden of proof was "justified, necessary and proportionate" in health and safety cases, and therefore compatible with the Convention.

1.136 Fourth, in the last analysis, it will be for the court to decide, as a question of fact, based on the evidence which can be adduced, whether or not something was reasonably practicable. In the crown court, this will be decided by the jury (*R v Nelson Group Services (Maintenance) Ltd* (see paragraph 3.80)). In the last resort, therefore, the issue can only be determined after the event when it has been tested in court.

1.137 For example, in *Martin v Boulton & Paul Ltd*, an employee of the defendants was injured while erecting a steel beam, and the defendants were prosecuted for failing to provide, so far as was reasonably practicable, a safe system of work. The magistrate found that the method adopted by the defendants was a universal practice adopted in the steel erection industry and dismissed the charge. On appeal by way of "case stated", the Divisional Court held that the existence of a universal practice did not, by itself, lead to the conclusion that there was no other reasonably practicable way of doing something. There may be evidence to suggest that despite the universal practice, there were other ways of doing the work that were safer and therefore reasonably practicable. Thus evidence of a universal practice does not discharge the burden of proof that lies on the defendant, though it is a factual matter that can be taken into account, along with all the other evidence.

1.138 Thus in *HSE v Norwest Holst Ltd* an employee was killed when, contrary to instructions, he had climbed over a guard rail which led to the collapse of a platform on which he was working. It was held that the employers were not guilty of an offence under s 2(1) of the Act. The accident was completely unforeseeable.

1.139   Indeed, it would not be impossible for different courts and tribunals to come to contrary conclusions on identical facts if perceptions differ. The passage of time, greater knowledge and experience, accident statistics, as well as the "inarticulate major premise" of those hearing cases, may account for a different end result. For example, an employment tribunal in *International Stores Ltd v Johns* quashed a prohibition notice imposed on an unguarded meat-slicing band saw, whereas in *Gateway Foodmarkets Ltd v Eastwood*, a similar notice on an identical machine was upheld.

1.140   We have seen that it is the duty of all Member States of the European Union to comply with and abide by European directives, and that the European Commission may bring proceedings before the European Court against any state which is in breach of EU law. Infraction proceedings were brought against the UK Government by the Commission (*Commission v United Kingdom* C-127/05), who argued that provisions in UK law which impose duties on employers "so far as is reasonably practicable" (eg see HSWA, s.2(l)) do not comply with the Framework Directive (89/391/EEC), which imposes responsibilities on employers for all accidents and incidences of ill health at work. The only permitted exception is "where occurrences are due to unusual and unforeseeable circumstances or to exceptional events, the consequences of which could not have been avoided despite the exercise of all due care unless there are very special circumstances" (Article 5(4) of the directive). It was submitted by the Commission that the test of "so far as is reasonably practicable" enables an employer to escape responsibility by using the balancing "cost/risk" test (see paragraph 1.133) which is a lesser standard, as it permits employers to take financial matters into account, and that this is contrary to the directive.

1.141   In its decision, the European Court pointed out that Article 5(1) of the directive does not impose no-fault liability for all accidents in the workplace. Article 5(4) provides that Member States can exclude or limit the employer's responsibility where occurrences are due to unusual or unforeseeable circumstances, beyond the employer's control, or to exceptional events, the consequences of which could not be avoided despite the exercise of all due care.

1.142   The ECJ thus accepted the view of the UK Government, but it is submitted that the matter has not yet been finally resolved. The Advocate General had queried whether the UK was right to allow economic factors to be taken into account, and argued that the test should be whether, objectively speaking, it is technically feasible to eliminate or reduce the risk to the health and safety of workers. He further held that the concept of what is "reasonably practicable" is incompatible with the scope that should attach to the general duty to ensure safety laid down in Article 5(1) of the Framework Directive. He concluded: "Even accepting the United Kingdom's point that a cost-benefit analysis of that nature will rarely, in practice, produce a result favourable to the employer, such an analysis does not seem to me to be permissible under the Community system of protecting the health and safety of workers, which appears to give priory to protecting the individual worker rather than financial enterprise".

1.143 The result could well be that if, in a subsequent case, an employer seeks to raise the cost/benefit argument of "so far as is reasonably practicable" as opposed to technical feasibility, it is possible for a court to disapply the UK provision and adopt a purposeful interpretation of EU law as set out in the directive.

"Relevant statutory provisions"

1.144 This means the provisions of Part 1 of HSWA (including health and safety regulations made under the Act), plus the following provisions, which are contained in schedule 1 of HSWA.

	Provisions which are relevant statutory provisions
The Explosives Act 1875	The whole Act except ss.30–32, 80 and 116–121
The Boiler Explosions Act 1882	The whole Act
The Boiler Explosions Act 1890	The whole Act
The Alkali, etc Works Regulation Act 1906	The whole Act
The Revenue Act 1909	Section 11
The Employment of Women, Young Persons and Children Act 1920	The whole Act
The Celluloid and Cinematograph Film Act 1922	The whole Act
The Public Health (Smoke Abatement) Act 1926	The whole Act
The Petroleum (Consolidation) Act 1928	The whole Act

The Hours of Employment (Conventions) Act 1936	The whole Act except s.5
The Petroleum (Transfer of Licences) Act 1936	The whole Act
The Ministry of Fuel and Power Act 1945	Section 1(1) so far as it relates to maintaining and improving safety, health and well-being of persons employed in and about mines and quarries in Great Britain
The Coal Industry Nationalisation Act 1946	Section 42(1) and (2)
The Radioactive Substances Act 1948	Section 5(1)(a)
The Alkali, etc Works Regulation (Scotland) Act 1951	The whole Act
The Agriculture (Poisonous Substances) Act 1952	The whole Act
The Mines and Quarries Act 1954	The whole Act except s.151
The Factories Act 1961	The whole Act except s.135
The Public Health Act 1961	Section 73
The Pipelines Act 1962	Sections 20–34, 37 and 42, schedule 5
The Offices, Shops and Railways Premises Act 1963	The whole Act
The Nuclear Installations Act 1965	Sections 1, 3–6, 22 and 24A
The Mines and Quarries (Tips) Act 1969	Sections 1 to 10
The Mines Management Act 1971	The whole Act
The Employment Medical Advisory Service Act 1972	The whole Act except ss.1 and 6 and schedule 1
The Mineral Workings (Offshore Installations) Act 1971	The whole Act
The Petroleum and Submarine Pipelines Act 1975	Sections 26, 27 and 32
The Petroleum Act 1978	Sections 11(2(2a)), 21–24
The Gas Act 1986	Sections 16, 47(3)–(4)

1.145 Since the passing of HSWA, many of the original provisions of schedule 1 have been repealed in whole or in part, or have been superseded in some way. A number of other Acts were added to this list by the Offshore Safety Act 1992 and by the Railways Act 1993, relating to the operation of railways.

"Prescribed"

1.146 If something is to be prescribed, it has to be specifically referred to at some future time. Thus, if a statute states that something shall be done "in prescribed cases" then the power exists for someone (eg the Secretary of State) to prescribe the cases where that thing shall be done, and until the power is exercised, nothing has happened. For example, s.2(7) of HSWA states that in prescribed cases an employer shall establish a safety committee, and the Safety Representatives and Safety Committees Regulations 1977 specify that this shall be done when at least two safety representatives request the employer, in writing, to establish such a committee. If something has to be prescribed under the Act, it will be done by regulations (s.53(1)).

"At work"

1.147   An employee is at work throughout the time when he is in the course of his employment, but not otherwise (s.52(1)(b)). The phrase "course of his employment" is not capable of precise definition and legal authorities based on civil cases have, as a matter of policy, given it a somewhat liberal construction. These authorities do not necessarily bind in criminal law. In *Coult v Szuba*, the defendant was employed to work at the Scunthorpe site of the British Steel Corporation. The site had 39 miles of roads. The defendant, who was due to start work at 0600, clocked in at 0541 and then drove along a road to the place where he was due to work. On the way, he was involved in an accident with another car due to the defendant's fault. He was prosecuted for an offence under s.7(a) of HSWA for failing to take reasonable care of the safety of himself and others while at work. The magistrates dismissed the charge, and their decision was upheld by the Divisional Court on appeal. On the facts of the case, it was not possible to say that the defendant was in the course of his employment at the time of the accident (this case may be contrasted with *Bolton Metropolitan Borough Council v Malrod Insulations Ltd*, paragraph 3.29).

1.148   It will be noted that trainees and others on work experience are "at work" for the purpose of s.52(1)(b) even though they are not employees in the legal sense (see paragraph 3.13).

Burden of proof

1.149   In criminal cases, the general rule is that it is for the prosecution to prove its case in the hallowed phrase "beyond reasonable doubt". However, in some circumstances, the burden of proof is on the defendant. For example, s.17 of HSWA requires the accused to show that he observed the specific statutory provision otherwise than by observing the Approved Code of Practice; s.40 of HSWA requires the accused to show that it was not practicable or not reasonably practicable to do more than in fact was done, etc. However, this burden can be discharged by proof on the balance of probabilities (*R v Carr-Briant*).

1.150 In civil cases, the rule is that the burden is upon the plaintiff to prove his case on the balance of probabilities. In this, he may be assisted by some principles of evidence.

(a) *Res ipsa loquitur*

1.151 If something is under the control of the defendant, and an accident occurs in circumstances such that it would not have happened unless there had been a want of care by the defendant, then a presumption is raised that the defendant has been negligent. The burden is then put on the defendant to explain the accident, and to show that there was no want of care on his part. In other words, "the facts speak for themselves". However, the defendant may be able to show a convincing reason why he was not negligent (eg the accident was caused by the fault of a third party) in which case the burden of proof is thrown back to the plaintiff to prove his case in the usual manner.

(b) Shifting presumptions

1.152 Sometimes, the mere statement of facts will give rise to an inferential presumption which may cause the burden of proof to shift from one party to the other, requiring it to be rebutted by evidence. For example, in *Gardiner v Motherwell Machinery and Scrap Co Ltd*, the plaintiff sued in respect of dermatitis which he alleged was contracted at work. Lord Reid said, "When a man who has not previously suffered from a disease contracts that disease after being subjected to conditions likely to cause it, and when he shows that it starts in a way typical of the disease caused by such conditions, he establishes a *prima facie* presumption that his disease was caused by those conditions." Thus if a person contracts bronchitis after working in dusty conditions, or suffers deafness after being exposed to excessively noisy conditions, an evidential presumption arises that those conditions caused the disease or injury in question.

The scope of the law

1.153 The United Kingdom consists of four countries, ie England, Wales, Scotland and Northern Ireland. A reference to Great Britain excludes Northern Ireland. As a general rule, it may be said that the

English common law, ie judge-made law, is applicable in all four countries, though there are some procedural and linguistic differences so far as Scotland is concerned. The situation is slightly more complicated so far as legislative provisions are concerned, following recent devolution policies, and we must distinguish between primary legislation, passed by Parliament, and secondary legislation, which generally speaking refers to regulations. So far as health and safety legislation is concerned, England, Wales and Scotland are governed by statute laws passed in the Westminster Parliament, in particular HSWA. In theory, Northern Ireland can pass its own legislation, and generally it follows the pattern in force in the other three countries. Devolved government for Northern Ireland has recently been restored.

1.154 Scotland now has its own Parliament and Executive, and may enact secondary legislation in certain areas. It retains its own legal system, which has certain distinctive terminology and procedure. Matters relating to health, the environment and certain other domestic matters are devolved to the Scottish Parliament, but there are circumstances when Acts of the Westminster Parliament have to indicate the extent to which they apply to Scotland (if at all). Sometimes it is necessary to enact further specific legislation bringing Scottish law into line with the rest of the UK (eg Sunday Working (Scotland) Act 2003). However, the Scottish Parliament is not able to make changes to the laws relating to employment, industrial relations and health and safety at work, as these powers are reserved for the Westminster Parliament (Scotland Act 1998, schedule 5).

1.155 The Welsh Assembly has no primary law-making powers, although it does have limited powers to enact secondary legislation, in particular with reference to how provisions passed at Westminster should be implemented in Wales.

1.156 An illustration of how devolution affects legislative powers can be seen from the way in which the recent legislative provision on smoking at work was implemented. The Health Act 2006 applied only to England and Wales, and came into force in England in July 2007 (see Smoke Free (Premises and Enforcement) Regulations 2006), whereas it came into force in Wales in April 2007. As health is a "devolved" issue, the Smoking, Health and Social Care (Scotland) Act 2005 came into force in March 2006.

1.157 There are also some differences in the way EU directives are implemented, although since the end result is usually the same, these differences have no practical importance.

1.158   The Isle of Man and the Channel Islands are not part of the UK (Royal and Parliamentary Titles Act 1927). However, s.54 of HSWA applies the Act to the Isles of Scilly as if it were a local government area of the UK. The Isle of Man, Jersey and Guernsey have adopted legislation based on the UK model.

1.159   By the Health and Safety at Work, etc Act 1974 (Application Outside Great Britain) Order 2001, the provisions of HSWA are extended to cover offshore oil and gas installations, pipeline work, offshore construction work, certain loading and unloading operations, and shipbuilding, repair work, floating accommodation vessels and diving operations that take place outside British territorial waters. This is additional to the provisions of the Mineral Workings (Offshore Installations) Act 1971, the Petroleum and Submarine Pipelines Act 1975 and regulations made thereunder. At the present time, approximately 40 sets of regulations apply to the offshore installation industry.

The Human Rights Act 1998

1.160   In order to prevent a recurrence of the horrors and atrocities that took place before and during the Second World War, the European Convention for the Protection of Human Rights and Fundamental Freedoms was signed in 1950. The Human Rights Act 1998 is designed to give effect to those rights and freedoms by effectively incorporating the Convention into UK law. Basically, there are four principles that apply.
1. When determining a question that arises in connection with a Convention right, a court or tribunal must take account of any judgment, decision, declaration or advisory opinion of the European Court of Human Rights.
2. So far as it is possible to do so, primary and subordinate legislation must be read and given effect to, in a way that is compatible with Convention rights.
3. If a court (not a tribunal) is satisfied that a provision of primary legislation is incompatible with the convention, it may make a declaration of incompatibility.
4. It is unlawful for public authority to act in a way which is incompatible with a Convention right.

1.161   So far as the law of health and safety at work is concerned, the Human Rights Act 1998 is likely to have very limited application. Article 6 of the Convention guarantees a person (which term includes an artificial legal body, such as a limited company) the right to a fair trial in civil and criminal proceedings (see *Davies v Health and Safety Executive*, paragraph 1.135). This means that each party to a case must have a reasonable opportunity of presenting his case; there must be a public hearing and judgment, with a reasoned decision; the hearing must take place within a reasonable time, and must be before an independent and impartial tribunal. There is no reason to suspect that the UK legal system is wanting in this respect. Article 8 of the Convention guarantees respect for private life, family life, home and correspondence, and although there have been cases before the European Court which have taken the view that state bodies could be in breach of Article 8 if they fail to take appropriate steps to prevent environmental harm, the likelihood of public authorities in the UK falling foul of this provision is somewhat remote.

1.162   In theory, if the Health and Safety Executive (HSE) refused to investigate a major injury, or failed to prosecute in respect of a serious offence, or failed to take some action which would have prevented a major injury, or failed to enforce a legal provision designed to prevent a major injury, then such actions may give rise to a complaint under the Human Rights Act 1998. There may well be cases where the powers of HSE inspectors will be challenged, and where a defendant complains that the right to a fair trial has been violated, but existing laws should be adequate to resolve such issues, and it will be rare to have to resort to the Human Rights Act 1998.

CHAPTER 2

The institutions of health and safety

The role of Government

2.1 The prime responsibility for overseeing health and safety legislation is a political function of the relevant government department. As a result of a reorganisation, all matters relating to health and safety at work are now with the Department for Work and Pensions. The head of the Department is a Secretary of State (with a seat in the Cabinet) assisted by various junior ministers, one of whom will have been designated as having a special responsibility for occupational health and safety matters. Other problems of health and safety, which are partly concerned with the occupation and partly of general concern to the whole community are dealt with by other departments. Powers relating to the control of industrial pollution are exercisable by the Environment Agency, created by the Environment Act 1995. The former responsibility of the Department of Energy for occupational health and safety on offshore installations has now been assigned to the Health and Safety Executive (HSE), but control of rail safety has been taken away from the HSE and passed to the Office of Rail Regulation (Railways Act 2005 (Commencement No. 5) Order 2006).

Health and Safety Executive

2.2 The Health and Safety Commission and the Health and Safety Executive were abolished by the Legislative Reform (Health and Safety Executive) Order 2008, and replaced by a new unitary organisation called the Health and Safety Executive. This consists of a chairman and nine non-executive members appointed by the Secretary of State. Three members will be appointed after consultation with employers' association, three members will be appointed after consultation with employees' associations, one member will be appointed after consultation with organisations representing local authorities, and between two and four members will be appointed after consultation with professional bodies and devolved administrations. The new HSE will appoint a chief executive. All the powers and functions of the old Commission and Executive have been transferred to the new organisation.

General purposes (HSWA, s.1(1))

2.3   The general duty of the HSE is to do such things and make such arrangements as it considers appropriate for the general purposes of Part 1 of the Health and Safety at Work, etc Act 1974. The "general purposes" are stated to be:
   (a) securing the health, safety and welfare of persons at work
   (b) protecting persons other than persons at work against risks to their health and safety arising out of or in connection with the activities of persons at work
   (c) controlling the keeping and use of explosive or highly flammable or otherwise dangerous substances, and generally preventing the unlawful acquisition, possession and use of such substances (s.1(1)).

2.4   The general purposes were further extended to protect the public from personal injury, fire, explosions and other dangers arising from the transmission or distribution of gas through pipes (Gas Act 1986, s.18 (1)), securing the health, safety and welfare of persons on offshore installations (Offshore Safety Act 1992, s.1(1)), and securing the proper construction and safe operation of railways (Railways Act 1993, s.117(2)).

2.5   It will be noted that the HSE is no longer responsible for controlling emissions into the atmosphere of noxious or offensive substances. Section 1(1) (d) of the Act was repealed as from December 1996 (Environmental Protection Act 1990 (Commencement no.18) Order 1996), and control over industrial pollution is now the responsibility of the Environment Agency or local authorities, depending on the type and size of the processes involved.

2.6   It shall also be the duty of the HSE to do such things and make such arrangements as it considers appropriate for the general purposes of the Health and Safety at Work, etc Act 1974. In particular, the HSE shall:
   (a) assist and encourage persons concerned with matters relevant to those purposes to further those purposes
   (b) make arrangements as it considers appropriate for the carrying out of research and the publication of the results of research, and the provisions of training and information, and encourage research and the provision of training and information by others
   (c) make arrangements to provide information and advisory services

to government departments, local authorities, employers, employees and their organisations, and other purposes concerned with matters relevant to the general purposes of the Act.

2.7   The HSE will submit proposals to the Secretary of State, submit particulars of which it proposes to do for the purpose of carrying out its functions, ensure that its activities are in accordance with proposals approved by, and give effect to any directions issued by the Secretary of State. However, the Secretary of State may not give directions with regard to the enforcements of the relevant statutory provisions in any particular case.

2.8   The HSE may carry out an investigation or hold an inquiry into any matter, occurrence or situation, in accordance with the Health and Safety Inquiries (Procedure) Regulations 1975. It will issue guidance to local authorities and work with them to establish best practice and consistency in the enforcement of health and safety law. The enforcement powers of the HSE and local authorities remain unchanged.

Powers (HSWA, s.13)

2.9   The HSE may do anything (except borrow money) that is calculated to facilitate, or is conducive or incidental to, the performance of its functions, and in particular may:

(a) enter into agreements with any government department or other person for that department or person to perform any function on behalf of the HSE (eg the HSE has made an "agency agreement" with the Radiation Protection Division of the Health Protection Agency for the latter to perform certain functions relating to ionising and other radiations)

(b) make agreements whereby the HSE performs functions on behalf of any other minister, government department or other public authority, being functions which, in the opinion of the Secretary of State, can appropriately be performed by the HSE (but not the power to make regulations or other legislative instruments)

(c) provide services or facilities which may be required by any government department or public authority

(d) appoint persons or committees to provide the HSE with advice (see paragraph 2.19)

(e) pay travelling and/or subsistence allowances and compensation for loss of remunerative time in connection with any of the functions of the HSE

(f) pay for any research connected with the functions of the HSE and to disseminate (or pay for the dissemination of) information derived from such research

(g) make arrangements for the making of payments to the HSE by other parties who are using facilities and services provided by the HSE.

Investigations and inquiries (HSWA, s.14)

2.10 If there is an accident, occurrence, situation or other matter that the HSE thinks necessary or expedient to investigate in order to fulfil any of the general purposes of the Act (above) or with a view to the making of regulations for those purposes, it may direct any other person to carry out that investigation and make a report (s.14(2)(a)).

2.11 As an alternative, and with the consent of the Secretary of State, the HSE may direct that an inquiry shall be held into the matter (s.14(2)(b)). The result of the investigation or inquiry may be made public, in whole or in part, as the HSE thinks fit.

2.12 The distinction between an investigation and an inquiry is that an inquiry is a formal, public affair into a matter in which there is general public interest as to its outcome, whereas an investigation is more informal and may be carried out in a manner determined by the investigator, though he must still observe the rules of natural justice, and receive evidence from any person who may be able to contribute worthwhile information.

2.13 The Health and Safety Inquiries (Procedure) Regulations 1975 (as amended), lay down the procedure for the conduct of inquiries under s.14(2)(b). The date, time and place shall be fixed (and may be varied) by the HSE, who shall also give 28 days' notice to every person entitled to appear whose name and address is known. It must also publish a notice of the intention to hold the inquiry in one or more newspapers (where appropriate, circulating in the district in which the subject matter of the inquiry arose) giving the name of the person who has been appointed to hold the inquiry and of any assessors appointed to assist.

2.14   The following persons shall be entitled to appear at the inquiry as of right:

(a) the HSE

(b) any enforcing authority concerned

(c) in Scotland, the Procurator Fiscal

(d) any employers' association or any trade union representing employers or employees concerned

(e) any person who was injured or who has suffered damage as a result of the incident, or his personal representatives

(f) the owner or occupier of any premises in which the incident occurred

(g) any person carrying on the activity which gave rise to the incident.

2.15   Other persons may appear at the inquiry, but only at the discretion of the person appointed to hold it. Anyone wishing to appear at an inquiry may do so in person, or may be represented by a lawyer or by any other person.

2.16   The person appointed to conduct the inquiry may, either on his own volition or on the application of any person entitled or permitted to appear, require the attendance of any other person in order to give evidence or to produce any document, and it is an offence, punishable by a fine of up to £5000 to fail to comply with such requirement.

2.17   The conduct of the inquiry will be the responsibility of the appointed person, and it will be held in public unless a Minister of the Crown directs that part or all of the inquiry shall be held in private because it would be against the interests of national security to allow certain evidence to be given in public. Also, a private session may be held if information is likely to be disclosed which relates to a trade secret, on an application made by a party affected. Otherwise, the procedure to be followed will be at the discretion of the appointed person, which he will state at the commencement of the proceedings, subject to any submissions made by any person appearing (or their representatives). He will also inform them as to any proposals he may have regarding an inspection of any site, will determine the order of the witnesses, permit opening statements, examination and cross-examination, hear evidence on oath, permit documents to be introduced as evidence and allow them to be inspected and copied. He may receive any written submissions, and if necessary, adjourn the proceedings from time to time.

2.18 After the inquiry has been concluded, a report containing the findings of fact and any recommendations will be made to the HSE.

Advisory committees

2.19 A number of advisory committees have been created in order to provide the HSE with specialised advice and information. These will usually consist of representatives from each side of industry, academic and industrial experts, and officials from the HSE. They will report to the HSE, and may make recommendations. Examples of existing Standing Advisory Committees dealing with specific subjects are as follows.

Advisory Committee on Toxic Substances

2.20 This committee was set up to advise the HSE on methods of controlling health hazards to persons at work (especially in connection with the COSHH Regulations, see paragraph 7.1) and also to the general public consequent on or arising from the use of toxic substances. The committee has representatives from industry, local authorities and other expert advisors.

Advisory Committee on Dangerous Substances

2.21 This committee considers methods of securing the safety of persons at work and related risks to the general public arising from the manufacture, import, storage, conveyance and use of materials which are flammable or explosive, and the transportation of a wide range of dangerous substances. Its membership includes representatives from industry, local authorities and other experts.

Nuclear Safety Advisory Committee

2.22 This committee advises on all aspects of nuclear safety. It is chaired by an independent member and has scientific and industrial advisors.

Advisory Committee on Dangerous Pathogens

2.23   This committee is viewed as having a wider remit than most HSE advisory committees, due to its broad terms of reference. It will advise the HSE and the Department of Health and Department for Environment, Food and Rural Affairs on matters relating to all classes of pathogens that are dangerous to human beings. As well as representatives from both sides of industry it has a number of medical and scientific experts. It will advise the HSE on the general standards of safe working to be observed in laboratories, point out any improvements necessary, consider new hazards, and make recommendations concerning proposed regulations, Approved Codes of Practice and guidance generally.

Scientific Advisory Committee on Genetic Modification

2.24   This committee gives guidance on the planned release of genetically manipulated organisms for agricultural and environment purposes, including risk assessment and notification of proposals to carry out such work. It also deals with guidelines for the health surveillance of persons involved in genetic manipulation in laboratories, etc and the setting up of safety committees.

Occupational Health Reference Group

2.25   As its name implies, this committee is concerned with all aspects of occupational health, and has professional as well as industry membership.

Ionising Radiations Health and Safety Forum

2.26   This body acts as a liaison group between the HSE and organisations with an interest in radiation protection. It deals with matters concerning the protection against exposure to ionising radiations at work and identifies significant issues for future action.

Advisory committees, boards and councils

2.27   The HSE has also set up a number of industry-based advisory committees, boards and councils with a view to stimulating action to promote the health and safety of workers within particular industries and to protect the general public from work-related hazards arising from such activities. As a general rule, the HSE provides the secretariat and chairmen, with the rest of the membership drawn from the main organisations in the respective industries. Each advisory committee will draw up its own plan of work (short term and long term) reviewing specific problems that need to be tackled, and reports submitted to the HSE, with proposals for action set out for consideration.

2.28 Currently, there are about 37 such bodies, together with a number of sub-committees, which may deal with health and safety issues that arise in a particular industry, or with hazards that may arise across a range of industry sectors. Thus there are committees on dangerous substances, biocides, dangerous pathogens, toxic substances, agriculture, asbestos, ceramics, chemicals, construction, engineering, local authority liaison, health services, higher and further education, ionising radiations, mining, motor repair, nuclear safety, occupational health, offshore industries, paper and board, printing, quarries, rubber, mines, schools, genetically modified organisms, shipbuilding, small businesses and textiles.

Strategic planning

2.29 The HSE is constantly updating its strategic planning, in an effort to prioritise its activities, as well as paying attention to its continuing aims. In a strategy statement issued in 2000, entitled *Revitalising health and safety*, it announced its targets for the next decade, to include a reduction in working days lost through work-related injury and ill health by 30%, a reduction in the incidence of people suffering from work-related ill health by 20%, and a reduction in the rate of fatal and major injury accidents by 10%. To achieve these targets, a ten-point strategy supported by a 44-point action plan was introduced, to provide incentives and practical support for employers, as well as new measures to be taken against those employers who do not meet their health and safety responsibilities. The HSE is currently consulting on a new strategy for health and safety, expected in June 2009.

2.30 Another example is the Workplace Health Connect scheme, run by the HSE, which provided businesses employing between 5 and 250 employees with confidential expert advice on health and safety, using a free telephone helpline, free worksite visits and a dedicated website. The pilot scheme finished in February 2008 and a final evaluation will take place in 2009.

2.31   The major part of the HSE's enforcement work is carried out by the Field Operations Directorate, with other divisions dealing with nuclear safety, hazardous installations, corporate science and analytical services, the health and safety laboratory, and so on.

2.32   Thus, although industry has to deal with one unified body, in practice specialists from the different branches may be encountered, as well as other enforcement bodies (eg fire authority, local authorities, see below). Each inspectorate will obviously deal with those matters in respect of which it has been assigned.

2.33   The HSE may charge a fee in respect of certain applications for licences, medical examinations, certificates, approvals, changes, etc (see Health and Safety (Fees) Regulations 2009).

Sector groups

2.34   The internal organisation of the HSE is designed to permit a greater degree of industrial specialisation. There are a number of sector groups that specialise in specific topics and that can be approached as required for specialist advice and information. These sector groups are:

(a) agriculture and food

(b) public services (health and social care, education, central and local government, fire, police and defence establishments)

(c) manufacturing (engineering, polymers and fibres, metals and minerals, woodworking)

(d) consumer and commercial services, transport and utilities (public transport, wholesale and retail trade, utilities)

(e) health unit (co-ordination of generic health issues relevant to all sectors)

(f) safety unit (co-ordination of generic safety issues).

Enforcement (HSWA, ss.20–26)

2.35   The HSE has a number of actual and potential powers whereby it may seek to ensure compliance with the relevant statutory provisions. Primarily, however, it will seek to give advice and assistance to any employer or other person who is seeking ways of meeting the necessary standards. Persuasion, rather than compulsion, has always been the style adopted by the inspectorate, for the object has always been to establish high standards of health and safety rather than to punish offenders. Thus an inspector may give verbal or written advice as to the steps which need to be taken to ensure compliance with the statutory duties. If remedial steps are not taken, or where the dangers are so obvious or imminent that immediate action is necessary, the powers of issuing improvement or prohibition notices may be exercised. As a last resort, criminal proceedings may be brought by an inspector (see *Campbell v Wallsend Slipway & Engineering Co Ltd*) which are usually instituted when there has been an incident, or after prior warnings have been given, or where the employer in question has a bad record of compliance. In other words, the inspectors will usually start off with advice, persuasion and encouragement. If these fail, it may be necessary to resort to compulsion or sanctions. For the principles of enforcement action, see paragraph 3.177.

2.36   Every enforcement authority has the power to appoint as inspectors (under whatever title they may think fit) such persons having suitable qualifications as it thinks necessary for enforcing the relevant statutory provisions within its field of responsibility, and may also terminate the appointment (HSWA, s.19). However, it is submitted that this does not take inspectors outside the protection of the relevant provisions of the Employment Rights Act 1996, particularly in respect of rights not to be unfairly dismissed.

Powers of inspectors (HSWA, s.20)

2.37   When an inspector is appointed, he will be given a document specifying which of the powers conferred on him by the relevant statutory provisions are to be exercisable by him, and he may only exercise those powers within the area of the responsibility of the enforcing authority which appointed him (see *Laws v Keane*). When seeking to exercise those powers, he must produce, on request, his instrument of appointment. The powers of inspectors are as follows.

1. At any reasonable time or, if there is a dangerous situation, at any time, to enter premises which he has reason to believe it is necessary to enter for the purpose of carrying into effect any relevant statutory provision.
2. To take with him a constable if he has reasonable cause to apprehend any serious obstruction in the execution of his duty.
3. To take with him any person duly authorised by the inspector's authority, and any equipment or materials required for any purpose for which the power of entry is being exercised.
4. To make such examination and investigation as may be necessary.

5. To direct that any premises or anything therein shall be left undisturbed so long as it is reasonably necessary for the purpose of examination or investigation.

6. To take such measurements and photographs and make such recordings as he considers necessary for the purpose of examination or investigation.

7. To take samples of any article or substance found in any premises and in the atmosphere in or in the vicinity of any such premises; the Secretary of State may make regulations concerning the procedure to be adopted in such cases.

8. In the case of any article or substance likely to cause danger to health or safety, to cause it to be dismantled or subjected to any process or test, but he may not destroy or damage it unless it is for the purpose of exercising his powers. If the person who has responsibilities in relation to those premises so requests, the inspector will exercise this power in that person's presence, unless he considers that it would be prejudicial to the safety of the state to do so. In any case, before exercising these powers, he must consult with appropriate persons for the purpose of ascertaining what dangers, if any, there may be in doing what he proposes to do.

9. In the case of any article or substance likely to cause danger to health or safety, to take possession of it, and detain it for so long as is necessary in order to examine it, to ensure that it is not tampered with before he has completed his examination, or to ensure that it will be available for use as evidence in any proceedings for an offence, or in respect of matters arising out of the issuing of an improvement or prohibition notice. He must leave a notice giving particulars of the article or substance, stating that he has taken possession of it and, if it is practicable to do so, leave a sample with a responsible person.

10. If he is conducting an examination or investigation under (4) above, to require any person whom he has reasonable cause to believe to be able to give any information to answer such questions as the inspector thinks to ask, whether orally or in writing (*R (Wandsworth LBC) v South Western Magistrates' Court*), and to sign a declaration of the truth of his answers. However, no answer given in response to an inspector's questions shall be admissible in evidence against that person or his husband or wife in any proceedings.

11. To require the production of, inspect, and take copies of any entry in any books or documents which are required to be kept, and of any

book or document which it is necessary for him to see for the purpose of any examination or investigation under (4) above, but not if the production is refused on the ground of legal professional privilege.

12. To require any person to afford him such facilities and assistance within that person's control or responsibilities, as are necessary for him to exercise his powers.

13. Any other power which is necessary for the purpose of exercising any of the above powers.

Obtaining information (HSWA, s.27)

2.38 In order to discharge their functions, the HSE or any other enforcing authority may need further information. To obtain this, s.27 gives power to the HSE, with the consent of the Secretary of State, to serve on any person a notice requiring him to furnish the HSE or any other enforcing authority with such information about such matters as may be specified in the notice, and to do this in such form and manner, and within such time, as may be specified.

Disclosure of information (HSWA, s.28)

2.39 No information obtained under this power shall be disclosed without the consent of the person by whom it was furnished, but this does not prevent the disclosure:

(a) to the HSE, a government department or any other enforcing authority

(b) by the recipient of the information to any person for the purpose of any function conferred on the recipient by any relevant statutory provision

(c) to an officer of a local authority, water authority, or river purification board, or to a constable, in each case to a person who is authorised to receive it

(d) by the recipient, as long as it is in a form which is calculated to prevent it from being identified as relating to a particular person or as a particular case

(e) of any information for the purpose of any legal proceedings or any investigation or inquiry held by virtue of s.14(2) (above) or any report made as a result thereof.

(f) where the recipient is a public authority for the purpose of the Freedom of Information Act 2000.

2.40   A person exercising powers of entry or inspection under s.14(4)(a), or general powers of inspection, etc under s.20 may not disclose any information obtained by him (including, in particular, any information with respect to any trade secret obtained by him in any premises into which he has entered by virtue of such powers) except:

(a) for the purpose of his functions
(b) for the purpose of any legal proceedings, or any investigation or inquiry held by virtue of s.14(2), or a report thereof
(c) with the consent of the person who furnished the information in pursuance of a requirement imposed under s.20, and with the consent of the person having responsibilities in relation to the premises where the information was obtained in any other case (s.28(7)).

2.41   However, an inspector is expressly authorised by s.28(8) to disclose information to employed persons or their representatives if it is necessary for him to do so for the purpose of assisting in keeping them adequately informed about matters affecting their health, safety or welfare. Normally, this information will be communicated to safety representatives, but in the absence of these, it can be to a shop steward, or to representatives of employee safety, or to individuals or even their legal representatives, should this be necessary. The information that can be disclosed is:

(a) factual information obtained by him as a result of the exercise of any of his powers under s.20 (above) or as a result of a person who is holding an inquiry under s.14 (above) exercising his right to enter and inspect premises (see s.14(4)(a)), as long as the information relates to the premises where the employees are employed, or to anything which was or is in there, or was or is being done there
(b) information with respect to any action which he has taken or proposes to take in or in connection with those premises.

2.42   If the inspector does give such information to employees or their representatives, he must also give the same information to the employer.

Disclosure for civil proceedings (HSWA, s.28(9))

2.43   Section 116 of the Employment Protection Act 1975 added a new subsection (s.28(9) to HSWA), which permits the disclosure by an inspector of information to a person who is likely to be a party to any civil proceedings arising out of an accident, occurrence or other situation. He will do this by providing a written statement of the relevant facts observed by him in the course of exercising any of his powers.

2.44 Thus, in a civil action for damages (see Chapter 12) either the plaintiff or the defendant may request the information from an inspector.

Additional powers

2.45 As we shall see, an inspector may serve a prohibition notice, an improvement notice, and in England and Wales may prosecute offenders. He may seize and render harmless any article or substance likely to be a cause of danger, and is responsible for the enforcement of the employer's duty to display the certificate of insurance under the provisions of the Employers' Liability (Compulsory Insurance) Act 1969 (see paragraph 5.1).

Power of an enforcing authority to indemnify inspectors (HSWA, s.26)

2.46 A person who is aggrieved by any action of an inspector who has exceeded his powers may always bring a civil action against him. If the circumstances are such that the inspector cannot legally claim the right of indemnity from the appointing authority, the latter may nonetheless indemnify him in whole or in part against any damages, costs, or expenses ordered to pay or incurred if the authority is satisfied that the inspector honestly believed that he was acting within his powers and that his duty as an inspector required or entitled him to do the act in question.

2.47 An aggrieved person may also pursue a complaint against an inspector or the HSE through the machinery laid down in the Parliamentary Commissioner Act 1967 (which created the investigatory role of the Ombudsman).

2.48 When an inspector is carrying out his functions as such, he owes no duty of care when giving advice about safety improvements, even though the fortunes of a business enterprise might be adversely affected. In *Harris v Evans and the HSE*, the plaintiff wished to use a mobile telescopic crane for bungee jumping, and was informed by the HSE to comply with the Code of Practice issued by the Standard Association of British Bungee. He did this, but subsequently another inspector advised the local authority that the crane should not be used unless it had been certified by the manufacturer or by a competent person appointed by the National Certification System for Insurance Inspection Bodies. Such certification proved to be impossible, but the local authority served a prohibition notice until he obtained certification. An appeal against the prohibition notice was dismissed by an employment tribunal. However, the Secretary of State for Employment indicated that there was no technical evidence to show that there was an unacceptable level of risk in using mobile cranes for bungee jumping, and that the advice given by the inspector to obtain certification was wrong. The local authority then withdrew the prohibition notice. The plaintiff sued for the financial loss he had suffered as a result of the (alleged) negligent advice given by the HSE inspector to the local authority. It was held that his claim must fail. The advice given was in pursuance of a statutory function, and did not give rise to a duty of care on the part of the inspector. The plaintiff had protection by way of an appeal to an employment tribunal, and it would not be right to permit an aggrieved person to recover via a negligence action the damage cause to his business by a notice which had been upheld by an employment tribunal.

2.49   The HSC leaflet, *What to Expect When a Health and Safety Inspector Calls*, is a guide for businesses, employees and their representatives.

Health and Safety Awareness Officers

2.50   HSE also employs Health and Safety Awareness Officers, whose role is to undertake proactive work among small and medium sized enterprises (firms with fewer than 50 employees) and specific target groups (eg young persons). These officers are not inspectors, and can only enter premises with the consent of the occupier. They will provide advice and guidance, as well as arrange seminars and workshops. They may also discuss health and safety issues with safety representatives. They have no powers other than to enforce non-compliance with the Employers Liability Compulsory Insurance legislation. However if, following a visit, they encounter obvious unsafe working practices that pose a risk to health and safety, they may advise the dutyholder to stop the activity and not to continue with it until a risk assessment has been carried out or a reference to HSE guidance has been undertaken. If the advice is ignored, the officer will make a report to an inspector.

Local authorities

2.51   One of the problems disclosed by the Robens Committee was the overlapping jurisdiction of the different enforcement authorities. Thus, a shoe repair shop — since it was both a factory *and* a shop — could be visited by the factory inspector and a local authority inspector, each concerned with his own responsibilities. To prevent this happening, s.18 of HSWA enables the Secretary of State, by regulation, to make local authorities responsible for certain prescribed activities, to facilitate the transfer of responsibilities between the HSE and local authorities, and to deal with uncertain areas.

2.52   For the purpose of enforcement of the relevant statutory provisions, a local authority in England is a county council or district council, a London borough council, the Common Council of the City of London, the Sub-Treasurer of the Inner Temple or the Under-Treasurer of the Middle Temple. In Wales, a local authority is a county council or county borough council, and in Scotland, a regional, islands or district council.

2.53   The enforcement functions are carried out by officials who have a number of different titles, although they are increasingly being known as Environmental Health Officers (EHOs). EHOs are usually members of the Chartered Institution of Environmental Health (CIEH), the qualification for which is either passing the institution's Diploma in Environmental Health, or obtaining a degree or post-graduate diploma in environmental health from a recognised institution of higher education. The CIEH has over 7000 members, most of whom are employed by local authorities throughout the country. EHOs have all the powers of an HSE inspector (see above).

2.54   The Health and Safety (Enforcing Authority) Regulations 1998 drew a clear line between the responsibilities of the HSE and local authorities. The regulations basically apply three principles, namely allocation of premises shall be based on the concept of the main activity carried on, dual inspection is to be avoided, and there shall be no self-inspection by enforcing authorities. Local authorities will be allocated responsibility for premises as specified in schedule 1 of the regulations.

Enforcement

Local authority enforcement

2.55   The following are the main activities which determine whether local authorities will be enforcing authorities.

1. The sale or storage of goods for retail or wholesale distribution except:
   (a) at container depots where the main activity is the storage of goods in the course of transit to or from dock premises, an airport or a railway
   (b) where the main activity is the sale or storage for wholesale distribution of any substance or preparation dangerous for supply
   (c) where the main activity is the sale or storage of water or sewage or their by-products or natural or town gas
   and, for the purposes of this paragraph, where the main activity carried out in premises is the sale and fitting of motor car tyres, exhausts, windscreens or sunroofs, the main activity shall be deemed to be the sale of goods.
2. The display or demonstration of goods at an exhibition for the purposes of an offer or advertisement for sale.
3. Office activities.
4. Catering services.
5. The provision of permanent or temporary residential accommodation including the provision of a site for caravans or campers.
6. Consumer services provided in a shop except dry cleaning or radio and television repairs, and in this paragraph "consumer services" means services of a type ordinarily supplied to persons who receive them otherwise than in the course of a trade, business or other undertaking carried on by them (whether for profit or not).
7. Cleaning (wet or dry) in coin-operated units in launderettes and similar premises.
8. The use of a bath, sauna or solarium, massaging, hair transplanting, skin piercing, manicuring or other cosmetic services and therapeutic treatments, except where they are carried out under the supervision or control of a registered medical practitioner, a dentist registered under the Dentists Act 1984, a physiotherapist, an osteopath or a chiropractor.

9. The practice or presentation of the arts, sports, games, entertainment or other cultural or recreational activities except where the main activity is the exhibition of a cave to the public.
10. The hiring out of pleasure craft for use on inland waters.
11. The care, treatment, accommodation or exhibition of animals, birds or other creatures, except where the main activity is horse breeding or horse training at a stable, or is an agricultural activity or veterinary surgery.
12. The activities of an undertaker, except where the main activity is embalming or the making of coffins.
13. Church worship or religious meetings.
14. The provision of car parking facilities within the perimeter of an airport.
15. The provision of childcare, or playgroup or nursery facilities.

Activities for which the HSE is the enforcing authority

2.56   Where the main activity carried on in non-domestic premises is not covered by schedule 1, the HSE is the enforcing authority. This would cover factories, etc. In addition, the HSE is the enforcing authority for local authorities' premises, police and fire authorities, international organisations, the Crown, s.6 of HSWA (manufacturers, etc, see paragraph 3.90) and the following activities, set out in Schedule 2.

1. Any activity in a mine or quarry in respect of which notice of abandonment has been given under s.139(2) of the Mines and Quarries Act 1954.
2. Any activity in a fairground.
3. Any activity in premises occupied by a radio, television or film undertaking in which the activity of broadcasting, recording or filming is carried on, and the activity of broadcasting, recording or filming wherever carried on, and for this purpose "film" includes videos.
4. The following activities carried on at any premises by persons who do not normally work in the premises:
   (a) construction work if:
      (i) regulation 7(1) of the Construction (Design and Management) Regulations 2007 (which requires projects that include or are intended to include construction work to be notified to the Executive) applies to the project which includes the work, or
      (ii) the whole or part of the work contracted to be undertaken by

the contractor at the premises is to be external fabric or other external part of a building or structure, or

(iii) it is carried out in a physically segregated area of the premises, the activities normally carried out in that area have been suspended for the purpose of enabling the construction work to be carried out, the contractor has authority to exclude from that area persons who are not attending in connection with the carrying out of the work and the work is not the maintenance of insulation on pipes, boilers or other parts of heating or water systems or its removal from them

(b) the installation, maintenance or repair of any gas system, or any work in relation to a gas fitting

(c) the installation, maintenance or repair of electricity systems

(d) work with ionising radiations except work in one or more of the categories set out in schedule 3 to the Ionising Radiations Regulations 1999.

5. The use of ionising radiations for medical exposure (within the meaning of regulation 2(1) of the Ionising Radiations Regulations 1999).

6. Any activity in premises occupied by a radiography undertaking in which there is carried on any work with ionising radiations.

7. Agricultural activities, and any activity at an agricultural show which involves the handling of livestock or working of agricultural equipment.

8. Any activity on board a seagoing ship.

9. Any activity in relation to a ski slope, ski-lift, ski-tow or cable-car.

10. Fish, maggot and game breeding, except in a zoo.

11. Any activity in relation to a pipeline within the meaning of regulation 3 of the Pipelines Safety Regulations 1996.

2.57   Where premises are multi-occupied, each part separately occupied is regarded as separate premises for the purpose of enforcement allocation.

2.58   It may be noted at this stage that the Offshore Safety Act 1992 transferred responsibility for health and safety on offshore installations from the Department of Energy to the HSE, following recommendations made in the Cullen Report, which enquired into the Piper Alpha disaster.

2.59   In order to establish a certain amount of consistency of approach, the HSE has established a Local Authority Unit (LAU), which prepares guidance for Environmental Health Officers (EHOs). The LAU provides the secretariat for the HSE local authority Enforcement Liaison Committee (HELA) which acts as a forum for the exchange of information and informal discussions and also attempts to arrive at practical co-operation between the HSE and local authorities. Additionally, each HSE area office has a liaison officer, whose task it is to maintain links with local authorities and provide advice and assistance, with particular reference to the provisions of training and the dissemination of information. The HSE has published a policy statement on the approach to be taken to enforcement of health and safety legislation by the HSE and local authority environmental health departments (HSE41: *HSE enforcement policy statement*, available from HSE Books).

Self-inspection

2.60   On the principle that there shall be no self-inspection, the HSE will inspect the premises of the local authorities, and the local authorities will inspect those belonging to the HSE (even though it is a Crown body). Although it might be expected that local authorities should be regarded as good employers and aware of their responsibilities, there have been several cases where they have been prosecuted by the HSE and convicted of offences under HSWA. Hopefully, this is an indication of human weakness within the organisation, rather than a wilful or neglectful disregard of the standards on health and safety.

Transfer of authority

2.61   Regulation 5 of the Health and Safety (Enforcing Authority) Regulations 1998 enables the responsibility for enforcement to be transferred in a particular case from the HSE to a local authority, or from a local authority to the HSE. This may be done by agreement between the enforcing authority which has current responsibility and the authority to which it is proposed to transfer. The new enforcing authority will then give notice of the transfer to persons affected by it.

2.62   In cases of uncertainty, in respect of any premises, part of premises or any activity, responsibility may be assigned to the local authority or the HSE as appropriate by the other enforcement authority.

Alternatively, either authority may apply to the Secretary of State and if he thinks that uncertainty exists, he will take into account the views expressed, inform each party of the views expressed by the other (*R v Health & Safety Commission, ex parte Spelthorne Borough Council*) and assign accordingly, giving notice to the authorities and persons affected by it. Any proposal to transfer the responsibility for premises occupied or controlled by the Crown can only be done with the combined agreement of the HSE, the local authority, and the government department concerned.

2.63   However, if there is a change in the main activity being carried on at the premises, there is an automatic transfer of responsibility from one enforcing authority to the other. It is not necessary to go through the formal procedure for effecting a transfer, because this would result in there being a period of time when there would be no one charged with the task of enforcement (*Hadley v Hancox*).

2.64   It will be recalled that responsibility for enforcing legislation relating to air pollution (including s.5 of HSWA) has been transferred to the Environment Agency, or local authorities, as appropriate (see paragraph 2.5).

Employment Medical Advisory Service (EMAS)

2.65   There has been a medical branch of the Factory Inspectorate since 1898, but a new streamlined medical service was created by the Employment Medical Advisory Service Act 1972, and it commenced operations in 1973. Its existence was continued by virtue of Part II of HSWA, and EMAS is now an integral part of the HSE.

2.66   The functions of EMAS are laid down in s.55 of HSWA, and are as follows:
   (a) securing that the Secretary of State, the HSE, employers' organisations, trade unions, and occupational health practitioners can be kept informed and adequately advised on matters of which they ought to take notice, concerning the safeguarding and improvement of the health of persons who are employed or who are seeking employment or training for employment
   (b) giving to employed persons and persons seeking employment or training for employment, information and advice on health in relation to such employment or training

(c) other purposes of the functions of the Secretary of State relating to employment.

2.67 EMAS is headed by a Director of Medical Services, with Senior Employment Medical Advisors to be found throughout the various regions of the country. There is also a Chief Employment Nursing Advisor, and specialist advisors in toxicology, respiratory diseases, pathology research, and the medical aspects of rehabilitation. From its head office, EMAS controls a force of Employment Medical Advisors (EMAs) who are qualified registered medical practitioners and Employment Nursing Advisors (ENAs) who are also qualified in occupational health.

2.68 In order to exercise its statutory functions, EMAS has responsibility for:
(a) advising the inspectorate on the occupational health aspects of regulations and Approved Codes of Practice
(b) regular examinations of persons employed on known hazardous operations
(c) other medical examinations, investigations and surveys
(d) giving advice to the HSE, employers, trade unions and others about the occupational health aspects of poisonous substances, immunological disorders, physical hazards (noise, vibrations, etc) dust, and mental stress, including the laying down of standards of exposure to processes or substances which may harm health
(e) research into occupational health
(f) advice on the provision of occupational medical, nursing and first aid services
(g) advice on the medical aspects of rehabilitation and training for and replacement in employment.

Powers of EMAS

2.69 An employment medical advisor has the same power of entry and investigation as inspectors have under s.20 (above) by virtue of an appointment as such. He can examine workers in those employments which regulations require that they shall be examined at regular intervals (eg Control of Lead at Work Regulations 2002), but he cannot force a person to be examined against his will. Nor will he prescribe any treatment, but will refer workers to their own family general practitioner.

2.70   Advice is also given on the medical aspects of employing young persons (ie below the age of 18).

2.71   Employment Nursing Advisors (ENAs) are an integral part of the service and will visit premises on request or as a result of a visit by an inspector, and give advice and assistance to employers, trade unions, safety officers, safety representatives, etc. They will also give advice to the Disablement Resettlement Officers and others about the advisability of employing someone who has a health problem, enforce the Health and Safety (First Aid) Regulations 1981 and undertake biological monitoring.

2.72   Thus information about suspected health hazards will reach EMAS from a number of sources, enabling an investigation to take place, and advice given on how hazards can be reduced or eliminated. EMAS is frequently used as an advisory service and is constantly engaged in research into health problems, in collaboration with the HSE.

Other institutions

Royal Society for the Prevention of Accidents

2.73   The Royal Society for the Prevention of Accidents (RoSPA) is the largest independent safety organisation in Europe. A major part of its activities are concerned with occupational health and safety and it publishes three journals on the subject: *Occupational Safety and Health*, *RoSPA Bulletin* and *Safety Express*. RoSPA also organises conferences and training courses, and gives advice and assistance to members. Its address is Edgbaston Park, 353 Bristol Road, Birmingham B5 7ST, tel: 0121 248 2000, website: *www.rospa.co.uk*.

British Safety Council

2.74   A non-profit-making independent body, financed entirely by subscriptions from its members, the BSC provides information and training on all aspects of health and safety, will undertake loss control surveys, issues posters and booklets, runs a National Safety Award scheme, and issues a Diploma in Safety Management. The BSC also publishes a magazine, *Safety Management*, and a newsletter, *HSWA Newsletter*. The address is 70 Chancellor's Road, Hammersmith, London W6 9RS, tel: 020 8741 1231, website: *www.britishsafetycouncil.co.uk*.

71

British Standards Institution

2.75   The British Standards Institution (BSI) was incorporated by Royal Charter in 1929, and has as its objectives:

(a) to co-ordinate the efforts of producers and users for the improvement, standardisation and simplification of engineering and industrial materials so as to simplify production and distribution and eliminate national waste of time and material in the production of unnecessary varieties of patterns and sizes of articles used for one and the same purpose

(b) to set up standards of quality and dimensions, prepare and promote the adoption of BSI specifications and schedules, revise, alter and amend these from time to time as experience and circumstances may require

(c) to register, in the name of the BSI, marks of all descriptions, and to approve, affix and license the affixing of such marks

(d) to take any other action as may be necessary or desirable to promote the objectives of the institution.

2.76   The BSI is governed by an executive board consisting of 35 members, who appoint a director general. Over 1000 technical committees perform the day-to-day work of developing appropriate standards. When these are agreed, the final standard can be adopted. The BSI is financed from government funds, sales revenue and individual subscriptions.

2.77   British Standards, in themselves, do not have the force of law. However, the courts may treat them as providing authoritative guidance on a particular topic, as long as they are not out of date. Also, a regulation may make compliance with British Standards compulsory, eg see Furniture and Furnishing (Fire) (Safety) Regulations 1988.

2.78   Manufacturers who adopt the approved standards are entitled to use the BSI Kite Mark, but must agree to supervision and sample testing.

2.79   The BSI increasingly works closely with the International Organization for Standardization (ISO) and other European organisations which have objects similar to its own. The BSI is a member of the European Committee for Standardisation (CEN) and the Committee for Electrotechnical Standardisation (CENELEC) (see paragraph 14.46).

Institution of Occupational Safety and Health

2.80   The Institution of Occupational Safety and Health (IOSH) is the professional body of health and safety practitioners. It has some 27,000 members and was incorporated by Royal Charter in 2003. Members who possess the appropriate qualifications and experience are entitled to call themselves "Chartered Safety and Health Practitioner". Members who have five years' experience of working with health and safety issues and hold appropriate qualifications can become "Technician Members".

British Safety Industry Federation

2.81   The British Safety Industry Federation is a trade body representing manufacturers, etc of safety equipment. It has direct links with government departments and is able to provide advice and information to its members.

CHAPTER 3

Health and Safety at Work, etc Act 1974

The scope of the Act

3.1   The Health and Safety at Work, etc Act 1974 (HSWA) is based on principles and details which are fundamentally different from other health and safety legislation. These differences are designed to bring about a greater awareness of the problems which surround health and safety matters, a greater involvement of those who are, or who should be, concerned with improvements in occupational health and safety and a positive movement away from the apathy and indifference which tended to surround the whole subject.

3.2   In the first place, the Act applies to people, not to premises. It covers all employees in all employment situations with minor exceptions, eg domestic servants. We will not be concerned with problems of interpretation as to whether or not certain premises are, or are not, a factory, a shop, an office, etc. The nature or location of the work is irrelevant. At one stroke, the Act brought within the ambit of protective legislation some 7–8 million people (the "new entrants") who were hitherto not covered by the various statutes then in force, eg Factories Act 1961. Subject only to the exception in respect of domestic employees (see paragraph 3.17) every employer needs to know and to carry out duties required under the Act. Further, the Act requires all employers to take account of the fact that persons who are not in their employment may be affected by work activities, and there are additional duties in this regard. Obligations are placed on those who manufacture, design, import or supply articles or substances for use at work to ensure that these can be used in safety and are without risks to health.

3.3   Next, the Act is basically a criminal statute, and does not give rise to any civil liability (but see paragraph 3.18). No tort action in respect of a breach of statutory duty can be brought; prevention and punishment (rather than compensation) is the keynote. However, to assist the courts when interpreting the Act, regard may be had to legal precedents which have arisen from civil as well as criminal proceedings, provided, of course, that it is appropriate to do so in the context. Additionally the inspectorates are given powers of enforcement in order to eliminate or minimise hazards before an incident occurs, rather than take action afterwards.

3.4 It should be noted that subject to the defence of reasonable practicability, the Act imposes absolute criminal liability. It is not possible, for example, for a corporate employer to avoid liability for an offence on the ground that the "directing mind" or senior management were not involved, or that they had delegated control or supervision of safety matters to competent persons. Under the Act, there is no defence of due diligence (see paragraph 1.119). Thus employers (whether incorporated or not) cannot escape liability on the grounds that they were not personally to blame for a breach of the Act (*R v British Steel plc*).

3.5 Finally, there are some provisions which are designed to bring about a greater personal involvement and individual responsibility so as to actively encourage and promote health and safety, being part of the greater self-regulatory system which the Robens Committee thought to be desirable. Safety policies, risk assessments, safety representatives and safety committees should increase the awareness that the main responsibility for the elimination of accidents and ill health in employment lies with those who create the dangers.

3.6 The requirement for employers to carry out risk assessments (see paragraph 11.197) will focus minds on key problem areas, health surveillance and monitoring should assist in dealing with certain illnesses at an early stage, and also act as a warning sign of possible deficiencies in health and safety practices. Employers are required to give information, training, etc not only to their own employees, but sometimes to non-employees. In other words, health and safety is now high on the agenda.

3.7 How successful the Act has been, or will be in the future, is something we may never know. It is impossible to state how many accidents did not happen as a result of this legislation. Statistics may illustrate trends, and perhaps even lead to some satisfaction, but these are notoriously inconclusive. New machinery, new processes, new designs, new substances, etc may decrease hazards irrespective of legislative arrangements. If nothing else, the Act should play a positive role in ensuring that technological change does not increase the exposure to risks at work. On the other hand, the increasing consciousness of the problems, the growing acceptance that health and safety is the concern of all from the most senior person in the organisation to the most junior, the vast increase in training opportunities and the general streamlining of legal rules should all have a considerable effect in reducing the annual accident figures progressively each year. There must be a limit, however, to the power of the law to influence human conduct, for a majority of accidents occur in situations where there is no actual breach of a legislative provision, but are regarded as common occurrences or human failings (slipping, tripping, falling, etc) which legal control can only prevent if it can induce a state of mind. A knowledge of the legal framework may make a positive contribution to this.

3.8 The Act is sometimes referred to as an "enabling Act". This is merely descriptive of the role envisaged by the Robens Committee, ie that all the old law should be progressively swept away, and replaced by a single statute, supplemented by regulations and Codes of Practice. Since 1974, this pattern has been adopted, so that by the turn of the century the major legislative provisions which were pre-1974 had considerably reduced significance or relevance.

3.9 The Act is divided into four parts. Part I will be the subject of this chapter; Part II provides for the continuation of the Employment Medical Advisory Service (see Chapter 2); Part III (now repealed) made amendments to the Building Regulations (and was the main reason for the curious addition of the word "etc" in the title of the Act) and Part IV contains some miscellaneous provisions. There are also 10 schedules to the Act (three of which have been repealed).

Application of the Act

3.10 The Act applies to all employment in Great Britain (ie England, Wales and Scotland) but not in Northern Ireland. However, by the Health and Safety at Work (Northern Ireland) Order 1978 the provisions of the Act have been repeated so far as Northern Ireland is concerned, with some modifications. The Act does not apply to the Isle of Man or to the Channel Islands, but does apply to the Isles of Scilly.

3.11 By the Health and Safety at Work (Application outside Great Britain) Order 2001 the provisions of the Act have been extended to cover persons working on offshore installations and pipeline work within British territorial waters or the UK sector of the continental shelf, as well as to certain diving and construction work carried on within territorial waters. These provisions are in addition to the Mineral Workings (Offshore Installations) Act 1971 and the regulations made thereunder, the Petroleum and Submarine Pipelines Act 1975, and the Offshore Safety Act 1992.

Application to the Crown

3.12 The provisions of Part I apply to the Crown with the exception of ss.21–25 and 33–42. This means that it is not possible to issue improvement or prohibition notices against the Crown or in respect of Crown premises. However, the Health and Safety Executive (HSE) has taken to issuing Crown Notices (see paragraph 3.115) which have a persuasive effect. Also, it is not possible to prosecute the Crown for any offence committed (based on the theory that the Queen cannot be prosecuted in her own courts), but s.48(2) provides that ss.33–42 (ie the criminal sanctions sections) shall apply to persons in the service of the Crown as they apply to other persons. This means that an individual Crown employee who commits an offence (eg under ss.7, 8, 37, etc) can be prosecuted if necessary. By the National Health Service and Community Care Act 1990, s.60, the National Health Service is not to be regarded as part of the Crown for the purpose of health and safety legislation. Thus prosecutions may be carried out and enforcement notices issued against the NHS.

Trainees

3.13 By the Health and Safety (Training for Employment) Regulations 1990 a person is to be treated as being at work for the purpose of HSWA if he is being provided with relevant training, which is defined as being work experience provided pursuant to a training course or programme, or training for employment, except training provided on a course run by an educational establishment, or training given under a contract of employment. In other words, for the purposes of HSWA, persons on all training for employment schemes (as opposed to training in employment) are to be regarded as employees at work, even though technically they are not employees. The employer, for the purpose of the regulations, is the person whose undertaking is providing the training.

Police

3.14 The Police (Health and Safety) Act 1997 applies the provisions of HSWA to holders of the office of constable (ie police, including police cadets), even though they are not employed under a contract of employment, the deemed employer being the chief officer of police, or Director General of the National Criminal Intelligence Service, or the National Crime Squad. The various provisions of the Employment Rights Act 1996 (ie ss.44, 48, 49 and 100, see paragraph 4.180) giving protection to employees when exercising health and safety rights also apply. The Police Federation is to be treated as a recognised trade union for the purpose of appointing safety representatives under s.2(4) of HSWA (see paragraph 4.110).

3.15 The Police (Health and Safety) Regulations 1999 provide that a person who holds the office of constable or appointment as a police cadet shall be treated as being an employee of the relevant officer for the purpose of all regulations made under HSWA, the only proviso being that a police officer shall be treated as being at work only when he is on duty. Various police staff associations are to be treated as recognised trade unions for the purposes of the Safety Representative and Safety Committees Regulations 1977. Regulation 4(1) of the Personal Protective Equipment at Work Regulations 1992 is amended so that where the characteristics of any policing activity are such that compliance with the duty to provide suitable protective equipment would inevitably conflict with the exercise of police powers or the performance of police duties, the requirement shall be complied with so far as is reasonably practicable. A minor amendment has also been made to regulation 4(4) of the Provision and Use of Work Equipment Regulations 1998, so that the requirements of suitability relating to work equipment used by the police for arrest, restraint, self-defence or as deterrent equipment will only apply to the health and safety of police officers and cadets.

3.16 The ACOP accompanying the Management of Health and Safety at Work Regulations 1999 has amended the earlier code so as to reflect the sometimes inherently dangerous work undertaken by the police, fire-fighters and other emergency service workers.

Domestic employees

3.17 Section 51 provides that none of the statutory provisions shall apply in relation to a person by reason only that he employs another, or is himself employed, as a domestic servant in a private household.

Civil liability (s.47)

3.18 As we have already noted, HSWA is essentially a criminal statute enforced by criminal sanctions. Section 47 specifically provided that nothing in Part I (which contains the relevant provisions so far as this book is concerned) shall be construed as conferring any right of action in any civil proceedings in respect of a failure to comply with any duty imposed by ss.2–7 or a contravention of s.8. Thus no civil action under HSWA can be brought for a breach of statutory duty as a result of an accident. However, if a prosecution is brought under the Act and is successful, it would appear, under the provisions of s.11 of the Civil Evidence Act 1968, that the fact of that prosecution may be raised and pleaded in an action for damages caused by negligence, leaving the defendant with the burden of proving that he was not negligent. Additionally, s.47(2) provides that any breach of duty imposed by health and safety regulations shall be actionable in a civil claim except in so far as the regulations provide otherwise. HSWA does not alter the present rights at common law (see Chapter 12), but does not add to them except as stated.

The general purposes (s.1)

3.19 The provisions of the Act shall have effect with a view to:
(a) securing the health, safety and welfare of persons at work
(b) protecting persons other than persons at work against risks to health or safety arising out of or in connection with the activities of persons at work
(c) controlling the keeping and use of explosives or highly flammable or otherwise dangerous or environmentally hazardous substances, and generally preventing the unlawful acquisition, possession and use of such substances.

3.20 It will be noted that by the Health and Safety at Work, etc Act 1974 (Application to Environmentally Hazardous Substances) Regulations 2002 (as amended) the reference in s.1(1)(c) of HSWA to dangerous substances shall include a reference to environmentally

hazardous substances, for the purpose only of making regulations under
s.15 in order to implement various EU directives, which are concerned
with the transportation by road or rail of dangerous goods, and
emissions from the storage and distribution of petrol.

3.21   The general purposes of the Health and Safety at Work, etc Act
1974 have been extended to include the following:
  (a) securing the safety, health and welfare at work of persons on
      offshore installations or engaged on pipeline works
  (b) securing the safety of such installations and preventing accidents
      on or near them
  (c) securing the proper construction and safe operation of pipelines
      and preventing damage to them
  (d) securing the safe dismantling, removal and disposal of offshore
      installations and pipelines (see Offshore Safety Act 1992, s.1,
      which has the effect of transferring responsibility for all aspects of
      offshore safety from the Department of Energy to HSE).

3.22   The general purposes of the Act shall also include safety matters
relating to on-shore pipelines, in particular:
  (a) securing the proper construction and safe operation of pipelines
      and preventing damage to them
  (b) ensuring that, in the event of an accidental escape or ignition of
      anything in a pipeline, immediate notice of the event will be
      given to persons who will or may have to discharge duties or take
      steps in consequence of the happening of the event
  (c) protecting the public from personal injury, fire, explosions and
      other dangers arising from the transmission, distribution, supply
      or use of gas (including liquid gas) (see Offshore Safety Act 1992,
      s.2(1), repealing, *inter alia*, s.18(1) of the Gas Act 1986).

3.23   Finally, the general purposes of the Act also include:
  (a) securing the proper construction and safe operation of railway
      systems, including locomotives, rolling stock and other vehicles
      used on such systems
  (b) protecting the public (whether passengers or not) from personal
      injury and other risks arising from the construction and operation
      of railway tramways or trolley vehicle systems (Railways Act
      1993, s.117(2)).

3.24   The general scheme of things is progressively to replace all the
enactments specified in schedule 1 of the Act (and regulations, etc made

thereunder) by a system of regulations and Approved Codes of Practice which are designed to maintain and improve standards of health, safety and welfare. Since 1974, this policy has been steadily followed. Virtually all of the Factories Act 1961 and the Offices, Shops and Railway Premises Act 1963 have been repealed in addition to other enactments. New regulations have been introduced, and Codes of Practice have been approved. It is, therefore, essential for all concerned to keep up to date with the latest developments with a field of law that is constantly changing.

The general duties (s.2(1))

3.25   *It shall be the duty of every employer to ensure, so far as is reasonably practicable, the health, safety and welfare at work of all his employees.*

3.26   This is the prime duty under the Act, in respect of which all the other subsequent duties imposed by s.2 are more detailed. As we have seen (see Chapter 1), what is reasonably practicable is a question of fact and evidence in each case (and see paragraph 1.128).

3.27   It must be borne in mind that the duty, placed fairly and squarely on the employer, is a strict one, subject to the defence of reasonably practicable. If the employer is an individual (or an identifiable group of individuals), it would not be difficult to place liability for a failure to comply with s.2(1). However, most employers are corporate bodies, and the question arises: is liability placed on the employer only for the acts or omissions of directors or senior management, or can the corporate body also be liable for the wrongful acts of more junior personnel? In *R v Gateway Foodmarkets*, there was a lift operating in a supermarket, and the company's head office had made arrangements with a reputable firm for regular maintenance and a call-out service. However, there was a faulty electrical contact, which frequently caused the lift to jam. The defect could be cured manually, and the contractors told the store personnel how to do it so as to avoid them having to be called out each time the lift jammed. This practice was unauthorised and no-one at the company's head office knew about it. Following a routine maintenance, contractors left open a trap door in the control room floor. The following day an employee went into the control room in order to free the contact. Unfortunately, he did not see that the trap door was open, and he fell to his death. The company was prosecuted for a breach of s.2(1).

3.28 For the company, it was argued that s.2(1) does not render them liable for the acts or omissions of an employee who could not be regarded as the embodiment of the company (in this case, the store manager who had carried out this practice). It was submitted that the section was limited to the acts or omissions of "the directing mind" of the company, ie senior management and/or head office personnel. However, the Court of Appeal decided to follow the general approach laid down in *R v Associated Octel Co Ltd* (see paragraph 3.73). The onus is on the employer to show that all reasonable precautions were taken by it and by its employees and agents on its behalf. There is no clear legal basis for distinguishing between "management" and other more junior employees. If all reasonable precautions have been taken, then it is not material that the acts of an individual are those of a senior or junior employee. Thus, although the company may have taken reasonable precautions at a senior level, there was a failure at store management level, for which the company was liable under s.2(1), and a conviction was upheld. However, the Court of Appeal left open the question whether an employer would be liable in circumstances where the only negligence or failure to take reasonable precautions had taken place at some more junior level.

3.29 The duty is owed to employees while they are in the course of their employment, but is not confined to the times when the employee is actually working. The duty is broken if the employer makes available unsafe plant or an unsafe system of work, etc even though these have not yet been put into operation or use. In *Bolton Metropolitan Borough Council v Malrod Insulations Ltd*, contractors were engaged to strip asbestos insulation, for which task a special decontamination unit was to be used. Before the work had commenced, an Environmental Health Officer (EHO) inspected the decontamination unit, and discovered several defects, which could have given rise to electric shocks. The contractors were prosecuted for a breach of ss.2(1) and 2(2) of the Act. In their defence, it was argued that no offence could be committed until the employees were "at work" using the decontamination unit. The argument was upheld in the crown court, but the decision was reversed by the Divisional Court. The employer's duty under s.2(2) was "to provide" safe plant and safe systems of work, and thus the duty arose in respect of employees who *will be* at work, as well as those who *are* at work. To hold otherwise would mean that an inspector who came on to the premises at the end of a working day and discovered breaches of the law would be powerless to take any action because the employees were not actually at work at the time of the inspection, a conclusion which is not consistent with the statutory health and safety provisions. Further, the duty under s.2(1) of the Act applies to the employer's duty to all his employees, not just to those employees who are engaged on a specific process. An employee can be exposed to a risk of injury from unsafe plant even though he is not engaged on the process or work being carried on.

3.30 It must be borne in mind that the Act does not prevent dangerous work; it is designed to ensure that work — even dangerous work — can be done in a way that is safe. Thus in *Langridge v Howletts Zoo & Port Lympne Estates Ltd*, a local authority issued a prohibition notice designed to prevent keepers entering an enclosure in a wild animal park where there were tigers roaming around freely. This followed an incident when a keeper had been mauled to death by a tiger. The notice would have prohibited keepers from entering the enclosure unless the tigers were anaesthetised, immobilised or otherwise made safe. The owners of the animal park argued that it was necessary for keepers to enter the enclosure in order to achieve "bonding", so that the tigers could be successfully released into the wild. An employment tribunal modified the notice to allow the previous practice to continue, albeit with a new system of work designed to reduce the risks to the keepers. On an appeal, the judge held that if the council's submissions were upheld, then certain types of dangerous work would be proscribed. The Act is not concerned with what work is being done, but with the manner of performing it. On the facts of the case, the council's appeal was dismissed.

3.31 The phrase "health, safety and welfare" is not defined. Clearly, "health" includes mental as well as physical health and "safety" refers to the absence of any foreseeable injury. Welfare, on the other hand, is a somewhat elusive concept. Schedule 3 of HSWA provides that regulations may be made for "Securing the provision of specified welfare facilities for persons at work, including, in particular, such things as adequate water supply, sanitary conveniences, washing and bathing facilities, ambulance and first aid arrangements, cloakroom accommodation, sitting facilities and refreshment facilities". It is clear that this list is not an exhaustive definition of welfare, and indeed, some of them may well be regarded as health matters. Social clubs may be generally regarded as being part of a firm's welfare facilities, but since employees do not use them in the course of their employment, they are not within the scope of the Act. There is no obligation on an employer to concern himself with health, safety or welfare matters that arise outside the employment, although this is being done increasingly as part of advanced personnel policies.

3.32 The duties of an employer under ss.2–6 are owed to each employee individually, as well as collectively. Thus, special care must be taken where employees with special needs are employed, eg persons with disabilities, young or inexperienced workers, pregnant women, etc (see Chapter 11).

Particular duties (s.2(2))

3.33 The above general duty is particularised by five specific duties placed on the employer, which spell out the general duty in detail. These duties, which as we have noted are essentially criminal in nature, are very similar to the duties of care which an employer owes to his employees at common law and which are frequently raised in civil actions (see Chapter 12). They must all be fulfilled "as far as is reasonably practicable". Thus, meanings which have been given to certain words and phrases in civil actions may be used as an aid in interpreting the words used in the Act, for although the issues in criminal and civil proceedings are different, the canons of statutory interpretations (see paragraph 1.121) generally apply to both types of proceedings.

3.34 It must further be borne in mind that the particular duties which follow are spelt out in even greater detail by the regulations outlined in subsequent chapters, ie Management of Health and Safety at Work, Provision and Use of Work Equipment, Workplace (Health, Safety and Welfare), Personal Protective Equipment at Work, Manual Handling Operations and Health and Safety (Display Screen Equipment). Thus, s.2 of HSWA must be read in conjunction with these and other regulations.

3.35 *To provide and maintain plant and systems of work that are, so far as is reasonably practicable, safe and without risks to health* (s.2(2)(a)).

3.36 An employer "provides" when the plant, etc is in a place where it can be easily come by, or when he gives clear directions as to where it can be obtained (*Norris v Syndic Manufacturing Co Ltd*). Thus, in *Woods v*

Durable Suites, the employee was working with a synthetic glue, which could cause dermatitis unless certain precautions were taken. The employers instructed the employee in the proper procedure to be followed and provided washing facilities and a barrier cream, but the employee did not take the necessary precautions and contracted dermatitis. It was held that the employers had fulfilled their common law duty of care, for they had provided the necessary precautions. They were under no duty to compel the employee to use the barrier cream or to stand over him to ensure that he used the washing facilities.

3.37 The duty to provide may be observed even though the employee does not use that which is provided. In certain cases, however, it has been held that the employers' common law duty may be something more than the passive one of providing and includes the more active duty of encouraging, persuading and even insisting on the use of the precautions (see Chapter 12). On other occasions the law may well go further and place an obligation on the employee *to use* the precautions supplied, eg under the Personal Protective Equipment at Work Regulations 1992 (see Chapter 6). But if the employer fails to provide the necessary equipment, or provides defective equipment, he will be in breach of his duty. In *Lovett v Blundells and Crompton & Co*, the employee erected a makeshift staging in order to do his work. This collapsed and he was injured. It was held that the employer had not provided adequate equipment for the work to be done in safety.

3.38 Once having provided the necessary plant, etc the employer must ensure that it is maintained and in a condition which makes it fit for use. Plant and systems of work are "maintained" safe when they are kept in efficient working order at all times. Thus if there is a single failure of a component, this will normally be sufficient evidence that the equipment has not been properly maintained. Under the absolute provisions of the Factories Act 1961 it was never a defence for an employer to argue that he could not have discovered the defect before an accident occurred (*Galashields Gas Co v O'Donnell*), but under s.2(2)(a) the burden on the employer is to fulfil his obligation so far as is reasonably practicable. Maintenance is a matter of forethought and foresight. There must be a proper system of regular inspection with the reporting of defects to a responsible person. In *Barkway v South Wales Transport Co*, a coach crashed owing to a burst tyre and the plaintiff's husband was killed. Although the defendants could show a system of testing and inspecting tyres, they did not require their drivers to report incidents which could produce impact fractures and were thus held liable for negligence.

3.39   Maintenance also requires the rectification of known defects, either by repairs or replacement, as necessary. In *Taylor v Rover Car Co Ltd*, the employee was injured when a splinter of steel flew from the top of a chisel he was using. The chisel had previously been used by a leading hand on the production line, who had himself been injured when a splinter had flown off, but this incident was not reported. It was held that the employers were liable, for they should have had a system whereby defective tools were reported and withdrawn from circulation and replaced by ones which were not defective.

3.40   Routine maintenance, as well as revealing defects, can prolong the life of the plant or machinery, etc thus creating a cost benefit for the employer as well as making it safe for the user. It is further suggested that manufacturers of articles for use at work should include maintenance schedules along with the articles they sell, as being part of "the conditions necessary to ensure that when put to use it will be safe and without risks to health".

3.41   Section 53(1) states that the term "plant" includes any machinery, equipment or appliance. In accordance with the *ejusdem generis* rule of interpretation, it is unlikely that the word includes "buildings" of any kind (contrary to the popular use of the word) as these would be covered by s.4 of the Act (see paragraph 3.82). But the definition is not exhaustive, and there is no indication of what else may be included. At common law, a van was held to be "plant" (see *Bradford v Robinson Rentals Ltd*, see paragraph 12.32).

3.42   Systems of work was defined by Lord Greene in *Speed v Thomas Swift & Co Ltd*, who said, "It may be the physical layout of the job — the setting of the stage, so to speak — the sequence in which the work is to be carried out, the provision in proper cases of warnings and notices, and the issue of special instructions." To this we may add the provision of safety equipment and the taking of adequate safety precautions. Whatever system of work is adopted, the employer must ensure, so far as is reasonably practicable, that it is a safe one.

3.43   *To ensure, so far as is reasonably practicable, safety and the absence of risks to health in connection with the use, handling, storage and transport of articles and substances (s.2(2)(b)).*

3.44   In appropriate cases, protective clothing, proper equipment and tools, etc must be provided in relation to use. The handling must be organised in a safe manner, eg excessive weights should be considered, contamination should be guarded against, dangerous parts should be covered, etc. Storage facilities must be adequate and safe, eg proper racks provided, fork-lift truck drivers must be instructed in proper stacking techniques. The transportation must be done in a safe manner: loads must be properly tied down, with an even distribution of weight, goods must be packed properly so as to be safe when being transported.

3.45   *To provide such information, instruction, training and supervision as is necessary to ensure, so far as is reasonably practicable, the health and safety at work of all employees (s.2(2)(c)).*

3.46   Thus, information must be given to employees about the hazards involved in the work, and the precautions to be taken to avoid them. Since the employer will, in most cases, be in a better position to know of those hazards, he must provide the information, not wait for the employees to request it. In addition to the general requirement of s.2(2), there are a number of specific statutory provisions which require an employer to provide detailed information to employees in particular circumstances (see Chapter 4).

3.47   The information which is provided must be accurate and meaningful. In *Vacwell Engineering Ltd v BDH Chemicals Ltd*, the plaintiff purchased a quantity of boron tribromide from the defendant. The chemical was delivered in ampoules which were labelled "Harmful Vapour". The chemical was poured on to some water, and an explosion resulted, causing damage to the plaintiff's premises. It was held that the defendants were liable for negligently labelling a dangerous substance. The information given was misleading and did not accurately describe the hazard.

3.48   Proper and clear instructions must be given as to what is to be done, and what must not be done, for workers performing routine tasks are frequently heedless of their own safety. Greater care must be taken when dealing with employees whose command of English is weak so that they understand clearly the nature of the dangers and the precautions to be taken. Young and inexperienced workers must be given clear instructions.

3.49   The employer's duty to provide information and instruction to ensure the health and safety of his own employees includes a duty to provide such information and instruction to the employees of a subcontractor where this is necessary to ensure the health and safety of the employees. In *R v Swan Hunter Shipbuilders Ltd*, the employers distributed a booklet to their employees giving practical rules for the safety of users of oxygen equipment, in particular warning of the dangers of oxygen enrichment in confined spaces. The booklet was not distributed to employees of a subcontractor except on request. A fire broke out on a ship which the appellants were building and because an employee of a subcontractor left an oxygen hose in the deck, the fire became intense because that part of the ship, which was badly ventilated, became oxygen enriched. As a result, eight workmen were killed. The appellants were prosecuted on indictment for a breach of s.2(2)(a) (failure to provide a safe system of work), s.2(2)(c) (failure to provide information and instruction) and s.3(1) (duty to non-employees). The appellants were convicted in the crown court, and an appeal was dismissed by the Court of Appeal. If the provision of a safe system of work for the benefit of an employer's own employees involved the provision of information and instruction as to potential dangers to persons other than his own employees, then the employer was under a duty to provide such information and instruction. In the circumstances, it was reasonably practicable to do so.

3.50   Training in safe working practices should be undertaken on a regular basis; where special courses are available, employees should be required, not merely encouraged, to go on them (eg for fork-lift truck drivers, or when handling heavy weights). Where appropriate, "in-house" training can be given. The employee is under a legal duty to co-operate with the employer (s.7(2), see paragraph 3.106), and hence a refusal to go on an appropriate training course, as well as being a possible offence under the Act, may well be grounds for fair dismissal (see Chapter 13). Sometimes regulations will specify the actual training to be given, including the syllabus, but otherwise the training may be carried out by the employer or an independent body. As long as it is adequate, the requirements of HSWA will be met.

3.51   A failure to provide training for employees could lead to an improvement notice being issued. In *Sunner v Radford*, a local authority inspector while inspecting a supermarket noticed that a fork-lift truck was not being operated correctly. He also discovered that the two employees who drove the truck had never received any formal training. He served an improvement notice requiring the employer to send the men on a course of training for fork-lift truck drivers and, on appeal, an employment tribunal upheld the notice. The employer had failed to provide such training as was reasonably practicable to ensure the safety of employees at work.

3.52   A suitable and satisfactory system of supervision must be provided with properly trained and competent supervisors who have authority to ensure that safety precautions are implemented, safety equipment used, and safe systems followed. Young and inexperienced employees in particular must be properly supervised.

3.53   *So far as is reasonably practicable, to ensure the maintenance of any place of work under the employer's control in a condition that is safe and without risks to health, and the provision and maintenance of means of access and exit that are safe and without such risks* (s.2(2)(d)).

3.54   Thus premises must be safe and maintained safe. Obstacles must be removed, dangerous wiring replaced, defective floors and stairs repaired, roads, pavements, pathways, doors, etc must all be safe.

3.55   *The provision and maintenance of a working environment that is, so far as is reasonably practicable, safe, without risks to health, and adequate as regards facilities and arrangements for the welfare of employees at work* (s.2(2)(e)).

3.56   Thus the employer must pay proper regard for systems of noise control, eliminate noxious fumes and dust, lighting must not be excessive or inadequate. Welfare arrangements and facilities must be adequate, eg toilet accommodation, washing facilities, cloakroom arrangements, etc. Ergonomic factors, such as seating, posture, reaching, etc may also need to be considered.

3.57   It will be recognised that the above statutory duties bear a strong resemblance to those duties owed by an employer to an employee at common law (see Chapter 12) spelt out in greater detail. Under s.2 of HSWA these duties may only be enforced by criminal sanctions or by the use of an enforcement notice (see paragraph 3.115).

3.58   The general nature of the employer's obligations under s.2(2) are spelt out in even greater detail by regulations, in particular the "six pack" regulations originally passed in 1992 in order to comply with EU directives (see Chapter 4 and Chapter 6).

Safety policies (s.2(3))

3.59   Every employer shall prepare (and as often as may be appropriate revise) a written statement of his general policy with respect to:

  (a) the health and safety at work of his employees
  (b) the organisation and arrangements in force for the time being for carrying out that policy

and bring the statement and any revision of it to the notice of all his employees.

3.60   However, this duty does not apply to any employer who carries on an undertaking in which for the time being he employs less than five employees (Employers' Health and Safety Policy Statements (Exception) Regulations 1975).

3.61   In *Osborne v Bill Taylor of Huyton Ltd*, the employer owned and controlled 31 betting shops. Each shop employed three people, but two of them were entitled to have a day off work each week, during which time relief staff were employed. An improvement notice was served on the employer requiring him to prepare a written safety policy and when he failed to do so he was prosecuted for contravening the notice. The Divisional Court held that the words "for the time being" meant "at any one time" and thus the relief staff were to be excluded when determining the number of employees employed for the purpose of the Exception Regulations. However, the further question to be asked was whether the employer was carrying on 31 separate businesses or one business in 31 different places. In the latter case, the employer would not be excluded from the duty to prepare a written safety policy. It was held that there was one business with more than five employees employed at any one time, and therefore the prosecution could succeed. To determine whether there is a single business run through a number of outlets, or whether a person has set up a series of separate businesses (albeit that each of those businesses are of the same nature) it is necessary to look at the manner in which the activities are run. If there is a series of separate legal bodies running each enterprise, almost certainly each will be a separate undertaking. Control from the centre is an indication that there is a single undertaking.

3.62 The drawing up of the safety policy is the beginning of the commitment of the employer to safety and health at work. There is no standard policy, no precedent which can be adopted. Each employer must work it out for himself, bearing in mind the nature of the hazards involved and the precautions and protections needed. General advice on the drawing up of safety policies may be sought from a number of sources (employers' associations, safety organisations, etc) but the responsibility is placed fairly and squarely on the shoulders of each employer. Studies have revealed that while some policy statements lay down a general commitment, they lack details of "the organisation and arrangements in force" for the carrying out of the policy. Moreover, there is a need to review and revise the policy statement regularly, particularly following any changes to working practices, organisational structure, etc.

3.63 The Act requires the statement to be brought to the notice of all employees. This is not done merely by affixing a policy statement to a notice board. Some employers issue the statement as a paper communication which conforms with the law but is not necessarily good practice, for sheets of paper are frequently lost or destroyed. Perhaps the best method is by introducing the policy statement on an induction course and publishing it together with the works rules or information handbook which is given to employees. Particular attention should be paid to those employees whose command of English is limited and steps must be taken to draw attention to the policy in a language they understand.

3.64 A safety policy can be drawn up in the following manner.

General statement

3.65 This will specify the commitment of the employer to a standard at least as high as that required by law. It should make clear that management considers it to be a binding commitment and that safety will rank as a prominent and permanent feature of all activities. The objectives should be spelt out, eg to reduce and eliminate accidents, to achieve a safe and healthy working environment, and so forth.

Organisation

3.66   The distribution of responsibility should be detailed, starting with the management board, through the different levels of management, supervision, safety officer and safety representatives, medical personnel and ending with the responsibilities of employees. Where there are a number of sites or departments, responsibilities should be fixed as appropriate. It is probably good practice to identify the person responsible in each case, either by name or by position. The lines of communication for dealing with grievances, complaints or suggestions about health and safety matters should be stated.

Arrangements in force

3.67   The existence of the arrangements must be stated in relation to the objectives to be achieved in each case. For example, on health, state details of the first-aid facilities, fire precautions, medical arrangements, etc. On safety, specify training, supervision, safety equipment, safety precautions, safety rules, maintenance practices, etc. On welfare, specify washing facilities provided, requirements relating to ventilation, heating, lighting, etc. Stress the need for all employees to be involved in good housekeeping, to co-operate with management and to report any defects or potential hazards.

Review

3.68   Safety policies should be reviewed (and revised if necessary) when there are changes in the law, new processes introduced, new hazards revealed, or when health and safety problems are revealed.

3.69   Safety policies cannot be adequately reviewed unless there is periodic monitoring. This may well be one of the functions of the safety committee but the prime responsibility must always rest with senior management. The statement should be dated and signed by the senior person in the organisation so that employees will recognise that it is an authoritative document and will note the ongoing commitment.

3.70   Safety policies should be seen to work. They should not be a mere formality to satisfy the curiosity of visiting inspectors.

General duties owed to others (s.3)

3.71   Every employer is under a duty to conduct his undertaking in such a way as to ensure, so far as is reasonably practicable, that persons not in his employment who may be affected thereby are not exposed to risks to their health and safety. A similar duty is imposed on self-employed persons, in respect of themselves and other persons not being their employees (s.3(2)). The Genetically Modified Organisms (Contained Use) Regulations 2000 provide that in relation to an activity involving genetic modification the reference to a self-employed person shall include a reference to any person who is not an employer or employee in relation to any activity involving genetic manipulation. This would include, for example, a research student.

3.72   Section 3 is designed to give protection to the general public or other non-employees to ensure that they are not at risk from workplace hazards, etc. Thus, it would be an offence under the Act (irrespective of any other heading of legal liability) if a construction firm were to permit an explosion to take place which causes windows to break in nearby houses, or for a firm to permit the seepage of a poisonous chemical into a private water supply. Visitors who come on to the employer's premises, subcontractors who come to work there, students who are on a university campus, etc are all within the class of persons who may be affected by the way the undertaking is being carried on. Whether such people have a right of civil action is irrelevant to the criminal liability of the employer in respect of a breach of the duty.

3.73   To establish criminal liability under s.3(1), it is not necessary to show that the employer had any control over the operation in question as part of his undertaking. It is sufficient to show that the operation in question came within the employer's conduct of his undertaking. The question of control, however, may be relevant to the defence of "reasonably practicable". Thus, in *R v Associated Octel Co Ltd*, the company had closed down production processes for pre-planned annual maintenance. The task of repairing the lining of a tank within the chlorine plant was entrusted to a specialist contractor. As the plant was designated a major hazard site under what is now the Control of Major Accident Hazards Regulations 1999 (see paragraph 7.82) the company was obliged to submit a safety case to the HSE. The case required contractors to conform to a permit-to-work system. However, this was not properly implemented, with the result that an employee of the contractor was seriously burned. The company was convicted of an offence under s.3(1). On appeal, it was argued that the company was not liable for the actions of independent contractors, and that it was the contractor who was conducting the undertaking. The latter should have been responsible for deciding how the work was to be done and the precautions to be taken. However, the Court of Appeal dismissed the appeal, and this decision was confirmed by the House of Lords. The term "undertaking" meant "enterprise" or "business". The cleaning, maintenance or repair of plant, machinery or buildings necessary for carrying on the business was part of the undertaking, whether carried out by the employer's employees or by independent contractors. Thus there was *prima facie* liability under s.3(1). The House of Lords also disapproved of an earlier decision in *RMC Roadstone Products Ltd v Jester*, which appears to suggest that the liability of an employer under s.3(1) for acts of subcontractors depended on there being actual or shared control over the conduct of the undertaking.

3.74 It is a question of fact in each case whether the activity can be described as being part of the employer's undertaking. Thus if an independent contractor comes on to an employer's premises to do some repair work to the employer's machinery, the work will fall within s.3. If, on the other hand, the independent contractor takes the machinery away for repair, and does it on his own premises, the employer will have no control over the way the work is done, and thus s.3 will not apply.

3.75 The House of Lords further pointed out that if an employer engages an independent contractor to do work which forms part of the employer's undertaking, he must stipulate for whatever conditions are needed to avoid those risks and are reasonably practicable. The employer cannot, having omitted to do so, say that he was not in a position to exercise control. Thus once the "undertaking" test has been satisfied, in the sense that the work is for the business or ancillary to it, the only defence for an employer is that he took such steps as were reasonably practicable. The form of control, if any, he has over the independent contractor is basically irrelevant. Thus if the employer has no control whatsoever over the way an independent contractor did the work, it might not be reasonably practicable for him to do other than rely on the contractor to take the necessary precautions, but it is possible to stipulate that such precautions must be taken, and to take whatever supervisory steps as are possible to ensure that those precautions are implemented. Further, if the employer is aware of special hazards, or the work involves the co-ordination of activities between several contractors, or between the contractor and the employer's employees, then again the employer must take reasonably practicable steps. A large organisation, with a high level of expertise, would have more control over the activities of a contractor than a small employer would. Some employers would have a higher level of competence or expertise than others. On the facts of the instant case, *Associated Octel* had assumed sufficient measure of control over the safety precautions as to bring them within s.3(1).

3.76 Further, "the risks" to which non-employees should not be exposed to include the possibility of danger or injury, and s.3(l) is not confined to actual accidents or instances of ill health. In *R v Board of Trustees of the Science Museum*, it was alleged that an air-conditioning system at the Science Museum exposed members of the public to risks to their health from *Legionella pneumophila* (LP), because there was a failure to institute a system of regular cleaning and disinfection, etc. For the museum it was argued that the prosecution had to show that members of the public actually inhaled the bacterium, but this argument was rejected by the Court of Appeal. The term "risk" conveys the notion of possible danger, not actual danger. This is in accordance with the purposive construction which the courts give to the Act so as to promote the preventative aims.

3.77 The duty imposed by s.3(1) is wide enough to include the duty to provide information and instruction to persons who are not in the employer's employment (*R v Swan Hunter Shipbuilders Ltd* (see paragraph 3.49)).

3.78 The words "conduct his undertaking" do not appear to apply to the effects which a deleterious product may have on an ultimate consumer, where the ordinary law of negligence (as in *Donoghue v Stevenson*) or the provisions of the Consumer Protection Act 1987 will apply.

3.79 A person may be "conducting his undertaking" even though his "business" is closed. In *R v Mara*, the accused was a director of a small cleaning company which had a contract to clean the premises of a supermarket each weekday morning. It was also agreed that the cleaning machines used by the company would be left on the supermarket's premises to be used by the latter's employees. The accused knew that an electric cable on a cleaning machine was defective.

An employee of the supermarket used the cleaning machine and because of the defect was electrocuted. The accused was charged with consenting to and conniving with (see s.37, *post*) a breach of the Health and Safety at Work, etc Act, s.3(1), in that the company had failed to conduct its undertaking in such a way as to ensure that persons not in its employment were not exposed to risks to their health and safety. For the accused it was argued that at the time of the accident the company was not carrying on its undertaking because it was closed and the only undertaking being carried on was that of the supermarket. This contention was rejected by the Court of Appeal. It was the business of the company to provide cleaning services. To do this it cleaned the premises on weekday mornings and left the cleaning machines for the use of employees of the supermarket. Those employees were clearly persons who may be affected by the way the company carried on its undertaking and the conviction was upheld.

3.80   The fact that the offence was committed by an employee, or an appointed safety advisor, will no longer amount to a defence for any contravention of any statutory provision. Thus, in *R v Nelson Group Services (Maintenance) Ltd*, the company was involved in the installation, servicing and maintenance of gas appliances. A fitter, who had been properly trained to perform his work competently, left a gas fitting in a condition which exposed the occupier of the house to health and safety risks. It was held that the employer had done everything reasonably practicable to ensure that the employee had a safe system of work laid down, had the appropriate skills and instruction, was subject to adequate supervision, and had been provided with safe plant and equipment for the proper performance of the work. An isolated act of neglect by the employee performing the work did not render the employer criminally liable. However, regulation 21 of the Management of Health and Safety at Work Regulations 1999 appears to have closed this line of defence. It provides that nothing in any relevant statutory provision shall operate so as to afford a defence in any criminal proceedings for a contravention of those provisions by reason of any act or default of an employee or a person appointed to provide health and safety assistance (see paragraph 4.28). But the ACOP accompanying the regulations states that in practice, enforcement inspectors will doubtless take into account the circumstances of the case before deciding on the appropriateness of enforcement action, including the fact that the employer has taken reasonable steps to satisfy himself of the competency of the employee or safety assistant concerned.

3.81 In such cases as may be prescribed, and in the circumstances and prescribed manner, it shall be the duty of every employer and every self-employed person to give to persons who are not his employees, but who may be affected by the way he conducts his undertaking, the prescribed information about such aspects of the way he conducts his undertaking as might affect their health or safety (s.3(3)). This subsection is clearly designed to ensure that persons living near to some hazardous operation have some form of advance notification of what they may expect if something goes wrong and the necessary action they should take. To date, no regulations requiring the disclosure of any such information have been made. However, under the Control of Major Accident Hazards Regulations 1999, operators who control installations carrying out certain dangerous activities must prepare a site emergency plan for dealing with any major accident and may be required to provide information to the public (see paragraph 7.82).

General duties of controllers of premises (s.4)

3.82 This section imposes duties on people who have the control over non-domestic premises, or of the means of access thereto or exit therefrom, or of any plant or substances therein, which are used by persons (who are not their own employees) as a place of work or as a place where they may use plant or substances provided there for their use. The duty is to take such measures as it is reasonable for a person in his position to take to ensure, so far as is reasonably practicable, that the premises, the means of access and exit, and any plant or substance in or provided for use there, is or are safe and without risks to health.

3.83 Residential premises are clearly domestic premises, but the common parts of those premises, ie those parts which are not exclusively used for domestic purposes, are non-domestic. In *Westminster City Council v Select Managements Ltd*, the defendants owned and managed a block of flats. An improvement notice was served on them relating to the lifts and electrical installations which serviced the common parts of the flats. They appealed against the notice, arguing that the lifts, etc were "domestic premises" within the meaning of s.4 of the Act. The validity of the notice was upheld by the Court of Appeal. The common parts of the block of flats (eg the hallway, lift, stairs, landing, etc) were non-domestic premises. These common parts were available to persons who were not in the employment of the flat owners as a place of work or as a place where they may use plant (eg the lifts). Thus an improvement notice could properly be served.

3.84 It would appear from this decision that premises will be regarded as being non-domestic if they are not in the exclusive occupation of the occupants of a private dwelling.

3.85 Section 4 is the criminal counterpart of the civil liability contained in the Occupiers' Liability Act 1957 (and the Occupiers' Liability (Scotland) Act 1960) (see paragraph 12.97) and would apply in those cases where an employee is using premises which are not controlled by the employer, eg a visiting window cleaner. However, the effect of the section is somewhat wider than that. Thus a coin-operated launderette would be covered, even though no one was employed there, for a customer would be using plant or substances provided for use. Universities would have a duty under this section to ensure that their premises (libraries, etc) are safe; schools have duties towards their pupils using laboratories, etc. In *Moualam v Carlisle City Council*, the defendant operated a children's play-centre, and was convicted following his failure to comply with a number of improvement notices. His appeal was dismissed. The premises were non-domestic, the children were using plant (ie equipment) there, and he had control over the premises. Section 4 is not limited to persons who are at work.

3.86 Further, a person who, by virtue of any contract or tenancy, has an obligation to maintain or repair any premises used by others as a place of work or as a place where they may use plant or substances, or to maintain the means of access or exit, or to ensure the safety or absence of risks to health arising from the use of such plant or substances, will be the person upon whom the above duty will lie, s.4(3). For example, a maintenance contractor who is responsible for the maintenance of plant, or a specialist advisor who has to deal with the control of a dangerous substance, will have those duties imposed by this section to persons other than his employees.

3.87 When a person makes available premises for the use of another person, the reasonableness of the measures taken to ensure the safety of those premises must be determined in the light of the controller's knowledge of the anticipated use of those premises and of his knowledge of the actual use. In *Austin Rover Group Ltd v Inspector of*

Factories, an employee of a firm of subcontractors was killed while working on the premises of Austin Rover. On the facts of the case, Austin Rover had given clear instructions, and the accident was caused by employees of the subcontractor acting contrary to those instructions. The prosecution of Austin Rover was dismissed. If premises are not a reasonably foreseeable cause of injury to anyone acting in a way in which a human being may reasonably be expected to act in circumstances which may reasonably be expected to occur, then it would not be reasonable to take further measures to prevent the occurrence of unknown and unexpected events.

3.88   For the purpose of s.4, the premises in question must be used by the person in control by way of a trade, business or other undertaking (whether for profit or not). The question may well arise as to whether the word "undertaking" is to be construed *ejusdem generis* (of the same species) with "trade or business", as implying some form of commercial activity.

Duty to prevent pollution (s.5)

3.89   Section 5 of HSWA deals with the duty of controllers of prescribed premises to prevent the emission into the atmosphere of noxious or offensive substances, and render harmless and inoffensive such substances as may be emitted. However, pollution control is no longer the responsibility of the HSE, but has been transferred to the Department for the Environment, Food and Rural Affairs (Defra), which now has responsibility for environment protection, food production and standards, agriculture, fisheries and rural communities. There are concordat agreements with the Scottish Government, the Cabinet of the National Assembly for Wales and representatives from the Northern Ireland Assembly insofar as these matters have been devolved. The Pollution Prevention and Control Act 1999 is designed to implement EU Directive 91/61 on integrated pollution prevention and control.

General duties of designers, manufacturers, importers and suppliers (s.6)

3.90   Section 6 lays down duties on any person who designs, manufactures, imports or supplies any article for use at work, and on any person who manufactures, imports or supplies any substance for use at work. The basic objective is to introduce safety measures at source, rather than leave this to the ultimate user. Before we consider the nature of these duties, we must first ascertain the scope of the above words.

3.91 "An article for use at work" is defined as being "any plant designed for use or operation (whether exclusively or not) by persons at work and any article designed for use as a component in any such plant". The word "plant" includes "any machinery, equipment or appliance". A "substance" is "any natural or artificial substance (including micro-organisms) whether in solid or liquid form, or in the form of gas or vapour" (s.53). "Work" in this connection means at work as an employee or as a self-employed person. Thus a sale to a "do-it-yourself" enthusiast is not within s.6, for although he may be working, he is not at work. If an article is being tested to determine whether or not it is suitable for use at work, and an injury results during the test, there is no breach of s 6, as the article was not being used by a person at work (*McKay v Unwin Pyrotechnics Ltd*). Consumer sales are not included within the Act, but since s.53 states that the article need not be exclusively designed for use at work, an item which is capable of being used at work is within the scope of the section even though it is also capable of being a consumer item. It may be that a test will emerge which asks if it was reasonably foreseeable that an employer would purchase the item for use at work.

3.92 The article or substance must be "for use". Thus if it is part of the stock-in-trade, or is purchased for resale purposes, the section does not apply. Nor does it apply to goods which are manufactured, etc for export, for the Act does not apply extraterritorially.

3.93 "Supply" in this connection means the supply of an article or substances by way of sale, lease, hire or hire purchase, whether as a principal or as an agent for another However, s.6(9) recognises the commercial nature of hire-purchase agreements, conditional sales agreements, and credit-sales agreements, and draws a distinction between the ostensible supplier and the effective supplier. The ostensible supplier is in reality merely financing the transaction even though in the course of the transaction he may become the legal owner of the goods in question. The liability under s.6 is on the effective supplier, ie the manufacturer, etc who sells to the finance company, who then sells to the customer. A similar provision is to be found in the

Health and Safety (Leasing Arrangements) Regulations 1992, whereby if the ostensible supplier is merely acting as a financier for a leasing arrangement made between the effective supplier and the customer, then, subject to certain conditions, the effective supplier and not the ostensible supplier will have the duties of s.6 imposed on him.

3.94   It will be noted that in respect of articles the designer has certain duties, as well as manufacturers, importers and suppliers. It is not clear whether this means the person who actually designs the product or the employer of the designer. It is likely that HSE policy will be to leave the employee to be prosecuted under s.7, and take action against the employer of the designer under s.6. This is because subsection (7) of s.6 reminds us that the duties only apply "to things done in the course of a trade, business or undertaking carried on by him" and presumably it is the employer of the designer who is carrying on the trade, business or undertaking. If the employer had no reason to suspect that the designer was incompetent, or had made a faulty design, presumably he could rely on the defence that he took all steps which were reasonably practicable.

3.95   Section 6 of HSWA was amended by the Consumer Protection Act 1987 (schedule 3). It is clear that there is a close connection between occupational safety and consumer safety generally, and indeed it will frequently occur that goods are manufactured, etc for consumers as well as for persons at work. It was recognised that it is strongly desirable to introduce enforcement at the earlier point of supply and the ultimate use for which the goods are intended should not be particularly relevant. In other words, safety has to be built into the design and manufacture of the product, rather than at the user end. Thus more extensive obligations were placed on those who put goods into circulation. A new subsection (6(1)A) was added relating to articles of fairground equipment, although this is more for the protection of the general public than for persons at work. Again, however, the obligations relating to safety were placed at the earlier point in time, ie with the manufacturer, etc.

3.96   Section 6 lays down six duties in respect of articles, and five duties in respect of substances.

Articles

3.97   The six duties in respect of articles are as follows.

1. It shall be the duty of any person who designs, manufactures, imports or supplies any article for use at work to ensure, so far as is reasonably practicable, that the article is so designed and constructed that it will be safe and without risks to health at all times when it is being set, used, cleaned or maintained by a person at work. However, s.6(10) goes on to state that the absence of safety or a risk to health shall be disregarded in so far as it is shown to be an occurrence which could not reasonably be foreseen. Further, in determining whether the duty has been performed, regard shall be paid to any relevant information or advice which has been provided by the designer, manufacturer, importer or supplier.

2. Designers, manufacturers, importers and suppliers must carry out (or arrange for the carrying out) of such testing and examination as may be necessary for the performance of the above duty, but there is no need to repeat any testing or examination which has previously been carried out, in so far as it is reasonable for him to rely on the results thereof.

3. Designers, manufacturers, importers and suppliers must take such steps as are necessary to ensure that the person supplied by them with the article is provided with adequate information about the use for which it has been designed or tested, and about any condition necessary to ensure that it will be safe and without risks to health when it is being set, used, cleaned or maintained.

4. Designers, manufacturers, importers and suppliers must take such steps as are necessary to secure, so far as is reasonably practicable, that persons who have been provided with information are also provided with any revisions of the information as are necessary by reason of it becoming known that there is a serious risk to health or safety.

5. It is the duty of designers and manufacturers (but not importers or suppliers) to carry out (or arrange for the carrying out of) any necessary research with a view to the discovery and elimination or minimisation of any risks to health or safety to which the design or article may give rise. Again there is no need to repeat any research which has already been done insofar as it is reasonable to rely on the results thereof.

6. It shall be the duty of any person who erects or installs any article for use at work in any premises where the article is to be used by persons at work, to ensure, so far as is reasonably practicable, that nothing about the way the article is erected or installed makes it unsafe or a

103

risk to health when it is being set, used, cleaned or maintained by a person at work. New duties have been placed on installers by the Provision and Use of Work Equipment Regulations 1998.

Substances

3.98   The five duties in respect of substances are as follows.

1. It shall be the duty of any person who manufactures, imports or supplies any substance to ensure, so far as is reasonably practicable, that the substance will be safe and without risks to health at all times when it is being used, handled, processed, stored or transported by a person at work or in premises to which s.4 of the Act applies (see paragraph 3.82). Again, the absence of risks to health or safety may be disregarded insofar as the occurrence was one which could not be reasonably foreseen, and regard shall also be had to any relevant information or advice provided by the person by whom the substance was manufactured, imported or supplied.

2. To carry out or arrange for the carrying out of such testing and examination as may be necessary to perform the above mentioned duty. However, it is not necessary to repeat any testing or examination which may have been previously carried out insofar as it is reasonable for him to rely on the results thereof.

3. To take such steps as are necessary to secure that persons supplied by him with the substance are provided with adequate information about any risks to health or safety to which the inherent properties of the substance may give rise, about the results of any relevant tests carried out and about any conditions necessary to ensure that the substance will be safe and without risks to health at all times when it is being used, handled, processed, stored, transported and disposed of.

4. To take such steps as are necessary to secure, so far as is reasonably practicable, that persons supplied with the information are provided with all revisions of the information as are necessary by reason of it becoming known that there is a serious risk to health or safety.

5. A manufacturer of a substance is under a duty to carry out (or arrange to carry out) any necessary research with a view to discovering and, so far as is reasonably practicable, the elimination or minimisation of any risks to health or safety to which the substance may give rise at all times when it is being used, handled, processed,

stored or transported. Again, there is no need to repeat any research which has been carried out previously insofar as it is reasonable to rely on the existing results.

3.99   The above duties only extend to a person in respect of things done in the course of a trade, business or other undertaking carried on by him (whether for profit or not) and to matters within his control, s.6(7). This appears to exclude employees from the scope of s.6 (though not, of course, from s.7). Whether the matters are within the control of a person is a question of fact. If he has the right of control, but fails or refuses to exercise it, the matters are still within his control.

Indemnity clauses (s.6(8))

3.100   Where a person designs, manufactures, imports or supplies an article to or for another person on the basis of a written undertaking by that other person to take specific steps sufficient to ensure, so far as is reasonably practicable, that the article will be safe and without risks to health when it is being set, used, cleaned or maintained; the undertaking will have the effect of relieving the first-mentioned person from the duty of ensuring that it is designed and constructed so as to be safe, to such an extent as is reasonable having regard to the terms of the undertaking. Thus if a person supplies second-hand machinery to another on the basis of that other's assurance that he will ensure that it is properly serviced and examined before being put to use, or where a manufacturer supplies machinery made specifically to certain specifications or to a certain design, the supplier or manufacturer may be relieved from legal responsibility under s.6(l)(a). However, there must be a written assurance that implies a specific commitment in the instant case, not a general standard commitment. Further, the exclusion is only from the liability under s.6(1)(a), not from the liability imposed by ss.6(1)(b) or 6(1)(c) or 6(2). In other words, the obligations to test, provide information and carry out research, remain. Further, the terms of the undertaking may be looked at to discover the extent to which the designer, etc is to be absolved. The HSE appears to take the view that this may lead to a partial relief, depending on the terms of the undertaking, but this may be misleading. A breach of s.6 is a criminal offence; either an offence has been committed or it has not. There is no such thing as "partially guilty". Mitigating circumstances can only arise if an offence has been committed, and the extent of the mitigation will be for the court to determine.

Further liability of importers

3.101   Nothing in ss.6(7) or (8) shall relieve an importer of any article or substance from any of his duties under the Act as regards anything done or not done which was within the control of a foreign designer or foreign manufacturer of an article or substance. Thus importers of unsafe products may be liable for the acts or omissions of foreign designers or manufacturers even though they have no control over their activities (s.6(8A)).

The effect of s.6

3.102   The exact scope and meaning of s.6 has still to receive authoritative judicial interpretation, for although there have been some prosecutions, there appears to be a marked reluctance on either side to challenge these findings in the High Court. The purpose is to try to ensure that acceptable levels of health and safety are built into articles and substances at the design and manufacturing stage, whether by way of compliance with new Approach Directives (see paragraph 14.45) or recognised standards (eg BSI) or HSE Guidance Notes or other acceptable tests. But the fact that the manufacturer, etc may be in breach of his duty under s.6 is irrelevant to the employer's liability under the general law to take reasonable care to ensure the health and safety of his employees, or the duty to fence or guard dangerous machinery (see regulation 11 of the Provision and Use of Work Equipment Regulations 1998). A modern practice is for purchasers of products for use at work to make the contract conditional upon compliance by the supplier with s.6 of HSWA, thus leaving it open for the purchaser to reject the product. It will be recalled that nothing in HSWA gives rise to any civil liability, but it would be an interesting argument if the purchaser rejected a product on the grounds that a failure to comply with the requirements of s.6 rendered the product not of satisfactory quality as required by the Sale and Supply of Goods Act 1994.

General duties of employees (s.7)

3.103   Two main duties are placed on an employee.

3.104   Section 7(1) *To take reasonable care for the health and safety of himself and of others who may be affected by his acts or omissions at work.*

3.105 Thus an employee who refuses to wear safety equipment or use safety precautions is liable to be prosecuted under this section. Further, if, through his carelessness or negligence someone else is injured, he could again be prosecuted. Thus an employee who is prone to horseplay or skylarking, with the result that he or another is injured, commits an offence. A supervisor who encourages an employee to take an unsafe short cut or to remove effective guards may equally be guilty under this section.

3.106 Section 7(2) *As regards any duty or requirement imposed on his employer or other person by or under any of the relevant statutory provisions, to co-operate with him insofar as is necessary to enable that duty or requirement to be performed or complied with.*

3.107 This duty to co-operate is potentially very wide. An employee who announces that he intends to refuse to wear a safety belt or refuses to use a safety precaution provided by his employer in pursuance of the latter's duty under s.2 is failing to co-operate with the employer and thus a prosecution may again succeed.

3.108 In addition, the Management of Health and Safety at Work Regulations 1999 impose further duties on employees to report dangerous situations and shortcomings in the employer's protection arrangements (see paragraph 4.54).

Interference or misuse (s.8)

3.109 *No person shall intentionally or recklessly interfere with or misuse anything provided in the interests of health, safety or welfare in pursuance of any of the relevant statutory provisions.*

3.110 This obligation is again wider than the corresponding provision in the Factories Act which referred to wilful conduct in the sense of being deliberate or perverse. Intentional or reckless conduct does not need to be perverse.

3.111 It should be noted that s.8 is not restricted to employees and could, for example, apply to visitors, burglars, etc.

Duty not to charge (s.9)

3.112 *No employer shall levy or permit to be levied on any employee of his any charge in respect of anything done or provided in pursuance of any specific requirement of the relevant statutory provisions.*

3.113 This provision originally applied only to the specific requirements of relevant statutory provisions, but most of these have now been repealed by virtue of the Personal Protective Equipment at Work Regulations 1992 (see paragraph 6.99). Section 9 now applies to all personal protective equipment deemed necessary by those regulations.

Enforcement of the Act

3.114 A breach of the Act or of health and safety regulations can be dealt with in two ways. First, there are the powers given to the inspectors to issue enforcement notices or to seize and destroy. Second, a prosecution may take place in respect of the commission of a criminal offence.

Enforcement notices (ss.21–24)

3.115 There are two types of enforcement notices which may be issued. These are (1) an improvement notice and (2) a prohibition notice (which may be immediate or deferred). In addition, the inspectorate have taken to issuing Crown Notices in respect of premises belonging to the Crown, but although there is no legal basis for such notices (it will be recalled that ss.21–24 do not bind the Crown) they have a moral and persuasive effect. A failure to comply with a Crown Notice would lead to an approach by the HSE to the government department concerned, and the Government has announced that in such circumstances, the necessary action would be taken to ensure compliance. Moreover, a copy of the Crown Notice will be given to the representatives of the employees, thus drawing attention to the hazard.

3.116 The HSE can also issue a Crown Censure, which is a formal recording of a decision that, but for Crown immunity, there was sufficient evidence to warrant the bringing of a prosecution against the Crown body concerned, for a breach of health and safety law.

3.117 Enforcement notices may be issued by HSE inspectors and Environmental Health Officers (EHOs) of a local authority, all of whom must act within the powers contained in the instrument of their appointment. However, it must be shown that the premises concerned are within the scope of the relevant legislation. In *Dicker & Sons v Hilton*, a notice was served requiring the appellant to comply with s.36 of the Factories Act, which laid down that air receivers shall be cleaned and examined by a competent person every 26 months. The notice was cancelled on appeal when the employment tribunal learned that the appellant ran a one-man business. Since his premises were not a factory (which is defined as being premises where persons are employed) the relevant statutory provision did not apply.

Improvement notice (s.21)

3.118   If an inspector is of the opinion that a person:
(a) is contravening a relevant statutory provision, or
(b) has contravened one or more provisions in circumstances that make it likely that the contravention will continue or be repeated,

then he may serve an improvement notice, which must state:

(a) that he is of that opinion
(b) the provisions in question
(c) particulars of the reasons for his opinion.

3.119   The improvement notice will also require that person to remedy the contravention or matters occasioning the contravention within such period as the notice may specify, but not earlier than 21 days after the notice has been served (which is the period in which the person affected may lodge an appeal against the notice).

3.120   In other words, if there is a statutory requirement that a certain thing shall be done (or not done) an inspector may serve a notice requiring the thing be done (or not done) any time after 21 days.

3.121   But the fact that a period of grace is permitted does not absolve the person concerned from any criminal or civil liability in respect of anything which may happen prior to the notice taking effect.

3.122   An inspector may (but is not bound to) attach a schedule of the remedial steps to be taken (s.23). If he does, and it is unclear or vague, this will not affect the validity of the notice (*Chrysler (UK) Ltd v McCarthy*) but the tribunal may clarify or alter the schedule.

3.123   If the requirement of the statutory provision is absolute, then there can be no defence in the case of a breach (*Ranson v John Baird*). If the statutory requirement is to do that which is reasonably practicable, the employment tribunal may exercise its own judgment in accordance with the circumstances of the case when hearing an appeal. Thus, in *Roadline (UK) Ltd v Mainwaring*, an improvement notice required an employer to provide heating in a transit shed. The employment tribunal thought that the cost of doing so was excessive in relation to the marginal improvement which would result.

3.124   Section 3(2) of the Act requires every self-employed person to conduct his undertaking so as to ensure, so far as is reasonably practicable, that he and other persons who may be affected are not exposed to risks to their health and safety. In *Jones v Fishwick*, an Environmental Health Officer served an improvement notice on a butcher requiring him to use a chain-mail apron while boning meat. Applying the "cost/risk" analysis the employment tribunal noted that there had been a number of serious accidents in that industry during boning out procedures, and the cost of acquiring a chain-mail apron was £32.40. Thus it was reasonably practicable to take the necessary precautions and the improvement notice was confirmed.

3.125   Before issuing an improvement notice, the inspector will discuss with the duty holder the breaches of law concerned, and the action needed to be taken by the duty holder to ensure compliance. The duty holder will be given the opportunity to discuss issues with the inspector before formal action is taken, and, if possible, resolve points of difference. If the inspector decides to issue the improvement notice, it must enable the recipient to know what is wrong and why. It must be clear and easily understood and should set out clearly how the inspector intends that what is wrong should be put right (*BT Fleet Ltd v McKenna*).

Prohibition notice (s.22)

3.126   If an inspector is of the opinion that activities are being carried on or are likely to be carried on in relation to which any of the relevant statutory provisions apply, and which involve or will involve a risk of serious personal injury, he may serve a prohibition notice. This will:
  (a) state that the inspector is of such an opinion
  (b) specify the matter which, in his opinion, is giving or will give rise to the risk of serious personal injury
  (c) if the matter also involves a contravention of a relevant statutory provision, he will state the statutory provision, and give particulars of the reason as to why he is of that opinion
  (d) direct that the activities to which the notice relates shall not be carried on by or under the control of the person on whom the

notice has been served unless the matters specified in the notice (and any associated contraventions of statutory provisions) have been remedied.

3.127 The prohibition notice will take effect immediately (immediate prohibition notice) if it so declares or at the end of the period specified in the notice (deferred prohibition notice). Again, the inspector may, but is not bound to, attach a schedule of the remedial steps to be taken. It will be noted that to issue a prohibition notice, the inspector need only be satisfied that the activities complained of give rise to a risk of serious personal injury and there is no need for there to be a breach of a relevant statutory provision (*Roberts v Day*). However, if he has little information on which to form such an opinion, the notice may be cancelled by the employment tribunal (*Bressingham Steam Preservation Co Ltd v Sincock*).

3.128 There must be substrata of fact on which an inspector can form his "opinion" that there has been a breach of the general duties under the Act, and ideally this should be demonstrable by a risk assessment carried out which is at least as thorough as that required by an employer under the Management of Health and Safety at Work Regulations 1999 (see Chapter 4) and other legislation. This would include a consideration of the risk, the nature of the hazard, the preventative measures already taken and the cost of further measures, and so on. Equally, the employer's own risk assessment is capable of being used to counter the inspector's opinion, by showing additional factors, such as the training given, the supervision employed, the use in actual practice, the low number of previous incidents, the search for suitable alternatives, and expert evidence (if available) as to the reasonably safe equipment or systems of work as appropriate. The employment tribunal will then be in a position to make an informed evaluation, and decide if the inspector's "opinion" is sustainable.

3.129 For the purpose of s.22, activities are still being carried out even though they have been temporarily interrupted or suspended as a result of an accident. Thus, the activities themselves may have ceased, and the state of inactivity may be prevailing, but this can be for any number of reasons. It is thus a question of fact and degree whether, because the activities have been temporarily suspended, they have ceased for the purpose of s.22. But as long as there is a risk, however remote, that the activities may be brought back into use, an inspector is entitled to issue a prohibition notice prohibiting the activity until remedial action has been taken (*Railtrack plc v Smallwood*).

Supplementary provisions (s.23)

3.130   As already noted, an improvement and prohibition notice may (but need not) include directions as to the measures to be taken to remedy any contravention, for the inclusion of details of the precise nature of the breach, and the remedial matters which will have to be taken to remedy it, is an option, not an obligation (*MB Gas Ltd v Veitch*). The measures to be taken may be framed by reference to any Approved Code of Practice or may give a choice as to different ways of taking remedial action. However, if the improvement notice refers to a building, or a matter connected with a building, the notice may not direct that measures shall be taken which are more onerous than the requirements of any building regulations applied in respect of new buildings. If the notice refers to the taking of measures affecting the means of escape in the case of fire, the inspector must first consult the fire authority.

3.131   In the case of an improvement notice or a deferred prohibition notice, these may be withdrawn at any time by the inspector before the date on which they are to take effect, and also the period for compliance may be extended by him provided an appeal is not pending.

3.132   Once the matter which has been the subject of an improvement or prohibition notice has been attended to, or the person to whom it is addressed has complied with any requirement contained therein, the activity may be carried on without any further need to contact the inspector, although prudence may well advise such a course in order to ensure that he is satisfied with the rectification. This is particularly important in view of the fact that a failure to comply with the requirements of an enforcement notice exposes the offender to potentially severe punishment. However, the prohibition notice does not lapse on compliance. It continues in force so long as the activities in question are being carried on, for there is no procedure to remove it, although appeals can be made.

Appeals against enforcement notices (s.24)

3.133   A person on whom a prohibition or improvement notice has been served may appeal to an employment tribunal within 21 days of its receipt, and the tribunal may confirm or cancel the notice. If it is confirmed, this may be done in its original form, or with such modifications as the employment tribunal thinks fit. An appeal may be made on a point of law or of fact.

Procedure for appeals

3.134 The Employment Tribunals (Constitution and Rules of Procedure) Regulations 2004, schedule 4, lay down the procedure to be followed for the making of an appeal against the decision of an inspector to issue a notice. The appellant shall send a Notice of Appeal to the Regional Office of Employment Tribunals, stating:
 (a) his name and address for service of documents
 (b) the date of the notice appealed against
 (c) the address of the premises concerned
 (d) the name and address of the respondent (ie the inspector)
 (e) particulars of the requirements or directions appealed against
 (f) the grounds for the appeal.

3.135 The appeal must be lodged within 21 days from the date the notice was served on the appellant, although the employment tribunal may extend the time limit on application if it is satisfied that it was not reasonably practicable to bring the appeal earlier. The 21-day time limit runs from the date of the receipt of the notice (*DH Tools Co v Myers*).

3.136 If the appeal is against the imposition of an improvement notice, the lodging of the appeal will automatically suspend the operation of the notice until the appeal is disposed of. If the appeal is against the imposition of a prohibition notice, the appellant may apply for it to be lifted pending the hearing of the appeal, although the notice will continue to take effect despite the fact that an appeal is pending. Since a prohibition notice which takes immediate effect can have serious repercussions on the employer's business, appeals against them are often heard as a matter of urgency, if necessary the very next day (*Hoover Ltd v Mallon*).

3.137 Employment tribunals have wide powers to deal with preliminary matters prior to the appeal. They can require further and better particulars of the application, grant disclosure of documents, issue attendance orders compelling witnesses to attend and so on. As a rule, at least 14 days' notice of the date of the hearing is given, unless a speedier hearing can be arranged by agreement between the parties. The hearing will normally be in public, unless a party applies for it to be heard in private on grounds of national security or if there may be evidence that, if disclosed, would be seriously prejudicial to the interests of the appellant's undertaking other than its effect on collective bargaining. Either side may be represented by a solicitor, barrister or any other person whom he desires to represent him, including a trade union official or the representative of an employers' association. If written submissions are made, these must be sent to the employment tribunal seven days prior to the hearing and a copy must be sent at the same time to the other party.

3.138 Each side is entitled to make an opening statement, give evidence on oath, call witnesses, cross-examine witnesses from the other side, introduce documentary or other evidence and make a closing submission. The tribunals do not appear (to date) to have found it necessary to appoint assessors to assist them, but they can, and do, visit the premises in order to make their own informed judgment (eg *Wilkinson v Fronks*).

3.139 The tribunal will then make its decision, which may be a unanimous one or by a majority. If the tribunal consists only of two members, the chairman has a casting vote. The decision may be given orally or in writing after consideration, but it will always be promulgated in writing and a copy sent to each side.

Grounds for appeal

3.140 An appeal may be lodged on the ground that the inspector lacked the legal power to impose an enforcement notice. This may be because the premises are not covered by the relevant statutory provisions (*Dicker & Sons v Hilton*, above) or because the inspector has misinterpreted the statutory provision in question. But the fact that the employer has complied with the requirements previously laid down by some official authority is not by itself sufficient objection to a subsequent requirement made on grounds of health or safety. In *Hixon v Whitehead*, the appellant had received permission from the district Environmental Health Officer to store 4000kg of liquified petroleum gas on the premises. As a result of complaints from local residents, another inspector issued a notice limiting the holding to 500kg. The notice was affirmed by the employment tribunal. There was no question of estoppel arising against the local authority, for the tribunal had to consider the avoidance of serious injuries to employees and to other persons who may be affected. Similarly, in *Williamson Cliff Ltd v Tarlington*, the company installed a tank containing 29,000 gallons of butane. Planning permission had been given for this after a fire hydrant had been installed. Subsequently another inspector insisted that a spray system be installed. Although the employment tribunal expressed sympathy with the company, which had installed the correct system initially only to find that it was now required to add another one even though there was no new knowledge in relation to safety, the improvement notice was confirmed. The overriding consideration was the safety of employees and other persons who were likely to be affected should an explosion occur.

Appeals against improvement notices

3.141 An improvement notice may be issued if there is a breach of a relevant statutory provision. This may be HSWA or any other appropriate legislation or regulations. The provision in question may be an absolute one, or prefaced by the requirement that something shall be done "so far as is reasonably practicable". In either case, the issues will be determined largely by the evidence which can be adduced.

3.142 In *Dundee City Council v Stephen* an inspector served an improvement notice on a local authority requiring them to install an occupational health management system. Such plans as the council had were largely aspirational and reactive. For the inspector, it was argued that the council were in breach of regulation 5 of the Management of Health and Safety at Work Regulations 1999 (see Chapter 4) by failing to "make and give effect to such arrangements as are appropriate ... for the effective planning, organisation, control and review of the preventative measures." For the council it was argued that the inspector had disregarded the HSE enforcement policy, and hence had acted unreasonably in issuing the notice. An employment tribunal upheld the validity of the notice. All that was required was for the inspector to hold an opinion that a relevant statutory provision is being contravened, and there was no abuse of his statutory powers. There was no need to import the concept of reasonableness into the exercise of the inspector's discretion when issuing an improvement notice.

3.143 The council argued further that the inspector had not produced any evidence which would indicate that there was an actual risk, but this argument was soon disposed of. What matters is whether persons might be exposed to a risk if such remedial actions were not taken (see *R v Trustees of the Science Museum*, paragraph 3.76).

3.144 Thus, in *Murray v Gadbury*, a farmer and his labourer used a rotary grass cutter for 26 years without incident. An inspector issued an improvement notice requiring the farmer to have the cutter guarded in accordance with the Agriculture (Field Machinery) Regulations 1962. It was argued that since the machine had been used for such a long time without accident, the notice was unnecessary. The employment tribunal rejected the appeal and confirmed the notice. The farmer appealed to the Divisional Court, claiming that the law only required him to do that which was reasonably practicable. Again, the appeal was dismissed. The provisions of the regulations were quite clear and were mandatory. On the other hand, in *Associated Dairies v Hartley*, the appellants, who used roller trucks, provided safety footwear for employees at cost price. One day the wheel of a truck ran over the foot of an employee who was not wearing protective footwear, causing a fracture. An inspector issued an improvement notice requiring the employers to provide suitable safety footwear free of charge. An appeal against this notice was allowed. There was no statutory requirement that such footwear should be provided and the obligation under s.2 of HSWA to make arrangements for securing safety at work is subject to the limitation "so far as is reasonably practicable". In determining whether or not a requirement was reasonably practicable, it was proper to take into account the time, trouble and expense of the requirement and to see if it was disproportionate to the risks involved. In this case, it would cost £20,000 in the first year to provide the boots, and £10,000 each year thereafter. On the other hand, the likelihood of such an accident occurring was fairly remote and there was no evidence that employees would use the boots if they were provided free. The tribunal concluded that the present arrangement whereby the employers made safety footwear available was satisfactory.

3.145 The fact that employees are content with existing arrangements is also irrelevant. In *File Tile Distributors v Mitchell*, the firm had a cold water supply, with a gas ring and kettle on which they could heat water. Employees used this method without complaint, but an improvement notice requiring the firm to provide running hot water was upheld. The statutory requirements are designed to improve facilities for employees and their acquiescence in lower standards must be discounted.

3.146   Nor is it relevant that there has not been a previous accident or dangerous occurrence. In *Sutton & Co Ltd v Davies*, the inspector issued an improvement notice requiring a machine to be fenced. The company produced evidence that there had not been an accident arising from this particular machine in 27 years. Nonetheless, the notice was affirmed. The requirements of the statute were absolute. One need not wait for an accident to happen before condemning a system as being dangerous or unsafe.

3.147   The fact that it is financially and physically possible to comply with an improvement notice does not mean that it is reasonably practicable to do so. In *West Bromwich Building Society v Townsend*, an inspector served an improvement notice on a branch of a building society requiring them to erect anti-bandit screens for the protection of employees. The society appealed to an employment tribunal and the inspector sought to treat the appeal as a test case for all building societies in the area. The employment tribunal held that the risks were more than minimal, and that the measures required were financially and physically possible. Thus the notice was confirmed. On a further appeal, the Divisional Court reversed the decision. The employment tribunal had concentrated on the general desirability of having anti-bandit screens, whereas they should have decided whether screens were needed for this particular office. Further, they had decided that it was physically and financially possible to erect the screens, instead of whether it was reasonably practicable to do so.

3.148   The statutory requirements are not met by providing substitutes, unless some other equally efficacious method is permitted by the legislation. In *Belhaven Brewery Co v McLean*, the inspector issued an improvement notice requiring the company to securely fence transmission machinery by the use of an interlocking device attached to the doors or gates. This would switch off the power when the doors were opened. The company argued that this would be very expensive and they wanted to deal with the problem by erecting safety screens. They would also put up a notice warning employees of the danger. Since the employees were of sufficient intelligence to see that the gates were in position while the plant was working, and since there was a high level of supervision, they wanted the notice cancelled or modified. The notice was confirmed without modification. The requirements of s.13 of the Factories Act could not be met by erecting a screen. Moreover, under s.2(1) of HSWA it was reasonably practicable to fit the interlocking device. The sacrifice in terms of cost was not disproportionate to the risk and dangers.

3.149 The employment tribunal may grant an extension of time for compliance in exceptional circumstances (*Otterburn Mill v Bulman*), but not if there is a risk of serious personal injury (*Nico Manufacturing Co v Hendry*).

3.150 In *Campion v Hughes*, an improvement notice was issued requiring the employer to make changes to the means of escape in the event of fire. It was held that the appeal would be allowed only for the purpose of extending the time for compliance. One of the requirements was that the fire escape be made on land which belonged to the local authority, and consent for doing the work had not been given. An extension of time for a further three months was given in order to enable the employer to obtain the appropriate consent.

3.151 Similarly, in *Porthole Ltd v Brown*, a firm enlarged its kitchen on the ground floor and this took away the stairway which led to the first floor lavatory used by employees. An outside stairway was erected to provide the necessary access to the lavatory, and an inspector issued an improvement notice requiring this to be covered. The operation of the notice was suspended to permit the firm to obtain the consent of the landlord and planning permission from the local authority.

3.152 An unusual extension of time arose in the case of *Cheston Woodware Ltd v Coppell*, where an improvement notice was issued requiring the appellant to fit an exhaust appliance to a planing machine used for thicknessing. The firm pointed out that if the machine was being used for thicknessing and surfacing, no such exhaust appliance would be required by the Woodworking Machines Regulations 1974. The tribunal agreed that this was somewhat odd, and postponed the operation of the notice to enable the appellant to apply for an exemption certificate.

3.153 As a general rule, an appeal cannot succeed merely because the employer is unable financially to comply with the requirements. In *Harrison (Newcastle-under-Lyme) Ltd v Ramsey*, an improvement notice was issued requiring the company to clean and paint its walls in accordance with s.1(3) of the Factories Act. The company appealed on the ground that it could not afford to spend the money on the work, in view of its grave financial position. The notice was confirmed by the tribunal. To hold otherwise would enable an employer to ignore the statutory requirements because of expense and undercut his competitors who were so complying.

3.154 However, the employment tribunals are not totally unsympathetic with the financial plight of firms, and will take into account the record of compliance in the past. In particular, they are more likely to postpone (as opposed to cancel) the operation of an improvement notice where the matter concerns a "health" rather than a "safety" aspect (*R A Dyson & Co. Ltd v Bentley*).

3.155 An improvement notice may be successfully challenged on the ground that the employer is in fact complying with the statutory requirements. In *Davis & Sons v Leeds City Council*, the tenancy of a flat above a small bakery shop was subject to a condition that employees at the shop could use the toilet facilities at all times. An improvement notice was issued requiring the shop occupiers to provide readily accessible sanitary facilities instead of this arrangement, in order to comply with s.9(1) of the Offices, Shops and Railway Premises Act 1963 (OSRPA). The employment tribunal allowed an appeal against the notice. Section 9(5) of the Act recognised that facilities might have to be shared with others, and in a circular addressed to local authorities the (then) Ministry of Labour had stated that the effect of s.9(5) would be that "workers in a lock-up shop might have to use the conveniences and facilities in adjacent premises". The tribunal, having visited the premises, concluded that the toilet facilities in the flat were conveniently accessible, and cancelled the notice.

3.156 A similar result was reached in *Alfred Preedy & Sons Ltd v Owens*, where an improvement notice was served alleging that a stone stairway leading to a storage room was in a dangerous condition. The tribunal cancelled the notice after hearing evidence from a witness with a long experience in property management and maintenance that the defects were minimal and of no practical significance.

3.157 A notice may be successfully challenged on the ground that the inspector has misunderstood the application of the statutory provision. In *NAAFI v Portsmouth City Council*, an improvement notice was served requiring the appellants to maintain a constant temperature of 55°F, so as to conform with s.6(1) of OSRPA. The appellants argued that as the premises were used for the storage of fresh food, a temperature of between 41°–50°F was adequate. The tribunal noted that s.6(3)(b) of the Act provides for an exception where it is a room in which the maintenance of a reasonable temperature would cause the deterioration of goods, provided employees had conveniently accessible means of keeping themselves warm. Since a warm room was provided, together with suitable clothing, the notice was cancelled.

3.158   Nor may an inspector impose a non-statutory requirement. In *Chethams v Westminster Council*, a notice was issued because the appellants were allegedly in breach of regulation 7(1) of the OSRPA (Hoists and Lifts) Regulations. The notice required that the latest British Standards for lifts be adopted. This requirement was struck out, because British Standards are merely a guide for new work and are not a statutory provision.

3.159   The fact that the breach in question is a trivial one is irrelevant. In *South Surbiton Co-operative Society v Wilcox*, an improvement notice required the employers to replace a wash basin which was cracked. On appeal, the notice was confirmed. The surface of the basin was not "impervious" as required by the Washing Facilities Regulations 1964, and consequently it was not "properly maintained" in accordance with s.10(2) of OSRPA. That the infringement was trivial was irrelevant to the validity of the notice.

3.160   Nor does the validity of the notice depend on the instructions for remedying the defect being precise. In *Chrysler (UK) Ltd v McCarthy*, two improvement notices were issued following a fire at the company's premises. Appeals were lodged on the ground that one of the notices was imprecise. On a preliminary point of law, the tribunal dismissed the appeal, and this was confirmed by the Queen's Bench Divisional Court. It was pointed out that employment tribunals have wide powers under s.24 of HSWA to modify the requirements of the notice as they think fit in the circumstances. However, when the matter was returned to the tribunal, it felt that they lacked sufficient information on which to make such a modification, and the notice was suspended to permit the parties to agree between themselves what requirements should be laid down.

3.161   When modifying the notice, an employment tribunal may add to the inspector's requirements as well as vary them (*Tesco Stores Ltd v Edwards*). If the requirements of the inspector are vague or imprecise, the employment tribunal may exercise its power to amend them (*Chrysler (UK) Ltd v McCarthy*), but there is no power which enables the employment tribunal to amend a notice so as to include further allegations that an employer is in breach of other provisions of the Act (*British Airways Board v Henderson*).

Appeals against prohibition notices

3.162   A prohibition notice may be issued if the inspector considers that there is a risk of serious personal injury, irrespective of whether or not there is a breach of any relevant statutory provision. Consequently, a certain amount of subjectivity is involved in the formation of such opinion and accordingly this assessment can be challenged. In *Nico Manufacturing Co Ltd v Hendry*, a power press operated by the company was examined and tested by a competent person who found certain defects. In accordance with the Power Presses Regulations 1965, he made a report to the company and to the inspector of factories. A few weeks later a director of the company operated the press, and when this came to the attention of the inspector, he issued a prohibition notice. An appeal was lodged on the grounds that the worn state of the press did not constitute a likely source of danger to the employees and that the deprivation of the use of the machine would cause a serious loss of production and endanger the jobs of other employees. It was held that the notice would be confirmed. The employment tribunal preferred the evidence of the expert witness called on behalf of the inspector insofar as his evidence as to the danger was in conflict with that of the company's technical director. Although there was a small likelihood that the press would break up, there was a danger that parts would fracture which would constitute a serious danger to operatives.

3.163   Thus if a defect could lead to a catastrophic failure, or there was a substantial risk of a serious injury, the employment tribunal is unlikely to be impressed by arguments of financial hardship or loss of profits. In *Grovehurst Energy Ltd v Strawson*, a prohibition notice was served on the company preventing it from using a receiver, which had been declared unsuitable for further use by a qualified engineer who had carried out a statutory inspection on the firm's boilers and receivers. The company was finding some difficulty in obtaining a replacement receiver and so it applied for the prohibition notice to be suspended. The managing director of the company (who was a qualified engineer) was confident that a replacement receiver would be available in a few weeks, and offered to take extra precautions until it arrived. If he were unable to use the existing receiver, he would suffer a considerable loss of profit.

Nonetheless, the employment tribunal affirmed the notice. The consequences of a catastrophic failure would have been very serious, and the receiver was a substantial risk of injury to anyone who happened to be passing at the time of a failure and to others who worked nearby.

3.164   However, if a machine or process has been in use for a long time without any history of accident or injury, it may be easier to challenge the inspector's view that the activities will involve a risk of serious personal injury. In *Brewer & Sons v Dunston*, an inspector issued a prohibition notice on a hand-operated guillotine. The company had used the machine for 18 years without incident and also had nine other similar machines. The tribunal, having visited the premises and seen the machine in operation, were satisfied that there was no risk of serious personal injury and cancelled the notice.

3.165   The employment tribunals take a similar attitude to appeals based on expense or a request for an extension of time as they do with improvement notices. Thus in *Otterburn Mill Ltd v Bulman*, the company operated four machines with no guards. After making a number of visits to the premises, the factory inspector insisted that the appropriate guards be fitted, and when this was not done, he issued deferred prohibition notices requiring the guards to be fitted within three months. The company appealed against the time limit imposed, and requested that they should be allowed to fence one machine every six months, as they did not have the necessary finance to make the improvements. This argument was rejected by the tribunal. It would not be right to insist that a prosperous company should do the work in a short time, while a struggling company should be given a much longer period. However, since it was a deferred notice, in that the risk was not imminent, the time taken to put the matter right was always a factor to be taken into account. As the last (and only) accident recorded at the factory was about nine years earlier, the tribunal was prepared to grant an extension of time in respect of one machine, in order to avoid serious embarrassment to the company.

3.166   The number of enforcement notices issued will, of course, vary from year to year, but there is little doubt that they are, and will continue to be, used increasingly by the enforcement authorities.

Application for review

3.167 An application may be made within 14 days after the promulgation of the decision to an employment tribunal to review its decision, on the grounds that:
(a) the decision was wrongly made as a result of an error on the part of the tribunal staff
(b) a party did not receive notice of the proceedings
(c) the decision was made in the absence of a party
(d) new evidence has come to light since the making of the decision, the existence of which was not previously known or foreseen
(e) the interests of justice require a review.

3.168 It must be remembered that an application for review is not an appeal against the decision of the employment tribunal, and thus it must fall strictly within one of the above five grounds. The application may be refused by a chairman of tribunals sitting on his own if he thinks that it stands no reasonable prospect of success. In making the application, the appellant should state the facts or evidence upon which he seeks to base his case. If the tribunal decides to hear the application, it may vary or revoke the original decision and order a rehearing, or dismiss the application.

Costs

3.169 Unlike other proceedings before employment tribunals, costs are normally awarded against the loser to the party who wins the case. The amount awarded may be a specific sum or, in default of agreement between the parties, the amount may be taxed in accordance with the County Court scales, as directed. However, the award of costs is always a matter for the discretion of the tribunal. Thus in *South Surbiton Co-operative Society v Wilcox* (see paragraph 3.159) an improvement notice was confirmed on appeal, but because the breach in question was a trivial one, the employment tribunal refused to make an order for costs.

3.170 HSE keeps a register of improvement and prohibition notices which have been issued, and which is available for public inspection under the provisions of the Environment and Safety Information Act 1988.

3.171　In 2007–2008 HSE issued 7740 enforcement notices as well as a few Crown Notices, and in the same period 6010 enforcement notices were issued by local authorities.

Further appeals

3.172　An appeal from a decision of an employment tribunal which relates to an enforcement notice can only be made to the Queen's Bench Divisional Court on a point of law.

Failure to comply

3.173　A failure to comply with the requirements of a prohibition notice or an improvement notice is a criminal offence under s.33(1)(g) of the Act. The offence is an absolute one, and it is no defence to argue that the accused had done that which was reasonably practicable in the circumstances. The question of reasonably practicable and allied matters must be raised on appeal to an employment tribunal, not as a defence in the magistrates' or crown court (*Deary (HM Inspectors of Factories) v Mansion Upholstery Hide Ltd*).

Power to deal with imminent danger (s.25)

3.174　Where an inspector finds any article or substance in any premises which he has power to enter, and has reasonable cause to believe that, in the circumstances in which he finds it, the article or substance is a cause of imminent danger of serious personal injury, he may seize it and cause it to be rendered harmless (whether by destruction or otherwise). Before doing so, if it is reasonably practicable to do so, he must take a sample and give it to a responsible person at the premises where it was found, marked in a manner sufficient to identify it. After the article or substance has been seized and rendered harmless, the inspector will prepare and sign a written report giving particulars of the circumstances in which the article or substance was seized and dealt with by him, and shall:

(a) give a signed copy to a responsible person at the premises where it was found

(b) unless that person is the owner, give a copy to the owner. If the inspector cannot ascertain the name or address of the owner, the copy will be given to the responsible person in question.

3.175   Additionally, for the purpose of facilitating the exercise of any power by an enforcing authority, a customs official may seize any imported article or substance, and detain it for not more than two working days (s.25A).

Prosecutions for criminal offences (ss.33–42)

3.176   Historically, the various branches of the inspectorate have always sought to ensure compliance with health and safety legislation by giving advice and using persuasion, rather than compulsion. Prosecutions for offences are generally used as the weapon of last resort. The HSE has produced a revised *Enforcement policy statement*, setting out the general principles and approach which health and safety enforcing authorities (HSE and local authorities) are expected to follow, based on principles of proportionality in applying the law and ensuring compliance, consistency of approach, targeting of enforcement action, transparency about how the regulator operates, and accountability for the regulator's actions. Enforcing authorities must use their discretion in deciding whether to initiate a prosecution. There must be a realistic prospect of a conviction, and the prosecution must be in the public interest. Factors which will be taken into account include:

(a) whether a death occurred as a result of a breach of legislation

(b) the gravity of the alleged offence, the seriousness of actual or potential harm, and the general record of the offender

(c) whether there has been a reckless disregard of health and safety requirements

(d) repeated or persistent poor compliance

(e) work carried out without, or in serious breach of, a licence

(f) any failure to comply with a written warning or improvement or prohibition notice

(g) any evidence of inspectors having been intentionally obstructed in the lawful course of their duties.

3.177   In addition, prosecution will be expected when:

(a) false information has been wilfully supplied, or there has been an intent to deceive

(b) there have been serious failures in the management of health and safety

(c) it is appropriate to draw general attention to the need for compliance with the law, and a conviction may deter others from similar failures

(d) a breach which gives rise to a significant risk has continued despite warnings from employees, their representatives or others affected by work activity.

3.178 The HSE has also developed an *Enforcement management model* which establishes a framework within which inspectors may make informed enforcement decisions, proportionate to the risks or seriousness of any breach, and assist in ensuring consistency of enforcement action.

3.179 The policy statement states that individuals should be prosecuted if it is considered that a prosecution is warranted, Account should be taken of the chain of command and the role of individual directors and managers.

3.180 In England and Wales, the decision to bring a prosecution rests with the enforcing authority, by an inspector, or by or with the consent of the Director of Public Prosecutions (s.38 of HSWA). An inspector, if authorised by the enforcing authority, may conduct the prosecution before a magistrates' court even though he is not a solicitor or a barrister (s.39). However, the inspector has no power to delegate the institution of those proceedings to someone else (eg a local authority's solicitor, see *R v Croydon Justices, ex parte WH Smith Ltd*). In Scotland, the decision is taken by the Procurator Fiscal, either on the recommendation of an enforcing authority or on the Procurator Fiscal's own initiative.

3.181 A refusal by enforcing authorities to take enforcement account can be challenged by judicial review proceedings (*R v Director of Public prosecutions, ex parte Timothy Jones*, 23 March 2000), but if the HSE takes a realistic view that a prosecution would not be successful they are entitled to decline to take such action (*R v HSE, ex parte Pullen* (2003) EWHC 2934).

3.182 It is not necessary for the prosecution to identify a specific breach of duty by a defendant. It is sufficient to prove that there was a risk of injury arising from a state of affairs at work. The burden of proof then passes to the accused under s.40 of the Act (see paragraph 3.196) to prove that they have done all that was reasonably practicable to avoid the risk. Thus, if there has been no risk assessment, or no training given, or no adequate safety precautions provided, it will be difficult for the accused to discharge that burden (*R v Chargot Ltd*). But the prosecution must prove that there was a real risk, as opposed to a fanciful or hypothetical risk. In *R v Porter* the headmaster of a private school was prosecuted following the death of a young pupil, who had fallen down some steps at school. His conviction was quashed on appeal, the incident being the tragic consequence of the hazards of everyday life, and the child in question had not been exposed to a real risk by the accused.

3.183   The HSE publishes in its Annual Report the names of all the companies and individuals who have been convicted in the previous 12 months of breaking health and safety legislation, following prosecutions by HSE. Their names will also appear on a website (to be found at *www.hse-databases.co.uk/prosecutions*).

3.184   Under a protocol agreed between the HSE, the Association of Chief Police Officers, the British Transport Police and the Crown Prosecution Services, a CID officer will have to attend the scene of any sudden death in the workplace to assess whether a charge of manslaughter may be brought.

3.185   Changes to the sentencing powers of all courts have been made by the Health and Safety (Offences) Act 2008, Schedule 3A, as follows:

Offence	Summary Conviction	On indictment
1. Failure to discharge a duty under ss.2–6	£20,000 and/or 12 months imprisonment	unlimited fine and/or two years imprisonment
2 Failure to discharge a duty under s.7	Statutory maximum fine and/or 12 months imprisonment	unlimited fine and/or two years imprisonment
3. Contravening s.8	£20,000 and/or 12 months imprisonment	unlimited fine and/or two years imprisonment
4. Offence under s.9	£20,000 fine	unlimited fine
5. Contravening health and safety regulations	£20,000 and/or 12 months imprisonment	unlimited fine and/or two years imprisonment

6. Contravening a requirement relating to investigations or obstructing anyone exercising powers under s.14	Fine up to Level 5 on the standard scale	
7. Contravening requirements under s.20 (powers of inspector)	£20,000 fine and/or 12 months imprisonment	unlimited fine and/or two years imprisonment
8. Contravening requirement under s.25 (power of inspector to seize and render harmless articles or substances likely to cause imminent danger	£20,000 fine and/or 12 months imprisonment	unlimited fine and/or two years imprisonment
9. Preventing a person from appearing before an inspector or from answering questions under s.20(2)	£20,000 fine and/or 12 months imprisonment	unlimited fine and/or two years imprisonment
10. Contravening a requirement imposed by a prohibition notice or an improvement notice	£20,000 fine and/or 12 months imprisonment	unlimited fine and/or two years imprisonment
11. Intentionally obstructing an inspector or customs officer under s.25A	51 weeks imprisonment and/or fine up to level 5 on the standard scale	
12. Contravening a notice served under s.27(1) requiring information	Fine not exceeding the statutory maximum	unlimited fine

13. Using or disclosing information in contravention of s 27(4) or s.28	Fine not exceeding the statutory maximum and/or 12 months imprisonment	unlimited fine and/or two years imprisonment
14. Making a false or reckless statement in purported compliance with a statutory provision, or for the purpose of obtaining a document under any statutory provision (s.33(1)(k))	£20,000 fine and/or 12 months imprisonment	unlimited fine and/or two years imprisonment
15. Making a false entry in any register, book or other document required to be kept (s.33(1)(l))	£20,000 fine and/or 12 months imprisonment	unlimited fine and/or two years imprisonment
16. With intent to deceive, using a document issued under a relevant statutory provision (s.33(1)(m)	£20,000 fine and/or 12 months imprisonment	unlimited fine and/or two years imprisonment
17. Falsely pretending to be an inspector	Fine not exceeding level 5 on the standard scale	
18. Failing to comply with an order of the court under s.42 (order to remedy)	£20,000 fine and/or 12 months imprisonment	unlimited fine and/or two years imprisonment

19. An offence under the existing statutory provisions for which no other penalty is specified (eg acting without a licence contravening a licence, acquiring using or possessing explosives contrary to the relevant statutory provisions, etc).	£20,000 fine and/or 12 months imprisonment	unlimited fine and/or two years imprisonment

3.186   **Note:** Currently, the 'statutory maximum' fine and a fine on Level 5 of the standard scale are both £5000).

3.187   In 2007/2008 the HSE prosecuted some 1028 offences, of which 839 resulted in a conviction. The average fine was £12,896, although when certain extremely high fines are excluded, the average figure is lower. In the same period, local authorities prosecuted 354 offences, of which 334 resulted in a conviction. The average fine was £5650, which figure does include a number of maximum fines.

3.188   In recent years, there have been signs that the courts are prepared to impose stiff penalties for breaches of health and safety law. There are several instances where custodial and suspended prison sentences have been imposed, for example for failure to comply with a prohibition notice. For example, a sentence of 12 months' imprisonment (as well as a fine) was imposed on a company director who failed to ensure that protective clothing was supplied to a worker who came into contact with a deadly chemical and who, in consequence, was killed. Substantial fines have also been imposed. In 2005 a fine of £15 million was imposed following a domestic gas explosion which killed four members of the same family (*Transco v HM Advocate*), and in 2004 a fine of £2 million was imposed following the Ladbroke Grove rail disaster (*Thames Trains Ltd v Health and Safety Executive*).

3.189   For many years critics have suggested that the level of fines imposed by the courts for breaches of health and safety legislation has been too low, but a 1999 decision by the Court of Appeal gave guidance on the criteria to be adopted by magistrates and judges, which will undoubtedly result in significantly higher fines being imposed. In *R v*

Howe & Sons (Engineers) Ltd, it was stated that a fine needs to be large enough to bring the message home to managers and shareholders that the purpose of enforcing health and safety legislation is to achieve a safe environment for those who work in a workplace and for other members of the public who may be affected. The court suggested a three-stage approach should be adopted: criteria, aggravating factors and mitigating factors.

3.190 The criteria to be adopted when assessing the gravity of the breach is for the court initially to see how far the defendant fell short of the appropriate standard of reasonably practicable. Sometimes, it will be a matter of chance whether death or serious injury results from a serious breach, but if death does result, the penalty should reflect the public disquiet at the unnecessary loss of life. A deliberate breach is to be regarded seriously. The size of a company and its financial strength or weakness cannot affect the degree of care that is required, because those firms lacking in-house expertise can obtain assistance from the HSE or other sources. The degree of risk, the extent of the danger, the extent of the breach (ie whether an isolated incident or one which continued over a period) and the defendant's resources and the effect of a fine on the business should all be taken into account. If a company wishes to make any submissions about its ability to pay a fine, it should produce its annual accounts prior to the hearing and these should be examined carefully. If the accounts are not produced, the court will draw any necessary conclusion about the company's ability to pay a fine.

3.191 The aggravating factors to be taken into account will include a failure to heed warnings and a defendant either specifically running a risk to save money or deliberately profiting financially from the failure to take necessary health and safety steps. A deliberate breach of health and safety legislation with a view to profit will always seriously aggravate the offence.

3.192 Mitigating factors which a court can take into account include a prompt admission of responsibility and a timely admission of guilt. It will also count in a defendant's favour if steps were taken immediately to remedy any deficiencies after these were drawn to his attention. A previous good safety record will also help by way of mitigation.

3.193 Subsequently, the Court of Appeal in *R v Friskies Petcare (UK) Ltd* gave further guidance on the approach to sentencing policies. It was suggested that the HSE should list, in writing, for the assistance of the court, the aggravating features alleged to exist, and the defendant should then be invited to outline the mitigating features which it says the court should take into account. In this way, both sides will know and understand the basis on which the court can make its appropriate decision. It was further suggested that large fines, in excess of £500,000, tend to be reserved for those cases where a major public disaster occurs, or where breaches of legislation put large numbers of the public at risk of serious injury. A high fine is appropriate where safety has been deliberately sacrificed for profit.

3.194   Fines for health and safety offences are increasing in severity, although this is mainly due to stiffer sentences being handed out in higher courts. It is thought that the programme of "naming and shaming" convicted offenders on the HSE's website may assist contracting organisations to look at tender bids and scrutinise potential job applicants, and generally enable investors to evaluate management competence.

3.195   As we have seen (paragraph 1.115), punishment for an offence under the Corporate Manslaughter and Corporate Homicide Act 2007 is likely to be severe, probably as a percentage of the company's annual global turnover. The existence of a previous warning would be an aggravating factor. As well as a remedial order requiring the organisation to take specified steps to remedy the breach, a publicity order, detailing the facts and circumstances of the conviction, may also be made.

Burden of proof (s.40)

3.196   As a general rule, it is for the prosecution to prove its case beyond reasonable doubt. However, s.40 provides that if the offence consists of a failure to comply with a duty or requirement to do something "so far as is practicable" or "so far as is reasonably practicable" or to "use the best practicable means", it shall be for the accused to prove that it was not practicable or not reasonably practicable to do more than was in fact done or that there was no better practicable means than was in fact used to satisfy the duty or requirement. However, when this burden is placed on the accused, he need only satisfy the court on the balance of probabilities that what he has to prove has been done (*R v Carr-Briant*).

3.197   The fact that s.40 reverses the burden of proof does not violate a person's rights under the Human Rights Act 1998. The Court of Appeal has held that it was necessary to balance the fundamental rights of the individual with the general interests of the community in ensuring health and safety at work, and the reversal of the burden of proof was necessary and proportionate, and thus compatible with the European Convention on Human Rights (*Davies v Health and Safety Executive*).

Offences due to the fault of another person (s.36)

3.198   Where the commission of an offence by any person is due to the act or default of some other person, that other person shall be guilty of an offence and may be charged and convicted, whether or not proceedings are taken against the first-mentioned person (s.36(1)). If an offence is committed by the Crown, but the Crown cannot be prosecuted (see paragraph 3.12) and the offence is due to the act or default of a person other than the Crown, that person shall be guilty of the offence and may be charged and convicted accordingly (s.36(2)). Thus employees of the Crown may be convicted, even though the Crown itself is immune.

Offences by directors, managers, secretaries, etc (s.37)

3.199   Where an offence committed by a body corporate is proved to have been committed with the consent or connivance of, or attributable to any neglect on the part of, any director, manager, secretary or other similar officer of the body corporate, or a person who was purporting to act in such capacity, then he, as well as the body corporate shall be guilty of that offence and shall be liable to be proceeded against (s.37(1)). A director consents to the commission of an offence when he is well aware of what is going on and agrees to it. He will be deemed to connive to an offence when he is equally well aware of what is going on but his agreement is tacit, not actively encouraging what happens, but letting it continue and saying nothing about it (*Huckerby v Elliot*). He will be committing an act of neglect if he is under a duty to do something and fails to do it, or if he does it in a negligent manner. This section was considered in *Armour v Skeen*, where the Strathclyde Regional Council and its Director of Roads were both prosecuted for a breach of safety regulations, lack of a safe system of work and failing to notify an inspector that certain work was being undertaken. As a result of these failures, an employee of the council was killed. The alleged neglect on the part of the Director of Roads was a failure to have a sound safety policy for his department, failing to provide information to his subordinates and a failure to provide training and instructions in safe working practices. He was convicted of the offences and the conviction was upheld on appeal. The fact that s.2 of HSWA imposes a duty on the employers to provide a safe system of work did not mean that there was no duty on his part to carry out that duty. Section 37(1) refers to "any neglect", not to the neglect of a duty imposed. The offences were committed by the body corporate, but were due to his neglect. Further, although his title as "Director of Roads" did not mean he was a "director" within the meaning of s.37(1), he was within the scope of the words "manager or similar officer".

3.200 Persons who purport to act as directors, managers, secretaries or similar officers are equally liable. Thus if a person acts as a director even though he has been disqualified from doing so under the Companies Act, he is purporting to act as such. Nor do the words "purporting to act" imply that there is a fraudulent or false intention in so acting. Anyone who acts in a managerial capacity may be held liable under s.37(1) whatever title he may have. If the affairs of the body corporate are being managed by its members (eg a workers' co-operative), then the acts of a member which are in connection with his managerial functions are within the meaning of this section (s.37(2)).

3.201 A director does not escape responsibility for health and safety matters by appointing a third party to carry out the necessary duties. The director must make sure that an independent third party is competent and properly supervised, but the director has to accept greater responsibility for the safety of employees and others than those who are engaged on a part-time basis to assist (*R v Ceri Davies*).

3.202 For a person to be convicted under this section, it must be shown that he has some responsibility for the making of management decisions, and be in a position of responsibility. In *R v Boal*, the accused was the assistant general manager of Foyle's bookshop. He had been given no management training, and in particular, none in health and safety matters, or fire precautions. He was, however, in charge of the shop while the general manager was away on a week's holiday. During this period, the premises were visited by officers from the local fire authority, who discovered that there were serious breaches of the fire certificate which had been issued. Foyle's and the accused were charged with a number of offences under the Fire Precautions Act 1971 — Foyle's as the "body corporate" and the accused because the 1971 Act provides that "...where an offence committed by a body corporate is proved... to be attributable to any neglect on the part of any director, manager, secretary or other similar officer of the body corporate, he as well as the body corporate shall be guilty of that offence...".

3.203 Foyle's were convicted on 11 counts, and were fined. The accused pleaded guilty to three counts and was found guilty of seven others. He was sentenced to three months' imprisonment, suspended for 12 months. He then appealed against the conviction on the ground that he was not a "... manager or other similar officer..." within the meaning of the Act.

3.204 The Court of Appeal (Criminal Division) allowed his appeal. A person was "a manager" if he had power of "... the management of the whole of the affairs of the company..." or was "... entrusted with power to transact the whole of the affairs of the company..." or was "managing in a governing role the affairs of the company itself". The court further thought that the intended scope of s.23 of the Fire Precautions Act was "... to fix with criminal liability only those who are in a position of real authority, the decision makers within the company who have both the power and responsibility to decide corporate policy and strategy. It is to catch those responsible for putting proper procedures in place; it is not meant to strike at underlings."

Additional powers of the court (s.42)

3.205 If a person is convicted of an offence under any of the relevant statutory provisions in respect of any matter which appears to the court to be something which is in his power to remedy, the court may (in addition to, or instead of, any other punishment) order him, within such time as may be fixed, to take specified steps to remedy the matter. An application may be made to the court for an extension of time within which to comply with the order.

3.206 If a person is convicted of an offence under s.34(4)(c) (acquiring, possessing or using an explosive article or substance in contravention of a relevant statutory provision), the court may order the article or substance to be forfeited or destroyed or dealt with in such other manner as the court may order. Before making a forfeiture order the court must give an opportunity to the owner (or any other person with an interest in the article or substance) an opportunity to show cause why the order should not be made.

3.207   A failure to comply with an order under s.42 (eg if a person fails to take the necessary remedial action) is punishable by a fine of up to £20,000, and/or six months' imprisonment on summary conviction, and an unlimited fine and/or two years' imprisonment if convicted in the crown court.

Disqualification of directors

3.208   Under s.2 of the Company Directors Disqualification Act 1986, the court may disqualify a person from being a director of a company if he is convicted of an indictable offence, whether on indictment or summarily, if the offence was in connection with the management of the company. A magistrates' court may impose a disqualification for up to five years, while the higher court may disqualify for up to 15 years. To date, ten directors have been disqualified as a result of serious health and safety offences (eg a failure to comply with a prohibition notice). The disqualification can be in addition to any other penalty imposed.

Time limits for prosecutions

3.209   By virtue of s.127 of the Magistrates' Courts Act 1980, a prosecution for a summary offence must be commenced by the laying of an information (ie issuing a summons) within six months from the date of the commission of the offence. However, s.34 of HSWA specifies that in certain cases an extension of the time limit may be possible. These are:
  (a) where there has been a special report made by a person holding an investigation under s.14(2)(a) (see paragraph 2.10)
  (b) where a report is made by a person holding an inquiry under s.14(2)(b) (see paragraph 2.11)
  (c) a coroner's inquest is held touching the death of a person which may have been caused by an accident happening at work, or a disease contracted at work
  (d) a public enquiry is held into a death so caused under Scottish legislation.

If it appears from the report, inquest or inquiry that a relevant statutory provision was contravened, then summary proceedings may be commenced at any time within three months from the making of the report, or the conclusion of the inquest or inquiry (s.34(1)).

3.210   If an offence is committed by a designer, manufacturer, importer or supplier (ie s.6 offences) then summary proceedings may be commenced at any time within six months from the date when the enforcing authority had sufficient evidence, in its opinion, to justify a prosecution (or, in Scotland, to justify the making of a report to the Lord Advocate). A certificate of an enforcing authority stating that such evidence came to its knowledge on a specified date shall be conclusive evidence of that fact (ss.34(3), (4), (5)). However, this provision appears to be superfluous since the passing of the Criminal Law Act 1977 (see *Kemp v Leibherr (GB) Ltd*) because s.6 offences are hybrid offences (ie triable either summarily or on indictment).

3.211   When an offence is committed by reason of a failure to do something within a fixed time, the offence shall be deemed to continue until that thing is done (s.34(2)).

Indictable offences

3.212   Because of the maxim "Time does not run against the Crown", a prosecution in respect of an indictable offence is never barred by time limits. Since most of the offences under HSWA are triable either way (ie potentially indictable), the six-month time limit has limited effect and applies to those offences which are summary only. Hybrid offences are deemed to be indictable offences so far as time limits for prosecution are concerned (*Kemp v Leibherr (GB) Ltd*).

3.213   However, it will be recalled that Article 6 of the European Convention on Human Rights (see paragraph 1.160) provides that in the determination of civil and criminal rights and obligations, everyone is entitled to a fair and public hearing within a reasonable time. It is therefore likely that a prosecution brought long after the enforcing authority was aware of the essential facts would be dismissed under the Human Rights Act 1998.

Alternative sanctions

3.214   The Regulatory Enforcement and Sanctions Act 2008 is designed to introduce a new system of regulatory enforcement and sanctions in respect of a wide range of matters which are the subject of regulatory control. A Local Better Regulation Office is created, which will enable a more consistent and co-ordinated regulatory enforcement regime to operate, while other regulators (eg the HSE) will also be given more flexible powers to deal with breaches of legal requirements. In brief, the Act will enable regulators to impose:

(a) fixed monetary penalties in respect of low-level instances of non-compliance

(b) variable monetary penalties, the value of which will be determined by the regulator

(c) compliance notices, requiring certain actions to be taken to bring the offender back into compliance

(d) restoration notices, which will require a person to undertake action to restore a position to the way it would have been had a regulatory non-compliance not occurred

(e) stop notices, requiring a person to cease an activity that is causing harm or presents a serious risk of injury

(f) enforcement undertakings, requiring a person to take specific action. These powers will be an alternative to prosecution.

3.215 It appears that the HSE is somewhat cool about the Act's provisions, the view being taken that there already exist sufficient powers to deal with infractions of health and safety law. It is thought that local authorities are more likely to use the new sanctions when dealing with minor or technical infringements.

CHAPTER 4

Health and safety management

4.1   In this chapter, we shall consider some of the legal requirements which are the minimum requirements of a health and safety management programme.

4.2   Successful health and safety management begins with a commitment by all concerned within an organisation, but in particular by the decision-makers, whose actions (or inaction) will have a powerful influence on the attitudes of the rest of the workforce. But the commitment should not be just lip-service. A structured and planned approach must be adopted and implemented and appropriate resources made available. Health and safety must always be regarded as a prime responsibility of all levels of management and not solely of those who have been given specific assignments. An attitude of indifference or a lack of knowledge displayed by those who are in senior positions will quickly percolate throughout the organisation.

4.3   The success of a health and safety management programme will be proportionate to the effort put into a structured approach to the problem. It is generally accepted that there are five steps to be adopted, and the input required at each stage will usually depend on the particular problems encountered and solutions adopted. The HSE has published a booklet HSG65: *Successful Health and Safety Management*, to which reference may be made. Also the British Standards publication BS 8800: 2004, *Guide to Occupational Health and Safety Management* and OHSAS 18001: 2007 *Occupational Health and Safety Management Systems Specification* may be of use.

1. *Policy:* The policy on health and safety should not be limited to the written statement, which needs to be given to all employees under s.2(3) of HSWA (see paragraph 3.59), but should be a policy which demands that health and safety considerations be given top priority by all levels of management, and a commitment to find the resources to meet that policy. Appropriate health and safety rules and procedures should be adopted not only with regard to systems of work, but for purchasing tools, equipment, materials, services, etc. All the activities of the organisation can be considered with a view to the implementation of the policy.

2. *Organisation:* The overall responsibility for overseeing the implementation of the policy should be a function of senior management, but particular responsibilities can be assigned in specific areas. Effective communication will be needed, competence established, and participation encouraged at all levels.

3. *Planning:* The actual implementation of the policy through the established health and safety organisation will be the subject of detailed planning. Risk assessments should be undertaken, training needs identified, shortcomings noted and rectified, control methods introduced, and so on. Each organisation will adopt the methods most suited to deal with its own particular problems, and find its own solutions.

4. *Measuring performance:* Once predetermined standards and objectives have been laid down, it will then be possible to measure performance, so as to identify those areas where further action needs be taken and further improvements made. It should also identify underlying causes or weaknesses, and generally tighten up on existing health and safety practices.

5. *Reviewing performance:* Health and safety audits, operated systematically and on a regular basis, will then reveal the success or otherwise of the health and safety management programme. Statistics can be analysed, incidents examined, lessons learned, and recommendations for further action made. New or developing knowledge can be noted and considered, and the experiences of other organisations taken into account. Successful health and safety management frequently depends on the ability to foresee problems before they arise, rather than dealing with them once they have arisen.

Management of Health and Safety at Work Regulations 1999

4.4   The original Management Regulations were passed in 1992 in order to implement the provisions of the Framework Directive (89/391/EEC) and the Temporary Workers Directive (91/383/EEC). The regulations were amended in 1994 in order to implement the Pregnant Workers Directive (92/85/EEC) and again in 1997 in order to implement the Protection of Young Persons at Work Directive (94/33/EC).

4.5 All these provisions are consolidated in the Management of Health and Safety at Work Regulations 1999, which came into force at the end of that year, with additional provisions relating to the general principles of prevention set out in Directive (89/391/EEC), and some further minor amendments to the Health and Safety (First Aid) Regulations 1981, Mines Miscellaneous Health and Safety Provisions Regulations 1995, Construction (Health Safety and Welfare) Regulations 1996, and Fire Precautions (Workplace) Regulations 1997. The regulations were further amended by the Management of Health and Safety at Work and Fire Precautions (Workplace) (Amendment) Regulations 2003, the Management of Health and Safety at Work and Health and Safety (Consultation with Employees) (Amendment) Regulations 2005, the Regulatory Reform (Fire Safety) Order 2005 and the Management of Health and Safety at Work (Amendment) Regulations 2006.

4.6 The regulations apply to all work activities to which HSWA applies, including offshore activities and trainees, but not to merchant shipping. The Secretary of Defence may, in the interests of national security, exempt the armed forces from certain obligations (other than regulations 16–18) and members of the armed forces from certain requirements (other than regulation 14).

4.7 The 1999 regulations were accompanied by a new Approved Code of Practice L21: *Management of Health and Safety at Work Regulations 1999* and Guidance Notes.

Risk assessment (regulation 3)

4.8 Every employer shall make a suitable and sufficient assessment of:
  (a) the risks to the health and safety of his employees to which they are exposed while they are at work, and
  (b) the risks to the health and safety of persons not in his employment arising out of or in connection with the conduct by him of his undertaking,

for the purpose of identifying the measures he needs to take to comply with the requirements and prohibitions imposed on him by or under the relevant statutory provisions and the Regulatory Reform (Fire Safety)

Order 2005. A similar duty is placed on self-employed persons, with regard to the risks to his own health and safety, and the safety of others not in his employment.

4.9   The assessment shall be reviewed by the employer or self-employed person if there is reason to suspect it is no longer valid, or there has been a significant change in the matters to which it relates. If on review, changes to the assessment are required, these are to be made.

4.10   An employer shall not employ a young person (ie under the age of 18) unless he has made or reviewed an assessment, taking particular account of:

   (a) the inexperience, lack of awareness of risks and the immaturity of young persons

   (b) the fitting out and layout of the workplace and the workstation

   (c) the nature, degree and duration of exposure to physical, biological and chemical agents

   (d) the form, range and use of work equipment and the way it is handled

   (e) the organisation of processes and activities

   (f) the extent of health and safety training provided or to be provided to young persons

   (g) the risks from agents, processes and work listed in the Annex to Council Directive (94/133/EC) on the protection of young people at work (Annex A deals with ionising radiation, work in high pressure atmosphere, biological and certain chemical agents, and certain types of work connected with explosives, high voltage electrical hazards, dangerous animals, dangerous gases, and work where there is a risk of a structural collapse, etc).

4.11   The requirement to make an assessment for young persons does not apply to occasional work or short-term working involving domestic service in a private household, or work regulated as not being harmful, damaging or dangerous to young people in a family undertaking.

4.12   If the employer employs five or more employees, he shall record the significant findings of the assessment, and any group of his employees identified by it as being specially at risk. Normally this would be done in writing, but it could be recorded by some other means (eg electronically) as long as it is retrievable for use or examination.

4.13   A failure to carry out a risk assessment, which would have identified a potential source of injury (eg the need to vary working practices so as to avoid work-related upper limb disorder) could be evidence of negligence in a civil claim for damages (*Godfrey v Bernard Matthews plc*). In a criminal case, if it is alleged that an employer failed to carry out an adequate and sufficient risk assessment so as to properly assess the risks involved, the prosecution must specify in what respects the risk assessment was alleged to be inadequate. It is not enough merely to rely on the fact that an accident happened (*Heermac VOF v Munro*).

4.14   Something is a "risk" if there is a chance or possibility of danger, loss, injury or other adverse consequence. Thus the extent of the risk will depend on the likelihood of harm occurring, the potential severity of that harm, and the person or persons who may be adversely affected.

4.15   A "hazard" is something with the potential to cause harm. Thus a risk assessment will establish the likelihood of potential harm from that hazard being realised. The ACOP to the Management Regulations states that "A risk assessment is carried out to identify the risks to health and safety to any person arising out of, or in connection with, work or the conduct of their undertaking. It should identify how the risks arise and how they impact on those affected. This information is needed to make decisions on how to manage those risks so that the decisions are made in an informed, rational and structured manner, and the action taken is appropriate".

4.16   When carrying out a risk assessment, all aspects of the work activity need to be examined, including routine and non-routine activities. The HSE has produced a Guidance Note — *Five Steps to Risk Assessment* — which states that there are no hard and fast rules, the emphasis being on flexibility and common sense.

4.17   A risk assessment will be "suitable and sufficient" if it enables the employer (or self-employed person) to identify the risks arising from work. To do this, employers should look at appropriate sources of information, eg relevant legislation, suppliers' manuals, manufacturers' instructions, the trade press, or seek advice from a competent source. The risk assessment should be appropriate to the nature of the work, and identify the period of time for which it is likely to remain valid. It should identify what the hazards are, who might be exposed to harm (and how) as well as evaluate the risks. This will enable the employer to prioritise the measures which need to be taken to comply with the relevant statutory provisions.

4.18   Risk assessments should be reviewed at regular intervals, but in particular when the nature of the work changes or there has been a further appreciation of hazards or risks. The monitoring of health and safety arrangements required by regulation 5 may reveal further hazards, which can be the subject of a revised assessment.

4.19   There are no fixed rules about how a risk assessment should be carried out, for this will depend on the nature of the undertaking and the type of hazards and risks present. For small undertakings it can be a simple process based on judgment and will require no specialist skills or complicated techniques. At the other extreme, it may be the basis for a complete safety case. In intermediate cases, specialist advice may be necessary in respect of unfamiliar risks. Separate assessment exercises may be necessary in particular operations or groups of hazards. The views of employees, safety representatives, advisors, etc, should be taken into account. A structured approach should always be adopted.

4.20   In particular, the ACOP suggests that a risk assessment should:
   (a) ensure that the significant risks and hazards are addressed
   (b) ensure that all aspects of the work activity are reviewed, including routine and non-routine activities, and those which are not under the immediate supervision of the employer, eg relating to contractors, loaned employees, the self-employed, homeworkers, mobile workers, etc
   (c) take account of non-routine operations, including maintenance, cleaning operations, loading and unloading of vehicles, emergency response arrangements, etc
   (d) take account of the management of incidents such as interruptions to the work activity, including the procedures which should be followed
   (e) be systematic in identifying the risks and hazards — activities should be looked at in groups, eg machinery, transport, substances, electrical, etc, and sometimes an operational approach is appropriate, eg production, despatch, office work, etc
   (f) take account of the way the work is organised, and the effect this can have on health
   (g) take account of the risks to the public

(h) take account of the need to consider fire risks — if necessary, a separate assessment should be carried out.

4.21   Where an assessment is required to be made under some other regulation (eg COSHH, etc, see paragraph 7.1) that will cover in part the obligation to make an assessment under the Management Regulations, it need not be repeated as long as it remains valid. On the other hand, an assessment under the Management Regulations may reveal that a further assessment should be made under the other regulation.

Principles of prevention to be applied (regulation 4)

4.22   Where the employer implements any preventative and protective measures, he shall do so on the basis of the principles set out in schedule 1 to the regulations. This involves:
(a) avoiding risks
(b) evaluating risks that cannot be avoided
(c) combating the risks at source
(d) adapting the work to the individual, especially as regards the design of the workplace, the choice of work equipment, and the choice of working and production methods, with a view, in particular, to alleviating monotonous work and work at a pre-determined work-rate and to reduce their effect on health
(e) adapting to technical progress
(f) replacing the dangerous with the non-dangerous or less dangerous
(g) developing a coherent overall prevention policy that covers technology, organisation of work, working conditions, social relationships and the influence of factors relating to the working environment
(h) giving collective protective measures priority over individual protective measures
(i) giving appropriate instructions to employees.

Health and safety arrangements (regulation 5)

4.23   Every employer shall make and give effect to such arrangements as are appropriate, having regard to the nature of his activities and the size of his undertaking, for the effective planning, organisation, control monitoring and review of the preventative and protective measures. Where the employer employs five or more employees, he shall record these arrangements.

4.24 The ACOP suggests that a health and safety management system should consist of five elements.

1. *Planning.* Once a systematic approach to the completion of a risk assessment has been adopted, priorities and objectives can be set for eliminating hazards and reducing risks. A programme should be adopted, deadlines set, risk control methods selected, and performance standards developed.

2. *Organisation.* This includes involving employees and their representatives in carrying out risk assessments, deciding on preventative protective measures, and implementing those requirements. Effective means of communication should be established, health and safety information communicated to employees, and competence secured by the provision of adequate information, instruction and training.

3. *Control.* Health and safety responsibilities should be well co-ordinated, those with responsibilities given time and resources to discharge them effectively, standards set, and adequate and appropriate supervision provided.

4. *Monitoring.* Adequate routine inspections and checks should ensure that preventative and protective measures are in place and are effective. The underlying causes of incidents and accidents should be adequately investigated, remedial action taken, and lessons learned.

5. *Review.* Priorities should be established for any necessary remedial action discovered necessary as a result of the monitoring, to ensure that suitable action is taken in good time and is completed. The whole management system needs to be reviewed to ensure that it remains effective.

Health surveillance (regulation 6)

4.25 Every employer shall ensure that his employees are provided with such health surveillance as is appropriate having regard to the risks to their health and safety which are identified by the assessment.

4.26 The ACOP suggests that once the risk assessment has been done, it should be possible to identify the circumstances when health surveillance is required by specific health and safety regulations (eg under COSHH, etc). Health surveillance should also be introduced when:

(a) there is an identifiable work-related disease or adverse health condition

(b) valid detection techniques are available

(c) there is a reasonable likelihood that the disease or condition may occur under the particular working conditions

(d) surveillance is likely to further the protection of the employees to be covered.

4.27   The object of surveillance is to detect adverse effects of ill health at an early stage, thus preventing further harm. Additionally, the effectiveness of control measures can be checked, as well as the accuracy of the risk assessment. If health surveillance is appropriate, individual health records should be kept. Health surveillance procedures will depend, for their suitability, on the circumstances.

Health and safety assistance (regulation 7)

4.28   Every employer shall employ one or more competent persons to assist him in undertaking the measures he needs to take to comply with the requirements of the relevant statutory provisions and the Regulatory Reform (Fire Safety) Order 2005. This does not apply to a self-employed person (who is not in partnership with another person), where he has sufficient training and experience or knowledge to undertake those measures himself. Nor does regulation 7 apply to a partnership which employs persons where at least one of the partners has sufficient training and experience or knowledge and other qualities to carry out the measures needed to ensure compliance with the statutory requirements and prohibitions, and can properly assist the partnership in carrying out those measures.

4.29   If the employer appoints more than one person, he shall make arrangements to ensure adequate co-operation between them. The number of persons appointed and the time and means made available to them to fulfil their functions shall be adequate having regard to the size of the undertaking, the risks to which employees are exposed, and the distribution of those risks throughout the undertaking.

4.30   The person designated to provide health and safety assistance need not be an employee of the employer. However, if an outside consultant is appointed, the employer must inform him of all the factors known to the employer of the conduct of the undertaking that may affect the health and safety of any person. The employer must also give the outside consultant access to the information referred to in regulation 10 (below), as well as details of persons working under a fixed-term contract or employed in an employment business. But if there is a competent person in the employer's employment, he shall be appointed as a safety assistant under regulation 7 in preference to an outside consultant.

4.31 A person shall be regarded as being competent if he has sufficient training and experience or knowledge and other qualities to enable him properly to assist in carrying out the measures which the employer needs to take in order to comply with the statutory provisions.

4.32 The ACOP states that it is the employer's responsibility to ensure that those who are appointed to assist with health and safety measures are competent to carry out the tasks assigned to them (taking into account the complexities of the work situation and the skills required), and to ensure that they are given adequate information and support. The appointment of a competent person should be included among the health and safety arrangements under regulation 5 (above), and safety representatives should be consulted on the arrangements for the appointment for competent assistance.

Procedures for serious and imminent danger and for danger areas (regulation 8)

4.33 Every employer shall establish, and give effect to, appropriate procedures to be followed in the event of serious and imminent dangers to persons at work in his undertaking. Competent persons shall be nominated to implement evacuation procedures. The procedures shall, so far as is practicable, require any persons at work who are exposed to serious and imminent danger to be informed of the nature of the hazard, and of the steps to be taken to protect them from it. They should be able to stop work and immediately proceed to a place of safety and, save in exceptional circumstances specified in the procedures (eg emergency services), require the persons concerned to be prevented from resuming work while there is a danger.

4.34 The employer shall ensure that none of his employees has access to any area occupied by him which it is necessary to restrict access on grounds of health and safety unless the employee concerned has received adequate health and safety instruction.

Contacts with external services (regulation 9)

4.35 Every employer shall ensure that any necessary contacts with external services are arranged, particularly as regards first aid, emergency medical care, and rescue work.

4.36 The ACOP states that procedures should be established for any worker to follow if situations presenting serious and imminent danger were to arise. This should set out the nature of the risk and how to respond to it, additional procedures to cover risks beyond those caused by fire and bombs (eg a release of toxic gases), the additional responsibilities of particular employees who may have specific tasks to perform (eg shutting down plant), the role, responsibilities and authority of the competent people nominated to implement detailed action, and details of how and when the procedures are to be activated so that employees can proceed in good time to a place of safety.

4.37 Emergency procedures should be written down, under regulation 5 (above) and made known to the safety assistants under regulation 7 (above), to employees under regulation 10 (below) and to non-employees under regulation 12 (below). They should form part of any induction course (regulation 13 below). Test exercises should be carried out.

4.38 Work should not be resumed after an emergency if a serious danger remains. After the emergency has passed, consideration should be given to a review of the risk assessment.

Information for employees (regulation 10)

4.39 Every employer shall provide his employees with comprehensible and relevant information on:
  (a) the risks to their health and safety identified by the assessment
  (b) the preventative and protective measures
  (c) procedures dealing with serious and imminent dangers, danger areas, and fire-fighting measures
  (d) the identity of persons nominated to implement evacuation procedures and fire-fighting measures

(e) the risks which have been notified to him by another employer with whom the workplace is shared.

4.40 Before employing a child (ie a person who is not above compulsory school-leaving age) the employer shall provide the child's parents with comprehensible and relevant information on:
(a) the risks to health identified by the assessment
(b) the preventative and protective measures
(c) any information provided to him by another employer with whom the workplace is shared concerning the risks to the employees' health and safety arising from the conduct by that other employer of his undertaking (regulation 11(1)(c)).

4.41 However, this requirement does not apply to occasional work or short-term work involving domestic service in a private household, or work regulated as not being harmful, damaging or dangerous to young people in a family undertaking.

4.42 The ACOP states that the information should be capable of being understood by the employees concerned and will thus take into account their level of training, knowledge and experience. Special attention should be given to persons with language difficulties or physical disabilities which may affect their receipt of information (eg blind persons, persons whose first language is not English, etc).

4.43 Persons who are on fixed-term contracts are required to have additional information (see regulation 15, below).

Co-operation and co-ordination (regulation 11)

4.44 Where two or more employers share a workplace (whether on a temporary or permanent basis), each employer shall:
(a) co-operate with other employers concerned so far as is necessary to enable them to comply with their statutory duties
(b) take all reasonable steps to co-ordinate health and safety measures with those which the other employers are taking to comply with statutory provisions
(c) take all reasonable steps to inform the other employers concerned of the risks to their employees' health and safety arising out of the conduct by him of his undertaking.

4.45 This regulation also applies to employers who are sharing the workplace with self-employed persons, and to self-employed persons who are sharing with other self-employed persons.

4.46 The ACOP points out that where a worksite is under the control of a main employer, other employers (or self-employed persons) on the site should assist in assessing shared risks and co-ordinating any necessary measures. Equally, the controlling employer will have to establish site-wide arrangements and this information should be passed on, as appropriate. If there is no employer in control, joint arrangements should be agreed and consideration given to the appointment of a health and safety co-ordinator.

Visiting workers (regulation 12)

4.47 Every employer, and every self-employed person, shall ensure that the employer of any visiting employees is provided with comprehensible information on:
  (a) the risks to the visiting employees' health and safety arising out of the conduct of the undertaking
  (b) the measures taken to ensure compliance with the statutory requirements insofar as they relate to those visiting employees.

4.48 The employer shall then ensure that every visiting worker is provided with appropriate instructions and comprehensible information regarding any risks to that person's health and safety which arise out of the conduct of the employer's undertaking. Employers must also ensure that the employer of any visiting employee, as well as the visiting employee, is provided with sufficient information to identify the person responsible for evacuation procedures.

4.49 In other words, an employer owes a duty to the employer of any visiting employee who comes on to his premises, and to the visiting employee as well.

4.50 The ACOP points out that the risk assessment should have identified risks to people who come on to the employer's premises. Thus, comprehensible information on those risks, and the measures to be taken to control them, should be given to visiting workers. If necessary, the information can be provided through a written permit-to-work system. Information provided to employees under regulation 10 should be provided to visiting workers either directly or through their own employer.

Capabilities and training (regulation 13)

4.51   When entrusting tasks to his employees, every employer shall take account of their capabilities as regards health and safety. The employer shall also ensure that his employees are provided with adequate health and safety training:
  (a) when they are recruited
  (b) on being exposed to new or increased risks because of being transferred, or given new responsibilities, or when new equipment, new technology, or new systems of work are introduced.

4.52   The training should be repeated periodically where appropriate, and adapted to take account of new or changed risks. Training should take place in working hours.

4.53   The employer should ensure that the demands of the job do not exceed the employees' ability to carry out the work without risk to themselves or others. Account should be taken of the employees' capabilities, and the level of their training, knowledge and experience. Managers should be aware of relevant legislation, and be competent to manage health and safety effectively. Health and safety training should take place during normal working hours, but if it is necessary to arrange training outside working hours, this should be treated as an extension of time at work and compensated accordingly.

4.54   The ACOP states that training needs are likely to be greatest on recruitment. Basic training should include the arrangements for first aid, fire and evacuation procedures, as well as general health and safety matters. Refresher training may be needed if particular skills are used infrequently.

Employees' duties (regulation 14)

4.55   Every employee shall use any machinery, equipment, dangerous substances, transport equipment, means of production or safety device provided to him, in accordance with any training received by him and any instructions provided to him by his employer in compliance with the statutory provisions.

4.56   Every employee shall inform his employer (or the person responsible for health and safety matters):
  (a) of any work situation which a person with his training and

instruction would reasonably consider to represent a serious and immediate danger to health and safety

(b) of any matter which a person with his training and instruction would reasonably consider represented a shortcoming in the employer's protection arrangements for health and safety.

4.57 This duty arises insofar as the situation affects the employee's own health and safety, or arises out of his own activities at work. Also, the matter must be one which has not previously been reported to the employer or his safety advisor.

4.58 The ACOP points out that employees have certain duties under s.7 of HSWA, but this regulation clearly goes much further. The employee must report to his employer any work situation which might give rise to a serious or imminent danger to himself or to others if it flows from the work activity. Further, he should report shortcomings in the employer's arrangements even when no danger exists, so that the employer can take remedial action. However, this does not reduce the responsibility of the employer to comply with his statutory duties.

Temporary workers (regulation 15)

4.59 If an employer engages a worker on a fixed-term contract, or engages a person employed by an employment business, the employer must provide that person with comprehensible information on:

(a) any special occupational qualification or skills required to be held by that employee if he is to carry out his work safely

(b) any health surveillance required to be provided to that employee.

4.60 This information is to be provided before the employee concerned commences his duties.

4.61 Where an employer is seeking to have work done by persons who will be provided by an employment agency, he must provide the person carrying on that business with comprehensible information on:

(a) any special occupational qualifications or skills required to be held by the employees if they are to carry out their work safely

(b) the specific features of the jobs to be filled by those employees in so far as those features are likely to affect their health and safety.

4.62 The person carrying on the employment agency shall pass on the information to the employees concerned.

4.63   The ACOP points out that both the user employer and the person carrying on the employment business have duties to provide information to the employees concerned.

Risk assessment for new or expectant mothers (regulation 16)

4.64   Where persons working in an undertaking include women of child-bearing age, and the work is of a kind which could involve risk to the health and safety of a new or expectant mother, or to that of her baby, from any processes or working conditions, or from physical, biological or chemical agents, including those specified in Annexes I and II of Directive 92/185/EEC on measures to encourage improvements in the health and safety at work of pregnant workers and workers who have recently given birth or who are breast-feeding, the assessment required by regulation 3(1) (above) shall include an assessment of such risks.

4.65   Annex I of the directive provides a non-exhaustive list of agents, processes and working conditions in respect of which an employer must make an assessment and decide what measures need to be taken. These include physical agents likely to cause foetal lesions and/or likely to disrupt placental attachment, particularly shocks, vibrations, handling of loads entailing risks, noise, ionising radiation, extremes of cold and heat, movements and posture, travel and mental and physical fatigue. Also specified are certain biological agents and certain chemical agents, insofar as it is known that they endanger the health of a woman or her foetus. Certain industrial processes and underground mine workings are also specified. Annex II to the directive provides for a non-exhaustive list of agents and working conditions to which a pregnant woman must not be exposed, and a further list of agents to which a woman who is breast-feeding must not be exposed.

4.66   The requirement to carry out such a risk assessment is not limited to when a woman is pregnant. The regulations require a risk assessment to be carried out when an employer employs a woman of child-bearing age even before she is pregnant. The assessment is designed to ascertain whether the work could be a risk to her health, or the health of her child should she become pregnant (*Day v T Pickles Farms Ltd*). What is not clear is at what age does a woman cease to be of child-bearing age. There does not appear to be a requirement to undertake an assessment under regulation 16 of a woman who has had a hysterectomy, because there would not be a risk to her as a new or expectant mother. However, a regulation 3 assessment would need to be carried out in the usual way.

4.67   Regulation 16(2)–(4) and regulation 17 make further provisions for the steps to be taken by an employer to alter a woman's working conditions or working hours, or to suspend her, or suspend her from night work, in certain circumstances (see paragraph 11.9). Regulation 18 makes it clear that the employer will not be required to take this action unless the employee has notified the employer in writing that she is pregnant, has given birth within the previous six months, or is breast-feeding.

4.68   The HSE has issued a Guidance Note (HSG122: *New and Expectant Mothers at Work: A Guide for Employers*) that includes a table of hazards to which employers should pay attention when carrying out risk assessments, and advice on subsequent action to be taken.

Protection of young persons (regulation 19)

4.69   Every employer shall ensure that young persons employed by him are protected at work from any risks to their health and safety which are a consequence of their lack of experience, or absence of awareness of existing or potential risks, or the fact that the young person has not yet fully matured.

4.70   No employer shall employ a young person for work:
  (a) which is beyond his physical or psychological capacity
  (b) involving harmful exposure to agents which are toxic or carcinogenic, cause heritable genetic damage or harm to the unborn child or which in any way chronically affects human health
  (c) involving harmful exposure to radiation
  (d) involving the risks of accidents which it may reasonably be assumed cannot be recognised or avoided by young persons owing to their insufficient attention to safety or lack of experience or training
  (e) in which there is a risk to health from:
    (i) extreme cold or heat
    (ii) noise
    (iii) vibration.

4.71 However, the above restrictions do not prevent the employment of a young person (who is not a child) for work:

(a) where it is necessary for his training
(b) where the young person will be supervised by a competent person
(c) where any risk will be reduced to the lowest level that is reasonably practicable.

4.72 Nor does regulation 19 apply to occasional work or short-term working involving domestic service in a private household, or work regulated as not being harmful, damaging or dangerous to young people in a family undertaking (regulation 2(2)).

Provisions as to liability (regulation 21)

4.73 In criminal proceedings for the contravention of any relevant statutory provision, it will not be a defence for an employer to argue that the contravention was due to the act or default of an employee of his, or of a person appointed as a health and safety assistant under regulation 7 (this regulation has effectively closed the escape route revealed in *R v Nelson Group Services*, see paragraph 3.80). The Guidance Notes state that, in practice, the enforcing authorities will take account of the circumstances of each case before deciding on the appropriateness of any enforcement action. Thus if an employer has taken reasonable steps to satisfy himself of the competence of the person concerned, this will be taken into account. In the event of a prosecution, such factors may be considered mitigating, but cannot affect liability.

Restriction on civil liability for breach of statutory duty (regulation 22)

4.74 A civil action for breach of statutory duty under the Management Regulations may be brought against an employer by an injured employee, but regulation 22 excludes any liability on the employer (and a self-employed person) for breach of statutory duty in respect of an action brought by a person not in his employment. The Management of Health and Safety at Work (Amendment) Regulations 2006 extend this protection to employees insofar as there is a duty imposed by regulation 14. In other words, a third party cannot use the Management Regulations to bring an action for breach of statutory duty owed by an employer or employee, or a self-employed person.

Hours of work

Working Time Regulations 1998 (as amended)

4.75 These regulations came into force in October 1998 and are designed to implement the provisions of the Working Time Directive (93/104/EC), and the Young Workers Directive (94/33/EC). Technically, these directives should have been implemented by 23 November 1996, and thus in theory those employers who are emanations of the state (see *Foster v British Gas*) and private employers were exposed to "*Francovitch*" type claims. In *Gibson v East Riding of Yorkshire*, it was held that article 7 of the directive, which provided for workers to have four weeks' holiday pay, was directly enforceable against the state because it was clear and precise and gave rise to no ambiguity or conditionality. The regulations have been subjected to a number of amendments.

4.76 Generally, the regulations give a series of new rights to "workers", a term that is wider than "employees" and applies additionally to a person working under a contract "to do or perform personally any work or services for another party to the contract whose status is not, by virtue of the contract, that of a client or customer of any profession or business undertaking carried on by the individual" (regulation 2(1)). This clearly covers casual, freelance and some self-employed workers, other than self-employed persons who are pursuing a professional or business activity on their own account. However, advantage has been taken of a number of derogations and exceptions permitted by the directive, and potentially by means of workplace or collective agreements.

4.77 The main provisions of the Working Time Regulations 1998 are as follows.
1. *Regulation 4 (maximum weekly working time).* Unless his employer has first obtained the worker's agreement in writing to perform such work, a worker's working time, including overtime, shall not exceed an average of 48 hours for each seven-day period in any applicable reference period. The reference period is 17 weeks, although in certain circumstances (regulation 21, special cases) the reference period can be 26 weeks, or 52 weeks if permitted by a collective agreement or a workforce agreement (regulation 23(b)). The opting out agreement may be for a specific period, or apply indefinitely. If there is no provision in the agreement to terminate it by notice, then

the worker may terminate it by giving seven days' notice. If the agreement can be terminated by notice, the notice period shall not exceed three months.

The employee's consent must be "individually, expressly and freely" given (*Pfeiffer v Deutsches Rotes Kreuz*). In *McLean v Rainbow Homeloans Ltd* the employee, who had not signed an agreement opting out of the regulations, was dismissed for refusing to work more than 48 hours a week. It was held that his dismissal was automatically unfair under s.101A of the Employment Rights Act 1996. The qualifying period of one year's employment does not apply in these circumstances.

To calculate the average hours in any reference period, the formula to be applied is: $(A + B) \div C$.

This requires some explanation. In any reference period, there will be days when the employee will not work, eg because of annual holidays, sick leave, or maternity, paternity, adoption or parental leave, etc. Clearly, to exclude those days from the calculation would distort the average hours worked. Therefore, those "excluded days" must be added back in to the calculation. "A" is the total number of hours worked during the reference period; "B" is the total number of hours worked immediately after the reference period during the number of days equivalent to the number of excluded days. "C" will be the number of weeks in the reference period. Thus the formula $((A + B) \div C)$ will give the average number of hours in the reference period, which will, in effect, be extended by the equivalent number of "excluded" days.

If a relevant agreement is provided for successive 17-week reference periods, then each reference period will be self-contained, for the purpose of calculating average working hours. In the absence of any such agreement, the reference period will be a "rolling" 17-week period, ie each week will be the start of a new 17-week reference period.

In *McCartney v Oversley House Management* the employee was the manager of a residential care home. She contracted to work for four days each week, with 24 hours on site cover, in return for a fixed salary and a flat in the home. Although her duties were mostly confined to working between 8am and 6pm she had to be available for emergencies, which tended to restrict what she could do in her non-working hours. It was held that the periods on-call had to be counted as working time. It was also held that she had been denied rest breaks, because such breaks have to have an ascertainable beginning and end. The fact that the employee could take such breaks was not sufficient if she was subject to instant recall whilst having a break.

2. *Regulations 5A, 6A, 7 (young workers).* The working time of a young worker (ie who has attained the age of 15 but not the age of 18 and who is over compulsory school leaving age) shall not exceed eight hours per day or 40 hours per week. A young worker shall not work during the restricted period, which is between 10pm and 6am or 11pm and 7am. An employer shall not assign a young worker to work during the restricted period unless the employer has ensured that the young worker will have the opportunity of a free assessment of his health and capacities before he takes up the assignment, and thereafter at regular intervals as may be appropriate in his case (see also paragraph 4.95).

3. *Regulation 6 (length of night work).* The normal hours of work for a night worker (defined in regulation 2) shall not exceed eight in any 24-hour period, again the average being assessed over a 17-week period (which can be fixed successive 17-week periods, as set out in a relevant agreement or, failing such agreement, a "rolling" 17-week period). In *R v Attorney General for Northern Ireland, ex parte Burns*, the applicant worked a cycle of 15 shifts of eight hours' duration. During five of these, at least three hours of her working time fell between 11pm and 6am. It was held that she was a night worker within the meaning of regulation 6. It was noted that the directive defined a night worker as a person who works at night "as a normal course", and this phrase was to be construed as meaning "as a regular feature".

An employer shall ensure that no night worker whose work involves special hazards or heavy physical or mental strain, works for more than eight hours in any 24-hour period. The work shall be regarded as involving special hazards or physical or mental strain if it is identified as such in a collective agreement or a workforce agreement, or in a risk assessment carried out under the Management of Health and Safety at Work Regulations 1999. Further, a night worker will be entitled to a free health assessment before he takes up the assignment, with further such assessments at regular intervals. If a registered medical practitioner advises the employer that a worker employed by him is suffering from health problems connected with night work, then, if possible, the employer should transfer the worker to other work for which he is suited, and undertaken at times so that he ceases to be a night worker.

To calculate the average working hours of a night worker, the normal working hours during the reference period must be divided by the number of working days in that period. The formula is: $A \div (B - C)$. Again, an explanation is required.

From the number of 24-hour periods during the reference period ("B") must be deducted the number of hours (divided by 24 to equate days) which comprise or are included in the weekly rest periods, as provided for in regulation 11 ("C"). The amount of the normal working hours during the reference period ("A") can thus be ascertained by dividing the normal working hours during the reference period by the number of working days in that period.

If a worker has worked for less than 17 weeks, the average will be calculated by reference to the period since the worker started to work for the employer.

4. *Regulation 8 (pattern of work)*. Where the pattern according to which the employer organises work is such as to put the health and safety of a worker employed by him at risk, in particular because the work is monotonous or the work-rate is predetermined, the employer shall ensure that the worker is given adequate rest breaks.

5. *Regulation 9 (records)*. The employer shall keep up-to-date records of all workers who have opted out of the maximum weekly working time (see regulation 4(2)), and records of the maximum weekly working time, length of night working, and health assessments, etc of night workers, in respect of each worker in relation to whom they apply, and keep such records for two years.

6. *Regulation 10 (daily rest)*. An adult worker is entitled to a rest period of not less than 11 consecutive hours in each 24-hour period during which he works for an employer, although a young worker is entitled to a rest period of 12 consecutive hours. In the Guidance to the Working Time Regulations the DTI stated that employers must make sure that workers are able to take their rest periods (as required by regs 10 and 11 of the regulations) but are not required to make sure that they actually do so. The European Court of Justice held that this was contrary to EC Law. An employer cannot force workers to take the rest periods due to them, but by letting it be understood that there was no obligation to ensure that they were able to exercise their rights, the guidelines were incompatible with the objects of the

Working Time Directive (*Commission of the European Communities v United Kingdom*; Case C-484/04).

7. *Regulation 11 (weekly rest periods)*. An adult worker is entitled to an uninterrupted rest period of not less than 24 hours in each seven-day period during which he works for his employer, although this can be changed to two uninterrupted periods of 24 hours in each 14-day period, or one uninterrupted period of 48 hours in each 14-day period. A young worker is entitled to a rest period of not less than 48 hours in any seven-day period, although this can be altered in certain circumstances.

8. *Regulation 12 (rest breaks)*. Where an adult worker's daily working time is more than six hours, he is entitled to a rest break, which shall be for an uninterrupted period of 20 minutes (unless a collective agreement or workforce agreement specifies otherwise), to be spent away from the workstation. A young worker who works for more than four and a half hours shall be entitled to a rest break of at least 30 minutes, spent away from the workstation.

In the Guidance to the Working Time Regulations the DTI (now the Department for Business, Innovation and Skills) stated that employers must make sure that workers are able to take their rest periods (as required by regulations 10 and 11) but are not required to make sure that they actually do so. The European Court of Justice held that this was contrary to EU law. An employer cannot force workers to take the rest periods due to them, but by letting it be understood that there was no obligation to ensure that they were able to exercise their rights, the guidelines were incompatible with the objectives of the Working Time Directive (*Commission of the European Communities v United Kingdom*; Case C-484/04).

9. *Regulation 13 (annual leave entitlement)*. A holiday year may be fixed by a relevant agreement, which can be a workforce agreement which meets the requirements of schedule 1 of the Working Time Regulations, or is a collective agreement with a recognised trade union, or a written contract of employment. In the absence of any such agreement, the holiday year will run from October each year or, in respect of workers who commenced work after 1 October 1998, from their start date and each subsequent anniversary. A worker is entitled to an annual holiday of 28 days each year and to receive his normal weekly pay during his holidays, calculated in accordance with ss.221–224 of the Employment Rights Act 1996 (ERA) (regulation 16). Where a worker is paid for a public bank holiday, this

will count towards entitlement to annual leave. If the employment is terminated during the leave year, the worker will be entitled to a proportionate pay in lieu. Leave entitlement is only in respect of the holiday year in which it is due, and may not be replaced by a payment in lieu except on termination of the worker's employment.

4.78   If a worker leaves his employment having taken less holiday than his entitlement at the time of leaving, he is entitled to be paid in respect of the untaken holiday period. If he leaves his employment having taken more holidays than his legal entitlement the relevant agreement may provide for a deduction in pay in respect of the excess holiday period.

4.79   To ascertain how much leave is owed on termination, the formula to use is $(A \times B) - C$ where "A" is the period of leave the worker is entitled to under the Regulations, "B" is the portion of the leave year which has expired prior to the effective date of termination, and "C" is the period of leave already taken by the worker. If a relevant agreement so permits, a worker who has already taken holiday entitlement in excess of his statutory entitlement can be required to compensate the employer, either by way of a payment, or by doing additional work.

4.80   In the first year of employment, entitlement will be based on one-twelfth of the annual leave entitlement in respect of each month's employment, with workers who work less than five days per week receiving a pro rata entitlement. If the accrued entitlement is more than a half day but less than a full day, entitlement is rounded up to a full day.

4.81   Where the contract of employment is terminated during the course of the leave year, and the employee has not taken his leave entitlement, regulation 14(3) provides that he shall receive a payment in lieu, which shall be such sum as is provided for in the relevant agreement or, if there is no such agreement, the formula $(A \times B) - C$ (above) will apply (but see *Witley & District Men's Club v MacKay*).

4.82   The ECJ has upheld the opinion of the Advocate General in the case of *Stringer v HMRC* that a worker who is on long-term sick leave is entitled to any holiday which accrues during his sickness absence, which he can presumably take on his return to work. If the employee is dismissed while on sick leave he is entitled to pay in lieu on any untaken leave which accumulated during his sickness absence.

4.83   It goes without saying that clauses sometimes found in existing employment contracts which specify that an employee dismissed for reason of gross misconduct shall not be entitled to accrued holiday pay are no longer valid.

4.84 The worker may give notice to the employer of the dates when he wishes to take his holidays, subject to the employer requiring the worker to take his holidays on particular dates. The worker must give twice the number of days' notice as days' leave he wishes to take. The employer can prevent the employee taking leave on a particular day by giving notice equivalent to the same number of days as the length of leave the employee wishes to take. However, the notice provisions are capable of being overridden by a relevant agreement, which may provide for longer (or shorter) periods of notice.

4.85 Entitlement to statutory holidays applies to all workers, not just those who are employees in the legal sense. Thus self-employed workers, casual employees, part-time employees, etc are all entitled to holidays with pay, the only exception being a person who is a client or customer of any profession or business undertaking. Agency workers are entitled to holiday pay from whichever of the agent or principal is responsible for paying the agency worker.

Special cases

4.86 There are a number of sectors of employment and specified activities that are partially or totally excluded from the regulations.

4.87 The regulations do not apply to certain sea-farers, workers in sea-going fishing vessels and workers aboard certain ships and hovercrafts. Non-mobile workers engaged in sea transport, inland waterways, lake transport and sea-fishing are covered. Police, armed forces and workers in civil protection services are also partially excluded where their activities are inevitably in conflict with the regulations.

4.88 The regulations apply to all rail workers, with certain derogations (daily rest breaks, weekly rest breaks and night work provisions). They also apply to workers in the aviation industry who are not covered by the sector-specific Aviation Directive. Special provisions apply to a crew member (cabin or flight) on board a civil aircraft (Civil Aviation (Working Time) Regulations 2004). Mobile workers who are not subject to the Road Transport Directive are entitled to an average 48 hours per week, 24 days paid annual leave, health assessments if working at night and adequate rest time. Mobile road transport workers who drive or travel in goods or passenger vehicles which are covered by European Council Regulation (EC) 561/2006 are covered in respect of maximum weekly working time, periods of availability, rest periods and night work (Road Transport (Working Time) Regulations 2005). Non-mobile workers in the transport industry are covered. Working hours of doctors in training will be reduced to 48 hours per week in 2009. The time spent by an on-call doctor who is required to be physically present at a hospital is working time, even though he is permitted to rest during periods when his services are not required (*Landeshaupstadt Kiel v Jaeger*).

4.89 *Regulation 19*: Domestic servants in a private household are excluded from regulation 4 (maximum weekly working time), regulation 6 (length of night work), regulation 7 (health assessment for night workers) and regulation 8 (safe pattern of work).

4.90 *Regulation 20*: Workers whose working time cannot be measured or predetermined or can be determined by the worker himself. In particular:

(a) managing executives or other persons with autonomous decision-making powers

(b) family workers

(c) workers officiating at religious ceremonies in churches and religious communities.

4.91 The above workers are excluded from regulation 4 (maximum weekly working time), regulation 6 (length of night work), regulation 10 (daily rest periods), regulation 11 (weekly rest period) and regulation 12 (rest breaks).

4.92 *Regulation 21*: There is a limited exclusion for the following group of workers:

(a) workers whose activities are such that his place of work and place of residence are distant from one another, or whose different places of work are distant from one another

(b) where a worker is engaged in security and surveillance activities requiring a permanent presence in order to protect property and persons, particularly security guards and caretakers or security firms

(c) workers whose activities involve the need for continuity of service or production, particularly:
   (i) services relating to the reception, treatment or care provided by hospitals or similar establishments, residential institutions and prisons
   (ii) work at docks or airports
   (iii) press, radio, television, cinematographic production, postal and telecommunications services and civil protection services
   (iv) gas, water and electricity production, transmission and distribution, household refuse collection and incineration
   (v) industries in which work cannot be interrupted on technical grounds
   (vi) research and development activities
   (vii) agriculture
(d) where there is a foreseeable surge of activity, particularly in:
   (i) agriculture
   (ii) tourism
   (iii) postal services
(e) where the worker's activities are affected by:
   (i) an occurrence due to unusual and unforeseeable circumstances, beyond the control of the worker's employer
   (ii) exceptional events, the consequences of which could not have been avoided despite the exercise of all due care
   (iii) an accident or the imminent risk of an accident
(f) railway transport workers whose activities are intermittent, whose working time is spent aboard trains or whose activities are linked to railway timetables and to ensuring the continuity and regularity of traffic.

4.93   In respect of the above group of workers, the following regulations do not apply, namely, regulation 6 (length of night work), regulation 10 (daily rest periods), regulation 11 (weekly rest periods) and regulation 12 (rest breaks). However, if a worker is required to work during what would normally be a rest period, the employer shall allow him to have a compensatory period of rest or, if this is not possible, afford him appropriate protection (regulation 24).

4.94   Regulation 23 provides that a collective agreement or a workforce agreement may modify or exclude the following regulations in relation to particular workers, namely regulation 6 (length of night work), regulation 10 (daily rest periods), regulation 11 (weekly rest period) and regulation 12 (rest breaks). So far as regulation 4 (maximum weekly working time) is concerned, such an agreement can substitute a different period over which the average can be worked out, not exceeding 52 weeks (in place of 17 weeks).

4.95   Although young workers are generally covered by regulations 5A, 6A and 7 (see paragraph 4.77), there are certain exceptions to those rules in sectors where there are particular operational requirements, eg hospitals, agriculture, hotels, postal services, newspaper deliveries, when there is a surge in demand, where no adult worker is available, the occurrence of a *force majeure*, and so on (see regulations 27 and 27A). There are limited exclusions in respect of shift workers, workers in the armed forces and offshore workers. There are also special rules for agricultural workers (schedule 2).

Enforcement

4.96   The regulations can be enforced in three ways. First, inspectors from the HSE (or, in appropriate circumstances, enforcement officers of local authorities) are responsible for the enforcement of the following relevant requirements (see regulation 28), namely:

(a) the duty of an employer to take all reasonable steps to ensure that the provisions relating to the 48-hour week have been complied with, and also to keep up-to-date records of workers who are subject to an opting-out agreement

(b) the duty of an employer to take all reasonable steps to ensure that a young worker's working time does not exceed eight hours per day and 40 hours in any week

(c) the duty of an employer to take all reasonable steps to ensure that a night worker's normal hours of work do not exceed an average of eight hours in each 24 hours

(d) the duty of an employer to ensure that no night worker whose work involves special hazards or heavy physical or mental strain works for more than eight hours in any 24-hour period

(e) the duty of an employer to ensure that a young worker does not work between 10pm and 6am (or 11pm and 7am)

(f) the duty of an employer to provide a free health assessment for a night worker and for a young worker who works at night and for the health assessment to be repeated at regular intervals

(g) the duty of the employer to provide adequate rest breaks when the work is monotonous

(h) the duty of the employer to keep adequate records and to retain them for two years

(i) where a young worker is permitted under the regulations to work at night, the duty of the employer to ensure that he is supervised by an adult worker and be allowed a compensatory period of rest

(j) where the application of the regulations to special cases or shift workers is excluded, the duty of the employer to ensure an equivalent compensatory period of rest

(k) where certain mobile workers are excluded from the regulations, the duty of the employer to ensure adequate rest.

4.97 It may be noted that although the above positions are generally enforced by the health and safety inspectors, it is the duty of the Civil Aviation Authority to enforce the provisions in respect of relevant civil aviation workers, and the duty of the Vehicle and Operator Services Agency to enforce the provisions in respect of relevant road transport workers.

4.98 In respect of the above matters, an employer may be prosecuted in the magistrates' courts, where a fine of up to £5000 may be imposed, or an unlimited fine imposed in the crown court. Enforcement officers may also issue an improvement notice, requiring the employer to rectify matters specified therein, in order to ensure compliance with the statutory requirements, and a failure to comply with such notice can lead to a fine of up to £20,000 and/or six months' imprisonment by the magistrates' court, or an unlimited fine and/or up to two years' imprisonment by the crown court. A prohibition order may also be issued.

4.99 The powers of inspectors to enforce the regulations are identical to those possessed by inspectors under the Health and Safety at Work, etc Act 1974 (see paragraph 2.35), as are the offences that may be committed by a person who obstructs, inhibits, gives false information, etc, while the inspector is exercising his powers (see regulation 29 and schedule 3).

4.100 The second way in which the regulations can be enforced is by way of a complaint by a worker to an employment tribunal, alleging that the employer has failed to comply with any of the following provisions:

(a) the daily rest periods for adult or young workers (regulation 10)

(b) the weekly rest periods for adult or young workers (regulation 11)

(c) rest break periods for adult or young workers (regulation 12)

(d) entitlement to annual leave (regulation 13)

(e) entitlement to equivalent compensatory rest, where the provisions of regulations 10, 11 and 12 have been excluded or modified

(f) entitlement to compensatory rest where the provisions of regulations 10 and 11 have been excluded in respect of special cases or shift workers or young workers

(g) the duty of the employer to pay a worker statutory annual leave pay, or pay for leave outstanding on the termination of employment (regulations 14 and 16).

4.101 A complaint to an employment tribunal must be brought within three months from the date on which it is alleged that the exercise of the right should have been permitted or, in the case of holiday pay, from the date when the payment should have been made, although the employment tribunal may extend the period if it was not reasonably practicable to bring the complaint earlier. If the complaint is well-founded, the employment tribunal may make a declaration, and may award compensation of such amount as the tribunal considers to be just and equitable, having regard to the employer's default in refusing to permit the worker to exercise the right in question, and any loss sustained by the worker attributable to that default. In the case of holiday pay, the amount due will be awarded.

4.102 A worker also has the right (s.45A Employment Rights Act (ERA)) not to be subjected to any detriment because:

(a) he refused to comply with a requirement that the employer imposed which would be in contravention of the regulations

(b) he refused to forgo a right conferred by the regulations

(c) he failed to sign a workforce agreement or an individual agreement opting out of the regulations

(d) he performed any functions or activities as a workforce representative, or as a candidate in an election for workforce representatives

(e) he brought proceedings against the employer to enforce a right conferred by the regulations

(f) he alleged that the employer had infringed a right conferred by the regulations.

4.103   An employee (not a worker) also has the right not to be unfairly dismissed for any of the above reasons (s.101A, ERA), and also the right not to be unfairly selected for redundancy (s.105(4A), ERA). Again, the complaint must be brought within three months from the date of the act complained of, with the usual extension of time if it was not reasonably practicable to bring the complaint earlier. If the complaint is upheld, the employment tribunal will make a declaration, and may make an award of compensation on just and equitable principles. If the employee was unfairly dismissed, no qualifying period of employment is required and the minimum basic award may be made in appropriate cases.

4.104   The third way of enforcing the regulations is to seek an appropriate remedy for breach of contract of employment. In *Barber v RJB Mining (UK) Ltd*, pit deputies, although contractually obliged to work for 42 hours a week, regularly worked a considerable amount of overtime, in excess of 48 hours. They were asked to sign an agreement opting out of their rights under the regulations, but refused, and they sought from the court a declaration to the effect that they need not work at all until such time as their average working hours fell below the limit specified in regulation 4(1). The High Court granted the declaration. It was held that it was clearly the intention of Parliament that their contract of employment should be read so as to provide that an employee should work no more than 48 hours a week during the relevant reference period. Thus regulation 4(1) created a free-standing right which took effect as a contractual term in the contracts of employment of the pit deputies.

4.105   When deciding whether psychiatric injury was foreseeable in respect of a claim for illness due to stress, it is proper to take into account the fact that the employee worked excessively. If the employer has breached the 48 hour per week and the daily rest provisions, it will be more difficult to argue that the stress illness was not reasonably foreseeable (*Hone v Six Continents Retail*). In *Pakenham-Walsh v Connell Residential* the employee voluntarily worked for seven days each week over a period of time. She claimed that working long hours had caused her psychiatric illness. Her claim under the Working Time Regulations failed. She had never complained about stress at work, the work itself was not stressful, she had volunteered to work additional days and there was no change in her behaviour which would have indicated that she was finding it difficult to cope with her work. Any illness she suffered was not reasonably foreseeable.

4.106   A claim for damages in respect of psychiatric injury caused by overwork must be based on foreseeability in order to succeed in a common law action, but no such claim can succeed if it is based on the tort of breach of statutory duty, as it clearly was not the intention of Parliament to create such a cause of action (*Sayers v Cambridgeshire County Council*). In other words, a claim cannot be based on regulation 4(2) of the Working Time Regulations, as these regulations have their own enforcement systems, and these are not to be added to by allowing employees to bring an action for breach of statutory duty at common law (see paragraph 12.9).

Safety representatives

4.107   One of the more important innovations to be found in HSWA is contained in s.2(4), which enabled the Secretary of State by regulations to provide for the appointment by recognised independent trade unions of safety representatives from among the employees, who will represent them in consultation with the employers and have other prescribed functions. It will then be the duty of every employer to consult with such representatives with a view to the making and maintenance of arrangements which will enable him and his employees to co-operate effectively in promoting and developing measures to ensure the health and safety at work of the employees, and in checking the effectiveness of such measures (s.2(6)).

4.108   The relevant regulations have been made (Safety Representatives and Safety Committees Regulations 1977, as amended by the Management of Health and Safety at Work Regulations 1992) together with an ACOP and non-statutory Guidance Notes. In addition, there is an ACOP on time off for the training of safety representatives. These are all published in one document, L146: *Consulting Workers on Health and Safety*.

4.109   It should be noted that the Health and Safety (Consultation with Employees) Regulations 1996 extend the consultation provisions to all employees, not merely to those who belong to recognised trade unions (see paragraph 4.151).

Appointment of safety representatives (s.2(4))

4.110   A safety representative may be appointed by an independent trade union which is recognised by the employer for the purpose of collective bargaining. To be a trade union, it must be on the list of trade unions maintained by the Certification Officer under s.2 of the Trade Union and Labour Relations (Consolidation) Act 1992. It will be an independent trade union if it has applied for and received a Certificate of Independence from the Certification Officer (issued if it can show that it is not under the domination or control of the employer, whether by way of the provision of financial benefits or otherwise) under s.6 of the same Act. It will be a recognised trade union if the employer recognises it for the purpose of negotiations relating to or connected with one or more of the matters specified in s.244 of the 1992 Act. There is no need to have a formal agreement concerning recognition; it is a question of fact, to be determined by the circumstances of each case as to whether or not the employer does recognise the trade union concerned (*National Union of Tailors and Garment Workers v Charles Ingram & Co Ltd*).

4.111   Only an independent trade union which is recognised for the purposes of collective bargaining is legally entitled to appoint safety representatives. In *Cleveland County Council v Springett*, union representatives, who were members of the Association of Polytechnic Teachers, claimed that they had been denied time off work with pay in accordance with legislation. The union was not formally recognised by the local authority that ran the polytechnic, although it was represented on the national Burnham Committee, a body that made recommendations on teachers' pay. It was held that this did not constitute recognition by the employer. Further, the fact that the union had had previous dealings with the employer when representing an individual employee of the polytechnic did not constitute recognition for the purpose of collective bargaining.

4.112   If an employer refuses to consult with the appointed safety representatives on the ground that he does not recognise the trade union concerned, it is likely that the HSE will invoke the aid of the Advisory Conciliation and Arbitration Service (Acas) to provide advice. The Trade Union and Labour Relations (Consolidation) Act 1992, schedule A1, provides for a statutory scheme whereby a trade union will have to be recognised when the majority of the relevant workforce so desires.

4.113   The system whereby the legal right to appoint safety representatives is confined to trade unions has been the subject of some criticism. It is argued that it tends to perpetuate the divisions in industry between "us" and "them". Safety, after all, should be the concern of all, be they employers, managers, employees, union officials, and so on, and it is wrong that safety representatives are to be seen against the backcloth of the battleground of industrial relations. Against this, it is argued that the disputes which may arise over the functions and rights of a safety representative can more readily be resolved within the existing framework of collective bargaining machinery, and that to place the safety representative outside that machinery is to leave no avenue available for the resolution of disputes.

4.114 Although a safety representative is appointed by the recognised trade union, he need not be a member of the trade union. The only requirements are that he shall, so far as is reasonably practicable, have been employed by his employer throughout the preceding two years or have had at least two years' experience in similar employment (Safety Representatives, etc Regulations, regulation 2). Again, this raises some argument in practice. Some trade unions will appoint shop stewards to be the safety representatives, on the grounds that they are better trained, will not be overawed by management, and can handle the appropriate dispute procedures. On the other hand, this can cause some problems for, as a shop steward, he may be subject to the processes of re-election, or there may be a conflict arising out of his functions as a shop steward and those he exercises as a safety representative. For example, if there are disciplinary proceedings being taken against an employee (see Chapter 13) who has acted in breach of safety rules, the shop steward who has to represent his member will have to reconcile his actions with his belief that the safety rules must be upheld. To avoid such conflict, some trade unions will refuse to appoint shop stewards and look to other members to carry out this important work. This has the added advantage of spreading the workload and training opportunities, and involving more members in the activities of the union. Clearly, no single pattern will meet all the circumstances, and the matter must be regarded from a pragmatic viewpoint.

4.115 Neither the regulations nor the ACOP specify how many safety representatives should be appointed by the trade union concerned, and certain difficulties may well exist in multi-union situations. The Guidance Notes attached to the regulations suggest that the appropriate criteria should be based on:
  (a) the total number of employees in the workplace
  (b) the variety of different occupations
  (c) the size of the workplace and the variety of workplace locations
  (d) the operation of shift systems

(e) the type of work activity and the degree and character of inherent dangers.

4.116   A person who has been appointed safety representative shall cease to be such when:

(a) the trade union which appointed him notifies the employer in writing that the appointment has been terminated

(b) he ceases to be employed at the workplace; however, if he was appointed to represent employees at more than one workplace, he shall not cease to be a safety representative so long as he continues to be employed at any one of them

(c) he resigns.

Consultations with safety representatives

4.117   Once an employer has been notified in writing by or on behalf of a trade union that a person has been appointed as a safety representative, and of the group of employees he is to represent, the safety representative shall have the right to be consulted by the employer with a view to the making and maintaining of arrangements which will enable the employer and his employees to co-operate effectively in promoting and developing measures to ensure the health and safety at work of the employees, and to check the effectiveness of those measures (HSWA, s.2(6)). The Management of Health and Safety at Work Regulations 1999 introduced new consultation provisions to the Safety Representative, etc Regulations which require the employer to consult with the safety representatives in good time with regard to:

(a) the introduction at the workplace of any measure which may substantially affect the health and safety of the employees who are represented by the safety representative

(b) his arrangements for appointing or nominating his safety assistant/advisor and person responsible for evacuation procedures

(c) any health and safety information required to be provided by the employer to the employees that the safety representative concerned represents

(d) the planning and organisation of any health and safety training required to be provided by the employer to the employees that the safety representative represents

(e) the health and safety consequences of the introduction of new technologies into the workplace.

4.118   The employer shall also provide such facilities and assistance as safety representatives may reasonably require for the purpose of carrying out their statutory functions.

Functions of safety representatives

4.119   Regulation 4 of the Safety Representatives and Safety Committees Regulations 1977 lays down a number of functions which a safety representative shall be entitled to perform. These are:

(a) to investigate potential hazards and dangerous occurrences at the workplace (whether or not they are drawn to his attention by the employees he represents) and to examine the causes of accidents at the workplace; this right is not confined to having time off work (with pay) to make the investigation inside the workplace, for there may be circumstances when it is necessary to go outside in order to investigate (eg to interview an injured employee at home, see *Dowsett v Ford Motor Co*, paragraph 4.138)

(b) to investigate complaints by any employee he represents relating to that employee's health, safety or welfare at work

(c) to make representations to the employer on the above matters

(d) to make representations to the employer on general matters affecting the health, safety or welfare at work of the employees at the workplace

(e) to carry out inspections (see below)

(f) to represent employees in consultations at the workplace with inspectors of HSE or any other enforcing authority

(g) to receive information from inspectors (see paragraph 2.44)

(h) to attend meetings of the safety committee where he attends in his capacity as safety representative in connection with any of the above functions.

4.120   As an employee, the safety representative is subject to the general requirements imposed by ss.7–8 of HSWA (see Chapter 3) but no function conferred on him as noted above shall impose any duty on him. This means that he cannot be prosecuted for a failure to perform his duty as a safety representative, or for performing his duties badly. Nor can he be sued civilly for a failure to perform his statutory duty, although he is subject to the ordinary law of negligence in the usual way (see Chapter 12).

4.121   A safety representative is expected to act responsibly and, in particular, he should not ignore established internal procedures. In *O'Connell v Tetrosyl Ltd*, a safety representative was dismissed because he made direct calls to the Factory Inspectorate concerning alleged breaches of safety regulations. The employers considered his actions to be misconduct because he should have drawn management's attention to the matters before going to an outside body. By a majority, an employment tribunal had found his dismissal to be fair and an appeal against that decision was rejected by the Employment Appeal Tribunal. The employers had reasonable grounds for believing that he had bypassed internal procedures by going to the outside body, and this conduct did constitute a fair reason for dismissal.

4.122 Following the enactment of the Trade Union Reform and Employment Rights Act 1993, safety assistants, safety representatives, members of safety committees and employees generally have protection against being subjected to a detriment or being dismissed, when taking certain actions connected with their functions as such, or health and safety generally (see Employment Rights Act 1996, paragraph 4.181).

Inspection of the workplace

4.123 Safety representatives are entitled to inspect the workplace or any part of it on three occasions.

4.124 First, if they have not inspected it within the previous three months. They must give reasonable notice to the employer in writing of their intention to do so. More frequent inspections may be carried out with the agreement of the employer.

4.125 Second, where there has been a substantial change in the conditions of work (whether by way of the introduction of new machinery or otherwise), or where new information has been published by the HSC or HSE relevant to the hazard since the last inspection. Then, after consulting with the employer, a further inspection may be carried out notwithstanding that less than three months have elapsed since the last inspection.

4.126 Third, where there has been a notifiable accident or dangerous occurrence (see Chapter 6) or a notifiable illness has been contracted there and:

(a) it is safe for an inspection to be carried out

(b) the interests of the group of employees represented by the safety representatives might be involved.

4.127 In these circumstances, the safety representatives may carry out an inspection of the part of the workplace concerned (and so far as is necessary to determine the cause, they may inspect any other parts of the workplace). Where it is reasonably practicable for them to do so, they shall notify the employer of their intention to carry out the inspection.

4.128 The duties of a health and safety representative are not confined to examination of accidents and records on the employer's premises. In *Healey v Excel Logistics Ltd*, the applicant was a safety representative. One of his colleagues had a serious accident while making a delivery to a supermarket, and he decided to visit the site in question, and also made an approach to the manager of the supermarket. The employer felt that this action was tantamount to gross misconduct, and so he was dismissed. An employment tribunal held that his dismissal was fair, because he was not carrying out an inspection of the workplace under the Safety Representative and Safety Committee Regulations 1977, but had gone to the supermarket to pry into health and safety matters without permission. On appeal, the Employment Appeal Tribunal (EAT) reversed the decision, and held the dismissal to be unfair. One of the duties of a safety representative was to investigate potential hazards and dangerous occurrences at the workplace. He had been dismissed because he wanted to look at the accident report book at the supermarket in order to examine the cause of an accident at the workplace, an activity which was within his function as a safety representative.

4.129 The employer shall provide such facilities and assistance as the safety representatives may reasonably require, including facilities for independent investigation by them and private discussions with employees, but the employer or his representative is entitled to be present in the workplace during the inspection.

Inspection of documents

4.130 For the performance of their duties, safety representatives are entitled, on giving reasonable notice to the employer, to inspect and take copies of any document relevant to the workplace or to employees they represent which the employer is required to keep by virtue of any relevant statutory provision. Thus, they can inspect and take copies out of the general register, reports of the examination of hoists, lifts, cranes, etc, but they are not entitled to inspect or take copies of any document consisting of or relating to any health record of an identifiable individual.

Disclosure of information to safety representatives

4.131 Safety representatives will be entitled to receive information from two main sources. First, regulation 7(2) requires the employer to make available information within his knowledge which is necessary to enable the safety representatives to perform their functions. However, the employer need not disclose:

(a) information the disclosure of which would be against the interests of national security

(b) any information which he could not disclose without contravening a prohibition imposed by or under an enactment

(c) any information relating specifically to an individual, unless that individual has consented to it being disclosed

(d) any information, the disclosure of which would, for reasons other than its effect on health, safety or welfare at work, cause substantial injury to the employer's undertaking or, where the information was supplied to the employer by some other person, to the undertaking of that other person

(e) any information obtained by the employer for the purpose of bringing, prosecuting or defending any legal proceedings.

4.132 Nor do the regulations require the employer to disclose any document or to allow the inspection of it if it does not relate to health, safety or welfare at work.

4.133 The restriction concerning the discovery of documents used for the purpose of legal proceedings was an issue before the House of Lords in *Waugh v British Railways Board* (see Chapter 12), where it was held that for a document to be privileged, the dominant purpose in preparing it must have been for its use in possible litigation. Thus, if an accident report is prepared as a matter of routine practice in order to establish the cause, and is subsequently required for the purpose of litigation, the safety representative will be entitled to see it, for the dominant purpose in preparing it was not for the purpose of litigation.

4.134 The Approved Code of Practice makes a number of recommendations concerning the nature of the information which should be disclosed to safety representatives. These include:

(a) information about the plans and performance of the undertaking and any changes proposed insofar as they affect the health and safety at work of employees

(b) information of a technical nature about the hazards to health and the precautions deemed necessary to eliminate or minimise them, in respect of plant, machinery, equipment, processes, systems of work, and substances in use at work, including any relevant information provided by consultants and designers, or the manufacturer, importer or supplier of any article or substance used at work

(c) information which the employer keeps relating to the occurrence of any accident, dangerous occurrence or notifiable disease, and any statistical records relating to those matters

(d) any other information specifically relating to matters affecting health and safety at work, including the results of any measurements taken by the employer (or person acting on his behalf) in the course of checking the effectiveness of his health and safety arrangements

(e) information on articles or substances which an employer issues to his homeworkers.

4.135 The second source of information for safety representatives may come from the inspector who, by virtue of s.28(8) of HSWA, may give information to employees or their representatives to ensure that they are adequately informed about matters affecting their health, safety or welfare (see above and paragraph 2.44). This may be factual information relating to the premises or anything therein, or information regarding any action taken or proposed to be taken by the inspector (eg the issuing of a prohibition or improvement notice). The inspector must give the like information to the employer.

Time off work for safety representatives

4.136 A safety representative is entitled to have time off work, with pay, during his working hours, for the purpose:

(a) of performing his functions as a safety representative

(b) to undergo training in aspects of those functions as may be reasonable having regard to the ACOP issued by the HSE.

4.137   If his pay does not vary with the amount of work done, then he shall be paid as if he had worked throughout the whole of the time. If his pay varies with the amount of work done, then he shall be entitled to be paid his average hourly earnings for his work or, if no fair estimate of his earnings can be made, the average hourly earnings for work of that description of persons in comparable employment or, if there are no such persons, then the average hourly earnings which are reasonable in the circumstances. A part-time employee, who goes on a full-time training course in health and safety matters, is entitled to be paid on the same basis as a full-time employee attending such courses (*Davies v Neath Port Talbot County Borough Council*).

4.138   The right to investigate hazards and dangerous occurrences is not confined to having time off (with pay) to make an investigation inside the workplace. In *Dowsett v Ford Motor Co*, an employee was injured in an accident. The applicant, who was the safety representative, investigated the incident, and concluded that no further action was necessary. Five weeks later, he attended a meeting of the works safety committee where the safety engineer gave a report on the incident. The applicant wanted to have time off work with pay to visit the employee at home in order to make further enquiries, but this was refused, so he made an application to the employment tribunal. It was held that the regulations were sufficiently wide to enable the safety representative to go outside the workplace if it was necessary to perform his functions. However, this was a question of fact and degree. In this case, he had not done anything for five weeks, and would not have acted had he not heard the report at the safety committee. Consequently, it was not necessary to make any further enquiries. In principle, however, the employment tribunal made it quite clear that there could be circumstances where it would be necessary to interview the injured person (or others) and to perform this function satisfactorily it may be necessary to go outside the workplace.

Training of safety representatives

4.139   The ACOP (L146: *Consulting Workers on Health and Safety*) on time off work for the training of safety representatives, states that as soon as possible after they have been appointed they should be permitted to have time off work to attend basic training facilities approved by the TUC or their own trade union. Further training, similarly approved, should be undertaken when they have special responsibilities, or when this is necessary because of changed circumstances or new legislation. The trade union should inform management of the course it has approved and supply a copy of the syllabus if the employer asks for it. The trade union should give a few weeks' notice, and the number of safety representatives attending at one time from the same employer should be that which is reasonable in the circumstances, bearing in mind the availability of the relevant courses and the operational requirements of the employer. Unions and management should endeavour to reach agreement on the appropriate numbers and arrangements, and refer any problems to agreed procedures. Health and safety training for safety representatives is not limited to training that is necessary to enable the representative to perform his functions. The issue is whether the training is reasonable for aspects of his functions (*Rama v South West Trains*).

4.140   It will be recalled that the status of the Code of Practice is not of a rule of law; it is guidance to good practice. Thus there is no absolute rule that training should be only on a union-approved course. In *White v Pressed Steel Fisher Ltd*, the applicant was appointed safety representative by the T&GWU. The union wanted him to go on a union-sponsored training course, but management wanted to provide an in-company course and refused to permit him to have time off work with pay to attend the union course. It was held by the EAT that the employers were not acting unreasonably in refusing him time off work to go on the union course. The provisions in regulation 4(2) were for such training as may be reasonable in all the circumstances. It was therefore necessary to consider all the circumstances, including the Code of Practice. The approval of a course by the trade union was a factor to be taken into account, but (unlike s.168 of the Trade Union and Labour Relations (Consolidation) Act 1992, which relates to time off work for training in trade union duties) the Safety Representative and Safety Committees Regulations do not require that the course must be approved by the TUC or by the trade union. If the course provided by the employer was adequate, and contained all the necessary material, including the trade union aspects of safety, then it could be perfectly proper for the employer to insist that the safety representative went on the in-house course.

4.141   Whether it is reasonable for a safety representative to have time off work for training depends on whether, looked at overall, it is reasonable for him to attend for training. It does not depend on management's view of what is reasonable. In *Gallagher v Drum Engineering Co Ltd*, two management members of a safety committee were sent on a training course dealing with the impending introduction of the COSHH Regulations and a third manager was due to go on another course. The union wanted to send three of its members who were on the safety committee to a course run by the TUC, but the company refused to permit this, although they were prepared to allow one union member to go. The applicant, one of those refused permission, applied to an employment tribunal alleging a breach of the Safety Representatives and Safety Committees Regulations, and his claim was upheld. There was no unreasonable expense involved, no operational problems arose out of allowing three union representatives to attend the course and the union members had a large part to play in applying the regulations. In all the circumstances, the employment tribunal thought that it was reasonable to allow the applicant time off work with pay to attend the TUC sponsored course.

4.142 In determining whether it is reasonable in the circumstances to have time off work with pay, the employer's decision is to be judged by standards of reasonableness which are similar to those used in unfair dismissal cases. For example, in *Scarth v East Hertfordshire District Council*, a safety representative applied for time off work, with pay, to attend a training course specifically designed for local government representatives. The request was refused, because the manager who made the decision thought it was not suitable, even though he had not seen the syllabus. Three days later he saw the syllabus, and granted the applicant three days' leave with pay. An employment tribunal held that at the date he made his decision, the manager had not acted reasonably because he had not seen the syllabus for the course. Further, the figure of three days' pay had been "plucked out of the air" without any particular reason. Thus it was held that the applicant had been unreasonably refused time off work, and her claim for a further three days' pay was upheld.

4.143 A part-time employee who goes on a full-time training course is entitled to be paid on the same basis as a full-time employee (*Davies v Neath Port Talbot County Borough Council*).

4.144 A decision by an employer to grant or refuse a request by a health and safety representative for time off work in order to undertake training in his duties should be based on what is reasonable in all the circumstances having regard to the Code of Practice. Factors to be taken into account include the contents of the course and how it relates to the particular health and safety function of the employee, and whether the training would assist him in performing those functions. The test is whether the training is reasonable in all the circumstances, not whether it was necessary (*Duthie v Bath & North East Somerset Council*).

4.145 The Code of Practice also gives guidance on the contents of a safety training syllabus. Basic training should provide for an understanding of the role of a safety representative, of safety committees, and of trade union policies and practices in relation to:
- (a) the legal requirements relating to health and safety at work
- (b) the nature and extent of workplace hazards, and of the measures necessary to eliminate or minimise them
- (c) the health and safety policy of the employer, and the organisation and arrangements necessary to fulfil these policies.

4.146 In addition, they will need to develop new skills, including how to carry out a safety inspection, how to make use of basic sources of legal and official information, etc.

4.147 A safety representative is entitled to go on a specialised training course in order to become familiar with hazards. In *Howard v Volex Accessories Division*, the applicant, who was a safety representative, found that the work involved coming into contact with lead and various chemicals. She applied for time off work to attend a TUC course on chemical hazards. Management refused the request because they took the view that they were doing everything that could be done by way of investigating and checking hazards. She decided to use two of her holiday days to go on the course, and then made a claim to an employment tribunal under regulation 4(2). The employment tribunal thought that she was entitled to learn more about the chemical and other hazards at work and that the TUC course would help her to acquire that knowledge. It was held that she was entitled to be paid for attending the course and she was also awarded £50 compensation for the loss of her two days' holiday.

4.148 However, it may be inappropriate for a newly-appointed safety representative to seek to go on a specialist training course before he has had his initial basic training (*Knight v Shell UK Ltd*).

4.149 If there are more safety representatives in the organisation than are warranted by the genuine safety needs of the firm, then the employer may well be justified in refusing time off work with pay in particular circumstances, because such time off will not be "necessary for the purpose of..." the performance of their functions as safety representatives (*Howard & Peet v Volex plc*).

Non-employees as safety representatives

4.150 The regulations specify that if the safety representatives have been appointed by the British Actors' Equity Association or the Musicians' Union, it is not necessary that they shall be employees of the employers concerned. This is because such people are performers in theatres, etc which are not owned by their employer, and are generally itinerant workers.

Health and Safety (Consultation with Employees) Regulations 1996

4.151 However, EC Directive 89/391/EEC (the "Framework Directive") applies to all employees, whether in recognised trade unions or not. Consequently, it became necessary to enact the Health and Safety (Consultation with Employees) Regulations 1996, which extend the consultation provisions to all employees, not merely those who belonged to trade unions.

4.152 Under the regulations, the employer has two choices with respect to those employees who are not represented by safety representatives under the 1977 regulations. He can either consult with the employees directly or consult with one or more persons of any group of employees who were elected for the purposes of consultation, and who are referred to as "representatives of employee safety". There is no provision in the regulations as to how the employer shall organise the election but this, apparently, is not necessary (*R v Secretary of State for Trade & Industry, ex parte Unison*).

4.153 The employer shall thus consult those employees (or the representatives) in good time, on matters relating to their health and safety at work and, in particular, with regard to:
   (a) the introduction of any measure at the workplace that would substantially affect the health and safety of those employees
   (b) his arrangements for appointing, or nominating, competent persons to assist him in undertaking the measures needed to ensure compliance with statutory requirements, and to

implement evacuation procedures (as required by regulations 7(1) and 8(1)(b) of the Management Regulations)

(c) health and safety information he is required to provide to employees under any statutory requirement

(d) the planning and organisation of any health and safety training he is required to provide

(e) the health and safety consequences for those employees of the introduction of new technologies into the workplace.

4.154   If the employer consults with employees directly, he must make available such information as is necessary to enable them to participate fully and effectively in the consultation. If the employer consults with representatives of employee safety, he must make available such information as is necessary to enable them to carry out their functions, and information contained in any records kept by virtue of RIDDOR that relate to the workplace or the group of employees represented by those representatives. However, the employer is not bound to disclose certain information (see paragraph 4.132).

4.155   Representatives of employee safety are entitled to:

(a) make representations to the employer on potential hazards and dangerous occurrences at the workplace that affect the group represented

(b) make representations on general matters affecting the health and safety at work of the group represented

(c) represent the group of employees in consultations with health and safety inspectors.

4.156   Representatives of employee safety are entitled to have time off work for training in respect of their functions, the employer paying for reasonable costs incurred (including travel and subsistence) and to have time off work with pay to perform their functions as such. They have the usual protections under the Employment Rights Act 1996 (see paragraph 4.181).

4.157   A representative of employee safety is entitled to be paid when carrying out his functions or being trained, the amount being calculated under schedule 1 of the regulations (ie normal pay, average hourly pay or a figure of average hourly earnings which is reasonable in all the circumstances). A complaint may be made to an employment tribunal that an employer has failed to permit the representative of employee safety to take time off to perform his functions or go for training, or has failed to pay him. The complaint must be presented within three months, and if the complaint is well founded, the employment tribunal will make a declaration to that effect, and award such compensation as is thought to be just and equitable, or the amount due.

4.158   A representative of employee safety is entitled not to have action short of dismissal taken against him by way of penalising him for, or deterring him from, performing his functions as such, and it will be an unfair dismissal to dismiss him for participating reasonably in any consultations with the employer.

4.159   A breach of duty imposed on an employer by these regulations shall not confer a right of action any civil proceedings insofar as that duty applies for the protection of a person not in his employment (Management of Health and Safety at Work (Amendment) Regulations 2006).

4.160   The HSE has published an ACOP to accompany these regulations, L146: *Consulting Workers on Health and Safety*.

Safety committees

4.161   The Safety Representatives and Safety Committees Regulations 1977 lay down (regulation 9) that the employer must establish a safety committee if requested to do so in writing by two union safety representatives. In order to do this, he must consult with the safety representatives who made the request and with the representatives of any recognised trade union whose members work in the workplace in respect of which he proposes to establish the committee. The duty is one of consultation, not negotiation or agreement, so that actual composition of the committee is a matter for the employer to determine. However, he must establish the committee within three months of the request. He must also post a notice stating the composition of the committee and the workplace covered by it, and the notice shall be posted in a place where it may easily be read by the employees.

4.162   Section 2(7) of HSWA states that the function of the safety committee shall be to keep under review the measures taken to ensure the health and safety at work of employees and such other functions as may be prescribed. Apart from this vague generalisation, neither the regulations nor the Code of Practice give any further indication as to its functions. However, the Guidance Notes give some very helpful information. The detailed arrangements necessary should evolve from discussions and negotiations between the parties who are best able to determine the needs of the particular workplace. Since the circumstances of each case will vary a great deal, no single pattern is possible.

4.163 Certain guides may be followed. The safety committee should have its own separate identity and not have any other function or tasks assigned to it. It should relate to a single establishment although group committees can play an additional role. Finally, its functions should be clearly defined. A suggested brief for the committee might go along the following lines:

(a) a study of the trends of accidents, dangerous occurrences and notifiable diseases, so that recommendations may be made to management for corrective action to be taken

(b) the examination of safety audit reports, to note areas where improvements can be made

(c) consideration of reports and factual information from the enforcing authority

(d) the consideration of reports made by the safety representatives

(e) assisting in the development of safety rules and safe systems of work

(f) an evaluation of the effectiveness of the safety content of employee training

(g) monitoring of the adequacy of health and safety communication and publicity

(h) acting as a link between the company and the enforcing authority

(i) evaluating the safety policy and making recommendations for its revision.

4.164 Safety committees are not specifically empowered to deal with welfare matters, though there is nothing to prevent this happening should the parties so decide.

Membership of the committee

4.165 The aim should be to keep the membership reasonably compact, with adequate representation from all interested parties. Management representatives should include persons involved in health and safety matters, eg works engineers, works doctor, safety officer, etc and there should be seen to exist some form of mechanism for the consideration and implementation of the recommendations by senior management. The committee must contain sufficient expertise to evaluate problems and come up with solutions. Outside specialists may be made *ex officio* members. There is no requirement that safety representatives should be members of the committee but it would clearly be desirable to have some representation, depending on the numbers involved. There is no provision for time off work to be paid for attendance at the meetings of the committee, but this should be obvious. It is also desirable that a senior member of the company attends the meetings and plays a leading role, eg the company chairman or a board director.

Meetings

4.166 The safety committee should meet on a regular basis, as frequently as necessary, depending on the volume of business. The date of the meetings should be notified well in advance, and provision should be made for urgent meetings. An agenda should be drawn up, minutes kept, with action taken noted. Probably the most important function of the committee will be to monitor action taken on any recommendations made.

Safety committees in non-unionised workplaces

4.167 The HSE has issued some guidance on safety committees in those premises where there is no recognised independent trade union. Since there is no formal trade union machinery, and no legal requirement to set up a committee, the initiative will presumably come from management. Again, there should be adequate representation of appropriate management skills, and the employee representatives should be chosen by their fellow employees. In cases of difficulty, the HSE will give further guidance.

Enforcement of the regulations

4.168 A safety representative may present a complaint to an employment tribunal that:
  (a) the employer has failed to permit him to take time off for the purpose of performing his functions as a safety representative or to permit him to go on a training course
  (b) the employer has failed to pay him for his time off.

4.169   The complaint must be presented within three months from the date when the failure occurred or, if it was not reasonably practicable to do so within that time, within such further period of time as the employment tribunal considers to be reasonable. If the employment tribunal upholds the complaint that the employer has failed to permit him to have time off, a declaration to that effect shall be made. Additionally, the employment tribunal may make an award of compensation to be paid by the employer to the employee, which shall be of such amount as the tribunal considers to be just and equitable in all the circumstances, having regard to the employer's default in failing to permit the employee to have the time off, and to any loss suffered by the employee as a result of that failure. The compensation awarded would normally be a modest amount, for it will be rare that an employee actually suffers any loss. In *Owens v Bradford Health Authority*, a trade union appointed as a safety representative a man who was within a year of retirement. He applied to go on a training course, but the employers refused, as they did not think it was reasonable for a safety representative so near to retirement to go on a training course. The employment tribunal upheld the employee's complaint, and awarded him £50 compensation. It is the prerogative of the trade union to make the appointment and a refusal to send someone on a training course because he was near to retirement was not justified.

4.170   If the complaint is that of a failure to pay for the time off work, and it is upheld by the employment tribunal, an award of the amount due to be paid will be made.

4.171   The enforcement of the other duties in the Act and the regulations is the responsibility of the appropriate enforcing authority. Thus if the employer fails to consult with the safety representatives, as required by s.2(4), or fails to set up a safety committee as required by s.2(7), or fails to provide the necessary information as required by regulation 7, he will be in breach of the law and thus commits a criminal offence. The HSE has issued Guidance Notes (Worker Consultation and Involvement July 2007) on how the enforcement of these matters should be dealt with. In three cases, they will not go to immediate enforcement, but will try other means. These are:

(a) the HSE must be satisfied that all voluntary means have been explored, including taking advice from or using the services provided by the Advisory Conciliation and Arbitration Service (ACAS)

(b) if there is some doubt as to whether or not the trade union has made a valid appointment as a safety representative for example, the employer may allege that the trade union is not recognised by him; this problem might be resolved by using the services of ACAS

(c) if the problem relates to time off work or a failure to pay, the specified remedy of using the machinery of the employment tribunal should first be explored.

4.172 Enforcement by the HSE might be appropriate in other cases, for example:

(a) if the trade union or safety representative complain that the employer is not carrying out his obligations after full use has been made of any consultative machinery or disputes procedure

(b) where the employer is refusing to acknowledge the existence of the safety representative who has been validly appointed

(c) where the employer refuses to make particular information available, or refuses to provide particular facilities to enable the safety representative to perform his functions

(d) where the employer has refused or failed to set up a safety committee after being requested to do so under regulation 9.

4.173 Since the employer will be in breach and is "contravening one or more of the relevant statutory provisions", it is possible that instead of prosecuting for such breaches, the inspector may issue an improvement notice under s.21. To date, this tactic does not appear to have been necessary. Indeed, it is a credit to all concerned that the implementation of the provisions relating to safety representatives has, despite original fears, proceeded with great smoothness.

4.174 Also in force are the Offshore Installations (Safety Representatives and Safety Committees) Regulations 1989, which require the election of safety representatives by the whole workforce (but who cannot represent more than 40 employees) and a mandatory safety committee. There are a number of other differences between these regulations and the 1977 regulations.

Employment protection in health and safety cases

4.175 The Offshore Safety (Protection Against Victimisation) Act 1992 gave protection against dismissal (or action short of dismissal) to safety representatives and members of safety committees who worked on offshore installations, and it was intended that such protection should be extended throughout industry. However, the Act was defective, in that it only applied to safety representatives who were appointed by recognised trade unions, whereas EC Directive (89/391/EEC) (the Framework Directive) requires that such protection should be given to all persons with health and safety responsibilities.

4.176 Consequently, the Act was repealed by the Trade Union Reform and Employment Rights Act 1993, and new rights were inserted into what is now the Employment Rights Act 1996. This Act provides that an employee has the right not to be subjected to any detriment (s.44) or be dismissed (s.100) on the grounds that:

(a) having been designated by the employer to carry out activities in connection with preventing or reducing risks to health and safety at work, he carried out (or proposed to carry out) any such activities

(b) being a representative of workers on matters of health and safety at work, or a member of a safety committee (whether under statutory or voluntary procedures) he performed (or proposed to perform) any functions as a representative or committee member

(c) the employee took part in consultation with the employer in an election of representatives of employee safety.

4.177 The above provisions will clearly protect an employee who is a safety assistant (appointed under the Management of Health and Safety at Work Regulations 1999, see above) as well as safety representatives and safety committee members, whether appointed by independent trade unions, or elected by the workforce, or nominated or appointed by the employer in non-union situations.

4.178 The protection for safety representatives is confined to those workers who are employees. In *Costain Building & Civil Engineering Ltd v Smith*, the claimant was an independent engineering consultant who worked for various agencies who supplied labour to building contractors. He was sent by an agency to work at a site being developed by Costain Building, and was appointed safety representative by a trade union in respect of work carried out at the site. After writing several critical safety reports, Costain Building informed the agency that they did not want him to work there any more. He claimed he had been unfairly dismissed for health and safety reasons. An employment tribunal upheld his claim, but the decision was reversed on appeal by the EAT. His contract was with the agency, and he was not an employee of Costain Building. The union's appointment of him as a safety representative was clearly ineffective in law. The protection afforded by s.100 of ERA was confined to those people who were employees.

4.179   The statutory provisions afforded to safety representatives do not confer on them a licence to be irresponsible, and are not designed to give blanket immunity. Thus if a safety representative acts in respect of matters which are not within the area of the workplace for which he is a representative, or acts outside the laid down procedure, or acts in bad faith, then it may be that he is not pursuing a genuine health and safety matter, but is pursuing a personal agenda in order to embarrass the employer. In such circumstances, he may be disciplined as appropriate (*Shillito v Van Leer (UK) Ltd*). Equally, the manner in which he performs his duties may be such as to take him outside the scope of his health and safety activities. This is a question of fact for the employment tribunal to decide (*Goodwin v Cabletel UK Ltd*). But if the safety representative is acting within his remit as such, he will not lose legal protection even if he goes "over the top", for he is entitled not to be overawed by management while exercising his proper functions (*Bass Taverns Ltd v Burgess*).

4.180   However, the statutory protection afforded to health and safety representatives, while designed to ensure that they are not disadvantaged because they exercise their functions, does not confer any advantage. Thus, in a redundancy exercise, they are entitled to have their performance assessed on the work they do under their normal contractual obligations, and the employer should not take into account the way they perform their health and safety functions. Indeed, to do this would amount to a positive discrimination in their favour, but discriminatory against other employees. The statutory protection is neutral (*Smiths Industries Aerospace & Defence Systems v Rawlings*).

Protection for employees in health and safety cases (Employment Rights Act 1996, s.100)

4.181   In addition, every employee will have the right not to be subjected to any detriment, or be dismissed, if:

(a) being at a place where there was no safety representative or safety committee (or where there was, but it was not reasonably practicable to go through those channels) he brought to the employer's attention, by reasonable means, circumstances connected with his work which he reasonably believed were harmful (or potentially so) to health or safety

(b) in circumstances of danger which he reasonably believed to be serious and imminent and which he could not reasonably be expected to avert, he left (or proposed to leave) or refused to return to (while the danger persisted) his place of work or any dangerous part of his place of work

(c) in circumstances of danger which he reasonably believed to be serious and imminent, he took (or proposed to take) appropriate steps to protect himself or other persons from danger.

4.182　The "other persons" (mentioned above) are not just employees, but can be members of the public. In *Masiak v City Restaurants Ltd*, a chef claimed he was dismissed because he refused to cook food which he believed to be unfit for human consumption. It was held that s.100(1)(e) did not limit the class of persons at risk to danger only to fellow employees, and the claim was remitted back to an employment tribunal for a decision on the merits.

4.183　Whether the steps were appropriate is to be judged by reference to all the circumstances, including his knowledge and the facilities and advice he had at the time. But if it was negligent for the employee to act as he did, action taken against him by the employer would not be a detriment or unfair dismissal, as the case may be.

4.184　In *Harris v Select Timber Frames Ltd*, the employee made a complaint about health and safety standards at his employment, which resulted in a visit from an HSE inspector. He was due to be examined by an Employment Medical Advisor, but shortly before the date of the examination he was dismissed. The employment tribunal thought that in the circumstances he had been dismissed because he had raised the issue of health and safety, and his dismissal was therefore unfair.

4.185　The employment tribunals have considered a number of issues arising out of the protections given by s.100 of ERA, for example, complaints by drivers about a possible breach of the Drivers' Hours Regulations, poor working conditions, lifting of heavy loads, confrontational representations made by employees who are not designated health and safety representatives, and action taken by employees to protect members of the public. An unusual case is *Harvest Press Ltd v McCaffrey*, where an employee walked out from his job because of the abusive and threatening behaviour of a colleague. Management interviewed the person responsible, but did not seek the claimant's version of events. It was held that the claimant had a reasonable belief that he was in serious and imminent danger. Section 100 was not confined to dangers which arise from the work or work premises, but covered any danger, no matter how it arose, including the actions or omissions of fellow employees. On the facts, he had been dismissed, and the dismissal was automatically unfair.

4.186 However, in order to claim the statutory protection, it must be shown that the employee's belief that there was a health or safety problem was based on reasonable grounds. Thus, in *Kerr v Nathan's Wastesavers Ltd*, the applicant was employed to drive a van collecting bags of waste from different locations. One day he refused to drive the van because he believed that it would become overloaded. He was dismissed, and claimed that the dismissal was unfair. It was accepted that he reasonably believed that the van would be overloaded by the time he finished his collections, and hence honestly believed that the circumstances were potentially harmful. However, he had failed to take into account the practice whereby drivers who found that their vehicles might be overloaded could return to the depot, or telephone to arrange for another vehicle to be sent. Thus he did not have reasonable grounds on which to sustain that belief, and hence his claim was dismissed by the employment tribunal and the Employment Appeal Tribunal (EAT).

4.187 In *Barton v Wandsworth Council*, the applicant was employed as an ambulance driver. His job involved transporting patients who had severe physical and mental disabilities. He was accompanied by an escort on each occasion. However, the escorts were not experienced or trained properly, and the applicant made several complaints about the problems he was experiencing, pointing out the risks that were being run. Management felt that the applicant was being aggressive and overbearing, and suspended him pending an investigation. He was eventually given a five-year warning about his behaviour, although following an internal appeal, this was reduced to two years. He claimed that the disciplinary action constituted a detriment. The employment tribunal upheld his complaint. He genuinely believed that the matters he complained about represented a serious and imminent danger to himself and to his patients. There was nothing unreasonable about his beliefs, for there had been a number of unfortunate incidents, and management had failed to address the problem with any sense of urgency. Finally, by transferring him to another centre, suspending him from work (with a consequent loss of overtime working) and imposing a two-year final warning, his employer had caused him to suffer a detriment.

4.188   There is an implied term in the contract of employment that the employer will take reasonable steps to ensure the safety of his employees. Thus if an employer fails to address genuine fears or investigate legitimate complaints, this could amount to a fundamental breach of contract by the employer, entitling the employee to resign and claim that he was constructively dismissed.

4.189   The aggrieved employee may bring a claim in an employment tribunal within the usual period of three months. In addition, if he is dismissed, the interim relief procedures will be available, in which case a claim must be brought within seven days.

4.190   Under the Public Interest Disclosure Act 1998 (sometimes referred to as the "Whistleblowers Act"), protection is given to workers (a wider term than employees) who make a "protected disclosure" in certain circumstances. The Act inserted various rights to protection into the relevant parts of the ERA. Thus workers have the right: not to suffer a detriment (ERA, s.47A); not to be dismissed (ERA, s.103A); and not to be made redundant (ERA, s.105(6A)) because they made a protected disclosure. As with all automatically unfair dismissals, no qualifying period of employment is required, and workers over the age of 65 may bring a claim.

4.191   A protected disclosure is one made by a worker which tends to show that:
  (a) a criminal offence has been, is being or is likely to be committed
  (b) a person has failed, is failing or is likely to fail to comply with a legal obligation
  (c) a miscarriage of justice has occurred or is likely to occur
  (d) the health or safety of any individual is being endangered
  (e) the environment has been, is being or is likely to be damaged
  (f) any of the above matters have been or are likely to be concealed.

4.192   The person making the disclosure must do so in good faith to his employer or other person in respect of whose conduct the above matters relate. However, there can be no protected disclosure in respect of legal privilege or confidentiality between client and professional advisor.

4.193 If disclosure is made to someone other than the employer, to be protected, the person making the disclosure must do so in good faith, reasonably believe the information is substantially true, and the disclosure must not be made for the purpose of personal gain. Thus disclosure could be made to a relevant regulatory body, or a legal advisor, or other responsible person. The worker must also believe that he will suffer a detriment if he makes the disclosure to the employer, or that the evidence will be destroyed or concealed, or he has already disclosed the information to his employer. In all the circumstances, it must be reasonable for him to make the disclosure. Thus, regard will have to be paid to the identity of the person to whom the disclosure was made, the seriousness of the matter, whether action was taken by the employer as a result of any previous disclosure, and whether the worker has complied with any procedure laid down by his employer.

4.194 BSI British Standards has produced a Whistleblowing Arrangements Code of Practice.

Safety assistance

4.195 Under the Management of Health and Safety at Work Regulations 1999 and the Regulatory Reform (Fire Safety) Order 2005 every employer shall appoint one or more competent persons to assist him in undertaking the protective and preventative measures which have been identified in consequence of an assessment as to the measures he needs to take in order to comply with the relevant statutory provisions (see paragraph 4.28). There is also a requirement to appoint safety supervisors or competent persons to ensure compliance with statutory requirements under certain regulations, eg the Ship Building and Ship-repairing Regulations 1960, the Diving at Work Regulations 1997, the Ionising Radiations Regulations 1999, and a planning co-ordinator under the Construction (Design and Management) Regulations 2007. No formal standards of training are laid down, the obligation is merely to ensure that he has sufficient time to discharge his duties efficiently, has the experience and expertise necessary to carry out those duties, and the authority to perform his duties. The Carriage of Dangerous Goods and Use of Transportable Pressure Equipment

Regulations 2007 require that any carrier, filler or loader involved in the carriage of dangerous goods by road or rail shall comply with the statutory provisions relating to the appointment and duties of safety advisors.

4.196 There are also a number of statutory provisions which require an employee to be "qualified" or "trained", and other provisions require that certain things may only be done by or under the supervision of a "competent person" (see paragraph 4.203). These phrases are usually left undefined, and it may well be that the burden is on the employer to show in any given case that the person who performed the task in question was qualified, trained or competent, as the case may be. The possession of some formal certificate or qualification would no doubt assist in discharging this burden but it may also be shown that the person concerned has pursued some approved course of training or instruction, as well as possessing practical experience of the work.

4.197 The existence of a safety officer, with details of his functions and powers, would be one of the things an employer would refer to in the written statement of his general policy on health and safety at work, as required by s.2(3) of HSWA, being part of the organisation and arrangements in force for the carrying into effect of that policy.

4.198 The relevant organisation for safety professionals is the Institution of Occupational Safety and Health (IOSH), which was formed in 1953, and has over 32,000 members. Two qualifications may be awarded by the National Examination Board in Occupational Safety and Health (NEBOSH).

1. *Certificate*. This examination consists of papers in Management of Health and Safety, Controlling Workplace Hazards and Health and Safety Practical Application.
2. *Diploma*. This examination consists of papers in Management of Health and Safety, Hazardous Agents in the Workplace, Workplace and Work Equipment Safety, Application of Health and Safety in Theory and Practice, Communication Skills and Training Skills.

4.199 A two-part National Diploma in Occupational Safety and Health was phased in from September 1997, replacing the former National Diploma. The new syllabus comprises five modules, the second part of the Diploma course dealing with subjects in greater depth. Part I of the course will satisfy Level 3 of the National Vocational

Qualification and Scottish Vocational Qualification in Occupational Health and Safety Practice. Part II of the course will satisfy Level 4.

4.200   A person who has passed the Diploma Part II and has the appropriate period of professional experience may apply to be admitted as a member of IOSH. There are several grades of membership, depending on a person's qualifications and experience (see paragraph 2.80).

4.201   There are about 50 educational and training establishments throughout the country which offer Certificate or Diploma courses.

4.202   The Occupational Health and Safety Lead Body and the Employment Occupational Standards Council have now merged to form the Employment National Training Organisation. This body will be responsible for the development and marketing of vocational qualifications and standards of competence in occupational health and safety.

"Competent person"

4.203   A number of legislative provisions require that certain types of work (inspections, testing, assessments, etc) shall only be done by a "competent person" but the phrase is rarely defined and little guidance is given as to the abilities or expertise which are required. Some help may be obtained from an ACOP but the provisions are usually in very general terms. The Management of Health and Safety at Work Regulations 1999 (see paragraph 4.4) provide that a person shall be regarded as competent "where he has sufficient training and experience or knowledge and other qualities to enable him properly" to do the task in question. The Code of Practice (L122) issued under the Pressure Systems Safety Regulations 2000 contains a detailed definition of a competent person for the purpose of those regulations. In practice, whether or not a person is competent will be determined by the courts retrospectively in any particular case (see *Brazier v Skipton Rock*).

4.204   It is clear that the obligation is on the employer to select a competent person and to ensure that either he is trained in the relevant tasks to be performed or that he receives the necessary training. Full information must be given of the tasks to be performed, and all necessary facilities. A competent person is one who has the necessary theoretical and practical knowledge and has the technical and practical experience to carry out the task, such experience being matched to the complexity of the work and the degree of the risk. The statutory provision itself may indicate what is required. Thus, if a statute requires an "inspection", this is something less than an "examination"; it may be that the latter should be carried out by someone with appropriate technical qualifications, whereas the former need not be (see *Gibson v Skibs*).

4.205　However, the appointment of a "competent person", though evidence that the employer is attempting to meet statutory responsibilities, does not, by itself, prove that those responsibilities have in fact been met. The employer's duty is to meet his statutory and common law obligations, by actually adopting measures to ensure the health and safety of his employees. If those measures are not adopted, the fact that a competent person was appointed will not, by itself, absolve the employer from responsibility (see *Bell v Department of Health and Social Security*).

4.206　One would expect a competent person to be able to produce some evidence of his claim to be such, as well as the requisite experience. He would be expected to display the qualities which an ordinary member of his profession would have, but the law "does not require of a professional man that he be a paragon, combing the qualities of a polymath and prophet" (per Lord Justice Bingham, in *Eckersley v Binnie and Partners*).

Safety consultants

4.207　As indicated (see paragraph 4.28) every employer shall appoint one or more persons to provide health and safety assistance. In most cases, the ideal appointment will be made in-house, from persons who are familiar with the firm, its organisation, products, hazards and problems, etc. If no such person is readily available, a suitable person may be trained into the job. Sometimes specialist in-house knowledge will need to be supplemented by reference to external sources, eg trade associations, professional organisations, etc.

4.208　However, there will obviously be occasions when a suitable external consultant will be needed and, in such circumstances, the employer must be quite clear of the precise nature of the need and the role to be played. A formal consultancy agreement should be drawn up, with a detailed brief and defined objectives. Responsibilities should be determined, time scales laid down, performance monitored, fees agreed, and so on. The choice of consultant will more likely be determined by the nature of the problem but, before an appointment is made, appropriate checks should be made on the applicant's qualifications, experience, references, etc. Once the appointment is made, the consultant will presumably make an initial review of the problems being faced, prepare a report on this, and suggest how he proposes to tackle them. Ideally, he should work towards the termination of his consultancy agreement, either by permanently resolving the problem, or putting in place proper procedures to prevent the problem from recurring, or training sufficient in-house staff in how to deal with the problem.

Occupational health services

4.209　The Management of Health and Safety at Work Regulations 1999 (regulation 6, see paragraph 4.25) require an employer to provide employees with such health surveillance as is appropriate having regard to the risks to their health and safety identified by the risk assessment which has been carried out, but this does not give rise to a general legal obligation to provide medical services at the place of work (but see Health and Safety (First Aid) Regulations 1981, Chapter 6). Many employers engage trained medical personnel to ensure the immediate treatment of injuries or illnesses which may occur during the employment, carry out pre-employment screening, investigate existing or potential medical hazards, or generally to provide a health care service for the benefit of employees. Occupational health services, by their very nature, are usually found in large firms, although there is a recent trend for smaller firms to pool together their resources and run a joint scheme. Sometimes the impetus comes from the need to reduce the incidence of accidents or ill health and consequently reduce the number of days lost through absenteeism. In other cases, the service may be part of the company's philosophy to provide additional welfare services on the premises for the use of all employees. Whatever the motive, occupational health services are on the increase.

4.210　Doctors and Registered General Nurses (RGNs) who practise occupational health may obtain their Associateship of the Faculty of Occupational Medicine (AFOM) from a recognised institution. Doctors may obtain a Diploma in Industrial Health (DIH) or an MSc in Occupational Medicine. Nurses may obtain a Certificate or Diploma in Occupational Health Nursing (OHNC or OHND).

4.211 The relationship between works doctors (or nurses), management, trade unions, the individual and his own family doctor is a complex one, for problems of confidentiality and conflicting interests may arise.

Directors' responsibilities

4.212 Health and safety is now a boardroom issue, along with other corporate functions, such as sales, marketing, finance, etc. A start may be made with the joint guidance issued by HSC and the Institute of Directors entitled "Leading Health and Safety at Work; leadership action for Directors and Board Members"which replaces the previous guidance "Directors responsibilities for health and safety".

4.213 The document sets out three essentials, namely: the need for active leadership; worker involvement; and assessment and review. Health and safety policies should be an integral part of the organisation's culture. Board members must take the lead in ensuring that there is a proper communication of health and safety duties and benefits throughout the organisation. Executive directors must develop policies which will avoid health and safety problems, and they should be able to respond quickly when difficulties arise and new risks are introduced. Board members must be aware of the significant risks faced by the organisation, and the safety policy should set out the board's own role and that of individual board members in leading health and safety policies throughout the organisation.

4.214 A four-point strategy is called for, based on planning, delivering, monitoring and reviewing. Health and safety should appear regularly on the agenda of board meetings, with the chief executive officer giving the clearest visibility of leadership. The presence of a director with health and safety responsibilities can be a strong signal that the issues are taken seriously, and their strategic importance understood. The board should set targets to help define what is being sought to achieve, and non-executive directors can act as scrutineers. Members of the board must ensure that health and safety arrangements are adequately resourced, and that they obtain competent advice on health and safety matters. Health and safety must also be a factor to take into account when making senior management appointments.

4.215 The board must ensure that risks assessments are carried out and that employees or their representatives are involved in decisions that affect them. The board must also consider the health and safety implications of introducing new processes, new working practices and new personnel, dedicating adequate resources and safety advice when necessary.

4.216 Health and safety issues must be regularly monitored, with the board receiving regular reports, including sickness absences and appraisals of the performance of senior managers. Finally, the board should review the health and safety performance of the organisation at least once a year, to ensure that risk management and health and safety structures have been effectively reported. Any shortcomings or weaknesses must be redressed.

CHAPTER 5

General health and safety requirements

Employers' liability insurance

5.1   Under the Employers' Liability (Compulsory Insurance) Regulations 1998–2008 (made under the Employers' Liability (Compulsory Insurance) Act 1969), every employer (subject to certain exceptions, see below) must take out and maintain an insurance policy with an authorised insurer against bodily injury or disease sustained by employees arising out of and in the course of employment. The policy must now provide cover of at least £5 million arising out of any one occurrence, although a "cap" of £10 million is usually imposed by the Association of British Insurers. Where the employer is a holding company, the insurance cover will be in respect of that company together with any subsidiaries as if they were a single employer. The actual policy may not contain certain exemption clauses (eg excluding liability if the employer does not take reasonable care to protect his employees against injury, or if he fails to perform a statutory duty, etc) but can require the employer to contribute a sum to the insurer in respect of the satisfaction of any claim made.

5.2   A contract of insurance is one of *uberrimae fidei*, ie of the utmost good faith, and the proposer must disclose all the information which would affect the mind of a prudent insurer. If, therefore, the employer fails to make such disclosure, the policy may be void and, as well as being without the necessary cover to meet a claim, the employer will be liable for a criminal offence. It must be stressed that the Act applies to every employer carrying on a trade or business, including sports and social clubs, as long as a person is an employee within the legal definition. It is not necessary to take out an insurance policy if the employer engages persons as independent contractors, domestic servants (who are not employed for the purposes of a business), close relatives and persons who are not normally resident in Great Britain and who are working here for fewer than 14 consecutive days.

5.3   The certificate of insurance must be in a form prescribed. The certificate (or copies) must be displayed at each place of business at which the employer employs any relevant employee of the class or description to which the certificate relates, and must be of such size and legibility that it may be easily seen and read. It must also be reasonably protected from being defaced or damaged. Alternatively, the certificate may be made available in electronic form as long as employees have reasonable access to it in that form.

5.4 An inspector can request to see the certificate of insurance, and also the policy itself (on reasonable notice being given). The inspector may also request sight of policies issued in previous years, so as to investigate possible past infringement. Employers are no longer required to keep the certificates for 40 years, although it would be prudent to do so in the event of a future claim, otherwise there may be personal liability.

5.5 There are a number of employers who are exempt from the requirements of the regulations, generally speaking, because they are big enough to carry out their own insurance (eg mutual insurance association for shipowners), or where claims can be settled out of public funds (eg magistrates' courts' committees) or are already under a statutory duty to insure (eg licensees under the Nuclear Installations Act 1965). A full list of exempt employers can be found in schedule 2 of the regulations. There are also special provisions for offshore installations (see Offshore Installations and Pipeline Works (Management and Administration) Regulations 1995).

5.6 Any employer who is not insured in accordance with the Act shall be guilty of an offence punishable by a fine of £1000 for each day when he is in default and if the offence is committed with the consent, connivance, or facilitated by the neglect of any director, manager, secretary or other officer, then he, as well as the employer (if a body corporate), shall be guilty of an offence and can be punished accordingly.

5.7 It is also an offence, punishable by a fine of £1000, to:
(a) fail to display the certificate or a copy of the insurance certificate
(b) fail to send the certificate or a copy to the inspector when so required
(c) fail to produce the certificate or a copy on demand by an inspector
(d) refuse to allow the inspector to inspect the actual policy document.

5.8 The fact that the employer has a valid policy in force does not confer any automatic right to compensation for an injured employee, as this must be determined by reference to the legal rights of the parties (see Chapter 12). However, it does mean that if an employee succeeds in his claim, there will be funds available with which to satisfy the judgment.

5.9 A failure by an employer to take out the necessary insurance, although a criminal offence, does not give rise to civil liability. In *Richardson v Pitt-Stanley*, the plaintiff was injured during the course of his employment. His employer, a limited company, had not taken out employers' liability insurance. The plaintiff obtained judgment against the company, but it went into liquidation, with no assets to satisfy the judgment. The plaintiff then brought an action against the company's director and company secretary, claiming that as they had consented to or connived with a breach of the Act, they were personally liable for the loss sustained by him. The Court of Appeal dismissed his claim. Whether a breach of statutory duty (see paragraph 12.9) which involved criminal liability also gave rise to a civil cause of action was a question of construction. There was no express provision in the Employers' Liability (Compulsory Insurance) Act 1969 creating civil liability on the part of the directors or secretary of a corporate body for failing to insure under the Act, and it was not possible to imply such liability. The Act only created a criminal offence.

Fire precautions

5.10 The Regulatory Reform (Fire Safety) Order 2005 came into force in October 2006. It applies to England and Wales. Provisions relating to fire precautions for Scotland are contained in the Fire (Scotland) Act 2005 and the Fire Safety (Scotland) Regulations 2006.

5.11 The Order replaces much of the existing legislation on fire safety law, including the Fire Precautions Act 1971, the Fire Precautions (Workplace) Regulations 1997, and repeals and revokes a number of other statutory provisions. It is designed to bring all fire safety law under one regime, and gives effect to EU Directive 89/391 and other amending directives.

5.12 The Order does not apply to domestic premises, nor to offshore installations, ships, fields and woodlands, aircraft, vehicles etc, a mine or boreholes.

The responsible person (article 3)

5.13   The Order imposes duties on the responsible person. This will be either:
- (a) in relation to a workplace, the employer, if the workplace is to any extent under his control
- (b) in relation to other premises, the person who has control of the premises (as occupier or otherwise) in connection with the carrying on by him of any trade business or other undertaking, or the owner, where the person in control of the premises does not have control in connection with the carrying on by that person of a trade, business or other undertaking.

General fire precautions (article 4)

5.14   In relation to premises, general fire precautions are:
- (a) measures to reduce the risk of fire on the premises and the risk of fire spreading
- (b) measures in relation to the means of escape
- (c) measures for securing that means of escape can be safely and effectively used
- (d) measures in relation to the means for fighting fire on the premises
- (e) measures in relation to the means for detecting fire on the premises and the giving of warnings in case of fire
- (f) measures in relation to the arrangements for action to be taken in the event of fire, including the instruction and training of employees and mitigating the effect of fire.

Risk assessment (article 9)

5.15   The responsible person must make a suitable and sufficient risk assessment for the purpose of identifying the general fire precautions he needs to take. The matters to be considered in risk assessments in respect of dangerous substances are set out in schedule 2 of the Order. The assessment must be reviewed regularly, particularly if there is reason to suspect that it is no longer valid or if there have been significant changes in the matters to which it relates. If changes are required, the responsible person must make them. He must not employ a young person unless, in relation to risks to young persons, he has made or reviewed the assessment, taking into account:

(a) the inexperience, lack of awareness of risks and immaturity of young persons
(b) the fitting out and layout of the premises
(c) the nature, degree and duration of exposure to physical and chemical agents
(d) the form, range and use of work equipment and the way it is handled
(e) the extent of safety training provided to young persons
(f) risks from chemical and biological agents.

5.16 When the risk assessment is complete, then if the responsible person employs more than five employees, he must record the significant findings (including the measures which have to be taken), and any groups of workers identified as being especially at risk. New work involving a dangerous substance may not commence unless a risk assessment has been made and measures required by the Order have been implemented.

5.17 The Department of Communities and Local Government has produced detailed advice and guidance on how to carry out a fire risk assessment with reference to a dozen different types of business premises, including offices, shops, factories, theatres, residential care premises, open air events, transport premises, and so on (*www.communities.gov.uk/fire/firesafety/firesafetylaw*).

Principle of prevention (article 10)

5.18 When the responsible person implements preventative and protective measures, he must do so in accordance with the principles of prevention set out in schedule 1. These are almost identical to those contained the Management of Health and Safety at Work Regulations 1999 (see paragraph 4.22).

Fire safety arrangements (article 11)

5.19 The responsible person must make fire safety arrangements as are appropriate, having regard to the size of his undertaking and the nature of its activities, for the effective planning, organisation, control, monitoring and review of preventative and protective measures. If he employs more than five employees, he must record these arrangements.

Risks from dangerous substances (article 12)

5.20 A dangerous substance is a substance which creates a risk to the safety of persons from fire. Where there is a dangerous substance on the premises, the responsible person must ensure that the risk to relevant persons is either eliminated or reduced so far as is reasonably practicable. A dangerous substance must be replaced with a substance or process which either eliminates or reduces the risk. If it is not reasonably practicable to do this, the risk must be controlled, and the detrimental effects of fire be mitigated. The responsible person must ensure the safe handling, storage and transport of dangerous substances and consequential waste.

Fire fighting and fire detection (article 13)

5.21 Where necessary, in order to safeguard the safety of relevant persons, the responsible person must ensure that the premises are equipped with appropriate fire-fighting equipment and with fire detectors and alarms, and that non-automatic fire-fighting equipment is easily accessible, simple to use, and indicated by signs. What is appropriate is to be determined by the size and use of the premises, the equipment contained therein, the physical and chemical properties of substances likely to be present, and the maximum number of persons who may be present at any one time. He must take measures for fire fighting in the premises, nominate competent persons to implement those measures, and ensure that their numbers, and the training and equipment available to them are adequate. He must also arrange any necessary contacts with external emergency services, particularly with regard to fire fighting, rescue work, first aid and emergency medical care.

Emergency exits and routes (article 14)

5.22 The responsible person must ensure that routes to emergency exits from premises and the exits themselves are kept clear at all times. They must lead to a place of safety, it must be possible for persons to evacuate the premises as quickly and as safely as possible, the numbers of emergency exits must be adequate having regard to the number of persons who may be present at any one time, emergency doors must open in the direction of escape, they must not be locked so that they cannot be easily and immediately opened, emergency routes and exits must be indicated by signs, and those requiring illumination must be provided with emergency lighting.

Procedures for serious and imminent danger (article 15)

5.23 The responsible person must give effect to appropriate procedures, including safety drills, in the event of a serious and imminent danger, and nominate a sufficient number of competent persons to implement those procedures in the event of evacuation from the premises. No person shall have access to any area to which it is necessary to restrict access on the grounds of safety unless he has received adequate safety instruction.

Dangerous substances (article 16)

5.24 If there is a dangerous substance on the premises, the responsible person must ensure that details of relevant work hazards, hazard identification arrangements and specific hazards likely to arise, are available. Suitable warning and other communication systems are to be established. Visual or audible warnings must be given before explosion conditions are reached, and where necessary, escape facilities provided. Information relating to safety drills and emergency arrangements, warnings and escape facilities is to be made available to the accident and emergency services, and displayed on the premises.

5.25 In the event of a fire, the responsible person must ensure that immediate steps are taken to mitigate the effects of the fire, restore the situation to normal, and inform persons who may be affected. Only persons who are essential for carrying out repairs are to be permitted in the affected area, and they must be provided with appropriate personal protective equipment, and any necessary specialised safety equipment. However, these measures are not required if the results of the risk assessment show that because of the quantity of each dangerous substance in the premises, there is only a slight risk to persons, and the measures taken to comply with article 12 (above) are sufficient to control that risk.

Maintenance (article 17)

5.26   The responsible person must ensure that the premises and any facilities, equipment and devices are subject to a suitable system of maintenance, and are maintained in an efficient state, in efficient working order and in good repair.

Safety assistance (article 18)

5.27   The responsible person must appoint one or more competent persons to assist him in undertaking the preventative and protective measures. The number of persons so appointed must have sufficient time available and adequate means for them to perform their functions. If the person so appointed is not in his employment, the responsible person must ensure that the person so appointed is informed of factors known by him to affect the safety of persons affected by the conduct of the undertaking, and has access to details relating to dangerous substances, any relevant safety data sheet, and legislative provisions which apply to the substance, and the significant findings of the risk assessment.

Provision of information to employees (article 19)

5.28   The responsible person must provide his employees with comprehensible and relevant information on:
- (a) the risks to them identified by the risk assessment
- (b) the preventative and protective measures
- (c) the procedures for dealing with serious and imminent danger
- (d) the identities of persons nominated to implement safety measures and safety procedures
- (e) information received from other persons about risks arising out of the conduct of that other person's undertaking.

5.29   If there is a dangerous substance on the premises, the responsible person must also inform his employees of details of any such substance, its name, the risk it presents, access to any safety data sheet and legislative provisions which apply to the substance, and the significant findings of the risk assessment.

Provision of information to others (article 20)

5.30   The responsible person must ensure that the employer of any employees from an outside undertaking who are working on the premises is provided with comprehensible and relevant information about the risk to those employees and the preventative and protective measures taken by the responsible person. He must also ensure that self-employed persons working on his premises are provided with appropriate instructions and comprehensible and relevant information regarding any risks to that person. The employer concerned and self-employed persons must also be provided with the identity of the person nominated to oversee evacuation procedures.

Capabilities and training (article 21)

5.31   The responsible person must ensure that his employees are provided with adequate safety training at the time when they are first employed, and on being exposed to new or increased risks. The training must deal with appropriate precautions, be repeated periodically when appropriate, be adapted to new or changed risks, be provided in an appropriate manner, and take place during working hours.

Co-operation and co-ordination (article 22)

5.32   Where two or more responsible persons share premises, they must co-operate with each other so far as is necessary to comply with the provisions of the Order, take all reasonable steps to co-ordinate measures, and take all reasonable steps to inform other responsible persons of risks arising out of the conduct of their undertakings.

General duties of employees at work (article 23)

5.33   Every employee must, while at work:
  (a) take reasonable care for the safety of himself and of other persons who may be affected by his acts or omissions at work
  (b) as regards any duty or requirement imposed on his employer, co-operate with his employer as far as is necessary to enable that duty or requirement to be complied with
  (c) inform his employer or any other employee with specific responsibility for the safety of his fellow employees of any work situation which his training and instruction would reasonably consider represents a serious and immediate danger to safety in the event of fire, and of any matter which he would reasonably consider represents a shortcoming in the employer's protection arrangements for safety in the event of fire, insofar as the matter

arises out of or in connection with his own activities at work, and has not been previously reported.

Enforcing authorities (article 25)

5.34 The Order is to be enforced by the fire authority for the area in which the premises are situated, or the Health and Safety Executive in respect of nuclear installations, ships under construction, and construction sites. The Secretary of State for Defence will be the enforcing authority for premises occupied by the armed forces and visiting forces, while the relevant local authority will be the enforcing authority for sports grounds, and fire inspectors will enforce the Order in respect of premises owned or occupied by the Crown and the premises of the United Kingdom Atomic Energy Authority.

5.35 Inspectors have wide powers to do anything necessary for the purpose of enforcing the Order (article 27) and may serve an "alteration notice".

Enforcement notice (article 30)

5.36 If the enforcing authority is of the opinion that the responsible person has failed to comply with any provision of the Order, an enforcement notice may be served:

(a) stating that the enforcing authority is of that opinion
(b) specifying the provisions which have not been complied with
(c) requiring that person to take steps to remedy the failure within such period as may be specified in the notice (being not less than 28 days).

5.37 The notice may include directions as to the measures necessary to remedy the failure (including different ways of remedying the contravention). A prohibition notice may also be served.

Offences, defences and appeals (articles 32-35)

5.38 The Order provides for various offences, which are punishable in some cases by a fine on summary conviction up to Level 3 on the standard scale, in other cases up to the statutory maximum fine, and on indictment an unlimited fine. It is a defence for a person charged to prove that he took all reasonable precautions and exercised all due diligence to avoid the commission of an offence. It will be for the accused to prove that it was not reasonably practicable to do more than was in fact done to satisfy the duty or requirement. An appeal against an alteration notice, an enforcement notice and a prohibition notice may be made to the magistrates' court, with a further appeal to the crown court.

Civil liability (article 39)

5.39 A breach of a duty imposed on an employer under the Order, insofar as it causes damage to an employee confers a right of action in civil proceedings.

Employee consultation (article 41)

5.40 The Safety Representatives and Safety Committee Regulations 1977 and the Health and Safety (Consultation with Employees) Regulations 1996 are amended so as to require an employer to consult with employees over fire fighting measures, nominating competent persons, and contacts with emergency services.

Fire (Scotland) Act 2005

5.41 The law of fire precautions in Scotland is based on a somewhat different regime. The Fire (Scotland) Act 2005 sets out the duties of the joint fire and rescue boards, with responsibilities in relation to fire and rescue services. These boards will have control over water supply, fire hydrants, etc and officers appointed will have wide powers in respect of investigation and inspection.

5.42 So far as safety at work is concerned, the Act has been implemented by the Fire Safety (Scotland) Regulations 2006. Employers and persons who have control of premises (including a person who has obligations by virtue of a contract or tenancy) shall make a risk assessment for the purpose of identifying risks to the safety of relevant persons in respect of harm caused by fire to the premises. They must also take such fire safety measures as in all the circumstances it is reasonable for a person in his position to take in order to ensure the safety of relevant persons in respect of harm caused by fire. The risk assessment shall be reviewed as necessary.

5.43 The fire safety measures to be taken are to be based on the following considerations:
   (a) avoiding risks

(b) evaluating risks which cannot be avoided
(c) combating risks at source
(d) adapting to technical progress
(e) replacing the dangerous with the non-dangerous or less dangerous
(f) developing an overall fire prevention policy which covers technology, organisation of work, and the influence of factors relating to the working environment
(g) giving collective fire safety protective measures priority over individual measures
(h) giving appropriate instructions to employees.

5.44 Every employee shall, while at work, take reasonable care for the safety in respect of harm caused by fire, of himself and any other person who may be affected by his acts or omissions, and co-operate with the employer insofar as is necessary for the purpose of enabling the employer to comply with the statutory requirements.

Safety notices

5.45 There are a number of legislative provisions that require the display of notices relating to issues of safety and/or health. These include the:
(a) Coal and Other Mines (Managers and Officials) Order 1956, which requires a danger sign around dangerous areas
(b) Stratified Ironstone, Shale and Fireclay Mines (Explosives) Regulations 1956, which require warning notices when shot-firing is being carried out
(c) Miscellaneous Mines (Explosives) Regulations 1959, which require notices warning that shot-firing is about to commence
(d) Quarries Regulations 1999, which require danger areas to be clearly marked
(e) Ionising Radiations Regulations 1999, which require the designation and demarcation of controlled areas
(f) Dangerous Substances and Explosive Atmospheres Regulations 2002, which require warning signs for places where explosive atmospheres may occur
(g) Control of Substances Hazardous to Health Regulations 2002, which require notices to be affixed to premises when certain fumigation is to be carried out, and removed when the premises are safe to enter

(h) Control of Noise at Work Regulations 2005, which require ear protection zones to be demarcated and identified by means of specific signs.

(i) Control of Asbestos Regulations 2006, which require the designation of asbestos areas and respiratory zones.

5.46 The former Health and Safety Commission (HSC) conducted a review of all the legal requirements relating to the display of posters and health and safety information, with the result that ss.138–139 of the Factories Act were repealed, and some 53 regulations revoked without replacement (Health and Safety Information for Employees (Modifications and Repeals) Regulations 1995), on the grounds that they no longer fulfilled any necessary health and safety function, and could distract attention from the employer's duties under more modern legislative provisions to provide information for employees and others.

Health and Safety (Safety Signs and Signals) Regulations 1996

5.47 In order to implement Directive 92/587/EEC on the minimum requirements for the provision of health and/or safety signs at work (which standardises signs throughout the EU), these regulations came into force in 1996, and signs that were lawfully in use prior to that date must comply with the regulations.

5.48 Regulation 4 of the 1996 regulations provides that where a risk assessment carried out by the employer under regulation 3 of the Management of Health and Safety at Work Regulations 1999 (see Chapter 4) indicates that, notwithstanding that he has adopted all appropriate techniques for collective protection and measures, methods or procedures used in the organisation of work, he cannot avoid or adequately reduce risks to employees, except by the provision of appropriate safety signs to warn or instruct employees of the nature of the risks and measures to be taken against them, then he shall provide and maintain any safety sign set out in schedule 1 of the regulations, or ensure that such a sign is in place, and also ensure, so far as is reasonably practicable, that the appropriate hand signal or verbal communication described in schedule 1 is used. If there are risks in connection with the movement of traffic (including risks to pedestrians) then the appropriate sign prescribed under the Road Traffic Regulation Act 1984 may be used.

5.49   It is permissible to use illuminated signs and acoustic methods as well as hand signals. Signs are required for fire exits and fire-fighting equipment, and road traffic signs are to be used in respect of roads within the workplace.

5.50   An employer must ensure that comprehensible and relevant information on the measures to be taken in connection with safety signs is provided to each of his employees, and that employees receive suitable and sufficient instruction and training in the meaning of safety signs and the measures to be taken in connection with safety signs.

5.51   Safety signs are to be regarded as the last resort in the hierarchy of control measures for health and safety at work, and should be used when there is an absence of any reasonable or suitable alternative.

5.52   There are five categories of signs, each with its own distinctive shape and colour.

Prohibitory signs

5.53   These will be circular with a red border and diagonal line over a black symbol on a white background. It is meant to indicate the prohibition of the depicted activity, eg "No Smoking".

Warning signs

5.54   These will be triangular in shape with a black border and symbol on a yellow background. It will denote the presence of the depicted danger in the area when the sign is displayed, eg "Caution".

Mandatory signs

5.55   These will be circular on a blue background with symbols in white. These will indicate specific instructions that must be obeyed, where there is an obligation to use safety equipment, eg "Hearing protection must be worn".

Emergency signs

5.56   These will be square or rectangular (depending on the size of the text or symbol) and will consist of a green background with white symbols. These will denote some safety consideration, eg "first aid post".

Fire-fighting signs

5.57 These will be rectangular or square, with a white pictogram on a red background.

5.58 As to shape, colour, placing and intrinsic features, etc safety signs must comply with the minimum requirements set out in schedule 1 to the regulations. The safety signs below may be used.

Examples of safety signs and their meanings

Prohibitory signs: Round with white background and red border and cross bar. Symbols must be black and placed centrally on the background without obliterating the cross bar. The signs mean that something must not be done, as follows:

Warning signs: Triangular with a yellow background and a black border. The symbol, placed centrally, must be black. These signs warn of a particular hazard as follows:

Flammable material or high temperature

Explosive material

Toxic material

Corrosive material

Radioactive material

Overhead load

Industrial vehicles

Danger: electricity

General danger

Laser beam

Oxidant material

Non-ionising radiation

Strong magnetic field

Obstacles

Drop

Biological risk

Low temperature

Harmful or irritant material

Mandatory signs: Round with a blue background and white symbol. These signs state what protective equipment must be worn, as follows:

Eye protection
must be worn

Safety helmet
must be worn

Ear protection
must be worn

Respiratory equipment
must be worn

Safety boots
must be worn

Safety gloves
must be worn

Safety overalls
must be worn

Face protection
must be worn

Safety harness
must be worn

Pedestrians must
use this route

General mandatory sign
(to be accompanied where
necessary by another sign)

Emergency signs: Square or oblong with white symbols on green background. These signs indicate safe conditions such as first-aid posts or emergency routes.

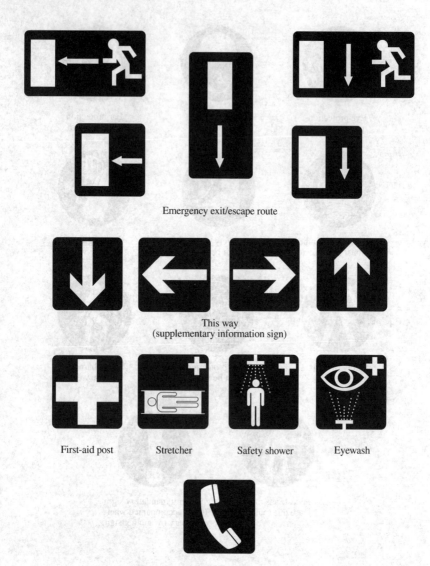

Emergency exit/escape route

This way
(supplementary information sign)

First-aid post   Stretcher   Safety shower   Eyewash

Emergency telephone for first-aid or escape

Fire-fighting signs: Rectangular or square shape with a red background and white symbol.

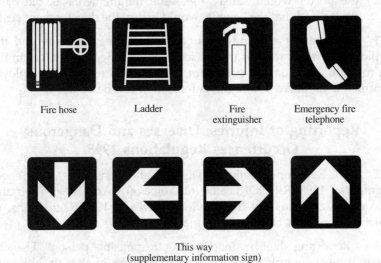

| Fire hose | Ladder | Fire extinguisher | Emergency fire telephone |

This way
(supplementary information sign)

Health and Safety Information for Employees Regulations 1989–2009

5.59　　These regulations dispense with the need to display abstracts of the Factories Act and Offices, Shops and Railway Premises Act, and instead require all employers to display a poster or distribute a leaflet entitled *Health and Safety Law: What You Should Know*, informing employees in general terms about the requirements of health and safety law. These can be obtained from HSE Books.

5.60　　The Health and Safety Information for Employees (Modifications and Repeals) Regulations 1995 have revoked a number of statutory requirements to display health and safety information, in particular those made with reference to specific industrial processes under s.139 of the Factories Act 1961. It was thought that these requirements no longer fulfilled any useful health and safety function. The new regulations also permit an employer to dispense with the current *Health and Safety Law* poster and, subject to HSE approval, permit the display or use of a particular form of poster or leaflet designed for a particular employment. The employer would have to show that:

(a) there was a clearly defined industry or group of employees
(b) there was a clear demand for the alternative poster
(c) the poster would satisfy the same requirements as the basic poster, and that the benefits would justify the development costs.

5.61   The names and addresses of the enforcing authority and the employment medical advisory service need no longer be written in the appropriate place on the poster (or leaflet), as long as the employer informs the employees how this information can be obtained.

Reporting of Injuries, Diseases and Dangerous Occurrences Regulations 1995

5.62   The Reporting of Injuries, Diseases and Dangerous Occurrences Regulations 1995 (RIDDOR) came into force on 1 April 1996. Their aim is to revise and simplify the previous RIDDOR 1985 Regulations, to which a number of changes were made.

5.63   Reporting shall be done by the "responsible person". Usually, this will be the employer or someone acting on his behalf, although more specific persons are identified as being responsible for reporting in mines, quarries, offshore and diving activities.

1. The following incidents must be reported forthwith by the quickest practicable means (usually this will be by telephone) and a report sent to the relevant enforcing authority on the approved form within 10 days:
   (a) where any person dies as a result of an accident arising out of or in connection with work
   (b) where any person at work suffers a major injury (defined below) as a result of an accident arising out of or in connection with work
   (c) where a person not at work suffers an injury as a result of an accident arising out of or in connection with work, and that person is taken to a hospital for treatment in respect of that injury
   (d) any person not at work suffers a major injury as a result of an accident arising out of or in connection with work at a hospital (excluding accidents arising from medical or dental treatment)
   (e) any dangerous occurrence (defined below).
2. The following injuries must be reported as soon as practicable, and a report sent to the relevant enforcing authority within 10 days on the approved form: where a person is incapacitated for work of a kind which he might reasonably be expected to do, for more than three

consecutive days (excluding the day of the accident but including days that would not have been working days), because of an accident arising out of or in connection with work.

3. Where an employee, as a result of an accident at work, has suffered an injury reportable under 1(a), (b) or (e) above, which is the cause of his death within one year from the date of the accident, the employer shall inform the relevant enforcing authority in writing of the death as soon as it comes to his knowledge, whether or not it was previously reported.

4. Where a person at work suffers from any of the occupational diseases specified in schedule 3 of the regulations, and the work involved one of the activities specified in the corresponding entry, the responsible person shall forthwith send a report to the relevant enforcing authority on an approved form. However, he need only do this if he has received a written statement prepared by a registered medical practitioner diagnosing the disease as one of those specified in schedule 3.

5. Also reportable are incidents arising out of the supply or distribution or installation of gas, failures in railway signalling and railway accidents, and accidents and occurrences, etc on offshore installations.

6. Road accidents are only reportable if:
   (a) a person was killed or injured as a result of exposure to a substance being conveyed on the vehicle
   (b) a person was engaged in, or was killed or injured as the result of the activities of another person who was engaged in work connected with the loading or unloading of any article or substance onto or off the vehicle
   (c) a person was engaged in, or killed or injured as a result of the activities of another person engaged in work on or alongside a road, being work concerned with the construction, demolition, alteration, repair or maintenance of the road (or markings or equipment thereon), or verges, fences, hedges or boundaries of the road, or pipes or cables on, under, over or adjacent to the road, or buildings or structures adjacent to or over the road
   (d) a person was killed or injured as a result of an accident in connection with the movement of a vehicle on a road which also involved a train.

7. Not reportable are deaths or injuries which arise from medical treatment or examinations carried out by a registered medical

practitioner or registered dentist. Nor is it necessary to report an occupational disease identified during health surveillance.

5.64   A major injury (see above) is defined as:
(a) any fracture, other than to the fingers, thumbs or toes
(b) any amputation
(c) dislocation of the shoulder, hip, knee or spine
(d) loss of sight (whether temporary or permanent)
(e) a chemical or hot metal burn to the eye, or any penetrating injury to the eye
(f) any injury from an electric shock or electric burn leading to unconsciousness or requiring resuscitation or admission to hospital for more than 24 hours
(g) any other injury leading to hypothermia, heat-induced illness, or unconsciousness, or requiring resuscitation, or admission to hospital for more than 24 hours
(h) loss of consciousness caused by asphyxia or by exposure to a harmful substance or biological agent
(i) acute illness or loss of consciousness caused by the absorption of any substance by inhalation, ingestion or through the skin
(j) acute illness resulting from exposure to a biological agent or its toxins or infected material.

5.65   A list of dangerous occurrences (see above) is contained in schedule 2 of the regulations. These include incidents involving the collapse or overturning of lifting machinery (or the failure of any load-bearing part), the failure of pressure systems, the failure of freight containers, incidents connected with overhead electric lines, electric short circuits or overloads which result in the stoppage of plant for more than 24 hours, incidents involving explosives, release or escape of biological agents, malfunctioning of radiation generators, malfunctioning of breathing apparatus while in use or being tested prior to use, incidents relating to diving operations, the collapse of scaffolding, train collisions, and incidents connected with wells, pipelines, fairground equipment, and the carriage of dangerous substances by road, the collapse of a building or structure, an explosion or fire, the escape of flammable substances, and the escape of any substance likely to cause injury, death or any other damage to the health of any person. There are specific definitions dealing with dangerous occurrences in mines, quarries, transport systems and offshore installations.

5.66 It should be noted that the term "accident" now includes non-consensual physical violence done to a person at work. Thus an assault on an employee is now reportable (subject to the above provisions), unless the incident is not work-related. Also included now are suicides on "relevant transport systems".

5.67 The HSE has published a guide (L73: *A Guide to the Reporting of Injuries, Diseases and Dangerous Occurrences Regulations 1995* (RIDDOR)) and a free leaflet on the regulations *(Everyone's Guide to RIDDOR'95)*, and new simplified accident reporting forms have been drawn up. The relevant form (F2508 for accidents and F2508A for diseases) must be sent to the local office of the HSE or to the environmental health office of the local authority, as appropriate.

5.68 The HSE, together with local authorities, has set up a new single Incident Contact Centre (ICC) to which all work-related health and safety incidents can be reported, as an alternative to local HSE or local authority offices. Users may telephone or fax their reports, complete a form on-line at *www.riddor.gov.uk*, or continue to use and send completed Forms F2508. Reports may be sent by post to Incident Contact Centre, Caerphilly Business Park, Caerphilly CF83 3GG. Telephone reports should be made to tel: 0845 300 9923. Fax reports should be made to fax: 0845 300 9924. Enquiries can be sent to the following e-mail address: *riddor@natbrit.com* or to the HSE Information Centre, e-mail: *hseinformationservices@natbrit.com*.

Obtaining further information

5.69 On having received a report, the HSE can require further information about the reported incident. This may be further details about the circumstances which gave rise to the incident, details about the plant (including its design), details of safety systems, qualification experience and training of staff, protection arrangements, tests, levels of exposure, etc.

Keeping records

5.70 Employers are required to keep records of all events reported under the regulations. No specific design is required, and the records may be in the form of photocopies of accident report forms, an accident book or stored on a computer. All that is necessary is to comply with the requirements laid down in schedule 4. In the case of a notifiable disease, the information must contain the occupation of the person affected, the name or nature of the disease, and the date of its diagnosis. In the case of a reportable accident or dangerous occurrence, the record must contain the date and time of the incident, the name, occupation and nature of any injury, the place where the injury or dangerous occurrence happened and a brief description of the circumstances.

Defences

5.71   If a person is prosecuted for an offence under the regulations, it will be a defence for him to show that he was not aware of the event which he was required to report or notify, and that he had taken all reasonable steps to have all such events brought to his notice.

Health and Safety (First Aid) Regulations 1981

5.72   The Health and Safety (First Aid) Regulations came into force on 1 July 1982. Four statutory provisions were repealed (Factories Act s.61, Mines and Quarries Act s.115 (in part), OSRPA s.24, and Agriculture (Safety, Health and Welfare Provisions) Act s.6(1)(4)). In addition, some 42 regulations and orders were revoked in whole or in part, and thus the new regulations (as amended), supported by an Approved Code of Practice and Guidance Notes, are now the main source of legal rules on this subject.

5.73   The regulations lay down four general requirements. First, an employer shall provide, or ensure that there are provided, such equipment and facilities as are adequate and appropriate in the circumstances for enabling first aid to be rendered to his employees if they are injured or become ill at work. A similar obligation applies to a self-employed person to enable him to render first aid to himself while he is at work.

5.74   Second, an employer shall provide (or ensure that there is provided) such number of suitable persons as is adequate and appropriate in the circumstances for rendering first aid to his employees if they are injured or become ill at work. A person shall not be regarded as being suitable for this purpose unless he has undergone:
   (a) such training and has such qualifications as the HSE may approve for the time being in respect of that case
   (b) such additional training, if any, as may be appropriate in the circumstances of that case.

5.75 However, where such a person is absent in temporary and exceptional circumstances, it is sufficient compliance if another person has been appointed to take charge of the situation relating to an injured or ill employee who will need help from a medical practitioner or nurse, and who is also in charge of the equipment and facilities. Further, where, having regard to the nature of the undertaking, the number of employees at work and the location of the establishment, it would be adequate and appropriate to appoint someone to take charge of the situation and equipment and facilities (who may not necessarily be trained or qualified as above), the employer meets the legal requirements by making such an appointment.

5.76 Third, the employer shall inform his employees of the arrangements that have been made in connection with the provision of first aid, including the location of equipment, facilities and personnel.

5.77 Fourth, any first aid room provided must be easily accessible to stretchers and to any other equipment needed to convey patients to and from the room, and signposted in accordance with the Health and Safety (Safety Signs and Signals) Regulations 1996.

First aid Approved Code of Practice and Guidance Notes

Assessment

5.78 The first step is for the employer to make an assessment of the first aid needs appropriate to the circumstances of each workplace. This should take into account factors such as:
  (a) workplace hazards and risks
  (b) the size of the organisation
  (c) the organisation's history of accidents
  (d) the nature and distribution of the workforce
  (e) the remoteness of the site from emergency services
  (f) the needs of travelling, remote and lone workers
  (g) employees working on shared or multi-occupied sites
  (h) annual leave and other absences of first aiders and appointed persons.

5.79 There is no requirement that the assessment shall be in writing, but it is suggested that it is advisable to do so. Appendix 1 to the regulations contains a checklist for assessing whether additional provisions should be made.

5.80   The assessment will reveal the appropriate steps for the employer to take in the circumstances. Thus, if there is a comparatively low risk to health and safety, the employer will only need to provide a clearly identified and well-stocked first aid container, and appoint a person to look after the first aid arrangements and take charge in emergencies. However, if the assessment reveals particular risks, eg if there are hazardous substances or dangerous tools or equipment, the employer will need to consider that a sufficient number of trained first aiders are always available, that they are trained in special procedures dealing with identifiable hazards, that local emergency services are informed of the site where hazardous substances or dangerous processes are used or carried on, and that first aid rooms are provided. The assessment will also note that there may be different requirements in different parts of the establishment, that there may be employees who are potentially at greater risk (disabled persons, trainees, young persons, etc) problems arising from working patterns (shift work, night work, etc) distances involved, the type of first aid or medical assistance that may be needed and so on. Like all assessments, the first aid assessment should be reviewed and, if necessary, revised periodically in the light of experience and new knowledge.

Personnel

5.81   First aiders should be provided in sufficient numbers and at appropriate locations. The ACOP suggests that where 50 or more employees are employed, at least one first aider should be provided unless the assessment justifies otherwise. However, there are no hard and fast rules; a small organisation, with comparatively low health and safety risks, may not need a first aider, but will need an appointed person. A high-risk organisation, or where there are scattered sites, might need additional first aiders. The employer must make an appropriate judgment in the light of all the circumstances.

5.82   A person should be selected to be a first aider, depending on his reliability, skills and aptitude, and on his ability to absorb knowledge, develop new skills and cope in emergencies. His normal duties should be such that he is able to respond immediately and rapidly to an emergency. He should hold a valid certificate of competence in first aid work (issued by an organisation approved by the HSE), be given time off work for training and refresher courses, and be put in touch with suitable sources of advice.

5.83   An appointed person is not necessarily a qualified first aider, but he should be given instruction on how to look after the first aid equipment and, as a minimum, should know what to do in emergency situations. The appointed person should be available to undertake his duties at all times when persons are at work. The ACOP suggests that as he is required to look after the first aid equipment, he should ideally know how to use it. Employers are strongly advised to consider the need for emergency first aid training for an appointed person, on such topics as:

(a) what to do in an emergency
(b) cardio-pulmonary resuscitation
(c) first aid for the unconscious casualty
(d) first aid for the wounded or bleeding.

Equipment and facilities

5.84   The minimum level of first aid equipment is a well-stocked and properly identifiable first aid container (with a white cross on a green background). These should be easily accessible and, if possible, near to hand-washing facilities. There is no mandatory list of contents, but the assessment should reveal any special requirements. The container should contain a leaflet giving guidance on first aid, individually wrapped sterile adhesive dressings, sterile eye pads, triangular bandages, safety pins, unmedicated wound dressings and disposable gloves. The contents of the container should be checked regularly and restocked after use. Additional material that may be needed may be stored separately, as long as they are available for use if required. Travelling first aid kits should be provided where necessary.

5.85   A suitable first aid room should be provided when the assessment identifies such a need. Again, it should contain essential first aid equipment and facilities and, if possible, should be reserved exclusively for the purpose of providing first aid. It should have a couch, be kept clean and tidy, be positioned near to a point of access for transport to hospital and display a notice on the door advising of the names, locations, etc of first aiders, with information on how they are to be contacted.

Information for employees

5.86   Employees must be informed of the nature and location of first aid facilities and first aiders. New employees may be given this information on an induction course. Suitable first aid notices and information concerning the location of first aiders should be displayed, with special attention being paid to the need to inform employees who are visually impaired or have language difficulties.

No smoking

5.87 The Health Act 2006 applies to Wales and England and Northern Ireland and came into force in 2007. Its provisions may be summarised as follows.

1. All work premises are to be "smoke free" if enclosed or substantially enclosed. Premises are substantially enclosed if they have a ceiling, unless more than 50% of the wall area is open to the outside.
2. A person who occupies or who is concerned with the management of smoke-free premises must display a "no smoking" sign. The sign must be at least A5 in size, and accompanied by the words "No Smoking. It is against the law to smoke on these premises".
3. An occupier or person concerned with the management of smoke-free premises who fails to display a prominent "no smoking" sign is liable to a fixed penalty of £200 (discounted to £150 if paid within 15 days). If the fine remains unpaid, he is liable to a fine of £1000 and a criminal conviction will be recorded.
4. An employer or visitor who is caught smoking in smoke-free premises is liable to a fixed penalty of £50 (discounted to £30 if paid within 15 days). If unpaid, he is liable to a fine up to £200 and a criminal conviction will be recorded.
5. It is the duty of a person who controls or manages a smoke-free premises to cause a person to stop smoking there and it is an offence to fail to do so, punishable by a fine of up to £2500. It is a defence if he took reasonable steps to cause that person to stop smoking, or that he did not know that the person was smoking, or on other grounds that it was reasonable for him not to comply with the duty.

5.88 The regulations also specify various exemptions from the Health Act 2006, including private residential accommodation and designated rooms in hotels and guest houses, care homes, hospices, prisons, etc. Private vehicles will also be exempt, not including work vehicles used by more than one person.

5.89 The Smoking, Health and Social Care (Scotland) Act 2005 came into force in March 2006, and makes it an offence for a person to smoke in no smoking premises and for a person who has the management or control of no smoking premises:

(a) to permit a person to smoke there

(b) to fail to display a "no smoking" notice in or approaching the premises.

5.90   No smoking premises are those which are wholly or substantially enclosed and:

(a) to which the public has access

(b) which are used wholly or mainly as a place of work

(c) which are used for the purposes of a club or other unincorporated association

(d) which are used for the provision of education or health or care services.

5.91   The Prohibition of Smoking in Certain Premises (Scotland) Regulations 2006 specify in greater detail the premises to which the Act applies, including restaurants, bars and public houses, hotels, libraries, cinemas, conference centres, offices, factories and other non-domestic premises in which one or more persons work, hospitals, airport terminals, and so on. Also specified are those premises which are exempt from the provisions of the Act, including residential accommodation, adult hospices, private vehicles, and so on. The penalties for non-compliance are the same as those in force in England and Wales.

CHAPTER 6

Health and safety at the workplace

6.1 In this chapter we shall consider the remaining five of the "six pack" regulations, which came into force following the adoption of EU Framework Directive 89/391/EEC (see paragraph 4.4).

6.2 Over the years, a number of amendments have been made to the "six pack" regulations, the most recent changes being made by the Health and Safety (Miscellaneous Amendments) Regulations 2002, which have been incorporated into the text. Some of these changes had to be made in order to ensure the full implementation of EU directives and to correct drafting problems.

Workplace (Health, Safety and Welfare) Regulations 1992

6.3 The objective of these regulations is to implement most of the requirements of Directive 89/654/EEC, while the remaining requirements will be dealt with by other legislative provisions (eg on fire precautions). It is also thought that some requirements of the directive are adequately dealt with by existing British law, and no changes are proposed in these areas (eg first aid). However, other existing legislation, though adequate, is not comprehensive enough, because it only applies to certain defined premises (eg factories, offices, shops and railway premises, etc). Thus most of these provisions have been repealed or revoked, replaced by comprehensive provisions which apply to all workplaces. The regulations are accompanied by an Approved Code of Practice with guidance, L24: *Workplace health, safety and welfare*.

6.4 The regulations apply to all workplaces, ie any premises (which are not domestic premises) that are made available to any person as a place of work, including any place within the premises to which a person working has access while at work, and any room, lobby, corridor, staircase, road or other place used as a means of access to or egress from the workplace, or where facilities are provided for use in connection with the workplace, other than a public road.

6.5   The application of the regulations is, therefore, very wide. They will apply not only to the traditional factories, offices and shops, but also to schools, hospitals, theatres, common parts of shared buildings, private roads on industrial estates, hotels, nursing homes, etc in fact almost anywhere people work other than domestic premises (homeworkers are thus not covered by the regulations).

6.6   There are, however, certain statutory exceptions where the regulations will not apply, or where only limited compliance is required. These are as follows:

(a) means of transport, including ships, aircraft, trains and road vehicles, although regulation 13 (below) will apply when these places are stationary inside a workplace or when a vehicle is not on a public road

(b) mines, quarries and other sites where minerals are being explored or extracted, including offshore sites and installations (these workplaces have their own separate legislation)

(c) sites where building operations or works of engineering construction are being carried out; if construction work is being carried on within a workplace, the site will be excluded if it is fenced off, otherwise the Construction (Design and Management) Regulations 2007 and the Workplace Regulations will both apply

(d) so far as temporary sites are concerned, the welfare provisions of the regulations (regulations 20–25, below) will apply "so far as is reasonably practicable"; a temporary site is one used for a short period or infrequently, eg a fairground

(e) so far as agriculture and forestry work is concerned, regulations 20–22 (below) apply so far as is reasonably practicable.

6.7   In general, the regulations place duties on employers in respect of workplaces under their control and where their employees work. In addition, duties are placed on controllers of premises in respect of matters within their control. For example, the owner of a multi-occupancy building will be responsible for the common provision of services and facilities (toilets, ventilation plant, etc) thus extending the legal obligations set out in s.4 of HSWA (see paragraph 3.82).

6.8   In *Donaldson v Hays Distribution Services Ltd* the Inner House of the Scottish Civil Court of Appeal held that the regulations do not extend to non-employees, such as visitors. Any such claim must be dealt with under the Occupiers Liability Act (see paragraph 12.97).

6.9 The regulations were examined by the Scottish Outer House in *Campbell v East Renfrewshire Council*, where the claimant was injured when he fell 20 feet down an embankment. It was held:
 (a) the embankment was a workplace
 (b) the embankment was not a floor in a workplace within regulation 12
 (c) the embankment had not been constructed within the provisions of regulation 12
 (d) regulation 13 (now Work at Height Regulations 2005) was designed to cover falls from a height, rather than falling to the ground and tumbling down an embankment
 (e) there was thus no claim for breach of statutory duty based on the regulations.

6.10 However, his claim for common law negligence could be proceeded with.

Stability and solidity (regulation 4A)

6.11 Where a workplace is in a building, the building must have a stability and solidity appropriate to the nature of the use of the workplace.

Maintenance of workplace, and of equipment, devices and systems (regulation 5)

6.12 The workplace and the equipment, devices and systems shall be maintained (including cleaned as appropriate) to an efficient state, in efficient order and in good repair.

6.13 This regulation applies to equipment, devices and systems, a fault in which is liable to result in a failure to comply with other regulations. Examples of equipment, devices and systems include mechanical ventilation systems, emergency lighting, equipment and devices intended to prevent or reduce hazards, fencing, fixed equipment used for cleaning windows, powered doors, escalators and moving walkways, etc.

6.14 The ACOP points out that regular maintenance shall be carried out at suitable intervals, dangerous defects remedied, and a suitable record kept.

Ventilation (regulation 6)

6.15   Effective and suitable provision shall be made to ensure that every enclosed workplace is ventilated by a sufficient quantity of fresh or purified air. Any plant used shall include an efficient device which gives a visible or audible warning of any failure.

6.16   Additional information on compliance with this regulation is given in the ACOP and guidance.

Temperature in indoor workplaces (regulation 7)

6.17   During working hours, the temperature in all workplaces inside buildings shall be reasonable. A method of heating shall not be used which results in the escape into the workplace of fumes, gas or vapour which may be injurious or offensive. A sufficient number of thermometers shall be provided. A workplace shall be adequately thermally insulated where it is necessary, having regard to the type of work carried out and the physical activity of the persons carrying out the work. Excessive effects of sunlight on temperature shall be avoided.

6.18   The ACOP suggests that the temperature should provide reasonable comfort without the need for special clothing. It should be at least 16°C unless the work involves severe physical effort, when it should be at least 13°C. These temperatures do not apply to workplaces where lower maximum room temperatures are impractical. The ACOP does not specify a maximum temperature, but this too must be reasonable (see HSWA s.2(2)(e)). Thus, if there is an exceptional heat wave, a reasonable temperature must still be observed.

Lighting (regulation 8)

6.19   Every workplace shall have suitable and sufficient lighting, which, so far as is reasonably practicable, shall be by natural light. Sufficient emergency lighting shall be provided in any room where persons are exposed to danger if artificial lighting fails.

6.20   The ACOP points out that lighting should also be placed at places of particular risk, eg pedestrian crossing points on traffic routes, dazzling lights and glare should be avoided, and light fittings should not cause a hazard. Lights should not be permitted to become obscured, they should be replaced, repaired or cleaned as necessary.

Cleanliness and waste materials (regulation 9)

6.21 Every workplace, and the furniture, furnishings and fittings therein shall be kept sufficiently clean. Surfaces of floors, walls and ceilings shall be capable of being kept sufficiently clean. So far as is reasonably practicable, waste materials shall not be allowed to accumulate except in suitable receptacles.

6.22 The ACOP states that floors and indoor traffic routes should be cleaned at least once each week. If dirt or refuse is not in suitable receptacles, it should be removed daily.

Room dimensions and space (regulation 10)

6.23 Every room where persons work shall have sufficient floor area, height and unoccupied space for purposes of health, safety and welfare.

6.24 The ACOP adopts the standard of $11m^3$ for each person, although it suggests ignoring space which is more than 3m high when making this calculation. There are exceptions in certain employment where space is limited, eg retail sales kiosks, attendants' shelters, etc. The number of persons who may work in a room at any particular point in time will also depend on the space taken up by furniture, equipment, etc.

Workstations and seating (regulation 11)

6.25 Every workstation shall be so arranged that it is suitable for the person at work and for any work likely to be done there. A workstation which is out of doors shall be so arranged that:
   (a) so far as is reasonably practicable, it provides protection from adverse weather
   (b) it enables any person at the workstation to leave it swiftly or be assisted in the event of an emergency
   (c) it ensures that any person at the workplace is not likely to slip or fall.

6.26 If a substantial part of the work can be done while the person at work is seated, then a suitable seat shall be provided. The seat must be suitable for the person and for the operations to be performed. A suitable footrest shall be provided where necessary.

6.27   The ACOP states that workstations should be so arranged that each task can be carried out safely and comfortably. The worker should have adequate freedom of movement, spells of work carried out in cramped conditions should be limited, seating should provide adequate support for the lower back, and so on.

Condition of floors and traffic routes (regulation 12)

6.28   Workplace floors and surface traffic routes shall be so constructed that they are suitable for the purposes. The floor or surface shall not have a hole or slope, or be uneven or slippery so as to expose a person to a risk to his health or safety and shall have effective means of drainage as appropriate. Suitable and sufficient handrails and guards shall be provided on all traffic routes which are staircases.

6.29   The ACOP gives some practical advice on the construction of floors, stairs, etc and pays particular attention to hazards from spillages and contamination by liquids. Appropriate control measures should be taken.

Tanks and pits (regulation 13(5))

6.30   The provisions in regulation 13 (1-4) relating to the prevention of persons likely to fall a distance or being struck by an object have been revoked, and replaced by the Work at Height Regulations 2005 (see paragraph 9.71). Regulation 13(5) requires that so far as is reasonably practicable, every tank, pit or structure where there is a risk of a person falling into a dangerous substance shall be covered or fenced.

Windows and transparent or translucent doors, gates and walls (regulation 14)

6.31   Every window, transparent or translucent surface in a wall, partition, door or gate shall, where necessary for reasons of health or safety, be of safety material or protected against breakage. It shall also be appropriately marked.

6.32   The HSE has recently approved a change in paragraph 147 of the ACOP so as to clarify more precisely the factors to be taken into account when assessing whether it is necessary, for reasons of health or safety, for transparent or translucent surfaces to be made of a safety material or be adequately protected against breakage.

Windows, skylights and ventilators (regulation 15)

6.33 Windows, skylights or ventilators shall not be opened, closed or adjusted in a manner which exposes any person performing such an operation to a risk to his health or safety. Nor must they pose a risk to health and safety when open.

Ability to clean windows, etc safely (regulation 16)

6.34 All windows and skylights in a workplace shall be of a design or so constructed that they may be cleaned safely.

Organisation, etc of traffic routes (regulation 17)

6.35 Every workplace shall be organised in such a way that pedestrians and vehicles can circulate in a safe manner. Traffic routes shall be suitable for the persons or vehicles using them, in sufficient number, in suitable position and of sufficient size. (For existing workplaces, this duty shall be complied with "so far as is reasonably practicable".) Suitable measures shall be taken to ensure that pedestrians or vehicles may use traffic routes without causing danger to persons at work nearby, and there is sufficient separation between vehicles and pedestrians. Traffic routes shall be suitably indicated.

6.36 The ACOP gives considerable advice on how safe traffic routes may be achieved. A safe circulation of movement of persons and vehicles requires a suitable combination of the physical layout and safe system of use.

Doors and gates (regulation 18)

6.37 Doors and gates shall be suitably constructed and fitted with any necessary safety devices. Sliding doors or gates shall have a device to prevent them from coming off tracks during use, an upward opening door or gate shall have a device to prevent it falling back, a powered door or gate shall have a suitable and effective feature to prevent it causing injury by trapping any person and shall be capable of being operated manually (unless it opens automatically if the power fails), and a door or gate which is capable of being pushed from either side shall provide, when closed, a clear view of the space close to both sides.

Escalators and moving walkways (regulation 19)

6.38 Escalators and moving walkways shall function safely, be equipped with any necessary safety device, and fitted with one or more emergency stop controls that are easily identifiable and readily accessible.

Sanitary conveniences (regulation 20)

6.39 Suitable and sufficient sanitary conveniences shall be provided at readily accessible places. They shall be adequately ventilated and lit, kept in a clean and orderly condition, and separate rooms containing conveniences shall be provided for men and women, except where each convenience is in a separate room, the door of which is capable of being secured from the inside.

6.40 So far as workplaces which were in use prior to 1 January 1993 are concerned, and which were subject to the provisions of the Factories Act 1961, it is sufficient compliance if the sanitary conveniences consist of at least one water closet for use by females only for every 25 females, and one for every 25 males (see schedule 1, Part 2 of the regulations).

Washing facilities (regulation 21)

6.41 Suitable and sufficient washing facilities, including showers if required by the nature of the work for health reasons, shall be provided at readily accessible places. These shall be provided in the immediate vicinity of sanitary conveniences (whether or not provided elsewhere) and include a supply of clean hot and cold or warm running water. Soap or other means of cleaning and towels or other suitable means of drying shall be provided. The rooms shall be sufficiently ventilated and lit, kept clean and orderly, and have separate facilities for men and women, except where they are provided in a room which is capable of being secured from inside.

6.42 The ACOP specifies the minimum number of sanitary conveniences and washing stations which should be provided and deals with, in particular, remote workplaces and temporary work sites.

Drinking water (regulation 22)

6.43 An adequate supply of wholesome drinking water shall be provided for all persons at work in the workplace. This shall be at readily accessible places and be conspicuously marked by an appropriate sign. A sufficient number of suitable cups or other drinking vessels shall be provided, unless the supply is from a jet from which persons can drink easily.

Accommodation for clothing (regulation 23)

6.44 Suitable and sufficient accommodation for clothing shall be provided for clothing not worn during working hours, and for special clothing worn at work which is not taken home. The accommodation must be in a suitable location, and where facilities to change clothing are required by regulation 24 (below) suitable security must be provided. There must be separate accommodation for clothing worn at work where necessary to avoid risks to health (or damage to the clothing), and, so far as is reasonably practicable, the accommodation must allow or include facilities for drying clothing.

Facilities for changing clothing (regulation 24)

6.45 Suitable and sufficient facilities shall be provided for any person at work in the workplace to change clothing where the person has to wear special clothing for the purpose of work, and he cannot, for reasons of health or propriety, be expected to change in another room. Facilities shall not be regarded as being suitable unless they include separate facilities for, or separate use of facilities by, men and women where necessary for reasons of propriety. The facilities must also be easily accessible, of sufficient capacity and provided with seating.

6.46 In *Post Office v Footitt*, it was held that "special clothing" was not restricted to clothing which is worn only at work, but could include clothing worn while travelling to and from work, as well as at work (such as a uniform). Further, the concept of propriety is not confined to gender separation, and that to require one female to undress or dress in the presence of another may offend against the principles of propriety. That many women would not object to changing in the presence of others of the same sex did not absolve the employer from providing facilities for those who may prefer privacy.

Facilities for rest and to eat meals (regulation 25)

6.47 Suitable and sufficient rest facilities shall be provided at readily accessible places. In the case of new workplaces, extensions or conversions, where necessary for reasons of health or safety, one or more rest rooms shall be provided. In other cases, a rest room or rest areas may be provided. Where food is eaten in a workplace which would otherwise become contaminated, suitable facilities for eating meals shall be provided.

6.48   Rest rooms and rest areas shall include suitable arrangements to protect non-smokers from discomfort caused by tobacco smoke. They should also be equipped with an adequate number of tables and adequate seating with backs, as well as seating which is adequate and suitable for disabled persons. Suitable facilities shall be provided for any person at work who is a pregnant woman or nursing mother to rest.

6.49   Suitable and sufficient facilities shall be provided for persons at work to eat meals, where meals are eaten regularly in the workplace.

6.50   The ACOP suggests that suitable seats should be provided as appropriate, eating facilities should be kept clean to a suitable hygiene standard, and general advice is further given on compliance with this regulation.

Disabled persons (regulation 25A)

6.51   Where necessary, those parts of the workplace (including, in particular, doors, passageways, stairs, showers, washbasins, lavatories and workstations) used or occupied directly by disabled persons at work shall be organised to take account of such persons.

Exemption certificates (regulation 26)

6.52   The Secretary of State for Defence may, in the interests of national security, exempt the armed forces and visiting armed forces from the requirements of the regulations, subject to conditions and a time limit.

Repeals and revocations (regulation 27 and schedule 2)

6.53   The following statutory provisions have been repealed.
1. Factories Act 1961, ss.1–7, 18, 29, 57–60, 69.
2. Offices, Shops and Railway Premises Act 1963, ss.4–16.
3. Agriculture (Safety, Health and Welfare Provisions) Act 1956, ss.3, 5, 25(3)(6).

6.54   Some 36 regulations and orders, dating from 1906 onward, have also been revoked, either in whole or in part.

Provision and Use of Work Equipment Regulations 1998

6.55   The Provision and Use of Work Equipment Regulations 1992 were passed to implement Directive 89/655/EEC on the minimum health and safety requirements for the provision and use of work equipment at the workplace. These regulations have now been revoked and replaced by the Provision and Use of Work Equipment Regulations 1998 (PUWER), which implement Directive 95/63/EC and generally extend the scope of the 1992 regulations to include mobile, self-propelled and remote-controlled work equipment and power presses. In consequence, s.19 of the Offices, Shops and Railway Premises Act 1963 was repealed, and some 12 sets of regulations revoked, including the Power Presses Regulations 1965, Abrasive Wheels Regulations 1970, and the Woodworking Machines Regulations 1974. The 1992 regulations repealed a number of familiar legal provisions, including ss.12–16, 17, and 19 of the Factories Act 1961, s.17 of Offices, Shops and Railway Premises Act 1963, and some 17 sets of regulations (in whole or in part) were revoked. The regulations are accompanied by an Approved Code of Practice and Guidance Notes (L22: *Safe Use of Work Equipment*).

6.56   To some extent there is an overlap between PUWER and provisions which implement a number of EU product directives, including the Supply of Machinery (Safety) Regulations 1992 (as amended). These "Supply" Regulations (listed in schedule 1 to PUWER) impose obligations on manufacturers and suppliers of work equipment to meet essential health and safety requirements (in line with s.6 of HSWA) and work equipment which is able to satisfy those requirements will to that extent be exempt from some of the specific requirements of PUWER, contained in regulations 11–19 and 22–29.

6.57   There is also an overlap between PUWER and a number of other legislative provisions. The general rule to be adopted is that compliance with specific legal requirements will be sufficient to comply with more general requirements. For example, regulation 19 of PUWER requires isolation from sources of energy but, so far as electrical power is concerned, the specific requirements of regulation 12 of the Electricity at Work Regulations 1989 would be the more appropriate legal rule to follow.

Application of the regulations

6.58 The regulations impose obligations on every employer in respect of work equipment provided for use by an employee at work, and also impose obligations on self-employed persons, and persons who have control to any extent of work equipment to the extent of that control. Duties are also placed on those who use, supervise or manage the use of work equipment or the way work equipment is used. Generally speaking, the regulations do not apply to a ship's work equipment, but they do apply to offshore installations. A breach of the regulations may give rise to civil and/or criminal liabilities.

6.59 Work equipment is defined as "any machinery, appliance, apparatus, tool or installation for use at work (whether exclusively or not)" (this definition differs materially from the definition in the 1992 regulations). The courts have adopted a very wide and liberal approach to the meaning of "work equipment", eg a bolt joining railway line (*Kelly v First Engineering Ltd*), a steel cabinet in a nursery area (*Duncanson v South Ayrshire Council*), a ship (*Coltman v Bibby Tankers Ltd*), a flagstone (*Knowles v Liverpool City Council*), a stair carpet (*Irvine v Metropolitan Police Commissioner*), a passenger lift (*PRP Architects v Reid*), a drinks dispensing machine (*Given v James Watt College*), a portable ladder attached to the top bunk of a bed (*Robb v Salamis*) and a door-closing device (*Spencer-Franks v Kellogg Brown & Root Ltd*) have all been held to be work equipment. It used to be thought that the regulations are generally concerned with what are loosely described as the tools of the trade provided by the employer, and did not apply to an object on which an employee is working (*Hammond v Metropolitan Police Comr*) but this opinion was dissented from by the House of Lords in *Spencer-Franks v Kellogg Brown & Root Ltd*(above), where it was held that the test was whether the object performs a useful, practical function in relation to the purposes of the business.

6.60 Work equipment is "in use" when there is any activity involving work equipment, including starting, stopping, programming, setting, transporting, repairing, modifying, maintaining, servicing and cleaning, etc. However, if an item of equipment which had not been supplied by the employer is being used at work, it will not be "work equipment" for the purpose of the regulations unless the employer has expressly or impliedly permitted its use or must be deemed to have permitted its use (*Couzens v McGee Group Ltd*).

6.61   The main provisions of the regulations are as follows.

Suitability of work equipment (regulation 4)

6.62   Work equipment shall be so constructed or adapted as to be suitable for the purpose. When selecting work equipment, every employer shall have regard to the working conditions and to the risks to the health and safety of persons which exist in the premises or undertaking in which that work equipment is to be used, and any additional risk posed by the use of that equipment. Work equipment shall be used only for operations for which, and under conditions for which, it is suitable. The target of achieving suitability of work equipment under regulation 4 of PUWER has to be measured by reference to such hazards to anyone's health and safety as are reasonably foreseeable. Thus, if work equipment only becomes unsafe as a result of the extraneous, deliberate, unpredictable or violent act of a third party, the employer will not be liable for an injury or accident in respect of an alleged breach of duty (*Horton v Taplin Contracts Ltd*).

6.63   In *Robb v Salamis* the claimant was injured when he descended from a portable ladder which was attached to the top bunk of his bed on an oil rig. Neither the ladder nor the fittings were defective, but the ladder had slipped because it was not properly connected to its mountings. It was held by the House of Lords that the ladder (which was work equipment) was not suitable for its purpose because a person replacing it might not replace it properly due to carelessness. In other words, an employer must anticipate situations which might give rise to accidents, and not wait for them to happen. They must take account of risks created by the careless actions of others in relation to work equipment (in the circumstances of the case, compensation was reduced by 50% to reflect the claimant's contributory negligence).

6.64   The ACOP and Guidance Notes point out that the risk assessment carried out under the Management of Health and Safety at Work Regulations 1999 (see paragraph 4.8) will help employers to select work equipment and assess its suitability for particular tasks. Ergonomic risks should be taken into account, and work equipment installed, located and used in such a way as to reduce risks to users and other workers. Energy and substances used or produced must be supplied and removed in a safe manner. If mobile work equipment has a combustion engine, there must be sufficient air of good quality.

Maintenance (regulation 5)

6.65   Work equipment shall be maintained in an efficient state, efficient working order and in good repair. Maintenance logs shall be kept up to date. This regulation imposes an absolute obligation. In *Stark v Post Office*, the plaintiff was employed as a delivery postman by the Post Office. He suffered serious injuries when, in the course of his employment, the front brake stirrup of his delivery bicycle broke, with the result that he was thrown over the handlebars. The employers were held liable. It was their duty to ensure that the work equipment was maintained in an efficient state, in efficient working order, and in good repair, and they were thus in breach of their statutory duty.

6.66   However, the duty to maintain can only apply to matters which are within the power of the employer to do something without obtaining someone else's consent, and could not therefore apply in respect of property belonging to a third person (*Smith v Northamptonshire County Council*).

6.67   The Guidance Notes state that maintenance should only be done by competent persons. Equipment should be checked frequently, maintenance management techniques used, and maintenance logs, if used, should be kept up to date.

Inspection (regulation 6)

6.68   Where the safety of work equipment depends on the installation conditions, it must be inspected before being put into service for the first time, or after assembly at a new site or location, to ensure that it has been installed correctly and is safe to operate. If work equipment is exposed to conditions causing deterioration which is liable to result in dangerous situations, it must be inspected at suitable intervals to ensure that health and safety conditions are maintained, and that deterioration can be detected and remedied in good time. Records of such inspections shall be kept.

6.69   The purpose of the inspection is to identify whether the equipment can be operated, adjusted, and maintained safely, and that any deterioration can be detected and remedied. The ACOP suggests that the extent of the inspection required will depend on the potential risks.

Specific risks (regulation 7)

6.70   If the use of work equipment is likely to involve a specific risk, the use shall be restricted to those persons who have been specifically designated to use it. Repairs, modifications, maintenance or servicing of work equipment shall be restricted to those persons who have been specifically designated to perform such operations. Such persons shall be given adequate training in the operations in question.

6.71   The ACOP states that risks shall be controlled:
(a) by eliminating the risk
(b) by using control measures
(c) by implementing safe systems and providing information, instruction and training.

Information and instruction (regulation 8)

6.72   Employers shall ensure that all persons who use work equipment, including those who supervise or manage the use of work equipment, have available adequate health and safety information and, where appropriate, written instructions. This includes information and instructions on the conditions in which, and the methods by which, work equipment may be used, any foreseeable abnormal situations likely to occur and the action to be taken if such a situation were to occur, and any conclusions to be drawn from experience in using the work equipment. The information and instructions shall be readily comprehensible.

6.73   The Guidance Notes point out that it is for the employer to decide whether the information should be given in writing or verbally, taking into account whether there are unusual or complicated circumstances, the degree of skill of the workers involved, their experience and training, the degree of supervision and the complexity and length of the particular job. Supervisors and managers need access to information and written instructions, which should be presented to workers in clear English or other languages where necessary. Special considerations should be given to workers with language difficulties or with disabilities which may make it difficult for them to understand what is required.

Training (regulation 9)

6.74 Employers must ensure that all persons who use work equipment, and employees who supervise or manage the use of work equipment, have received adequate training for the purposes of health and safety, any risks which such use may entail, including the precautions to be taken.

6.75 The Guidance Notes point out that the requirements for adequate training will be determined by the nature of the job requirements and the work equipment. Special attention should be paid to the needs of young persons. The ACOP draws attention to the need to train drivers of self-propelled equipment and chainsaw operators.

Conformity with Community requirements (regulation 10)

6.76 Every employer shall ensure that an item of work equipment conforms, at all times, with the essential requirements, ie requirements relating to the design and construction of work equipment in compliance with any enactment which implements the EU Product Directives (a list of the relevant regulations is set out in schedule 1). The most significant relevant directive is the Machinery Directive, which has been implemented by the Supply of Machinery (Safety) Regulations 1992 (as amended).

6.77 The Guidance Notes point out that employers should check that adequate operating instructions have been provided with the equipment, that there is information about residual hazards, such as noise or vibration, and check for obvious faults. Products should carry a CE marking and be accompanied by relevant certificates or declarations.

Dangerous part of machinery (regulation 11)

6.78 Employers shall take effective measures to prevent access to any dangerous part of machinery, or to stop the movement of any dangerous part of machinery before any part of a person enters a danger zone. This can be achieved by fixed guards where it is practicable to do so, but where or to the extent it is not, then other guards or protection devices should be used, with jigs, holders, pushsticks, etc as a last resort. Additionally, the employer must provide such information, instruction, training and supervision as is necessary. Guards and protection devices shall be suitable for the purpose, of good construction, sound material and adequate strength, be maintained in an efficient state, not give rise to any increased risk to health or safety, not easily bypassed or disabled, be situated at sufficient distance from the danger zone, not unduly restrict the view of the operating cycle of the machinery (where such view is necessary), be so constructed that operations to fit replacement parts and maintenance work can be carried out without having to dismantle the guard or protection device.

6.79 Again, the risk assessment should identify the hazards from machinery, and determine what risk reduction measures are needed. Attached to the Guidance Notes is Appendix 2, which sets out various requirements for guards and protective devices.

Protection against specified hazards (regulation 12)

6.80 Where certain specified hazards are likely to occur, measures shall be taken to ensure that exposure is prevented, or adequately controlled, by measures other than the use of personal protective equipment, as well as by minimising the effects of the hazard and reducing the likelihood of it occurring. The specified hazards are:

(a) articles or substances falling or being ejected from the work equipment

(b) rupture or disintegration of parts of work equipment

(c) work equipment catching fire or overheating

(d) the unintended or premature discharge of any article or substance which is produced, used or stored in the work equipment

(e) the unintended or premature explosion of work equipment or any article or substance produced, used or stored in it.

6.81 However, this regulation does not apply where the following regulations apply: Ionising Radiations Regulations 1999, Control of Asbestos Regulations 2006, Control of Noise at Work Regulations 2005, Construction (Head Protection) Regulations 1989, Control of Lead at Work Regulations 2002 and Control of Substances Hazardous to Health Regulations 2002.

6.82 In general, the risk assessment will identify the likely hazards, eg material falling from equipment, or being ejected, pieces of equipment breaking away, overheating, explosions due to pressure build-up, etc. The primary aim is to prevent the occurrence, but if this is not possible, steps must be taken to reduce the risks. Thus the discharge or ejection of materials intentionally, or inevitably (eg sawdust from woodworking, grit-blasting of castings) is not prohibited as such, but risks must be controlled.

High and very low temperature (regulation 13)

6.83   Where work equipment, or articles or substances produced, used or stored in work equipment, is at a very high or very low temperature, protection must be afforded so as to prevent injury to any person by burn, scald or sear.

6.84   The Guidance Notes point out that although engineering methods should be considered first, other forms of protection may be necessary, eg warning signals, alarms, personal protective equipment, etc.

Starting controls (regulation 14)

6.85   Controls that require a deliberate action (except normal cycles of automatic devices) shall be provided for starting work equipment, or controlling changes in speed pressure, etc where a change results in a greater risk to health and safety. It should not be possible to start or change speed except by a deliberate action on a control, although this does not apply to re-starting or changing operating conditions as a result of the normal operating cycle of an automatic device.

6.86   The Guidance Notes state that controls should be designed and positioned so as to prevent inadvertent or accidental operation.

Stop controls (regulation 15)

6.87   Readily accessible stop controls shall be provided which will bring the work equipment to a safe condition in a safe manner, if necessary, for reason of health and safety, to a complete stop, and sources of energy switched off. Stop controls shall act in priority to other controls.

Emergency stop controls (regulation 16)

6.88   Work equipment shall be provided with readily accessible emergency stop controls, unless this is not necessary by reason of the nature of the hazard, and the time taken to come to a complete stop using other controls.

Controls (regulation 17)

6.89   All controls must be clearly visible and identifiable, and not in a position which exposes the operator to a risk to his health or safety. The control operator must be able to ensure from the position of control that no person is in a place where he would be exposed to any risk to his health or safety, as a result of the operation of the control, but where this is not reasonably practicable, the systems of work shall be effective to ensure that when work equipment is about to start, no person is in any such place or, where this is not reasonably practicable, audible, visual or other suitable warnings are given. Any person who is in a place where he would be exposed to a risk as a result of stopping or starting work equipment shall have sufficient time and suitable means to avoid the risk.

Control systems (regulation 18)

6.90   Every employer shall ensure, so far as is reasonably practicable, that all control systems of work equipment are safe, and are chosen making due allowance for the failures, faults and constraints to be expected in the planned circumstances of use. A control system will not be considered safe unless:
  (a) its operation does not create any increased risk to health or safety
  (b) it ensures, so far as is reasonably practicable, that any fault in, or damage to, any part of the control system, or loss of supply of any source of energy, cannot result in any additional or increased risk to health or safety
  (c) it does not impede the operation of any stop or emergency stop controls.

Isolation from sources of energy (regulation 19)

6.91   Where appropriate, work equipment must be provided with suitable means to isolate it from all its sources of energy, and reconnection must not expose any person to any risk.

251

Stability (regulation 20)

6.92 Work equipment shall be stabilised or clamped where necessary for purposes of health or safety.

Lighting (regulation 21)

6.93 Suitable and sufficient lighting, which takes into account the operations to be carried out, shall be provided at any place where a person uses work equipment.

Maintenance operations (regulation 22)

6.94 Appropriate measures shall be taken to ensure that, so far as is reasonably practicable, maintenance operations shall be carried out while the work equipment is shut down, or otherwise carried out without exposing persons to risk. Appropriate measures shall also be taken to ensure that a person carrying out maintenance is not exposed to risk to his health or safety.

Markings (regulation 23)

6.95 Work equipment shall be marked in a clearly visible manner, with any marking appropriate for reasons of health and safety.

Warnings (regulation 24)

6.96 Warnings or warning devices shall be provided, where appropriate for reasons of health or safety. Warnings shall be unambiguous, easily perceived and easily understood.

Mobile work equipment (regulations 25–30)

6.97 There are detailed requirements in respect of mobile work equipment (including fork-lift trucks and self-propelled work equipment). Steps shall be taken to minimise the risk of roll-over, by stabilising the equipment, or providing structures or devices which give protection. Fork-lift trucks shall be adapted or equipped to reduce the risk to safety from overturning. Steps shall be taken to prevent unauthorised persons from starting self-propelled work equipment, minimising the consequences of collision, provide braking devices, and ensuring the driver's vision is adequate. Remote controlled self-propelled work equipment shall stop automatically once it is out of its control range, and have features to guard against the risks of crushing or impact.

Power presses (regulations 31–35)

6.98 There are detailed provisions for power presses (excluding power presses detailed in schedule 2). Power presses, guards and protection devices shall be thoroughly examined when put into service for the first time, to make sure they have been installed correctly, are safe to operate, and any defects are remedied. Further thorough examinations shall take place every 12 months where there are fixed guards, or every six months in any other case. Power presses shall not be used after setting, re-setting or adjustment of its tools, unless every guard and protection device has been tested while in position by a person who is competent or is undergoing training under the supervision of a competent person. A certificate of inspection and testing must be signed. A person making a thorough inspection shall notify the employer forthwith of any defect which could become a danger to persons, and make a report of the thorough examination, containing the information set out in schedule 3. (See also the Approved Code of Practice and guidance, L112: *Safe Use of Power Presses.*)

Personal Protective Equipment at Work Regulations 1992

6.99 These regulations are designed to implement Directive 89/656/EEC on the Minimum Health and Safety Requirements for the Use of Personal Protective Equipment at the Workplace. They came into force on 1 January 1993.

Note: The Personal Protective Equipment Regulations 2002 implement the PPE Product Directive (89/686/EEC), which lays down conditions governing the placing on the market of PPE, including the free movement of products and the basic safety requirements that PPE must satisfy in order to ensure health protection and safety of users. If PPE satisfies EU-type examination procedures, it will bear the CE mark. These regulations must not be confused with the Personal Protective Equipment at Work Regulations 1992.

6.100   There are in existence a number of health and safety regulations made under HSWA relating to PPE: the Control of Lead at Work Regulations 2002, Ionising Radiations Regulations 1999, Control of Substances Hazardous to Health Regulations 2002, Control of Noise at Work Regulations 2005, Construction (Head Protection) Regulations 1989 and Control of Asbestos Regulations 2006. These regulations will continue in force, although they have been modified slightly so as to conform with the PPE Regulations.

6.101   On the other hand, there are a large number of pre-HSWA regulations which deal with PPE, and most of these have been revoked (including the familiar Protection of Eyes Regulations) as they are no longer necessary. Certain legislative provisions which deal with specialised subjects (eg docks, electricity, construction and offshore installations) are retained, and are complemented by the new regulations. Also, the new regulations do not apply to the master or crew of a seagoing ship, to ordinary clothes or uniforms which do not specifically protect the health and safety of the wearer, portable devices for detecting risks and nuisances, PPE used for protection while travelling on a road, equipment used during the playing of competitive sports or an offensive weapon used for self-defence or deterrence.

6.102   PPE is defined as being all equipment (including clothing affording protection against the weather) which is intended to be worn or held by a person at work and which protects him against one or more risks to his health or safety. The Guidance Note (L25: *Personal Protective Equipment at Work*) suggests that PPE includes protective clothing (aprons, waterproof clothes, gloves, safety footwear, safety helmets, high visibility waistcoats, etc) and protective equipment (eye protectors, life jackets, respirators, underwater breathing apparatus and safety harnesses). Ordinary working clothes and protective clothing used for the purpose of hygiene would not be included.

6.103   A breach of the regulations may give rise to civil and/or criminal liabilities.

Provision of personal protective equipment (regulation 4)

6.104   Every employer shall ensure that suitable PPE is provided to his employees who may be exposed to a risk to their health or safety while at work, except where and to the extent that such risk has been adequately controlled by other means which are equally or more effective. A similar obligation is imposed on self-employed persons in respect of their own activities.

6.105 PPE shall not be suitable, unless:

(a) it is appropriate for the risks involved, the conditions at the place where exposure to the risk may occur, and the period for which it is worn

(b) it takes account of ergonomic requirements and the state of health of the person or persons who may wear it, and of the characteristics of the workstation of each such person

(c) it is capable of fitting the wearer correctly (if necessary after adjustment)

(d) so far as is practicable, it is effective to prevent or adequately control the risks involved without increasing overall risk

(e) it complies with any enactment which implements relevant EU directives applicable to that item of PPE.

6.106 Where it is necessary to ensure that PPE is hygienic and otherwise free from risks to health, every employer must ensure that PPE provided to a person is provided only for that individual's use.

6.107 The Guidance Notes suggest that PPE should be regarded as a "last resort". Engineering controls and safe systems of work should first be considered, so that risks are controlled or prevented at source. PPE should be readily available, and generally supplied to employees on an individual basis, although there may be circumstances where it can be shared (eg if required for only a limited period).

6.108 No charge may be made for the provision of PPE (HSWA, s.9, see paragraph 3.113), even if the employer permits the use by the employee outside working hours.

6.109 When considering the provision of PPE, it is important to bear in mind the need to avoid "overkill". For example, if there is a noise hazard, the protection must match the volume of noise which is hazardous, but not eliminate harmless (or even useful) noise, for this could result in a greater hazard being created. An employee who wears every single item of protective clothing provided by his employer would probably resemble someone from outer space, and is likely to be a positive menace to himself and to others.

6.110 PPE must be suitable for each employee to use or wear, for the legal duty is owed to them as individuals, not collectively (*Paris v Stepney Borough Council*).

6.111 The legal problems involved in enforcing the use of PPE will be examined in Chapter 13.

Compatibility of personal protective equipment (regulation 5)

6.112 Every employer shall ensure that where the presence of more than one risk makes it necessary for his employee to wear or use simultaneously more than one item of PPE, such equipment is compatible and continues to be effective against the risks in question. A similar obligation is placed on self-employed persons.

Assessment of personal protective equipment (regulation 6)

6.113 Before choosing PPE, employers (and self-employed persons) shall ensure that an assessment is made in order to determine whether the PPE he intends to provide is suitable. The assessment shall include:
  (a) risks which have not been avoided by other means
  (b) the definition of the characteristics which the PPE must have in order to be effective
  (c) a comparison of the characteristics of the PPE available with those needed to avoid the risk
  (d) a determination as to whether the PPE is compatible with other PPE which is in use and which an employee would be required to wear simultaneously.

6.114 Employers (and self-employed persons) shall review any such assessment if they have reason to believe that it is no longer valid, or if there has been a significant change in the matters to which it relates. If any changes are required as a result of the review, these shall be made.

6.115 The Guidance Notes (Appendix 1) give a specimen risk survey table which may be used to determine whether or not PPE is required. There is also considerable advice given on the selection, use and maintenance of PPE in widely different circumstances.

Maintenance and replacement of personal protective equipment (regulation 7)

6.116 Every employer shall ensure that any PPE provided to his employees is maintained in an efficient state, in efficient order, in good repair and is replaced or cleaned as appropriate (see *Fytche v Wincanton Logistics*, paragraph 12.12). A similar obligation is placed on self-employed persons.

6.117 The Guidance Notes suggest that PPE should be examined when issued, before it is used or worn, and it should not be used or worn if found to be defective or unclean. A sufficient stock of spare parts should be available, and maintenance programmes should include, where appropriate, cleaning, disinfection, examination, repair, testing and record-keeping. Manufacturers' maintenance schedules and instructions should normally be followed.

Accommodation for personal protective equipment (regulation 8)

6.118 Every employer shall ensure that appropriate accommodation is provided for PPE when it is not being used.

6.119 The Guidance Notes point out that accommodation may be simple, as long as it is appropriate. It should protect PPE from contamination, loss or damage.

Information, instruction and training (regulation 9)

6.120 Where PPE is provided, employers shall ensure that the employee is provided with such information, instruction and training as is adequate and appropriate to enable the employee to know:
  (a) the risks which the PPE will avoid or limit
  (b) the purpose for which, and the manner in which the PPE is to be used
  (c) any action to be taken by the employee to ensure that it remains in an efficient state, in efficient working order and in good repair.

6.121 Employers must ensure that this information is kept available to employees. The information and instructions given will not be adequate and appropriate unless they are comprehensible to the persons to whom they are provided.

6.122 The employer shall, where appropriate, and at suitable intervals, organise demonstrations in the wearing of PPE.

6.123 The Guidance Notes point out that the extent of the training will vary with the complexity of the equipment. Training should be both theoretical and practical, and its duration and frequency will depend on the individual circumstances. Refresher training should be considered if necessary.

Use of personal protective equipment (regulation 10)

6.124 Every employer shall take all reasonable steps to ensure that any PPE provided to his employees is properly used.

6.125 Every employee shall use PPE provided to him in accordance with the training given to him and the instructions respecting its use. Self-employed persons shall also make full and proper use of PPE. Employees and self-employed persons shall take all reasonable steps to ensure that PPE provided is returned to the accommodation provided for it after use.

Reporting loss or defect (regulation 11)

6.126 Every employee who has been provided with PPE shall forthwith report to his employer any loss or obvious defect.

Exemption certificates (regulation 12)

6.127 The Secretary of State for Defence may exempt the armed forces and visiting armed forces from the regulations, subject to conditions and/or limitations of time.

Extension outside Great Britain (regulation 13)

6.128 The regulations apply to those activities carried out in British territorial waters and off-shore installations, eg oil and gas installations, mobile installations, diving support vessels, heavy lifting barges, pipe laying barges, etc (see Health and Safety at Work, etc Act 1974 (Application Outside Great Britain) Order 2001).

Repeals, revocations and modifications (regulation 14)

6.129 The regulations revoke some 20 old regulations dealing with personal protective equipment, repeal s.65 of the Factories Act 1961, and modify six regulations (see paragraph 6.95) so that they harmonise with the new law.

Manual Handling Operations Regulations 1992

6.130 These regulations are designed to implement Directive 90/269/EEC on the minimum health and safety requirements for the manual handling of loads. They are accompanied by a Guidance Note (L23: *Manual Handling*), and came into force on 1 January 1993.

6.131 Accidents caused by manual handling of loads account for some 25% of all reportable accidents. The cost to industry in terms of lost time, compensation payments, etc and the cost to the State by way of medical attention, social security benefits, etc is huge. Accidents of this nature occur in all types of employment and to all categories of workers. Previous legislation had a somewhat limited application, and was usually framed in a general manner. Some specific industries did have actual weight limits, but these were neither effective nor justifiable, because they failed to take into account individual capabilities.

6.132 Consequently, the new regulations have repealed a number of statutory provisions, including Factories Act 1961 (s.72), Offices, Shops and Railway Premises Act 1963 (s.23(1)), and Agriculture (Safety, Health and Welfare Provisions) Act 1956 (s.2). In addition, the Agriculture (Lifting of Heavy Weights) Regulations 1959 were revoked, as was regulation 55 of the Construction (General Provisions) Regulations 1961.

Application of the regulations

6.133 The regulations apply to all employers in respect of their employees at work, including offshore installations, pipelines, etc (see paragraph 1.159). They also apply to self-employed persons in respect of their own activities. However, they do not apply to the master or crew of a seagoing ship.

6.134 The phrase "manual handling operations" is defined as any transporting or supporting of a load (including the lifting, putting down, pushing, pulling, carrying or moving) by hand or by bodily force. A "load" includes any person or animal. However, an injury does not include any contact with a corrosive or toxic substance.

6.135 A breach of the regulations may give rise to civil and/or criminal liability.

Duties of employers (regulation 4)

6.136 Every employer shall, so far as is reasonably practicable, avoid the need for his employees to undertake any manual handling operations which involve a risk of their being injured.

6.137 It should be noted that the Manual Handling Regulations require an employer to avoid manual handling operations so far as is reasonably practicable. If this cannot be done, the employer must take appropriate steps to reduce the risk of injury to the lowest level reasonably practicable. This does not mean that all risk will be eliminated. In *King v Sussex Ambulance NHS Trust*, an ambulance worker assisted a colleague to bring a patient down some steep stairs in a carry chair. The colleague momentarily loosened his grip, which meant that the claimant was left bearing the entire weight of the patient and, in consequence, suffered various injuries. A county court judge awarded the claimant damages but the decision was reversed by the Court of Appeal. Whereas a commercial organisation can turn down a job involving hazardous handling operations, the ambulance service cannot do so. An employee must not be exposed to an unacceptable risk, but here the work to be done was of considerable social utility and there was no other way of doing the job. Although, in *Ogwo v Taylor*, it was held that the duty of care still existed even though the work might involve elements of urgency or danger, and in *Watt v Hertfordshire County Council* it had been held that the saving of life or limb justifies taking considerable risk. It is all a question of balancing the risk against the end to be achieved.

6.138 If there is a foreseeable possibility of injury (not a foreseeable probability) the manual handling operation should be avoided, so far as is reasonably practicable. If it is not possible to do this, a risk assessment must be carried out and a decision made as to what measures — if any — would reduce or avoid that risk (*Koonjul v Thameslink Healthcare Services Ltd*). The assessment must also take into account the factors specified in schedule 1 to the regulations and a consideration of the associated questions (see paragraph 6.142). The employer must also take appropriate steps to reduce the risk of injury arising out of manual handling operations to the lowest level reasonably practicable.

6.139 To determine whether manual handling operations involve a risk of injury, and the appropriate steps to reduce that risk, regard shall be had in particular to:

(a) the physical suitability of the employee to carry out the operations

(b) the clothing, footwear or other personal effects the person is wearing

(c) the person's knowledge and training

(d) the results of any risk assessment carried out

(e) whether the employee has been identified by that assessment as being especially at risk

(f) the result of any health surveillance carried out.

6.140 It should be noted that the regulations impose an almost unqualified duty to assess and reduce the risk of injury, as well as to provide employees with information about manual handling operations (*Swain v Denso Marston Ltd*). Thus a failure to carry out a manual handling assessment, or to train employees in safe lifting techniques can make an employer liable for back injuries suffered in consequence of lifting moderately heavy loads (*Stone v Commissioner of Police for the Metropolis*).

6.141 In *Hawkes v London Borough of Southwark*, the plaintiff had to carry a heavy door (weighing over 32kg) up a flight of stairs. While trying to manoeuvre round a half-landing, he was knocked off balance, and fell injuring his ankle. The Court of Appeal held that it was not reasonably practicable to avoid doing the lifting other than by manual handling, and so a proper risk assessment should have been carried out by the employer. This would have revealed that there was a risk of injury, the risk was slight (there had been no previous similar accidents), but the cost of reducing that risk (by providing a second worker to assist) was also small. Thus the risk was not insignificant in relation to the cost to the employers of reducing the risk to the lowest level reasonably practicable, and they were held liable for damages.

6.142 The factors and the questions to be taken into account are as follows.

Factors to be taken into account	Questions

1. The tasks	Do they involve:
	• holding or manipulating loads at distances from the trunk?
	• unsatisfactory bodily movement or posture, especially:
	  – twisting the trunk?
	  – stooping?
	  – reaching upwards?
	• excessive movement of loads, especially:
	  – excessive lifting or lowering of loads?
	  – excessive carrying distances?
	• excessive pushing or pulling of loads?
	• risk of sudden movement of loads?
	• frequent or prolonged physical effort?
	• insufficient rest or recovery periods?
	• a rate of work imposed by a process?

2. The loads	Are they: • heavy? • bulky or unwieldy? • difficult to grasp? • unstable, or with contents likely to shift? • sharp, hot or otherwise potentially damaging?
3. The working environment	Are there: • space constraints preventing good posture? • uneven, slippery or unstable floors? • variations in level of floors or work surfaces? • extremes of temperature? • conditions causing ventilation problems or gusts of wind? • poor lighting conditions?
4. Individual capability	Does the job: • require unusual strength, height, etc? • create a hazard to those who might reasonably be considered to be pregnant or to have a health problem? • require special information or training for its safe performance?
5. Other factors	Is movement or posture hindered by personal protective equipment or by clothing?

6.143　Thus, having regard to those factors, and the answers to the questions posed, the employer shall take appropriate steps to reduce the risk of injury to those employees to the lowest level reasonably practicable.

6.144　The employer shall also provide general indications and precise information (where it is reasonably practicable to do so) on the weight of the load, and the heaviest side of any load whose centre of gravity is not positioned centrally. The assessment which has been carried out shall be reviewed if there is reason to believe that there has been a significant change in the operations, and such revisions made as are appropriate in the circumstances.

6.145 The Guidance Notes which accompany the regulations are extremely informative, and will repay detailed study. It is noted that the regulations set no specific requirements such as weight limits. Instead, they focus on the needs of the individual, based on a range of relevant factors which are used to determine the risk of injury, and indicate the remedial action which should be taken. It is pointed out that the aim of the regulations is to prevent injury to any part of the body, and thus account must be taken of the external properties of the load (eg slipperiness, sharp edges, etc) as well as its weight, size, bulk, etc. Hazards from the contents of the load (eg corrosive substances) are not generally covered, although this should be considered under other appropriate legislation, (eg COSHH Regulations, etc). The load may be animate or inanimate, but generally will not be a tool or instrument.

6.146 The first task of the employer is to avoid manual handling where possible and, where this is not possible, the next task is to make an assessment, taking into account the matters already mentioned. Proper records should be kept, and any evidence which reveals an indication of a relationship between manual handling and ill health (eg absenteeism due to some form of back injury) should be noted. Employees and safety representatives should be involved in redesigning the systems of work, loads should be reduced to a manageable size or otherwise made risk-free, and the capabilities of each employee assessed.

6.147 When it is alleged that there has been a breach of the Manual Handling Operations Regulations 1992, which has resulted in an injury, the judge should first consider whether there was such a breach, and then the nature of the breach, in order to assess whether or not the breach caused the injury. Thus, if an employee suffers an injury and it is shown that there was a failure to train employees in the correct techniques of manual handling, then a causal link has been established between the breach and the failure to train (*O'Neill v DSG Retail Ltd*).

Duties of employees (regulation 5)

6.148   Each employee while at work shall make full and proper use of any system of work provided for his use by his employer in compliance with the latter's duty to take appropriate steps to reduce the risk of injury.

6.149   This duty should be read together with the employee's duty under s.7 of HSWA. Also of relevance is regulation 14 of the Management of Health and Safety at Work Regulations 1999 (see paragraph 4.55), which requires employees to use appropriate equipment provided.

Exemption certificates (regulation 6)

6.150   The Secretary of State for Defence may, in the interests of national security, exempt the armed forces and visiting armed forces from the requirements of certain parts of the regulations, subject to conditions and/or time limits.

Health and Safety (Display Screen Equipment) Regulations 1992

6.151   These regulations are designed to implement Directive 90/270/EEC on the minimum health and safety requirements for work with display screen equipment. They are accompanied by Guidance Notes, L26: *Display Screen Equipment at Work.*

6.152   Currently, there are no other legislative provisions on this topic, other than the general duties laid down by HSWA. However, the advent of modern technology in this field has brought in its wake a number of health and safety problems, including musculo-skeletal injuries, visual fatigue and mental stress. Such illnesses are not an inevitable consequence of working with display screen equipment, but the introduction of sound ergonomic techniques can reduce the incidence.

6.153   However, there is no scientific evidence that visual display units (VDUs) pose any hidden health risk to the user (in particular to pregnant women) and generally VDUs have been given a clean bill of health following a number of investigations, including a recent study by the National Radiation Protection Board (now the Radiation Protection Division of the Health Protection Agency).

Application of the Regulations (regulation 1)

6.154 The term "display screen equipment" refers to any alphanumeric or graphic display screen, regardless of the display process involved. The Guidance Notes state that this definition covers cathode ray tube and liquid crystal displays. As well as the typical office visual display terminals, non-electronic display systems such as microfiche are covered, but not screens used to show television or films, unless the main purpose is to display text, numbers and/or graphics.

6.155 The regulations are generally for the benefit of every person "who habitually uses display screen equipment as a significant part of his normal work". Clearly, the interpretation to be given to the words "habitually uses" and "significant part" is going to be crucial. The Guidance Notes suggest that a person will be covered by the regulations if most or all of the following criteria apply:

(a) whether the individual has to depend on the display screen equipment to do his job, because alternative means are not readily available for achieving the same results

(b) whether the individual has no discretion in using it

(c) whether the individual has had special training and/or particular skills in the use of the equipment

(d) whether the individual normally uses the equipment for continuous spells of an hour or more at a time on a more or less daily basis

(e) whether the fast transfer of information is an important requirement of the job

(f) whether the performance requirements of the system demands high level of attention and concentration.

6.156 The Guidance Notes give a list of examples of persons who are definitely users, eg word processing pool worker, data input operator, air traffic controller, and so on. Some possible users would be airline check-in clerks, customer support officers at a building society, depending on the circumstances. Persons who would not be users include receptionists who only use display screens occasionally.

6.157 Portable laptops will be exempt from the regulations if they are not in prolonged use, but if portable equipment is habitually used as a significant part of normal working, the regulations may well apply. In any case, various safety considerations can still apply to laptop users, bearing in mind such problems as cramped working conditions (trains, aeroplanes), unsuitable seating and desks, inadequate lighting (dimly lit hotel rooms), etc. Risk assessments and proper training techniques can help to avoid problems arising.

6.158   Generally, the regulations are for the protection of two classes of persons, namely "users" and "operators". The former will be an employee, whether working at his employer's workstation, a workstation at home, or at another employer's workstation. Risks to homeworkers must be assessed, regardless of whether or not the workstation is provided by the employer. The term "operator" refers to a self-employed person who habitually uses display screen equipment as a significant part of his normal work.

6.159   The regulations also cover "the workstation", which means the actual display screen equipment, optional accessories, peripheral equipment (disk drive, telephone, modem, printer, chair, desk, etc) and the immediate environment.

6.160   The regulations do not apply to:
    (a) drivers' cabs or control cabs for vehicles or machinery
    (b) display screen equipment on board a means of transport
    (c) display screen equipment mainly intended for public use
    (d) portable systems not in prolonged use
    (e) calculators, cash registers or any equipment having a small data or measurement display
    (f) window typewriters.

6.161   A breach of the regulations may give rise to civil and/or criminal liability.

Analysis of workstations (regulation 2)

6.162   Every employer shall perform a suitable and sufficient analysis of those workstations which:
    (a) (regardless of who has provided them) are used for the purposes of his undertaking by users, or
    (b) have been provided by him and are used for the purposes of his undertaking by operators

for the purpose of assessing the health and safety risks to which those persons are exposed in consequence of that use. This analysis must include all known health problems that may be associated with display screen work, including training, workplace practices and hours of work (*Denton Hall Legal Services v Fifield*).

6.163 The assessment shall be reviewed if the employer has reason to believe it is no longer valid, and if revisions are required as a result, these shall be made. Risks which have been identified shall be reduced to the lowest extent reasonably practicable.

6.164 The Guidance Notes state that in simple and obvious cases, there is no need to record the assessment, ie if no significant risks are indicated. However, records are useful to ensure continuity and accuracy, and to check on risk reduction methods. The views of the individual users are an essential part of any assessment. Remedial action should be taken when risks are disclosed, especially postural problems, visual problems and fatigue and stress.

Requirements for workstations (regulation 3)

6.165 Every employer shall ensure that any workstation used for the purpose of his undertaking meets the requirements set out in the schedule to the regulations.

6.166 The schedule requires that attention should be given to all the factors which might affect the health and safety of the user or operator, including:
(a) the display screen (monitor)
(b) the keyboard
(c) the work desk or work surface
(d) environmental requirements, such as space, lighting, reflection and glare, noise, heat, radiation and humidity
(e) interface between the computer and operator or user, etc.

6.167 The Guidance Notes provide some useful advice on compliance with these requirements.

Daily work routine of users (regulation 4)

6.168 Every employer shall so plan the activities of users at work in his undertaking that their daily work on display screen equipment is periodically interrupted by such breaks or changes in activity as reduce their workload at that equipment.

6.169   The Guidance Notes suggest that spells of intensive screen work should be broken by activities which do not require broadly similar use of the arms or hands, or which are not equally visually demanding. Further guidance is given on the taking of rest breaks, which should be designed to prevent the onset of fatigue.

Eyes and eyesight (regulation 5)

6.170   Where a person is a user in the undertaking in which he is employed, or is to become a user, the employer shall, if so requested by that person, ensure that an appropriate eye and eyesight test is carried out by a competent person, as soon as practicable after the request by the user or, in the case of a person who is to become a user, before he so becomes. Thus an agency who supplies workers for other employers' undertakings must provide appropriate tests for its workers if requested. The tests shall be repeated at regular intervals, the timing of which should be influenced by the clinical judgment of the optometrist or doctor, and may vary in accordance with relevant factors, including age, etc. Further eye tests should be carried out if the user experiences visual difficulties which may reasonably be considered to be caused by work on display screen equipment. However, an eye test cannot be provided against an employee's will.

6.171   Further, every employer shall ensure that each user employed by him is provided with special corrective appliances, eg glasses, appropriate for the display screen work being done by the user where:
  (a) normal corrective appliances cannot be used
  (b) the result of any eye and eyesight test the user has had under this regulation shows such provision to be necessary.

6.172   The special corrective appliances need only be supplied where normal corrective appliances cannot be used. The Guidance Notes suggest that only a small minority of the working population would need the special appliances. Anti-glare screens, VDU spectacles, etc are not included within this category. The employer's liability is to pay for the cost of a *basic* appliance necessary for the display screen work.

Provision of training (regulation 6)

6.173   Every employer shall ensure that each user (and a person about to become a user) shall receive adequate health and safety training in the use of the workstation on which he is required to work, and also when the workstation is substantially modified.

6.174 The Guidance Notes point out that the purpose of training in health and safety requirements is to minimise the risks of musculo-skeletal injuries, visual fatigue and mental stress. The aspects of training which should be covered are outlined.

Provision of information (regulation 7)

6.175 Every employer shall ensure that operators and users at work in his undertaking are provided with adequate information about:

(a) all aspects of health and safety relating to their workstations
(b) the measures taken by the employer to analyse the workstation (under regulation 2 above) and the measures taken to comply with the requirements of regulation 3 and the schedule.

6.176 Further, every employer shall provide users (ie his employees) with adequate information about the measures he has taken to periodically interrupt the work activity (regulation 4), to provide eye and eyesight testing (regulation 5) and to provide training (regulation 6).

Exemption certificates (regulation 8)

6.177 The Secretary of State for Defence may, in the interests of national security, exempt home forces and visiting armed forces from the requirements of the regulations, subject to conditions and any limits of time.

CHAPTER 7

Substances

Control of Substances Hazardous to Health Regulations 2002 (COSHH) (as amended)

7.1   The Control of Substances Hazardous to Health Regulations 2002 (COSHH) re-enact, with modifications, the Control of Substances Hazardous to Health Regulations 1999, as well as implementing a number of EU directives. They are designed to protect workers against the risks of exposure to any substance considered to be hazardous to health, the use of which arises out of or in connection with work undertaken under the control of an employer.

7.2   Minor changes have been made by the Control of Substances Hazardous to Health (Amendment) Regulations 2004, which revoke the terms "maximum exposure limits" and "occupational standards limits" and replace them with a single "workplace exposure limit", which is an exposure limit approved by the HSE and is contained in publication EH40: *Workplace Exposure Limits* as updated from time to time.

7.3   The regulations are accompanied by an Approved Code of Practice and Guidance Notes (L5: *Control of Substances Hazardous to Health*, fifth edition).

7.4   Apart from certain specified substances, such as asbestos, lead and inhalable dust in coal mines, all of which have their own specific legislative provisions, and risks that flow from the administration of medical treatment, COSHH applies to all substances that are hazardous to health. This means:

(a) a substance which is listed in Part I of the Approved Supply List as dangerous for supply within the meaning of the Chemicals (Hazard Information and Packaging for Supply) Regulations 2002 (CHIP 3) and for which an indication of danger specified for the substance is very toxic, toxic, harmful, corrosive or irritant

(b) a substance for which the HSE has approved a workplace exposure limit

(c) a biological agent

(d) dust of any kind, when present at a concentration in air equal to or greater than specified limits

(e) a substance which, because of its chemical or toxicological properties and the way it is used, creates a risk to health.

7.5   Thus, a substance is hazardous if it is a potential cause of harm. Whether there is a risk from the substance will depend on the circumstances in which it is being used or controlled. A substance with a low hazard can have a substantial risk if poorly controlled, whereas the most hazardous substance can have a low risk if adequately controlled. COSHH does not apply to a substance with flammable or explosive or radioactive properties unless they additionally fall within the definition of a substance hazardous to health (see paragraph 7.4).

Prohibitions relating to certain substances (regulation 4)

7.6   The use of certain substances (see schedule 2 of COSHH) for certain purposes is prohibited, as is the importation of certain substances and articles. The supply of these substances or articles is also prohibited.

Assessment of the risk to health (regulation 6)

7.7   An employer shall not carry out work which is liable to expose any employees to a substance which is hazardous to health unless a suitable and sufficient assessment of the risk created by that work to the health of those employees has been made, as well as steps that need to be taken to eliminate or reduce that risk. The employer must also implement those steps. The risk assessment must include consideration of:

(a) the hazardous properties of the substance
(b) information on health effects provided by the supplier, including any relevant information contained in a safety data sheet
(c) the level, type and duration of exposure
(d) the circumstances of the work, including the amount of substance involved
(e) activities, such as maintenance, where there is the potential for a high level of exposure
(f) any relevant workplace exposure limit
(g) the effect of preventative and control measures
(h) the results of relevant health surveillance
(i) the results of monitoring of exposure

(j) the risk presented by exposure to substances in combination, if the work will involve exposure to more than one substance hazardous to health

(k) the approved classification of any biological agent

(l) any additional information the employer may need in order to complete the risk assessment.

7.8 The risk assessment must be reviewed regularly, and promptly if there is reason to believe it is no longer valid, or there have been significant changes in the work to which it relates, or the results of monitoring carried out show that it is necessary. Where the employer employs more than five employees, the significant findings of the risk assessment must be recorded, as well as the steps taken to prevent or control exposure to such substances.

Prevention or control of exposure to substances hazardous to health (regulation 7)

7.9 Every employer shall ensure that the exposure of employees to substances hazardous to health is either prevented or, where this is not reasonably practicable, adequately controlled. The duty under regulation 7(1) of COSHH is an absolute one, ie to prevent exposing employees to hazardous substances. If prevention is not reasonably practicable, then it must be adequately controlled. The qualification of reasonably practicable applies to prevention, but not to the issue of adequate control (*Dugmore v Swansea NHS Trust and Anor*). The employer must avoid, where reasonably practicable, the use of a substance hazardous to health by substituting a substance or process which either eliminates or reduces the risk to the health of employees. If it is not reasonably practicable to prevent such exposure, the employer shall ensure:

(a) the design and use of appropriate work processes, systems and engineering controls, and the provision and use of suitable work equipment and materials

(b) the control of exposure at source, including adequate ventilation systems and appropriate organisational measures

(c) the provision of suitable personal protective equipment

(d) arrangements for the safe handling, storage and transport of such substances hazardous to health, and of waste containing such substances, at the workplace

(e) the adoption of suitable maintenance procedures

(f) the reduction, to the minimum required for the work concerned, of the number of employees subject to exposure, the level and duration of exposure, and the quantity of substances hazardous to health present at the workplace

(g) the control of the working environment, including appropriate general ventilation

(h) appropriate hygiene measures, including adequate washing facilities.

7.10 If it is not reasonably practicable to prevent exposure to a carcinogen or mutagen, the employer shall apply the following additional measures:

(a) totally enclosing the process and handling systems

(b) prohibiting eating, drinking and smoking in areas that may be contaminated by carcinogens or mutagens

(c) cleaning floors, walls and other surfaces at regular intervals

(d) designating those areas that may be contaminated by carcinogens or mutagens and using suitable and sufficient warning signs

(e) storing, handling and disposing of carcinogens and mutagens safely, including using closed and clearly labelled containers.

7.11 Special additional safety procedures shall be applied where there is the potential of exposure to biological agents giving effect to the Biological Agents Directive (90/679/EEC).

7.12 Where there is exposure to a substance hazardous to health, control of that exposure shall only be treated as being adequate if the following principles of good practice are observed. The employer must:

(a) design and operate processes and activities to minimise emission, release and spread of substances hazardous to health

(b) take into account all relevant routes of exposure-inhalation, skin absorption and ingestion when developing control measures

(c) control exposure by measures that are proportionate to the health risk

(d) choose the most effective and reliable control options which minimise the escape and spread of substances hazardous to health

(e) where adequate control of exposure cannot be achieved by other means, provide, in combination with other control measures, suitable personal protective equipment

(f) check and review regularly all elements of control measures for their continuing effectiveness

(g) inform and train all employees on the hazards and risks from the substances with which they work and the use of control measures developed to minimise the risks

(h) ensure that the introduction of control measures does not increase the overall risk to health and safety

(i) particular attention must be paid to a substance which is carcinogenic, or a potential cause of occupational asthma.

7.13 In addition, the employer must ensure that any workplace exposure limit for that substance is not exceeded as detailed in the HSE publication, EH40: *Workplace Exposure Limits*.

Use of control measures (regulation 8)

7.14 Every employer who provides any control measure shall take all reasonable steps to ensure that it is properly used or applied as the case may be. Every employee must make full and proper use of any control measure provided and, where relevant, shall take all reasonable steps to ensure that it is returned after use to any accommodation provided for it. The employee shall report any defects discovered to the employer.

Maintenance, examination and testing of control measures (regulation 9)

7.15 Every employer who provides any control measure shall ensure that:

(a) in the case of plant and equipment (including engineering controls and personal protective equipment) it is maintained in an efficient state, in efficient working order, in good repair and clean condition, and

(b) in the case of the provision of systems of work and supervision and of any other measure, it is reviewed at suitable intervals and revised if necessary.

7.16 Where engineering controls are provided, the employer shall ensure that a thorough examination and testing is carried out at suitable intervals, including regard to respiratory protective equipment (other than disposable types). Exhaust plant shall be tested at least once each 14 months. Suitable records of examinations and tests shall be made and kept for five years. Personal protective equipment must be properly stored in a defined place, checked at suitable intervals and, if discovered to be defective, repaired or replaced before further use.

Monitoring exposure at the workplace (regulation 10)

7.17 Where a risk assessment indicates that it is necessary, the employer shall ensure that the exposure of employees to substances hazardous to health is monitored in accordance with a suitable procedure. The monitoring shall take place at regular intervals and also when any change occurs which may affect that exposure. If the record is representative of the personal exposure of identifiable employees, a suitable record shall be kept for 40 years and, in any other case, for five years. If an employee is under health surveillance, an individual record shall be made. The employee shall be allowed access to that record, and copies given to the HSE on request.

Health surveillance (regulation 11)

7.18 Where appropriate, the employer shall ensure that employees who are exposed or liable to be exposed to substances hazardous to health are placed under health surveillance. It will be appropriate to do so if the employees are exposed to a substance and engaged in a process specified in schedule 6, and there is a reasonable likelihood that an adverse health effect will result from that exposure. Additionally, health surveillance will be required if the exposure is such that an identifiable disease or adverse health effect may occur, or there is a reasonable likelihood that it would occur under the particular conditions of work, and there are valid techniques for detecting indications of the disease or effects. A health record must be kept for 40 years. If the employee is exposed to a schedule 6 substance, medical surveillance shall be carried out under the supervision of a relevant doctor at intervals of not more than 12 months. If, as a result of medical surveillance, the doctor certifies that the employee shall not be engaged in work which exposes the individual to the substance, the employer shall not permit the employee to be engaged in such work. If, in consequence of the medical surveillance, the employee is found to have an identifiable disease or an adverse health effect, the employer must ensure that the employee is notified accordingly. In such cases, the risk assessment must be reviewed, compliance methods reassessed, and the employee assigned alternative work where there is no risk of further exposure to that substance. Finally, a review should be undertaken of any other employees who may have been similarly exposed.

Information, instruction and training (regulation 12)

7.19   Every employer who undertakes work which is liable to expose an employee to a substance hazardous to health must provide that employee with suitable and sufficient information, instruction and training. This shall include the following.

1. The details of the substances in question, the name of the substances, and the risk which they present to health, as well as any relevant workplace exposure limit. The employer shall also give the employee access to any relevant data sheets and detail any legislative provisions which concern the hazardous properties of the substances.
2. The significant findings of the risk assessment.
3. The appropriate precautions to be taken.
4. The results of any monitoring of exposure. If a workplace exposure limit has been approved, then the employee or employee representative shall be informed immediately if the monitoring shows that the limit has been exceeded.
5. The collective results of any health surveillance undertaken.
6. Where employees are working with a Group 4 biological agent, the provision of written instructions and, if appropriate, the display of notices which outline the procedures for handling such an agent.

Arrangements to deal with accidents, incidents and emergencies (regulation 13)

7.20   In order to protect the health of employees from an accident, incident or emergency related to the presence of a substance hazardous to health at the workplace, the employer shall ensure that:

(a) procedures, including the provision of appropriate first aid facilities and relevant safety drills, have been prepared which can be put into effect when such an event occurs
(b) information on emergency arrangements is available
(c) suitable warning or other communication systems are established to enable an appropriate response to be made immediately.

7.21   The employer must ensure that information on procedures and systems is made available to relevant accident and emergency services, and displayed at the workplace if appropriate. Should such an event occur, the employer must take immediate steps to mitigate the effects, restore the situation to normal and inform those employees who may be affected.

Defence (regulation 21)

7.22 Subject to regulation 21 of the Management of Health and Safety at Work Regulations 1999 (see paragraph 4.73), in any proceedings for an offence consisting of a contravention of the regulations, it will be a defence for any person to prove that all reasonable precautions were taken and all due diligence was exercised to avoid the commission of that offence.

Control of asbestos

7.23 The Control of Asbestos Regulations 2006, together with an Approved Code of Practice, came into force in October 2006, and give effect to the Asbestos Worker Protection Directive 83/477/EEC (as amended). The regulations revoke the Control of Asbestos at Work Regulations 2002, the Asbestos (Licensing) Regulations 1983 and the Asbestos (Prohibitions) Regulations 1992. The new regime departs from the earlier "action level" requirements, and requires that notification of work to the enforcing authority and medical surveillance will not apply to certain specific types of work where the worker's exposure to asbestos fibres is sporadic and of low intensity, and it is clear from the risk assessment that the control limit will not be exceeded. The regulations apply to employers, employees and self-employed persons.

Duty to manage asbestos in non-domestic premises (regulation 4)

7.24 The dutyholder will be the person who has an obligation to maintain or repair non-domestic premises or has control of any part, including the means of access and egress. Every person shall co-operate with the dutyholder so far as is necessary to enable him to comply with his duties under the regulations. The dutyholder shall ensure that a suitable and sufficient assessment is carried out as to whether asbestos is present on the premises, taking into account the building plans and age of the premises, and an inspection of those parts which are reasonably accessible. If asbestos is found to be present, the dutyholder will make a determination of the risk, prepare a written plan identifying those parts, and specifying the measures to be taken for managing the risk, including monitoring, removal and making the information available to every person liable to disturb it and the emergency services.

Identification of the presence of asbestos (regulation 5)

7.25 Every employer shall not undertake work in demolition, maintenance or other work which is liable to expose his employees to asbestos unless either he has carried out a suitable and sufficient assessment as to whether asbestos is present on the premises, or, if there is some doubt, he assumes that asbestos is present and that it is not chrysotile alone.

Assessment of work which exposes employees to asbestos (regulation 6)

7.26 An employer shall not carry out work which is liable to expose his employees to asbestos unless he has made a suitable and sufficient assessment of the risks created by that exposure, identified the steps to be taken to meet the requirements of the regulations, and has implemented those steps. The significant findings of the risk assessment are to be recorded, and the assessment reviewed if it is suspected no longer to be valid, or if there a significant change in the work to which it relates, or if the results of any monitoring show it to be necessary. The risk assessment will identify the type of asbestos, the nature and degree of exposure, consider the effect of control measures, set out the steps to be taken to prevent exposure or reduce it to the lowest level reasonably practicable, and consider the results of relevant medical surveillance.

Plan of work (regulation 7)

7.27 An employer shall not undertake any work with asbestos unless he has prepared a suitable written plan of work, dealing with how that work is to be carried out. A copy of the plan of work shall be kept at the premises where the work is being carried out, and will include details of the nature and probable duration of the work, the location where it is being carried out, the methods to be applied, the characteristics of equipment used for protection and decontamination of those carrying out the work, and the protection of other persons on or near the worksite. So far as is reasonably practicable, the employer shall ensure that the work is carried out in accordance with the plan of work.

Licensing of work with asbestos (regulation 8)

7.28 Unless the exposure to asbestos is sporadic and of low density, and it is clear that the exposure will not exceed the control limit, (see regulation 3(2)), an employer shall not undertake work with asbestos unless he holds a licence from the HSE. The licence may be issued on such terms as the HSE considers appropriate, and may be varied, amended or revoked as necessary.

Notification of work with asbestos (regulation 9)

7.29 Before undertaking work with asbestos (except for work to which regulation 3(2) above applies) an employer shall notify the HSE in writing of the name, address and usual place of business of the notifier, the location of the worksite, the type(s) of asbestos to be handled, the maximum quantity of asbestos to be handled at any one time, the activities and processes involved, the number of workers involved, the measures taken to limit exposure, and the date of the commencement of the work and its expected duration. Any material changes in the work shall also be notified.

Information, instruction and training (regulation 10)

7.30 Every employer shall ensure that adequate information, instruction and training is given to those of his employees who are liable to be exposed to asbestos, so that they are aware of the properties of asbestos and its effect on health (including its interaction with smoking) the types of products likely to contain asbestos, the operations which could result in asbestos exposure, and the importance of preventative controls to minimise exposure. The training, etc shall inform on safe working practices, control measures, protective equipment, the proper use of respiratory equipment, emergency procedures, hygiene requirements, decontamination procedures, waste handling procedures, medical examination requirements, the control limit and the need for air monitoring. The information, instruction and training shall be given at regular intervals, adapted to take account of any significant changes in the type of work carried out, and provided in an appropriate manner.

Prevention or reduction of exposure to asbestos (regulation 11)

7.31 Every employer shall prevent the exposure of his employees to asbestos so far as is reasonably practicable. If it is not reasonably practicable to do so, the employer shall take measures to reduce exposure to the lowest level reasonably practicable by means other than the use of respiratory protective equipment, including the design of work processes, systems and engineering controls, and the provision of suitable work equipment and materials in order to avoid or minimise the release of asbestos, including control at source and adequate ventilation systems. Suitable respiratory protective equipment shall be provided. The employer shall ensure that no employee is exposed to asbestos in a concentration in the air inhaled which exceeds the control limit. If the control limit is exceeded, he shall inform the employees concerned (and their representatives) and work must not continue in the affected area until adequate measures have been taken to reduce such exposure. The reasons for the control limit being exceeded must be identified, and the effectiveness of measures checked by carrying out air monitoring.

Use of control measures (regulation 12)

7.32   Every employer who provides any control measure shall ensure, so far as is reasonably practicable, that it is properly used or applied. Every employee shall make full and proper use of any control measure provided, and return it after use to any accommodation provided for it. If there is a defect he shall report it forthwith to his employer.

Maintenance of control measures (regulation 13)

7.33   Every employer shall ensure that plant, equipment, engineering controls and personal protective equipment is maintained in an efficient state, in efficient working order, in good repair and in a clean condition. Where exhaust ventilation equipment or respiratory protective equipment is provided, these must be thoroughly examined, and tested at suitable intervals by a competent person. Records of such examinations must be kept for five years.

Provision and cleaning of protective clothing (regulation 14)

7.34   Every employer shall provide adequate and suitable protective clothing for such of his employees who are liable to be exposed to asbestos, unless no significant quantity of asbestos is liable to be deposited on the clothes of his employees while at work. Protective clothing provided must be disposed of as asbestos waste or adequately cleaned at suitable intervals. If a significant quantity of asbestos is deposited on personal clothing, it shall be treated as if it were protective clothing and dealt with accordingly.

Arrangements to deal with accidents, incidents and emergencies (regulation 15)

7.35 The employer shall ensure that procedures, including safety drills, are prepared which can be put into effect in order to protect his employees from any accident, incident or emergency. Information on emergency arrangements shall be available, including relevant work hazards and hazard identification arrangements, and suitable warning and other communication systems are established to enable an appropriate response to be made immediately when such an event occurs. This information shall also be made available to relevant accident and emergency services, to enable them to prepare their own response procedures and precautionary measures. In the event of an accident, incident or emergency relating to the unplanned release of asbestos at the workplace, the employer shall ensure that immediate steps are taken to mitigate the effects of the event, restore the situation to normal, and inform any person who may be affected.

Duty to prevent the spread of asbestos (regulation 16)

7.36 Every employer shall prevent (or where this is not reasonably practicable, reduce to the lowest level reasonably practicable) the spread of asbestos from any place where work under his control is carried out.

Cleanliness of premises and plant (regulation 17)

7.37 Every employer who undertakes work which exposes his employees to asbestos shall ensure that the premises and the plant used in connection with that work are kept in a clean state, and where such work has been completed, the premises are thoroughly cleaned.

Designated areas (regulation 18)

7.38 Every employer shall ensure that any area in which work under his control is carried out is designated as an asbestos area (except where regulation 3(2) above applies) where any employee would be liable to be exposed to asbestos in that area, and a respirator zone where the concentration of asbestos fibres in the air in that area would be liable to exceed the control limit. Such areas or zones shall be clearly and separately demarcated and identified by notices, and in the case of a respirator zone, that respiratory protective equipment must be worn. Only competent persons shall enter a respirator zone. The employer must also ensure that employees do not eat, drink or smoke in an area designated as an asbestos area or respirator zone, and arrangements must be made for them to eat or drink in some other place.

Air monitoring (regulation 19)

7.39   Unless the exposure of an employee to asbestos is not liable to exceed the control limit, every employer shall, at regular intervals, monitor the exposure of his employees to asbestos by measurement of asbestos fibres in the air. The employer shall keep a suitable record of such monitoring. If the exposure is such that a health record is required (see regulation 22) the monitoring record shall be kept for 40 years, otherwise it shall be kept for five years. The employer shall allow an employee access to his personal monitoring record, and provide the HSE with such copies as may be required. If he ceases to trade, he shall notify the HSE forthwith in writing and make available to the HSE all monitoring records kept by him.

Standards for air testing and site clearance certificates (regulation 20)

7.40   Every employer who carries out any measurement of the concentration of asbestos fibres present in the air shall ensure that he meets the criteria equivalent to those set out in ISO 17025 which cover organisation, quality systems, control of records, personnel accommodation and environmental conditions, test and calibration methods, method validation, equipment, handling of test and calibration items, and reporting results. The person carrying out such measurements must be accredited by an appropriate body.

Standards for analysis (regulation 21)

7.41   Every employer who analyses a sample of material to determine whether it contains asbestos shall ensure that he meets the criteria set out in ISO 17025.

Health records and medical surveillance (regulation 22)

7.42 Subject to regulation 3(2) above every employer shall ensure that a health record, containing approved particulars, relating to each of his employees who is exposed to asbestos is maintained, and a copy kept in a suitable form for 40 years. Such employees must also be subject to adequate medical surveillance by a relevant doctor. The medical surveillance shall include a medical examination at intervals of not more than two years and include a specific examination of the chest. The relevant doctor shall issue a certificate stating that the employee has been examined and the date of the examination, which the employer shall keep for at least four years from the date on which it was issued. The employee shall present himself during working hours for such examination, and provide the relevant doctor with such information concerning his health as may be reasonably required. Where an employee is found to have an identifiable disease or adverse health effect as a result of exposure to asbestos at work, the employer shall ensure that the employee is informed, review the risk assessment, review the prevention measures (see regulation 11) consider assigning the employee to alternative work, and provide a review of the health of every other employee who may have been similarly exposed.

Washing and changing facilities (regulation 23)

7.43 Every employer shall ensure that for any employee who is exposed to asbestos, there is provided adequate washing and changing facilities, adequate facilities for changing protective clothing and personal clothing not worn during working hours, and adequate facilities for storing respiratory protective equipment. Such facilities shall be separate from each other.

Storage, distribution and labelling of raw asbestos and asbestos waste (regulation 24)

7.44 Every employer who undertakes work with asbestos shall ensure that raw asbestos or asbestos waste is not stored, or received into or despatched from any place of work, or distributed within any place of work, except in a totally enclosed distribution system, unless it is in a sealed container clearly marked. Raw asbestos shall be labelled in accordance with provisions contained in schedule 2, and waste containing asbestos shall be labelled either in accordance with the Carriage of Dangerous Goods and Use of Transportable Pressure Equipment Regulations 2007 (see paragraph 7.78) or schedule 2.

Prohibitions of exposure to asbestos (regulation 26)

7.45 No person shall undertake asbestos spraying or working procedures involving low density (less than lg/cm^3) insulating or soundproofing materials which contain asbestos. Every employer shall ensure that no employees are exposed to asbestos during the extraction of asbestos, or during the manufacture and processing of asbestos products.

Exemption certificates (regulation 32)

7.46 The HSE may issue exemption certificates relating to persons or products subject to conditions, if it is satisfied that the health and safety of persons who are likely to be affected will not be prejudiced in consequence. Where an exemption applies (either under schedule 3 or regulation 32) the product must be labelled in accordance with schedule 2. Where the exceptions in schedule 3 or the exemptions in regulation 32 apply, the employer shall ensure that the quantity of asbestos used in a work process is reduced to the lowest level reasonably practicable.

Defence (regulation 36)

7.47 In any proceedings for an offence under the regulations, it shall be a defence for any person to prove that he took all reasonable precautions and exercised all due diligence to avoid the commission of that offence.

7.48 So far as civil liability is concerned in respect of developing pleural plaques due to exposure from asbestos, see *Grieves v FT Everard & Sons and others*, paragraph 12.14 and see paragraph 12.52.

Control of Lead at Work Regulations 2002

7.49 These regulations came into force on 21 November 2002 and are designed to give greater protection to the health of workers exposed to lead. The regulations re-enact, with modifications, the previous 1998 regulations. Ten other regulations dealing with the use or manufacture of lead products and the production of pottery have earlier been revoked. Also repealed are ss.74, 128, 131 and 132 of the Factories Act 1961. A revised Approved Code of Practice and Guidance has been issued (L132: *Control of Lead at Work*, third edition).

7.50   As with the previous regulations, the objective is to protect the health of workers who are exposed to lead dust, fume or vapour by controlling and reducing the amount of absorption to an absolute minimum level, and to monitor the amount of lead absorbed by a worker so that he may be removed or temporarily suspended from work before health is adversely affected. The new regulations also give effect to parts of Directive 82/605/EEC (on the protection of workers from risks relating to exposure to metallic lead and its ionic compounds at work) and Directive 80/1107/EEC (on the protection of workers from the risks relating to exposure to chemical, physical and biological agents at work) as well as to Directive 98/24/EC (on the protection of the health and safety of workers from risks related to chemical agents at work) insofar as it relates to health from exposure to lead.

Duties of the employer (regulation 3)

7.51   The regulations place a number of duties on an employer in respect of his employees. In addition, the employer shall, so far as is reasonably practicable, be under a like duty in respect of any other person, whether at work or not, who may be affected by the work carried on by the employer. Thus, a duty is owed not only to employees and workers but, for example, to members of an employee's family who may be exposed to significant risks of lead poisoning consequent on the employee's own exposure (see *Hewett v Alf Brown's Transport Ltd*, paragraph 12.60). However, this duty does not apply in respect of medical surveillance to persons who are not his employees (other than employees of another employer who is working under the direction of the first-mentioned employer). Nor do the duties relating to air monitoring and provision of information, instruction and training apply to persons who are not his employees, unless such persons are on the premises where the work is being carried on. The regulations also apply to self-employed persons as if they were both an employer and employee, except the provision relating to air monitoring.

Prohibitions (regulation 4)

7.52   There is an absolute prohibition on the use of glaze (other than leadless glaze or low solubility glaze) in the manufacture of pottery.

Further, an employer shall not employ a young person or a woman of reproductive capacity in certain specified occupations in lead smelting and refining processes and lead-acid manufacturing processes (see schedule 1).

Assessment of the risk to health (regulation 5)

7.53   An employer shall not carry out work which is liable to expose any employee to lead unless he has made a suitable and sufficient assessment of the risk created by that work, and of the steps that need to be taken to meet the requirements of the regulations, and implemented these. The risk assessment must include consideration of:

(a) the hazardous properties of the lead
(b) information on health effects provided by the supplier
(c) the level, type and duration of the exposure
(d) the circumstances of the work, including the amount of lead involved
(e) activities, such as maintenance, where there is a potential for a high level of exposure
(f) any relevant occupational exposure limit, action level and suspension level
(g) the effect of preventative and control measures to be taken under regulation 6
(h) the results of relevant medical surveillance
(i) the results of monitoring of exposure according to regulation 9
(j) the risk presented by the combination of lead and another substance hazardous to health
(k) whether the exposure of any employee to lead is liable to be significant
(l) such additional information as the employer may need in order to complete the assessment.

7.54   The risk assessment shall be reviewed regularly and promptly if:

(a) there is reason to suspect that it is no longer valid
(b) there has been a significant change in the work
(c) the results of air monitoring show it to be necessary
(d) the blood-lead concentration of any employee under medical surveillance equals or exceeds the action level.

7.55   Where the employer employs five or more employees, he must

287

record the significant findings of the risk assessment, and of the steps taken to meet the requirements of regulation 6 (see below).

Prevention or control of exposure to lead (regulation 6)

7.56 Every employer shall ensure that the exposure of employees to lead is either prevented or, where this is not reasonably practicable, adequately controlled. Substitution is to be preferred, by replacing the use of lead with substances or processes which either eliminate or reduce the risks to health. Where it is not reasonably practicable to prevent exposure to lead, the employer must apply protection methods appropriate to the activity and consistent with the assessment, including:

(a) the design and use of appropriate work processes, systems and engineering controls, and the use of suitable work equipment and materials

(b) the control of exposure at source, including adequate ventilation systems

(c) where adequate control of exposure cannot be achieved by other means, the provision of suitable personal protective equipment in addition to the steps outlined in (a) and (b) above.

7.57 If the exposure to lead is liable to be significant, the employer shall provide the employee with suitable and sufficient protective clothing, and any personal protective equipment provided must comply with the Personal Protective Equipment Regulations 2002 or be of a type approved by the HSE. Employers must take all reasonable steps to ensure that control measures are properly used or applied, and every employee must also make full and proper use of control measures provided. Where relevant, employees must take all reasonable steps to ensure that things provided in accordance with these regulations, eg clothing, are returned after use to any accommodation provided. Employees should also report any defects discovered to the employer.

Eating, drinking and smoking (regulation 7)

7.58 Every employer must ensure, so far as is reasonably practicable, that employees do not eat, drink or smoke in any place which is, or is liable to be, contaminated with lead. This does not prohibit the use of proper drinking facilities, which are required for the welfare of employees who are exposed to lead, as long as the facilities are not contaminated. Employees are forbidden to eat, drink or smoke in any such contaminated place.

Maintenance, etc of control measures (regulation 8)

7.59   The employer shall ensure that control measures provided by him are maintained in a clean condition, in an efficient state, in efficient working order, and in good repair. If engineering controls are used, these shall be thoroughly examined and tested, at least every 14 months in the case of local exhaust ventilation plants, at suitable intervals in any other case. Respiratory equipment (other than the disposable variety) shall be thoroughly examined and tested as appropriate, at suitable intervals. Records of testing and examinations shall be kept for five years. Personal protective equipment, including clothing, should be properly stored in a defined place, checked at suitable intervals and, when discovered to be defective, repaired or replaced before further use. Personal protective equipment that may be contaminated by lead must be removed on leaving the working area, and kept apart from uncontaminated clothing and equipment. The equipment must also be subsequently decontaminated or, if necessary, destroyed.

Air monitoring (regulation 9)

7.60   Where employees are liable to receive a significant exposure to lead, the employer shall monitor the concentration of lead in the air, in accordance with EU standards set out in Directives 82/1605/EEC and 80/1107/EEC. In principle, the monitoring shall be carried out every three months, but the period may be increased to 12 months (except for exposure to lead alkyls) where:
(a) there has been no material change in the work or conditions of exposure since the last occasion of monitoring, and
(b) the lead in the air for each group of workers or work area has not exceeded 0.10 mg/m^3 on the two previous occasions on which monitoring was carried out.

7.61   The employer shall keep a suitable record of any monitoring carried out, and the records, or a suitable summary, shall be kept for at least five years.

7.62   If an employee is under medical surveillance as required by regulation 10 (below), an individual record of air monitoring must be kept in respect of that employee. The employer should allow an employee access to the personal monitoring record, and copies should be provided to the HSE on request.

Medical surveillance (regulation 10)

7.63   Every employer shall ensure that each of his employees who is, or is liable to be, exposed to lead is under suitable medical surveillance by an appointed doctor or an employment medical advisor, where:

(a) the exposure of the employee to lead is or is liable to be significant (ie where any employee is liable to be exposed to a concentration of lead in the atmosphere exceeding half the occupational exposure limit for lead, or where there is a substantial risk of an employee ingesting lead, or where there is a risk of contact between the skin and lead alkyls or other substance containing lead which can be absorbed through the skin), or

(b) the blood lead concentration is equal to or exceeds:
   (i) 20µg/dl in respect of a woman of reproductive capacity, or
   (ii) 35µg/dl in respect of any other employee, or

(c) the urinary lead concentration is equal to or exceeds:
   (i) 20µg Pb/g creatinine in respect of a woman of reproductive capacity, or
   (ii) 40µg Pb/g creatinine in respect of any other employee, or

(d) the appointed doctor or employment medical advisor certifies that the employee should be under medical surveillance.

7.64   Medical surveillance shall commence either before an employee starts work, or within 14 days of such commencement. It shall further be carried out at intervals of not more than 12 months. Biological monitoring shall also be carried out in respect of young persons and women of reproductive capacity at intervals not greater than three months, and for other employees at least every six months (see schedule 2).

7.65   Adequate health records of the results of such surveillance shall be made and maintained and kept for a least 40 years from the date of the last entry. If the medical surveillance is carried out on the employer's premises, the employer shall ensure that suitable facilities are made available.

7.66 An employee shall, when required to do so by his employer, and at the cost of his employer, present himself during his working hours for such medical surveillance, and shall furnish the relevant doctor with such information concerning his health as the doctor may reasonably require. For the purpose of carrying out his functions, the doctor may inspect any workplace or any records kept for the purpose of these regulations. In respect of every female employee whose exposure to lead is liable to be significant, the employer shall ensure that the doctor makes an entry in the health record indicating whether she is of reproductive capacity.

7.67 Where the doctor certifies by an entry in the health record of any employee that, in his professional opinion, the employee should not be engaged in work that exposes him to lead, or should only be so engaged under specified conditions, the employer shall not permit the employee to be engaged in work which exposes him to lead, except in accordance with the conditions, if any, specified in the health record. Once the entry has been cancelled by the doctor, the employee may resume such workings.

7.68 Either the employer or the employee may appeal to the HSE for a review of the decision by the doctor:
   (a) that the employee is a female of reproductive capacity, or
   (b) that the employee should not be engaged in work which exposes him to lead. The result of that review will be entered into the health record.

Action levels (regulation 2)

7.69 When the blood-lead concentration for any employee equals or exceeds the appropriate action level, the employer shall take steps to determine the reasons for the high level of lead in blood, and shall, so far as is reasonably practicable, give effect to measures designed to reduce the blood-lead concentration of that employee to a level below the action level.

7.70 The appropriate action levels are a blood-lead concentration of:
   (a) in respect of a woman of reproductive capacity, 25µg/dl
   (b) in respect of a young person, 40µg/dl
   (c) in respect of any other person, 50µg/dl.

Suspension levels (regulation 2)

7.71   The appropriate suspension levels are as follows:
  (a) a blood-lead concentration of:
   (i) in respect of a woman of reproductive capacity, 30μg/dl
   (ii) in respect of a young person, 50μg/dl
   (iii) in respect of any other employee, 60μg/dl, or
  (b) a urinary lead concentration of:
   (i) in respect of a woman of reproductive capacity, 25μgPb/g creatinine
   (ii) in respect of any other employee, 110μgPb/g creatinine.

7.72   If the blood-lead concentration or urinary-lead concentration reaches the appropriate suspension level, the employer shall ensure that an entry is made in the health record of the employee by a relevant doctor. The doctor will certify whether in his professional opinion the employee should be suspended from any work which is liable to expose that employee to lead. If the doctor does not so certify, he may specify the conditions under which the employee may continue to be employed in such work.

Information, instruction and training (regulation 11)

7.73   Every employer who undertakes work which is liable to expose any of his employees to lead shall provide that employee with such information, instruction and training as is suitable and sufficient for him to know:
  (a) the risks to health created by such exposure
  (b) the precautions that should be taken.

7.74   The employer shall also provide the employee with:
  (a) information on the results of any monitoring of exposure to lead carried out under regulation 9 (above)
  (b) information on the collective results of any medical surveillance undertaken in accordance with regulation 10 (above), in a form which prevents it from identifying any particular person,
  (c) an explanation of the significance of the above information.

7.75   The employer must also ensure that any person (whether or not his employee) who carries out any work in connection with the employer's duties under these regulations has the necessary information, instruction and training.

Arrangements to deal with accidents, etc (regulation 12)

7.76 In order to protect the health of employees from an accident, incident or emergency relating to the presence of lead at the workplace, the employer must ensure that procedures and relevant safety drills have been prepared, that information on emergency arrangements is available, and suitable warning and other communication systems are established to enable an appropriate response, including remedial actions and rescue operations, to be made immediately when such an event occurs. This information must be made available to relevant accident and emergency services to enable them to prepare their own response procedures and precautionary measures. The information should also be displayed at the workplace, if appropriate. If an accident, incident or emergency does happen, the employer must take immediate steps to mitigate the effects of the event, restore the situation to normal, and inform those employees who may be affected. Only persons who are essential for carrying out repairs or other necessary work are to be permitted in the area affected, and they should be provided with appropriate personal protective equipment and any necessary specialised safety equipment and plant.

Application of the regulations

7.77 The regulations apply to offshore workings covered by the Health and Safety at Work Act 1974 (Application Outside Great Britain) Order 2001 (as amended) but do not apply to the master or crew of a seagoing ship. The HSE may issue exemption certificates, subject to conditions.

Dangerous Substances (Notification and Marking of Sites) Regulations 1990 (as amended)

7.78 These regulations require the notification and marking of sites where there is a total quantity of 25 tonnes or more of dangerous substances present at the site. A dangerous substance is any substance which is dangerous for carriage within the meaning of the Carriage of Dangerous Goods and Use of Transportable Pressure Equipment Regulations 2007. There must be notification to the fire authority and to the enforcing authority, with the specified information. Safety signs must be displayed which give adequate notice to firemen that a dangerous substance is present and access and location markings displayed.

Notification of Installations Handling Hazardous Substances Regulations 1982 (as amended)

7.79   These regulations require a person who stores, manufactures, processes, uses or transfers a specified minimum quantity of substance defined in the regulations as being hazardous to supply relevant information to the HSE. This will enable the HSE to define priorities in their inspection programme, notify local planning authorities so as to assist in development control, give necessary advice to emergency services and enable all persons concerned to be made aware of special hazards involved.

7.80   The notification must state the name of the person making it, the address of the site, the area of the site, the date when the activity will commence, a general description of the activity, the name of the local planning authority, and the name and the maximum quantity of each hazardous substance likely to be on the site. The information must be given at least three months before the commencement of the activity (or, if the hazardous substance consists of ammonium nitrate, four weeks).

7.81   Regulations made under the Planning (Hazardous Substances) Act 1990 limit the quantity of hazardous substances which may be kept, until the appropriate authority has had an opportunity to assess the risks of an accident, and the likely consequences for the inhabitants of surrounding areas.

Control of Major Accident Hazards Regulations 1999 (as amended)

7.82   Growing public concern in the UK, Europe and indeed throughout the world following a number of industrial disasters has led to demands for more stringent control over the use and storage of dangerous substances which, if uncontrolled, could lead to major personal and environmental damage. The major accidents that took place at Buncefield, Flixborough, Seveso, Mexico City, Bhopal, etc have highlighted the need not only to reduce the likelihood of such occurrences in the future, but also to establish co-ordinated emergency plans in the event of such major accidents. Thus the Control of Major Accident Hazard Regulations 1999 lay down a comprehensive new set of control systems with the aim of preventing major accidents, or mitigating the consequences should one occur.

7.83 These regulations are designed to impose certain requirements with respect to the control of major accident hazards arising out of the presence of dangerous substances. Although they follow the same fundamental principles as the Control of Industrial Major Accidents Hazards Regulations 1984 (now revoked), there are some significant changes, which stem largely from the implementation of the Seveso II Directive (96/82/EC). The regulations were amended in 2005 to comply with Directive 2003/105/EC, which is basically concerned with a reduction in the thresholds set out in Parts 2 and 3 of schedule 1 (which determines whether or not the regulations apply to a particular site).

7.84 The regulations apply to an establishment where certain dangerous substances are present in the specified quantities (see schedule 1 of the regulations). The old distinction between storage and use has been abolished, different materials with similar hazards are to be aggregated (even if the individual quantities of each are below the thresholds), and materials classified as being dangerous to the environment are now included. The general duties apply to all operators who control establishments where the dangerous substances are present in the specified quantities. Additional duties (regulations 7–14 below) apply to the so-called top-tier operators, ie where the dangerous substances are in quantities equal to or in excess of the amounts specified in column 3 of parts 2 and 3 of schedule 1.

7.85 The basic obligation is on the operator to take all measures necessary to prevent major accidents and limit their consequences to persons and the environment (regulation 4). The "operator" is the person who is in control of an establishment or installation. Regulation 5 requires the operator to prepare and keep a document setting out his policy with respect to the prevention of major accidents, designed to guarantee a high level of protection for persons and the environment by appropriate means, structures and management systems, taking into account the principles set out in schedule 2. If there is a modification of the establishment or installation, the processes carried on there, or nature or quantity of dangerous substances which could have significant repercussions, the operator shall review and revise the major accident prevention policy document.

7.86 Regulation 6 provides that prior to the start of construction of an establishment (or prior to the start of the operation of the establishment, as the case may be) the operator shall send to the competent authority (the HSE, Environment Agency or Scottish Environment Protection Agency) a notification, containing the prescribed particulars. Details must also be sent of any significant increase in the quantity of dangerous substances, any significant change in the nature or physical form of substances so notified, the processes employing them or changes in other information previously notified.

7.87 Regulation 7 provides that in respect of top-tier sites, the operator must also send to the competent authority (the HSE and the Environment Agency) a safety report containing the relevant information specified in schedule 4, and shall not start construction of an establishment or commence operations until the competent authority has sent its conclusions. The safety report must be reviewed every five years, or as necessary if new facts or new technical knowledge become available, or if there has been a change in safety management systems. A similar revision of the safety report shall take place if there is a modification of the establishment or installation, or the process carried on, or the nature or quantity of dangerous substances, any of which could have significant repercussions with respect to the prevention of major accidents or the limitation of the consequences of major accidents to persons or to the environment.

7.88 The operator of a top-tier site must also prepare an emergency plan adequate for securing the containment and control of incidents, so as to minimise the effects, and to limit damage to persons, the environment and property, implementing measures necessary to protect persons from the effects of major accidents, communicating the necessary information to the public and to the emergency services and authorities concerned in the area, and providing for the restoration and clean-up of the environment following a major accident (regulation 9 and schedule 5). The plan will also give the names or positions of persons authorised to set emergency procedures in motion, co-ordinate on-site mitigatory action, and other information prescribed in schedule 5. Local authorities, in whose area there is an establishment shall also prepare an off-site emergency plan (regulation 10). Emergency plans shall be reviewed at least every three years, and revised when necessary. The local authority, emergency services and operator shall endeavour to reach agreement as to how off-site emergency plans are to be tested (regulation 11).

7.89 The operator of an establishment shall ensure that persons who are likely to be in an area likely to be affected by a major accident, including every school, hospital or other establishment serving the public, are regularly provided with information, in the most appropriate form, and without their having to request it, on the safety measures at the establishment, and on the requisite behaviour in the event of a major accident occurring. The information shall be made permanently available to the public (regulation 14).

7.90 The regulations also specify the functions of the competent authority, which will be the HSE, Environment Agency or Scottish Environment Protection Agency (regulations 17–22). The competent authority will examine safety reports, and can prohibit the operation of an establishment or installation if the measures for the prevention or mitigation of major accidents are seriously deficient. The authority will also have an ongoing system of inspection of establishments and control measures and, if a major accident has been notified, obtain all relevant information from the operator, ensure that urgent, medium and long-term measures proven necessary are taken, make a full analysis of the accident and collect any appropriate information, ensure that the operator takes remedial action, make recommendations for the future, and in the event of certain types of accidents, notify the European Commission, together with specified information.

Genetically Modified Organisms

7.91 The Genetically Modified Organisms (Contained Use) Regulations 2000 (as amended) implement Directives 90/219/EEC, 94/51/EC and 98/81/EC, and replace the 1992 regulations. Any activity involving genetic modification of micro-organisms is prohibited unless the person undertaking the activity has ensured that a risk assessment has been carried out. The person carrying out the assessment is required to establish a safety committee to advise. Before the first use of any premises involving such activity, the HSE must be notified, and certain specified information provided. The consent of the HSE must be obtained before the work commences, which may be varied or revoked.

A person who carries out an activity which involves the genetic modification of micro-organisms, or organisms other than micro-organisms, must apply the appropriate containment measures. All waste containing genetically modified micro-organisms must be made inactive, and there is a requirement for enhanced public access to information via an expanded public register of notifications.

Dangerous chemicals

7.92 The Chemicals (Hazard Information and Packaging for Supply) Regulations 2009 (CHIP 4) revoke and replace earlier regulations on this topic. The regulations implement a number of EU directives and basically deal with the supply and packaging of substances and preparations which have a potential hazard. A supplier (including an importer) must ensure that the substances or preparations are classified in accordance with one of the categories specified in the regulations, which can be explosive, oxidising, extremely flammable, highly flammable, flammable, very toxic, toxic, harmful, corrosive, irritant, carcinogenic, mutagenic, toxic to reproduction, and dangerous to the environment. For each category, an identifiable symbol letter is to be used. Reference can be made to the Approved Supply List for the appropriate classification. The supplier must provide a safety data sheet, which contains sufficient information to enable the recipient to take the necessary measures relating to health and safety at work. The supplier must also ensure that the substance or preparation is in a package that is suitable and which prevents the contents from escaping.

7.93 The earlier version of the regulation (CHIP 3) will be amended so as to allow alignment with the European Regulation on the Classification, Labelling and Packaging of Substances and Mixtures which adopt an internationally agreed Globally Harmonised System (GHS) on the classification of labelling of chemicals.

REACH

7.94 REACH is an acronym for the Registration, Evaluation and Authorisation of Chemicals Regulation (1907/2006/EC) which came into force in June 2007. The regulations, adopted by the EU Council of Ministers, have direct effect in the UK.

7.95 The regulations require the registration of all chemicals produced or imported in volumes of more than one tonne a year, a process which is to be phased over a period of eleven years, beginning with the most toxic substances and those produced in the largest quantities. Manufacturers and importers must submit a dossier to the new European Chemicals Agency based in Helsinki which must contain details of the substance's properties.

7.96 The pre-registration process has now been completed, and a list of pre-registered substances has been published. Downstream users do not have to register or pre-register provided that their suppliers/manufacturers have included the downstream users' exposure/use scenarios in the registration. New substances which are not in the European List of Notified Chemical Substances (ELINCS) need to be registered.

7.97 The REACH Enforcement Regulations 2008 specify the various authorities who are to enforce the REACH provisions.

7.98 The European Chemical Agency will carry out an evaluation of the product, and substances of very high concern may need to be authorised for specific uses. Authorisation will be granted if the product is deemed to be safe as long as the risks are adequately controlled, and the importance of the use of the substance outweighs the risks to human health and the environment. No authorisation for use will be granted unless there is a substitution process and safer alternatives or, if these do not exist, a research and development plan. Restrictions may be placed on a given hazardous substance, and it shall not be manufactured or used or put on the market unless it complies with the conditions of the restrictions.

7.99 A Safety Data Sheet should accompany the product throughout the supply chain so that users of the chemical can ensure it is safely managed. It should equally be possible for information to be passed up the supply chain so that manufacturers and suppliers can be informed about any hazards brought about by the product.

Dangerous Substances and Explosive Atmospheres Regulations 2002

7.100 These regulations, in force since 9 December 2002 with some minor exceptions, impose requirements for the purpose of eliminating or reducing the risks to safety from fire, explosion or other events arising from the hazardous properties of a dangerous substance in connection with work. A number of older regulations dealing with risks arising from potential fire hazards have been revoked. The regulations implement Directives 98/24/EC and 99/92/EC.

7.101   A dangerous substance is defined as being "a substance or preparation which meets the criteria in the Approved Guide to the Classification and Labelling of Dangerous Substances and Dangerous Preparations (fifth edition), which is explosive, oxidising, extremely flammable, highly flammable or flammable". A dangerous substance may also be a substance or preparation which, because of its physico-chemical properties and the way it is used, creates a risk, or any dust which can form an explosive mixture with air, or an explosive atmosphere.

Risk assessment (regulation 5)

7.102   Where a dangerous substance is present or liable to be present at the workplace, the employer must make a suitable and sufficient assessment of the risks to employees which arise from that substance. The risk assessment shall include consideration of:
  (a) the hazardous properties of the substance
  (b) information on safety provided by any supplier, including a relevant data sheet
  (c) the circumstances of the work, including the work processes, the amount of substance used, the risk presented by the use of substances in combination, the arrangements for the safe handling, storage and transport of dangerous substances and waste containing dangerous substances
  (d) activities, such as maintenance, where there is the potential for a high level of risk
  (e) the effect of measures taken under these regulations
  (f) the likelihood that an explosive atmosphere will occur
  (g) the likelihood that ignition sources will be present and become active
  (h) the scale of the anticipated effects of a fire or an explosion
  (i) any places which can be connected via openings to places where an explosive atmosphere may occur
  (j) such additional safety information as the employer may need in order to complete the risk assessment.

7.103 The risk assessment shall be reviewed regularly, particularly if the employer suspects that it is no longer valid, or if there has been a significant change, for example in the work or work processes to which it relates. If the employer employs five or more employees, the assessment must be recorded in writing. The written assessment needs to include the measures which have been or will be taken to meet the requirements of the regulations. Sufficient information shall be contained in the written assessment to show that the workplace and work processes are designed, operated and maintained with due regard for safety, and that the requirements of the Provision and Use of Work Equipment Regulations 1998 are met regarding safe use of work equipment.

Elimination or reduction of risks from dangerous explosions (regulation 6)

7.104 Every employer has a duty to ensure that risks from dangerous substances are either eliminated or reduced, so far as is reasonably practicable. The preferred method is by substitution. This means the employer should avoid, so far as is reasonably practicable, the presence or use of a dangerous substance at the workplace, by replacing it with a substance or process which either eliminates or reduces the risk. If it is not reasonably practicable to eliminate the risk, the employer must apply control measures to mitigate against the harmful effects of fire or explosion. This will include:
  (a) reducing the quantity of dangerous substances to a minimum
  (b) avoiding the release of the dangerous substance at source
  (c) controlling the release at source
  (d) preventing the formation of an explosive atmosphere, including the application of ventilation
  (e) ensuring that any release of a dangerous substance is collected, safely contained and moved to a safe place
  (f) avoiding ignition sources or adverse conditions
  (g) the segregation of incompatible dangerous substances.

7.105 Further methods include:
  (a) the reduction, to a minimum, of the number of employees exposed
  (b) the avoidance of the propagation of fires or explosions
  (c) the provision of explosion relief arrangements

(d) the provision of explosion suppression equipment and of plant likely to withstand the pressure produced by an explosion

(e) the provision of suitable personal protective equipment.

7.106 The employer shall also arrange for the safe handling, storage and transport of dangerous substances.

Places where explosive atmospheres may occur (regulation 7)

7.107 Where an explosive atmosphere may occur, the employer shall classify places at the workplace into hazardous or non-hazardous zones. Places classified as hazardous must be marked with signs at the point of entry. Appropriate work clothing which does not give rise to electrostatic discharges must be provided for use in such places.

Arrangements to deal with accidents, incidents and emergencies (regulation 8)

7.108 In order to protect the safety of employees from an accident, incident or emergency relating to the presence of a dangerous substance at the workplace, the employer must ensure that:

(a) procedures (including the provision of first aid facilities and relevant safety drills) have been prepared which can be put into effect should such an event occur

(b) information on emergency arrangements is available

(c) suitable warning and other communication systems are established to enable an appropriate response, including immediate remedial action and rescue operations

(d) visual or audible warnings are given, before explosive conditions are reached

(e) escape facilities are provided to ensure that, in the event of danger, employees can leave endangered places promptly and safely.

7.109 Relevant information must be made available to accident and emergency services to enable them to prepare their own response and precautionary measures. If an accident, incident or emergency does occur, the employer should take immediate steps to mitigate the effect of the event, restore the situation to normal, and inform those employees who may be affected. Only persons who are essential for carrying out repairs or other necessary work shall be permitted in the affected area, and they must be provided with appropriate personal protective equipment as well as any necessary safety equipment and plant.

Information, instruction and training (regulation 9)

7.110   Where there is a dangerous substance present in the workplace, the employer must provide each employee with:
  (a) suitable and sufficient information, instruction and training on the appropriate precautions and action to be taken in order to safeguard himself and other employees at the workplace
  (b) the details of any such substance including its name, the risk it presents, access to relevant safety data sheets, legislative provisions, and the significant findings of the risk assessment.

Duty of co-ordination (regulation 11)

7.111   Where two or more employers share the same workplace where an explosive atmosphere may occur, the employer responsible for the workplace shall co-ordinate the implementation of all measures required by these regulations.

CHAPTER 8

Physical agents

Ionising Radiations Regulations 1999

8.1 There are two types of radiation: ionising and non-ionising. The more dangerous type of ionising radiation comes from X-rays and radioactive material. (Non-ionising radiation can stem from laser beams, arc-welders, infra-red and ultra-violet sources, microwave ovens, etc.) The effect of ionising radiation exposure will vary according to the dose and exposure time, but it is accepted that serious illnesses and even death can result, as well as damage being caused to a person's genetic structure, causing stillbirths and malformation in newborn children. The exposure limits at present adopted in this country are those recommended by the International Commission on Radiological Protection, and those limits vary with the area of the body exposed. However, there appears to be no valid proof that the thresholds recommended are in fact safe and any radiation exposure must therefore be regarded as being potentially damaging. Proper shielding is therefore essential (principally by the use of lead material), the equipment must be properly maintained so as to prevent leakage, radiation film badges should be worn at all times when there is a likelihood of exposure in order to measure the amount (or a dosimeter used), and whole body counts should be made when there is a danger that an affected person may have absorbed or ingested radiation.

8.2 The Ionising Radiation Regulations 1999 supersede and consolidate the Ionising Radiation Regulations 1985 and the Ionising Radiation (Outside Workers) Regulations 1993. The regulations implement in part Council Directives 96/29/Euratom, 90/641/Euratom and 97/43/Euratom, which generally lay down basic safety standards for the protection of persons who work with ionising radiations and the general public against the dangers arising from radiation, particularly in relation to medical exposure. The regulations apply to employers, employees, self-employed persons and trainees.

8.3 A radiation employer (ie a person who in the course of business carries out work with ionising radiation) shall not carry out certain specified practices (use of X-rays and accelerators) without prior authorisation from the HSE, unless the practice is of a type that has been approved by the HSE. Before carrying out certain specified work with ionising radiation for the first time, the radiation employer must notify the HSE, and provide specified particulars. Before commencing work with radiation, the employer shall make a risk assessment of the hazards likely to arise from that work, for the purpose of identifying the measures he needs to take to restrict the exposure of an employee or other person to ionising radiation. Hazards with the potential to cause a radiation accident need to be identified, and the nature and magnitude of the risks evaluated. All reasonably practicable steps shall be taken to prevent an accident, or limit the consequences should one occur, and employees must be provided with the information, instruction and training and the equipment necessary to restrict their exposure to radiation.

8.4 Every radiation employer shall take all necessary steps to restrict so far as is reasonably practicable the extent to which his employees and other persons are exposed to ionising radiation, by means of engineering controls, design features, safety features and warning devices. These must be properly maintained with thorough examination and tests carried out at suitable intervals. Personal protective equipment shall be provided where appropriate. Pregnant women must not be exposed to a dose which exceeds 1mSv. An investigation shall be carried out if any employee receives a dose in excess of 15mSv for the first time in any calendar year.

8.5 Radiation employers must consult with suitable radiation protection advisors (except in respect of work specified in schedule 1). Employees must be given suitable information and instruction so that they know the risks to health from exposure and the precautions that should be taken. Controlled or supervised areas shall be designated and local rules set down in writing. Employees who are likely to receive a dose in excess of 6mSv shall be designated as classified persons and an assessment made and recorded of all doses likely to be significant. Dose records shall be kept until the employee reaches age 75 or for 50 years from when they are made. Outside workers shall be provided with a radiation passbook, with particulars kept up to date. Classified persons and employees who receive an over-exposure shall be under adequate medical surveillance, with a health record kept. If an appointed doctor or employment medical advisor certifies that an employee shall not be engaged in work with ionising radiation, the employer shall not permit him to do so.

8.6   If a radiation employer suspects that any person has received an over-exposure, he shall immediately investigate and notify the HSE, the employer of the employee (where appropriate) and the appointed doctor or employment medical advisor.

8.7   Employees must not knowingly expose themselves or any other person to ionising radiation, to a greater extent than is reasonably necessary, shall make full and proper use of any personal protective equipment, report defects to his employer, and ensure that personal protective equipment is returned after use to accommodation provided. If he has reasonable cause to believe that he has received an exposure, he will notify his employer forthwith.

8.8   The regulations and the Approved Code of Practice and Guidance (L121: *Working with Ionising Radiation*) also deal with arrangements for the control of radioactive substances, articles and equipment, the approval of dosimetry services by the HSE, and a new criteria of competence for individuals or organisations who wish to act as radiation protection advisors.

8.9   The Ionising Radiation (Medical Exposure) Regulations 2000 (as amended in 2006) lay down basic measures for the protection of individuals against the dangers of ionising radiation in respect of medical exposure. Duties are imposed on an employer (which refers to any natural or legal person who, in the course of trade, business or other undertaking, carries out medical exposures at a given radiological installation) to ensure that the practitioner or operator protects persons undergoing medical exposure, whether as part of:

(a) their own medical diagnosis or treatment
(b) occupational health surveillance
(c) a health screening programme
(d) a voluntary medical, diagnostic or therapeutic research programme
(e) medico-legal procedures.

8.10   The regulations require the employer to lay down procedures and written protocols for standard radiological practices, establish recommendations for referral criteria, quality assurance programmes, diagnostic reference levels, and dose constraints. Practitioners and operators must undertake continuous training after qualification, and comply with the employer's procedures.

8.11 The Radiation (Emergency Preparedness and Public Information) Regulations 2001 lay down basic safety standards for the protection of the health of workers and the general public against dangers arising from ionising radiation. They also impose requirements on operators of premises where radioactive substances are present and in quantities which exceed specific thresholds. Similar requirements are placed in carriers of radioactive substances. Operators and carriers must carry out risk assessments as to hazard identification and risk evaluation, and take all reasonably practical steps to prevent a radiation accident or limit the consequences should an accident occur. If the assessment reveals a reasonably foreseeable radiation emergency arising, emergency plans must be prepared.

Electricity at Work Regulations 1989

8.12 The Electricity at Work Regulations 1989 replaced a range of inflexible and out-of-date legislation with a comprehensive and systematic set of main principles covering electrical safety in all work activities. They apply to work on or near electricity. They are supported by two Approved Codes of Practice relating to mines and quarries, and a Memorandum of Guidance for other workplaces. Some of the regulations contain absolute requirements, so that civil liability (based on the tort of breach of statutory duty) is retained, but so far as a criminal prosecution is concerned, it will be a defence for the accused to show that he used "due diligence".

8.13 In a number of ways, the 1989 regulations differ from the approach taken by the previous law. There is no voltage threshold, no exemption for electrothermal operations, or for testing and research. The regulations apply in all circumstances where it is necessary to avoid danger, defined as meaning a risk of injury. This, in turn, means "death or personal injury from electrical causes, fire or explosion associated with the transmission, rectification, conversion, conduction, distribution, control, storage, measurement or use of electrical energy". Consequential or indirect injuries due to electrical malfunction are not generally included.

8.14 The regulations impose duties on employers and self-employed persons in relation to matters within their control. Further, employees are under a duty to comply with the provisions insofar as they relate to matters within their control, and they are also under a duty to co-operate with their employer so far as is necessary to enable the duties to be carried out. Persons who have control of non-domestic premises (see HSWA, s.4) come within the regulations because they will be either employers or self-employed persons.

8.15 Electrical systems must, so far as is reasonably practicable, be constructed and maintained so as to be safe, as must the work activity and the adequacy of protective equipment. There is an absolute duty not to exceed the strength and capability of electric equipment so as to cause danger. If there are adverse or hazardous environmental circumstances, exposure is limited to that which is reasonably foreseeable. There are provisions relating to insulation, protection, placing and earthing of conductors, and installing switches or other devices in neutral conductors. Excess current protection must be efficient and suitably located, and there must be provision for cutting off the supply and isolating it.

8.16 Working space, means of access and lighting shall be adequate, so as to prevent injury.

8.17 Probably the most significant feature of the regulations is the general prohibition on live working. This will only be permitted if *all* three of the following conditions are met:
  (a) it is unreasonable in all the circumstances for the system to be dead
  (b) it is reasonable in all the circumstances for the work to be carried out live
  (c) suitable precautions are taken to prevent injury.

8.18 There are no specific age restrictions on those who work with electricity, but those who do this type of work must have sufficient technical knowledge and experience to prevent danger and avoid injury, and if they do not have such expertise, they must be supervised as appropriate, having regard to the nature of the work.

8.19 The regulations apply to offshore installations (Offshore Electricity and Noise Regulations 1997).

Noise at work

8.20 Although it has long been recognised that excessive noise levels at work could cause deafness (boiler-makers' deafness was well-known in the 19th century), it is only in comparatively recent times that the law has begun paying attention to the problem. It is now accepted that excessive exposure to noise levels in excess of 90dB(A) will cause permanent damage to a person's hearing, as will exposure to louder impact noises (explosions, hammer guns, etc). However, not every deaf person can complain of the hazards of his occupation, for there are other causes of deafness, including presbyacusis, which is brought on by old age. Since noise is a common feature of everyday living, it cannot be assumed that occupational noise is the sole cause of deafness.

8.21   Occupational deafness was not given serious treatment by the authorities until the mid-1960s, when the various scientific evidence began to percolate through to industry. Several legislative provisions were enacted to deal with specific problems, eg the Woodworking Machines Regulations 1974, the Agriculture (Tractor Cabs) Regulations 1974 (as amended) the Offshore Installations (Construction and Survey) Regulations 1974, and the Offshore Installations (Operational Safety, Health and Welfare) Regulations 1976. The Department of Employment issued a Code of Practice in 1972, and it occasioned little surprise when the EU passed a directive in 1986 (86/188/EEC). Following this, the Noise at Work Regulations 1989 were enacted, which are now replaced by the 2005 regulations.

8.22   The problem of noise at work can be tackled in four ways. First, by reducing the noise at its source. This involves new design techniques, new technology, new materials, etc. Consultations can take place with manufacturers (reminding them of their obligations under s.6 of HSWA).

8.23   Second, noise reduction techniques can be implemented. This may involve isolating the source of the noise, so that workers are unaffected by it, or blanketing walls and ceilings with noise absorbing materials which will have the effect of reducing noise levels, and so on.

8.24   Third, ear protection should be provided, appropriate to the dangers present. This can be achieved by ear plugs, ear muffs, helmets, etc but it is important that the correct protection is provided in each case, depending on the level of noise present. The object must be to reduce harmful sound, not sound itself, for it is essential to retain the latter (eg as a warning of danger or to receive instructions, etc). Ear plugs should initially be fitted by a qualified person (occupational nurse, etc) otherwise the selection of a wrong size may render the protection ineffective. Ear muffs must be comfortable to wear, aesthetically acceptable to the wearer and must not interfere with the work or other protective equipment.

8.25   Fourth, exposure time to excessive noise can be reduced by allowing rest periods in rest rooms away from the noise, or operating a rota system.

8.26   The civil remedy in respect of occupational deafness is a claim for compensation based on common law negligence (see *Berry v Stone Manganese and Marine Ltd*). The existence of a duty of care is now well recognised, and while a failure to provide the necessary precautions will clearly amount to a breach of that duty, there is some room for argument as to the duty to compel, exhort or propagandise in order to ensure that they are used. An employee may not readily realise the insidious nature of the danger of working without the precautions or the fact that he may suffer permanent damage. Something more positive is required from the employer than the passive duty to provide ear muffs, plugs, etc. It also follows that if an employee fails to use the precautions after being instructed in their proper use, any compensation awarded can be reduced in respect of his contributory conduct. Compensation awards have been awarded in the region of £4000–£8000, depending on the extent of the deafness (see *Smith v British Rail Engineering Ltd*). Any claim must be brought within three years from the damage (Limitation Act 1980), but since deafness is a process which takes place over the years, an affected person may not know in the early stages of the nature or extent of the damage caused (see paragraph 12.77).

8.27   The Social Security (Industrial Injuries) (Prescribed Diseases) Regulations 1985 (as variously amended) enable a worker to obtain industrial injuries disablement benefit (see paragraph 12.102) if he suffers from occupational deafness. The worker must have been employed in the prescribed occupation for more than 10 years, and he must suffer from an average hearing loss of at least 50 decibels in both ears. In at least one ear, the loss must be due to noise at work.

Control of Noise at Work Regulations 2005

8.28   These regulations are designed to implement the provisions of the Physical Agents (Noise) Directive (2003/10/EC) and came into force on 15 February 2006. They revoke and replace the Noise at Work Regulations 1989. The main changes are a reduction by 5dB in the exposure levels at which specific action is to be taken, the introduction of a new exposure limit value of 87dB(A) as a weekly personal noise exposure (to be used when exposure to noise varies from day to day), and a specific requirement on health surveillance. Below is an overview of the main provisions.

8.29   If work exposes employees to noise at or above a lower exposure action value of a daily or weekly noise exposure level of 80dB(A) (or a peak sound pressure level of 135dB(C)), the employer shall carry out a suitable and sufficient risk assessment, identifying the measures which need to be taken to meet the requirements of the regulations. If the work is liable to expose employees to noise at or above the upper exposure action level of 85dB(A) (or a peak sound pressure level of 137dB(C)), the risk assessment shall include measurement of the level of noise exposure.

8.30   There is a general requirement to ensure that risk from exposure to noise is either eliminated at source or, where this is not reasonably practicable, reduced to a minimum. If an employee is likely to be exposed to noise at or above an upper exposure action value, the employer shall reduce exposure to a minimum by establishing and implementing a programme of organisational and technical measures (excluding the provision of personal hearing protectors) which is appropriate to the activity and consistent with the risk assessment.

8.31   If an employee is exposed to noise at or above the lower exposure action level, the employer shall make personal hearing protectors available upon request to any employee who is so exposed. If the employer is unable to reduce the level of exposure to below the upper exposure action level, he shall provide personal hearing protectors to any employee who is so exposed. Further, if there is an area in which an employee is likely to be exposed to noise at or above the upper exposure action level, the employer shall ensure that:
  (a) the area is designated as a hearing protection zone
  (b) the area is identified and demarcated as specified for the purpose of indicating that ear protection shall be worn, and
  (c) access to the area is restricted where this is technically feasible and the risk of exposure justifies it.

8.32   Every effort shall be made to ensure that no employee enters that area unless personal ear protectors are worn. The employer shall select personal hearing protectors so as to eliminate or reduce the risk, and ensure that they are maintained in an efficient state, efficient order and in good repair. Every employee shall make full and proper use of personal hearing protectors, and of any other control measures provided, and report any defect to his employer. Hearing protection supplied must conform with the Personal Protective Equipment Regulations 2002.

8.33   If the risk assessment indicates that there is a risk to the health of employees who are exposed to noise, health surveillance, including audiometric testing, shall be carried out. Copies of the health record shall be kept in a suitable form, and, on request, an employee must be allowed access to it. Copies shall be provided to an enforcement authority as required. If the employee is found to have identifiable hearing damage which is likely to be the result of exposure to noise, the employee shall be examined by a doctor.

8.34   Where employees are exposed to noise which is likely to be at or above the lower exposure action level, the employer shall provide employees (and their representatives) with suitable and sufficient information, instruction and training.

8.35   Part 2 of the Guidance Notes issued by the Health and Safety Executive sets out simple "listening tests" based on a one metre and two metre rule.

Test	Probable noise level
Have to shout or have difficulty being heard clearly by someone about one metre (three feet) away	90dB
Have to shout or have difficulty being heard clearly by someone about two metres (six feet) away	85dB
Noise level sounds about as loud as a voice when talking at a normal conversation distance	80dB

8.36   This simple listening test is designed to enable employers and employees to identify whether or not there is likely to be a problem, and thus take appropriate measures.

8.37   The Control of Noise at Work Regulations 2005 came into effect in the music and entertainment industry as from April 2008, and a

313

Guidance Note has been produced giving advice on compliance. A Sound Advice web update is also available.

Control of Vibration at Work Regulations 2005

8.38   The Control of Vibration at Work Regulations came into force in July 2005. They implement EU Directive 2002/44/EC.

8.39   The most common form of vibration illnesses is vibration white finger, which is a disorder caused by the constriction of the blood supply to the fingers, due to working with vibrating tools, such as pneumatic drills, hammers, etc, although these can also cause damage to the sensory nerves, muscles and joints in the hands and arms. Whole body vibration can be caused by vibration transmitted through the seat or feet, and regular long-term exposure could affect drivers of some mobile machines, including tractors, fork-lift trucks and quarrying or earth-moving machinery. In the majority of cases the illness does not prevent a person from continuing to work, although it may cause considerable discomfort, especially during cold weather conditions.

8.40   For the evidential problems in determining whether or not a claimant is suffering from Hand Arm Vibration Syndrome (HAVS) see *Whalley v Montracon Ltd*, in which the court had to decide whether the claimant was suffering from HAVS, based on his own description of the symptoms.

Risk assessment (regulation 5)

8.41   Every employer who carries out work which is liable to expose any employees to risk from vibration shall make a suitable and sufficient risk assessment of the risk to health and safety, and of the steps that need to be taken to meet the requirements of the regulations.

Eliminating or reducing exposure (regulation 6)

8.42   The employer shall ensure that the risk to exposure to vibration is either eliminated at source or, if that is not reasonably practicable, reduced to a minimum. There are a number of steps which shall be taken if the exposure action value is exceeded, including other methods of working, choosing equipment which produces the least possible vibration, the provision of auxiliary equipment, appropriate maintenance programmes, the design and layout of the workplace, suitable and sufficient information and training for employees, limiting the duration of exposure, appropriate work schedules with adequate rest periods and the provision of clothing to protect employees from cold or damp.

8.43 Exposure shall not exceed the exposure limit value, but if it does, action must be taken to reduce vibration to below that level, the reason for exceeding the limit be identified, and organisational and technical measures taken to prevent the limit being exceeded again.

Health surveillance (regulation 7)

8.44 If the risk assessment indicates that there is a risk to health to employees who are liable to be exposed to vibration, and if employees are exposed to vibration in excess of the exposure limit value, employees must be under suitable health surveillance. A health record must also be kept, to which the employees shall have access. If a doctor, or other occupational health professional, considers that an employee has an identifiable disease or adverse health effect as the result of exposure to vibration, the employer shall ensure that a suitably qualified person informs the employee accordingly. Consideration shall be given to re-assigning the employee to alternative work where there is no risk of further exposure. The risk assessment and compliance measures will need to be reviewed.

Information, instruction and training (regulation 8)

8.45 Where employees are exposed to risk from vibration, the employer shall provide them and their representatives with suitable and sufficient information, instruction and training. This shall include details of the organisational measures taken, the exposure limit values and action values, the significant findings of the risk assessment, why and how to detect and report signs of injury, entitlement to appropriate health surveillance, and safe working practices to minimise exposure to vibration.

8.46 Exposure limits will not apply until July 2010 (2014 for agriculture and forestry) where work equipment is used which was first provided to employees prior to 2007.

8.47 A Guidance Note accompanies the regulations.

CHAPTER 9

Construction work

Construction industry

9.1 Section 127 of the Factories Act 1961 applies the relevant provisions of that Act to building operations and works of engineering construction undertaken by way of trade or business, or for the purpose of any industrial or commercial undertaking and to any line or siding used in connection therewith which is not part of a railway. The relevant provisions are:

(a) Part V (formal investigation of accidents and cases of disease)
(b) Part X with respect to general registers and the preservation of records and registers (ss.140, 141)
(c) Part XI relating to certain duties of district councils (s.153)
(d) Part XII relating to offences (ss.155–171)
(e) Part XIII (ss.172, 174)
(f) Part XIV (ss.175, 176).

9.2 The legal rules relating to health and safety in the construction industry are:

(a) Construction (Head Protection) Regulations 1989
(b) Construction (Design and Management) Regulations 2007.

9.3 In addition, there are a number of relevant regulations that were passed in order to comply with EU directives on type examination certificates of approval. These include:

(a) Construction Plant and Equipment (Harmonisation of Noise Emission Standards) Regulations 1988 (as amended)
(b) Falling Object Protective Structure for Construction Plant (EC Requirements) Regulations 1988
(c) Roll-over Protective Structures for Construction Plant (EC Requirements) Regulations 1988.

Construction (Design and Management) Regulations 2007

9.4 These regulations came into force in April 2007 and implement in Great Britain the requirements of Directive 92/57/EEC, with the exception of certain requirements which are implemented by the Work at Height Regulations 2005 (see paragraph 9.71). The regulations revoke and replace the Construction (Design and Management) Regulations 1994 and revoke and re-enact, with modifications, the Construction (Health, Safety and Welfare) Regulations 1996. An Approved Code of Practice and Guidance Notes, L144: *Construction (Design and Management) Regulations 2007*, have been issued by HSE to assist all concerned to understand their obligations under the regulations and give guidance on actions to be taken.

9.5   Part 2 of the regulations (regulations 4–13) set out the general management duties which apply to construction projects, including the duties of clients, designers and contractors. Part 3 (regulations 14–24) imposes additional duties on clients, designers and contractors when a notifiable project is being undertaken. A project is notifiable when the construction phase is likely to involve more than 30 days or 500 person days of construction work. There are a number of significant changes made as compared with the 1994 regulations. Part 4 (regulations 25–44) sets out the duties relating to health and safety on construction sites and to prevent danger from a number of specified hazards.

Definitions (regulation 2)

9.6   This regulation defines a number of terms used, including a substantial definition of the phrases "construction work", "contractor", "designer", "project", "structure", etc.

Competence (regulation 4)

9.7   A person who is appointing a CDM co-ordinator (see paragraph 9.22), designer, principal contractor or contractor shall take reasonable steps to ensure that the person appointed or engaged is competent. A person who accepts such appointment must be competent, and a worker who carries out or manages design or construction work must be competent or under the supervision of a competent person. All such persons must be competent only in their ability to perform any requirement or avoid contravening any prohibition imposed by any relevant statutory provision.

Co-operation (regulation 5)

9.8   Every person concerned with a project shall seek the co-operation of any other person concerned, and actually co-operate with any other person so concerned, in any project involving construction work at the same or an adjoining site so far as is necessary to enable that person to perform any duty or function under these regulations.

Co-ordination (regulation 6)

9.9 All persons concerned in a project on whom a duty is placed by these regulations shall co-ordinate their activities with one another in a manner which ensures, so far as is reasonably practicable, the health and safety of persons carrying out or affected by construction work.

General principles of prevention (regulation 7)

9.10 Every person on whom a duty is placed by these regulations in relation to the design, planning and preparation of a project shall take account of the general principles of prevention in the performance of those duties during all stages of the project. The "general principles of prevention" are those set out in schedule 1 of the Management of Health and Safety at Work Regulations 1999 (see paragraph 4.22).

Election by clients (regulation 8)

9.11 Where there is more than one client in relation to a project, one or more clients may elect to be treated as the only client or clients. When this happens, no other client who has agreed in writing to such election shall be subject to any duties owed by a client under these regulations. However, this exclusion will not apply to the duty to co-operate (regulation 5, s.1(b)), providing pre-construction information (regulation 10, s.1), and the provision of pre-construction information (regulation 15) and health and safety information (regulation 17, s.1). Such duties will still apply to a client who has "opted out".

Managing the project (regulation 9)

9.12 Every client shall take reasonable steps to ensure that the arrangements made for managing the project by persons with a duty under these regulations are suitable to ensure:
- (a) the construction work can be carried out so far as is reasonably practicable without risk to the health and safety of any person
- (b) the provisions relating to welfare facilities set out in schedule 2 are complied with

(c) any structure designed for use as a workplace meets the requirement of the design and materials provisions contained in the Workplace (Health, Safety and Welfare) Regulations 1992 (see paragraph 9.17).

Pre-construction information (regulation 10)

9.13 Every client shall ensure that every person designing the structure, and every contractor appointed by the client, is provided with pre-construction information. This will consist of all the information in the possession of the client, including information about or affecting the site or the construction work, the proposed use of the structure as a workplace, the minimum amount of time before the construction phase allowed to the contractors for planning and preparation for construction work, and any relevant information in any existing health and safety file.

9.14 The purpose of providing this pre-construction information is to ensure the health and safety of persons engaged in construction work and others liable to be affected by the way the work is carried out, and also for the benefit of those who will use the structure as a workplace. This information will also assist the contractor to perform his duties under the regulations, and to determine the resources for the management of the project.

Duties of designers (regulation 11)

9.15 No designer shall commence work in relation to a project unless any client for the project is aware of his duties under these regulations. When preparing or modifying a design which may be used in construction work, every designer shall avoid foreseeable risks to the health and safety of any person:
- (a) carrying out construction work
- (b) liable to be affected by such construction work
- (c) cleaning any window or transparent or translucent wall, ceiling or roof
- (d) maintaining the permanent fixtures and fittings of a structure, or
- (e) using a structure designed as a workplace.

9.16 Collective measures are to have priority over individual measures.

9.17 In designing any structure to be used as a workplace, the designer shall take account of the Workplace (Health, Safety and Welfare) Regulations 1992 which relate to the design of and materials used in the structure.

9.18 The designer must also take all reasonable steps to provide with his design sufficient information about aspects of the design of the structure or maintenance as will adequately assist clients, other designers and contractors to comply with their duties under the regulations.

Designs prepared abroad (regulation 12)

9.19 If the design is prepared or modified outside Great Britain for use in construction work, the person who commissions it (if he is established in Great Britain) or the client shall ensure that the above provisions in regulation 11 are complied with.

Duties of contractors (regulation 13)

9.20 Every contractor shall plan, manage and monitor construction work carried out by him or under his control in a way which ensures that, so far as is reasonably practicable, it is carried out without risks to health and safety. The contractor shall also supply every worker with information and training needed for the particular work to be carried out safely and without risks to health, including:

(a) suitable site induction
(b) information on risks to their health and safety identified by the risks assessment made under regulation 3 of the Management of Health and Safety at Work Regulations (see paragraph 4.8), or arising out of the conduct by another contractor of which he ought reasonably to be aware
(c) the measures which have identified by the contractor in consequence of the risk assessment as the measures he needs to take to comply with the requirements and prohibitions imposed on him by relevant statutory provisions
(d) any site rules
(e) the procedure to be followed in the event of serious and imminent dangers to such workers, and
(f) the identity of the persons nominated to implement those procedures.

9.21   The contractor must also provide his employees with any health and safety training as required by regulation 13(2)(b) of the Management of Health and Safety at Work Regulations (see paragraph 4.51), and work shall not commence on a construction site unless reasonable steps have been taken to prevent access by unauthorised persons to that site.

Appointments by the client (regulation 14)

9.22   The client shall appoint a CDM co-ordinator as soon as practicable after the initial design work or preparation for construction work has begun. He shall then appoint the principal contractor as soon as he knows enough about the project to be able to select a suitable person. These appointments are to be changed or renewed as necessary to ensure that at all times until the end of the construction phase there is a CDM co-ordinator and a principal contractor. For any period when there are no such appointments, the client will be deemed to be so appointed, and subject to the duties set out in these regulations.

Client's duty to provide information (regulation 15)

9.23   The client shall provide the CDM co-ordinator with pre-construction information, consisting of any information about the site, the proposed use of the structure, minimum planning time and health and safety file (see regulation 10(2) above), and any further information which is relevant to the CDM co-ordinator to ensure the health and safety of persons engaged in the construction work, others liable to be affected, and those who will use the structure as a workplace (see regulation 10(3)).

Client's duty in relation to the start of construction phase (regulation 16)

9.24   The client will ensure that the construction phase does not start unless the principal contractor has prepared a construction phase plan (see regulation 23) and he is satisfied that the requirements relating to welfare facilities will be complied with during the construction phase.

Client's duty in relation to health and safety file (regulation 17)

9.25 The client will ensure that the CDM co-ordinator is provided with all the health and safety information in the client's possession which is likely to be needed for inclusion in the health and safety file. After the construction phase is completed, the file shall be kept for inspection, although if the client disposes of his entire interest in the structure he must deliver it to the person who acquires his interest.

Designer's additional duties (regulation 18)

9.26 No designer shall commence work (other than initial design work) unless a CDM co-ordinator has been appointed for the project. The designer shall take all reasonable steps to provide with his design sufficient information about aspects of the design of the structure or its construction or maintenance as will adequately assist the CDM co-ordinator to comply with his duties under these regulations.

Additional duties of contractors (regulation 19)

9.27 No contractor shall carry out construction work unless he has been provided with the name of the CDM co-ordinator and principal contractor, been given access to such part of the construction phase plan as is relevant to the work to be performed by him, and notice has been given to HSE by the CDM co-ordinator (see regulation 21).

9.28 Every contractor shall give to the principal contractor any information which might affect the health and safety of any person carrying out construction work or who may be affected by it, or which might justify a review of the construction phase plan, or has been identified for inclusion in the health and safety file (see regulation 22). The contractor will identify any sub-contractor appointed, will comply with site rules, and provide the principal contractor with any information in relation to death, injury, condition or dangerous occurrence which the contractor is required to notify under RIDDOR.

General duties of CDM co-ordinators (regulation 20)

9.29 The CDM co-ordinator will give suitable and sufficient advice and assistance to the client to enable the client to undertake the measures he needs to take to comply with these regulations (in particular regulations 9 and 16 above).

9.30 The CDM co-ordinator will also ensure that suitable arrangements are made and implemented for the co-ordination of health and safety measures during the planning and preparation for the construction phase, including facilitating co-operation and co-ordination between persons concerned in the project and the application of the general principles of prevention set out in schedule 1 of the Management of Health and Safety at Work Regulations 1999 (see paragraph 4.22). The CDM co-ordinator will also take all reasonable steps to identify and collect the pre-construction information and provide this information in a convenient form to every person designing the structure, and every contractor who may be or has been appointed. He will ensure co-operation between the designer and the contractor, prepare and review the health and safety file, and, at the end of the construction phase, pass this file to the client.

Notification of the project to HSE (regulation 21)

9.31 As soon as practicable after his appointment, the CDM co-ordinator shall ensure that notice of the project is given to HSE, containing the particulars specified in schedule 1. This will include the exact address of the construction site, the name of the local authority, a brief description of the project, contact details of the client, CDM co-ordinator and principal contractor, start date, time allowed for planning and preparation, planned duration of the construction work, estimated maximum number of persons at work on the construction site, number of contractors, name and address of any contractor and designer already appointed, and a declaration signed by or on behalf of the client that he is aware of his duties under the regulations. If the principal contractor has not been appointed, the particulars shall be given as soon as practicable after his appointment.

Duties of principal contractor (regulation 22)

9.32 The principal contractor shall plan, manage and monitor the construction phase in a way which ensures, so far as is reasonably practicable, it is carried out without risks to health or safety. This will include:

(a) facilitating co-operation between the various persons concerned in the project

(b) applying the general principles of prevention (see paragraph 4.22)

(c) liaising with the CDM co-ordinator

(d) ensuring that welfare facilities are sufficient

(e) drawing up appropriate site rules

(f) giving reasonable directions to other contractors on the site

(g) ensuring that contractors are informed of the minimum amount of time which will be allowed for planning and preparation and ensuring that he has sufficient time to prepare properly for the work

(h) identifying the information relating to the contractor's activities which is likely to be required by the CDM co-ordinator for inclusion in the health and safety file

(i) ensuring that the particulars which have been sent to HSE (see paragraph 9.31) are displayed where they can be read by any worker engaged in the construction work

(j) taking reasonable steps to prevent access by unauthorised persons to the site.

9.33 He will also take all reasonable steps to ensure that every worker carrying out construction work is provided with suitable site induction, information and training.

Duties in relation to the construction phase plan (regulation 23)

9.34 Before the start of the construction phase, the principal contractor shall prepare a construction phase plan, so as to ensure that the construction work is, so far as is reasonably practicable, without risks to health or safety. From time to time he will update, review and refine the construction phase plan so that it continues to be sufficient for this purpose. The construction phase plan is to be implemented in a way which will ensure the health and safety of all persons carrying out the construction work as well as those who may be affected by the work. The construction phase plan must identify the risks to health and safety arising from the work, and include suitable and sufficient measures to address such risks.

Co-operation and consultation (regulation 24)

9.35 The principal contractor shall make and maintain arrangements which will enable him to co-operate with the workers engaged in the construction work in promoting and developing measures to ensure the health, safety and welfare of workers, and checking the effectiveness of such measures. He will also consult those workers (or their representatives) in good time on matters connected with the project which may affect their health, safety or welfare, and ensure that workers or their representatives can inspect and take copies of any information which the principal contractor has which relates to the planning or management of the project, or which otherwise may affect their health, safety or welfare. However, the principal contractor need not disclose information relating to national security, or which he is prohibited by law from disclosing, or which relates specifically to an individual, or which could cause substantial injury to the undertaking, or which has been obtained for the purpose of bringing, prosecuting or defending legal proceedings.

Application of regulations 26–44 (regulation 25)

9.36 Part 4 of the regulations sets out the duties relating to health and safety on construction sites. These duties are placed on every contractor and every other person in so far as they carry out construction work under his control. In particular every person at work on construction work who is under the control of another person shall report to that person any defect of which he is aware which may endanger the health and safety of himself or another person.

Safe places of work (regulation 26)

9.37 So far as is reasonably practicable, there shall be suitable and sufficient safe access and egress from every place of work, and to and from every other place provided for the use of any person while at work. Such access and egress shall be properly maintained. Every place of work shall, so far as is reasonably practicable, be made and kept safe and without risks to health to any person at work there. Every place of work shall, so far as is reasonably practicable, have sufficient working space and be so arranged that it is suitable for any person who is working there, taking into account any necessary work equipment present.

Good order and site security (regulation 27)

9.38 Every part of a construction site shall, so far as is reasonably practicable, be kept in good order, and every part of a construction site which is used as a place of work shall be kept in a reasonable state of cleanliness. Where necessary in the interests of health and safety, a construction site shall, so far as is reasonably practicable, and in accordance with the level of risk posed, either have its perimeter identified by suitable signs, or be fenced off, or both. Timber and other material with projecting nails shall not be used in any work or be allowed to remain in any place if they may be a source of danger to any person.

Stability of structures (regulation 28)

9.39   All practicable steps shall be taken, where necessary to prevent danger to any person, to ensure that any new or existing structure which may become unstable or in a temporary state of weakness or instability due to the carrying out of construction work does not collapse. Any buttress, temporary support or temporary structure must be of such design and so installed and maintained as to withstand any foreseeable loads which may be imposed on it, and must be used for the purpose for which it is so designed, installed and maintained. No part of any structure shall be so loaded as to render it unsafe to any person.

Demolition or dismantling (regulation 29)

9.40   The demolition or dismantling of a structure shall be planned and carried out in such a manner as to prevent danger, or to reduce danger to as low a level as is reasonably practicable. The arrangements for carrying out such demolition or dismantling shall be recorded in writing before the work begins.

Explosives (regulation 30)

9.41   So far as is reasonably practicable, explosives shall be stored, transported and used safely and securely. An explosive charge shall be used or fired only if suitable and sufficient steps have been taken to ensure that no person is exposed to risk of injury from the explosion or from projected or flying material caused thereby.

Excavations (regulation 31)

9.42   All practicable steps shall be taken, where necessary to prevent danger to any person, to ensure that any excavation does not collapse, no material from a side or roof of an excavation is dislodged, and no person is buried or trapped in an excavation which is dislodged or falls. Suitable and sufficient steps shall be taken to prevent any person, work equipment or any accumulation of material from falling into any excavation.

9.43   Construction work shall not be carried out in an excavation where any support or battering has been provided unless the excavation and any work equipment and materials which affect its safety have been inspected by a competent person at the start of the shift, after any event likely to affect the strength or stability of the excavation, and after any material unintentionally falls or is dislodged, and the person who carries out the inspection is satisfied that the work can be carried out there safely.

Cofferdams and caissons (regulation 32)

9.44   Every cofferdam or caisson shall be of suitable design and construction, be appropriately equipped so that workers can gain shelter or escape if water or materials enter it, and be properly maintained. A cofferdam or caisson may only be used in construction work if it has been inspected by a competent person at the start of any shift and after any event likely to have affected its strength or stability.

Reports of inspections (regulation 33)

9.45   A person who carries out an inspection under regulations 31 and 32 (above) shall, if he is not satisfied that the construction work can be carried out safely, inform the person for whom the inspection was carried out of any matters about which he is not satisfied, and prepare a report (see schedule 3). The latter shall keep the report available for inspection by an HSE inspector until three months after the work has been completed.

Energy distribution installations (regulation 34)

9.46   Energy distribution installations shall be suitably located, checked and clearly indicated. Power cables shall be directed away from the area of risk, or isolated and earthed. Measures which shall be taken include barriers, suspended protection, etc in order to ensure safety.

Prevention of drowning (regulation 35)

9.47   Suitable and sufficient steps shall be taken to prevent a person from drowning, including suitable rescue equipment. Any vessel used to carry persons by water to or from a place of work shall not be overcrowded or overloaded.

Traffic routes (regulation 36)

9.48   Every construction site shall be organised in such a way that, so far as is reasonably practicable, pedestrians and vehicles can move safely and without risks to health. Traffic routes shall be suitable for persons and vehicles, in sufficient number, in suitable positions and of sufficient size. Every traffic route shall be indicated by suitable signs where necessary for reasons of health or safety, regularly checked and properly maintained.

Vehicles (regulation 37)

9.49   Suitable and sufficient steps shall be taken to prevent or control the unintended movement of any vehicle. If a person is likely to be endangered by the movement of a vehicle, warnings shall be given. A person may only ride on a vehicle in a safe place provided thereon, and steps shall be taken to prevent any vehicle from falling into any excavation, pit, water, or overrunning the edge of any embankment or earthwork.

Prevention of risk from fire (regulation 38)

9.50   Suitable and sufficient steps shall be taken to prevent, so far as is reasonably practicable, the risk of injury to any person during the carrying out of construction work from fire, explosions, flooding, or any substance likely to cause asphyxiation.

Emergency procedures (regulation 39)

9.51   Where necessary in the interests of health and safety of any person on a construction site, there shall be prepared suitable and sufficient arrangements for dealing with any foreseeable emergency, including evacuation procedures. Account shall be taken of the type of work, the characteristics and location of the site and the number and location of places of work on the site, the work equipment used, the number of persons likely to be present at any one time, and the physical and chemical properties of any substance or materials on the site. Steps shall be taken to ensure that persons are familiar with these arrangements, and that they are tested at suitable intervals.

Emergency routes and exits (regulation 40)

9.52　A sufficient number of emergency routes and exits shall be provided to enable any person to reach a place of safety quickly in the event of danger. The emergency route or exit shall lead as directly as possible to an identified safe area, shall be kept clear and free from obstruction, and where necessary shall be provided with emergency lighting. Such routes shall also be indicated by suitable signs.

Fire detection and fire-fighting (regulation 41)

9.53　There shall be provided suitable and sufficient fire-fighting equipment and fire detection and alarm systems, which shall be suitably located. These shall be tested and examined at suitable intervals and properly maintained. Every person at work on a construction site shall, so far as is reasonably practicable, be instructed in the correct use of fire-fighting equipment, particularly if the work activity gives rise to a particular risk of fire.

Fresh air (regulation 42)

9.54　Suitable and sufficient steps shall be taken to ensure, so far as is reasonably practicable, that every place of work has sufficient fresh or purified air. Any plant used for this purpose shall include an effective device to give visible or audible warning of any failure of the plant.

Temperature (regulation 43)

9.55　Suitable and sufficient steps shall be taken to ensure, so far as is reasonably practicable, that during working hours the temperature at any place of work indoors is reasonable having regard to the purpose for which it is used. Every place of work outdoors shall be so arranged that having regard to the purpose for which that place is used and any protective clothing or work equipment provided for use, it provides protection from adverse weather.

Lighting (regulation 44)

9.56   Every place of work and approach thereto, and every traffic route shall be provided with suitable and sufficient lighting, which shall be, so far as is reasonably practicable, by natural light. The colour of any artificial lighting provided shall not affect or change the perception of any signs or signals provided for the purpose of health and safety. Secondary lighting shall be provided where there would be a risk to health and safety in the event of a failure of primary artificial lighting.

Civil liability (regulation 45)

9.57   A breach of duty imposed by these regulations shall not (with certain exceptions) confer a right of action in any civil proceedings insofar as that duty applies for the protection of a person who is not an employee of the person on whom the duty is placed.

Welfare facilities (schedule 2)

Sanitary conveniences

9.58   Suitable and sufficient sanitary conveniences shall be provided or made available at accessible places. These are to be adequately ventilated and lit, kept clean and orderly. Separate rooms shall be provided for men and women.

Washing facilities

9.59   Washing facilities shall be provided in the immediate vicinity of every sanitary convenience and changing rooms. There shall be a supply of clean hot and cold or warm water, soap or other suitable means of cleaning, and towels or other suitable means of drying. Such rooms must be sufficiently ventilated and lit, kept clean and orderly, with separate facilities for men and women (unless the facilities provided are for washing hands, forearms and face only).

Drinking water

9.60   An adequate supply of wholesome drinking water shall be provided or made available, with a sufficient number of suitable cups or other vessels unless the water supply is from a jet.

Changing rooms and lockers

9.61   Suitable and sufficient changing rooms shall be provided at accessible places if a worker has to wear special clothing for his work and cannot be expected to change elsewhere. Changing rooms shall be provided with seating and include, where necessary, facilities to enable a person to dry such special clothing and his own clothing. Lockers shall also be provided for any such special clothing which is not taken home, or a worker's own clothing which is not worn during working hours, and his personal effects.

Rest rooms

9.62   Suitable and sufficient rest rooms or rest areas shall be provided and made available at readily accessible places. These shall include suitable arrangements to protect non-smokers from discomfort caused by tobacco smoke, and be equipped with an adequate number of tables and adequate seating with backs. Where necessary suitable facilities for pregnant women or nursing mothers shall be included, and suitable arrangements to ensure that meals can be prepared and eaten, including the means for boiling water. Rest rooms shall be maintained at an appropriate temperature.

Construction (Head Protection) Regulations 1989

9.63   The Construction (Head Protection) Regulations 1989 are designed to give protection to persons who work on construction sites, which are defined as being works of building operations and engineering construction. Employers must provide and maintain head protection and replace it whenever necessary. An identical obligation lies on self-employed persons. The head protection must be suitable, ie conform to British Standard EN 397, be compatible with the work or activity and comply with relevant EU "product" directives. Head protection must be worn at all times during construction work unless there is no risk of injury to the head from falling objects. Employers, self-employed persons and employees who control others (eg foremen) must ensure that the head protectors are worn. A person who has control of a site may make rules governing when and where helmets shall be worn. Such rules shall be in writing and brought to the attention of those affected by them.

9.64   Sikhs are exempted from the requirements of the regulations at any time when they are wearing their turbans while working on construction sites and thus they cannot be required to wear safety helmets in such circumstances (Employment Act 1989, s.11). In consequence, an employer will not be liable to tort in respect of any injury or damage caused because he failed to comply with the statutory duty. A Sikh who is injured because of failure to wear the safety helmet will only be able to recover damages to the extent the injury or damage would still have occurred had he been wearing a safety helmet.

Confined Spaces Regulations 1997

9.65   The Confined Spaces Regulations 1997 came into force on 28 January 1998 and implement part of Directive 92/57/EEC on minimum safety and health requirements on temporary or mobile construction sites. Various relevant items of legislation are, in consequence, repealed or revoked, including s.30 of the Factories Act 1961 and parts of certain regulations relating to processes that involved working in confined spaces, including ship-building, agriculture, breathing apparatus, etc.

9.66   The regulations define a confined space as being any place, including chamber, tank, vat, silo, pit, trench, pipe, sewer, flue, well or similar space in which, by virtue of its enclosed nature, there arises a reasonably foreseeable specified risk. The "specified risks" are risks of:
(a) serious injury to any person at work arising from a fire or explosion
(b) the loss of consciousness of any person at work arising from an increase in body temperature, or the loss of consciousness or asphyxiation of any person at work arising from gas, fume, vapour or lack of oxygen
(c) drowning of any person at work arising from a free-flowing solid or the inability to reach a respirable environment due to entrapment by a free-flowing solid ("free-flowing" solid means any substance consisting of solid particles and which is of, or is capable of being in, a flowing or running consistency, including flour, grain, sand, sugar or other similar material).

9.67   The duty to ensure compliance with the regulations is placed on the employer, in respect of any work carried out by his employees, and to ensure compliance, so far as is reasonably practicable in respect of any work carried out by persons other than his employees, in so far as the provisions relate to matters which are within his control. Self-employed persons are under similar obligations with respect to their own work carried out by other persons.

Work in confined spaces (regulations 4–5)

9.68   No person at work shall enter a confined space to carry out work for any purpose unless it is not reasonably practicable to achieve that purpose without such entry. If such entry is necessary, no person shall enter or carry out any work in or (except in an emergency) leave a confined space otherwise than in accordance with a system of work which, in relation to any specified risks (see above), renders that work safe and without risks to health. A person shall not enter or carry out work in a confined space unless suitable and sufficient arrangements have been prepared for the persons in the event of any emergency, whether or not arising out of specified risk. Those arrangements must also reduce the risks to the health and safety of any person required to put rescue arrangements into operation, and include the provision and maintenance of resuscitation procedures.

Exceptions

9.69   The regulations do not apply to activities on seagoing ships, work below ground in mines, and diving operations. The HSE may also grant exemption certificates, subject to certain stringent conditions, if satisfied that the health and safety of persons who are likely to be affected by the exemption will not be prejudiced in consequence.

9.70   The regulations are supplemented by an Approved Code of Practice and Guidance Notes, L101: *Safe Work in Confined Spaces*. In particular, the ACOP emphasises the need for a risk assessment to be carried out under regulation 3 of the Management of Health and Safety at Work Regulations 1999 (see paragraph 4.8), and details a wide range of risks that are commonly associated with work in confined spaces.

Work at Height Regulations 2005 (as amended)

9.71   These regulations implement several EU directives (2001/4/EC, 89/391/EEC, 92/57/EEC) and came into force on 6 April 2005. Section 24 of the Factories Act 1961 is repealed, and regulations 13(1–4) of the

Workplace (Health, Safety and Welfare) Regulations and regulations 6–8 of the Construction (Health, Safety and Welfare) Regulations 1996 are revoked.

9.72 "Work at height" means any place (including at or below ground level) where a person could fall a distance liable to cause personal injury (thus the standard used in the Construction (Health, Safety and Welfare) Regulations, which requires certain measures to be taken in respect of work over two metres in height has been replaced). The regulations impose duties on an employer and self-employed person in relation to work by an employee or any person under his control.

9.73 Falls from height are the biggest cause of fatal injuries at work, and a major cause of serious injuries. The construction industry alone accounts for half of these. Falls from ladders account for about a quarter of these grim statistics, caused by over-reaching, over-balancing, failure or misuse of equipment, unexpected movement, falls from fragile surfaces, etc. It therefore needs to be stressed that the use of ladders is not banned by the regulations. They can be used when all other safe alternatives for work at heights have been ruled out. If a risk assessment shows that the task is one of low risk and short duration, or that the site features are such that other items of equipment are not appropriate, then ladders may be used, provided, as with most matters, appropriate safety precautions are taken.

Planning of work at height (regulations 4–5)

9.74 Every employer shall ensure that work at height is properly planned, appropriately supervised and carried out in a manner which is so far as reasonably practicable safe. Any person who is engaged in any activity in relation to working at height must be competent to do so.

Avoidance of risks (regulation 6)

9.75 Employers shall take account of risk assessment under regulation 3 of the Management of Health and Safety at Work Regulations 1999, and ensure that the work shall not be carried out at height where it is reasonably practicable not to do so. Suitable and sufficient measures shall be taken to prevent, so far as is reasonably practicable, any person falling a distance liable to cause personal injury. These include ensuring that places of work at height (eg ladders, scaffolding, cradles, etc) and means of access and egress, are stable, of sufficient strength and stability, and rest on a stable and sufficiently strong surface. They must also be of sufficient dimensions to permit safe passage of persons and safe use of any plant or materials, possess suitable and sufficient means of preventing a fall, possess a surface which has no gap through which a person or object could fall, not give rise to risks of injury to other persons, and be so constructed and maintained as to prevent, so far as is reasonably practicable, the risk of slipping, or tripping or prevent any person from being caught between it and any adjacent structure (see schedule 1). If these measures do not eliminate the risk of a fall occurring so far as is reasonably practicable, sufficient work equipment shall be provided to minimise the distance and consequences of a fall, or such additional training and instruction and sufficient measures to prevent any person from falling a distance liable to cause personal injury.

Selection of work equipment (regulation 7)

9.76 In selecting work equipment for use at height, the employer shall take account of the working conditions, the distance for access and egress, the distance and consequences of a fall, the duration and frequency of use, and the need for easy and timely evacuation and rescue in the case of emergency. The characteristics of work equipment (including dimensions) shall be appropriate to the nature of the work and foreseeable loadings.

Requirements for particular work equipment (regulation 8)

9.77 Guard-rails, toe boards and barriers shall comply with the requirements of schedule 2. Thus they must be of sufficient dimensions and of sufficient strength and rigidity, and be so placed as to ensure that they do not become accidentally displaced, and so placed as to prevent the fall of any person or material or object. In construction work, the top guard-rail must be at least 950mm above the edge. Nets, airbags or other collective safeguards and other personal fall protection systems must comply with the requirements of schedule 5.

Fragile surfaces (regulation 9)

9.78 No person shall pass across or near a fragile surface where it is reasonably practicable to carry out work safely and under ergonomic conditions without his doing so. If it is not reasonably practicable to do so, the employer shall ensure that sufficient and suitable platforms, coverings, or guard-rails are provided but if, despite these measures there is still a risk of a person falling, suitable and sufficient measures shall be taken to minimise the distances and consequences of a fall. Prominent warning notices shall be affixed to the approach of a fragile surface or persons made aware of it by other means.

Falling objects (regulation 10)

9.79   Every employer shall take sufficient and suitable steps to prevent the fall of any material or object. If this is not reasonably practicable, steps must be taken to prevent a person from being struck by a falling object which is liable to cause personal injury. No material or object shall be thrown or tipped from height in circumstances where it is liable to cause injury to any person.

Danger areas (regulation 11)

9.80   Every employer shall ensure that where there is a risk of a person falling a distance, or being struck by a falling object which is liable to cause personal injury, the workplace shall be equipped with devices preventing unauthorised person froms entering such an area. The area must be clearly indicated.

Inspection of work equipment (regulation 12)

9.81   Work equipment is not to be used after installation or assembly unless it has been inspected. If work equipment is exposed to conditions causing deterioration which is liable to result in a dangerous situation, it must be inspected at suitable intervals, and each time that the exceptional circumstances occur. Working platforms used in construction work, from which a person could fall two metres or more, must not be used unless they have been inspected. A record of the inspection must be kept until the next inspection.

Inspection of places of work at height (regulation 13)

9.82   So far as is reasonably practicable, every employer shall ensure that the surface of every parapet, permanent rail or other fall protection measure of every place of work at height are checked on each occasion before the place is used.

Duties of persons at work (regulation 14)

9.83   Every person, where working under the control of another person, shall report to that person any activity or defect relating to work at height which he knows is likely to endanger the safety of himself or another person. Also, he shall use any work equipment or safety device provided to him for work at height, in accordance with the training received by him, and the instructions respecting that use which have been provided for him.

9.84   There are eight schedules to the regulations, as follows.

Schedule 1   Requirements for existing places of work and means of access and egress at height

Schedule 2   Requirements for guard-rails, toe boards, barriers and similar means of protection

Schedule 3   Requirements for working platforms

Schedule 4   Requirements for collective safeguards

Schedule 5   Requirements for personal fall protection systems

Schedule 6   Requirements for ladders

Schedule 7   Particulars to be included in a report of inspection

Schedule 8   Revocation of instruments

Lifting Operations and Lifting Equipment Regulations 1998

9.85   These regulations give effect to certain provisions of Directive 89/665/EEC as amended by Directive 95/63/EC, and deal with the particular risks posed by the provision and use of lifting equipment and the management of lifting operations. Existing sector-based legislation on this topic has been repealed, including 17 sets of regulations (in whole or in part) and ss.22, 23, and 25–27 of the Factories Act 1961. The regulations are accompanied by an Approved Code of Practice, L113: *Safe Use of Lifting Equipment*.

9.86   The regulations impose duties on employers in respect of lifting equipment provided for use at work, and also to self-employed persons and to persons who have control to any extent of lifting equipment to the extent of their control. Generally speaking, they do not apply to a ship's work equipment, which is generally covered by merchant shipping legislation.

Strength and stability (regulation 4)

9.87   Lifting equipment shall be of adequate strength and stability for each load.

9.88   The Guidance Notes point out that particular attention should be paid to mounting or fixing points, and account should be taken of any combination of destabilising forces.

Lifting equipment for lifting persons (regulation 5)

9.89   Lifting equipment must ensure that a person cannot be crushed, trapped, struck or fall from the carrier and, if it is not possible to have a suitable device to prevent the risk of the carrier falling, the carrier must have an enhanced safety coefficient rope or chain, which is inspected by a competent person every working day.

9.90   The ACOP suggests that the lift car should be fully enclosed when in use, and the floor of any carrier should be slip-resistant.

Positioning and installation (regulation 6)

9.91   Lifting equipment must be positioned or installed in such a way as to reduce the risk of the lifting equipment (or a load) striking a person, or from a load drifting, falling freely or being released unintentionally, and is otherwise safe.

9.92   The ACOP states that the positioning of lifting equipment should be such as to minimise the need for loads to be lifted over people. If a load moves along a fixed path, there should be a suitable and substantial enclosure; if the lifting equipment moves along a fixed path (less than two metres above the ground level) barriers or gates should be provided, to prevent a person being endangered by the underside of the lifting equipment or any fitting attached to it.

Marking of lifting equipment (regulation 7)

9.93   Machinery for lifting loads shall be clearly marked to indicate their safe working loads, including safe working loads for each configuration.

9.94 The Guidance Notes point out that a "safe working load" is a value or set of values based on the strength and/or stability of the equipment when lifting. Guidance is also given on handling safe working loads that vary in accordance with the configuration.

Organisation of lifting operations (regulation 8)

9.95 Every lifting operation must be properly planned by a competent person, appropriately supervised, and carried out in a safe manner.

9.96 The ACOP points out that the person planning the operation should have adequate practical and theoretical knowledge and experience of planning lifting operations. The risk assessment should reveal the risks, identify the resources required, the procedures and responsibilities. Measures should be taken to prevent lifting equipment from tilting, overturning, moving or slipping. If lifting equipment is to be used in the open air, meteorological conditions should be considered, and lifting operations halted if the integrity of the equipment could be affected, or persons exposed to danger.

Thorough examination and inspection (regulation 9)

9.97 Before lifting equipment is put into service for the first time, it must be thoroughly examined for any defect (unless it has not been used before and has an EC declaration of conformity). There must be a thorough examination after installation, and if it is likely to be exposed to conditions causing deterioration, thoroughly examined every six months if used for lifting persons and lifting accessories, otherwise every 12 months, and also whenever exceptional circumstances have occurred which are likely to jeopardise its safety.

9.98 The Guidance Note states that the thorough examination should be by a competent person who is independent and impartial, so that an objective decision can be made. Deterioration (which can take place for a number of reasons, such as wet, abrasive or corrosive environments) should be detected, and there should be a further examination when a significant change of circumstances has occurred (eg an accident, change of use, long period of disuse, etc).

Reports and defects (regulation 10)

9.99   A person making a thorough examination shall notify the employer of any defect in lifting equipment, make a report containing the information set out in schedule 1, which shall be sent to the employer and any person from whom the equipment was hired or leased. If there is a defect involving an existing or imminent risk of serious personal injury, send a copy of the report to the relevant enforcing authority. Once notified of a defect, the employer shall not use the lifting equipment until the defect is remedied.

Keeping of information (regulation 11)

9.100   If the employer has an EC declaration of conformity, he shall keep it for so long as he operates the equipment. The length of time other reports shall be kept will depend on the purposes for which they were made, which generally will be either until the employer ceases to use the equipment or for two years in other cases.

CHAPTER 10

Miscellaneous provisions

Health, safety and welfare in factories

10.1   As has been noted, one of the main objects of the Health and Safety at Work, etc Act 1974 (HSWA) was the repeal of much of pre-1974 legislation, to be replaced by new regulations and codes of practice. A prime candidate for repeal was the Factories Act 1961, which, although a major source of civil and criminal litigation, only gave statutory protection to those working in factories (as defined). Much of the Act has already been repealed, and replaced by regulations applicable to all employment situations (eg first aid, fire precautions, removal of dust and fumes, use of lead compounds, etc). Following the introduction of the "six pack" regulations in 1992 (see Chapter 4 and Chapter 6), further parts of the Act were repealed, and are only of relevance insofar as they concern litigation arising out of incidents which occurred when they were in force.

10.2   The latest provisions to be repealed are s.137 (notice of intention to occupy premises as a factory) and s.140 (requirement to keep a General Register), see Factories Act 1961 and Offices, Shops and Railway Premises Act 1963 (Repeals and Modifications) Regulations 2009.

10.3   The Factories Act 1961 only applies to factories as defined under the Act (s.175, and see *J & F Stone Lighting and Radio Ltd v Haygarth*). Its provisions were designed to protect all persons who worked in a factory, whether or not they were employed by the owner, occupier or employer, including self-employed persons, visitors, etc.

10.4   The following provisions of the Factories Act will remain in force for the time being.

Medical examinations (s.10A)

10.5   If an Employment Medical Advisor (EMA) (see Chapter 2) is of the opinion that a person's health has been or is being injured (or that it is possible that he is or will be injured) by reason of the work he is doing, the EMA may serve a notice on the factory occupier requiring the occupier to permit a medical examination of that person to take place. The notice will state the time, date and place of the examination, which must be at reasonable times during working hours. Every person to whom it relates shall be informed of its contents and of the fact that he is free to attend for that purpose. If the examination is to take place in the factory, suitable accommodation shall be provided.

Water-sealed gas holders (s.39)

10.6　Every gasholder which has a storage capacity of at least $140\text{m}^3/5000$ cubic feet shall be of sound construction and properly maintained. They must be examined externally by a competent person at least every two years, and a record containing the prescribed particulars entered into or attached to the general register (see the Gasholders (Record of Examinations) Order 1938).

Certificate of fitness (s.119)

10.7　If an inspector is of the opinion that the employment of a young person in a factory or a particular process is prejudicial to his health or to the health of other persons, he may serve a written notice to this effect on the occupier. The latter will not be able to continue to employ that young person in that place or on that process until the employment medical advisor has examined him and certified that he is fit to work in the factory or on the process.

Special applications (ss.121–127)

10.8　These sections make special provisions for applying the requirements of the Act (with appropriate modifications) to parts of buildings let off as a separate factory, electrical stations, charitable or reformatory institutions, docks, wharves, warehouses, ships, building operations and works of engineering construction.

Enforcement of the Act (s.155)

10.9　The main liability for criminal penalties is placed on the occupier of the factory or, in certain cases, the owner. If a person contravenes the provisions of a regulation or order made under the Act which expressly imposes a duty on him, then that person shall be guilty of an offence, and the owner or occupier shall not be guilty of an offence unless it is proved that he failed to take all reasonable steps to prevent the contravention (s.155(2)). The onus is on the prosecution to prove that the occupier or owner failed to take all reasonable steps to prevent the contravention (*Wright v Ford Motor Co Ltd*).

Penalties

10.10   The Factories Act 1961 is one of the existing statutory provisions for the purpose of s.33(3) of HSWA (see schedule 1), and if no other penalty is specified, offences will be punishable in accordance with the provisions of the Health and Safety (Offences) Act 2008, see paragraph 3.185.

Application to the Crown

10.11   The Act applies to factories belonging to or in the occupation of the Crown and to building operations or works of engineering construction undertaken by or on behalf of the Crown (s.173).

Health, safety and welfare in offices, shops and railway premises

10.12   Most of the provisions of the Offices, Shops and Railway Premises Act 1963 were repealed with the passing of the "six pack" regulations (see Chapter 6) (except in relation to registrars of births, marriages and deaths and members of a police force, when the Act will still apply).

10.13   The Act applies to offices, shops and railway premises, defined in s.1 as being premises wherein persons are employed under a contract of employment (or apprenticeship) for a total of 21 or more hours a week. Thus if only voluntary labour is used, the Act does not apply (however, other replacement legislation will, eg Workplace Regulations or PUWER). Nor does the Act apply if the only persons employed are close family members. Also excluded are premises of home workers, premises which form part of a factory, premises to which an exemption order applies, or premises used for a temporary or transitional purpose of not more than six weeks in the case of a fixed structure or six months in the case of a moveable structure.

10.14   The following provisions remain in force for the time being.

Multi-occupancy buildings (s.42)

10.15   A building which is under the ownership of one person but parts of which are leased or licensed to another must have clean common parts, and all furniture, furnishings and fittings in such common parts shall be kept in a clean state. Effective provision shall be made for securing and maintaining in common parts suitable and sufficient lighting (whether natural or artificial), and all glazed windows and skylights shall, so far as is reasonably practicable, be kept clean on both sides and free from obstruction (except when whitewashed or shaded for the purpose of reducing heat or glare). Floors, stairs, steps, passages and gangways shall be of sound construction and properly maintained, and shall, so far as is reasonably practicable, be kept free from any substance likely to cause any person to slip. Staircases shall be provided with a substantial handrail or handhold, and any open stairway shall be guarded by the provision and maintenance of efficient means of preventing any person from accidentally falling through the space.

10.16   In the event of a contravention of this section, the owner of the building will be guilty of an offence.

Offences (s.63)

10.17   Since most of the obligations imposed by the Act are placed on the occupier of the premises, it is he who will be primarily liable. If the Act provides that some other person shall be held responsible as well as the occupier, then both shall be liable. The owner is liable in certain multi-occupancy situations (see above).

Defences (s.67)

10.18   It shall be a defence for a person charged with an offence under the Act or a regulation to prove that he used all due diligence to secure compliance with that provision (see paragraph 1.119). This defence is, of course, applicable to criminal proceedings, not to civil liability, although in the latter case a plea of "no negligence" may equally succeed. "Due diligence" and "reasonable care" are similar concepts. In *J H Dewhurst Ltd v Coventry Corporation*, the defence of due diligence failed, for although the defendants had given the boy instructions, put up notices, and had received regular visits from the inspectors without adverse comment, the court considered that in view of the statutory prohibition, there was a special obligation to provide the necessary supervision. However, the defence succeeded in *Tesco Supermarkets Ltd v Natrass* (see paragraph 1.119).

Power to modify agreements (s.73)

10.19 If a person is prevented from doing any structural or other alteration to the premises necessary to comply with a provision of the Act because of the terms of a lease or agreement, he may apply to the local county court, which may make an order modifying or setting aside the terms of that lease or agreement as the court thinks just and equitable. If such alterations do become necessary, the court may also apportion the expense of doing so between the parties having an interest in the premises.

Application of the Act (s.83)

10.20 Insofar as the Act imposes duties which may give rise to civil liability (based on an action in tort) the Act is binding on the Crown (except in respect of the Armed Forces). So far as enforcement is concerned, although the HSE can inspect Crown premises, it is not possible to prosecute the Crown in the criminal courts.

Protection of the environment

10.21 Basically, health and safety legislation is concerned with the protection of workers and those affected by work activity. There is an obvious link between these objectives and the need for general environmental protection, and in many cases there is an overlap. As governments became more aware of the need to prevent pollution of the environment, both on a national and international level, new strategies have been developed, and complex legislative provisions enacted.

Food safety

10.22 The provisions of the Food Safety Act 1990 are peripheral to health and safety at work legislation, but are mentioned here in brief for the sake of completeness. Generally speaking, local authorities are to be the "food authorities" and they will appoint "authorised officers" (usually Environmental Health Officers (EHOs)) to act in matters arising under the legislation. It is an offence to render food so as to be injurious to health (eg by adding or abstracting anything), or to sell food not complying with food safety requirements. An authorised officer may inspect and seize suspected food and may also serve improvement and/or prohibition notices. In many ways the Act is an enabling Act, and the precise measures to be taken in order to deal with its provisions will be found in regulations. The Food Hygiene (England) Regulations 2006, the Food Hygiene (Wales) Regulations 2006 and the Food Hygiene (Scotland) Regulations 2006 provide that no person shall use any premises for the purpose of a food business on five days or more in any period of five consecutive weeks unless the food premises are registered. The regulations require food proprietors to ensure that food preparation, processing, manufacturing, packaging, storing, transportation, distribution and sale are carried out in a hygienic manner. The regulations also contain provisions relating to training, personal hygiene of food handlers, reporting of diseases capable of being transmitted through food, and require proprietors to carry out food safety risk assessments. The temperature of food is controlled by schedule 4 of the regulations, which define certain temperatures that must be achieved during various food-related processes.

Product safety

10.23 The General Product Safety Regulations 2005 are designed to implement Directive (92/59/EEC), and impose requirements concerning the safety of products intended for consumers, placed on the market by producers or supplied by distributors. There is a general obligation that a product shall not be placed on the market unless it is safe, the producer must provide information to the consumer informing of any risks the product might present, and the measures to be taken to counter those risks. Distributors must act with due care to ensure the product is safe and the relevant information is provided. The regulations do not apply to second-hand products which are antiques, or products supplied for repair or reconditioning before use, or where there are EU rules governing the safety of the particular product.

Working in agriculture

10.24 Every year a number of people are killed working in agriculture and related industries. There are thousands of non-fatal accidents, but it is suspected that there is considerable under-reporting in the industry.

10.25   Agricultural workers frequently work alone in remote places where immediate attention is not readily available. Supervision is minimal. The industry is highly mechanised, yet the general working environment is far from ideal and many dangerous substances are used. These facts illustrate the need for strong protective legislative measures and a greater need for educating workers in safe practices and procedures. The annual reports from the HSE's Agricultural Inspectorate discuss many of the hazards which arise while working on farms and considers some of the special problems. The Agricultural Industry Advisory Committee is engaged in a wide programme of work in looking at improvements which can be made to increase safety in the industry generally.

10.26   Following the introduction of the "six pack" regulations (see Chapter 4 and Chapter 6), most of the relevant provisions of the Agriculture (Safety, Health and Welfare Provisions) Act 1956 have been repealed. It is an offence to cause or permit a child to ride on or to drive a vehicle or machine or agricultural implement in contravention of the Prevention of Accidents to Children in Agriculture Regulations 1998. These provide that no child (ie a person below the age of 13) shall ride on certain agricultural vehicles while they are being used in the course of agricultural operations. The vehicles in question are tractors, self-propelled agricultural machines, trailers, trailers into which a conveyor mechanism is built, machines mounted on or towed by tractors, binders or mowers drawn by animals. A child may ride on the floor of a trailer or on any load carried by a trailer, provided it has four sides each of which is higher than the load. A child shall not drive a tractor or self-propelled vehicle or machine while it is being used in the course of agricultural operations, or ride on agricultural implements.

10.27   The HSE has issued a Code of Practice and Guidance Notes on this issue (L116: *Preventing Accidents to Children in Agriculture*).

10.28   The Health and Safety (Repeals and Revocations) Regulations 1996 have repealed (under the Deregulation and Contracting Out Act 1994) a number of legislative provisions relating to agriculture; these were outdated and have been superseded by the "six pack" regulations. Thus, regulations that specifically dealt with threshers and balers, ladders, field machinery, workplaces, poisonous substances, etc are no longer in force.

Offshore Safety Act 1992

10.29   This Act makes existing offshore safety legislation "relevant statutory provisions" for the purpose of HSWA. The effect is to transfer responsibility for offshore safety from the Department of Energy to the HSC/HSE, thus making the HSE responsible for the enforcement of all safety legislation relating to offshore activities. Further, the reform of existing offshore legislation can now be achieved by means of health and safety regulations made under s.15 of HSWA.

10.30   The Offshore Installations (Safety Case) Regulations 2005 replace the 1992 regulations and implement EU Directive 92/91/EEC. They require the preparation of safety cases for offshore installations, which cannot be put into operation until the safety case is accepted by the HSE. A safety case is a document containing specific information relating to the management of health and safety and the control of major accident hazards. The licensees must ensure that any operator they appoint is capable of carrying out his functions and discharging his duties satisfactorily, and there are various minimum requirements for improving the safety and health protection of workers in the mineral-extracting industries through drilling.

Pressure Systems Safety Regulations 2000

10.31   These regulations re-enact, with amendments, the Pressure Systems and Transportable Gas Containers Regulations 1989, which have consequently been revoked. Also repealed were ss.34–38 of the Factories Act 1961. The regulations apply to plant containing a "relevant fluid" (eg all steam systems, and a gas or fluid which has a vapour pressure greater than 0.5 bar above atmospheric pressure), which is used or intended to be used at work. The requirements or prohibitions imposed by the regulations on employers in respect of his employees also extend to a self-employed person in respect of his own activities at work. Requirements or prohibitions which are imposed on designers, manufacturers, importers or suppliers of components only extend to those matters for which such persons have within their control.

10.32   Designers, manufacturers, importers or suppliers of any pressure system or any article intended to be a component of a pressure system, must ensure that the system or article is properly designed, and constructed from suitable material. The design should be such that all necessary examinations can be carried out and, if there is means of access to the interior of a pressure system, access must be without danger. All necessary protective devices shall be provided. Designers and suppliers must provide written information concerning the design, construction, examination, operation and maintenance of pressure systems or articles intended to be a component. Manufacturers shall ensure that the pressure vessel has attached to it the manufacturer's name, a serial number, date of manufacture, standard to which the vessel was built, the maximum allowable pressure, the minimum allowance pressure (other than atmospheric) and the design temperature.

10.33   The installer of a pressure system shall ensure that nothing about the way it was installed gives rise to danger or impairs the operation of any protective device or inspection facility, and the user shall not operate the system until he has established the safe operating limits, and drawn up a written scheme for periodic examination by a competent person. The user will ensure that the competent person does in fact examine the system in accordance with the scheme, and the competent person shall make a written report of such examination as soon as is practicable after the examination. If the competent person is of the opinion that the pressure system will give rise to imminent danger unless certain repairs or modifications are carried out, he will make a report to that effect and send a copy to the local enforcing authority. The user shall not operate the system until the appropriate repairs, modifications or changes have been made.

10.34   The user of a pressure system will keep records of the last report made by the competent person, as well as previous reports if they contain information which will assist in assessing whether the system is safe to operate.

10.35   In proceedings for an offence under the regulations, it will be a defence to prove that the commission of the offence was due to the act or default of another person, and that all reasonable precautions were taken and due diligence exercised in order to avoid the commission of the offence. The regulations are accompanied by an Approved Code of Practice (L122: *Safety of Pressure Systems*).

Transportable Pressure Vessels Regulations 2001

10.36 The Transportable Pressure Vessels Regulations 2001 give effect to the Transportable Pressure Equipment Directive (1999/36/EC) and apply to any transportable pressure vessel used at work and manufactured on or after 1 July 2001, or vessels used or manufactured prior to that date which are subject to a reassessment of conformity. No person shall place on the market or use at work any transportable pressure vessel unless it is safe and suitable for the purpose, and designed and tested in accordance with specified standards. Valves must have been designed, manufactured and tested according to the specified standards, be safe and suitable for the purpose, assessed in accordance with relevant conformity assessment procedures and bear conformity markings or CE markings as appropriate. The owner of a transportable pressure vessel shall ensure that it is periodically inspected. In any proceedings for an offence in respect of contravention of the regulations, it will be a defence for the accused to show that the commission of the offence was due to the act or default of another person not being one of his employees, and that all reasonable precautions were taken and due diligence exercised to avoid the commission of the offence.

Metrication

10.37 All unmetricated health and safety legislation (apart from certain offshore legislation) must now be expressed in metric units of measurement (see Health and Safety (Miscellaneous Provisions) (Metrication, etc) Regulations 1992, which implement Directive 80/181/EEC. However, special provision has been made for the measurement of temperature and humidity in humid textile factories, where use is made of wet and dry bulb temperatures. The regulations also harmonise the flashpoint test measures in the Petroleum (Consolidation) Act 1928 and supporting regulations with the Chemicals (Hazard Information and Packaging for Supply) Regulations 2002 (as amended).

CHAPTER 11

Particular health and safety issues

Employment of women

11.1 All restrictions on the hours of work which women may work have now been abolished, as well as most of the restrictions on the type of work they may perform (Employment Act 1989, ss.4–9 and schedules 1 and 2). The remaining restrictions are as follows.

1. Under the Maternity and Parental Leave Regulations 1999 (regulation 7), a woman shall not be permitted to work by her employer during the period of two weeks beginning with the date of her confinement, and a breach of this provision is punishable by a fine not exceeding level 2 on the standard scale. Also, a woman must not be employed in a factory within four weeks of childbirth (Factories Act 1961, schedule 5; Public Health Act 1936, s.205).
2. Under the Control of Lead at Work Regulations 2002 (see paragraph 7.49), a woman of reproductive capacity is prohibited from being employed in certain processes and activities involving lead and lead products. These are:
   (a) in lead smelting and refining processes:
       (i) work involving the handling, treatment, sintering, smelting or refining of ores or materials containing not less than five per cent of lead
       (ii) the cleaning of any place where any of the above processes are carried out
   (b) in lead-acid battery manufacturing processes:
       (i) the manipulation of lead oxides
       (ii) mixing or pasting in connection with the manufacture or repair of lead batteries
       (iii) the melting or casting of lead
       (iv) the trimming, abrading or cutting of pasted plates in connection with the manufacture or repair of lead-acid batteries
       (v) the cleaning of any place where any of the above processes are carried out.

3. The Ionising Radiations Regulations 1999 (see paragraph 8.1) set lower dose limits for exposure to ionising radiation for women who are still of reproductive capacity and for pregnant women than the limit set for men.

4. There are restrictions on the employment of pregnant women as aircraft flight crew, air traffic controllers, and on merchant ships while at sea (Air Navigation Order 1995; Merchant Shipping (Medical Examination) Regulations 1983).

11.2   Indeed, it is lawful to discriminate against a woman in so far as it is necessary to comply with the above restrictions (Employment Act 1989, s.4).

11.3   There are a number of biological substances which may affect women adversely, particularly pregnant women, including rubella (German measles) and various hazards associated with working with animals, eg Chlamydia (working with sheep) and Brucellosis (working with cattle). Excessive noise and long periods of standing may also be injurious to a woman's health, and work equipment and personal protective equipment must be suitable. The need for a comprehensive risk assessment is apparent.

11.4   As a general rule, it can be stated that the critical exposure of a pregnant woman to deleterious substances is not so much in terms of the quantity or amount, but in the timing of exposure. The first six weeks of pregnancy when the foetus is being formed (and when possibly the woman might not even know she is pregnant) might well be the most critical time of all, together with the last three months of pregnancy when the brain of the foetus is being formed. An American organisation — the National Institute of Occupational Safety and Health (NIOSH) — has issued guidelines which may usefully be followed when a woman is exposed to potentially harmful substances. (Similar guidance is available from the Society for Occupational Medicine.) The NIOSH guidelines cover:

(a) when a pregnant woman may continue to work

(b) when she may continue to work but with environmental modifications to accommodate her working

(c) when she should not work at all.

11.5   An employer must make a general risk assessment if his workforce consists of women of childbearing age. Once the employer is aware that a woman employee is pregnant, or is breastfeeding, a second risk assessment needs to be made in respect of that woman, to ascertain what measures need to be taken to avoid the risk to her health. These risks could be heavy lifting, prolonged standing, night work, early shift work, work-related stress, threats from customers, exposure to nauseating smells, working excessive hours, lack of rest breaks, and so on. If measures cannot be taken to avoid the risk, the employer must alter her working hours or, if this is not feasible or would not avoid the risk, she should be offered alternative employment or put on paid leave of absence (ERA s.67, and regulation 16(3) of the Maternity, etc Regulations). The risk assessment does not need to be in writing when relating to a particular individual, because it is the employer's "thought process" which is relevant (*Stevenson v J M Skinner & Co*). Avoiding the risk does not mean eliminating it altogether. It means reducing the risk to the lowest acceptable level (*New Southern Railways Ltd v Quinn*).

Maternity rights

11.6   The Employment Rights Act 1996 (ERA) provides that a woman employee who is pregnant has a number of statutory rights.

11.7   First, if, on the advice of a registered general practitioner or midwife or health visitor, she has made an appointment to attend an ante-natal clinic, she has the right not to be unreasonably refused time off work to attend. She must produce documentary evidence of such an appointment (though not for the first appointment), and she is entitled to be paid at her appropriate hourly rate (ERA, s.55).

11.8   Second, she may be suspended from work on maternity grounds where, in consequence of:
   (a) any requirement imposed by an enactment (including regulations), or
   (b) any recommendation in an Approved Code of Practice (ACOP)

she is entitled to be suspended because she is pregnant, has recently given birth, or is breast-feeding a child (ERA, s.66).

11.9   The Suspension from Work (on Maternity Grounds) Order 1994 (as amended) specifies regulation 16–18 of the Management of Health and Safety at Work Regulations 1999 to be the relevant statutory provision for the purpose of s.66. There are thus two grounds for maternity suspension:
   (a) if the risk assessment of women of child-bearing age (see

paragraph 4.62) reveals a risk which cannot be avoided, the employer shall, if it is reasonable to do so, and would avoid such risks, alter her working conditions or hours of work; if it is not reasonable to do so (or if doing so would not avoid the risk) the employer shall suspend her from work for as long as is necessary to avoid such risk (regulation 16 of the Management Regulations). However, the employer is not required to take any such action unless the woman informs him, in writing, that she is pregnant, or has given birth within the previous six months, or that she is breast-feeding (regulation 18)

(b) where a new or expectant mother works at night, and a certificate from a registered general practitioner or midwife shows that it is necessary for her health or safety that she should not be at work for any period of such work, the employer shall suspend her for as long as is necessary (regulation 17).

11.10   These provisions were considered by an employment tribunal in *Hickey v Lucas Services* where, following a finding of dissatisfaction with the applicant's performance, she was told that she had to transfer to work as a stores assistant in a warehouse. She discovered that she was pregnant, and because the new work would have involved her lifting heavy objects, she was advised by her doctor that this could constitute a risk to her health and to the health of her unborn child. Consequently, she went off work sick and was paid statutory sick pay. She complained to an employment tribunal that she should have received her full pay, as she had been effectively suspended from work on maternity grounds, and was thus entitled to her usual remuneration under s.68 of the ERA. Her claim was upheld. The employers had not carried out a risk assessment as required by the Management Regulations and, had they done so, they would have realised that the risks to her health could not be avoided by preventative or protective measures. Thus they should have altered her working conditions or suspended her on full pay under ss.66–67 of ERA.

11.11   Before suspending the woman from work under the above provisions, the employer, where he has suitable alternative work for her, must offer her such work. The work must be suitable for her and appropriate in the circumstances, and the terms and conditions, if they differ from those which normally pertain to her work, must not be substantially less favourable than those which previously applied (ERA, s.67). Otherwise, she is entitled to be paid her normal remuneration, unless she is offered suitable alternative employment which she unreasonably refuses (s.68).

11.12 Third, irrespective of her period of continuous employment, she is entitled to 26 weeks' ordinary maternity leave, followed by a further period of 26 weeks' additional maternity leave. Statutory maternity pay (SMP) will be paid for 39 weeks, which the employer can recoup from the amount of national insurance contributions which are paid to HM Revenue & Customs. During her period of ordinary and additional maternity leave she is entitled to all the benefits of her terms and conditions of employment, except those relating to the payment of remuneration.

11.13 Fourth, if she does not qualify for SMP because she lacks the relevant period of continuous employment, she may be entitled to Maternity Allowance payable by the Department for Work and Pensions.

11.14 Fifth, the Maternity and Parental Leave Regulations 1999 (regulation 20) provides that it will be unfair to dismiss a woman because:
  (a) she was pregnant
  (b) she gave birth to a child
  (c) she was suspended from work because of a requirement set out in regulation 16 of the Management of Health and Safety at Work Regulations 1999 (see paragraph 4.63) or a recommendation contained in a Code of Practice issued by the HSE
  (d) she took ordinary or additional maternity leave
  (e) she failed to return to work after maternity leave when the employer did not notify her when her leave would end
  (f) she refused to work during her maternity leave period, or
  (g) she was made redundant and not offered a suitable vacancy.

11.15 It will also be recalled (see paragraph 6.48) that under the Workplace Regulations suitable rest facilities for pregnant and breast-feeding workers shall be provided and under the Management of Health and Safety at Work Regulations 1999 a risk assessment must be carried out in respect of new or expectant mothers (see paragraph 4.62). Indeed, the failure by an employer to carry out such a risk assessment in relation to a pregnant woman who is required to do heavy lifting work can amount to unlawful sex discrimination (*Hardman v Mallon (t/a Orchard Lodge Nursing Home)*).

11.16   The HSE has issued some guidance documents, HSG122: *New and Expectant Mothers at Work: A Guide for Employers* and *Infection Risks to New and Expectant Mothers: A Guide for Employers* (ISBN 0 7176 1360 7).

11.17   It is generally accepted that English law would not provide a remedy for any injury suffered to a foetus while *en ventre sa mère*, there being no duty owed in tort and no statutory duty applicable. The thalidomide tragedy highlighted this problem, and the Congenital Disabilities (Civil Liability) Act 1976 was passed. It was intended to be a temporary measure, pending legislation consequent on the report of the Pearson Commission, but as the recommendations of the latter are unlikely to be the subject of Parliamentary action in the foreseeable future, the Act remains.

11.18   It provides that a child who is born disabled as a result of any breach of duty (whether through negligence or breach of statutory duty) to either parent, will be able to bring a civil action against the person responsible. In practice this will mean that if something happens to a woman while she is pregnant which results in her child being born disabled, the child will have a separate right of action. Since the Limitation Act 1980 does not apply to a minor (ie one under the age of 18) he may be able to bring a claim any time within three years from attaining his majority, ie potentially 21 years after the event which caused the disability. There must be a breach of duty to the child's parent, but it is not necessary that the parent be injured. The disability may be something which happened to either parent which prevents the mother from having a normal child, or an injury to the mother while she is pregnant, or an injury to the foetus during pregnancy.

11.19   If the person responsible would have been liable to the parent, he is liable to the child. The child must be born alive, for there is no duty to the foetus as such. It is not relevant that the person responsible knew that the woman was pregnant, as long as a duty was owed to her. Thus if a woman is working with a chemical which causes her to have a disabled child as a result of ingesting minute particles, an action will lie against the employer by the child.

11.20   This can cause some concern among those employers who regularly use chemicals, for there are a number of substances which are suspect so far as pregnant women are concerned, eg vinyl chloride, benzene, mercury, lead, etc. Molecules of almost any substance can pass through the placenta, and therefore any woman may, by ingesting, inhaling, or through skin absorption, pass a deleterious ingredient into her baby.

11.21 The Act poses problems for employers who have to balance delicately between the law against sex discrimination on the one hand and liability to unknown potential plaintiffs on the other.

Working alone

11.22 There are some situations where there is a serious risk to a person if he is injured while working alone, because he is unable to summon help.

11.23 There are a number of legal provisions which specify systems of working that require more than one person. These include:
- (a) Work in Compressed Air Regulations 1996
- (b) Diving at Work Regulations 1997
- (c) Control of Substances Hazardous to Health Regulations 2002
- (d) Carriage of Dangerous Goods and Use of Transportable Pressure Equipment Regulations 2007
- (e) Electricity at Work Regulations 1989.

11.24 There are other provisions that require work to be done "under the immediate supervision of a competent person" or similar wording, which would suggest that the work, although carried out by one person, must be done in the presence of another.

11.25 Persons particularly at risk include those whose activities involve handling cash (eg rent collectors), persons working with vulnerable clients (eg carers, health visitors, etc), and persons whose work takes them to remote locations (home visitors, etc). A Lone Worker Policy should be drawn up, taking into account the findings of a risk assessment, giving advice on how to deal with challenging behaviour, the development of communication skills to diffuse confrontational situations, and equipment and/or procedures for obtaining help and assistance.

11.26   For example, the Government recently announced that it will provide some 30,000 lone NHS workers with personal security alarms in an effort to improve the health and security of staff. Initially these will be given to workers who work with patients and their families and/or associates who have a history of violence or drug abuse or a clinical condition which heightens the risk to the lone worker and to those who work in areas of high crime and social deprivation.

11.27   The Health and Safety Executive (HSE) has produced a leaflet, *Working Alone in Safety*, to which reference may be made.

Working abroad

11.28   An employer may send an employee to another country to work, perhaps for a temporary period, and the question then arises as to the employer's duty to ensure the employee's health and safety. The Health and Safety at Work Act does not apply in foreign countries, where local laws will be relevant. But since the employer's duty is to take reasonable care, and does not involve an absolute guarantee, the circumstances of each case must be considered. In *Cook v Square D Ltd*, the plaintiff worked for the defendant company. Part of his duties took him to Saudi Arabia, where he worked on the premises of a reputable oil company. Also working on the site was a reputable main contractor. The plaintiff was working in a computer control room, the floor of which consisted of large tiles. One of these tiles had been lifted by the main contractor, and the plaintiff tripped and injured his knee. He claimed damages from his employers arguing that they had been negligent. A High Court Judge found in his favour, arguing that his employers had not taken proper steps to ensure his safety, but this decision was reversed by the Court of Appeal. It was noted that both the occupier of the premises and the main contractor were reputable companies, and it was not for the defendants to advise them of the need to take precautions against the type of hazard which caused the plaintiff's injury. Further, it was stated that "the suggestion that the home-based employer has any responsibility for the daily events of a site in Saudi Arabia has an air of unreality".

11.29   Nonetheless, it was suggested that if an employee is being sent to a foreign site to work there for a considerable period of time, an employer may be required to inspect the site and satisfy himself that the occupiers are conscious of their obligations concerning the health and safety of people working there.

11.30   Although an employer is required to take out compulsory insurance for the benefit of his employees (see paragraph 5.1) there is no duty to do so in respect of employees who are working abroad. Nor need an employer advise an employee to take out his own insurance cover. In *Reid v Rush & Tompkins Group plc*, the claimant worked for the defendants in Ethiopia. He received severe injuries in a road accident which was the fault of the other driver, for whom the defendants had no responsibility. The claimant was unable to recover damages from the other driver, as there was no third party insurance in Ethiopia, and so he sued his employers in the UK. His statement of claim was struck out. The employer owed no duty to inform or advise on the potential danger of suffering economic loss in the form of uncompensated injuries.

Working at height

11.31   About two-fifths of all serious injuries at work are caused by workers falling from a height, and such falls are the commonest cause of fatalities. The proper planning of working premises and systems of work would obviate the need for certain types of work (maintenance, servicing, etc) to be done in circumstances where there is a risk of falls, and plant and equipment should be installed with the problem in mind. The Construction (Design and Management) Regulations 2007 (see paragraph 9.4) place specific duties on designers and architects to ensure that health and safety features are considered at the earliest stage of a project, and these features must be applied during all subsequent stages of the project up to completion.

11.32   The relevant statutory provisions are now contained in the Work at Height Regulations 2005 (see paragraph 9.71), which lay down a full and comprehensive code on methods to be adopted to prevent injuries from falls or falling objects, and dangers from working on or near fragile surfaces.

11.33   There are a number of ways the risks of falling from height can be prevented. First, there is the provision of adequate information about the nature of the risk and the precautions to be taken. There should be clear and accurate instructions given about safe systems of work and safety rules to be followed. Employees should be thoroughly trained not only in the nature of the work to be done, but also in how to do the work safely. Competent supervisors should ensure that safe working practices are followed.

11.34   Second, there should be proper planning in the use and provision of proper access equipment. Included in this category are ladders, scaffolding, mobile towers, or powered equipment, each of which has its own hazard if proper care is not taken in the use or maintenance.

11.35   Third, access to areas where employees may fall can be restricted by the use of fencing, covers for tanks and pits, guard-rails, toe boards, barriers, etc.

11.36   Fourth, fall restraint equipment should be provided if there is no other suitable alternative method of preventing a fall. This includes harnesses (with suitable anchor points) safety nets, safety belts, etc.

11.37   Foresight of the risk can, more often than not, reduce or eliminate the risk totally.

Immigrant workers

11.38   There is no evidence to suggest that immigrant workers are more prone to accidents than any other group of employees, although since immigrants tend to be employed in those industries where there are greater dangers, obviously they may have a higher than average accident rate. The problem must be tackled by means of adequate training and language and cultural factors must be taken into account. Safety instructions may have to be prepared in the language of the worker concerned and signs and posters which need little translation should be used to indicate the hazards and/or the precautions to be taken. Several health and safety regulations, eg Management of Health and Safety at Work Regulations 1999, require employers to provide employees with "comprehensible" information, which implies that account should be taken of language difficulties. Indeed, if an employee has a limited command of the English language, there is need for a greater degree of training, instruction and supervision (*Tasci v Pekpal of London Ltd*). In *James v Hepworth and Grandage Ltd*, the employers put up a notice which stated that spats should be worn. Unknown to them, the claimant could not read English and he was injured through not wearing spats. His claim for compensation failed. He had observed other workmen wearing spats and his failure to make any enquiries about them led to the conclusion that he would not have worn them anyway. However, this case cannot be regarded as authority for the proposition that an employer fulfils his legal duty by merely drawing attention to a precaution (see Chapter 12) and if there is a risk of a more serious injury, greater steps must be taken to ensure the use of protective clothing, etc. Further, in *Hawkins v Ian Ross (Castings) Ltd*, an employee was injured partly because he was working alongside an immigrant who had a limited command of English and who misunderstood a warning shout. The court held that in such circumstances, a higher standard of care is required on the employers when considering the layout of the work and the steps to be taken to avoid accidents.

11.39 Language barriers may not be used as a device to exclude immigrants from employment and attempts to impose language tests have resulted in allegations of racial discrimination. The problem will no doubt be with us for many years, for although we tend to equate immigration with the influx from Asian or African countries, as a result of Article 48 of the Treaty of Rome concerning the free movement of workers throughout the European Union there has been an influx of non-English speaking workers from Europe. Training for safety officers may well include some form of instruction in foreign languages in the not-too-distant future.

11.40 The Race Relations Act 1976 makes it unlawful to discriminate on grounds of colour, race, nationality, ethnic or national origins, in the recruitment, employment or dismissal of any person. But if a requirement or condition is applied to all employees, irrespective of the racial, ethnic or national origins, then although it may be indirectly discriminatory of a particular group, such indirect discrimination is capable of being objectively justified and hence not unlawful under the Act. Thus, in *Dhanjal v British Steel General Steels*, all employees were required to wear hard hats. The applicant refused to do so because, as a Sikh, his religion did not permit him to remove his turban. In consequence, he was dismissed. An employment tribunal held that the company's desire to conform to health and safety legislation justified the discriminatory action, and that the dismissal was fair. (It should be noted that there is an exemption for Sikhs from wearing hard hats on building sites, see paragraph 9.64).

11.41 The Immigration, Asylum and Nationality Act 2006 makes it a criminal offence to employ a person who has not been granted leave to enter or remain in the UK, or who is subject to a condition prohibiting employment.

11.42 The HSE has produced a basic health and safety guide written in 29 different languages for the benefit of ethnic minorities, and a number of publications have been translated into languages other than English.

Sick building syndrome

11.43 Sick building syndrome is a convenient term which is sometimes used to describe certain mild symptoms, somewhat similar to the common cold, together with headaches, low concentration, and a general feeling of irritability and lethargy. It is usually associated with office work, and the symptoms tend to disappear when away from the building. It has nothing to do with illnesses generally associated with more specific hazards, nor to identifiable physical conditions brought on by environmental factors. It is not a recognised illness and its causes are unknown. Its presence is likely to be indicated by an increase in absenteeism, reduced efficiency and a general lowering of morale.

11.44 If sick building syndrome is suspected, the first step should be to ensure that all the requirements of the Workplace (Health, Safety and Welfare) Regulations have been complied with, together with the advice given in the Approved Code of Practice (ACOP) (L24: *Workplace Health, Safety and Welfare*). Consultation with employees may reveal their concerns, and possibly lead to a reorganisation of job factors, office design or the changing of furnishings and fittings, etc. Cleaning, ventilation, mild pollutants in the atmosphere (tobacco smoke, unpleasant smells from various sources, etc) should be attended to. Redecoration, designed to create a warm, friendly atmosphere, may also assist.

11.45 The HSE has produced a Guidance Document, HSG132: *How to Deal with Sick Building Syndrome: Guidance for Employers, Building Owners and Building Managers*, to which reference may be made.

Drug abuse

11.46 Generally, it is not the concern of an employer what an employee does outside working hours, but this rule may not necessarily apply if those actions have some effect or impact on work activities. There are a number of telling signs which may indicate whether an employee is having a drug problem, including frequent absenteeism, poor performance, erratic behaviour, lateness, repetitive minor illnesses, etc. Management can be trained in recognition techniques, although it may be advisable to have assistance from the police when it comes to training in identifying the actual substances. Once the signs have been recognised, help by way of counselling, medical examinations, etc can be offered.

11.47   However, it is always better to pre-empt a problem before it arises than to have to deal with it after it has caused difficulties. The first step is to have a clearly worded policy statement, drawn to the attention of all employees, setting out the employer's prohibition on having illegal substances on the premises, and noting that employees who take such substances outside working hours will be disciplined if their actions (a) have a deleterious effect on work performance, or (b) bring the employer's business into disrepute.

11.48   In cases of minor infringements of the company's rules on the taking or possession of drugs, the disciplinary procedure should be invoked and warnings, etc given, but in serious cases, stronger measures should be taken.

11.49   Thus, in *Mathewson v RB Wilson Dental Laboratories Ltd*, the applicant, during his lunch break, purchased a small amount of cannabis for his own use, but was arrested by the police. His employers dismissed him because they felt that they could no longer employ a person who was using drugs. They also thought that he might adversely influence younger members of staff. An employment tribunal held that his dismissal was fair, and this was upheld on appeal. The decision to dismiss fell within the range of reasonable responses of a reasonable employer.

11.50   It is an offence under the Misuse of Drugs Act 1971 for an occupier knowingly to permit the possession of certain controlled drugs on his premises. Thus, if an employee is known to possess drugs on his person, it may be a ground for dismissal (*Mathewson v RB Wilson Ltd* above).

Alcohol at work

11.51   Similar considerations apply to alcohol abuse. These matters are best dealt with by a clearly defined policy statement or in the works/staff rules.

11.52   As a general rule, an employer owes no duty of care towards an employee to prevent him consuming an excess amount of alcohol which results in the employee suffering an injury or even death, although the normal duty of care would arise if it is necessary to provide medical care and/or assistance should he collapse while at work (*Barrett v Ministry of Defence*).

11.53   The HSE has published a guidance document, *Don't Mix It — A Guide for Employers on Alcohol at Work.*

Policies for alcohol and drug abuse

11.54   There are many employment positions where it is inherently unsafe for employees to take unlawful drugs or excessive quantities of alcohol. Airline pilots, lorry drivers, employees who work with dangerous substances or machinery are but a few examples. No one would care to be operated on by a surgeon whose breath smelt of drink; no one would care to be a passenger in a vehicle driven by an individual who has been taking cocaine.

11.55   The first problem for the safety conscious employer who wishes to stamp out substance abuse, and ensure safety for employees and for others, is that of detection. It cannot be sufficient to rely on the suspicions (however well-founded), of supervisors, managers, etc. Should disciplinary action (including dismissal) take place, the employee will doubtless plead innocence. The fact that the supervisor thought that the employee's breath smelt of alcohol will be challenged; seeing an employee staggering about will be put down to a trip or stumble. Employment tribunals require solid proof and are not always consistent. They are not likely to be sympathetic to precipitous actions, even those taken for the best of motives.

11.56   Currently, the main method of detection is by the taking of blood or urine samples. These are intrusive, and require the services of an expert, such as a doctor or occupational nurse who is skilled in taking and handling the sample. If the testing is done on a substantial scale, there must be secure procedures, so that there can be no doubt that samples have not been mixed up.

11.57   Finally, the employee must consent to the taking of a blood or urine sample. To do this without such consent would be an assault, and the person responsible could incur criminal penalties. If the employee refuses to give consent, the employer may possibly need to consider disciplinary proceedings. The action taken will also depend on the status of the individual, ie whether an employee, a subcontractor or an employee of a subcontractor. These are difficult issues with no ready answers.

11.58 However, there are a number of common law and statutory provisions to which the employer must pay attention, including the Health and Safety at Work, etc Act 1974, the Misuse of Drugs Act 1971, the Transport and Works Act 1992, the Railways and Transport Safety Act 2003, the various regulations outlined in Chapter 4 and Chapter 6, as well as the common law duties. Thus, as well as criminal liabilities for permitting an employee to work who has had an excess of alcohol or who is known to be taking unlawful drugs, civil liabilities may also exist if an accident occurs and someone (not necessarily the drug or alcohol user) is injured. There is also the adverse effect on the employer's business to consider, should an incident attract publicity, depending, of course, on the nature of that business.

11.59 There is some scope to argue that the employer should treat the matter as a health problem, rather than institute disciplinary proceedings against the employee concerned. In other words, the employee should be encouraged to seek medical assistance rather than face dismissal. This sympathetic approach may work if the health and safety risks involved are not likely to be very great, or if no dangerous incident has happened. However, it is unlikely to be a satisfactory solution if drink or drugs can be seen to have caused an accident or injury, and employment tribunals generally will take a fairly robust approach to claims of unfairness made by the person responsible. Nevertheless, forethought and prevention is the preferable approach.

11.60 Modern science has come up with one solution which could well be of considerable assistance to employers wishing to take a firm stand on drug and alcohol abuse. Oral fluid testing is a technique which is simple to use, and accurate in its results. A specially treated pad is used to collect fluid from all areas of the mouth until the swab is saturated. This can then be tested to give an almost instant reading of the level of alcohol and/or drugs present in the subject's system. It can be used by anyone with a minimum of training, and is reliable and effective.

11.61 However, employers must be aware of the need to follow proper procedures. Ideally, there should be full consultation with representatives of trade unions or other employee representatives of safety, although the agreement of such bodies is not essential. Each employee should be asked, in advance, to sign a consent form, agreeing to undergo such tests on a random basis, either before starting work, during work or immediately after ceasing work. Specific persons should be nominated to operate the testing procedures, and disciplinary proceedings which follow should be fair and consistent. There should also be warnings that severe disciplinary action (including dismissal) will follow if the employee is found to have used unlawful drugs and/or has been drinking alcohol. The level of tolerance must be related to the activity and the risks. Thus, whereas zero tolerance may be the benchmark for airline pilots who are about to commence duty, or lorry drivers who are about to drive their vehicles (or who have been driving, etc), perhaps a more lenient approach may be taken in the case of an office worker or someone whose activities are unlikely to cause injury.

11.62 A major difficulty will arise if the employee refuses to sign such a consent form. The employee may seek to invoke the provisions of the Human Rights Act 1998 (see paragraph 1.160). Article 8 of the European Convention states that "Everyone has the right to respect for his private and family life..." and the employee may argue that what is done in non-working hours is no concern of the employer. This may be true, but if what an employee does impinges on the employer's business, different considerations would apply. Article 8 specifically excludes from that right actions taken in accordance with the law, in the interests of public safety and for the protection of health and morals. Thus the employee's argument is unlikely to succeed — but can the employer enforce the consent form by taking disciplinary action against recalcitrant employees? There is no direct legal authority on the point, but it is submitted that if consultation and persuasion do not succeed, and if the employer can show a genuine concern for the safety and health of others, or that there would be an adverse effect on the business should an incident occur, it is likely that disciplinary action, including dismissal, will be held to be fair. For new employees, the matter should be made part of the contractual obligations entered into, to remove this potential issue altogether.

Other illnesses

11.63   There are a number of contagious diseases which call for special consideration if contracted by an employee or, indeed, in appropriate circumstances, when an employee comes into contact with an infected person during the course of his employment. These include hepatitis, HIV/AIDS, herpes, other sexually transmitted diseases, tuberculosis, typhoid, rubella, chicken pox, etc. A full assessment of the health risks should be made, in consultation with medical advisors, and consideration should be given to a period of suspension so as to minimise the risks revealed.

11.64   There are some occupations where employees are particularly vulnerable, eg health workers, laboratory workers, and those in contact with animals or animal products, etc (see Directive 2000/54/EC).

11.65   Certain occupational diseases are reportable under the Reporting of Injuries, Disease and Dangerous Occurrences Regulations 1995. For a disease to be reportable, the person at work (including a self-employed person) must be suffering from a disease specified in column 1 of Part II of schedule 3 of the regulations, and the work must involve one of the corresponding activities in column 2. However, the disease is only reportable in the case of an employee if the responsible person receives a written statement from a registered medical practitioner diagnosing the disease as one of those specified.

Acts of violence against employees

11.66   Recent studies have indicated that acts of violence against employees while carrying out their employment duties are on the increase, and the matter is clearly becoming a factor in health and safety policies. Such acts may be committed by fellow employees, customers or third parties. So far as acts perpetrated by employees are concerned, these should be dealt with within the confines of the disciplinary procedures (see paragraph 13.42), and generally an employee would be left to pursue his own legal remedies, either criminal or civil, for assault.

11.67   The possibility of an employee suffering an act of violence while at work should be included in the risk assessment. There may be organisations where there is no history of such acts, but if it can be shown that the risk is not negligible, either in that particular type of industry or because of special features of the organisation, ways of avoiding or mitigating against such acts should be considered. Employees particularly at risk include those who handle cash in isolation (eg all-night petrol stations, rent collectors in certain housing estates), those who come into contact with violent people who are affected by drink or drugs (eg social workers, carers), those who have to deal with dissatisfied customers or complainants (eg clerks in Benefits Agency offices) those who handle or transport cash or valuables (eg cashiers, diamond merchants) and so on.

11.68 So far as acts committed by others are concerned, the general test of the conduct of the reasonable employer has to be applied and the question posed, has the employer taken reasonable care to see that his employees are not exposed to the risk of injury, even by criminals? The employer must take precautions against risks which he knows of or which he ought to know. Thus, in *Houghton v Hackney Borough Council*, a rent collector, employed by the defendants, was attacked while collecting rents on a housing estate. He alleged that the council had been negligent in failing to take proper precautions to protect him from injury. On the facts of the case, his claim for damages failed. The council had taken a number of precautionary steps, such as arranging for an estate porter to be around when rents were being collected, inviting the police to keep a watchful eye on the estate, and arranging for the claimant to be collected by car in order to take all the monies to the bank. In the circumstances, it was not negligent.

11.69 There are some employments where the risk of being assaulted is not a negligible one, for example, when dealing with violent offenders or mentally disturbed people. This does not mean that the employee voluntarily accepts the risk of being injured (see paragraph 12.68), and the employer must still exercise reasonable care to ensure appropriate protection and assistance (see *Michie v Shenley and Napsbury General Hospital Management Committee*).

11.70 But if an employee is injured while engaging in horseplay, the defence of consent to the risk of being injured may be raised. A duty of care will arise only if the conduct of one party amounts to recklessness or a very high degree of carelessness (*Blake v Galloway*).

11.71 It should finally be noted that if the employer fails to institute the necessary precautions to protect an employee from violence, the employee may resign his employment, and claim constructive dismissal (see paragraph 13.34).

11.72   Although there are no statutory provisions on this subject, reference may be made to s.2(1) of HSWA (see paragraph 3.25) and the Management of Health and Safety at Work Regulations 1999 (see paragraph 4.8) which require an employer to make an assessment of the risks to the health and safety of employees to which they are exposed while at work, and arrangements for dealing with that risk must be put into effect. As has been noted, these provisions do now give rise to civil liability (see paragraph 4.74).

11.73   Once the risk has been determined, appropriate measures can be taken. The working environment can be changed as appropriate, systems of work can be monitored and made safe, security measures can be introduced, and appropriate training given on how to counter acts of violence, or the effects thereof.

11.74   An act of violence at work which causes an injury to an employee and is associated with work activity is reportable under the Reporting of Injuries, Diseases and Dangerous Occurrences Regulations 1995 (see paragraph 5.62).

Agency workers

11.75   An agency worker may be an employee of the agency which hired him (*McMeecham v Secretary of State for Employment*), an employee of the client company where he works (*Franks v Reuters Ltd*), or an employee of neither, ie a self-employed independent contractor (*Bunce v Postworth Ltd*).

11.76   In practice, there are three different scenarios to consider when dealing with the status of agency workers. The first arises out of employment legislation, when it has to be determined whether or not the worker is legally an employee, for such issues as unfair dismissal, redundancy payments, and other rights which exist for employees. So far as employment status is concerned, there have been a number of recent cases on this topic. The fact that the arrangement has existed for a considerable length of time does not, by itself, give rise to an employment relationship (*James v Greenwich Council*) and generally speaking the tribunals and courts have taken the view that contractually expressed intentions will be preferred over the way in which the arrangement works in practice (*Astbury v Gist*) unless the documentation is totally unrealistic (*Consistent Group Ltd v Kalwak*).

11.77   The second issue arises when prosecutions are considered under the Health and Safety at Work, etc Act 1974 and associated regulations, which generally speaking only apply to employees, although under the Management of Health and Safety at Work Regulations 1999 an employer also owes duties to visiting workers and temporary workers.

11.78   If the worker is an employee of the agency, the latter should ensure that the employee is suitable to carry out the tasks assigned to him by the client. The agency also has all the responsibilities which arise from health and safety legislation, including training, risk assessments, the provision of protective equipment, etc. However, under regulation 12 of the Management of Health and Safety at Work Regulations, an employer shall ensure that employees from an outside undertaking are provided with comprehensive information on risks arising from the employer's activities, and the measures taken by him to comply with the relevant statutory provisions. In other words, the client employer owes duties in addition to those owed by the agency employer.

11.79   If the worker is an employee of the client company, then obviously the latter has all the duties placed on the employer by the legislation. Difficulties sometimes arise when the worker is an employee of neither the agency nor the client. Many of the duties imposed by the Act on employers also apply to self-employed persons. Thus self-employed workers have a duty under regulation 11(2) to co-operate with other employers so far as is necessary to enable them to comply with the various statutory provisions, under regulation 12 to provide comprehensible information on the risks to health and safety arising from his conduct, and under regulation 15(2)–(3) to provide comprehensible information on any special occupational qualifications or skills needed by employees of the employer.

11.80   Thirdly, claims for injuries based on common law negligence or vicarious liability are sometimes treated by the courts in a more relaxed manner, as the real defendant is the insurance company, not the employer! The courts are more likely to find in favour of an injured workman irrespective of who owes the common law duty of care. Usually, the client-employer owes an overall duty to co-ordinate the activities of all persons working on his premises, irrespective of whether such persons are his employees, or agency employees, or self-employed sub-contractors. Thus in *McArdle v Andmac Roofing Co* the claimant worked for one of several sub-contractors who were employed converting a building at a holiday camp. The site owners (Pontins (Contractors) Ltd) made no arrangements for safety precautions with the sub-contractors, and as a result the claimant suffered an injury when he fell off a roof. It was held that Pontins, as the main contractors, assumed the responsibility for co-ordinating the work and were therefore under a duty to ensure that reasonable safety precautions were taken by all those working on the site, even though they were not their employees.

11.81 To ensure compliance with health and safety legislation and common law duties, the agency and the client-employer should clarify in the relevant documentation the legal situation and allocate responsibilities accordingly. It should be made clear who would be responsible for the provision of PPE, first aid, training, risk assessments, information, reporting of injuries, etc.

Homeworkers

11.82 There is a growing tendency for more and more employees to work from home, where the work can be done this way efficiently. From the employer's point of view, there is a saving in working space and overheads, the employee gains by having to avoid spending time and money travelling, and can enjoy any relevant home comforts. The use of computers and other modern communication aids means that there can be an immediate exchange of information; employees working from home are no less in touch than employees who work on the employer's premises.

11.83 Nonetheless, the employer's responsibility for the health and safety of his employees, particularly as set out in s.2(2) of the Health and Safety at Work, etc Act 1974 (HSWA), still exists in respect of homeworkers, and such employees should not be disregarded by those concerned with health and safety. As always, the first step is to carry out a risk assessment (see paragraph 4.8), with particular attention to the potentially unusual and/or unexpected problems which could arise. For example, employees who work in a home environment could have their working area or equipment affected by children or visitors, etc. Ideally, segregation from the rest of the house would avoid many problems (eg in a separate room which was locked, or keeping work equipment in a locked cupboard, etc), but if this is not possible steps must be taken to ensure that neither the employee nor others who come into his house are adversely affected by any work activity. Equipment used by the worker must also meet the statutory requirements (see Chapter 6), and this applies not only to the technology used (computers, machines, etc) but also to ordinary items such as desks and chairs, even though these are initially provided by the employee.

11.84 Electrical equipment generally must comply with the requirements of the Electricity at Work Regulations 1989 (see paragraph 8.12), any hazardous substances used or provided must be assessed and identified under the COSHH Regulations (see paragraph 7.1) and training and instruction given as appropriate. The Health and Safety (Display Screen Equipment) Regulations 1992 (see paragraph 6.151) will be of particular importance, and the employer must ensure that, for example, the desks, chairs, etc supplied by the employee are suitable, and do not give rise to any risks. Other relevant legislation which will need to be considered includes provisions relating to first aid, reporting of accidents, etc.

11.85 Similar considerations apply to those employees who work in someone else's home. There is a growing army of professional carers who provide various services in the homes of the elderly, sick and disabled. Such carers are frequently at risk in relation to back injuries (when lifting or trying to move patients), violence (dealing with the mentally disturbed people who have been discharged into the community), simple domestic hazards (caused by the untidy nature of the premises), and so on. A full risk assessment is necessary, together with whatever training and supervision may be found necessary in the circumstances. If the risk assessment identifies a potential problem, appropriate precautions should be taken, eg the provision of personal security alarms, ensuring that employees are accompanied, training given in self-defence methods, the provision of a breakdown recovery service (for employees who may become stranded in vehicles) or mobile telephones, and so on.

11.86 The HSE has issued a Guidance Note, *Homeworking: Guidance for Employers and Employees on Health and Safety.*

Bullying at work

11.87 One of the more frequent causes of stress and other work-related illnesses arises from bullying at work, which would normally, but not necessarily, stem from the actions by senior members of the workforce. Frequently, this is caused by some form of interpersonal conflict, and can take a number of different forms, apart from physical violence. Subtle forms of bullying can take place when someone in authority deliberately withholds essential information or makes belittling remarks; unwarranted criticism, public humiliation, unnecessary threats, veiled hints of inadequacies, and generally undermining confidence are other examples which can have an adverse reaction on the person bullied (see *Hetherington v Darlington Borough Council* for an example). The end result can be an increase in work-related illnesses, causing absenteeism, low morale, poor performance and possibly accidents. The problem is probably more widespread than is generally realised.

11.88 There is no legal concept of "bullying" *per se*, but recent cases have established that an employer may be vicariously liable for acts of harassment, committed by one employee against another, which in some respect is similar to the idea of bullying. Under the Protection from Harassment Act 1997, a person must not pursue a course of conduct which:

(a) amounts to harassment of another, and

(b) he knows or ought to know amounts to harassment of that other.

11.89 To establish the tort, it must be shown that:

(a) the harassment must be intentional

(b) the alleged offender must have known that he was harassing another person (if a reasonable person would so regard that conduct), and

(c) the conduct must have caused alarm or distress to the other person.

11.90 The conduct complained of may include speech. In *Banks v Ablex Ltd*, a single act of verbal abuse was held not to constitute harassment, because the Act requires there to be a course of conduct. Nor were the employers vicariously liable in negligence for alleged depressive illness caused by the conduct in question because the illness in question was not reasonably foreseeable.

11.91 There are a number of advantages in bringing a claim for bullying under the Protection from Harassment Act, as opposed to bringing a claim under the various anti-discrimination regulations, which would normally, but not always, be the case. In *Majrowski v Guy's* *and St Thomas's NHS Trust* the House of Lords held that if Parliament enacts a criminal statute, civil liability for a statutory tort may also arise unless this is expressly excluded. The result is that an employer may be vicariously liable for the actions of those who harass others, with the following advantages.

1. The employer is more likely to be able to pay damages, rather than the individual whose acts amounted to harassment.
2. The statutory defence that the employer took all reasonable steps to avoid the harassment does not apply (this is a potential defence in discrimination cases).
3. The limitation period of six years will apply, as opposed to the three or six months limitation period for bringing employment tribunal claims, or three years for claims based on negligence.
4. Harassment claims under the Act can be made without reference to anti-discrimination legislation, eg race, sex, disability, etc. Thus bullying *per se* may well be actionable.

11.92 Liability for harassment or bullying is not confined to the typical paradigm of abuse of authority by senior members of staff over more junior employees. In *Green v DB Group Services (UK) Ltd*, the claimant claimed that she had suffered psychiatric illness as a result of a campaign of bullying and harassment by some junior employees. Although some of the incidents were in themselves unimportant, the cumulative effect had a serious impact on the claimant's general health. Her employer had been aware of what was going on, but had done little to prevent the incidents. The court found that the conduct of one of the claimant's colleagues was domineering, disrespectful, dismissive, confrontational, and designed to undermine and belittle the claimant. The conduct in question took place over a period of time, and thus constituted bullying and harassment. The employer was held to be liable in negligence, in that there had been a failure to take the necessary steps to prevent the claimant from suffering a breakdown, and was thus vicariously liable for the acts of the employees. Vicarious liability was also established under the Protection from Harassment Act. In the particular circumstances of the case, damages of over £800,000 were awarded.

11.93 Harassment can also result in a claim for constructive dismissal, on the basis that the mutual trust and confidence which should exist between employer and employee has broken down (*Blackburn with Darwen Borough Council v Stanley*). To determine whether harassment has occurred for the purpose of civil proceedings, the test is whether the gravity of the alleged misconduct would sustain criminal liability under s.2 of the Act. In *Conn v Sunderland City Council* an unmeritorious claim, based on two trivial incidents, was dismissed by the Court of Appeal. In reversing a finding of the trial judge, it was stated that the courts are well able to recognise the boundary between conduct which was unattractive, even unreasonable, and conduct which was oppressive and unacceptable. Doubts were also expressed as to whether boorish and ill-tempered behaviour could seriously be regarded as criminal.

11.94 There is no statutory definition of harassment. Case law suggests that it can be conduct targeting an individual which is calculated to produce alarm or distress, humiliation, exposure to ridicule, etc, and which is intimidating, degrading, hostile, oppressive and unreasonable (eg see *Thomas v News Group Newspapers Ltd*).

11.95 There appears to be some increase in awareness of a problem caused by "bullying" at work, which may have a sexual implication, although not always confined to such. To permit or tolerate this sort of behaviour may have health and safety implications under s.2(1) of HSWA, as well as a claim for constructive dismissal (see *Harvest Press Ltd v McCaffrey*, see paragraph 4.185).

11.96 Harassment is also unlawful if it is committed on the grounds of sex, sexual orientation, gender reassignment, race, disability or age.

Slips and trips

11.97 Over a third of all reported major injuries result from slips and trips, including 20% of over 3-day injuries to employees. Yet most of these are avoidable if the right care and attention is paid by employers, employees and others whose activities create potential hazards.

11.98 The first step is to acknowledge the legal requirements. The most important of these are:
  (a) Health and Safety at Work, etc Act 1974, s 2(1) (see paragraph 3.25)
  (b) Management of Health and Safety at Work Regulations 1999, reg 3 (see paragraph 4.8), regulation 14 (see paragraph 4.55)
  (c) Workplace (Health, Safety and Welfare) Regulations 1992, regulations 8, 9, 10,12, etc
  (d) Manual Handling Operations Regulations 1992, regulation 4

(e) Occupiers Liability Acts 1957–1984 and Occupiers Liability (Scotland) Act 1960 (see paragraph 12.97)
(f) Common law negligence (see paragraph 12.15).

11.99 The next step is to make a proper and thorough risk assessment. Forethought and foresight is essential. Good housekeeping is an excellent place to start. Floors must be kept clean, dry, free from obstructions and, of suitable construction. Goods and materials must be properly stored and kept secure, waste materials disposed of in proper containers, adequate lighting provided, footwear must be suitable, and so on. A system of regular inspection should ensure that spillages are cleared up immediately and obstacles or potential hazards are removed or prevented from arising. Remedial action should be given a priority, eg the replacement of worn carpets, removal of trailing wires, leaking machinery fixed, rainwater prevented from entering the premises, etc.

11.100 Human factors need to be considered. Employees rushing around, or carrying large objects, or being distracted, can also cause accidents. Some employees are at greater risk, eg persons with limited vision or who have a physical problem with mobility. Special attention needs to be taken when dealing with external factors, such as icy roads and surfaces.

11.101 A culture of awareness needs to be fostered. Safety is the responsibility of everyone. Employees should be consulted about the actual or potential hazards perceived, and are the persons most likely to be aware of hazards as well as being the ones most likely to suffer injuries in consequence. They should be encouraged to take action if hazards are observed without waiting for someone else to do something. This is no more than required by the legal duty set out in regulation 14 of the Management Regulations (see paragraph 4.55).

Disabled employees

11.102 The Disability Discrimination Act 1995 was passed for the protection of disabled persons in relation to employment and access to employment. Substantial amendments to the Act have been made by the Disability Discrimination Act 1995 (Amendment) Regulations 2003, in order to ensure compliance with Directive 2000/78/EC and the Disability Discrimination Act 2005. The Act is supplemented by various regulations and a Code of Practice and Guidance Notes. In particular, the guidance must be taken into account when a tribunal is reaching a decision on whether a person is suffering from a disability (*Goodwin v Patent Office*).

Definition of disabled person

11.103 A person will be regarded as being disabled for the purposes of the Act if he has "a physical or mental impairment that has a substantial and long-term adverse effect on his ability to carry out normal day-to-day activities". There are three elements to consider.

1. *Physical or mental impairment.* The physical impairment must be real and not the result of functional overlay (ie where symptoms are imaginary manifestations of an individual's psychological state (*Rugamer v Sony Music Entertainments UK Ltd*)). But if there are physical symptoms, the existence or non-existence of a physical cause is irrelevant (*College of Ripon and York St John v Hobbs*). A medical advisor can express an opinion about diagnosis, prognosis and observation of day-to-day activities, but it is for the employment tribunal to determine whether or not a person is disabled and not for them merely to adopt the opinion of the medical advisor (*Abedah v British Telecommunications plc*).

The requirement that a mental impairment had to be a clinically well-recognised illness has been repealed by the Disability Discrimination Act 2005, and the test will now be that of a substantial impairment having a long-term adverse effect. Vague expressions such as "depression", "anxiety", or "nervous debility" will not, by themselves lead to a conclusion that a mental impairment exists if there is no evidence of the long-term adverse effect of the illness.

Addictions to alcohol, nicotine or other substances do not amount to an impairment for the purpose of the Act, although if there is a physical or mental impairment, the fact that it was caused by such an addiction is not relevant (*Power v Panasonic UK Ltd*). What matters is the impairment, not how it is caused. Tendencies towards pyromania, kleptomania, physical or sexual abuse, exhibitionism or voyeurism are not impairments. Seasonal allergic rhinitis (hay fever) is excluded but not if it aggravates another condition. Also excluded are tattoos or the piercing of the body by objects for decorative or non-medical purposes (Disability Discrimination (Meaning of Disability) Regulations 1996).

2. *Substantial and long-term adverse effect.* Any impairment must have lasted for at least 12 months or be reasonably expected to last for that period or reasonably be expected to last for life. If the impairment ceases to have a substantial effect on a person's ability to carry out day-to-day activities, it will still be treated as having that effect if it is likely to recur (eg a mental illness) except in prescribed circumstances (s.2). Persons who suffer from cancer, HIV and multiple sclerosis will be deemed to be disabled from the moment of diagnosis, rather than from the time the illness takes a long-term effect. The Disability Discrimination (Blind and Partially Sighted People) Regulations 2003 provide that anyone certified or registered blind or partially sighted is deemed to be disabled for the purpose of the Act, and will no longer be required to establish that being blind or partially sighted has a substantial adverse effect on day-to-day activities. A severe disfigurement is to be treated as having a substantial effect on the ability of a person to carry out normal day-to-day activities.

Whether an impairment has a substantial effect on a person's ability to carry out normal day-to-day activities should not be judged by reference to whether he is able to carry out his job (*Goodwin v Patent Office*), but evidence as to how he carries out his duties at work can be relevant in assessing the employee's credibility, provided that the duties carried out can be regarded as being normal day-to-day activities (*Law Hospital NHS Trust v Rush*). If the effect of the impairment fluctuates and is exacerbated by conditions at work, then an employee's ability to perform normal day-to-day activities both while at work and while not at work is to be taken into account when assessing whether the impairment has a substantial and long-term adverse effect (*Cruickshank v VAW Motorcast Ltd*).

To assess whether or not an impairment has a substantial adverse effect, a tribunal should concentrate on what a claimant cannot do or can only do with difficulty, and not on what he can do (*Leonard v Southern Derbyshire Chamber of Commerce*). It is the effect of the impairment that must be substantial, not the severity of the impairment. Thus a person with dyslexia may only have a moderate impairment but it could have a substantial effect on his day-to-day activities. Minor impairments, which, taken together, have a cumulative effect, can lead to a substantial impairment.

3. *Normal day-to-day activities.* An impairment is to be taken as affecting normal day-to-day activities if it affects a person with regard to mobility, manual dexterity, physical co-ordination, continence, ability

to lift, carry or move everyday objects, speech, hearing, eyesight, memory or ability to concentrate, learn or understand, or perception of risks of physical danger (see schedule 1). The fact that a person is disabled within the meaning of other legislation (eg for the purpose of disability living allowance) does not mean that he comes within the definition of disability within the meaning of the Act. The playing of games or sports does not constitute "normal day-to-day activities" because such activities are only normal for a particular group of persons. But it is normal for a woman to put rollers in her hair and apply make-up to her face (*Ekpe v Metropolitan Police Commissioner*). The Guidance Notes give specific examples of normal day-to-day activities and reference should be made to these notes when reaching a decision in any particular case.

11.104 There is a danger of adopting a stereotype approach to disabled persons. Only a relatively small proportion of the disabled community is visibly disabled, ie in wheelchairs or carrying white sticks or other aids. The vast majority of disabled persons have a physical or mental disability that may not be immediately obvious, and will only come to light when they fail to do that which a non-disabled person can do. Thus in deciding whether a claimant's impairment is substantial, a purposive approach should be taken by the employment tribunal, having regard to the Guidance Notes and the Code of Practice issued by the Secretary of State. The focus of the Act is on the activities which the claimant cannot do (or can only do with difficulty), rather on the things he can do. "Substantial" means "more than minor or trivial" rather than "very large" (*Goodwin v Patent Office*). But the list of examples in the Guidance Notes are illustrative, not exhaustive. In *Vicary v British Telecommunications*, the employers had relied largely on the opinion of their medical officer who was of the opinion that the claimant's disabilities were not substantial, and did not affect her normal day-to-day activities, a conclusion which the employment tribunal appeared to adopt. On appeal it was held that a medical expert is entitled to express an opinion based on observation and examination, but it was for the employment tribunal to make this finding of fact, based on their own assessment of the evidence.

What is discrimination? (s.3A)

11.105 A person discriminates against a disabled person if:

(a) for a reason which relates to the person's disability, he treats him less favourably than he treats others to whom that reason does not apply

(b) he cannot show that the treatment is justified (s.3A(1)).

11.106 In *Clark v TDG Ltd* (t/a Novocold) the Court of Appeal held that in disability discrimination cases, there is no requirement that the comparator be in the same, or not materially different, circumstances as those which apply to the complainant. For example, it used to be thought that if an employee is dismissed because of a lengthy sickness absence which related to his disability, he should be compared with the dismissal of an employee who had not been absent at all, rather than to another employee who was absent for a reason unrelated to his disability. However, the House of Lords has now ruled that this approach is wrong. The correct approach was to compare the treatment of the complainant with that of a non-disabled person who was otherwise in the same circumstances as the complainant (*London Borough of Lewisham v Malcolm*).

11.107 The House of Lords in this case also reviewed the issue as to whether or not an employer needed to have actual or imputed knowledge of a complainant's disability in order to be found responsible for disability- related discrimination (see *HJ Heinz Co Ltd v Kenrick*). In their Lordships' view, disability-related discrimination does require the alleged discriminator to have actual or imputed knowledge of the disability, unless it could be said that the alleged act was inherently discriminatory.

11.108 It will also amount to discrimination if an employer fails to make reasonable adjustments to the premises or disabled person's working conditions (see below).

11.109 It will be noted that the burden of proof is on the employer to show that the less favourable treatment is justified, but the reason must be both material to the circumstances of the particular case and substantial. Depending on the circumstances, one may assume that less favourable treatment is capable of being justified if:

(a) the disabled person is not suitable for employment

(b) the disabled person is less suitable for employment than another person, and that other person is given the job

(c) the nature of the disabled person's disability significantly impedes the performance of any of his duties

(d) in the case of training, the nature of the disabled person's disability would significantly reduce the value of the training.

11.110 However, each individual circumstance must be taken into account. One should not assume that all blind persons are unable to type or use computers. A person who is off work sick because of a disability is not to be dismissed solely for that reason, if his level of absenteeism is not substantially more than other employees. Blanket concern for health and safety requirements should not override the need to consider the individual circumstances of a disabled person.

11.111 Discriminatory treatment will be justified if it arises from performance-related pay, eligibility for and contributions to occupational pension schemes, and permits for incapacitated persons under the agricultural wages legislation (see Disability Discrimination (Employment) Regulations 1996).

11.112 A person also discriminates against a disabled person if, on the ground of his disability, he treats the disabled person less favourably than he treats a person not having that particular disability whose relevant circumstances are the same or not materially different from those of the disabled person (s.3A(5)).

11.113 The distinction between these two forms of discrimination is as follows. Under s.3A(l) a comparison must be made with a person to whom the disability-related reason does not apply, ie he can be disabled or non-disabled, whereas under s.3A(5) an employer is making a generalised assumption about disability or its effects. Under s.3A(l), justification may be a defence in appropriate circumstances, whereas under s.3A(5) a "blanket ban" on disabled persons in general is incapable of being justified.

Discrimination against disabled workers (s.4)

11.114 It will be unlawful for an employer to discriminate against a disabled person:
(a) in the arrangements made for determining to whom he should offer employment
(b) in the terms on which he offers employment
(c) by refusing to offer, or deliberately not offering, employment.

11.115 Further, it will be unlawful to discriminate against a disabled person:

(a) in terms and conditions of employment
(b) in opportunities for promotion, transfers, training or any other benefit
(c) by dismissing him or subjecting him to any detriment.

11.116 It is also unlawful to subject a disabled person who is in employment or who is applying for employment to harassment, ie the unwanted conduct that has the purpose or effect of violating the disabled person's dignity or creating an intimidating, hostile, degrading, humiliating or offensive environment for him (see paragraph 11.87).

Duty of employer to make adjustments (s.4A)

11.117 Where a provision, criterion or practice applied by the employer or any physical feature of premises occupied by the employer places the disabled person at a substantial disadvantage in comparison with persons who are not disabled, it is the duty of the employer to take such steps as it is reasonable, in all the circumstances of the case, for him to have to take in order to prevent the provision, criterion or practice or feature having that affect. However, there is no such duty on an employer if he did not know, and could not be reasonably expected to know, that the disabled person is or may be an applicant for employment or that the person has a disability and is likely to be affected by the provision, criterion or practice or physical features of the premises.

11.118 An employer cannot be expected to make reasonable adjustments if he does not know the employee has a disability (*Ridout v TC Group*), and the adjustments must be related to the job, not to personal services required by the disabled person (eg going to the toilet, see *Kenny v Hampshire Constabulary*).

11.119 The Disability Discrimination (Employment Field) (Leasehold Premises) Regulations 2004 deal with the situation where the employer needs to obtain the consent of another person before he can make alteration to the premises.

11.120 The Code of Practice is comprehensive, and gives advice on all aspects of the nature of discrimination, recruitment, employment arrangements (including steps to make reasonable adjustments), and generally setting up management systems to avoid discrimination. The code can be taken into account should an action be brought in an employment tribunal.

Reasonable adjustments (s.18B)

11.121 In determining whether it is reasonable for a person to have to take a particular step in order to comply with the duty to make reasonable adjustments, regard shall be had to:
  (a) the extent to which taking the step would prevent the effect in relation to which the duty is imposed
  (b) the extent to which it is practicable for him to take the step
  (c) the financial and other costs that would be incurred by him in taking the step, and the extent to which taking it would disrupt any of his activities
  (d) the extent of his financial and other resources
  (e) the availability to him of financial or other assistance with respect to taking the step
  (f) the nature of his activities and the size of his undertaking
  (g) where the step would be taken in relation to a private household, the extent to which it would disrupt the household or disturb any person residing there.

11.122 The following are examples of the steps that a person may take in order to comply with the duty to make reasonable adjustments:
  (a) making adjustments to the premises
  (b) allocating some of the disabled person's duties to another person
  (c) transferring him to fill an existing vacancy
  (d) altering his hours of work or training
  (e) assigning him to a different place of work or training
  (f) allowing him to be absent during working hours or training hours for rehabilitation, assessment or treatment
  (g) giving, or arranging for, training or mentoring
  (h) acquiring or modifying equipment
  (i) modifying instructions or reference materials
  (j) modifying procedures for testing or assessment
  (k) providing a reader or interpreter
  (l) providing supervision or other support.

11.123 It should be noted that justification is no defence to a failure to make reasonable adjustments. The test is simply whether or not the adjustments which could be made are reasonable.

11.124 But the provisions of the Disability Discrimination Act are subordinate to health and safety law. In *Farmiloe v Lane Group plc* the claimant worked in a warehouse. He could not wear safety boots because he suffered with psoriasis. A local authority health and safety officer required him to wear safety boots, and threatened enforcement action if he failed to do so. The employers approached various footwear manufacturers, but none could provide suitable safety footwear. As there was no other employment available for him, he was dismissed. It was held that even though he had been discriminated against because of his disability, the principles of health and safety law overrode the principles behind the Disability Discrimination Act. The employers had made an effort to provide a reasonable adjustment, and as there was none available, and no other suitable employment for him, the claimant was fairly dismissed.

11.125 The Act also deals with the liability of principals in respect of contract workers, office holders, partnerships, barristers and advocates. A number of exclusions that were formally found in the 1995 Act have now been repealed.

Remedies

11.126 A complaint of disability discrimination may be made to an employment tribunal, which has the same powers as those that exist for complaints of race or sex discrimination. The time limits are the same, and there is a questionnaire procedure.

Commission for Equality and Human Rights

11.127 The CEHR will work towards the elimination of discrimination against disabled persons, promote equalisation of opportunities, take such steps as it considers appropriate with a view to encouraging good practice in the treatment of disabled persons and keep the workings of the Disability Discrimination Act 1995 under review. The Commission may make proposals or give advice to the minister or any other government agency as to the practical application of the law, and undertake (or arrange for support of) the carrying out of research or the provision of advice or information.

11.128 The Commission may prepare Codes of Practice (which must be approved by the Secretary of State and laid before Parliament) in order to give practical advice to employers and other service providers, give assistance to persons who propose to bring claims for unlawful discrimination, carry out formal investigations and issue non-discrimination notices.

To act reasonably

11.129 Once a disabled person has been taken into employment, he can of course be dismissed on health or safety grounds, but there is a high burden on the employer to show that he made a full appraisal of all the facts, and in particular that he searched around for suitable alternative employment before contemplating dismissal (see *Milk Marketing Board v Grimes*, see paragraph 13.56). The employer must familiarise himself with the job, the disability and the hazard *(Littlewood v AEI Cables)*, and extra efforts must be made to accommodate a disabled person. In *Cannon v Scandecor*, when the applicant, who was registered disabled, was employed it was recognised that her output would not be too high. She then had a series of illnesses and a car accident, and when she returned to work her daily output was that which she had previously achieved in an hour. She was dismissed, but this was held to be unfair. Much too short a period had elapsed between her return to work and her dismissal, and sufficient time had not been allowed in order to enable her to make a full recovery. She should have been given a reasonable trial period and then, if her output had not reached her previous performance, her dismissal would have been fair.

11.130 It has been held that the failure to place a disabled person on a shortlist for interview did not, by itself, indicate that the employer had discriminated unlawfully, for frequently there are a large number of applicants for a particular job, and it is inevitable that only a limited number of applicants can be called for interview. In another case, an employee developed multiple sclerosis and it was held that the employer acted unreasonably in dismissing him without taking heed of a report from a neurologist, who thought that the employee's prospect of working should be assessed on a "try and see" basis. By and large, the employment tribunals appear to be applying the same tests under the new Act towards the dismissal of a disabled person as they did before the Act came into force, ie did the employer act reasonably in dismissing this employee for the reason put forward? (See *Pascoe v Hallen &*

Medway). Therefore, a consideration of alternatives, proper consultation, a review of attendance and performance, providing additional support facilities, obtaining a full and up-to-date medical report are all steps that a reasonable employer would take.

11.131 Particular attention must be paid to regulation 25A of the Workplace (Health Safety and Welfare) Regulations (see paragraph 6.51) concerning adapting work premises to the needs of disabled persons.

11.132 It will thus be evident that employers who take on a disabled person have a special responsibility to do more than they would normally do to give him a period of time in which to reach acceptable standards. Some companies meet the problem by excluding disabled employees from departmental budgets, so as to ensure that they are not regarded as a drain or millstone by management seeking to reach targets. Certainly, a great deal can be done and although safety hazards must not be ignored, these are not always insuperable obstacles. There is no substitute for a careful assessment of the nature of the work, the risks associated with it and a measured judgment based on an investigation into the nature of the disability matched against the risks involved.

11.133 Clearly, disabled persons will always pose special problems so far as health and safety matters are concerned. Deaf persons will not always be able to hear fire alarms or warning cries, blind persons will not find their way to escape routes, physically disabled persons will not be able to react with the necessary speed to emergency situations, and so on. Since the duties owed by an employer to his employees are personal to each employee, special attention should be paid to these problems when disabled persons are involved.

11.134 Even so, there must come a point in time when safety factors will override all other considerations, although the duty of the employer is to act reasonably when handling employees who have any type of disability. Usually this will mean taking medical advice and looking round for suitable employment. In *McCall v Post Office* the applicant, unknown to his employers, suffered from epilepsy. He was employed as a cleaner, but had several fits which were of short duration. The personnel department took medical advice and were told that he should be employed in a "no risk" area. Unfortunately there was no suitable vacancy and he was dismissed. This was held to be fair. On medical advice the employee had to be moved to a safe area, and as there was none available it was in his interests and in the interests of other employees that he be dismissed.

Work-related upper limb disorders

11.135 This is a generic term for a group of musculo-skeletal injuries that affect the muscles, tendons, joints and bones usually in the hand or arm or shoulder, and is generally caused or aggravated by repetitive work. A variety of illnesses can result, including tenosynovitis, tendinitis, carpal tunnel syndrome, epicondylitis capullitus, peritendinitis, spondylosis bursitis, etc. From a legal point of view, an employee who suffers from this complaint may be able to sue for a breach of statutory duty and/or for common law negligence (see Chapter 12). For example, in *McSherry v British Telecommunications plc*, the claimant worked as a data processing officer. Her job was to key telephone meter readings into a computer controlled data system. She would be expected to reach a speed of some 13,000 key depressions an hour, and her work was regularly monitored to ensure that she maintained this speed. After doing this for about four years she began to feel pain in her hands, wrists, arms and shoulders, and her doctor diagnosed bilateral tenosynovitis (tennis elbow). It was established that these symptoms were attributable to the nature of the work. The main cause was poor postural positioning, due to unsuitable chairs and a modesty panel beneath her desk, which prevented her from stretching her legs. It was held that the employers were liable for a breach of statutory duty under the Offices, Shops and Railway Premises Act 1963 (OSRPA), s.14 (failure to provide suitable seating together with a footrest) and for common law negligence (failure to foresee that the sort of posture adopted by the plaintiff would, in the course of time, be likely to cause serious musculo-skeletal injury).

11.136 Although there is well-documented evidence of the disorder existing in specific industries and processes, it is now acknowledged that work-related upper limb disorders (WRULD) can occur in any particular occupation, and is therefore not confined to a particular sector of industry or commerce. Indeed, many of the more recent cases of claims for compensation appear to arise as a result of modern technology.

11.137 A failure by management to respond adequately to the dangers of WRULD can have a number of consequences, eg high levels of sickness and absenteeism, reduced output, complaints by employees of pain, poor-quality work, civil claims for compensation and, ultimately, a prosecution for failing to comply with s.2(1) of the Health and Safety at Work, etc Act 1974 and/or health and safety regulations (eg Health and Safety (Display Screen Equipment) Regulations 1992).

11.138 There are a number of possible causes of WRULD, including awkward posture (affecting the hand, wrist, shoulder or body), repeated forceful movements (usually by the hands or arms), frequent repetitive movements (eg keyboard work) and so on. Prevention techniques include:

(a) recognising the risk
(b) identifying the cause
(c) removing the risk by redesigning the work using ergonomic techniques, providing suitable tools, introducing adequate rest breaks in the work, teaching correct postures, introducing job rotation, and so on.

11.139 The first step is to identify whether or not the problem exists. An initial assessment should be carried out, which should reveal the nature and extent of WRULD in the workplace. If further action is needed, a more detailed assessment should be undertaken with a view to seeking solutions. These can be achieved in a number of ways, which vary from making minor adjustments to a major overhaul of the systems of work and/or equipment and materials used. Finally, as with every risk assessment, there should be a periodic review of the action taken, and further remedial steps implemented, as required.

11.140 A phrase frequently used to describe certain musculo-skeletal illnesses is "repetitive strain injury" (RSI), but there is considerable controversy over the use of the term, and disagreement between medical practitioners as to whether or not such an illness actually exists. In *Mughal v Reuters Ltd*, the plaintiff spent at least 50% of his time typing on a keyboard. He received no advice on working posture, the need to take breaks, the importance of keeping his wrists parallel to the keyboard, nor for the need to have his eyes at a proper angle to the screen. He then transferred to another job with the same firm, doing similar work. After a month he felt tingling and numbness in his fingers and hands, which then moved up his forearm. For two years thereafter he consulted a number of medical practitioners, and eventually a consultant physician diagnosed tenosynovitis. However, another consultant neurologist was unable to find any clinical symptoms. The employee brought a claim for damages against the employers alleging they had been negligent (see paragraph 12.15). Although the judge accepted that there was a well-known condition called tenosynovitis, with a defined pathology and cause, he held the term "repetitive strain injury" was meaningless, and had no place in the medical books. Its use could only lead to speculation and confusion. Any resultant pain could arise from psychological or emotional disturbance. Further, the judge held that there had been no breach of duty by the employers. Each keyboard operator employed by them had to establish a comfortable position by trial and error, and the employers had fulfilled their legal duty by providing British Standards equipment.

11.141 However, there has always been a disagreement within the medical profession as to whether RSI had organic or psychogenic causes, and the existence of RSI was consequently accepted in a number of other legal cases (eg *Bettany v Royal Doulton (UK) Ltd*). There have also been a number of substantial out-of-court settlement of RSI claims. On the other hand, the existence of RSI was doubted by the House of Lords in *Pickford v Imperial Chemical Industries*.

11.142 In this case, the claimant worked for ICI as a secretary from 1984. In 1986, she estimated that she spent 50% of her time typing, the remaining time being spent on various other secretarial duties. By 1988 she estimated that she spent 75% of her time typing. However, she was able to plan her own workload. She then experienced a strange feeling on the back of her hands, and went to see her doctor, who could find nothing wrong. She was referred to an orthopaedic surgeon, who said that her symptoms were work-related, but there was nothing he could do for her. She contacted the Repetitive Strain Injury Association, who referred her to several specialists, only one of whom suggested that the injury might be psychological in origin. Her works doctor suggested that she should be redeployed, but after working for three days as a filing clerk her hands became sore and painful, and she could not continue with that work. There being no other work available for her, her employment was eventually terminated. She issued a writ for damages, claiming that she had contracted prescribed industrial disease PDA4 in the course of her employment as a secretary (PDA4 is defined in the Social Security (Industrial Injuries) (Prescribed Diseases)

Regulations 1985 as being "cramp of the hand or forearm" caused by any repetitive movements, which might arise from "any occupation involving prolonged periods of handwriting, typing, or other repetitive movements of the fingers, hand or arm, eg typists, clerks and routine assemblers..."). She claimed that the illness was organic in origin caused by excessive typing without being advised to have rest periods, and that the defendants were negligent in not giving her any instructions about the need to have rest breaks.

11.143 The trial judge held that PDA4 may have an organic or psychogenic cause, but he was not satisfied, on the evidence, that the claimant's cramp was organic in origin. He further held that it was not reasonably foreseeable, considering the amount of typing the claimant did, that she was likely to suffer from PDA4, that she could intersperse her typing with other secretarial work, and that the defendants were not negligent in failing to advise her to take rest pauses from typing. Her claim was therefore dismissed. On appeal, the Court of Appeal reversed the decision, and held that the defendants were liable for negligence.

11.144 On a further appeal, the House of Lords reversed the decision, and restored the finding of the trial judge that the defendants had not been negligent. Because PDA4 is a condition that is not easily identifiable and not well understood, great caution should be exercised before laying down a duty that warnings of the risks to health should be given, because these could do more harm than good, and might even bring about the very condition it was designed to prevent. Nor was it the practice in the industry to give any such warnings, other than advice to see the works doctor in the event of experiencing unusual pain or discomfort. The employers had carefully taken steps to advise all their word processor operators of the need to have correct hand positions when typing, and to have breaks and rest pauses. Bearing in mind that the claimant did not work all the time on typing, and that she could intersperse her typing with other work, it was not foreseeable that she would suffer this particular injury.

11.145 It was stated in the House of Lords that the term "repetitive strain injury" was a familiar expression, but medical experts agree that as a medical term it is unhelpful. It covers so many conditions that it is of no diagnostic value as a disease.

11.146 Nonetheless, it is likely that diffuse work-related upper limb disorder can be caused by repetitive work carried out under intense pressure, with insufficient work breaks and poor arm posture. If the judge thinks that the case for psychogenic cause has not been proven, it follows that there must be a physical cause, and the employer could well be liable (*Alexander v Midland Bank plc*).

11.147 It would appear that "RSI" is a somewhat loose and vague description of a complaint which may have a psychogenic cause, or may be physical. A term which is sometimes used, non-specific arm pain (NSAP) is perhaps more descriptive and accurate. It is often stress-related, for in many cases no muscular, tendon or neurological abnormality can be found. In other cases, magnetic resonance scans have revealed reduced median nerve movement in the carpal tunnel, suggesting some form of nerve entrapment. Some doctors have defined RSI as a cumulative trauma disorder which results from the over-repetitive use of the muscles in the fingers, hands, arms and shoulders. Certainly there are a number of occupations where it is recognised that repetitive use of the fingers and hands, etc will produce symptoms which are clearly related to the occupation (musicians, keyboard operators, packers, machine operators, etc). It would seem that compensation claims will have to rely on the factual and medical evidence that can be adduced in each case.

11.148 There are a number of known health problems connected with display screen equipment work which should be identified by a risk assessment and followed up with a system whereby the employer can ensure that safe working practices are adopted. As well as ensuring correct equipment, this will include adequate training and a monitoring system to ensure prevention of upper limb disorders. It is not sufficient to rely on the employee to adopt safe working practices because they may not appreciate the importance of taking regular breaks, changing their routine, ensuring correct posture, having suitable seating arrangements, and so on (*Denton Hall Legal Services v Fifield*).

Vibration white finger

11.149 Vibration white finger (VWF) disorder is caused by a constriction of the blood supply to the fingers, due to working with vibrating tools, such as pneumatic drills, hammers, etc. In the vast majority of cases it does not prevent a person from continuing to work, although it may cause considerable discomfort, particularly in cold conditions. The precise causes of the injury are not clear and thus it is not possible to lay down specific safe exposure limits.

11.150 The first recorded civil action for damages in respect of VWF was in 1946 (*Fitzsimmons v Ford Motor Co Ltd*), where a successful claim was brought under the Workman's Compensation Act. Later claims floundered because it could not be shown that the employer had been in breach of a duty to take reasonable care or because the trivial nature of the problem did not warrant preventative measures (eg *Joseph v Ministry of Defence*). Employers were entitled to follow the recognised and generally accepted practice, and there was nothing in the literature to make them aware of any danger (see *Walker v Wafco Automative Ltd*). Further, even if an employee had been warned of the risk, he would still have continued to work. However, more recently, a number of claims for damages have succeeded, for the illness is now widely recognised, and appropriate precautionary measures can be taken (see *Shepherd v Firth Brown Ltd*). An employer who fails to reduce vibration levels, or to provide training, give warnings, implement job rotation, etc materially increases the risk of injury (*Brown v Corus (UK) Ltd*).

11.151 In *Armstrong v British Coal Corporation*, the defendants did carry out some investigation into the existence of VWF in the coal industry. Although it was discovered that there were some employees who had the complaint, they failed to carry out a wider investigation. The judge held that had they done so, they would have realised by 1973 that there was a problem which needed to be addressed, and would have set up a system of preventative measures. A compensation fund of some £500 million has been created for the benefit of thousands of former coal miners who were found to be suffering from VWF.

11.152 A useful summary of the legal and medical background of VWF, with a guide on the assessment of compensation, can be found in a decision of the Northern Ireland High Court in the case of *Bowman v Harland & Wolffe plc*. The HSE has produced a Guidance Note on hand-arm vibration (HSG88: *Hand-arm Vibration*).

11.153 Under the Supply of Machinery (Safety) Regulations 2008, suppliers must provide information on vibration levels from hand-held tools and hand-guided machinery that produce a vibration level of a magnitude exceeding the prescribed level.

11.154 VWF is now a prescribed disease for certain categories of workers under the Social Security (Industrial Injuries) (Prescribed Diseases) Regulations 1985.

11.155 The Control of Vibration at Work Regulations 2005 (see paragraph 8.38) set out the measures which need to be taken in order to deal with hand-arm and whole-body vibration.

Acquired Immune Deficiency Syndrome (AIDS)

11.156 Acquired Immune Deficiency Syndrome (AIDS) is caused by a virus which attacks the body's natural defence system, thus leaving it vulnerable to a number of infections and cancer. However, not all those who have the Human Immunodeficiency Virus (HIV) develop AIDS, although medical statistics on the extent of the disease are still in their infancy. At the present time there is no known cure. HIV can only be transmitted through sexual intercourse with an infected person, by being inoculated with infected blood or (possibly) by drinking breast milk from an infected person and by sharing infected needles. There is no evidence at present to suggest that the virus can be transmitted in any other way and certainly not by other physical contact with an infected person. This means that there is no grounds for refusing employment to a person who has the virus and the fact of infection is not a ground for dismissal.

11.157 However, there are some groups who are clearly at risk. These include doctors, nurses, dentists and others who, by the nature of their work, could come into contact with blood, etc and face the possibility of infection through a cut or accidental injection. These persons must take additional precautions in order to reduce the risk. Many employers have issued policy statements which, as well as indicating a refusal to discriminate against someone who has the virus, state the counselling services and other support which will be available.

Epileptics

11.158 Reconciling safety with social responsibility is one of the more difficult tasks of recruitment officers, and it is essential that judgments be made on the basis of informed opinion. This is particularly true of epilepsy, about which there is a great deal of ignorance. There is no reason in principle why an epileptic cannot be employed in most types of work, provided a full appraisal is made of the situation. Epilepsy does not conform to a single pattern; it varies in type, frequency, severity and timing. A candidate for a job who has all the necessary qualifications and experience should not be excluded from consideration on the ground of epilepsy without a full investigation, in which, of course, medical assessment would be invaluable.

11.159 A person who has a history of epilepsy cannot be permitted to drive a heavy goods vehicle or passenger vehicle (unless free from an attack for two years), or work as a specialist teacher of physical education. Other than these restrictions, objections to appointing an epileptic should be based on sound functional reasons. Once employed, safety considerations obviously become important, and if there is any risk to the employee or to his fellow employees, attempts must be made to find suitable employment where the risks are minimised. In the last resort, however, firmer action must be taken. For example, in *Harper v National Coal Board*, the applicant had three epileptic fits in a period of two years. During these fits he was, quite unknowingly, violent to other workers. He was then medically examined, and it was recommended that he be retired on medical grounds, under a mine workers' pension scheme. He refused to accept retirement and was dismissed. This was held to be fair. The employers owed a duty to their other employees to ensure their safety as well. The applicant was working alongside other disabled employees and they were clearly at risk.

11.160 Epilepsy is likely to be a long-term disability under the Disability Discrimination Act 1995, although this will not necessarily be so if the attacks are infrequent or only occur during sleep. As such, the provisions of that Act will apply, and any less favourable treatment is unlawful unless it can be justified. A full review of the medical evidence, together with a consideration of re-deployment away from areas of potential risk, will be necessary. A number of cases relating to epileptics have been considered by employment tribunals, with varying results (eg *Alexander v Driving Standards Agency, Jewell v Stoke Mandeville Hospital NHS Trust*, etc).

11.161 Advice on the employment of epileptics can be obtained from the British Epileptic Association (also known as Epilepsy Action) and the Employment Medical Advisory Service may also be contacted when necessary (see also *McCall v Post Office*, see paragraph 11.134).

Mental illness

11.162 This term encompasses a wide range of medical and psychological problems, but from the point of view of health and safety, an employer has to consider:

(a) whether to employ someone who has, or who has had, mental illness

(b) if he is employed, what steps should be taken to ensure that he is not a health or safety hazard to himself or to others

(c) whether or not a past or present illness is sufficient ground for dismissal.

11.163 The problem is one of medical evidence, and recruitment should be done in consultation with such specialists as are available (eg company doctor, nurse, etc) so that a full and satisfactory assessment can be made of the illness and the risks involved in employing the applicant. Generally, mental illnesses are of two types, namely psychoneurosis and psychosis. The former is a species of "bad nerves", the latter is more serious and involves a lack of contact with reality. So far as psychoneurosis is concerned, the recovery rate is good, and a person who has had a previous history of this sort of mental illness, but who is now fit and well, is no more likely to have a recurrence of the illness than a person who has no previous history is likely to have a mental breakdown. The prognosis for psychosis, however, is mixed, depending on the severity of the illness and the medical evidence which can be adduced.

11.164 Many companies, while they may be unwilling to take on persons with a history of mental illness, adopt a policy of social responsibility to existing employees and seek to provide suitable employment, rehabilitation units, and encourage the employee to obtain medical treatment. Satisfying work, of course, is a great therapy. The problem is one which requires sympathetic handling, involving the co-operation of all those who can contribute some expertise, as well as employees and management generally. Progress should be monitored, risks assessed, work planned and adequately supervised, and so on. Once the nature of the illness can be established, it may be possible to match it with employment where safety can be observed.

11.165 The fact that an employee "tells a lie" on a job application form and denies that he has ever had any history of mental illness is not *per se* grounds for dismissal should the previous history come to light

(*Johnson v Tesco Stores Ltd*), but if it can be shown that there is a good, sound, functional reason why the person cannot be employed, it may be fair to dismiss him. In *O'Brien v Prudential Assurance Co Ltd*, when the applicant was interviewed for a job he was given a medical examination and asked specific questions about his mental health. He made no mention of the fact that he had had a long history of mental illness, including psychosis, which necessitated the taking of drugs and a period of hospitalisation. When the truth came to light, the company consulted various medical experts and a decision was taken to dismiss him. He brought a claim for unfair dismissal, but it was held that the dismissal was fair for some other substantial reason. It was the company's policy not to appoint as district agents persons who had long histories of mental illnesses, as the job involved going into people's homes. Clearly, there was a risk that an unpleasant incident could occur which would seriously tarnish the company's image and thus the policy was not an unreasonable one. Had the company been aware of his long history of mental illness he would never have been appointed to the job.

11.166 The greater the risk of a serious incident occurring, the more management should consider dismissing the employee. In *Singh-Deu v Chloride Metals*, the applicant was sent home from work after complaining that he felt unwell. His doctor diagnosed paranoid schizophrenia and when the company could not obtain a satisfactory assurance from a specialist that there would not be a recurrence, he was dismissed. This was held to be fair. If he had an attack of this illness during working hours, a catastrophic accident could have happened. There was no other suitable alternative employment for him, and the company could not be expected to wait until an accident occurred before taking some action (see *Spalding v Port of London Authority*).

11.167 The need to exercise caution when dealing with employees who have a mental illness can be seen from the decision of the Employment Appeal Tribunal in *Goodwin v The Patent Office*. The appellant was a paranoid schizophrenic who had auditory hallucinations which interrupted his power of concentration. He was dismissed after complaints from female staff about his disturbing behaviour. An employment tribunal held that he was not a disabled person within the meaning of the Disability Discrimination Act 1995, because it was felt that his impairment did not have a substantial adverse effect on his normal day-to-day activities, as required by s.1(1) of the Act. The Employment Appeal Tribunal upheld an appeal, and remitted the case for rehearing by a fresh tribunal. The appellant was unable to carry on a normal day-to-day conversation with work colleagues, which was evidence that his capacity to concentrate and communicate was adversely affected in a significant manner. The Act is primarily concerned with things the applicant cannot do (or can only do with difficulty) rather than on the things he can do.

11.168 If a mental impairment is claimed, the onus of proof is on the claimant. Basing a claim on loose terms, such as anxiety or depression, is not sufficient. A medical report from a suitably qualified medical practitioner should be obtained, showing the diagnosis of a clinically well-recognised mental illness, which is either specified in the World Health Organization's International Classification of Diseases (WHOICD) or some other authoritative source. The medical evidence should cover not only the illness, but how it would manifest itself so as to put the employer on notice for the purpose of making work adjustments (*Morgan v Staffordshire University*). However, such clinical diagnosis is not essential for the purpose of establishing a mental impairment (see paragraph 11.104).

Stress at work

11.169 While most illnesses caused by work activities have a physical pathology, recent research appears to indicate that the somewhat more vague claims of mental stress or depression can have their origin in the workplace. These illnesses can be brought on by excessive working hours, pressures to meet deadlines, poor communications, office politics, uncertainties about job security, lack of guidance and/or training, demands for high standards or increased production, and so on. The end result is sometimes absence from work or even a mental breakdown.

11.170 In recent years, there has been an increasing awareness of work-related stress syndrome, which has resulted in a new and fertile source of litigation, whether by way of common law claims, claims for constructive or unfair dismissal, or as an aspect of claims for race and/or sex discrimination. Precise statistics are hard to come by, and may well vary from year to year. However, some estimates indicate that stress-related absenteeism results in the loss of some 90 million working days each year, and that some 250,000 people are affected annually. It is the second largest cause of occupational illness.

11.171   There is no medical or legal definition of stress. It is unlikely that stress *per se* will be regarded as a clinically well-recognised illness within the meaning of schedule 1 paragraph 1(1) of the Disability Discrimination Act 1995, though the line dividing it from other mental illnesses, eg depression, is somewhat fine. To come within the Act, there must be an impairment which has a substantial and long-term adverse effect on a person's ability to carry out normal day-to-day activities. However, there can be a progression from stress to anxiety, depression, clinical depression, post-traumatic stress disorder and other associated mental illnesses, which could well fall within the scope of the Act.

11.172   The causes of stress are many. It can arise as the result of unhappy personal circumstances or from a variety of workplace problems. Sometimes the one may be exacerbated by the other. It can affect employees differently, because some will be more vulnerable than others. For example, one employee may find a boring, monotonous job stressful, whereas another may prefer its routine nature. What is acceptable pressure for one person may be unacceptable stress for another. Some may prefer to have control over their work situation, others may find responsibility too much for them. The general low morale in the firm, lack of knowledge of career prospects, inter-personal relationships with fellow employees, conflicts between demands of work and personal factors affecting one's home life, and so on, may all play a part in creating stress which can have an impact on an employee's working life.

11.173   Signs to look for include changes in patterns of behaviour, deteriorating relationships, an increase in drinking, smoking, drug taking, irritability, lateness, absenteeism, poor work performance, trivial complaints, lack of concentration, stammering, and so on. There may also be identifiable physical symptoms, including headaches, visual problems, muscular pains, tiredness, insomnia, etc. Low productivity, high staff turnover, higher accident rates and an increase in customer complaints may also signify the existence of a problem which needs to be investigated.

11.174   At the present time, there is little by way of health and safety legislation that may be invoked. The risk assessment carried out under regulation 3 of the Management of Health and Safety at Work Regulations 1999 should contain an assessment of risks from work-related stress, pressures, etc particularly in occupations that demand that a high level of targets and deadlines are met, or where highly skilled and demanding work needs to be carried out under less than favourable conditions. (According to a recent report, the highest stress occupations were teaching, nursing and management.) The pressures which may be causing stress should be identified, the risks from stress assessed, reasonably practical measures should be taken to alleviate the problem, and the effectiveness of any preventative measures reviewed as appropriate. This will involve checking on morale generally, monitoring absenteeism and lateness, checking on improvements in quality, service and productivity, noting improvements in staff relationships and so on. Although not legally binding, in 2004 the HSE did issue the Management Standards for work-related stress. Their purpose is, as the HSE states, "to provide a yardstick against which organisations can measure their progress in tackling work-related stress and target action where it is most needed."

11.175 Stress can produce physical symptoms (headaches, tiredness, real or imaginary aches and pains), behavioural symptoms (increase in alcohol consumption or smoking, irritability, inability to cope) and psychological problems (feelings of anxiety, depression, paranoia), all of which will result in poor performance, increasing absenteeism, a potentially higher rate of accidents, and general inefficiency. The first step in dealing with the problem is to recognise that it exists; the next step is to consider the remedial action which needs to be taken. Finally, measures should be taken to prevent any recurrence, whether in respect of any particular individual, or the whole organisation.

11.176 In order to combat stress at work problems, a stress reduction programme should be considered where necessary. Job ambiguities should be noted, and proper job descriptions issued. There should be adequate training in the job requirements, monotonous work routines eliminated or reduced if possible, team-focused work introduced, and personality conflicts dealt with where possible. Health education may be introduced, and managers should be trained in effective management skills. Counselling may help and, in the last resort, medical advice taken or given. A well-structured stress reduction programme should produce a significant reduction in sickness absenteeism, as well as facilitate improvements in organisational efficiency.

11.177 In appropriate circumstances, an affected employee may be able to bring an action for damages at common law in respect of stress suffered from work activities, although much will depend on the facts of each case. In *Petch v Commissioners of Customs and Excise* such a claim was dismissed but in *Walker v Northumberland County Council*, the claimant was successful. Although there is a duty at common law on an employer to take reasonable care that an employee will not suffer from mental (as well as physical) injury, the extent of the precautionary steps to be taken by the employer may well be determined partly by the knowledge of the risk, but also by the perceived resilience of the employee, together with his stability of character, mental strength, the nature of the job, the financial and physical resources available, and so on. Each case is likely to give rise to complex evidential problems of causation and foreseeability.

11.178 However, as a result of a recent legal decision, the courts are likely to adopt a more cautious approach to claims for damages in respect of psychiatric injury caused by stress. In *Sutherland v Hatton*, the Court of Appeal heard appeals by employers in four unconnected cases against awards of damages to employees who had stopped work because of stress-induced psychiatric illness. Three of the appeals were allowed, while the fourth was dismissed "not without some hesitation". The court laid down a number of practical propositions designed to help other courts deal with future claims. While conceding that it was the employer's duty to take reasonable steps to ensure the physical and mental health of his employees, it was held that in order for an employer to be liable, the stress-induced injury must be sufficiently foreseeable to be plain enough for any reasonable employer to realise that he should do something about it. The Court of Appeal stated that there were no occupations which are intrinsically dangerous to mental health, that employers are entitled to assume that employees can withstand the normal pressures of the job (unless they know of some particular problem or vulnerability), and that an employee who returns to work after being absent through sickness is implying that he is fit for work, and the employer is entitled to take that at its face value. To trigger a duty to take steps, the indications of impending harm to health arising from stress at work had to be plain enough for any reasonable employer to realise that he ought to do something about it, and the employer will only be liable if he fails to take reasonable steps, bearing in mind the magnitude of the risk, the gravity of the harm, the costs and practicability of preventing it, and the justification for running the risk. Thus, it might be possible for the employer to suggest that the employee takes a sabbatical period of leave, or a transfer to other work, or a redistribution of the work, etc. Extra help may be provided, or a mentoring scheme introduced. But such assistance will depend very much on the employer's resources, and the interests of other employees at the workplace. An employer who offers a confidential advice service, with a referral to appropriate counselling or treatment services, is unlikely to be found in breach of a duty to take care although this is not a blanket defence in the absence of evidence about how such services would have helped (*Daw v Intel Corporation (UK) Ltd*).

11.179 The court went on to point out that it is not enough that the occupational stress has caused the harm. It must be shown that it was the employer's breach of duty to take reasonable care for the health of his employees that has caused or materially contributed to the harm. An employer can only reasonably be expected to take steps which are likely to do some good, and if the only reasonable steps an employer could take in order to remove the employee from a job which is causing stress is to demote the employee or dismiss him, and the employer will not be in breach of his duty for allowing a willing employee to continue in his job. If there is no alternative solution, it is for the employee to decide whether or not to continue in the job, and risk a breakdown in his health, or whether to leave the employment and look for work elsewhere. Finally, the consequence of the breach of duty may be only one of many stressful events which affected an employee's state of health, and the employer should only pay for that proportion of the harm which is attributable to his wrongdoing.

11.180 One of the cases in *Sutherland v Hatton* was appealed to the House of Lords (under the name of *Barber v Somerset County Council*). Here it was held that the outcome in every such case will depend on its own facts, but it was stressed that the best statement of general principles was outlined in *Stokes v Guest Keen and Nettlefold (Bolts and Nuts) Ltd*, where Swanwick J held that "… the overall test is still the conduct of the reasonable and prudent employer, taking positive thought for the safety of his workers in the light of what he knows or ought to know".

11.181 Liability for psychiatric injury caused by stress at work is, in general, no different in principle from liability for physical injury. The test is whether there was a foreseeable risk of injury flowing from the employer's breach of duty of care. It does not automatically follow that because an employee suffers from stress at work, the employer is in some way in breach of duty in allowing that to occur and thus automatically liable (*Hartman v South Essex Mental Health and Community Care NHS Trust*).

Private vehicles/private equipment

11.182 The fact that an employee used his own private vehicle for the purpose of the employer's business does not exonerate the employer from health and safety responsibilities. There is still a need to ensure that safety training is carried out, and safety procedures put in force. For example, there appears to be an increase in two-wheeled delivery drivers (fast food chains, document exchanges, etc) and steps should be taken to minimise or eliminate road accidents, by ensuring that such vehicles are subjected to regular periodic checks, maintenance carried out, and are taxed, appropriately insured, and roadworthy. Safety procedures require that riders must have suitable experience, delivery times must not be so unrealistic as to put pressure on riders to take risks or ride at excessive speed, and should be capable of being modified in accordance with traffic and weather conditions.

11.183 Under the Road Vehicles (Construction and Use) (Amendment) (No. 4) Regulations 2003, it is an offence to drive a motor vehicle on a public road if the driver is using a hand-held telephone or similar device. It is also an offence to cause or permit another person to drive a motor vehicle while that other person is using either instrument. This may have consequences for employers who provide such equipment for their employees and require them to keep in contact or to phone in for instructions, etc while driving a vehicle.

11.184 The prosecution of the Royal Mail over the death of a young delivery postal worker focused attention on the need to ensure that permission should be sought and given before vehicles are used on a regular basis for the employer's business. Employers should then carry out the usual risk assessment, and implement appropriate action. This is particularly important if the riders/drivers are young or inexperienced, if vehicles are being used for the purpose for which they may not have been intended (eg carrying heavy or awkward loads) or if they are so old or in such poor condition as to expose the driver/rider or other road users to the risks of an accident.

11.185 Privately-owned vehicles are not, by themselves, work equipment within the meaning of the Provision and Use of Work Equipment Regulations 1998, and in general are covered by road traffic legislation. However, motor vehicles which are owned by employees but used for the purpose of the employer's business could well come within the scope of the regulations. Additionally, motor vehicles can be "a place of work" (*Bradford v Robinson Rentals*, see paragraph 12.32). Section 2(2)(a) of HSWA requires employers to ensure that plant and systems of work must be maintained and, at common law, a vehicle is "plant" for the purpose of assessing the employer's common law duty of care. The risk assessment provisions of the Management Regulations must also be considered to be appropriate, in respect of activities involving the use of vehicles whether on or off the public highway.

11.186 Similar principles apply to the use by an employee of his own tools or equipment for the purpose of his employer's business. Risk assessments should be made, appropriate safety policies should be drawn up in accordance with the level of risk assessed, spot checks made to ensure that the tools or equipment are in good working order, maintained as appropriate, and are not likely to be the cause of injury or damage to any person.

Young persons

11.187 A young person is any person who has not attained the age of 18 and, therefore, includes children of any age. This is not to be confused with a young worker (a term used, for example, in the Working Time Regulations 1998), which refers to a person who has attained the age of 15 but not the age of 18 and who is over compulsory school age.

11.188 The Management of Health and Safety at Work Regulations 1999 (regulation 19) require every employer to carry out a risk assessment before employing a young person. The employer must also ensure that young persons employed by him are protected at work from any risks to their health and safety which are a consequence of their lack of experience, or the absence of awareness of existing or potential risks, or the fact that young persons have not yet fully matured.

11.189 In particular, an employer shall not employ a young person for work:
(a) that is beyond his physical or psychological capacity
(b) that involves harmful exposure to agents which are toxic or

carcinogenic, or cause heritable genetic damage or harm to an unborn child, or which in any other way chronically affect human health

(c) involving harmful exposure to radiation

(d) involving the risk of accidents which may reasonably be assumed cannot be recognised or avoided by young persons owing to their insufficient attention to safety, or lack of experience, or training

(e) in which there is a risk from extreme cold, heat, noise or vibration.

11.190   However, it is permissible to employ a young person who is not a child in the above work where it is necessary for his training, provided he is supervised by a competent person, and any risks have been reduced to the lowest level that is reasonably practicable.

11.191   There are special provisions in the Working Time Regulations 1998 (see paragraph 4.75) concerning free health assessments for young workers who work at night. There are also restrictions on night work (see paragraph 4.77).

11.192   There are other restrictions on the employment of young persons, including certain activities when working with lead (Control of Lead at Work Regulations 2002, schedule 1), certain work in buildings where explosives are present (Manufacture and Storage of Explosives Regulations 2005), employment on staging on or in any part of a ship (Shipbuilding and Ship Repairing Regulations 1960), and so on.

11.193   A young and/or inexperienced employee must be given proper training, clear instructions and suitable work equipment (*Fraser v Winchester Health Authority*). The HSE has issued a leaflet, *Young People at Work, A Guide for Employers*.

11.194   The Children (Protection at Work) Regulations 1998 deal with the employment of children below the minimum school leaving age, and amend the provisions of the Children and Young Persons Acts 1933 and 1963 and the Children and Young Persons (Scotland) Act 1937, in order to implement the requirements of Directive 94/33/EC on the Protection of Young Persons at Work.

11.195   The general principle is that a child under the age of 15 may not be employed in any work, other than as an employee of his parent or guardian in light agricultural work or horticultural work on an occasional basis. However, children over the age of 13 may be employed in categories of light work specified in local authorities' byelaws. Light work is defined as being work which does not jeopardise a child's safety, health, development, attendance at school or participation in work experience. Children have the right to have a two-week break from any employment in school holidays and there are restrictions on the times when they can work, on the number of hours they can work and on weekend working. Local authorities have the power to prohibit the employment of children who are employed in a manner which may be prejudicial to their health, or render them unfit to obtain the benefit of full-time education, and they may impose restrictions on such employment in terms of s.559 of the Education Act 1996.

11.196 The above legislation, together with the Children (Performances) Regulations 1968 (as amended), extends controls on the employment of children in performances, including sport, advertising and modelling. A licence may be obtained from any Justice of the Peace if it is proposed to take a child abroad for these purposes. (See also Children (Performances) (Amendment) (Wales) Regulations 2007.)

Risk assessments

11.197 There are a number of regulations that require an employer (sometimes also a self-employed person) to carry out a risk assessment. The nature of the duty and the obligations to be performed will vary in each case. The HSE has produced a leaflet, *Five steps to risk assessment*, which gives useful guidance on this subject. However, while a failure to carry out a proper risk assessment may be an offence, in criminal proceedings the prosecutor must specify in what respect the risk assessment is alleged to be inadequate, for making the allegation, by itself, is not sufficient (*Carmichael v Marks & Spencer plc*). In normal circumstances, there will have been a detailed investigation after an accident prior to charges being brought, and thus the prosecutor will have sufficient information to enable the inadequacies of the risk assessment to be identified.

11.198 On the other hand, in civil proceedings a failure to carry out a risk assessment will only be relevant if the result would have revealed a risk that was significant so that some form of control measures would have been put in place. In *Spencer v Boots the Chemist Ltd*, the claimant was employed as a pharmacist at a busy store. He began to suffer from an aching shoulder, which was diagnosed as work-related pericapulitis. He claimed damages from his employer, arguing:

(a) a breach of the Management Regulations (failure to carry out a risk assessment) and

(b) a breach of the Manual Handling Regulations (repetitive nature of his duties at the prescription counter).

11.199　His claim failed. Even if the hazard had been identified by a risk assessment, it would have shown that there was a foreseeable but not significant risk of injury. A risk assessment would not have resulted in any change in the employer's working practices.

11.200　The importance of carrying out a risk assessment cannot be over-emphasised. There is the obvious benefit of identifying risks and hazards, and thus helping to reduce the incidence of accidents and ill-health. Should an accident occur and no risk assessment has been made, it is likely that a prosecution for breach of the relevant regulations would follow. Additionally, the absence of a risk assessment has been used in the courts and employment tribunals leading to some other heading of legal liability. Three such instances can be cited.

1. In *Godfrey v Bernard Matthews plc*, the claimant had to clean between 800–1000 trays in an eight-hour shift, with three rest breaks. After a few weeks he was diagnosed as suffering from tenosynovitis, which subsequently developed into reflex sympathetic dystrophy. It was held that the injuries were work-related, and foreseeable. A risk assessment, had it been performed, would have led to some form of job rotation, which may have prevented the injury. Compensation of £212,000 was awarded.

2. In *Buxton v Equinox Design*, the employee developed multiple sclerosis. The employer was advised by the Employment Medical Advisory Service to carry out a risk assessment, but this was not done, and the employee was subsequently dismissed. The employment tribunal upheld his claim for unfair dismissal and disability discrimination, the failure to carry out a risk assessment defeating a defence of justification which had been raised. An award of £7627 compensation was made, although on appeal this matter was remitted to the tribunal for reconsideration, based on what would have been the outcome had a risk assessment been made.

3. In *Day v T Pickles Farms Ltd*, a woman was employed in a sandwich shop. She became pregnant, and the constant smell of food made her feel nauseous at work. She became unfit for work and resigned her employment. The Employment Appeal Tribunal held that she had been discriminated against on grounds of sex, in that she had

suffered a detriment because of the employer's failure to carry out a risk assessment, under the Management of Health and Safety at Work Regulations 1999. That obligation applies whenever an employer employs a woman of child-bearing age, as well as when a woman is pregnant. The claim was remitted back to the employment tribunal for reconsideration.

On the other hand, it is unrealistic to carry out a risk assessment for a mundane everyday task (*Koonjul v Thameslink Healthcare Services*), and an employer will not be liable for an injury if the carrying out of a risk assessment would not have prevented the accident (*Hawkes v London Borough of Southwark*). The following regulations require a risk assessment to be carried out.

4. *Management of Health and Safety at Work Regulations 1999* (see paragraph 4.4). Every employer shall make a suitable and sufficient assessment of the risk to the health and safety of his employees to which they are exposed at work, and the risks to the health and safety of persons not in his employment arising out of the conduct by him of his undertaking, for the purpose of identifying the measures which the employer needs to take in order to comply with the requirements and prohibitions imposed on him by any relevant statutory provision. A similar assessment shall be made by every self-employed person. The assessment shall be reviewed by the employer (or self-employed person) if there is reason to suspect it is no longer valid, or there has been a significant change in the matters to which it relates. Where the employer employs five or more employees, he shall record the significant findings of the assessment and identify any groups of his employees who are especially at risk. A risk assessment should also be made of the fire precautions in the workplace (see paragraph 5.15).

   The ACOP attached to the regulations gives further guidance on the matters to be given attention when carrying out the assessment, the general principles of risk assessment, and the follow-up with preventative and protective measures.

5. *Regulation 16 of the Management of Health and Safety at Work Regulations 1999*. Where an employer employs a woman of child-bearing age and the work is of a kind which could involve risk to her if she were pregnant, or nursing a baby, or involved risk to her baby, from any processes or working conditions, including those specified in Annexes I and II of Directive 92/85/EEC (which sets out a non-exhaustive list of certain physical, biological and chemical

agents and certain industrial processes), then the employer shall make an assessment of such risks. If the employer cannot take action under relevant statutory provisions to avoid that risk then, if it is reasonable to do so and would avoid such risks, he shall alter her working conditions or hours of work. If this is not possible, then he shall suspend her from work for so long as is necessary to avoid such risk. An employer is not required to take such action unless the woman informs him in writing that she is pregnant, has given birth to a child within the previous six months, or is breast-feeding. A guidance document accompanies the regulations (see paragraph 11.14).

6. *Regulation 19 of the Management of Health and Safety at Work Regulations 1999*. An employer shall carry out a risk assessment in respect of young persons employed by him, and the assessment shall be reviewed. The assessment will take particular account of:

   (a) the young person's inexperience, immaturity and lack of awareness of risks

   (b) the fitting-out and layout of the workplace and workstation

   (c) the nature, degree and duration of exposure to physical, biological and chemical agents

   (d) the form, range and use of work equipment and the way in which it is handled

   (e) the organisation of processes and activities

   (f) the extent of the health and safety training provided, or to be provided, to young persons

   (g) the risks from agents, processes and work listed in the Annex to Directive 94/33/EEC (which deals with ionising radiation, work in high-pressure atmosphere, biological and certain chemical agents, certain types of dangerous work connected with explosives, high-voltage electrical hazards, dangerous animals, dangerous gases, where there is a risk of structural collapse, etc). (See Chapter 4.)

7. *Control of Lead at Work Regulations 2002* (see paragraph 7.49). The employer shall not carry on any work which is liable to expose employees to lead at work unless he has made a suitable and sufficient assessment of whether the exposure of any employee to lead is liable to be significant. The requirement is without prejudice to the matters set out in regulation 3 of the Management of Health and Safety at Work Regulations 1999 (see paragraph 4.8). The

Approved Code of Practice gives further guidance on how the assessment is to be carried out, by whom, and the matters which should be considered, etc.

8. *Control of Asbestos Regulations 2006* (see paragraph 7.23). An employer shall not carry out any work which exposes any of his employees to asbestos unless he has made an adequate assessment of that exposure, identifying the type of asbestos, determining the nature and degree of exposure, and setting out the steps to be taken to prevent or reduce this to the lowest level reasonably practicable. The assessment shall be reviewed regularly, and a new assessment substituted, when there is reason to suspect that the existing assessment is no longer valid, or where there is a significant change in the work to which the assessment relates.

An Approved Code of Practice (ACOP) accompanies the regulations, which spells out the tasks to be performed when making an assessment in greater detail.

9. *Control of Substances Hazardous to Health Regulations 2002* (see paragraph 7.1). An employer shall not carry on any work which is liable to expose any employees to any substance hazardous to health unless he has made a suitable and sufficient assessment of the risks created by that work to the health of those employees, and of the steps that need to be taken to meet the requirements of the regulations. The assessment shall be reviewed regularly or if there is reason to suspect that it is no longer valid or there has been a significant change in the work to which it relates, and changes shall be made in the assessment as required.

A number of Approved Codes of Practice have been issued, and the HSE has produced a number of guidance documents.

10. *Manual Handling Operations Regulations 1992* (see paragraph 6.130). Where it is not reasonably practicable to avoid the need for employees to undertake any manual handling operations which involve a risk of their being injured, every employer shall make a suitable and sufficient assessment of all such manual handling operations undertaken by the employees. Then, having regard to the questions specified in schedule 1 to the regulations (see paragraph 6.142) the employer shall take appropriate steps to reduce the risk of injury to the lowest level reasonably practicable, and take appropriate steps to provide those employees with general indications and precise information on the weight of each load and the heaviest side of any load whose centre of gravity is not

positioned centrally. The assessment shall be reviewed when the employer suspects it is no longer valid, or there has been a significant change in the manual handling operations to which it relates, and changes will be made to the assessment as are appropriate in the light of the review.

The regulations are accompanied by comprehensive Guidance Notes, L23: *Manual Handling*.

11. *Personal Protective Equipment at Work Regulations 1992* (see paragraph 6.99). Before choosing any personal protective equipment (PPE) required by regulation 4 (see paragraph 6.104) an employer (or self-employed person) shall make an assessment to determine whether the PPE he intends to provide is suitable. The assessment shall consist of:

(a) risks which have not been avoided by other means

(b) the definition of the characteristics which the PPE must have in order to be effective against the above risks

(c) a comparison of the characteristics of the PPE with the characteristics of the PPE needed to be effective against those risks.

The assessment shall be reviewed forthwith if there is reason to suspect that any element of it is no longer valid, or there has been a significant change in the work to which the assessment relates. If, as a result of the review, changes in the assessment are required, these shall be made.

The regulations are accompanied by detailed Guidance Notes, L25: *Personal Protective Equipment at Work*.

12. *Health and Safety (Display Screen Equipment) Regulations 1992* (see paragraph 6.151). Every employer shall analyse the workstations in his undertaking for the purpose of assessing the risks to the health and safety of any user which arise out of or in connection with a person's use of those workstations. Any risks identified by the assessment shall be reduced to the lowest extent reasonably practicable.

The regulations are accompanied by Guidance Notes (L26: *Display Screen Equipment Work*) which give further information on the form, method and purpose of the assessment.

13. *Genetically Modified Organisms (Contained Use) Regulations 2000* (as amended) (see paragraph 7.91) require a risk assessment to be carried out before the premises are first used and before undertaking any activity involving genetic modification. The

organisms shall be classified, and decisions made about the level of confinement. The assessment shall be reviewed if it is no longer valid, or if there has been a significant change in the activity.

14. *Ionising Radiations Regulations 1999* (see paragraph 8.1). Before commencing a new practice involving work with ionising radiations in respect of which no risk assessment has been made, a radiation employer shall make a suitable and sufficient assessment of the risk to any employee and other person, for the purpose of identifying the measures he needs to take to restrict the exposure of that employee or other person to ionising radiation. Work shall not commence with ionising radiations unless the assessment is sufficient to demonstrate that all hazards with a potential to cause a radiation accident have been identified, and the nature and magnitude of the risks to employees and to other persons have been evaluated.

15. *Dangerous Substances and Explosive Atmospheres Regulations 2002* (see paragraph 7.100). Where a dangerous substance is present at the workplace, the employer should make a suitable and sufficient assessment of the risks to employees which arise from that substance. The risk assessment must include consideration of:
    (a) the hazardous properties of the substance
    (b) information on safety provided by the supplier, including information contained in any relevant data sheet
    (c) the circumstances of the work
    (d) activities such as maintenance
    (e) the effect of measures which will be taken
    (f) the likelihood that an explosive atmosphere will occur
    (g) the likelihood that ignition sources will be present and become active
    (h) the scale of the anticipated effects of a fire or explosion
    (i) any places which are connected via an opening to places where an explosion may occur
    (j) any additional information needed to complete the risk assessment.

16. *Control of Vibration at Work Regulations 2005* (see paragraph 8.38). An employer who carries out work which is liable to expose any employees to risk from vibration shall make a suitable and sufficient assessment of the risk created by that work to the health and safety of those employees and of the steps that need to be taken to meet the requirements of the regulations.

17. *Regulatory Reform (Fire Safety) Order 2005* (see paragraph 5.10). The responsible person must make a suitable and sufficient assessment of the risks to which relevant persons are exposed for the purpose of identifying the general fire precautions he needs to take to comply with the requirements and prohibitions imposed on him under the Order.

18. *Control of Noise at Work Regulations 2005* (see paragraph 8.28). An employer who carries out work which is likely to expose any employees to noise at or above the lower exposure action level shall make a suitable and sufficient assessment of the risk created by that work to the health and safety of those employees, and the risk assessment shall identify the measures which need to be taken to meet the requirements of the regulations.

Health surveillance

11.201 Under the Management of Health and Safety at Work Regulations 1999 (regulation 6) every employer shall ensure that his employees are provided with such health surveillance as is appropriate having regard to the risks to their health and safety which are identified by the risk assessment. The general requirement to introduce health surveillance applies when the assessment reveals an identifiable disease or health condition arising from the work, and there is a reasonable likelihood that the disease or condition will occur under the particular working conditions. A health record should be kept, any symptoms noted and examined by an occupational nurse or doctor, biological monitoring carried out, and techniques developed for detection.

11.202 Under the Control of Substances Hazardous to Health Regulations 2002 (regulation 11) suitable health surveillance is required in respect of employees who are, or who are likely to be, exposed to substances hazardous to health, ie if there is exposure to one of the substances specified in column 1 of schedule 6, and engaged in a process set out in column 2 of that schedule (unless the exposure is not significant) or if the exposure to a substance hazardous to health is such that an identifiable disease or adverse health condition may be related to the exposure. There must be a reasonable likelihood that the disease or effect may occur under the particular conditions of work, and that there are valid techniques for detecting indications of the disease or the effect. If the exposure is to column 1 of schedule 6 substances and the employee is engaged in column 2 of schedule 6 processes, the health surveillance must include a medical surveillance under the supervision of an employment medical advisor or appointed doctor at intervals of not more than 12 months or at such shorter intervals as may be required.

11.203   Under the Control of Lead at Work Regulations 2002 (regulation 10) every employer shall ensure that each of his employees who is or who is likely to be exposed to lead is under suitable medical surveillance by a relevant doctor, where the exposure is likely to be significant or a relevant doctor certifies that the employee should be under medical surveillance. So far as is reasonably practicable, the medical surveillance shall be carried out before the employee commences any work which gives rise to exposure to lead or in any event within 14 working days, and thereafter at intervals of not more than 12 months or such shorter intervals as the relevant doctor may require. Biological monitoring shall be carried out on employees (except women of reproductive capacity and young persons) every six months unless on two previous occasions the lead-in-air exposure and blood-lead concentration was below certain limits, in which case the biological monitoring can be carried out once a year. Biological monitoring shall also be carried out at least every three months on women of reproductive capacity and young persons. A relevant doctor is an appointed doctor or an employment medical advisor.

11.204   Under the Ionising Radiations Regulations 1999 (regulation 24) the employer shall ensure that each of his employees to whom the regulation applies is under adequate medical surveillance by an appointed doctor or employment medical advisor for the purpose of determining the fitness of each employee for work with ionising radiations. This regulation applies to classified persons (and persons who are to be designated as classified), employees who have received an overexposure and are not classified persons, and employees who are engaged in work with ionising radiations subject to conditions imposed by an appointed doctor or employment medical advisor. A health record shall be kept (containing the prescribed particulars, see schedule 7) and a copy kept until the person to whom it relates reaches the age of 75, or in any event for at least 50 years from the date of the last entry. If the appointed doctor or employment medical advisor is of the opinion that the employee should not be engaged in work with ionising radiations, the employer shall not permit this (except in accordance with any specified conditions).

11.205 Under the Control of Asbestos Regulations 2006, every employer shall ensure that each of his employees who is exposed to asbestos is under adequate medical surveillance by an employment medical advisor or appointed doctor unless the exposure does not exceed the action level. The employer should also keep a health record, containing approved particulars, which must be kept for 40 years. On reasonable notice being given, an employee is entitled to have access to his health records.

11.206 Health surveillance is also required under the Control of Vibration at Work Regulations 2005 (see paragraph 8.38) and the Control of Noise at Work Regulations 2005 (see paragraph 8.28).

Accident, incident and emergency procedures

11.207 There are several regulations that impose requirements on an employer to ensure that proper and comprehensive arrangements are made in order to deal with accidents, incidents and emergencies. The Management of Health and Safety at Work Regulations 1999 (regulation 8) requires employers to establish procedures for serious and imminent danger and for danger areas and to ensure that any necessary contacts are arranged with external services, particularly as regards first aid, emergency medical care and rescue work. The requirements laid down in the Control of Substances Hazardous to Health Regulations 2002 (regulation 13) are somewhat more comprehensive and include safety drills, information on emergency arrangements, suitable warnings and the provision of information to the emergency services. Similar provisions are to be found in the Control of Asbestos Regulations 2006 (regulation 15), the Control of Lead at Work Regulations 2002 (regulation 12) and the Dangerous Substances and Explosive Atmospheres Regulations 2002 (regulation 8).

Provision of instruction, information and training

11.208 There are a number of legislative provisions which require, in one form or another, an employer to provide the necessary information, instruction and training. Information requires the provisions of facts; instruction is basically teaching; and training is a more structured form of instruction. Whereas generally these requirements apply to employers in respect of their own employees, information may be additionally required to be given to others affected by work activities.

11.209 To be effective, training should be tailored to the needs of the employer and the nature of the work. It can be done in classrooms, on the job, or by means of external courses or distance learning programmes, for example, taking into account the risks of the job and the methods of avoiding those risks. Training should be updated as appropriate. In particular, an employee should be trained (or retrained) when an area of incompetence is revealed, if this is appropriate together with or as an alternative to taking disciplinary action.

11.210 Provisions which, in particular, should be noted include:
  (a) regulations 10–15 of the Management of Health and Safety at Work Regulations 1999
  (b) regulation 9 of the Personal Protective Equipment at Work Regulations 1992
  (c) regulations 6–7 of the Health and Safety (Display Screen Equipment) Regulations 1992
  (d) regulations 8–9 of the Provision and Use of Work Equipment Regulations 1998
  (e) regulation 12 of the Control of Substances Hazardous to Health Regulations 2002
  (f) regulation 11 of the Control of Lead at Work Regulations 2002
  (g) regulation 10 of the Control of Asbestos Regulations 2006
  (h) regulation 9 of the Dangerous Substances and Explosive Atmospheres Regulations 2002
  (i) regulations 4–5 of the Health and Safety Information for Employees Regulations 1989
  (j) regulation 27 of the Safety Representatives and Safety Committees Regulations 1977
  (k) regulation 7 of the Health and Safety (Consultation with Employees) Regulations 1996
  (l) regulation 6(b) of the Work at Height Regulations 2005
  (m) regulation 8 of the Control of Vibration at Work Regulations 2005
  (n) regulation 10 of the Control of Noise at Work Regulations 2005
  (o) regulations 19-21 of the Regulatory Reform (Fire Safety) Order 2005.

11.211 If there is a failure to train or to provide proper instructions and information and there is an accident, injury or dangerous occurrence in consequence of that failure, this may result in either criminal or civil proceedings being brought, as appropriate.

417

11.212 It is not sufficient for the training to deal with the risks which the employer knows about. The test for the adequacy of training is what is needed in the light of the risks that the employer ought to know about arising from the activities of his business (*Allison v London Underground Ltd*).

Keeping records

11.213 Problems can be incurred by anyone who has responsibilities for health and safety within an organisation due to the amount of record-keeping which has to be done. In the fullness of time, filing cabinets become overloaded, files misplaced, new personnel have great difficulties in locating previous records, and so on. Doubtless computerised information may alleviate the situation, but storing such information may take time and expertise.

11.214 There are three problems to consider. The first concerns the nature of the records that need to be kept. Clearly, certain documentation is required by law, including employers' liability insurance certificates, safety policies, risk assessments, certain medical and health surveillance records, working time records, atmospheric monitoring, records of accidents and diseases, etc. Other documents need to be kept as evidence that certain things have been done, eg minutes of safety committee meetings, inspection systems, maintenance logs, safety rules and procedures, safety audits, requests for information from suppliers, and so on. The value of such documentation will largely be proportionate to the use to which it is put. Collecting statistics for their own sake is a pointless exercise. Collecting them for the purpose of showing trends or problems in health and safety procedures can be of value, if positive action is thereby provoked. Obviously, adequate and complete records will be of great value in proving a point in an employment tribunal or High Court in the event of litigation arising. Many a case has been won or lost on the basis of good or poor records.

11.215 The next problem to arise concerns the length of time such documents need to be kept. Apart from specific statutory requirements (see below), there is no easy solution. A worker who has been injured and who wishes to claim compensation from his employer must generally bring a claim within three years of the accident or injury in question, and to that extent records of any such event could be destroyed once that period has passed. However, the Limitation Act

1980 (see paragraph 12.77) also contains a provision that the court may extend the time for bringing a claim to three years from the date when the employee knew, or ought to have known, that his employer was in breach of an alleged legal duty. Thus certain medical conditions, like bladder cancer, pneumoconiosis, asbestosis, etc may take many years to develop into full-blown illnesses, and records going back many years, concerning the nature of the employment (eg was the employee exposed to the alleged hazard?) and the precautions that were taken (eg was he provided with information, instruction, training, protective clothing, etc?) could well have a determinant effect on the outcome of the case. Claims brought before an employment tribunal must normally be brought within three months from the alleged act or default of the employer, but again, the tribunals have a wide discretion in allowing claims out of time if it was not reasonably practicable to have brought the claim earlier. In criminal matters, proceedings in respect of summary offences must be brought within six months from the alleged offence, but "time does not run against the Crown" and proceedings in respect of an indictable offence may be brought many years after the commission of the alleged offence. The ability to produce records to an HSE inspector, showing that safe systems of work, safe operating procedures, etc were in place, and that the legal requirements relating to training, supervision, provision of information, etc were complied with, may well pre-empt a decision to prosecute or, alternatively, strongly influence a jury's decision in criminal proceedings.

11.216 The final problem is how to ensure that adequate and accurate records are kept, whilst at the same time ensuring compliance with the provisions of the Data Protection Act 1998. Under that Act, there are various constraints on the manner and contents of data that can be held by an employer, whether in manual or electronic form. Workers have the right to obtain a copy of any information that an organisation has on them, and may apply to the court to obtain an order requiring a data controller to correct inaccurate information thereon, and seek compensation where damage or distress has been caused. The Act created the post of Information Commissioner, who has produced an Employment Practices Data Protection Code, which gives guidance on how employment matters can be dealt with under the provision of the Data Protection Act. The code is in four parts:

(a) recruitment and selection

(b) employment records

(c) monitoring at work

(d) information about workers' health.

11.217 The code itself is not legally binding and any enforcement action has to be based on a breach of the Act. However, the relevant benchmarks would be cited by the Commissioner in such proceedings and a disregard of those requirments is likely to mean that an employer does not comply with the Act.

11.218 Part 1 of the code deals with advertising, applications and verifications, shortlisting and interviews of applicants, pre-employment vetting, and retention of recruitment records.

11.219 Part 2 of the code deals with procedures and penalties for storing personal data about employees and job applicants, as well as the processes for subject access requests.

11.220 Part 3 of the code deals with monitoring at work. It covers the use of CCTV cameras, automatic checking software to monitor the use or mis-use of e-mails, recording telephone calls and videoing workers who are on sickness leave to ensure that they are not malingering. Since a balance must be drawn between the worker's right to privacy and the employer's monitoring requirements, workers must be clearly informed of the purpose of those arrangements and the employer must be satisfied that the particular arrangement is justified by the benefits that will ensue. The decision whether to monitor or not should be made by a senior member of staff and it should be done with a minimum of intrusiveness, with spot-checks and annual audits being preferred to continuous monitoring. All employees should, as far as possible, be treated equally.

11.221 Part 4 is entitled *Information About Workers' Health* and covers such topics as occupational health schemes, medical examinations and testing, drug and alcohol testing and genetic testing.

11.222 The HSE has issued a new Accident Book, which has been approved by the Information Commissioner, in order to ensure compliance with the Data Protection Act. This will allow accidents to be recorded while the details of individuals concerned can be stored separately in a secure location.

11.223 Sometimes, relevant information may be requested by an external body, although as a general principle the employer may not necessarily have a legal obligation to provide such information. For example, a request may come from the Benefits Agency for information as to the nature of the work (and/or work processes used) carried out by an employee (or ex-employee) in order that a claim for industrial injuries benefit may be determined, arising out of the use of certain tools or equipment or exposure to certain substances, which are set out in schedule 1 of the Social Security (Industrial Injuries) (Prescribed Diseases) Regulations 1985 (as amended). On such a claim, the employer is basically a disinterested party.

11.224 Certain legislative provisions require documents or records to be kept for a specified period of time. These include the following.

Statutory provision	Records to be kept	Length of time
Social Security (Claims and Payments) Regulations 1979	Accident Book (Form B1510)	3 years from date of an entry
Control of Asbestos Regulations 2006	Health records; Certificate of medical information	40 years
	Examination and tests of exhaust ventilation equipment and respiratory protective equipment (except disposable respiratory protective equipment).	At least 5 years from the date on which such tests and examinations were made
Control of Explosives Regulations 1991	Possession of explosives	3 years from last date of entry
Offshore Installations (Safety Case) Regulations 2005	Safety case; Copy of audit report and written statement	As long as is current; 3 years after being made
Reporting of Injuries, Diseases and Dangerous Occurrences Regulations 1995	Record of reportable injuries and dangerous occurrences	3 years from date when made
	Record of diseases	3 years from date when made
Offshore Installations and Pipeline Works (Management and Administration) Regulations 1995	Onshore record of persons working on installation	28 days after ceasing to work

Statutory provision	Records to be kept	Length of time
Construction (Design and Management) Regulations 2007	Report of inspection	3 months from completion of work
Work in Compressed Air Regulations 1996	Health record	40 years from date of last entry
	Exposure to compressed air	40 years from date of last entry
Control of Lead at Work Regulations 2002	Record of examinations and tests of control measures and respiratory equipment	5 years from date when made
	Air monitoring	5 years
	Adequate health record	40 years from date of last entry
Provision and Use of Work Equipment Regulations 1998	Reports of power press examinations	2 years from date when made
Lifting Operations and Lifting Equipment Regulations 1998	Reports of thorough examination of lifting equipment	Until employer ceases use of lifting equipment
Working Time Regulations 1998	Maximum weekly working time; Exclusion from maximum weekly working time; Length of night work	2 years from date when made
	Health assessment for night workers and young workers	Not specified
Control of Substances Hazardous to Health Regulations 2002	List of employees exposed to Group 3 or Group 4 biological agents	10 years from last known exposure or 40 years if exposure may result in infection
	Examination and tests of control measures	5 years from date when made

Statutory provision	Records to be kept	Length of time
	Monitoring of specified substances or processes	40 years from personal exposure of identifiable employees
	Health record	40 years from date of last entry
Ionising Radiations Regulations 1999	Dose assessment after accident	50 years (or until the age of 75)
	Health record	50 years (or until the age of 75)
	Examination of respiratory protective equipment	2 years
	Dose record	2 years
Pressure Systems Safety Regulations 2000	Report made by competent person	Until next report
Railways (Safety Case) Regulations 2000	Safety case for train operators	So long as is current
	Reports and records	5 years after made
Regulatory Reform (Fire Safety) Order 2005	Record of fire safety arrangements	Ongoing
Control of Noise at Work Regulations 2005	Health record	Not specified
Control of Vibration at Work Regulations 2005	Health record	Not specified
Work at Height Regulations 2005	Inspection of work equipment	Until next inspection

CHAPTER 12

Compensation for injuries at work

12.1 Inevitably, an employee who is injured in the course of employment will seek some form of compensation from the person (if any) who was responsible for those injuries, or look to the state to provide some assistance. If an employee is killed, his dependants will also be seeking some form of financial recompense for themselves. It is this area of the law which in the past has tended to dominate all other considerations of health and safety, as compensation, rather than prevention, became the main function of the law. This attitude prompted the Robens Committee to attempt some shift in the impact of the legislation.

12.2 It is a truism to say that legal decisions reflect the current social and economic forces of the day and this explains some of the changes in judicial attitudes which have taken place from time to time. Further, the impact of state and private insurance schemes (especially employers' liability insurance) has cast a powerful shadow over strict legal reasoning, for there is a natural tendency to seek some way in which the injured employee can be assisted financially and, after all, if an insurance company had to foot the bill, this could easily be recouped by a minute increase in general premiums. This benevolent attitude even reached employers, and there are many cases where liability is admitted or where valiant attempts were made to admit their own negligence so as to enable an injured employee to obtain compensation (eg see *Hilton v Thomas Burton (Rhodes) Ltd*). But there were limits, too, on judicial credulity, which compelled some judges to hold that they could no longer equate the relationship between employer and employee with that of nurse and imbecile child (Lord Simmonds in *Smith v Austin Lifts Ltd*) or that of schoolmaster and pupil (Devlin LJ in *Withers v Perry Chain Ltd*).

12.3 The basis of the employer's duty towards his employees stems from the existence of a contract of employment. It is an implied term of that contract that the employer will take reasonable care to ensure the safety of his employees (*Matthews v Kuwait Bechtel Corporation*), and an employer who fails to fulfil that duty is in breach of that contract (*British Aircraft Corporation v Austin*). The express terms of the contract must be capable of co-existing with the implied terms. In *Johnstone v Bloomsbury*

Health Authority, Dr Johnstone was required by his contract of employment to work a basic 40-hour week, and to be "on call" for a further 48 hours each week. He claimed that the number of hours he had to work were intolerable, depriving him of sleep, with consequent depression, stress and anxiety, which could result in the risk of mistakes or inefficient treatment of patients. He sought a declaration that he could not lawfully be required to work for so many hours in excess of his standard working week as would foreseeably injure his health. At a preliminary hearing, the Court of Appeal held that he had established an arguable case to warrant a full trial of the issues. The court, however, were not unanimous in their views, but it appears that the employer's right to require Dr Johnstone to work up to 48 hours "on call" was subject to the implied duty of the employer to take care that the employee's health was not damaged as a result. Further, it was held that it was arguable that the term (that he should work for up to 88 hours a week) was void under the Unfair Contract Terms Act 1977, which prohibits a contract term which excludes or restricts liability for personal injury caused by negligence. Since the offending term could be said to restrict or limit the ambit of the duty of care owed by the employers, the claimant was permitted to proceed with that aspect of his claim.

12.4 However, from the point of view of an injured employee there is little advantage in suing in contract. Practically all modern cases are brought under the law of tort, in particular for the tort of negligence which, since the famous case of *Donoghue v Stevenson* in 1932 consists of three general ingredients, namely (a) there is a general duty to take care not to injure someone whom one might reasonably foresee would be injured by acts or omissions, (b) that duty is broken if a person acts in a negligent manner, and (c) the breach of the duty must cause injury or damage. The existence of a duty-situation between employer and employee has been long recognised, and most of the cases turn on the second point, ie was the employer in fact negligent?

12.5 The liability of the employer may come about in two ways. First, he will be responsible for his own acts of negligence. These may be his personal failures or (since many employers nowadays are artificial legal entities, ie limited companies or other types of corporations) due to the wrongdoings of the various acts of management acting as the *alter ego* of the employer. Second, the employer may be liable vicariously for the wrongful acts of his employees which are committed in the scope of their employment and which cause injury or damage to others.

12.6   Compensation may be obtained under one or more of three headings. The first is for the injured employee (or his personal representatives, if he has died) to bring an action at common law. This will be for either (a) a breach by the employer of a duty laid down by statute, or (b) a breach of the duty owed by the employer at common law to ensure the health and safety of his employees. Frequently, a claim will be presented under both headings simultaneously. With two strings to his bow, it matters not if he wins under either heading, or both. (Of course, if he wins under both, he will only get one lot of damages.) It is regarded as a misfortune if he fails under both headings, for he has then lost his main financial solace. It was the uncertainties of litigation in this area of the law, the difficulties of establishing satisfactory evidential standards in court hearings held years after an incident had occurred, the legal expenses and complexities, and the social injustices caused, which were among the main reasons for the appointment of the Pearson Commission in 1974. Its report, however, did not recommend any major changes in the compensation system.

12.7   The second remedy for an injured employee is the automatic recourse to the National Insurance (Industrial Injuries) scheme operated by the state in one form or another since 1911 (see now the Social Security (Contributions and Benefits) Act 1992), which provide for a pension in respect of an injury at work or a prescribed disease which causes permanent disabilities. This scheme is in addition to the right to sue at common law, although benefits payable will be taken into account when fixing damages. However, the state scheme operates as of right, irrespective of the existence of fault or blame on the part of any person, including the injured worker.

12.8   Third, in appropriate circumstances, there are other schemes which may be resorted to, such as those operated by the Criminal Injuries Compensation Authority, the Motor Insurers' Bureau or (rarely used) the power of the courts to award compensation.

Claims at common law

Breach of statutory duty

12.9   When Parliament lays down a duty for a person to perform, it will usually ensure that there is an appropriate sanction to enforce that duty. This sanction will normally take the form of some sort of punishment in the criminal courts. The further question will thus arise; can a person who has been injured by the failure of another to perform that statutory duty bring a civil action based on that failure? After some hesitation, British courts upheld an action for the tort of breach of statutory duty, although the full extent of legal liability is not entirely settled. There is no automatic presumption that all breaches of statutory duties are actionable in civil courts; it is necessary to examine the purposes and objects of the statute in question, seek the intentions of Parliament (it is now permissible to look at Hansard in order to ascertain those intentions, see *Pepper v Hart*, paragraph 1.121) and ascertain the class of persons for whose benefit the Act was passed. If the injured party has suffered the type of harm the Act was designed to eliminate, it would not be unreasonable to grant him a remedy in respect of a breach of the statutory duty. The first case in which these propositions were accepted was *Groves v Lord Wimborne*, where a statute provided that an occupier of a factory who did not fence dangerous machinery was liable to a fine of up to £100. A boy employed in the factory was caught in an unfenced cog wheel, and his arm was amputated. It was held that the criminal penalty was irrelevant to civil liability, and the claim for a breach of statutory duty succeeded.

12.10   However, not every breach of statutory duty is actionable (eg see *Richardson v Pitt-Stanley*, paragraph 5.9), and though the point appears to be well-settled so far as health and safety legislation is concerned, there are one or two areas where there may still be an element of doubt. Certain legal problems were encountered when dealing with the welfare provisions of the Factories Act 1961 and the Offices, Shops and Railway Premises Act 1963 (eg see *Ebbs v James Whitson & Co Ltd*), but as those provisions have now been repealed the point need no longer be of concern.

12.11   No civil action may be brought in respect of a breach of the provisions contained in ss.2–8 of HSWA, but if an employee is injured because his employer has failed to observe the requirements of a health and safety regulation, this will amount to the tort of breach of statutory duty, in respect of which the employee may be able to recover damages (eg *Hawkes v London Borough of Southwark*, see paragraph 6.141). This is so in respect of all such regulations, eg COSHH, manual handling, personal protective equipment, control of lead, and so on, unless there is a specific exclusion of civil liability.

Elements of the tort of breach of statutory duty

12.12   In order to succeed in a claim for breach of statutory duty, a claimant must show four things.

1. That he is within the class of person that the statute or regulations were designed to protect. Thus, since the Management of Health and Safety at Work Regulations 1999 are generally designed to protect employees, it is only employees who will be able to sue for a breach. Contractors, agency workers, members of the public, etc will not have such a right. In *Ricketts v Torbay Council*, the claimant tripped on an uneven surface in a council car park. She sued for damages, arguing that the car park was a workplace, and under regulation 12 of the Workplace (Health, Safety and Welfare) Regulations 1996 there was a requirement that every floor in a workplace and the surface of every traffic route shall be suitable for the purpose and that floors and surfaces must be free from anything that may cause any person to slip, trip or fall. She argued that "any person" meant any person who was there lawfully. Her claim was dismissed by the Court of Appeal. The regulations were designed to protect persons at work in the workplace (see also *Donaldson v Hays Distribution Services Ltd*, paragraph 6.8). Similarly, in *Reid v Galbraith's Stores*, it was held that the provisions of the Offices, Shops and Railways Premises Act 1963 did not apply to a customer who was visiting the shop as the Act was concerned with the protection of persons who were at work in the shop. It follows that when statutory provisions are made for the benefit of a particular class of person, only those who are in that class can take advantage of the statutory provisions (*Canadian Pacific Steamship Ltd v Byers*).

2. An action for breach of statutory duty can only succeed if the breach is one against which the statute is designed to protect (*Gorris v Scott*) and not some other unconnected risk. In *Fytche v Wincanton Logistics plc*, the claimant was employed to drive a 32-tonne articulated bulk tanker collecting milk from farms. He was provided with steel-capped safety boots designed to protect his feet against injury from heavy, sharp or hard objects. The boots were changed every six months. He suffered from frostbite in his toe, caused by working in extremely cold weather conditions because, unknown to anyone, there was a tiny hole in the boots that permitted water to seep in. He brought an action for damages, alleging a breach of regulation 7 of the Personal Protective Equipment at Work Regulations. His claim

failed. The regulations only applied to those risks against which the equipment was designed to provide protection, and the boots were ordinarily satisfactory for the work he was employed to do. His only remedy would be an action for common law negligence, but as the judge found that there had been no breach of the common law duty of care because the defect was not known to the employers and could not reasonably have been discovered by them, his claim failed.

Similarly, in *Close v Steel Company of Wales*, a worker was injured by a piece of machinery that flew out of a machine. His claim, based on a breach of s.14 of the Factories Act 1961 (duty to fence dangerous parts of machinery) failed. The object of s.14 was to prevent the worker from coming into contact with the machine, not to stop parts of the machine from coming into contact with the worker. The purpose of fencing was not to keep the machine or its products inside the fence.

So far as the Management Regulations are concerned, there are some general provisions that are likely to be relevant in civil litigation, including regulation 3 (risk assessment), regulation 6 (health surveillance), regulation 8 (procedures for serious and imminent danger), regulation 10 (information for employees), regulation 13 (capability and training) and regulation 14 (duties of employees), etc. Thus a failure to carry out a proper risk assessment under regulation 3 of the Management Regulations or to carry out health surveillance under regulation 6 may give rise to civil liability where an employee suffers from a physical illness or psychiatric illness caused by stress at work. Other regulations have more specific requirements, a breach of which may, in appropriate circumstances, give rise to civil liability.

3. That there was a failure to carry out that duty. If the duty imposed by the statute or regulation is an absolute one, there can be no defence if there is a breach (*Stark v Post Office*). On the other hand, if the provisions require an employer to do all that is reasonably practicable, a failure to note a trivial risk would not give risk to such liability (*Furness v Midland Bank plc*). It is a question of fact in each case as to whether or not a defendant has complied with the relevant standard.

4. The damage or injury must actually be caused by the breach. This is the causation rule. Thus, if an accident occurs and no risk assessment has been carried out, it is a likely conclusion that the breach was in some way responsible for the accident or injury (*Griffiths v Vauxhall*

Motors Ltd). In *McWilliams v Sir William Arrol & Co Ltd*, the employers provided safety belts for steel erectors on a site. As the belts were not being used, they were taken to another site. A steel erector on the first site fell from a scaffolding and was killed. Although the employers were clearly in breach of their statutory duty to provide the safety belts, they were not liable for damages. Even if they had provided the belts, there is nothing to suggest that this worker (who had never used them before) would have worn them on the day he was killed. Thus, the breach of duty did not cause the damage; it would have occurred anyway.

12.13 But if an injury is caused by the act of the injured employee, which would not have occurred if the employer had performed his statutory duties, then the employer will be liable for damages unless the act of the employee was an unnatural and improbable consequence of the breach. For example, in *McGovern v British Steel Corporation*, the plaintiff was walking along a gangway made from scaffold boards. He saw a toe board which had fallen from the upright position and which was obstructing the walkway. He attempted to pick it up but, because it was jammed, it "whiplashed" causing him to suffer from a slipped disc. It was held that the employer was liable. The injury was not caused by the employee tripping or falling over the obstruction, but by the employer's breach of duty in failing to remove it. It was natural that the employee should attempt to do this, and the injury was not unforeseeable. Thus the injury was a natural and probable cause of the breach and the conduct of the employee was not such as to break the chain of causation.

12.14 A curious point about what constitutes actionable damage arose in the recent "pleural plaques" cases (see *Grieves v FT Everard & Sons*, paragraph 7.48). The claimants had been negligently exposed by their employers to asbestos dust. This caused them to develop pleural plaques, which were localised thickening on the membrane which facilitated the movement of the lung in the course of respiration. However, this condition is in no way debilitating, but there is a risk of developing one or more long-term asbestos-related diseases, and there is also the anxiety at the prospect that the claimants might suffer such a disease in the future. The Court of Appeal held that the claimants had not shown a sufficient cause of action. The mere presence of pleural plaques did not, by itself, justify an award of compensation, because these were symptomless and had no adverse effect on bodily functions.

In other words, there was no actual damage caused by the employer's negligence. Neither did the fact of the potential for future damage justify an award, and the anxiety which at least one of the claimants suffered from was not a foreseeable consequence of the employer's negligence. Thus each of the claimant's claims failed, and the court further held that there was no legal precedent for aggregating the three heads of claim, each of which would have been unsuccessful, into one successful head of claim. (See also *Rothwell v Chemical and Insulating Co Ltd*, paragraph 12.49.)

Negligence

12.15   At common law the employer is under a duty to take reasonable care for the health and safety of his employees. This duty is a particular aspect of the general law of negligence, which requires everyone to ensure that his activities do not cause injury or damage to another through some act of carelessness or inadvertence (see *Donoghue v Stevenson*, paragraph 12.4). The court must decide whether the wrongdoer (or tortfeasor) could have reasonably foreseen the injury (whether physical or psychological) to the victim (*Alcock v Chief Constable of Yorkshire*).

12.16   The employer must protect against personal injury, which can be physical or psychiatric, such as a nervous breakdown caused by stress of overwork in employment (see, eg *Daw v Intel Corp. (UK) Ltd*), but does not necessarily extend to the employee's personal property (*Deyong v Shenburn*), nor to the relatives of the employee in the absence of foreseeability (*Hewett v Alf Brown's Transport Ltd*).

The personal nature of the duty

12.17   The duty at common law is owed personally by the employer to his employee, and he does not escape that duty by showing that he has delegated the performance to some competent person. In *Wilsons and Clyde Coal Co v English*, the employer was compelled by law to employ a colliery agent who was responsible for safety in the mine. Nonetheless, when an accident occurred, the employer was held liable. Thus it can never be a defence for an employer to show that he has assigned the responsibility of securing and maintaining health and safety precautions to a safety officer or other person. He can delegate the performance, but not the responsibility.

12.18   Further, the duty is owed to each employee as an individual, not to employees collectively. Greater precautions must be taken when dealing with young or inexperienced workers and with new or untrained employees than one might take with more responsible staff. The former may require greater attention paid to their working methods or may need more supervision (*Byers v Head Wrightson & Co Ltd*). In *Paris v Stepney Borough Council*, the plaintiff was employed to scrape away rust and other superfluous rubbish which had accumulated underneath buses. It was not customary to provide goggles for this kind of work. However, the plaintiff had only one good eye, and he was totally blinded when a splinter entered his good eye. It was held that the employers were liable for damages. They should have foreseen that there was a risk of greater injury to this employee if he was not given adequate safety precautions and the fact that they may not have been under a duty to provide goggles to other employees was irrelevant.

12.19   A higher standard of care is also owed to employees whose command of the English language is insufficient to understand or comply with safety instructions, to ensure that as a result they do not cause injuries to themselves or to others. In *James v Hepworth and Grandage Ltd*, the employers put up large notices urging employees to wear spats for their personal protection. Unknown to them, one of their employees could not read, and when he was injured he claimed damages from his employer. His claim failed. He had observed other workers wearing spats and his failure to make any enquiries led the court to believe that even if he had been informed about the contents of the notice, he would still not have worn the spats. But with the growth of foreign labour in British industry, the problem is one for obvious concern, especially as immigrants tend to concentrate in those industries which are most likely to have serious safety hazards. The task of the safety officer to ensure the health and safety of such employees is likely to be very onerous in practice (see *Hawkins v Ian Ross (Castings) Ltd*).

12.20   The duty is owed by the employer to his employees, but this latter term is not one that is very precise, and a number of problems have arisen. In *Ferguson v John Dawson & Partners (Contractors) Ltd*, a man agreed to work on the "lump", ie as a self-employed bricklayer, but when he was injured, he sued, claiming the employers owed a duty to him as an employee. By a majority, the Court of Appeal upheld his claim, holding that it was the substance of the relationship, not the form, which was the determining factor in deciding whether or not a person was an employee in the legal sense.

12.21   As a general rule, each employer must ensure the safety of his own employees, and is not responsible in his capacity as an employer for the safety of employees of other employers. However, where a number of employees from different firms are employed on one job, there is a duty to co-ordinate the work in a safe manner (*McArdle v Andmac Roofing Co*).

12.22   The employer's duty of care persists even when an employee is "loaned" to work for another employer. Thus in *Morris v Breavenglen Ltd*, the claimant worked for a firm called Anzac Construction, and during the course of his employment he was permitted to drive a dumper truck, although he was not trained or licensed to do so. He was then sent to work at a prison farmyard, the main contractors being a firm called Sleeman Construction. On being informed that he could drive a dumper truck, he was instructed by Sleeman to dump some soil at a tipping site. While doing this, the dumper went over the edge, and he was injured. It was held that his main employer, Anzac, were liable for damages in respect of injuries received. They still owed him a duty of care under his contract of employment, and were in breach of that duty in failing to ensure that precautions were not taken to prevent the accident from occurring. An employer is not released from his duty of care which exists under the contract of employment merely because the employee is required to work under the direction and control of another employer. By failing to provide him with proper training and instruction in using the dumper truck, and by permitting him to use one when not properly instructed, they had exposed him to an unnecessary risk of injury. In this case, the Court of Appeal drew a distinction between those circumstances when a loaned employee injures himself, and when he injures a third party. In the latter case it is permissible to ascertain whether there had been a transfer of the legal obligations from one employer to the other (see *Mersey Docks and Harbour Board v Coggins and Griffiths (Liverpool) Ltd*) and the issue is usually which of the two employers will be vicariously liable for that injury. But when a loaned employee himself has been injured, either or both employers may be liable, for either or both could be in breach of their common law duties. Thus, in this case, there was no contract of employment between the employee and Sleeman, and thus Anzac, as the employer of the claimant still owed a duty not to expose him to unnecessary risks. If an employee is loaned from the general employer to a temporary employer, the question sometime arises as to which employer will be liable if the employee is subsequently injured whilst at work. The legal principles are not entirely clear on this point, but in general it may be said that the employer who has right of control bears the burden of responsibility. This control includes the ability to tell the loaned employee not only what to do, but the method of doing it (*Garrard v A E Southey & Co*). But if there is some evidence of joint control (eg where a skilled employee is loaned together with a complex or valuable piece of machinery) it is not impossible to hold that both employers should share liability equally (*Viasystems (Tyneside) Ltd v Thermal Transfers (Northern) Ltd*).

The extent of the duty

12.23   The standard of care which must be exercised by the employer is "The care which an ordinary prudent employer would take in all the circumstances" (*Paris v Stepney Borough Council*). The employer does not give an absolute guarantee of health or safety, he only undertakes to take reasonable care and will be liable if there is some lack of care on his part or in failing to foresee something which was reasonably foreseeable. The employee, for his part, must be prepared to take steps for his own safety and look after himself and not expect to be able to blame the employer for everything which happens. In *Vinnyey v Star Paper Mills Ltd*, the claimant was instructed by the foreman to clear and clean a floor area which had been made slippery by a viscous fluid. The foreman gave him proper equipment and clear instructions. The claimant was injured when he slipped on the floor while doing the work, and it was held that the employers were not liable. There was no reasonably foreseeable risk in performing such a simple task, and they had taken all due care. In *Lazarus v Firestone Tyre and Rubber Co Ltd*, the claimant was knocked down in the general rush to get to the canteen. It was held that this was not the sort of behaviour which could be protected against.

12.24   If the danger is one which the employer neither knew nor ought to have known he will not normally be liable for any resulting accident or injury (*Joseph v Ministry of Defence*). But knowledge will be imputed to the employer if the danger has been referred to in trade journals or other publications, or if it is known throughout the industry (*Morris v West Hartlepool Steam Navigation Co*). The ordinary and prudent employer should acquire knowledge from reading safety literature which is common in the trade (*Graham v Co-operative Wholesale Society*). In *Down v Dudley, Coles Long Ltd*, an employee was partially deafened by the noise which came from a cartridge-assisted hammer gun. At the then state of medical knowledge (ie in 1964) a reasonable employer would not have known of the potential danger in using this particular piece of equipment without providing adequate safety precautions and the employer was held to be not liable for the injury. Clearly, with the wide dissemination of literature on noise hazards nowadays, a different conclusion would be drawn on these facts although the general principle of law remains the same.

12.25 In recent years, there has been no shortage of cases dealing with the liability of an employer for various forms of psychiatric illness suffered by employees, whether brought about by overwork (*Johnstone v Bloomsbury Health Authority*), stress (*Petch v Commissioners of Customs & Excise*) and so on. However, if an employer has no reason to anticipate that the job is likely to cause psychiatric illness, that employer cannot be said to have been negligent in failing to prevent it (*Pratley v Surrey County Council* and *Sutherland v Hatton* (see paragraph 11.180)). The test, as always, is whether there was a foreseeable risk of injury flowing from the employer's breach of duty of care (*Hartman v South Essex Mental Health and Community Care NHS Trust*).

12.26 As a general rule, an employer will not incur liability for a first breakdown in physical and/or mental health, because an employee is expected to withstand the normal pressures of a job, and it will be rare that such illness is reasonably foreseeable. However, once a breakdown has occurred, which would generally be caused by the pressures of the job or by overwork, a recurrence may well be reasonably foreseeable unless steps are taken to alleviate the situation. In *Garrod v North Devon NHS Primary Health Care Trust*, the claimant was a health visitor. She suffered with stress and depression caused by having to cover for an absent colleague. After six months' absence, she returned on a phased return programme, with a reduction in her contractual hours, but again the pressures of work were increased because of absent colleagues, with the result that she had a second breakdown. She returned to work once more, following a promise by the Health Trust not to burden her with added case loads, but she had to cover for a colleague who had gone on maternity leave, with the result that she suffered a third and final breakdown in her health. The High Court held that once the employer had notice of the claimant's vulnerability, the subsequent failure to maintain the return-to-work programme meant that her illness was foreseeable, and thus the employer was liable for the tort of negligence.

12.27 An employer cannot ignore the possibility that an employee may injure himself through an error of judgment, or momentary forgetfulness, or tiredness, or carelessness, particularly when working on repetitive jobs. Thus even though a risk of injury may be obvious, the employer must still devise and implement safety systems and proper precautions where possible. Sometimes these precautions may be required in circumstances when they would not otherwise be called for (*Thurogood v Van den Berghs & Jurgens*). An employer is entitled to expect employees to look after their own safety, particularly when performing simple tasks, or where the employee is a skilled workman (*Baker v T Clarke (Leeds) Ltd*). But the employer must always be prepared to give clear and accurate instructions, particularly when young persons are at work, or where the work involves unusual risks, or where the employee would not be in a position to evaluate the risk (*Ping v Esselte-Letraset*). Similarly, there must be adequate supervision and enforcement of precautionary measures (*Pape v Cumbria County Council*).

12.28 Once a danger has been perceived, the employer must take all reasonable steps to protect the employees from the consequences of those risks which have hitherto been unforeseeable. In *Wright Rubber Co Ltd, Cassidy v Dunlop Rubber Co Ltd*, the employers used an anti-oxidant known as Nonox S from 1940 onwards. The manufacturers then discovered that the substance was capable of causing bladder cancer and informed the defendants that all employees should be screened and tested. This was not done for some time, and thus the employers, as well as the manufacturers, were held to be liable to the claimants.

12.29 The matter was summarised by Swanwick J in *Stokes v GKN Ltd*.
1. The employer must take positive steps to ensure the safety of his employees in the light of the knowledge which he has or ought to have.
2. The employer is entitled to follow current recognised practice unless in the light of common sense or new knowledge this is clearly unsound.
3. Where there is developing knowledge, the employer must keep reasonably abreast with it, and not be too slow in applying it.
4. If he has greater than average knowledge of the risk, he must take more than average precautions.

5. He must weigh up the risk (in terms of the likelihood of the injury and possible consequences) against the effectiveness of the precautions to be taken to meet the risk and the cost and inconvenience.

12.30   Applying these tests, if the employer falls below the standards of a reasonable and prudent employer he will be liable.

The threefold nature of the duty

12.31   There is only one single duty on the part of the employer, namely to take reasonable care. However, we may conveniently analyse that duty under three categories.
1. Safe plant, appliances and premises.
2. Safe system of work.
3. Reasonably competent fellow employees.

Safe plant, appliances and premises

12.32   First, all tools, equipment, machinery and plant that the employee uses or comes into contact with and all the employer's premises shall be reasonably safe for work. Thus a failure to provide the necessary equipment (*Williams v Birmingham Battery and Metal Co*) or providing insufficient equipment (*Machray v Stewarts and Lloyds Ltd*) or providing defective equipment (*Bowater v Rowley Regis Corporation*) will amount to a breach of the duty. There must be a proper and adequate system of inspection and testing, so that defects can be discovered and reported (*Barkway v South Wales Transport Co*) and then remedied (*Monaghan v WH Rhodes & Son*). In *Bradford v Robinson Rentals*, a driver was required to go on a 400-mile journey during a bitterly cold spell of weather in a van which was unheated and had cracked windows. He suffered frostbite and his employers were held liable for failing to provide suitable plant. Before putting second-hand machinery into use, it should be checked to make sure that it is serviceable (*Pearce v Round Oak Steel Works Ltd*). If unfenced machinery is liable to eject parts of the machine or materials used by the machine, then a failure to erect suitable and effective guards may well constitute negligence at common law (*Close v Steel Co of Wales*) irrespective of any liability for a breach of the Work Equipment Regulations (*Kilgollan v William Cooke & Co Ltd*). If the equipment is inherently dangerous, extra precautions must be taken (*Naismith v London Film Productions Ltd*).

12.33 However, if an employer purchases tools or equipment from a reputable supplier and has no knowledge of any defect in them, he will have performed his duty to take care and cannot be held liable for negligence (see *Davie v New Merton Board Mills*). An employee who was injured in consequence could only pursue his remedy against the person responsible for the defect under the general law of negligence (*Donoghue v Stevenson*). In practice, this would frequently be difficult or impossible. The employee would not have the time or resources to do this; it may be that the negligence was due to the acts of a foreign manufacturer, or stevedores at the docks, etc. In view of these problems, the law was changed with the passing of the Employers' Liability (Defective Equipment) Act 1969. This provides that if an employee suffers a personal injury in the course of his employment in consequence of a defect in equipment provided by his employer for the purposes of his employer's business, and the defect is attributable wholly or partly to the fault of a third party (whether identified or not), then the defect will be deemed to be attributable to the negligence of the employer. Thus, in such circumstances, the injured employee would sue the employer for his "deemed" negligence, and the latter, for his part, would attempt to recover the amount of damages he has paid out from the third party whose fault it really was. Since the insurance company is the real interested party in such matters, it is they, rather than the employer, who will attempt to make such recovery. The Employers' Liability (Compulsory Insurance) Act was also passed in 1969 to ensure that all employers have valid insurance cover to meet personal injuries claims from their employees, and a certificate to this effect must be displayed at the employers' premises (see paragraph 5.3).

12.34 The Employers' Liability (Defective Equipment) Act was considered by the House of Lords in *Knowles v Liverpool City Council*, where the claimant was employed as a "flagger" by the highway authority. He was injured when a flagstone he was handling broke. The flagstone had not been cured properly by the makers. He sued his employers, arguing that the flagstone was "equipment provided by the employer for the purpose of the employer's business", and his claim was upheld. The House of Lords refused to draw a distinction between "equipment" and materials, for to do so would create unjustifiable inconsistencies. There is little doubt that the decision represents a purposive construction of the Act.

12.35 If an employer is aware of any defect in tools, etc which have been purchased from outside he should withdraw them from circulation. In *Taylor v Rover Car Co Ltd*, a batch of chisels had been badly hardened by the manufacturers. One had, in fact, shattered without causing an injury, but the rest of the batch were still being used and another chisel shattered, injuring the claimant in his eye. The employers were held liable.

12.36   The employer must also ensure that the premises are reasonably safe for all persons who come on to the premises (under the Occupiers' Liability Act 1957–1984) as well as for his employees in particular. In *Paine v Colne Valley Electricity Supply Co Ltd*, an employee was electrocuted because a kiosk had not been properly insulated and the employers were held liable. However, it must be stressed that the employer need only take reasonable care, and this is a question of fact and degree in each case. In *Latimer v AEC Ltd*, a factory floor was flooded after a heavy storm, and a mixture of oil and water made the floor slippery. The employers put down sand and sawdust, but there was not enough to treat the whole of the factory in this way, and the claimant was injured when he slipped on an untreated part of the floor. It was held that the employers were not liable. The danger was not grave enough to warrant closing down the whole factory, which would have been an unreasonable thing to do in the circumstances, bearing in mind that the risk was minimal.

12.37   The employer does not absolutely guarantee the safety of his employees. Thus there are probably as many legal authorities where an employer was held to be liable for an injury caused when an employee slipped on an icy surface (eg *McDonald v BTC*) as there are cases when the employer was held not to be liable (eg *Thomas v Bristol Aeroplane Co Ltd*). It all depends whether or not the employer has done what is reasonable in the circumstances.

12.38   The employer cannot be responsible for the premises of other persons where his employees have to work, but as he still owes to them a duty of care, he must ensure that a safe system of work is laid down.

Safe system of work

12.39   Second, the employer is responsible for the overall planning of the work operations so that it can be carried out safely. This includes the layout of the work, the systems laid down, training and supervision, the provision of warnings, protective clothing, protective equipment, special instructions, etc. Regard must be had for the fact that the employee will be forgetful, careless, as well as inadvertent, but the employer cannot guard against outright stupidity or perversity.

12.40   A reasonable employer will frequently be expected to be aware of the existence of risks to health and safety even though they arise out of commonplace activities. In *Pape v Cumbria County Council*, the claimant was employed as a part-time cleaner. During her work, she used various chemical cleaning agents. The employer made available rubber gloves, but never advised her to use them, nor warned of the dangers of the risks of working without them. She contracted dermatitis and eczema on her hands, which then spread to other parts of her body, and she was forced to give up her employment. She sued for damages. It was held that the employer should have warned her of the dangers arising from the use of chemical cleaning agents, instructed her to use the rubber gloves provided, and taken reasonable steps to ensure that those instructions were carried out. The knowledge of the risk was not so well known to employees that the mere provision of rubber gloves was sufficient performance of the employer's duty of care.

12.41   Examples of a failure to provide a safe system of work abound. In *Barcock v Brighton Corporation*, the claimant was employed at an electric substation. A certain method of testing was in operation which was unsafe and in consequence the employee was injured. The employers were held liable. If there are safety precautions laid down, the employee must know about them; if safety equipment is provided, it must be available for use. In *Finch v Telegraph Construction and Maintenance Co Ltd*, the claimant was employed as a grinder. Goggles were provided for this work, but no one told him where to find them. The employers were held liable when he was injured by a piece of flying metal. Whether a system is safe in any particular case will be a question of fact, to be decided on the evidence available.

12.42   The more dangerous the process, the greater is the need to ensure that it is safe. On the other hand, the employer cannot be expected to take over-elaborate precautions when dealing with simple and obvious dangers (*Vinnyey v Star Paper Mills*). A situation which gives rise to some legal difficulties is where the employer provides safety precautions or equipment, but the employee fails or refuses to use or wear them. Is the duty a mere passive one, to provide and do no more? Or is it a more active one, to exhort or even compel their use? It is suggested that the answer to these questions can be summarised in four propositions.

12.43 (1) If the risk is an obvious one, and the injury which may result from the failure to use the precautions is not likely to be serious, then the employer's duty is a mere passive one of providing the necessary precautions, informing the employees of their presence, and leaving it to them to decide whether or not to use them. In *Qualcast (Wolverhampton) Ltd v Haynes*, an experienced worker was splashed by molten metal on his legs. Spats were available, but the employers did nothing to ensure that they were worn. The injury, though doubtless painful, was not of a serious nature, and the employers were held not liable.

12.44 Similarly, in *Smith v Scott Bowyers Ltd*, the claimant had been provided with wellington boots to protect against the risk of slipping on a wet floor. The soles of the boots had worn smooth, and he asked for and was given another pair. These also wore smooth but he did not seek a replacement pair. He then slipped on the wet floor and was injured. The trial judge held that the employers were liable, as they had taken no steps to emphasise to employees the importance of wearing boots with soles in good condition, but the decision was reversed on appeal. The employee knew why the boots were provided and he knew they would be replaced if the soles were worn. The Court of Appeal cited with approval a dictum from *Qualcast (Wolverhampton) Ltd v Haynes* that "there may be cases in which an employer does not discharge his duty of care towards his workmen merely by providing an article of safety equipment, but the courts should be circumspect in filling out that duty with the much vaguer obligation of encouraging, exhorting or instructing workmen or a particular workman to make regular use of what is provided."

12.45 However, it is submitted that the employer must not only provide the safety precautions, but also inform the employee of the relevant work risks involved. Thus in *Campbell v Lothian Health Board*, the claimant was a cleaner in a hospital. She was provided with rubber gloves, but was not told about the risks from using detergents, or how these risks could be reduced by using the gloves provided. The employers were thus held liable when she contracted dermatitis.

12.46 (2) If the risk is that of a serious injury, then the duty of the employer is a higher one of doing all he can to ensure that the precautions are used. In *Nolan v Dental Manufacturing Co Ltd*, a tool setter was injured when a chip flew off a grinding wheel. Because of the seriousness of the injury should one occur, it was held that the employers should have insisted that protective goggles should be worn.

12.47 (3) If the risk is an insidious one, or one the seriousness of which the employee would not readily appreciate, then again, it is the duty of the employer to do all he can by way of propaganda, constant reminders, exhortation, education, etc to try to get the employees to use the precautions. In *Berry v Stone Manganese and Marine Ltd*, the claimant was working in an environment where the noise levels were dangerously high. Ear muffs had been provided, but little effort was made to ensure their use. It was held that the workmen would not readily appreciate the dangers of injury to their hearing if they did not use the ear muffs and the employers were liable for failing to take further steps to impress on the claimant the need to use the protective equipment.

12.48 A number of problems have arisen out of cases of mesothelioma. This is an invisible injury, which cannot be attributed to any particular exposure, and is not made worse by any number of exposures. It is a major cause of death, but it may have a latency period of up to 50 years. A victim may have had several employers during that time, or he may have had a period of self-employment. It would be virtually impossible to prove which employer was responsible for the negligent exposure. In *Fairchild v Glenhaven Funeral Services Ltd*, it was held that the dependants of a man who had died of mesothelioma after negligent exposure to asbestos by more than one employer could recover compensation from any of them, even though it was not possible to identify the precise time when the fatal exposure had occurred. However, in *Barker v Corus (UK) Ltd*, the House of Lords ruled that workers who develop mesothelioma after being exposed to asbestos when working for multiple employers could only recover compensation from those employers (or their insurers) who were traceable and solvent, and these would only be liable for a proportion of the compensation that would be otherwise payable. The Government quickly responded to this decision by adding a new section to the Compensation Act 2006, which provides that where the responsible person has negligently, or in breach of a statutory duty, caused or permitted a person to be exposed to asbestos which causes mesothelioma, then any responsible person who can be traced will be liable for the whole of the damage caused, jointly and severally liable with any other responsible person. It will be for the responsible person to claim contribution from any other responsible person who can be found or identified (see also Mesothelioma Lump Sum Payment (Conditions and Amounts) Regulations 2008).

12.49   Employees who suffer from pleural plaques following exposure to asbestos will not be able to claim compensation from their employer, according to a decision of the House of Lords in *Rothwell v Chemical and Insulating Co Ltd*. Pleural plaques cause a localised thickening or fibrosis of the lung pleura, and are evidence of exposure to asbestos. However, they are symptomless, and do not give rise to a physical ill health condition. The absence of symptoms did not constitute an injury, even when combined with anxiety and the risk of possible further asbestos-related illnesses.

12.50   The Scottish Parliament has recently passed the Damages (Asbestos-related Conditions) (Scotland) Act 2009 which will ensure that people with pleural plaques caused by wrongful exposure to asbestos will be able to bring an action for damages. It is felt that although pleural plaques do not cause an impairment of a person's physical condition, it is a personal injury which is not negligible and consequently constitutes actionable harm for the purpose of bringing an action for damages for personal injuries. It is expected that the English Parliament will pass similar legislation in the near future.

12.51   (4) When the employer has done all he can do (and in the context of safety and health, this means doing a great deal), when he has laid down a safe system, provided the necessary safety precautions and equipment, instructed on their use, advised how they should be used properly, pointed out the risks involved if they are not used, and given constant reminders about their use, then he can do no more and he will be absolved from liability. Admittedly, this does not solve the problem, which is how to ensure that employees are protected from their own folly. Various ways of dealing with the enforcement of safety rules are discussed in Chapter 13.

12.52   If an employee is working on the premises of another employer, the employer must still take reasonable care for that employee's safety. There may well be some limits to what he can do, but this does not absolve him from doing what he can. In particular, he must ensure that a safe system of working is laid down, give clear instructions as to how to deal with obvious dangers, and tell him to refuse to work if there is an obvious hazard. In *Wilson v Tyneside Window Cleaning Co*, the claimant was a window cleaner who had, in the course of his employment over a period of 10 years, cleaned certain windows at a brewery on a number of occasions. One day he pulled on a handle, which was rotten, and fell backwards, sustaining injuries. His claim against his employers failed. He knew the woodwork was rotten and he had been instructed not to clean windows if they were not safe. This may be contrasted with *General Cleaning Contractors Ltd v Christmas*, where in almost identical circumstances, the employee succeeded in his claim. The distinction appears to be that in *Christmas*, the employers provided safety belts, but there were certain premises where these could not be used and there was a failure to instruct the employees to test for defective sashes before the work could proceed. Further, the employers could have provided ladders or taken other steps to ensure that the work could be performed safely.

Reasonably competent fellow employees

12.53 Finally, if an employer engages an incompetent employee whose actions injure another employee, the employer will be liable for a failure to take reasonable care. In *Hudson v Ridge Manufacturing Co Ltd*, an employee was known for his habit of committing practical jokes. One day he carried one of his pranks too far and injured a fellow employee. The employer was held to be liable. The practical answer in such cases is, after due warning, to firmly dispense with the services of such a person, for he is a menace to himself and to others. On the other hand, an employer will not be liable if he has no reason to suspect that practical jokes are being played, for such acts are outside the scope of the employee's employment, and not done for the purpose of the employer's business (*Smith v Crossley Bros*). In *Coddington v International Harvester Co of Great Britain Ltd*, an employee, for a joke, kicked a tin of burning thinner in the direction of another employee. The latter was scorched with flames and in the agony of the moment kicked the tin away so that it enveloped the claimant, causing him severe burns. The employers were held not liable. There was nothing in the previous conduct of the guilty employee to suggest that he might be a danger to others and his act was totally unconnected with his employment.

12.54 If an employer appoints an inexperienced person to perform highly dangerous tasks, he may be liable if through lack of experience another employee is injured (*Butler v Fife Coal Co*).

Proof of negligence

12.55   As a general rule, the burden is upon the claimant in an action to affirmatively prove his case. In other words, he must show that the defendant owed to him a duty to take care, that the defendant was in breach of that duty by being negligent and that as a result of that negligence the claimant suffered damage. To assist him in such an action, there are a number of rules of evidence and procedure, designed to enable each side to clarify the issues in dispute and to avoid surprises at the actual court of trial (see paragraph 12.122). Thus the court may make an order for inspection of the premises or machinery, it can order one party to disclose documents, records, etc to another, it can order that a party should make further and better particulars of his case, and so on. In *Waugh v British Railways Board*, the claimant's widow sued for damages, alleging that the defendant's negligence caused the death of her husband. She sought the disclosure of an accident report which was prepared by the defendants, partly for the purpose of establishing the cause of the accident and partly to assist their legal advisors to conduct the proceeding before the courts. The defendants resisted the disclosure on the ground of professional privilege, but it was held that the report should be disclosed. A document is only privileged if the dominant purpose of making it in the first place was for the purpose of legal proceedings. If the document had a dual purpose, it would not be covered by professional privilege. The implications of this case in practice can be very wide. Thus if an accident report is made as a result of an employee being away from work for more than three days because of an accident, it will not be privileged. If a safety officer makes a report of an accident, it will also not be privileged. However, once legal proceedings have been commenced, or are imminent, a report prepared for the exclusive use of the company's legal advisors would be privileged.

12.56   Further assistance can be obtained from the inspector under s.28(9) of HSWA, which enables him to disclose any factual information about any accident to persons who are a party to any civil proceedings arising from the accident.

12.57   Another rule of evidence which may be of considerable assistance to a claimant is *res ipsa loquitur* (let the facts speak for themselves) (see Chapter 1). This will apply when the circumstances are such that an accident would not have occurred unless there had been some want of care by the defendant. Thus if a barrel of flour fell out of a building and injured a person walking below, the latter would find it extremely difficult to show that someone was negligent (*Byrne v Boadle*). In practice, he would not need to do so. He would invoke the rule *res ipsa loquitur*, barrels of flour do not normally fall out of buildings unless someone was negligent, and thus the burden of proof is thrown back to the other party to show that he had, in fact, taken reasonable care. *Res ipsa loquitur* is a rule of evidence, not a rule of law. It creates a rebuttable presumption that there was negligence. If the presumption is rebutted by evidence then the burden of proof is thrown back to the claimant to prove his claim in the usual way.

12.58 If an accident occurs in circumstances where there is no statutory duty involved, the ordinary principles of negligence will apply. However, the existence of a statutory duty may have some relevance to the standard of care required at common law, for that fact should alert an employer to the possibility of some danger (*NCB v England*). Equally, the absence of a statutory duty may relieve the employer of liability (*Qualcast v Haynes*).

Defences to an action for damages

12.59 Only one action may be brought against an employer in respect of injuries which arise out of one incident. The claimant, therefore, must plead his case in such a manner that all possible legal headings are covered. Thus, where appropriate, he should claim in respect of a breach of statutory duty and common law negligence, for each is a separate cause of action. The defendant, for his part, must also be prepared to defend each heading where liability is claimed.

12.60 Since there is no automatic right to compensation, the following defences may be raised.

Statutory defence

12.61 Recent years have seen such an increase in negligence claims that many worthwhile activities (such as school outings, etc) have been abandoned or restricted because of fears of potential litigation. To counter these fears, the Compensation Act 2006 provides that a court considering a claim in negligence or breach of statutory duty may, in determining whether the defendant should have taken particular steps to meet a standard of care (whether by taking precautions against a risk or otherwise), have regard to whether the requirement to take those steps might prevent a desirable activity from being undertaken at all, to a particular extent or in a particular way, or discourage persons from undertaking functions in connection with a desirable activity. Further, an apology or an offer of treatment or other redress shall not by itself amount to an admission of negligence or breach of statutory duty. The Act only applies to England and Wales.

Denial of negligence

12.62   The employer may deny that he has failed to take reasonable care, or claim that he did everything which a reasonable employer would have done in the circumstances (see *Latimer v AEC Ltd*, above). For example, in *Brown v Rolls Royce Ltd*, the claimant contracted dermatitis owing to the use of an industrial oil. The employers did not provide a barrier cream on the advice of their chief medical officer, who doubted its efficacy. The employers were held not to be negligent in failing to provide the barrier cream. They were entitled to rely on the skilled judgment of a competent advisor and no more could be expected. Indeed, the medical officer had instituted his own preventative methods, as a result of which the incidence of dermatitis in the factory had steadily decreased.

12.63   An employer can only take reasonable care within the limits of the knowledge which he has or ought reasonably to have. After all, not every firm (particularly the smaller employer) can have available the resources of specialist expertise. Nonetheless, they must pay attention to current literature which may be available, either from their trade or employers' associations or from other sources. In *Graham v Co-operative Wholesale Society Ltd*, the claimant worked in a furniture workshop where an electric sanding machine gave off a quantity of fine wood dust. This settled on his skin and caused dermatitis. No general precautions were taken against this, although the manager received all the information which was commonly circulated in the trade. It was held that the employers were not liable. They had fulfilled their duty to take reasonable care by keeping up to date with current knowledge, and were not to blame for not knowing something that only a specialist advisor would have known.

12.64   An employer will not be liable for an injury if he does not owe a duty of care to the injured person. In *Hewett v Alf Brown's Transport Ltd*, the claimant's husband was a lorry driver. He was employed to drive a lorry which contained lead oxide. While working he wore overalls and boots. When he returned home, the claimant would bang the overalls against a garden wall and bang or wipe his boots. While doing this she either inhaled lead oxide powder or came into contact with it. She was subsequently diagnosed as suffering from lead poisoning and sued her husband's employers for personal injuries suffered.

12.65   It was held that the action would be dismissed. It was accepted that if there was a foreseeable risk to the family of an employee from clothing, etc worn by the employee at work which became contaminated, then the employers owed a duty of care to those family members. However, in the circumstances of this case, the claimant's husband had not been exposed to any risk while removing the lead oxide waste from the site, and therefore the employers were not in breach of their duty to the claimant's husband either under the Control of Lead at Work Regulations 1980 or at common law. Consequently, there was no breach of duty to the claimant. (It should be noted it is arguable that nowadays a different decision would be given in this case under regulation 3 of the Control of Lead at Work Regulations 2002 (see paragraph 7.49), which provides that where a duty is placed on an employer, that employer should, so far as is reasonably practicable, be under a like duty in respect of any other person, whether at work or not, who may be affected by the work carried out.)

The sole fault of the employee

12.66   If it can be shown that the injury was the sole fault of the employee, again the employer will not be liable. In *Jones v Lionite Specialities (Cardiff) Ltd*, a foreman became addicted to a chemical vapour from a tank. One weekend he was found dead, having fallen into the tank. The employers were not liable. In *Brophy v JC Bradfield*, a lorry driver was found dead inside a boiler house, having been overcome by fumes. He had no reason to be there and the employers had no reason to suspect his presence. Again, they were not liable. And in *Horne v Lec Refrigeration Ltd*, a tool setter had been fully instructed on the safety precautions to be followed when operating a machine, but was killed when he failed to operate the safety drill. The employers were held not liable, even though they were in breach of their statutory duty to ensure secure fencing.

12.67   If the claim is based on a breach of statutory duty, the employee cannot, by his own actions, put his employer in breach and then try to blame the employer for that breach. Provided the employer has done all that the statute requires him to do, ie provided the proper equipment, given training, provided adequate supervision, laid down safe systems, and so on, there will come a point when the injured workman will only have himself to blame. In *Ginty v Belmont Building Supplies Ltd*, the claimant was working on a roof. He knew that it was in a defective state and that he should not work without boards. The employer provided the boards for use, but the claimant failed to use them and fell through the roof. It was held that the employers were not liable for his injuries. They had done all they could do, and the accident was the sole fault of the claimant.

12.68 In the 19th century, the courts were inclined to the view that a worker accepted the risks which were inherent in the occupation and had to rely on his own skill and care, but this view was firmly discounted in the leading case of *Smith v Baker & Sons* and the defence of *volenti non fit injuria* (a person consents to the risk of being injured) is no longer applicable. The fact that the employee knows that there is a risk in the occupation does not mean that he consents to that risk because the employer has been negligent in failing to guard against it. This must apply, *a fortiori*, if the employer is under a statutory duty to guard against the risk. However, if the statutory duty is placed on the employee, and he disregards it, the employer is entitled to raise the defence of *volenti*. In *ICI Ltd v Shatwell*, the Quarries (Explosives) Regulations 1959 provided that no testing of an electrical circuit for shot firing should be done unless all persons in the vicinity had withdrawn to shelter. This duty, which was imposed in order to avoid risks from premature explosions, was laid on the employees. The employers had also prohibited such acts. Two employees were injured when they acted in breach of the regulations and the employers' instructions, and it was held that the employers could successfully raise the defence of *volenti*.

12.69 The payment of "danger money" to certain types of employees (eg stunt artistes) may indicate that there is an inherent risk in the occupation which cannot be adequately guarded against, but the real question to be asked is, was the employer negligent? Further, the Unfair Contract Terms Act 1977 states that a person cannot, by reference to a contract term or prominently displayed notice, exclude or restrict his liability for death or personal injury resulting from negligence.

12.70   In the 19th century there were reports of unscrupulous employers requiring their employees to sign "blood chits" which effectively excluded the employers from liability for injuries at work. Such signed waivers are virtually unknown today, but a problem does arise when the employer provides all the necessary health and safety precautions and/or equipment, and the employee deliberately refuses to use/wear them. As long as the employer has done all he can do, by way of encouragement, persuasion, provision of information, etc and complied with his common law and statutory duties, the employee would have no come-back if consequently he suffers an injury. An employer should keep any necessary records indicating the efforts made to ensure that compliance and the employee's responses and, if sued, plead *volenti non fit injuria* as a defence.

Fault of a third party

12.71   An employer will not be liable if the injury is caused by a new intervening act, ie by a person or event over which or whom the employer has no control. In *Horton v Taplin Contracts Ltd*, the claimant was standing on the platform of a scaffolding tower. A fellow worker, with whom he had previously had an altercation, deliberately pushed the tower over and the claimant suffered serious injuries. He claimed damages from his employer, alleging a breach of regulations 5 and 20 of PUWER (work equipment must be suitable for the purpose and work equipment must be stabilised), as well as regulation 5 of the Construction (Health, Safety and Welfare) Regulations (employers must keep the workplace safe for any person at work there). The claim failed. Under regulation 5 of PUWER, the suitability of work equipment was to be measured by taking into account those hazards that were reasonably foreseeable. The obligation to stabilise the equipment under regulation 20 only arose when this was necessary for the purpose of health and safety, which introduced considerations of foreseeability. Finally, the scaffolding tower was a safe place of work; it only became unsafe as the result of the deliberate, violent and unpredictable act of a third party.

12.72   Similarly, in *Yorkshire Traction Co v Searby*, a bus driver, while sitting in his driver's seat, was assaulted by a passenger. A county court judge held that the employers had been negligent in not inserting a screen to separate the driver from passengers and thus there was a failure to provide work equipment that was "suitable". This decision was reversed by the Court of Appeal. In the first place, his trade union had strongly objected to the insertion of such screens as these were considered to be a safety hazard. Indeed some drivers had taken action to have the screens removed from their buses. It was further found that the risk of injury to bus drivers was very low. Thus the measure of the risk, the perceived disadvantages, and the attitude of the workforce was such that the failure by the employers to fit screens did not amount to negligence at common law. So far as a breach of statutory duty is concerned, the regulations do not require complete and absolute protection. In assessing the suitability of work equipment, the test for liability involved a consideration of the degree of risk. Since the incidence of injury to drivers from passengers had been very low, it could not be said that the work equipment (ie the bus) was unsuitable.

Causation

12.73 Although the employer may be negligent, it must still be shown that the injury resulted from that negligence. If the injury would have happened had the employer not been negligent, then the breach of the duty to take care has not caused the damage (see *McWilliams v Sir William Arrol & Co Ltd*, paragraph 12.12). Where a breach of statutory duty is alleged, the same principles apply. In *Bonnington Castings Ltd v Wardlaw*, the claimant was subjected to a silica dust in premises where there was inadequate ventilation. It was held that the fact that there was a breach of statutory duty (to provide ventilation, Factories Act, s.4) and the fact that the employee suffered from pneumoconiosis did not by itself lead to the conclusion that the breach caused the injury. There must be sufficient evidence to link the one with the other. However, a more liberal view was taken in *Gardiner v Motherwell Machinery and Scrap Co Ltd* (see paragraph 1.147) where the court took the view that evidential presumptions may arise in such cases.

Contributory negligence

12.74 This defence is based on the Law Reform (Contributory Negligence) Act 1945, which provides that if a person is injured, partly because of his own fault, and partly due to the fault of another, damages shall be reduced to the extent the court thinks fit, having regard to the claimant's share in the responsibility for the damage. This defence is successfully raised in many cases. The employer will argue that even if he were negligent, the employee failed to take care for his own safety, and the court may well decide to reduce the damages awarded. There is no scientific basis for determining the percentage reduction and appeal courts may well take a different view of the apportionment of the blame between the parties (see, for example, *Anderson v Newham College of Further Education*).

12.75 Thus in *Badger v Ministry of Defence* the claimant developed asbestosis due to his employer's negligence. However, he smoked 20 cigarettes a day for 50 years. Medical experts agreed that the risk of developing lung cancer is significantly higher for a smoker than for a non-smoker. His compensation award was cut by 20%, to reflect his own contributory negligence.

12.76 Although in *Jayes v IMI (Kynoch) Ltd* the Court of Appeal had held that there was no principle in law that rules out a finding of 100% contributory negligence, the case was disapproved by a more recent decision of the court in *Anderson v Newham College of Further Education*. There is a distinction between arguing that a claimant is 100% contributory negligent and arguing that an accident was entirely due to the fault of the claimant. Thus, if there has been a breach of a statutory duty by an employer, it must be shown not only that the worker's breach of the same statutory duty was as great as that of the employer, but also that the employer did all he could to ensure compliance by the worker. If there is no breach of statutory duty by the employer, no question of contributory negligence arises (*Anderson v Newham College of Further Education*).

Limitations of actions

12.77 Any action for personal injury or death must be commenced within three years from the date of the accident (Limitation Act 1980, s.11; Prescription and Limitations (Scotland) Act 1973). This means that the actual writ must be issued within the three-year period, although the date of the court hearing may be considerably delayed thereafter. In accident cases the date of the incident is usually ascertainable, but in some circumstances, where the injury is a result of a constant exposure to the hazard, eg noise which causes deafness (*Berry v Stone Manganese and Marine Ltd*) or exposure to dangerous substances which can cause cancer (*Wright Cassidy v Dunlop Rubber Co Ltd*) or pneumoconiosis (*Cartwright v GKN Sankey Ltd*), it is not possible to fix a date, or the claimant will be unaware of the date. In such circumstances, s.14 of the Limitation Act 1980 provides that the three-year period shall begin to run from the date on which the cause of action accrued or the date when the claimant had knowledge of the fact that the injury was significant and that this was due to the employer's negligence. Knowledge in this connection means actual or constructive knowledge, ie knowledge which the claimant had or ought to have had. For example, if he has received medical advice which indicated an injury, he should know of the likely cause. The Act permits the court to exercise its discretion and allow the action to proceed even though it is outside the limitation period, if it is equitable to do so, having regard to the factors which brought about the delay, the effect it may have on the credibility of witnesses after such a period of time, the disability suffered by the claimant, and whether he acted promptly once he realised that he may have a cause of action having regard to any expert advice he may have received.

12.78   Thus in *Barrand v British Cellophane Ltd*, the claimant alleged that he had suffered noise-induced deafness through working in excessively noisy conditions between 1958 and 1980. He was aware of his condition from 1982, but did not start his legal action until 1990. The Court of Appeal thought that it was wrong for the trial judge to permit him to proceed with the action. The delay was entirely his fault, the defendants would be substantially prejudiced because of the passage of time, and it would have been inequitable to disapply the usual time limits.

12.79   A different conclusion was reached in *Irshad Ali v Courtlands Textiles Ltd*, where the claimant suffered exposure to excessive noise from 1969 to 1988. It was not until 1991 that he was told that his deafness could be work-related, and he obtained a medical report in 1992 which confirmed this. He issued proceedings in 1995. The trial judge held that his knowledge dated from 1991, and that proceedings were outside the limitation period, but the decision was reversed by the Court of Appeal. The claimant's personal circumstances were relevant. He spoke little English, and could not read or write either in English or his native language. He had no contact with his trade union, and he was thus isolated from potential knowledge. A suspicion that he might have had a cause of action was not enough to confer knowledge on him that he had a cause of action.

Damages

12.80   If an employee is killed in the course of his employment, an action may be brought by his personal representatives for the benefit of the estate of the deceased, under the provisions of the Law Reform (Miscellaneous Provisions) Act 1934. Damages will be awarded under the following headings:

(a) loss of expectation of life (this is usually a fairly modest sum)
(b) pain and suffering (if any) up to the time of death
(c) loss of earnings up to the time of death.

12.81   A further action may be brought simultaneously by his dependants for their own benefit under the Fatal Accidents Act 1976 based on the loss of financial support suffered by, for example, his wife, children or other dependants. Any other money due to the estate is not taken into account, eg personal insurances, pensions payable to the widow, etc but any award made under the 1934 Act will be taken into account. In other words, the one action is brought for the benefit of the deceased's estate, the other for the benefit of his family dependants. The two claims are invariably settled together.

12.82   The quantum of damages awarded is frequently a matter of speculation. No amount of money can compensate for the loss of a faculty (arm, leg, eyesight, etc) but the courts must try to do their best and awards will take account of inflation, the permanency of the injury, the effect of earning capacity, additional expenses incurred, and so on.

Rights against insurers

12.83   In normal circumstances, any damages awarded to an injured employee would be paid by the employer's insurance company. If the employer is no longer in business (eg because he has died, gone bankrupt or gone into liquidation, etc) then, provided his liability has been established, it is possible to pursue a claim against the insurance company under the provisions of the Third Parties (Rights against Insurers) Act 1930. But if, at the time of the claim, the employer's liability has not been established, this is not possible. For example, in *Bradley v Eagle Star Insurance Co Ltd*, the claimant claimed that she contracted byssinosis while working in a mill from 1933–1970. The employer company had been dissolved in 1976, but her claim was not made until 1984. It was not possible to resurrect the company in order to establish liability and hence her claim failed.

12.84   However, by s.1029 of the Companies Act 2006, it is possible to make an application to have a company re-registered and its dissolution declared void. Once this is done the action may be proceeded with in the normal way and if liability is shown, the insurance company (who will in any case be the real defendant) will be obliged to pay any damages awarded.

Vicarious liability

12.85   The tort of vicarious liability arises when one person (who has not committed a wrongful act) is legally liable for the acts of another person which cause injury or damage to a third person. Of course the actual wrongdoer is always personally liable, but in practice he is unlikely to have sufficient financial resources to meet any claim and so the injured party will seek to make the first person vicariously liable. There are two general circumstances to consider.
1. The liability of an employer for the wrongful acts of his employees which are committed in the course of their employment.
2. The liability of the employer for the acts of an independent contractor.

12.86   In recent years there has been a significant change in the law, brought about by judicial creativity. The general principle used to be that an employer would be liable for the acts of his employee which injure a third party if the employee, when doing the act, was acting in the course of his employment, in the sense that he was doing that which he was employed to do. Thus in *Century Insurance Co v Northern Ireland Road Transport Board* the employee was the driver of a petrol tanker. While he was discharging petrol at a garage forecourt, he lit a cigarette, and the subsequent explosion caused damage to the garage. It was held that the employer was liable. The act (of lighting a cigarette) was a negligent way of doing that which he was employed to do, namely to discharge petrol from the tanker, and he was therefore still acting in the course of his employment.

12.87   Vicarious liability existed even though the employer expressly prohibits an employee from doing the act in question. In *Rose v Plenty*, the employer prohibited milkmen from permitting children to ride on milk floats. In breach of this instruction a milkman engaged a young boy to help him deliver and collect milk bottles, and as a result of negligent driving by the milkman, the boy was injured. It was held that the employer, nonetheless, was liable for the injury, for the act (of permitting the boy to ride on the vehicle) was done for the purpose of the employer's business, and hence was within the course of the milkman's employment.

12.88   It now appears that if an employee commits an act which is unauthorised or prohibited, the test for vicarious liability is the closeness of the connection between the nature of the employment and the employee's wrongdoing. Thus in *Lister v Helsey Hall Ltd* a warden was found guilty of a series of sexual abuses against children at the defendant's children's home. One of the victims sued the defendant organisation as being vicariously liable. Clearly, the warden could hardly be said to have committed acts in the course of his employment, nor were they reasonably incidental thereto. On the contrary, the acts were completely contrary to his duties, which were to care for the well-being of the children. Nonetheless, the House of Lords held that the defendants were liable. The new test was formulated as follows; were the acts so closely connected with the employment that it would be fair and just to hold the employer liable?

12.89   Earlier cases, where it was argued that the employee "was on a frolic of his own" must now be treated with considerable reserve, if there is an albeit tenuous connection with the employment. Thus in *Mattis v Pollock* a nightclub owner was held liable for a physical assault by a bouncer on a customer who was seeking entry, even though there was a large element of personal animosity present, and the level of violence went far beyond that which was reasonably necessary to evict the claimant. A similar conclusion was reached in *Fennelly v Connex SE*, where a railway company was held vicariously liable for the acts of an over-zealous ticket inspector, who assaulted a commuter who had refused to permit the inspection of his rail ticket. The inspector's job was to check tickets, not to fight with passengers, but nonetheless the employer was held vicariously liable.

12.90   Vicarious liability is now appearing in a number of different areas of employment law, including sex discrimination (*Chief Constable of Lincolnshire v Stubbs*), race discrimination (*Jones v Tower Boot Co Ltd*), harassment (*Majrowski v Guy's and St Thomas NHS Trust*), and so on. Liability will frequently depend on whether, in a particular case, there is "a close connection" between the act and the employment, and whether it is thought to be "fair and just" to hold an employer vicariously liable. A large element of judicial discretion has now been introduced into this tort.

12.91   If an employee is travelling to and from work in a vehicle (whether or not provided by his employer) he will be acting in the course of his employment if, at the material time, he is going about his employer's business. The duty to turn up to work must not be confused with being on duty while travelling to work. In *Smith v Stages and Darlington Insulation Co*, the House of Lords laid down a series of propositions.

1. An employee travelling to work is not generally in the course of his employment, but if he is obliged by his contract of employment to use the employer's transport he will normally be regarded as being in the course of his employment while doing so.
2. Travelling in the employer's time between workplaces, or in the course of a peripatetic occupation will be in the course of employment.
3. Receipt of wages (but not a travelling allowance) will indicate that the employee is travelling in the employer's time and for his benefit and will be in the course of employment, and the fact that the employee has a discretion as to the mode and time of travelling will not generally affect this.
4. An employee travelling in his employer's time from his ordinary residence to a workplace other than his regular place of work or in the course of a peripatetic occupation or to the scene of an emergency will be acting in the course of his employment.
5. A deviation or interruption of the journey (unless merely incidental to the journey) will, for the time being, take the employee out of the course of his employment. Thus if the employee is driving in the course of his employment, and then departs from his normal route, he will be engaged "on a frolic of his own" (*Storey v Ashton*), and once he seeks to rejoin his normal route, it is a question of fact and degree as to whether or not he is in the course of his employment.
6. Return journeys are to be treated on the same footing as outward journeys.

12.92 These propositions are always subject to any express arrangements which may be made between the employer and employee, and do not always apply to salaried employees, with regard to whom the touchstone of payment made in the employee's time is not generally significant.

12.93 An employer is not generally liable for the wrongful acts of an independent contractor. The main difficulty here is to distinguish between an independent contractor and an employee, the former being employed under a contract *for* services, the latter employed under a contract *of* service. However, an employer may be liable:

(a) if he authorises the act
(b) if the independent contractor is carrying out a hazardous activity over which the employer has some control (see *Holliday v National Telephone Co*)
(c) if he co-ordinates or controls the activities of a number of independent contractors (*McArdle v Andmac Roofing Co*), or
(d) if he fails to show that he has exercised reasonable care in the selection of a competent contractor (*McTeare v Dooley*).

12.94   The reality of the situation is frequently to decide which insurance company is going to pay the damages. In road accidents, the dispute will usually be between one company holding the employers' liability insurance and another company holding the road traffic insurance; so far as independent contractors are concerned, the dispute will usually be between the insurance companies holding the respective employers' liability insurance. However, there are many situations that occur when one (or neither) of the parties will be insured and liability must be established in accordance with the above principles.

Liability of others

12.95   Hitherto we have considered the liability of an employer for his failure to take reasonable care for the health and safety of his employees. There are, additionally, a number of other people who are not employers but who may, in the particular circumstances of the case, owe a duty of care to ensure that another person (including, for our purposes, the employees of an employer) is not injured or does not suffer damage. This is merely a further application of the general law of negligence. Sometimes, the injured party will sue the employer and the other alleged wrongdoer jointly, leaving it to the court to apportion blame and responsibility accordingly. For example, in *Driver v William Willett (Contractors) Ltd*, a building contractor engaged a firm of safety consultants to advise on safety requirements and compliance with the relevant regulations. They failed to advise the employers to discontinue the unsafe use of a hoist, with the result that an employee was injured. He sued his employers and the safety consultant. The former were held to be 40% to blame for the accident, the latter 60%. Further, the employers were entitled to recover from the safety consultants the sum which they were liable to pay the injured employee.

12.96   This principle can be extended to other circumstances, eg a main contractor who employs a number of subcontractors (*McArdle v Andmac Roofing*, see paragraph 12.21), manufacturers who fail to provide adequate and meaningful information about the dangers associated with their products (*Cook v Englehard Industries Ltd*), occupiers of premises, and so on. As Lord McMillan stated in *Donoghue v Stevenson*, "the categories of negligence are never closed".

Occupiers' liability

12.97   At common law, an occupier of premises owed legal duties to those people who came on to his premises, but the extent of those duties varied in accordance with the legal status which was ascribed to them, ie contractual invitee, invitee, licensee, etc. Because of the unnecessary legal complications which arose, the common law rules were swept away by the Occupiers' Liability Act 1957, which introduced a common duty of care to all lawful visitors (see also Occupiers' Liability (Scotland) Act 1960).

12.98   The Act provides that an occupier is to take such care in all the circumstances as is reasonable to ensure that a visitor will be reasonably safe in using the premises for the purposes for which he was invited or permitted to be there.

12.99   However, it was recognised that a person exercising his calling would be expected to appreciate risks ordinarily incidental to the work (eg a window cleaner, see *General Cleaning Contractors Ltd v Christmas*, see paragraph 12.52). An occupier must expect children to be less careful than adults, and if he puts up some form of warning, this will not discharge his legal duty unless in all the circumstances it is sufficient. As a general rule, an occupier is not liable for the risks that have been created by an independent contractor.

12.100   The position with regard to trespassers was left unaltered by the Act, the common law rule being that the occupier owed no duty of care to such persons. However, in *British Railways Board v Herrington*, the House of Lords held that if an occupier knew that trespassers were on the land, and knew of physical facts in relation to the land which would constitute a serious risk to those trespassers, he would owe a duty to take reasonable steps to enable the trespasser to avoid the danger. Common humanity dictated that the occupier should not ignore the problem.

12.101 Following *Herrington*, Parliament passed the Occupiers' Liability Act 1984, which provides that an occupier of premises owes a duty to trespassers if:

(a) he knows there is a risk because of the state of the premises

(b) he knows the trespasser will be on the premises

(c) the risk was one which the occupier could reasonably be expected to provide some protection against.

State insurance benefits

12.102 From October 2008 the employment and support allowance, introduced by the Welfare Reform Act 2007, replaced incapacity benefit and income support for new claimants who are out of work because of incapacity for work or disability. A new test, the work capability assessment, is applied, and replaces the personal capability assessment. A claimant will have to satisfy the national insurance contribution test or an income-related test. The work capability assessment will look at a claimant's physical and mental abilities, and assess what a person can do, rather than what they cannot do. The assessment phase will generally last for 13 weeks, after which the claimant will be entitled to either a "work-related activity component" or a "support component" for claimants with severe disabilities. In order to receive a full entitlement, a claimant (other than those in the support group) may be required to attend for a work-focused health related assessment, or a work-focused interview, or work-related activity. If a claimant fails to undertake such assessments, interviews or activity without good cause, his benefits may be reduced.

12.103 The right to claim is independent of any right of action which may or may not exist at common law for negligence or breach of statutory duty, or indeed any other remedy, for the state scheme is a form of insurance policy, paid for partly by contributions from the employer and employee. Further, questions of fault, blame, contributory conduct, etc are irrelevant to the issue of claiming benefits, provided the employee is within the scope of the relevant provisions.

Industrial injuries

12.104 The basic outline of the industrial injuries scheme is to provide compensation for a person who suffers a personal injury caused by an accident arising out of and in the course of his employment (Social

Security Contributions and Benefits Act 1992, s.94), or a prescribed disease or personal injury due to the nature of that employment (s.108). Provided certain criteria are met, a claimant may be able to claim certain benefits.

Prescribed diseases and injuries

12.105 A person who suffers from a prescribed disease or injury, which is a disease or injury due to the nature of the employment, is also entitled to claim benefits under the Act. The disease or injury must be one which has been prescribed as such by the Secretary of State (Social Security (Industrial Injuries) (Prescribed Diseases) Regulations 1985, as variously amended), if he is satisfied that it ought to be treated as a risk of the occupation (and not just a risk common to all employments) and that it is attributable to the nature of the employment (s.108).

12.106 There is a presumption that if the employee works in the prescribed employment and he contracts the prescribed disease or suffers the prescribed injury, the disease or injury will be regarded as being due to the nature of the employment unless the contrary is proved (s.109).

12.107 The Secretary of State may also make special provision by regulations for cases of pneumoconiosis, which is accompanied by tuberculosis, emphysema and chronic bronchitis, and for occupational deafness and byssinosis.

Benefits under the Act

12.108 There are a number of benefits which may be payable. These include the following.

12.109 (1) Disablement benefit (s.103). This is payable as a pension if as a result of the relevant accident or prescribed disease there is a loss of a physical or mental faculty amounting to not less than 14%. The assessment of the extent of the disability and questions as to whether the disability results from the relevant accident or employment are to be determined by the medical authorities. The pension is payable after 15 weeks from the date of the accident.

12.110 (2) Constant attendance allowance (s.104). If there is a 100% loss of a faculty, so that the claimant requires constant attendance, a constant attendance allowance is payable.

12.111 (3) If constant care allowance is paid at the maximum rate, and the claimant is likely to be permanently in need of attendance, then exceptionally severe disablement allowance is payable (s.105).

12.112 Also payable in appropriate circumstances are:
(a) exceptionally severe disablement allowance
(b) reduced earnings allowance
(c) unemployability supplement.

Claims for benefit

12.113 These will be dealt with initially by the local insurance officer. There is a right of appeal from his decision to the local Social Security Appeal Tribunal, to which matters may also be referred by the insurance officer. An appeal will then lie with the commissioner. Certain matters may be referred by the insurance officer direct to the Secretary of State.

12.114 Questions that relate to disablement pensions, such as whether or not the applicant has lost a faculty or the degree of disability, are referred to the medical board, with a right of appeal to a medical appeal tribunal.

Other legal remedies

12.115 An employee who is injured by an act which amounts to a criminal offence on the part of some person may find that he is unable to sue his employer for compensation, for the employer will not have broken any legal duty towards him.

12.116 For example, in *Charlton v Forrest Printing Ink Co*, the claimant was a manager at the defendant's works. One of his duties was to collect the wages from the bank. In 1974 there was an unsuccessful attempt to snatch the wages and thus the managing director gave instructions to those who were to collect the wages that they should take precautions, such as varying the route taken each week, using different modes of transport and sending different people. Despite these instructions, a pattern of collection tended to develop. In 1977, when the claimant was returning from the bank, he was attacked by bandits who threw ammonia into his face, causing severe damage to his eyesight. He claimed damages from his employers, arguing that they had failed to take reasonable care for his safety. In the High Court, the judge accepted the argument that although the sum of money involved was only small

(£1500), in view of the previous robbery, it would have been reasonable to use a professional security firm for this task and hence the employers were in breach of their common law duty to take sensible precautions to protect employees who were involved in a hazardous task. This decision was reversed by the Court of Appeal. Proper steps had been taken to instruct the employees to vary their methods used for collecting the wages. It was unreasonable to expect the employers to guard against a possibility which would not influence the mind of a reasonable man. Statistics showed that the majority of firms of this size did not employ specialist security firms. Hence, the employers were not negligent. However, Lord Denning went on to point out that the applicant would no doubt have a good claim if he applied to the Criminal Injuries Compensation Board.

12.117   Formerly, a claim for compensation in respect of injuries caused by a criminal offence could be made to the Criminal Injuries Compensation Board, but the board has now been abolished, and has been replaced by a new authority, following the enactment of the Criminal Injuries Compensation Act 1995. Under the new scheme, if a person suffers a personal injury directly attributable to a crime of violence, or while trying to arrest an offender, he will be able to receive compensation on a scale laid down in a predetermined tariff, ranging from £1000 to £250,000, according to the nature of the injury. There will also be additional payments for special expenses and loss of earnings or earning capacity for those who are incapacitated for more than 28 weeks, and dependency and support provisions if death results. The award will initially be made by a claims officer, from whose decision there is a right of appeal to an independent Adjudicator. Certain types of injury, eg traffic accidents, are excluded from the scheme.

12.118   Another type of scheme is operated by the Motor Insurers' Bureau, which was set up in 1969 by an agreement between insurance companies and the Ministry of Transport. If a person suffers death or injury arising out of the use of a motor vehicle, and he is unable to trace the person responsible, or the person responsible is unable to pay compensation (usually because he is uninsured), then the board will accept the liability to compensate the injured party, the damages to be assessed in a like manner as a court applying the normal legal principles would assess. In practice, the bureau nominates an insurance company to accept the risk and the latter will then seek to recover the damages paid (in so far as they are able to do so) from the wrongdoer.

12.119 The Pneumoconiosis, etc (Workers' Compensation) Act 1979 provides for lump sum payments to be made to persons who are disabled by industrial lung diseases (pneumoconiosis, byssinosis and diffuse mesothelioma) (see Pneumoconiosis, etc (Workers' Compensation) (Payment of Claims) Regulations 1988 (as amended)). The conditions are that the claimant must be entitled to disablement benefit under the Social Security Contributions and Benefits Act 1992 (paragraph 12.109), he must be unable to recover damages from his employer because the latter has gone out of business and no legal action has been brought or compromised. This scheme is an interesting example of the state providing compensation to injured workers in circumstances where tort liability claims would not be met. A similar scheme for victims of pneumoconiosis has been in force on a voluntary basis for coal miners since 1974 and is operated by the National Coal Board. In *Fairchild v Glenhaven Funeral Services Ltd*, it was held that mesothelioma sufferers who were exposed to asbestos by more than one employer were unable to claim compensation because it was not possible to identify which employer was responsible for the particular fibre which caused the disease. Immediately following the decision, it was announced that as an interim measure, the Government would extend benefit under the Pneumoconiosis (Workers' Compensation) Act 1979 to cover all workers affected by the *Fairchild* ruling, pending consideration of what further action is need to redress what was perceived to be a major injustice. However, the decision in *Fairchild* was subsequently reversed by the House of Lords, and the affected workers will receive compensation in the normal course of events.

12.120 Finally, under the Powers of Criminal Courts Act 1973, the criminal courts (including magistrates' courts) are empowered to make an award of compensation to a person who has been injured or suffered any loss or damage as a result of the commission of a criminal offence. This is in addition to any other punishment which the court may impose. The maximum amount of compensation which may be awarded is (currently) £5000. Thus, in strict theory, if an employer was prosecuted for an offence under HSWA or other legislation for an offence which caused personal injury or damage to an employee's property, the latter could apply to the court for a compensation order to be made at the same time. Indeed, the court can make such an order on its own volition. If the injured person subsequently brings civil proceedings, any compensation awarded in the criminal court will be taken into account. Although this is a useful provision for dealing with claims in respect of minor personal injuries, very little use appears to have been made of it.

Disclosure statement in civil claims

12.121 It will be recalled (see paragraph 1.96) that the Woolf reforms of civil procedure have made considerable changes in the way civil litigation is to be conducted in the future. There will be a premium on full and proper disclosure of all relevant matters by both sides (by nature of the claims, the burden will fall largely on the employer), and this will have particular relevance to health and safety documentation.

12.122 It is highly likely that the health and safety manager will have considerable responsibilities under the new system. If an accident or injury occurs, a report should be made in the internal accident report book, Form F2508 (report of injury or dangerous occurrence) should be completed and sent to the HSE, the names and addresses of any witnesses obtained, photographs taken as appropriate, and medical certificates and/or medical reports kept. Once a claim has been made, a supervising officer should be appointed (this could well be the person responsible for health and safety management), who will be responsible for gathering together all documentation relating to the claim (including videos, tape recordings, photographs, etc) and signing a disclosure statement. So far as workplace claims are concerned, the suggested standard disclosure is of the following documents:
- accident book
- first aider's report
- surgery record
- foreman's/supervisor's accident report
- safety representative's accident report
- RIDDOR report to the HSE
- other communications between the defendant and the HSE
- minutes of health and safety committee meeting(s) where the incident was considered
- report to the Department for Work and Pensions (DWP) (formerly the Department of Social Security (DSS))
- documents listed above relative to any previous accident or matter identified by the claimant and relied upon as proof of negligence
- information relating to the earnings of the claimant at the time of the accident.

12.123 The following additional documents should be disclosed as a matter of routine, where applicable.

12.124 Documents produced in order to comply with the Management of Health and Safety at Work Regulations 1999:
- pre-accident risk assessment (regulation 3)
- post-accident risk assessment (ie, on review, regulation 3)
- accident investigation report prepared in implementing the requirements of regulations 5, 7 and 11
- health surveillance records (regulation 6)
- information provided to employees (regulation 10)
- health and safety training records relating to the employee (regulation 13).

12.125 Documents produced in order to comply with the Workplace (Health, Safety and Welfare) Regulations 1992:
- repair and maintenance records (regulation 5)
- housekeeping records (regulation 9)
- hazard warning signs or notices (regulation 17).

12.126 Documents produced in order to comply with the Provision and Use of Work Equipment Regulations 1998:
- manufacturer's specifications establishing suitability (regulation 4)
- maintenance logs and records (regulation 5)
- information and instructions to employees (regulation 8)
- records of adequate training (regulation 9)
- notices, signs and documents dealing with controls and control systems (regulations 14–18)
- instructions and training documents dealing with maintenance operations (regulation 22)
- work equipment markings (regulation 23)
- warning signs or devices (regulation 24).

12.127 Documents produced in order to comply with the Personal Protective Equipment at Work Regulations 1992:
- assessment of PPE (regulation 6)
- maintenance and replacement of PPE (regulation 7)
- records of maintenance procedures (regulation 7)
- records of tests and examinations of PPE (regulation 7)
- records of providing information, instruction and training for PPE (regulation 9)

– instructions for using PPE (including manufacturer's instructions) (regulation 10).

12.128 Documents produced in order to comply with the Manual Handling Operations Regulations 1992:
– manual handling risk assessment (regulation 4)
– post-accident re-assessment (regulation 4)
– information given to employees in relation to the load, and heaviest side of the load (regulation 4)
– training records in respect of manual handling operations.

12.129 The pre-action protocols also provide lists of other documents which need to be disclosed where other regulations are likely to be in issue, eg Construction (Design and Management) Regulations 2007.

12.130 The above lists are for guidance as to what documents should be disclosed as appropriate in the circumstances, provided they are in existence. They do not have to be specially created for disclosure purposes. A reasonable and proportionate search should be made for relevant documents, depending on the numbers involved, the complexity of the proceedings, the expense of retrieval, and the significance of them if found. If it is unreasonable to search for certain documents (eg relating to an incident which occurred many years ago) that fact should be stated. The duty is to disclose documents which are in the party's control, and if certain documents have been destroyed, an explanation given. If further documents come to light during the proceedings, they must be produced. Some documents may be privileged and advice should be taken before disclosing them.

12.131 A disclosure statement should then be signed by a representative of the party making the disclosure, containing a list of the documents submitted, and stating:
  (a) the extent of the search that has been made to locate documents which he is required to disclose
  (b) that he understands the duty to disclose documents
  (c) that to the best of his knowledge he has carried out that duty
  (d) his official position
  (e) why he is an appropriate person to make the statement.

12.132 A pre-action protocol has also been issued in respect of personal injury claims where the injury is not as a result of an accident, but takes the form of an illness or disease, which includes any illness (physical or psychological) any disorder, ailment, affliction, complaint, malady or derangement. Again, the approach to be adopted is that of "cards on the table" in order to ensure a better and earlier exchange of information, to enable the parties to be in a position to settle cases fairly and early without litigation, and to enable court proceedings to run efficiently.

12.133 In appropriate cases the potential claimant would request occupational records, including health records and personnel records prior to sending a Letter of Claim. Following such request, the potential defendant should disclose any other relevant document which may resolve a causation issue. If such documents are not forthcoming, the potential claimant can then apply for pre-action disclosure. The potential claimant should also obtain additional records from third parties, eg medical records from a GP or consultant, etc. A Letter of Claim should then be sent to the proposed defendant, with a clear summary of facts, the main allegations of fault, and an outline of the financial loss incurred. The defendant should then reply, indicating if the claim is admitted in full or in part, or not at all. The defendant should also supply documents in his possession which are material to the issues, and which would be likely to be ordered to be disclosed by the court, either on an application for pre-action disclosure, or for disclosure during the proceedings. Where relevant, reference should be made to the documents which are annexed to the personal injury protocol.

12.134 The protocol is less prescriptive on the use of experts by either side, although a less adversarial expert culture is advised.

12.135 Any failure to observe the spirit, if not the letter of the protocols, either by failing or refusing to disclose relevant documents or make factual admissions, or failing to respond to reasonable requests in a reasonable time, or by adopting delaying or other unfair tactics, etc is likely to be visited by an award of costs against the party concerned, irrespective of the ultimate outcome of the claim.

CHAPTER 13
Enforcing health and safety rules

13.1   The duty to ensure that health and safety policies are observed falls on all those who are involved in the work processes: on the employer, management, safety officer, shop steward, safety representative, supervisor and employees generally. Each must play his own special role in ensuring that health and safety policies are laid down, adequately promulgated and, perhaps the most important of all, carried out in practice.

13.2   The basis for these duties is the contract of employment, which is essentially mutual agreement. It follows that a breach of contract by either side entitles the other party to pursue whatever remedy is appropriate in the circumstances. Thus, on the one hand, if the employee commits a breach of contract, the employer may terminate the contract and in theory at any rate sue for any damage he has suffered. On the other hand, there is an implied term of the contract that the employer will take reasonable care to ensure the health and safety of his employees while at work (*Matthews v Kuwait Bechtel Corporation*); if he is in breach of that term the employee may "accept" the breach and resign (this is the doctrine of constructive dismissal). If he has suffered damages, he may claim in respect of these. Additionally, if the employer's breach has caused injury, he may sue in tort for a breach of duty imposed by law (see Chapter 12).

Appointment procedures

13.3   Health and safety policies begin with appointment procedures. In theory, the employer should ensure that all his employees are fit and healthy and not suffering from any disability which renders them liable to an accident or which would make them a hazard to the safety of themselves or to others. To this aim, pre-employment medicals may be used.

13.4   A medical practitioner retained by an employer to carry out a pre-employment medical assessment owes no duty of care to a job applicant when assessing that person's suitability for employment, because there is no proximity of relationship such as to give rise to a duty of care. Consequently, a disappointed job applicant, who is refused employment as a result of a doctor carrying out an independent medical examination on behalf of an employer, cannot claim damages from that doctor for negligence (*Kapfunde v Abbey National plc*).

13.5   Pre-medical screening must be related to a particular hazard. Judgment must be made on medical and safety grounds, not on the ground of general health. Epileptics can do a useful job at work, depending on the degree of their illness and the nature of the danger they face at work. Disabled employees can do a range of jobs if the work is matched to their abilities and care is taken to ensure their safety. Dedication to health and safety does not mean the exclusion of a large section of the population from employment opportunities. The provisions of the Disability Discrimination Act 1995 (see paragraph 11.102) must also be borne in mind by those responsible for making appointments. Thus the object of pre-medical employment must not be to exclude certain people, but to place employees in the appropriate niche.

13.6   Nonetheless, critical situations may require extreme measures. In *Jeffries v BP Tankers Ltd*, it was the company's policy not to employ people as radio operators on ships if they had any history of cardiac disease. They dismissed a radio officer who had suffered a heart attack, even though he had made an excellent recovery. His dismissal was held to be fair, for the policy was one which had to be rigorously enforced for reasons which the employers were satisfied were necessary.

13.7   Health considerations are equally relevant. In *Panesar v Nestlé Co Ltd*, the claimant, a Sikh, enquired about a job with the respondents. He was told that there was a company rule prohibiting beards and, since he was not prepared to shave off his beard, he was not interviewed for the job. He claimed that he had been unlawfully discriminated against on grounds of race (see Race Relations Act 1976, s.4). It was conceded that he had been indirectly discriminated against, in that the proportion of applicants of his race who could comply with the requirement that they should not wear a beard was smaller than the proportion of applicants from other racial groups (Race Relations Act, s.1(1)(b)). However, the requirement or condition was capable of being justified on grounds other than race, namely hygiene considerations and his claim failed before the employment tribunal, the EAT and the Court of Appeal. It should be noted that it would be discriminatory on grounds of race to refuse employment to (or to dismiss from employment) a Sikh who refuses to wear a head protection helmet on a building site, as long as he is wearing a turban (see paragraph 9.64).

Works rules

13.8   A rule book is a valuable source of information and guidance, and should in particular lay down precise rules concerning all aspects of health, safety and welfare. The contents of the rule book should be incorporated into the contract of employment, they should be updated in accordance with developments and experience and should be contained in a booklet which can be retained by the employee. Somewhat strangely, s.1 of the Employment Rights Act 1996 (which requires employers to give to their employees written particulars of their terms and conditions of employment) includes a requirement to provide information relating to disciplinary and grievance procedures, but specifically states that this does not apply to rules, disciplinary decisions, grievances or procedures relating to health or safety at work. This exclusion is even more surprising when it is realised that health and safety matters probably constitute the biggest single cause of disciplinary problems. It is to be hoped that this gap in the law is remedied in the near future. However, the Code of Practice issued by the Advisory Conciliation and Arbitration Service (ACAS) entitled *Disciplinary and Grievance Procedures* states that "When drawing up disciplinary rules the aim should be to specify clearly and concisely those that are necessary for the efficient and safe performance of work...".

13.9   Particular attention should be paid to publicising the contents of the rule book to new employees on some form of induction course. Those rules which are mandatory can be highlighted and disciplinary procedures and sanctions that will follow a breach can be spelt out. Attention can be paid to ways of communicating the rules to immigrant employees and others whose command of English is less than perfect, so that they are unable to plead ignorance. Records can be kept of when and how the rules were communicated to each individual concerned.

13.10   Rules that relate to health and safety are designed to protect employees individually and collectively and should therefore contain sanctions in the event of a breach. The matter was expressed forcefully by Stephenson LJ in *Bux v Slough Metals Ltd*, when he said "The employer must make the law of the land the rule of the factory". In other

473

words, the employee should be informed as to the legal requirements and warned that he is breaking the law if he fails to wear or use the precautions provided, for which he can be prosecuted. He can also be warned that he faces disciplinary action or even dismissal if he acts in breach of the safety rules or the legal requirements.

13.11   To achieve consistency in procedure, certain principles must be observed. First, the rules must be promulgated. This means that they must be brought to the attention of the employees in a suitable form. It is no longer regarded as being sufficient to post rules on a notice board or hide them in the personnel office. In *Pitts v Rivertex Ltd*, the employee was dismissed for breaking a works rule, a copy of which could be found on the notice board. It was held that if a rule was so important that a breach would be visited by instant dismissal, it should have been expressly communicated to all the employees concerned.

13.12   Second, rules must be reasonable. An employer may impose his own standards, but they must have a sound functional basis and not be old-fashioned, out-of-date or based on prejudice. In *Talbot v Hugh M Fulton Ltd*, the applicant was dismissed for having long hair in breach of the company's rules. The dismissal was held to be unfair. Management did not specify the length of hair which was acceptable, it was not shown that long hair was a safety hazard and the rule did not appear to apply to women with long hair. Clearly, it was an act of prejudice against the hair style of the day. By contrast, we can cite *Marsh v Judge International*, where a youth had hair that was two feet six inches long, reaching down to his waist. The factory inspector told the employers that they would be prosecuted if the youth caught his hair in any machinery and was injured, and so, after due warnings to cut his hair (which he ignored) the youth was dismissed. This was held to be fair. The rule, in the nature of an instruction, was perfectly reasonable and in the interests of safety. It follows that an employer can lay down suitable safety standards provided they are functional and reasonable (*Singh v Lyons Maid Ltd*).

13.13   Third, the rules must be consistently enforced. If a rule is generally disregarded, or no severe sanction is imposed for a breach, then it may be unfair to act on it without giving some indication that there was to be a change in enforcement policy. Thus in *Bendall v Paine and Betteridge*, the applicant had been employed for 15 years. From time to time he was told to put out a cigarette he was smoking, as there was a fire risk. One day, he was summarily dismissed for smoking and this was held to be unfair. In the past he had been warned without it being brought home to him that he was risking instant dismissal. He should have been given a final, written warning before he was dismissed.

13.14 Health and safety rules should therefore be drawn up in accordance with the hazards perceived. This requires a careful assessment of the likely risks, based on the nature of the firm, its processes, the workforce, and all other relevant considerations. The following are some examples of the more common rules which should be considered.

Smoking

13.15 If there is a risk of fire (*Bendall v Paine and Betteridge*) or a health hazard (*Unkles v Milanda Bread Co*), clear rules should be laid down informing employees that anyone caught smoking in the prohibited area will be instantly dismissed. Additionally, the employer must pay attention to the statutory provisions that prohibit smoking. These include the following.

Control of Lead at Work Regulations 2002	An employer shall take such steps as are adequate to ensure that employees do not smoke in any place which is or is likely to be contaminated with lead; there is also a prohibition on employees smoking in any place which an employer has reason to believe is contaminated with lead.
Control of Asbestos Regulations 2006	Employees should not smoke in any "designated asbestos area".
Gas Safety (Installation and Use) Regulations 1998	No person shall smoke in any area designated as a controlled area.
Ionising Radiations Regulations 1999	No employee shall smoke in any area designated as a controlled area.
Explosives Act 1875, s.10	Smoking is prohibited.

Control of Substances Hazardous to Health Regulations 2002	Smoking is prohibited in areas contaminated by carcinogens.

13.16   A number of older statutory provisions have been revoked either by the Control of Substances Hazardous to Health Regulations 2002 or by the Dangerous Substances and Explosive Atmospheres Regulations 2002. It should also be noted that the Workplace (Health Safety and Welfare) Regulations 1992 require that rest rooms and rest areas include suitable arrangements to protect non-smokers from discomfort caused by tobacco smoke (see paragraph 6.48).

13.17   As has been noted (see paragraph 5.87), smoking in enclosed workplaces is now prohibited altogether.

Eating and drinking

13.18   The following provisions prohibiting the partaking of food or drink are in force.

Control of Lead at Work Regulations 2002	An employee shall not eat or drink in any place which he has reason to believe to be contaminated by lead.
Control of Asbestos Regulations 2006	Employees should not eat or drink in any "designated asbestos area".
Ionising Radiations Regulations 1999	No employee shall eat or drink in any area designated as a "controlled area".
Control of Substances Hazardous to Health Regulations 2002	Eating and drinking is prohibited in areas contaminated by carcinogens.
Railways and Transport Safety Act 2003	A person commits an offence if he performs an aviation function (or an ancillary activity) at a time when his ability to do so is impaired because of drink or drugs. (There are similar provisions which apply to masters of ships and other seamen.)

Fighting

13.19 This can lead to a serious accident occurring, and the rule should lay down that anyone caught fighting will be subject to disciplinary proceedings. It cannot be right to state that fighting will lead to instant dismissal; after all, if two people are fighting, one may be merely defending himself, or the one who started the fight may have been provoked. A careful investigation of the circumstances is therefore called for. Further, two people may be fighting in a no-risk area, which may invoke a disciplinary sanction less than dismissal. The rule, therefore, should indicate the discretionary power of management. In *Taylor v Parsons Peebles Ltd*, the applicant had been employed for 20 years by the company and was dismissed after he was involved in a fight. It was the company's policy to dismiss automatically any employee who deliberately struck another employee. The employment tribunal held that the dismissal was fair, because the policy was applied consistently and the other employee who was fighting was also dismissed. On appeal, the decision was reversed by the EAT. In determining whether a decision to dismiss was reasonable, the proper test was not the employer's policy, but what the reaction would be of a reasonable employer in the circumstances. The employer's rules of conduct must be considered in the light of how it would be applied by a reasonable employer. Taking into account the fact that the employee had been employed for 20 years with no serious disciplinary record against him, a reasonable employer would not have applied the rigid sanction of automatic dismissal. In other words, the employer must be consistent in his procedures, but flexible in his punishment. He must consider the gravity of the offence, and the circumstances of the offender. The employee must always be given at least an opportunity to plead mitigating circumstances, although the weight to be attached to such a plea is for the employer to decide, bearing in mind the gravity of the incident. In the *Taylor* case, because the employers had applied a policy consistently without taking into account relevant factors, the dismissal was unfair. However, it was also held that the employee had contributed towards his dismissal, and compensation was reduced by 25%.

Drunkenness

13.20 If an employee is found to be drunk on the premises or to have been drinking alcohol, it may be good policy to escort him off the premises, for the fact of drinking *per se* may not be sufficient to warrant dismissal (*McGibbon v Gillespie Building Co*). However, disciplinary proceedings should normally be instituted. If the drunkenness is such as to cause or constitute a serious safety hazard, different considerations would apply. In these circumstances, the matter should be dealt with as a serious disciplinary offence and the procedure should be activated immediately. In *Abercrombie v Alexander Thomson & Son*, the claimant was found to be in an intoxicated state while in charge of a crane. A decision was taken to dismiss him, but this was not implemented until two weeks had elapsed, during which time he was permitted to carry on working. The dismissal was held to be unfair. By delaying the taking of action, the employers had condoned the offence.

13.21 A person who has symptoms of alcoholism should not be put through the disciplinary procedure immediately. Rather, his condition should be treated as an illness, and medical advice should be sought as to his condition and the likelihood of recovery or obtaining treatment.

13.22 There are some statutory provisions which also need to be borne in mind. These include the Work in Compressed Air Regulations 1996 (no person employed shall consume alcohol while in compressed air). There are a number of regulations which prohibit the consumption of food and drink while engaged in certain processes or activities, and these could certainly cover drinking alcohol (see paragraph 13.20).

Skylarking

13.23 The dangers from employees who indulge in horseplay or skylarking have already been noted (see Chapter 12 and see *Harrison v Michelin Tyre Co Ltd*), and the rules should state that such conduct will not be tolerated. Employees, particularly the young or inexperienced, should be given final written warnings, indicating that any repetition will result in instant dismissal. In *Hudson v Ridge Manufacturing Co Ltd*, the plaintiff was injured as a result of a prank played upon him by an employee who was known for horseplay. The employers were held to be liable. It was stated that "If a fellow workman by his habitual conduct is likely to prove a source of danger to his fellow employees, a duty lies fairly and squarely on the employer to remove the source of danger."

Breach of safety rules

13.24 Again, this will be dealt with in accordance with the hazard incurred. In *Martin v Yorkshire Imperial Metals*, the claimant tied down a lever on an automatic lathe with a piece of wire. This had the effect of bypassing the safety device, for the machine could only be used if the operator used both hands. It was held that his dismissal was fair. He knew that he would be dismissed if he neglected to use the safety device. In *Ashworth v John Needham & Sons*, the claimant acted in flagrant breach of safety rules by putting a fence around a hole in the ground instead of replacing a plate. After the matter had been discussed with the company's safety officer and a trade union official he was dismissed. This was held to be fair, as a serious accident could have happened.

Failure to use safety equipment

13.25 Again, the gravity of the consequences should be a factor which determines the severity of the sanction and the rules should be flexible enough to deal with this situation. Thus in *Frizzell v Flanders*, the employee was provided with a gas mask while working in a tank. He was seen working without the mask and was dismissed. This was held to be fair. It was essential to enforce rigorously the use of safety equipment. On the other hand, in *Henry v Vauxhall Motors Ltd*, the employee discovered that his safety helmet was missing. He was provided with another one which, he claimed, was uncomfortable. He therefore worked without the helmet and persisted in his refusal after being instructed to wear it by the foreman. He was dismissed, but this was held to be unfair. There was no proper enquiry into the reasons for his refusal. Nonetheless, the employment tribunal thought that he had contributed substantially to his dismissal and reduced his compensation award by 60%.

Hygiene observance

13.26 It may be necessary to enforce standards of hygiene because there is a risk of contamination to the product or a health hazard to employees. For example, in *Gill v Walls Meat Co*, the claimant, who was a Sikh, was employed to work with open meat. He did not have a beard at the time he commenced employment, but at some later stage he grew a beard. He was subsequently told that he could not be employed on that particular job while wearing his beard, but he refused to shave it off. He was offered alternative employment where he would be permitted to have his beard, but he refused and was dismissed. This was held to be fair. Similarly, the rules should provide that employees who have been suffering from or in contact with a contagious disease should be encouraged to report to the appropriate medical advisor before commencing work to ensure that they are "clear" and do not transmit the disease or illness to other employees or do not cause contamination of the product. Personal hygiene is also important. In *Singh v John Laing & Sons*, a company rule provided that anyone misusing the toilet facilities would be liable to instant dismissal. The applicant was seen urinating in a room he had been instructed to clean and he was thus dismissed. This was held to be fair. He knew of the rule, had a good command of English and could offer little by way of explanation. After all, employers are legally bound to maintain toilet facilities in clean and proper condition and thus it is not wrong to enforce high standards of hygiene (*Singh v Elliotts Bricks*).

Health generally

13.27   In some circumstances, general ill-health must be reported and noted, so as not to cause a hazard. In *Singh-Deu v Chloride Metals Ltd*, the employee worked in a lead smelting factory where it was essential to remain alert in view of the dangerous processes that were being carried on. He was sent home by the works doctor after complaining of feeling unwell. He visited his own doctor who diagnosed paranoid schizophrenia. He was then examined by a specialist, after which he attempted to return to work. However, the works doctor would not allow him to return unless the specialist gave an assurance that there would be no recurrence of the illness. This assurance was not forthcoming and so he was dismissed, as the works manager, mindful of the inherently dangerous processes being carried on in the lead factory, was not prepared to take the responsibility of allowing him back at work. The dismissal was held to be fair. It was not reasonable to continue to employ him in a delicately balanced job which called for a high degree of concentration. The effect of a relapse on the claimant and on others could have been devastating had a mistake or error been made. A similar result was reached in *Balogun v Lucas Batteries Ltd*, where the claimant, who was working with lead, suffered from hypertension. Medical evidence clearly indicated that this type of work can be harmful, especially to those who have an existing predisposition to certain types of illnesses, including hypertension. Efforts were made to find him alternative work, but there was no suitable job and he was dismissed. This was held to be fair. His continued employment constituted a risk to himself and to others.

13.28 However, an employee with a health problem may well have a long-term disability within the meaning of the Disability Discrimination Act 1995, and the employer may be under a duty to make reasonable adjustments so as to enable the disabled employee to do his work safely (see paragraph 11.102). A careful risk assessment should be carried out, and ways of enabling the employee to continue in employment without being a risk to himself or others should be investigated, before dismissal is contemplated.

Vandalism

13.29 An employee who misuses the company's property or interferes with anything provided for the use of employees generally can be disciplined. This is especially true if there is an interference or misuse of anything provided for health, safety and welfare, for there is also a breach of s.8 of HSWA. In *Ferodo Ltd v Barnes*, an employee was dismissed after the company decided he had been committing an act of vandalism in the lavatories. The employment tribunal decided that the dismissal was unfair, as they were not satisfied that in fact the employee had committed this act. This was reversed on appeal. It is not the duty of the employment tribunal to re-try the case. It was their duty to see that management acted reasonably and as long as there had been a fair and proper investigation, the employment tribunal should not substitute their judgment for that of management.

Neglect

13.30 An employee who is incompetent or neglectful in his work may cause some damage to the work processes and the matter should be regarded as a disciplinary problem. The first duty of management is to ensure that the employee has been trained properly, supervised adequately, has sufficient support staff and sufficient facilities to do the job in question. An employee who is suffering from irredeemable incompetence can be offered alternative employment, failing which a dismissal will be fair. If he is suffering from neglectful incompetence, he should be warned, in accordance with the gravity of the case. However, if the neglect is of such a dangerous nature that there is the likelihood of serious injury to persons or damage to property, then the matter becomes a health and safety issue and can be dealt with as such. This could result in a disciplinary sanction appropriate to the case, and even dismissal. In *Taylor v Alidair Ltd*, an airline pilot landed his aeroplane in a manner which caused some concern and consternation among the rest of the crew and passengers. After a full investigation it was decided that he had been negligent and he was dismissed. This was held to be fair. There are some activities the consequences of which are so serious and grave that it is not possible to risk a repetition. Nor does it matter if the neglect causes a risk of injury to fellow employees or to the public or customers of the employer. Thus if an employee fails to follow the prescribed safety checks (*Wilcox v HGS*) or the work is done in a negligent manner which creates a risk (*McGibbon v Gillespie Building Co*) he may be dismissed.

Sleeping on duty

13.31   Whatever may be the position in other work situations, it has always been recognised that safety considerations must be regarded as being paramount. In *Jenkins v British Gypsum Ltd*, the claimant was employed on the night shift checking and taking the temperature of a gas-fired kiln. He was found asleep on duty and was dismissed, even though there was no specific rule to cover this situation. Nonetheless, his dismissal was held to be fair. It was essential for him to monitor the temperature regularly as a safeguard, and the fact that he had to be woken in order to do his work constituted gross misconduct. "Alertness is essential from the safety angle", commented the employment tribunal.

Training

13.32   Since the employer is under an obligation to train his employees in safety and health matters, and since also the employee is obliged to co-operate with the employer in the performance of the statutory duties, an employee who refuses to be trained may be fairly dismissed. In *Minter v Willingborough Foundries Ltd*, the claimant was a nurse employed at the employer's factory. There were complaints about her standards of medical care and she was asked to go on a training course, but she refused. Subsequently, there were further complaints and she was again asked to undertake further training, and again she refused. Because the employers were concerned about their obligations under HSWA, she was dismissed. The EAT upheld the finding of the employment tribunal that the dismissal was fair. The course would not have involved her in any expense or inconvenience and she did not give an adequate explanation for her refusal.

Other dangerous practices

13.33 No list of actions that is to be the subject of disciplinary sanctions can be exhaustive and each employer must try to complete the list in accordance with his own situation, as well as covering the unexpected. Thus, it should be fairly obvious that it is an extremely dangerous practice to light a bonfire near to flammable material (*Bussey v CSW Engineering Ltd*) or to fire air guns while at work, even though this is during the lunch hour (*Shipside (Ruthin) Ltd v T&GWU*), to smoke in a wood and paint shop (*Bendall v Paine and Betteridge*), to walk out, leaving a high-pressure steam boiler on (*Gannon v JC Firth Ltd*), to drive a vehicle without being qualified to do so, or to drive a vehicle so badly that the brakes overheat (*Potter v WJ Rich & Sons*), all of which are examples of conduct capable of attracting disciplinary sanctions, including dismissal. The list can be extended almost indefinitely.

Enforcing safety rules: action by the employee

13.34 If there is an actual injury to an employee, he can, of course, pursue whatever remedy is available to him at common law (see Chapter 12). If there is a threatened injury, the situation is more delicate. Since it is an implied term of the contract of employment that the employer will ensure the health and safety of his employees, the employer will be in breach of contract if he fails to take the necessary steps. In these circumstances, the employee will accept the breach, and resign but, in law, since he was entitled to resign by virtue of the employer's conduct, it is the employer who has "dismissed" the employee. In technical terms, even though the employee has resigned, he may bring a claim for "constructive dismissal" and, provided he has the requisite period of continuous employment (or is asserting a statutory right, for which no period of continuous employment is required), he can bring his claim before the employment tribunal for compensation. For example, in *British Aircraft Corporation v Austin*, the employee asked her supervisor for a pair of prescription safety glasses. After waiting several months, during which time she heard nothing further, she resigned and claimed constructive dismissal. Her claim succeeded. It was an implied term of the contract that the employers would ensure her safety, and by failing to investigate her request and provide the necessary safety precaution they had broken the contract. It will be noted at this stage that the inaction was the fault of the supervisor, yet it was the employer who was held responsible.

13.35 A constructive dismissal claim does not need to be based on an actual injury (see *Knight v Barra Shipping Co Ltd*); the fear of the possibility is sufficient. In *Keys v Shoefayre Ltd*, the employee worked in a shop which was robbed in the daytime by a gang of youths. The manager was asked by the employee to do something about the security of the premises, but he replied that there was nothing he could do. A further daytime robbery took place, and the employee resigned and claimed constructive dismissal on the ground that the premises were no longer safe to work in. Her claim succeeded. The employers were obliged to take reasonable steps to operate a safe system of work and to provide safe premises. The employment tribunal thought that it might have been possible to install a telephone, or to employ a male assistant, etc.

13.36 However, the contractual obligation of the employer is no higher than the duty owed in tort, which is to take reasonable care only. The employer does not guarantee absolutely the safety of his employees. In *Buttars v Holo-Krome Ltd*, the employee was injured when a blank flew out of a machine and struck his safety glasses. A lens broke and injured his eye. When he returned to work he asked for a guard to be fitted to the machine, but the employers claimed it was safe. He resigned and claimed constructive dismissal, but the claim was rejected. The accident had been reported to the factory inspector who agreed that the machine was safe and proposed to take no further action on the incident. There was no duty on the part of the employer to fence, for this duty does not apply to parts of the machine or materials used by the machine which fly out (*Nicholls v F Austin (Leyton) Ltd*). The accident was a freak one, it was not usual to fit guards on this type of machine. In these circumstances, the employment tribunal thought that the employers had not broken the contract, and hence there was no constructive dismissal.

13.37 The fact that an employee genuinely believes that his health and safety is at risk will not, by itself, support a claim for constructive dismissal. In *Wojcik v Amtico Co Ltd*, the claimant suffered a minor back injury while working on a machine. He did not take the matter further, either with his health and safety representative or with the safety committee. He asked to be supplied with a back support, but the company's medical officer advised against this, arguing that the medical evidence indicated that this would do more harm than good. The company arranged for the machine to be examined by a consultant engineer and, following a report, made some minor adjustments to it.

The employee subsequently resigned, claiming that he had been constructively dismissed, alleging that the employer had broken the implied term of trust and confidence, by failing to take seriously his concerns about the safety of the machine. An employment tribunal dismissed his claim, stating that he had become obsessed with the whole matter. Health and safety concerns had been largely theoretical, and very minor. The employers had taken the complaint seriously, modifying the machine following the receipt of the consultant's report, and acted as a responsible employer. In the circumstances, the employer had not broken any implied term of trust and confidence.

13.38 More difficult is the situation where the employee responds to the employer's breach by action other than resignation. In *Mariner v Domestic and Industrial Polythene Ltd*, some workers discovered that the temperature in the workplace was 53°F. There was no fuel left for heating, as the employer had allowed his supplies to run down in anticipation of the warmer weather. The workers therefore went home, and the following day, when they reported for work, they were dismissed for going on strike. At that time, a complaint of unfair dismissal, brought about because a person is taking part in a strike or other industrial action could not normally be entertained by the employment tribunal (Trade Union and Labour Relations (Consolidation) Act 1992, s.238) but, in this case, the employment tribunal decided that the workers had not been on strike for they had not withdrawn their labour in breach of their employment contracts. It was the employer who was in breach, for he had allowed the temperature to fall below the statutory minimum and there is an implied term in the contract of employment that the employer will perform his statutory obligations. If he fails to do so, the employees are merely responding to the breach, not acting themselves in breach.

13.39 A claim based on constructive dismissal must be tested by employment tribunals in accordance with the principles of employment law relating to the reasonableness of the employer's conduct, not in accordance with the principles of health and safety law relating to the employer doing something so far as is reasonably practicable. In *Dutton & Clark Ltd v Daly*, the employee worked in the office of a building society agency. The employers had installed protective safety devices, including screens, partitions and alarm buttons. However, the premises were subjected to two armed robberies in a space of two months and the employee resigned. She claimed that the safety measures were inadequate and that she was too frightened to work in the premises, and she alleged that by failing to provide adequate security the employers were in breach of a fundamental term of the contract which entitled her to resign and claim that she had been dismissed. An employment tribunal upheld her claim, but on appeal the EAT remitted the case to another tribunal for further consideration. The test to be applied is whether the safety precautions taken were those that a reasonable employer would have taken. This duty is not as high as ensuring safety so far as is reasonably practicable.

13.40   It is interesting to note that the original test, formulated in *Western Excavating (EEC) Ltd v Sharp* by the Court of Appeal was "has the employer broken the contract?". The more modern approach appears to be, "did the employer evince an intention to break the contract?". This is slightly different, and employees who imagine that minor things that go wrong in their daily employment automatically give them a right to claim constructive dismissal should be cautioned about such a false assumption. Further, it must be borne in mind that while constructive dismissal is, in law, a "dismissal", it is not necessarily an unfair dismissal (*Industrial Rubber Products v Gillon*).

13.41   The Employment Act 2008 has now been passed by Parliament. The provisions relating to statutory dispute resolution procedures set out in the Employment Act 2002 have been repealed from 6 April 2009, as well as s .98A of the Employment Rights Act 1996, thus reviving the position set out in *Polkey v A E Dayton Services Ltd*. However, the repeal will not affect issues which arose on or before 5 April. The complex transitional provisions can be found in the Employment Act 2008 (Commencement No. 1 Transitional Provisions and Savings) Order 2008.

13.42   The revised ACAS Code of Practice on Disciplinary and Grievance Procedures has been issued. When in force following the repeal of the statutory dispute resolution procedures (from April 2009) a failure by either party to follow the provisions of the Code can lead to a increase or decrease in any award made by up to 25%. The Code is accompanied by a detailed Guidance (more than double its existing length!).

Enforcing safety rules: action by the employer

13.43   Safety rules can be enforced within the context of existing disciplinary procedures. These may be drawn up by management, in consultation with the trade unions or workforce if possible, without their co-operation or agreement if necessary. Details should be given to each employee explaining the steps to be followed, the sanctions which may be applied in accordance with the gravity of the case and the method of appeal. Further reference should be made to the ACAS *Code of Practice on Disciplinary and Grievance Procedures*.

13.44   A disciplinary procedure should have five characteristics.
1. There must be a full and proper investigation into the incident. This should be undertaken as soon as possible (*Abercrombie v Alexander Thomson & Son*), and consideration should be given to a short period of suspension (with or without pay, in accordance with the contract and/or procedure) pending such investigation.
2. The offender must be told of the charge against him. It is no bad thing to put this in writing, particularly if his command of English is weak, or the charge is a serious one, so that he can obtain advice from any available source.
3. He should be given an opportunity to state his case, to plead that he did not do it, or if he did, it was not his fault, or if it was, there were mitigating circumstances which ought to be taken into consideration, etc.
4. He is entitled to be represented by a single companion (ie a trade union official or a fellow worker), see Employment Relations Act 1999, ss.10–15.
5. He should be given the right of appeal, to a level of management not previously involved in the decision-making process.

13.45   Obviously, the nature of the disciplinary procedure will vary with the size and resources of the firm. One does not expect the same formalities in a small firm as might exist in a large firm. Equally, the sanction which will be imposed will depend on the nature and seriousness of the offence, the circumstances of the individual, and so forth. The purpose of disciplinary sanctions is to improve the conduct of the offender, to deter others from doing the same or similarly wrongful acts, and to protect the individual, other employees, the public and ultimately, the employer. Thus no simple pattern emerges; sometimes the sanction will be corrective in nature, sometimes it will be designed to encourage others not to break the rules. The gravity of the sanction will reflect the objectives to be achieved. In the case of a minor offence, a minor sanction will be imposed, such as a warning, which may be verbal. A repetition of the offence, or a different kind of offence, or a serious offence, would be dealt with by a written warning, which should detail the offence, warn as to the consequences which may flow from a repetition of the offence, or any other offence of a similar or dissimilar nature. A very serious offence should be dealt with by a final warning, or by dismissal.

13.46   No matter how serious the breach, how dangerous the practice, nor how strong the evidence is, an employer must always carry out a proper investigation into the incident, give the employee an opportunity to respond to any allegations made, and take account of any mitigating circumstances, before dismissing an employee. A failure to do so will invariably lead to a finding that the dismissal was unfair, despite whatever merits the decision would otherwise have. Due weight should be given to any previous warning, but as a general principle a warning which has expired should be ignored (*Diosynth Ltd v Thomson*). An employment tribunal may decide to reduce any compensation award on the grounds of contributory conduct, but they are not bound to do so (*OCS Cleaning Scotland Ltd v Oag*).

13.47   Depending on the nature of the offence and the circumstances of the offender, other sanctions might be imposed. Thus, consideration could be given to a period of suspension without pay (provided the disciplinary procedure confers this power), a transfer to other work, or even a "fine" (eg if an employee is failing to use safety equipment), which has been agreed as a recognised type of punishment (perhaps with the proceeds going to an appropriate charity).

Dismissal

13.48   The final power left to the employer is to dismiss the employee. This may be done for a number of reasons.

13.49   First, the circumstances may be so serious that a dangerous situation was created which put the employee or others at risk of serious injury. There are some activities where the degree of safety required is so high, and the consequences of a failure to achieve those standards so potentially serious, that a single departure from them could warrant instant dismissal. For example, in *Taylor v Alidair Ltd* (see above) it would be totally unrealistic to give the pilot a final warning saying "If you land your aeroplane in such an incompetent manner again we will dismiss you", etc. The driver of an express train, the scientist in charge of a nuclear power station, the driver of a vehicle carrying a dangerous chemical, etc must all display the highest standards of care. In *Wilcox v HGS*, the employee was employed as a converter, changing gas appliances from town gas to natural gas. He was instructed that before he left premises he had to undertake a mandatory safety check, but he failed to do so and was dismissed. The dismissal was held to be fair by the employment tribunal, although on appeal the case was remitted for reconsideration. If, as he alleged, the employers had persistently ignored the safety regulations, then such acquiescence was a relevant factor to be taken into account in determining whether or not a final warning should have been given.

13.50 Second, an employee may be at serious risk of injury to himself. In *Finch v Betabake (Anglia) Ltd*, an apprentice motor mechanic was found to have defective eyesight. A report from an ophthalmic surgeon stated that the individual could not be employed without undue danger to himself and to others and he was therefore dismissed. This was held to be fair. The fact that the employee is willing to take a risk that he may be injured is irrelevant, for the employer may expose himself to civil or criminal liabilities by continuing the employment (*Marsh v Judge International*).

13.51 Third, the situation may arise where the employee's physical condition is such that it amounts to a health or safety hazard. This must be handled carefully; there must be a full investigation, preferably backed with medical reports, there should be consultation with the employee and alternative employment should be considered. In *Spalding v Port of London Authority*, the employee failed a medical examination after it was discovered that he was suffering from deafness. It was recommended that he worked with a hearing aid, but this did not prove to be satisfactory and he was dismissed. This was held to be fair; the company's medical standards were not unnecessarily high, and were justified in order to ensure the safety of the employee and his fellow employees. In *Yarrow v QIS Ltd*, the employee was dismissed after it was discovered that he was suffering from psoriasis. Because he had to work with radiography equipment, he was subject to the Ionising Radiation (Unsealed Sources) Regulations 1969, which made it unsafe for him to be employed. This dismissal too was held to be fair. The employers were in danger of breaking the law if they continued to employ him. And in *Parsons v Fisons Ltd*, the company's medical advisor noted that the employee had poor vision and only narrowly averted several possible accidents. After a full discussion with the group medical advisor and her general practitioner, the employee was dismissed. This too was held to be fair. There was no other suitable job for her, and it was not necessary to wait until an accident occurred before taking appropriate action.

13.52 It is important to bear in mind the health and safety of other employees as well as their general comfort and working environment. In *Kenna v Stewart Plastics Ltd*, the employee had a series of epileptic fits in an open-plan office. The dismissal was held to be fair. The employer had a duty to ensure that other employees could do their work in reasonable working conditions that were physically and mentally conducive to work.

13.53 Fourth, the employee may be dismissed if he refuses to observe the safety instructions or wear the appropriate safety equipment. In *Frizzell v Flanders*, the employee was provided with a gas mask while working in a tank. He was seen working without the mask and was dismissed. This was held to be fair. It was essential to enforce the safety precautions rigorously both for his own sake and for the sake of others, and his dismissal would serve as a warning that flagrant breaches of the safety instructions would not be tolerated.

13.54 An over-zealousness on the part of the employee to be cossetted against the risks of the employment can also result in his fair dismissal. In *Wood v Brita-Finish Ltd*, the employee had been provided with acid-proof gloves, goggles, wellingtons and a protective apron, all of which had been approved by the Factory Inspectorate. He refused to work unless he was also provided with an overall and was dismissed This was held to be fair. Overalls had proved to be ineffective in the past and contributed nothing to the safety of the employee. In *Howard v Overdale Engineering Ltd*, the employee refused to work in a new factory because of dust caused by engineers drilling cables into the floor. The employment tribunal found that the employers were not in breach of any statutory obligation to prevent impurities from getting into the air or to prevent employees from being subjected to harmful substances, and his dismissal was held to be fair for refusing to obey a lawful order.

13.55 Fifth, an employee may be dismissed for a serious breach of the company's rules, particularly when there is a health or safety hazard. In *O'Flynn v Airlinks the Airport Coach Co Ltd*, the employers introduced a zero-tolerance policy on drug taking and also introduced random drug testing procedures. Reporting for duty with drugs in the system would be regarded as gross misconduct and would be a dismissible offence. When reporting for work one day, the claimant's drugs test proved positive. At a disciplinary hearing, she agreed that she was aware of the company's policy and she knew that a positive drugs test would result in her dismissal. An employment tribunal held that her dismissal was fair, and the decision was upheld by EAT. A further argument on her behalf was that her rights under Article 8 of the Human Rights Act 1998 (right to privacy) had been violated, but this point was also dismissed on appeal. First, the Convention on Human Rights only applies to actions by a public authority, which the employers in this case were not. Second, interference with the right to privacy under Article 8 was not wrong if it was in accordance with the law and is necessary in a democratic society in the interests of public safety. The employer's decision to introduce a zero-tolerance policy was not disproportionate.

13.56   Although an employer is entitled to dismiss if he genuinely and conscientiously believes that there is a health or safety hazard, such dismissals should only be carried out with a full investigation of all the relevant circumstances. A procedural failure is likely to result in a wrong decision being reached and hence an unfair dismissal. In *Milk Marketing Board v Grimes*, the employee was the driver of a milk float. He was almost completely deaf and could only communicate with his employers by means of written questions and answers. Fearing that there may be an obvious safety hazard, the employee was sent for an examination by the company's occupational health advisor, who reported that the employee was unfit to drive while deaf and that a hearing aid would not materially improve matters. He was thus dismissed. Before the employment tribunal, the employee produced a consultant's report who concluded that the use of a hearing aid would restore his hearing to a tolerable level, which would be adequate for safe driving. Further, he was able to show that he had been driving for 34 years without an accident. Because the employers had not given the employee an opportunity to deal with the question of his incapacity, and because the procedure leading to the dismissal was flawed, the dismissal was held to be unfair.

13.57   It is not the function of the employment tribunal to determine whether or not the employer is in breach of his common law or statutory duties, as they would not always have sufficient evidence available on which to make such a finding. In *Lindsay v Dunlop Ltd*, workers in the tyre-curing department became concerned about the possible carcinogenic nature of fumes and dust. As a temporary measure, it was agreed to resume normal working with masks being provided. The claimant, however, refused to adopt this course, maintaining that his continued exposure to fumes would endanger his health. His subsequent dismissal was held to be fair. Whether or not the employers were in breach of their obligations under s.63 of the Factories Act was a matter which could only be determined by the courts and, in the circumstances, the employers had not acted unreasonably.

13.58 If the employee refuses to do the work unless he is provided with the necessary safety precautions, it is up to the employers to make a full and informed investigation into the reasons for the refusal, consideration of whether or not there is justification for the refusal and a communication of the results of the investigation to the employees before the decision to dismiss is taken. If employees make a complaint about the lack of safety precautions that is sensible, *bona fide* and not frivolous, the employer must take all necessary steps to reassure the employees, and should not just treat the refusal to work as being *per se* a ground for dismissing from employment (see *Atlas Products & Services v Jones*).

13.59 To establish that it is fair to dismiss an employee for refusing to follow the safety rules or to wear or use the precautions provided, it must be shown that:

(a) the employee knew of the requirement

(b) the employer was consistent in his enforcement policies, and

(c) the precautions were suitable for the employee and for the work he was doing. Again, a full investigation into the circumstances is called for.

13.60 In *Mayhew v Anderson (Stoke Newington) Ltd*, an insurance company recommended that the employee be asked to wear protective glasses, stating that the company's insurance cover would be withdrawn if she did not do so. The employers purchased a pair of safety goggles for 78p but she refused to wear them because they were not comfortable. She was warned that if she persisted with her refusal she would be dismissed, and ultimately the threat was carried out. Her dismissal was held to be unfair. She had never refused to wear reasonable eye protectors, only this particular type, which irritated her eyes and were uncomfortable. Custom-made eye protectors were available at a cost of £33, and the employment tribunal thought that these should have been provided for her, even at the risk of creating a precedent.

13.61 Finally, other reasons prompted by a genuine concern for health and safety can justify dismissal. In *Wilson v Stephen Carter Ltd*, the claimant was dismissed after refusing to go on a training course which involved staying away from home for a week and this was held to be fair.

13.62 If lesser disciplinary sanctions do not succeed, the employer may ultimately dismiss a recalcitrant employee, but some employers do not consider this to be a satisfactory solution, as they would rather have the workers working than have the problem of obtaining new staff and training them all over again. At this stage it may be possible to invoke the assistance of the HSE inspectorate, who could issue a prohibition notice on the employee, which would effectively prevent him from working in contravention of the matters contained in the notice. A failure to comply with this is punishable by a fine or even imprisonment, and this may yet prove to be an effective way of dealing with the problem. At the same time, an employee could be warned that he is acting in breach of his duty under ss.7 or 8 of HSWA, which again is a criminal offence.

13.63 It has long been held that, as a general rule, there is no onus on an employer to remove an employee from unsafe work, the onus being on the employee to decide for himself whether to continue to take on the work (*Withers v Perry Chain Co Ltd* and *Henderson v Wakefield Shirt Co Ltd*). Still less is there an obligation on the employer to dismiss the employee if that was the only alternative. Indeed, in *Sutherland v Hatton* it was stated that if the only reasonable and effective step would have been to dismiss or demote the employee, the employer would not be in breach of his duty in allowing a willing employee to continue in the job. It is for the employee to decide whether or not to carry on in the employment and take the risk of a breakdown in his health. But there may well be cases where, despite the employee's desire to remain at work notwithstanding the risk he ran, the employer would be under a duty in law to dismiss him for his own good so as to protect him from physical danger (see *Coxall v Goodyear GB Ltd*). In unfair dismissal proceedings, the employer would have to plead some other substantial reason, ie the common law duty. If disability discrimination proceedings were brought, the defence of reasonable adjustments would have to be raised.

13.64 It will be recalled (see Chapter 4) that employees and safety representatives have protection in certain cases from suffering a detriment or being dismissed in health and safety cases.

Suspension on medical grounds

13.65 Section 64 of the Employment Rights Act 1996 provides that where an employee is suspended from work on medical grounds in consequence of:

(a) any requirement imposed by or under the provision of any enactment, or

(b) any recommendation contained in a Code of Practice issued under HSWA

which, in either case, is a provision specified in s.64(3) of the Act, then that employee shall be entitled to be paid during the suspension for up to 26 weeks. The present provisions are as follows:

(a) Control of Lead at Work Regulations 2002 (regulation 10)

(b) Ionising Radiations Regulations 1999 (regulation 24)

(c) Control of Substances Hazardous to Health Regulations 2002 (regulation 11).

13.66 It will be noted that there must be a suspension on medical grounds. This means the potential effect on the health of the employee, not the actual effect. In other words, the provisions of s.64 are not relevant if an employee is actually off work sick. Nor is the suspension on medical grounds if he is unable to work because a prohibition notice has been imposed. Medical suspension payments can only be claimed when there is a suspension from work in order to comply with a requirement in any of the above provisions, but if he is incapable of working because of any physical or mental disablement, he has no legal entitlement (s.65(3)).

13.67 If he is dismissed because of one of the above requirements, he can bring a claim for unfair dismissal as long as he has been employed for a period of four weeks, instead of the more usual period of one year.

Whether such dismissal would be fair will obviously depend on the circumstances. For example, it may be shown that the employee's job became redundant, etc.

13.68 Medical suspension pay is not meant to be a top-up for, or a substitution for, statutory sick pay. It is designed to meet the situation where employees are fit for work, but are prevented from doing so because of a health hazard, in particular following a recommendation that they should cease work made by a doctor from the Employment Medical Advisory Service. In *Stallite Batteries Co Ltd v Appleton and Hopkinson*, an employee fell into a skip containing lead waste. In consequence, his blood-lead concentration level rose dramatically to 93μg/100 ml, which was in excess of the limits laid down under the Control of Lead at Work Regulations 1998. The level decreased over the following months, but his own doctor certified that he was still unfit for work. Eight months after the incident he was dismissed and he claimed compensation for unfair dismissal and medical suspension pay. The Employment Appeal Tribunal held that as he was not available for work because of sickness, he was not entitled to medical suspension pay by virtue of the provisions of s.65(3).

13.69 If the employer still needs someone to do the work, he may decide to take on a temporary replacement. He should inform the latter in writing that his employment will be terminated at the end of the period of suspension. If, therefore, he has to dismiss the temporary employee in order to permit the first employee to return to work, the dismissal will be for "some other substantial reason" but without prejudice to the rule that the employer will still have to show that he acted reasonably in treating that reason as a sufficient ground for dismissal (s.106 of the Employment Rights Act 1996). However, since the medical suspension period is unlikely to last long enough to enable the temporary employee to obtain a sufficient qualifying period of employment, this provision is unlikely to be relevant.

13.70 To qualify for medical suspension payments, the employee must have been employed for more than four weeks. Further, he will not be entitled to be paid if the employer has offered him suitable alternative work (whether or not the employee was contractually obliged to do that type of work) and he unreasonably refuses to perform that work. The employee must also comply with reasonable requirements imposed by the employer with a view to ensuring that his services are available. In other words, as the employer is paying the employee wages during the suspension, the employer may require the employee to do other work, or hold himself in readiness for work. The amount of pay to be made is calculated in accordance with ss.220–225 of the Act, which depends on the contractual arrangements for pay.

13.71   An employee may complain to an employment tribunal that the employer has failed to pay him in accordance with the above provisions. The complaint must be presented within three months of the failure, and if the complaint is upheld, the employment tribunal will order the employer to pay the amount due.

13.72   For the provisions relating to suspension on maternity grounds, see paragraph 11.6.

CHAPTER 14

The impact of international obligations

European Union

14.1   In 1951, by the Treaty of Paris, the European Coal and Steel Community (ECSC) was established when six countries (France, West Germany, Italy, Belgium, Holland and Luxembourg) agreed to pool their coal and steel resources and create a common commercial market for their products. Subsequently, the Mines Safety and Health Commission was created to work for the elimination of occupational risks to health and safety in coalmines.

14.2   In 1957 the European Atomic Energy Commission (EURATOM) was established in order to co-ordinate and develop the peaceful uses of nuclear energy, and strong emphasis was placed on the need to ensure the protection of the health of workers as well as the community at large from dangers arising from radiation hazards.

14.3   Also in 1957, by the Treaty of Rome, the European Economic Community (EEC) was established. This has the wider objective of establishing a common market for its economic activities by the elimination of customs duties, creating common customs tariffs, permitting the free movement of capital and workers, laying down common agricultural and transport policies, harmonising the laws of Member States to ensure that competition is not distorted and to facilitate the anticipated economic expansion.

14.4   In 1967 these three institutions were merged into the European Community (EC), with the fusion of their executive institutions, and the result is that although the three organisations have a separate existence, they are all now under the one umbrella. By the European Communities Act 1972, the UK signified its accession to the Treaty of Rome, including its laws, which by s.2(1) of the Act are to be given legal effect without further enactment. The European Community now consists of 27 Member States (see paragraph 1.46).

The working of the European Union

14.5   The nature of European law and the structure of EU institutions have already been considered in Chapter 1. As noted, initial proposals are made by the Commission, there is a consultative process with interested parties (including the European Parliament) and final approval is given by the Council of Ministers.

14.6   Article 137 of the Treaty of Rome calls for the improvement of the working environment to protect workers' health and safety. Following the adoption of the Framework Directive 89/391/EEC, (see paragraph 1.12), an EU strategy on health and safety at work was adopted in 2002. The Commission operates through 27 Directorates-General, each appointed by a Member State. Empl D4 is a branch of the Employment and Social Affairs Directorate, and is responsible for implementing the EU strategy on health, safety and hygiene at work. It is assisted by an advisory committee on health and safety at work, on which each government appoints a member and a representative of trade unions and of employers' associations.

14.7   The terms of reference of the Advisory Committee are as follows.
1. To assist the Commission in the preparation, implementation and evaluation of activities in the fields of safety and health at work.
2. Specifically, the committee will:
   (a) exchange views and experiences regarding existing or planned regulation
   (b) help to devise a common approach to problems and identify priorities
   (c) draw the Commission's attention to areas where there is a need for new knowledge, suitable training and research measures
   (d) define action programmes
   (e) inform national administrations, trade unions and employers' associations of EU measures in order to facilitate co-operation
   (f) give an opinion on plans for EU initiatives and an opinion on the annual programme and the rotating four-year programme of the European Agency for Safety and Health at Work.

14.8   The European Foundation for the Improvement of Living and Working Conditions was set up in 1975 to contribute to the planning and design of better living and working conditions in Europe. It provides information, advice and expertise of living and working conditions, industrial relations and managing change. The foundation produces an annual management plan.

Consultative bodies

14.9   Before EU legislation is passed, a tremendous amount of consultative work takes place. There are a number of External Advisory Groups, consisting of experts from all EU countries. Their role is to be consulted on the scientific and technical content of the thematic programmes put forward. Proposals need to be supported by relevant scientific or technical data or surveys, national experts are consulted, advisory committees are asked for opinions and initial proposals will then be drawn up. These are then transmitted to the European Parliament, to the Economic and Social Committee and to the Council of Ministers. At all stages, representations can be made by national groups representing employers, trade unions and other interested parties.

14.10   When proposals reach the UK, the government department (generally known as the "lead department") most closely concerned with the proposal will take charge of the consultative process. Usually, on health and safety matters, this will be the Department for Work and Pensions, but it may be some other department which has a major interest in the proposals (eg Department for Business, Innovation and Skills). Discussions will continue with the TUC, CBI, trade associations, etc and an explanatory memorandum will be prepared by the lead department and submitted to Parliament for consideration by the scrutiny committee of each House. These committees may call for written or oral evidence, make recommendations for change or request a Parliamentary debate. Once the Government has formulated its views, the matter can be transmitted back to the Council of Ministers for consideration by a working group. Here, the respective views are collated, the text may be revised, and the final proposals formulated and ultimately adopted. Not surprisingly, it can take many years before an initial proposal is finally transformed into a binding directive.

Procedure for making directives

14.11   In order to adopt a directive under Article 137 of the Treaty of Rome, the "co-operation procedure" must be followed. The Commission submits proposals to the Council of Ministers. The European Parliament and the Economic and Social Committee are then consulted and give their opinion. The Commission may then amend the proposals (but is not obliged to do so) and they are resubmitted to the Labour and Social Affairs Council of the Council of Ministers. A "common position" is then adopted, if necessary by a qualified majority vote. This is then reconsidered by the European Parliament, which may then:

(a) approve the common position

(b) propose further amendments

(c) reject them, in which case the proposals must be adopted by the Council of Ministers unanimously.

14.12   Once a directive relating to health and safety at work has been adopted, the HSE draws up the necessary legislative proposals in order to implement it. Again, it will engage in a series of consultations with interested parties, but since all concerned should have been involved in the earlier discussion, the subject matter will occasion little surprise, and the only problems that are likely to arise will stem from the detailed arrangements which may be necessary in order to ensure that the final legislative proposals (usually made by regulations) will meet the European standards. Indeed, the HSE takes pride in considering that it already anticipates European legislation as part of its own ongoing programme, and is thus in a favourable position to influence the European standards. Indeed, "the aim in negotiations is to influence the shape of EU proposals during their embryonic stages and where practicable to advance UK policy and practice as a model for adoption across the Community" (*Annual Report* 1989/1990, page 1).

EU directives

14.13   As already noted (see paragraph 1.46) the Treaty of Rome was amended in 1986 by the Single European Act, which aimed to create a Europe without economic barriers by the end of 1992. One of the amendments was the inclusion of a new Article 118A, which read as follows.

1. The Member States shall pay particular attention to encouraging improvements, especially in the working environment, as regards the health and safety of workers, and shall set as their objective the harmonisation of conditions in this area, while maintaining the improvements.

2. In order to help achieve the objective laid down in the first paragraph, the Council, acting by a qualified majority on a proposal from the

Commission and after consulting with the European Parliament and the Economic and Social Committee, shall adopt, by means of directives, minimum requirements for gradual implementation, having regard to the conditions and technical rules obtaining in each of the Member States. Such directives shall avoid imposing administrative, financial and legal constraints in a way which would hold back the creation and development of small and medium-sized undertakings.

3. The provisions adopted pursuant to this Article shall not prevent each Member State from introducing more stringent measures for the protection of working conditions compatible with the Treaty.

14.14 The result was the adoption by the Council of a directive on the introduction of measures to encourage improvements in the health and safety of workers at work, the so-called "Framework Directive" (89/391/EEC). Its provisions were given effect by the Management of Health and Safety at Work Regulations 1992 (now replaced by the 1999 regulations — see Chapter 4). In addition, a number of "daughter" directives were adopted, ie Workplace Directive (89/654/EEC), Use of Work Equipment Directive (89/655/EEC), Personal Protective Equipment Directive (89/656/EEC), Manual Handling of Loads Directive (90/269/EEC) and Display Screen Equipment Directive (90/270/EEC). The provisions of these directives have been implemented by the respective regulations outlined in Chapter 4 and Chapter 6.

14.15 Several further directives on health and safety at work have been adopted by the Council, which have either been implemented by respective regulations, or are under active consideration. These include the following.

Adopted directives

(1) Carcinogens Directive (2004/37/EC)

14.16 This directive addresses the control of carcinogens and mutagens in the workplace. This directive was implemented by the Control of Substances Hazardous to Health Regulations 1994 (now replaced by the Control of Substances Hazardous to Health Regulations 2002), together with a revision of the supporting Approved Codes of Practice. The directive applies to substances which may cause cancer, mutagens, substances that change genetic information and to certain further substances and processes specified in Annex 1 of the directive. Employers must make an assessment of the risk of exposure and, dependent on that assessment, replace the substance with a less harmful or less dangerous substance or use the substance in a closed system. If this is not possible, exposure must be reduced to as low a level as is possible. There must be suitable procedures for dealing with situations of abnormal exposure and emergency conditions, monitoring and health surveillance must be adopted, and the employer must provide adequate training, information and instructions concerning the risks to the health of workers, the precautions to be taken, and the results provided of any health surveillance. The European Commission is proposing an amendment to the Carcinogens and Mutagens Directive. This is expected to extend the scope of the directive to cover substances classified as Category I and Category II Toxic to Reproduction and to review the existing exposure limits and to add new exposure limits for carcinogenic, mutagenic and toxic to reproduction substances.

(2) Asbestos Worker Protection Directive (91/382/EEC)

14.17 This was implemented by the Control of Asbestos Regulations 1987 and the Asbestos (Prohibitions) Regulations 1992 (as amended) (see now the Control of Asbestos Regulations 2006). The directive amends and updates the EC directive on the protection of workers from risks relating to exposure to asbestos at work (83/477/EEC). Generally it increases the protection afforded to workers using asbestos and, in particular, it requires employers to draw up a plan of work before starting on the removal from buildings of asbestos-containing products. Specific essential features of the plan are to be communicated to the competent authority. This directive was amended in 2003 (2003/18/EC).

(3) Temporary Workers Directive (91/383/EEC)

14.18 This directive was implemented by the Management of Health and Safety at Work Regulations 1992 (now replaced by the Management of Health and Safety at Work Regulations 1999). The directive applies to all workers with fixed-duration contracts, and also to those who are seconded from one employer to another. Employers must give appropriate training and information to temporary workers, and they must receive medical surveillance on the same basis as permanent employees. The transferee's employer is to be responsible for the health and safety of workers who are seconded to him.

(4) Biological Agents Directive (2000/54/EC)

14.19 This Biological Agents Directive, which replaces the Biological Agents Directive (90/679/EEC) and its amending directives, deals with the protection of workers from the risks related to exposure to biological agents while at work, although it does draw a distinction between exposure which is incidental to work activity (eg health care, farming, etc) and where there is a conscious decision to work with such agents, eg a micro-biological laboratory. Employers must make a risk assessment, reduce the risks of exposure, provide training, instruction and information to workers, provide health surveillance, notify their activities to competent authorities and take special measures related to health care. The directive has also been implemented by an amendment to the COSHH Regulations, which were consolidated in 1994 and again in 1999 and 2002.

(5) Genetically Modified Organisms Directives

14.20 The Council has adopted two directives on genetically modified micro-organisms. Council Directive 2001/18/EC on the deliberate release into the environment of genetically modified organisms, which replaces Directive 1990/220/EC (as amended) has been implemented by the Genetically Modified Organisms (Deliberate Release) Regulations 2002 (as amended). Council Directive 90/219/EC (as amended) on the contained use of genetically modified micro-organisms has been implemented by the Genetically Modified Organisms (Contained Use) Regulations 2000 (as amended).

(6) Construction Sites Directive (92/57/EEC)

14.21 This directive applies to building and civil engineering works and any site at which the construction, equipping, alteration, renovation, repair, upkeep, maintenance and demolition of all types of buildings or structures is taking place. A project manager has to be appointed to ensure that health and safety is considered from the concept of the project to its completion. Work plans will be required, with particular reference to specific hazards. There are duties on designers and developers to ensure that the work is done in a safe manner, with additional reference to the safety of the end users. This directive has been implemented by the Construction (Design and Management) Regulations 2007.

(7) Safety Signs Directive (92/58/EEC)

14.22   This directive replaces Directive 77/576/EEC, which was given effect to in the UK by the Safety Signs Regulations 1980. The new directive requires employers to use a safety sign whenever there is a risk which cannot be adequately controlled by other means, taking into account the risk assessments made. In addition, the term "safety sign" includes other means of communication, such as hand signals, coding of pipework, marking of traffic routes, acoustic signals (eg fire alarms) and luminous signs. The number of conventional signs has been increased (with particular reference to identifying fire fighting equipment). The directive has been implemented in the UK by the Health and Safety (Safety Signs and Signals) Regulations 1996.

(8) Pregnant Women Directive (92/85/EEC)

14.23   This directive is designed to protect the health and safety of women workers who are pregnant or who have recently given birth or who are breast-feeding. An assessment will have to be made of the chemical, physical and biological agents and industrial processes which are considered to be hazardous for such workers. Reference will have to be made to movement and posture, mental and physical fatigue, and other types of stress connected with the work. An assessment will also have to be made of any risks to health and safety which could arise from an appended list of agents, processes or working conditions, and pregnant women are to be informed of the result of the assessment. If it is revealed that there is a risk to health or safety, or that there would be an effect on pregnancy or breast-feeding, the employer will be required to avoid the risk either by making a temporary adjustment to the working conditions or moving the worker to another job. If such methods are not possible, the worker is to be given leave for the period necessary to ensure her health and safety. Pregnant women, or those who have recently given birth, must not be obliged to do night work if they produce a medical certificate stating that this would be detrimental to their health or safety.

14.24   The directive contains further provisions concerning the employment rights of pregnant women, including maternity pay, maternity leave of absence, and protection from dismissal because of pregnancy. The directive was implemented in the UK by the Management of Health and Safety at Work (Amendment) Regulations 1994, now revoked and incorporated into the Management of Health and Safety at Work Regulations 1999. The employment rights aspects of the directive have been met by various amendments to the law, now found in the Employment Rights Act, ss.66–85 (see paragraph 11.6).

(9) Working Time Directive (93/104/EEC)

14.25 In *UK v Council of European Union*, the European Court dismissed a challenge that the Working Time Directive (93/104/EEC) was not valid, and held that it was properly made under Article 118A of the Treaty of Rome (which enables directives dealing with health and safety matters to be passed by the majority voting procedure). Strictly speaking, the directive was due to have been implemented by 23 November 1996, which exposed those employers who are "emanations of the State" (see *Foster v British Gas*) to "Francovitch" type claims (which must be brought in the ordinary courts, see *Gibson v East Riding of Yorkshire*). However, the European Court did hold that the requirement in the directive that a weekly rest period shall in principle include Sunday was not valid, there being no evidence to suggest that Sunday was more closely connected with health and safety that any other day of the week.

14.26 The directive, which provided for maximum working hours, rest breaks, rest periods, annual holidays and limits on night work, etc was implemented by the Working Time Regulations 1998 (as amended) (see paragraph 4.75).

14.27 Directive 2000/34/EC extends the provisions of the Working Time Directive to those in the following previously excluded sectors: road, rail, sea, inland waterway and lake transport, sea fishing, offshore oil and gas, and doctors in training. The Working Time Regulations have been amended in order to give effect to this directive.

14.28 When the directive was adopted it contained derogations, including an option of not applying the maximum weekly working week of 48 hours. When the directive was implemented as the Working Time Regulations 1998, the UK made use of this opt-out. A proposal for an amendment to the Working Time Directive, including phasing-out the individual's right to opt-out of the 48-hour working week over three years. However, the European Parliament and Member States were unable to resolve their differences over whether to retain the opt-out or not and the Directive will remain as it is.

(10) Young Workers Directive (94/33/EEC)

14.29   The Protection of Young People at Work Directive (94/33/EEC) has been adopted, and was required to be implemented by Member States by 1996. The directive requires that the minimum working age for children is 15, although children under that age may be permitted in certain circumstances to undertake work experience/training, or certain light work for a limited number of hours each week. The directive is not likely to pose many difficulties so far as UK law is concerned, as there is already a well-defined scheme regulating the employment of children and young persons (see paragraphs 11.187–11.196).

14.30   The Health and Safety (Young Persons) Regulations 1997, which amended the Management of Health and Safety at Work Regulations 1992, were passed to implement this directive. These regulations have now been revoked by and incorporated into the Management of Health and Safety at Work Regulations 1999 (see paragraph 4.69). Provisions of the directive on the hours of work for young workers have been implemented by the Working Time Regulations (see paragraph 4.75).

(11) Use of Work Equipment Directive (95/63/EC)

14.31   This directive amends the original directive on the provision and use of work equipment (89/655/EEC). It deals principally with the hardware requirements for mobile and lifting equipment. The Provision and Use of Work Equipment Regulations 1998 and the Lifting Operations and Lifting Equipment Regulations 1998 implement this directive. The directive was further amended in 2001 (2001/45/EC).

(12) Seveso II Directive (96/82/EC)

14.32   This directive repeals the original Seveso Directive (82/501/EC and 87/716/EC) following a fundamental review of the problems revealed in dealing with major accident hazards. The object is to prevent such incidents by providing a stringent control regime, and to limit the consequences of any such incident for people and the environment. The directive removes the distinction between "process" and "storage", improves on the generic categories of substances to include, for example, substances that are dangerous to the environment, and extends cover to land planning. Operators are required to draw up a major accident prevention policy, and the competent authority is required to examine safety reports and set up an inspection system. Emergency plans must be implemented and tested. The directive has been implemented by the Control of Major Accident Hazards Regulations 1999 (COMAH).

14.33 The new EU Regulation on the Classification, Labelling and Packaging of Substances and Mixtures (CLP) which came into force on 20 January 2009 (see paragraph 7.93) will be phased in over a transitional period, and will break the legislative link between Seveso and the current classification system. A new method of defining the scope of the Directive will be needed and will necessitate an amendment to the Directive.

(13) Basic Safety Standards Directive (96/29/Euratom)

14.34 This directive lays down the basic safety standards for the protection of the health of workers and the general public against the dangers arising from the use of ionising radiation. Other directives deal with dangers to outside workers (90/641/Euratom) and the protection for individuals liable to medical exposure as a result of work with ionising radiations (97/43/Euratom). The Ionising Radiations Regulations 1999 implement these directives.

14.35 Provisions for emergency preparedness in respect of premises, transport by rail, and transport through a public place have been implemented through the Radiation (Emergency Preparedness and Public Information) Regulations 2001.

14.36 The European Commission intends to bring forward a formal proposal for a new Basic Safety Standard Directive that will be based on a consolidation of five existing directives and will take into account a scientific review of the directives.

(14) Physical Agents Directives

14.37 The Council has adopted four directives:
  (a) the Physical Agents (Vibration) Directive (2002/44/EC)
  (b) the Physical Agents (Noise) Directive (2003/10/EC)
  (c) the Physical Agents (Electromagnetic Field) Directive (2004/10/EC)
  (d) the Physical Agents (Artifical Optical Radiation) Directive 2006/25/EC.

14.38   The Vibration Directive, which lays down minimum standards for the health and safety of workers exposed to hand-arm and whole body vibration, has been implemented by the Control of Vibration at Work Regulations 2005. There is a provision in the directive for Member States to delay the coming into force of the exposure limit values until 6 July 2010 for equipment in use before 2007.

14.39   The Physical Agents (Noise) Directive repeals the existing 1986 Noise Directive (86/188/EEC) and has been implemented by the Control of Noise at Work Regulations 2005, which repeal the Noise at Work Regulations 1989.

14.40   A third directive is the Physical Agents (Electromagnetic Fields) Directive (2004/10/EC) which lays down the minimum health and safety requirements for workers exposed to electromagnetic fields. The implementation of this directive has been postponed until 2012.

14.41   The fourth directive, the Physical Agents (Artifical Optical Radiation) Directive has to be implemented in the UK by 27 April 2010.

Proposed directives

14.42   A number of directives with health and safety implications are currently being discussed at the various stages of procedure (see Appendix C).

Product safety directives

14.43   In addition to directives under Article 137, the EU is attempting to harmonise the laws of Member States on product safety and supporting standards. These directives are made under Article 95 of the Treaty — sometimes referred to as "New Approach" directives. These will depend on the availability of harmonised European standards because different laws in the various Member States could cause technical barriers to trade.

14.44   Directive 83/189/EEC requires Member States to inform the Commission of any new technical regulation, which is then circulated to other Member States for comment. If it is thought that the proposed regulation would create a barrier to the free movement of goods, the state may not implement it for a period, and the Commission may then decide to propose or adopt a directive on the subject of notification.

14.45 "New Approach" directives set out essential requirements (eg on safety) which must be complied with before products may be sold anywhere in the Community. They also state how manufacturers are to meet those essential requirements. Once these are complied with, the product may carry the "CE" marking, which means that it can be sold anywhere in the EU.

14.46 There are two European bodies that prepare European Standards. One is the European Committee for Standardisation (CEN), the other is the European Committee for Electrotechnical Standardisation (CENELEC). These bodies work with the national standards organisation in the respective states. In the UK, this body is the British Standards Institution (see paragraph 2.75). The European Committees achieve an acceptable consensus, and the standard is then adopted by the weighted majority system (see paragraph 1.49).

14.47 The following "New Approach" directives have a particular interest to those involved in health and safety matters.
1. *Personal Protective Equipment Directive (89/686/EEC) (PPE)*. This directive covers any device or appliance designed to be worn or used or held by an individual for protection against one or more safety or health hazards. It also covers combined PPE and interchangeable components which are essential to its satisfactory functioning.

   PPE must preserve the health and ensure the safety of users, and must not harm other people, domestic animals or goods when properly maintained and used for its intended purpose. This directive was implemented by the Personal Protective Equipment (EC Directive) Regulations 1992, now revoked and replaced by the Personal Protective Equipment Regulations 2002 (see paragraph 6.99).
2. *Machinery Safety Directive (89/392/EEC and 91/368/EEC, now consolidated by 98/37/EC)*. Machinery must satisfy the essential health and safety requirements set out in the directive, including the materials used in the construction, lighting, design, controls, stability, hazards relating to moving parts, fire, noise, vibration, radiation, emission of dust and gases, maintenance, warnings and instruction handbooks. This directive has been implemented by the Supply of Machinery (Safety) Regulations 1992. On 29 June 2006 a new directive (2006/42/EC) came into force which must be implemented in the EU by 29 December 2009 when the previous directive (98/37/EC) will be

revoked and the new Directive will be implemented by the Supply of Machinery (Safety) Regulations 2008.

14.48 Other "New Approach" directives deal with such topics as mobile machinery and lifting equipment, non-automatic weighing instruments, gas appliances, medical devices, and so on (see Appendix C).

International Labour Organization

14.49 The International Labour Organization (ILO) was formed in 1919. It consists of representatives of national governments, employers' and workers' organisations and is now an agency of the United Nations. It has worked consistently to improve international labour standards relating to such matters as conditions of work, training, freedom of association, social security, industrial relations, and many other similar topics. It holds international conferences, provides technical advice and assistance to individual countries, and generally acts as an international forum for the promotion and improvement of standards throughout the world.

14.50 A major part of the work of the ILO consists of adopting conventions and recommendations. These are submitted to national governments for consideration, for they are not automatically binding. A convention may be ratified by a nation state, which amounts to a pledge to implement its provisions. However, any state is free to denounce a convention it has adopted, and is then free to ignore its provisions. A recommendation does not require ratification, but merely serves as a guide if national action is to be taken on a particular topic.

14.51 Since its inception, the ILO has passed over 150 conventions, many relating to occupational health and safety matters. It has also passed over 160 recommendations covering similar topics, and has published a large number of reports and studies.

14.52 The ILO also produces research papers, suggests international classification standards, and issues Codes of Practice giving guidance on practical measures which may be taken to safeguard workers' health against occupational hazards.

APPENDIX A
Useful Addresses

HEALTH AND SAFETY EXECUTIVE (HSE)

Information Services

HSE Information Services

General enquiries and information are available from a national telephone public service called HSE Infoline (tel: 0845 345 0055). Open 8.00am to 6.00pm, Monday to Friday. Queries can also be sent by fax: 0845 408 9566 or e-mail: *hseinformationservices@natbrit.com*. There is also an HSE website at *www.hse.gov.uk*.

Written enquiries should be sent to:

HSE Infoline
Caerphilly Business Park
Caerphilly CF83 3GG

HSE Knowledge Centre

HSE Information Centres are for personal callers who want to consult the information held there. Opening hours are 8am to 5.30pm, Monday to Friday.

Knowledge Centre
Health and Safety Executive
(1G) Redgrave Court
Merton Road
Bootle
Merseyside L20 7HS

HSE Publications

All HSE publications can be obtained from:

HSE Books
PO Box 1999
Sudbury
Suffolk CO10 2WA
Tel: 01787 881165.
Fax: 01787 313995
E-mail: hsebooks@prolog.uk.com
Website: *www.hsebooks.co.uk*

Many of the HSE's free leaflets are
available online at: *www.hse.gov.uk.*

Offices of the Health and Safety Executive

Contact details for the HSE's head and regional offices are provided
below.

Headquarters

London

Rose Court
2 Southwark Bridge
London SE1 9HS

Liverpool

Redgrave Court
Merton Road
Bootle
Merseyside L20 7HS

Regional offices

Inspectors are based in offices organised into divisions. The asterisk (*)
shows an office where inspectors dealing with the manufacture,
processing and storage of chemicals and onshore major hazards
including gas transmission and distribution, pipelines and the road
transport of dangerous substances may be contacted.

Wales and South West Division

Covers: Wales, Cornwall, Devon, Somerset, North Somerset, Bath and North East Somerset, Gloucestershire, South Gloucestershire, Bristol, Dorset, Swindon and Wiltshire.

Government Buildings*
Phase 1
Ty Glas
Llanishen
Cardiff CF14 5SH
Tel: 029 2026 3000
Fax: 029 2026 3120

4th Floor, The Pithay
All Saints Street
Bristol BS1 2ND
Tel: 01179 886000
Fax: 01179 262998

Ballard House
West Hoe Road
Plymouth PL1 3BL
Tel: 01752 246300
Fax: 01752 226024

Unit 7 & 8 Edison Court
Ellice Way
Wrexham Technology Park
Wrexham
Clwyd LL13 7YT
Tel: 01978 316000
Fax: 01978 355669

3rd Floor*
Darkgate Buildings
3 Red Street
Carmarthen
Dyfed SA31 1QL
Tel: 01267 244230
Fax: 01267 223267

14 New Fields*
Stinsford Road
Nuffield Industrial Estate
Poole
Dorset BH17 0NF
Tel: 01202 634400
Fax: 01202 667224

East and South East Division

Covers: Bedfordshire, Berkshire, Buckinghamshire, Cambridgeshire, Essex, Hampshire, Hertfordshire, Isle of Wight, Norfolk, Suffolk, Oxfordshire, Kent, East and West Sussex, and Surrey

AW House
6–8 Stuart Street
Luton LU1 2SJ
Tel: 01582 444200
Fax: 01582 444320

Priestley House
Priestley Road
Basingstoke
Hampshire RG24 9NN
Fax: 01256 404100

Wren House*
Hedgerows Business Park
Colchester Road
Springfield
Chelmsford CM2 5PF
Tel: 01245 706200
Fax: 01245 706222

Phoenix House
23–25 Cantelupe Road
East Grinstead RH19 3BE
Tel: 01342 334200
Fax: 01342 334222

Lakeside 500
Old Chapel Way
Norwich
Norfolk NR7 0WQ
Tel: 01603 828000
Fax: 01603 828055

International House
Dover Place
Ashford
Kent TN23 1HU
Tel: 01233 653900
Fax: 01233 634827

London Division

Covers: all London Boroughs

Rose Court
2 Southwark Bridge
London SE1 9HS
Tel: 020 7556 2100
Fax: 020 7556 2102

Midlands Division

Covers: West Midlands, Leicestershire, Northamptonshire, Warwickshire, Derbyshire, Lincolnshire, Nottinghamshire, Hereford and
Worcester

1 Hagley Road*
Birmingham B16 8HS
Tel: 0121 607 6200
Fax: 0121 607 6349

900 Pavilion Drive
Northampton Business Park
Northampton NN4 7RG
Fax: 01604 738333

City Gate West
Level 6 (First Floor)
Toll House Hill
Nottingham NG1 5AT
Tel: 01159 712800
Fax: 01159 712802

Lyme Vale Court
Lyme Drive
Parklands Business Park
Newcastle Road
Trent Vale
Stoke on Trent ST4 6NW
Tel: 01782 602300
Fax: 01782 602400

Haswell House
St Nicholas Street
Worcester WR1 1UW
Tel: 01905 743600
Fax: 01905 723045

Yorkshire and North East Division

Covers: Cleveland, Durham, North Yorkshire, Northumberland, West
Yorkshire, Tyne and Wear, Humberside and South Yorkshire

Marshalls Mill*
Marshall Street
Leeds LS11 9YJ
Tel: 0113 283 4200
Fax: 0113 283 4382

Edgar Allen House*
241 Glossop Road
Sheffield S10 2GW
Tel: 0114 291 2300
Fax: 0114 291 2379

Arden House*
Regent Centre
Regent Farm Road
Gosforth
Newcastle Upon Tyne NE3 3JN
Tel: 0191 202 6200
Fax: 0191 202 6300

North West Division

Covers: Cheshire, Cumbria, Greater Manchester, Lancashire and
Merseyside

Grove House*
Skerton Road
Manchester M16 0RB
Tel: 0161 952 8200
Fax: 0161 952 8222

Marshall House*
Ringway
Preston PR1 2HS
Tel: 0161 952 8200
Fax: 01772 836 222

2 Victoria Place
Carlisle CA1 1ER
Tel: 01228 634100
Fax: 01228 548482

Scotland

Covers: all the Scottish unitary authorities and island councils

Belford House*
59 Belford Road
Edinburgh EH4 3UE
Tel: 0131 247 2000
Fax: 0131 247 2121

1st Floor
Mercantile Chambers
53 Bothwell Street
Glasgow G2 6TS
Tel: 0141 275 3000
Fax: 0141 275 3100

Lord Cullen House
Fraser Place
Aberdeen AB25 3UB
Tel: 01224 252500
Fax: 01224 252525

Offshore Safety Division
Lord Cullen House
Fraser Place
Aberdeen AB25 3UB
Tel: 01224 252500
Fax: 01224 252525

Longman House
28 Longman Road
Longman Industrial Estate
Inverness IV1 1SF
Tel: 01463 723260
Fax: 01463 713459

HSE contact points for specific activities

Construction Division

Covers London Division, East and South East, Midlands, Wales and South West, Yorkshire & North East Division, North West Division and Scotland

Rose Court
2 Southwark Bridge
London SE1 9HS
Tel: 020 7556 2100
Fax: 020 7556 2109

Nuclear industry

Nuclear Safety Directorate
Redgrave Court
Merton Road
Bootle
Merseyside L20 7HS
Tel: 0151 951 3484

Chemical safety directorate (CRD)

PSD
Mallard House
King's Pool
3 Peasholme Green
York YO1 7PX
Tel: 01904 455775
Fax: 01904 455733

Hazardous Installations Directorate

Manufacture, processing and storage of chemicals and other onshore major hazards including gas transmission and distribution, pipelines, the road transport of dangerous goods, major hazards, the mining industry, offshore oil and gas industry and the manufacture, transport, handling and security of explosives

Hazardous Installations Director-
ate Secretariat
Redgrave Court
Merton Road
Bootle
Merseyside L20 7HS

Agriculture, construction and factories

See HSE Regional Offices above.

Commercial, office and retail

Contact your local authority.

Health and Safety Laboratory

Harpur Hill
Buxton
Derbyshire SK17 9JN
Tel: 01298 218000

APPENDIX B

Publications

Approved Codes of Practice and legislative guidance

The following have been approved or authorised by the Health and Safety Commission. Copies are available from HSE Books (tel: 01787 881165), along with a free catalogue of all HSE priced and free guidance documents. British Standards may be ordered from the British Standards Institution (tel: 020 8996 9000).

Accidents and emergencies

L73 *A Guide to the Reporting of Injuries, Diseases and Dangerous Occurrences Regulations 1995*
L74 *First Aid at Work*

Agriculture

L116 *Preventing Accidents to Children in Agriculture*
HSG89 *Safeguarding Agricultural Machinery (Revised)*

Asbestos

L127 *The Management of Asbestos in Non-domestic Premises*
L143 *Work with Materials Containing Asbestos*
HSG189/2 *Working with Asbestos Cement*
HSG210 *Asbestos Essentials: Task Manual; Task Guidance Sheets for the Building, Maintenance and Allied Trades*
HSG213 *Introduction to Asbestos Essentials: Guidance on Working with Asbestos in Building, Maintenance and Allied Trades*
HSG227 *A Comprehensive Guide to Managing Asbestos in Premises*
HSG247 *Asbestos: The Licensed Contractors' Guide*

Confined spaces

L101 *Safe Work in Confined Spaces*

Construction

L96 *A Guide to the Work in Compressed Air Regulations 1996*
L102 *Construction (Head Protection) Regulations 1989*
L144 *Managing Health and Safety in Construction: Construction (Design and Management) Regulations 2007: Approved Code of Practice*
HSG33 *Health and Safety in Roofwork (Revised)*
HSG47 *Avoiding Danger from Underground Services (Revised)*
HSG141 *Electrical Safety on Construction Sites*
HSG144 *Safe Use of Vehicles on Construction Sites*
HSG149 *Safe Handling in Construction*
HSG150 *Health and Safety in Construction (Revised)*
HSG151 *Protecting the Public — Your Next Move*
HSG168 *Fire Safety in Construction Work*
HSG185 *Health and Safety in Excavations: Be Safe and Shore*

Dangerous substances

L5 *Control of Substances Hazardous to Health 2002 (as amended): Approved Code of Practice and Guidance (Revised)*
L8 *Legionnaires' Disease*
L60 *Control of Substances Hazardous to Health in the Production of Pottery*
L130 *The Compilation of Safety Data Sheets: Approved Code of Practice (Revised)*
L131 *Approved Classification and Labelling Guide (Fifth Edition) (Revised) for Substances and Preparations Dangerous for Supply*
L132 *Control of Lead at Work: Approved Code of Practice and Guidance*
L142 *Approved Supply List (Eighth Edition). Information Approved for the Classification and Labelling of Substances and Preparations Dangerous for Supply*
HSG97 *A Step-by-Step Guide to COSHH Assessment (Revised)*
HSG193 *COSHH Essentials: Easy Steps to Control Chemicals (Revised)*
HSG228 *CHIP for Everyone*
HSG251 *Health and Safety Guidance for Employers and Technicians Carrying Out Fumigation Operations*
HSG258 *Controlling Airborne Contaminants at Work: A guide to Local Exhaust Ventilation*

Display screen equipment

L26 *Display Screen Equipment Work (Revised)*
HSG90 *The Law on VDUs: An Easy Guide to the Regulations (Revised)*

Diving

L103 *Commercial Diving Projects Offshore*
L104 *Commercial Diving Projects Inland/Inshore*
L106 *Media Diving Projects*
L107 *Scientific and Archaeological Diving Projects*

Docks

COP 25 *Safety in Docks (Docks Regulations 1988)*
HSR27 *A Guide to the Dangerous Substances in Harbour Areas Regulations 1987*
HSR28 *A Guide to the Loading and Unloading of Fishing Vessels Regulations 1988*
HSG177 *Managing Health and Safety in Dockwork*
HSG186 *The Bulk Transfer of Dangerous Liquids and Gases between Ship and Shore*

Electricity and electrical systems

HSG85 *Electricity at Work: Safe Working Practices (Revised)*
HSG87 *Safety in the Remote Diagnosis of Manufacturing Plant and Equipment*
HSG107 *Maintaining Portable and Transportable Electrical Equipment*
HSG118 *Electrical Safety in Arc Welding*
HSG180 *Application of Electro-sensitive Protective Equipment Using Light Curtains and Light Beam Devices to Machinery*
HSG230 *Keeping Electrical Switchgear Safe*
HSR25 *Memorandum of Guidance on the Electricity at Work Regulations 1989*

Explosives

L10 *A Guide to the Control of Explosive Regulations 1991*
L66 *Guide to the Placing on the Market and Supervision of Transfers of Explosives Regulations (POMSTER) 1993*
L139 *Manufacture and Storage of Explosives: Manufacture and Storage of Explosives Regulations 2005. Approved Code of Practice and Guidance*

First aid

L74 *First Aid at Work*
L123 *Health Care and First Aid on Offshore Installations and Pipeline Works*

Flammable materials

L134 *Design of Plant, Equipment and Workplaces. Dangerous Substances and Explosive Atmospheres Regulations 2002. Approved Code of Practice and Guidance*
L135 *Storage of Dangerous Substances. Dangerous Substances and Explosive Atmospheres Regulations 2002. Approved Code of Practice and Guidance*
L136 *Control and Mitigation Measures. Dangerous Substances and Explosive Atmospheres Regulations 2002. Approved Code of Practice and Guidance*
L137 *Safe Maintenance, Repair and Cleaning Procedures. Dangerous Substances and Explosive Atmospheres Regulations 2002. Approved Code of Practice and Guidance*
L138 *Dangerous Substances and Explosive Atmospheres Regulations 2002. Approved Code of Practice and Guidance*
HSG51 *The Storage of Flammable Liquids in Containers (Revised)*
HSG103 *Safe Handling of Combustible Dusts (Revised)*
HSG139 *The Safe Use of Compressed Gases in Welding, Flame Cutting and Allied Processes*
HSG140 *The Safe Use and Handling of Flammable Liquids*
HSG158 *Flame Arresters*
HSG168 *Fire Safety in Construction Work*
HSG176 *The Storage of Flammable Liquids in Tanks*
HSG178 *The Spraying of Flammable Liquids*

Food/catering

HSG156 *Slips and Trips: Guidance for the Food Processing Industry*

Gas and oil-fired equipment

COP20 *Standards of Training in Safe Gas Installation*
L56 *Safety in the Installation and Use of Gas Systems and Appliances (Revised). The Gas Safety (Installation and Use) Regulations 1998*
L81 *The Design, Construction and Installation of Gas Service Pipes*

Healthcare

HSG137 *Health Risk Management: A Practical Guide for Managers in Small and Medium-sized Enterprises*
HSG174 *Anthrax: Safe Working and the Prevention of Infection*

Health services

The Management of Occupational Health Services for Healthcare Staff
Violence and Aggression to Staff in the Health Services: Guidance on Assessment and Management
Manual Handling in the Health Services

Ionising radiation

L121 *Work with Ionising Radiations: Approved Code of Practice and Guidance*
HSG94 *Safety in the Use of Gamma and Electron Irradiation Facilities (Revised)*

Lead

L132 *Control of Lead at Work: Approved Code of Practice and Guidance*

Leisure

A Report into Safety at Outdoor Activity Centres
HSG112 *Health and Safety at Motor Sport Events*
HSG154 *Managing Crowds Safely*
HSG179 *Managing Health and Safety in Swimming Pools*
HSG195 *The Event Safety Guide: A Guide to Health, Safety and Welfare at Music and Similar Events*

Lifts

L113 *Safe Use of Lifting Equipment: Approved Code of Practice and Guidance Notes. Lifting Operations and Lifting Equipment Regulations 1998*

Lift trucks

L117 *Rider Operated Lift Trucks: Operator Training*
HSG6 *Safety in Working with Lift Trucks (Revised)*
HSG136 *Workplace Transport Safety: Guidance for Employers*

Management of occupational health

L21 *The Management of Health and Safety at Work (Revised)*
L146 *Consulting Workers on Health and Safety: Approved Code of Practice*
HSG65 *Successful Health and Safety Management (Revised)*
HSG101 *The Costs to Britain of Workplace Accidents*
HSG137 *Health Risk Management: A Practical Guide for Managers in Small and Medium-sized Enterprises*

Manual handling

L23 *Manual Handling (Revised)*
HSG115 *Manual Handling: Solutions You Can Handle*
Manual Handling in the Health Service

Mines

COP28 *Safety of Exit from Mines Underground Workings*
L42 *Shafts and Winding in Mines*
L43 *First Aid at Mines*
L44 *The Management and Administration of Safety and Health at Mines*
L45 *Explosives at Coal and Other Safety-lamp Mines*
L46 *The Prevention of Inrushes in Mines*
L47 *The Coal Mines (Owners' Operating Rules) Regulations 1993*
L71 *Escape and Rescue from Mines Regulations 1995*
L128 *The Use of Electricity in Mines: Electricity at Work Regulations 1989; Approved Code of Practice*

New and expectant mothers

HSG122 *New and Expectant Mothers at Work: A Guide for Employers (Revised)*

Noise

L108 *Controlling Noise at Work: The Control of Noise at Work Regulations 2005: Guidance*
HSG232 *Sound Solutions for the Food and Drink Industries: Reducing Noise in Food and Drink Manufacturing*

Offshore

L65 *Prevention of Fire and Explosion, and Emergency Response on Offshore Installations*
HSG125 *A Brief Guide on COSHH for the Offshore Oil and Gas Industry*
HSG142 *Dealing with Offshore Emergencies*

Personal protective equipment

L25 *Personal Protective Equipment at Work*
HSG262 *Managing Skin Exposure at Work*
HSG53 *Respiratory Protective Equipment: A Practical Guide for Users*

Petroleum spirit

COP6 *Plastic Containers with Nominal Capacities up to 5 Litres for Petroleum Spirit: Requirements for Testing and Marking or Labelling*

Pressure systems

L122 *Safety of Pressure Systems: Pressure Systems Safety Regulations 2000: Approved Code of Practice*

Quarries

L118 *Health and Safety in Quarries: Quarries Regulations 1999: Approved Code of Practice*

Safety representatives and committees

L146 *Consulting Workers on Health and Safety: Approved Code of Practice*

Safety signs

L64 *Safety Signs and Signals*

Stress

HSG218 *Managing the Cause of Work-related Stress*

Vibration

L140 *Hand-arm Vibration*
L141 *Whole-body Vibration*
HSG170 *Vibration Solutions: Practical Ways to Reduce the Risk of Hand-arm Vibration Injury*

Violence

HSG133 *Preventing Violence to Retail Staff*
Violence and Aggression to Staff in the Health Services: Guidance on Assessment and Management (Revised)

Work equipment

L22 *Work Equipment (Revised)*
L112 *Safe Use of Power Presses*
L113 *Safe Use of Lifting Equipment*
L114 *Safe Use of Woodworking Machinery*

Workplace

L8 *The Prevention or Control of Legionellosis (Including Legionnaires Disease): Approved Code of Practice*
L24 *Workplace Health, Safety and Welfare*
HSG *Controlling Airborne Contaminants at Work*
HSG38 *Lighting at Work (Revised)*
HSG57 *Seating at Work*

HSG60 *Upper Limb Disorders in the Workplace*
HSG132 *How to Deal with Sick Building Syndrome*
HSG155 *Slips and Trips: Guidance for Employers on Identifying Hazards and Controlling Risks*
HSG194 *Thermal Comfort in the Workplace*
HSG202 *General Ventilation in the Workplace*
HSG256 *Managing Shift Work*

Young persons

HSG165 *Young People at Work: A Guide for Employers*

APPENDIX C

List of EU directives relating to health and safety

Available in the Official Journal Legislation series (OJ L) from The Stationery Office (tel: 0870 600 5522).

* These directives have been implemented by UK regulations.

Framework directive

89/391/EC* Directive concerning the minimum safety and health requirements for the workplace (Workplace Directives) OJ L183, 29.6.89

Daughter directives

Enacted as part of the "six pack".

89/654/EC* Directive concerning the minimum safety and health requirements for the workplace (Workplace Directive) OJ L393, 30.12.89
89/655/EC* Directive concerning the minimum safety and health requirements for the use of work equipment by workers at work (Use of Work Equipment Directive) OJ L335, 30.12.95 (this has been amended by Directives 95/63/EC and 2001/45/EC)
89/656/EC* Directive on the minimum safety and health requirements for the use by workers of personal protective equipment at the workplace (Personal Protective Equipment Directive) OJ L399, 30.12.89
90/269/EC* Directive on the minimum safety and health requirements for the manual handling of loads where there is a risk particularly of back injury to workers (Manual Handling of Loads Directive) OJ L156, 21.6.90
90/270/EC* Directive on the minimum safety and health requirements for work with display screen equipment (Display Screen Equipment Directive) OJ L156, 21.6.90

Hazardous materials

67/548/EEC* Directive on the approximation of laws, regulations and administration provisions relating to the classification, packaging and labelling of dangerous substances (Dangerous Substances Directive) OJ L196, 16.8.67 (this directive has been amended by 31 separate Adaptations to Technical Change).

The Directive is being replaced by Regulation (EC) No 1272/2008 on classification, labelling and packaging of substances and mixtures, and amending Directive 67/548/EEC and Regulation (EC) No 1907/2006 which is being phased in.

76/769/EEC* Directive on the approximation of laws, regulations and administration provisions of the Member States relating to restrictions on the marketing and use of certain dangerous substances and preparations OJ L262, 27.9.76 (this directive has so far been amended by 21 Adaptations to Technical Change)

83/477/EEC* Directive on the protection of workers from the risks related to exposure to asbestos (Asbestos Directive) OJ L263, 24.9.83 (this directive has been amended by Directive 91/382/EEC* OJ L203, 29.7.91 and in 2003 by Directive 2003/18/EC OJ L97/48, 15.4.2003)

90/219/EEC* Directive on the contained use of genetically modified micro-organisms OJ L117, 10.1.90 (this directive has been amended by Directive 98/81/EC* OJ L330, 5.12.98)

90/679/EEC* Directive on the protection of workers from the risks related to exposure to biological agents at work (Biological Agents Directive) OJ L374, 31.12.90 (this directive has been amended by Directive 2000/54/EC)

96/82/EC* Directive on the control of major-accident hazards involving dangerous substances OJ L10, 14.1.97, amended by Directive 2003/105/EC, OJ L345/97, 31.12.2003

98/8/EC* Directive concerning the placing of biocidal products on the market OJ L123, 24.4.98

98/24/EC Directive on the protection of workers from the risks related to chemical agents at work

99/45/EC Directive concerning the approximation of the laws, regulations and administrative provisions of the Member States relating to the classification, packaging and labelling of dangerous preparations (this directive has been amended by an Adaptation to Technical Change 2001/60/EEC)

99/92/EC Directive on minimum requirements for improving the safety and health protection of workers potentially at risk from explosive atmospheres OJ L023/57, 28.1.2000

2000/39/EC Directive establishing a first list of indicative occupational exposure limit values (1st IOELV Directive) OJ L142/47, 16.6.2000

2004/37/EC Directive on the protection of workers from the risks related to the exposure to carcinogens or mutagens at work OJ L229/23, 29.6.2004

2006/15/EC Directive establishing a second list of indicative occupational exposure limit values in implementation of Council Directive 98/24/EC and amending Directives 91/322/EEC and 2000/39/EC, 29.6.2004, OJ L38/36, 9.2.2006

Regulation (EC) 1907/2006 concerning the Registration, Evaluation, Authorisation and Restriction of Chemicals (REACH), establishing a European Chemicals Agency, amending Directive 1999/45/EC and repealing Council Regulation (EEC) 793/93 and Commission Regulation (EC) 1488/94 as well as Council Directive 76/769/EEC and Commission Directives 91/155/EEC, 93/67/EEC, 93/105/EC and 2000/21/EC (OJ L396, 30.12.2006)

Regulation (EC) No 1272/2008 on classification, labelling and packaging of substances and mixtures, and amending Directive 67/548/EEC and Regulation (EC) No 1907/2006 (OJ L354, 31.12.2008)

Transport of dangerous goods

94/55/EC* Directive on the approximation of the laws of Member States with regard to the transport of dangerous goods by road OJ L319, 12.12.94 (this directive has been amended six times, the latest amendment by Directive 2006/89/EC)

95/50/EC* Directive on uniform procedures for the checks on the transport of dangerous goods by road OJ L249, 17.10.95 (this has been amended by Directive 2004/112/EC OJ L367)

96/35/EC* Directive on the appointment and vocational qualifications of safety advisors for the transport of dangerous goods by roads, rail and inland waterways OJ L145, 19.6.96

96/49/EC Directive on the approximation of the laws of the Member States with regard to the transport of dangerous goods by rail OJ L235, 17.9.96 (this directive has been amended seven times)

Construction

92/57/EEC* Directive on the implementation of minimum safety and health requirements at temporary or mobile construction worksites OJ L245, 26.8.92

Safety signs

92/58/EEC* Directive on the minimum requirements for the provision of safety and/or health signs at work (Safety Signs Directive) OJ L245, 26.8.92

Temporary workers

91/383/EEC* Directive on the measures to encourage improvements in the safety and health of temporary employees (Temporary Workers Directive) OJ L206, 20.7.91

Pregnant and young workers

92/85/EEC* Directive on the introduction of measures to encourage improvements in the safety and health at work of pregnant workers and workers who have recently given birth or are breast-feeding (Pregnant Workers Directive) OJ L348, 28.11.92
94/33/EC* Directive on the protection of young people at work (Young Workers Directive) OJ L216, 20.8.94

Ionising radiations

96/29/Euratom* Directive laying down the basic safety standards for the protection of the health of workers and the general public against the dangers arising from ionising radiation OJ L159, 19.6.96
2003/122/Euratom Directive on the control of high activity sealed radioactive sources and orphan sources OJ L346, 31.12.03

Physical agents

2002/44/EC Directive on the minimum health and safety requirements regarding the exposure of workers to the risks arising from physical agents (vibration) OJ L177/13, 6.7.2002

2003/10/EC Directive on the minimum health and safety requirements regarding the exposure of workers to the risks arising from physical agents (noise) OJ L042/38, 15.2.2003

2004/40/EC Directive on the minimum health and safety requirements regarding the exposure of workers to the risks arising from physical agents (electromagnetic fields) OJ L159/01, 30.4.2004 amended by Directive 2008/46/EC (OJ L114/88, 26.4.2008)

2006/25/EC Directive on the minimum health and safety requirements regarding the exposure of workers to the risks arising from physical agents (artificial optical radiation) OJ L114/38, 27.4.2006

Other relevant EU documents

90/326/EEC *Recommendation* concerning the adoption of a European schedule of occupational diseases OJ L160, 26.6.90

Regulation (EC) 2062/94 *Regulation* on establishing a European agency for safety, hygiene and health at work (Safety Agency) OJ L216, 20.8.94

Proposed EU directives

Currently there are considerations about:
- developing of further EC legislation covering all musculoskeletal disorders
- amending the Seveso II Directive (96/82/EC)
- amending the Carcinogens and Mutagens Directive (2004/37/EC)
- simplifying and reviewing the Radiation Protection directives including Basic Safety Standards (BSS) and Outside Workers directives
- reviewing the Pressure Equipment Directive (PED) (97/23/EC)
- a proposal for a regulation setting out the requirements for accreditation and market surveillance in relation to the marketing of products, and a proposal for a decision of the European Parliament and of the Council on a common framework for the marketing of products (New approach directive).

New Approach Technical directives

The following table shows the main New Approach Technical directives and the regulations that implement those directives.

Reference	Directive	UK Implementing Regulations
2006/95/EC	Low Voltage	Electrical Equipment (Safety) Regulations 1994 (SI 1994 No. 3260)
87/404/EEC	Simple Pressure Vessels	Simple Pressure Vessels (Safety) Regulations 1991 (SI 1991 No. 2749) (as amended)
88/378/EEC	Toy Safety	Toys (Safety) Regulations 1995 (SI 1995 No. 204) (as amended)
89/106/EEC	Construction Products	Construction Products Regulations 1991 (SI 1991 No. 1620)
89/336/EEC	Electromagnetic Compatibility	Electromagnetic Compatibility Regulations 2006 (SI 2006 No. 3418) (as amended)
98/37/EC (To be replaced by 2006/42/EC December 2009.)	Machinery	Supply of Machinery (Safety) Regulations 2008 (SI 2008 No. 1597)
89/686/EEC	Personal Protective Equipment	Personal Protective Equipment Regulations 2002 (SI 2002 No. 1144) (SI 1994 No. 2063 and SI 2005 No. 831)
90/384/EEC	Non-automatic Weighing Instruments	Non-automatic Weighing Instruments Regulations 2000 (SI 2000 No. 3236) as amended
90/385/EEC	Active Implantable Medical Devices	Medical Devices Regulations 2002 (SI 2002 No. 618 as amended)
90/396/EEC	Appliances Burning Gaseous Fuels	Gas Appliances (Safety) Regulations 1992 (SI 1992 No. 711) and the Gas Appliances (Safety) Regulations 1995 (SI 1995 No. 1629)
1999/5/EC	Radio Equipment and Telecommunications Terminal Equipment and the Mutual recognition of their conformity	Radio Equipment and Telecommunications Terminal Equipment Regulations 2000 (SI 2000 No. 730)

Reference	Directive	UK Implementing Regulations
92/42/EEC	New hot water boilers fired with liquid and gaseous fluid (efficiency requirements)	Boiler (Efficiency) Regulations 1993 (SI 1993 No. 3083) as amended
93/15/EEC	Explosives for civil uses	Placing on the Market and Supervision of Transfers of Explosives Regulations 1993 (SI 1993 No. 2714) (except Art. 10)
93/42/EEC	Medical Devices	Medical Devices Regulations 2002 (SI 2002 No. 618) as amended (SI 2005 No. 2909 and SI 2007 No. 400)
94/9/EC	Equipment and protective systems intended for use in potentially explosive atmospheres	The Equipment and Protective Systems Intended for Use in Potentially Explosive Atmospheres Regulations 1996 (SI 1996 No. 192) (as amended by SI 2001 No. 3766 and SI 2005 No. 830)
95/16/EC	Lifts	Lifts Regulations 1997 (SI 1997 No. 831)
97/23/EC	Pressure Equipment	Pressure Equipment Regulations 1999 (SI 1999 No. 2001 as amended by SI 2002 No. 1267)
98/79/EC	In Vitro Diagnostic Medical Devices	The Medical Devices Regulations 2002 (SI 2002 No. 618 as amended)

APPENDIX D

GLOSSARY

This glossary of technical legal terms is designed for use by non-legal professionals in order to make the body of the text more accessible. In particular, it covers words with legal meanings that may differ from their everyday meanings. The glossary is intended to meet the demands of those concerned with health and safety at work.

Absolute:	Without conditions; complete. In criminal law absolute or strict liability means that an offence may be committed even though there is no intention to commit it.
Accessory:	A person who is involved in a criminal offence to a lesser extent than the principal offender.
Acquiescence:	Consent which is expressed or implied from conduct.
Amenity:	Something which is conducive to comfort or convenience.
Appellant:	A person making an appeal.
Apportionment:	Division into proportionate parts.
Body corporate:	A company or corporation.
Breach:	The infringement of a legal right or duty.
Case stated:	A procedure whereby an appeal is made on a point of law from a magistrates' court to the Divisional Court.
Causation:	The relationship between cause and effect, subject to detailed legal rules. In criminal cases it must be proved beyond reasonable doubt that the accused caused the unlawful act.
Chattel:	Technically, anything other than freehold land.
Child:	A person who has not attained the age of 18 (formerly infant/minor).
Citation:	1. A summons ordering a person to appear before a court. 2. Reference to case law in support of an argument.
Civil (action court/law):	Civil courts are those which deal with private rights as distinct from those which deal with allegations of crime. See also "Crime, Criminal" below.

Claimant:	A person making a legal claim (formerly plaintiff).
Claim form:	The document on which the claim is made (formerly writ).
Clause:	A subdivision of a document or a Parliamentary Bill.
Common law:	The meaning used in this book is that body of law created by judicial decision rather than by Parliament.
Consolidation:	A procedure whereby all relevant statutory provisions are brought together in one statute or regulation (no changes in the law are made by this process).
Construction, rules of:	Principles established by the courts for ascertaining the meaning of words and phrases in documents and legislation.
Contract:	The law of contract is the body of rules governing agreements intended to create legal obligations.
Corporeal:	Visible; tangible.
Corpus delicti:	The facts amounting to a breach of law.
Crime, Criminal:	An act, deemed to be an offence against the State, which is punishable.
Curtilage:	A garden, yard, field or other piece of ground included within an area belonging to a dwelling-house.
De minimis (non curat lex):	The law is not concerned with trifles.
Deemed:	Supposed.
Defendant:	A person against whom a legal claim is brought.
Derogation:	The restriction of the strength of an obligation or right.
Dictum:	A statement by a judge in the course of a decision. See also " *Obiter dictum*", below.
Disclosure:	An order that relevant documents, etc in the possession of one party be disclosed to another party (formerly discovery of documents).
Egress:	Means of exit.

Enactment:	An Act of Parliament or part of an Act, including bye-laws and regulations made under an Act.
Estoppel:	A rule of evidence which prevents a party from denying the validity of certain facts.
Exemption clause:	Part of an agreement excluding the liability of the parties in specific circumstances.
Express:	Clearly stated as opposed to implied.
Further information:	Requests made by one party to the other party for further information as to the nature of the claim or defence (formerly interrogatories/request for further and better particulars).
Held:	Decided.
Hereditament:	An inheritable interest in land. A mere licence to use land is not a hereditament because it is a personal right and would not pass to an heir. A corporeal hereditament is a physical object. An incorporeal hereditament is a right, for example a right of way.
In private:	A hearing before a judge in his private chambers (formerly *in camera*).
Indemnity:	A contract of indemnity is created when a person promises to give security against injury or loss which might be suffered by another.
Indictable, indictment:	An indictment is a written statement accusing a person of a criminal offence which is to be tried in the crown court before a judge and jury.
Ingress:	Means of entry.
Injunction:	A court order requiring a person to do or refrain from doing a particular thing.
Inspection:	An order whereby the court or a party to the proceedings may inspect documents, etc in the possession of the other party.
Instituted:	Commenced.
Inter alia:	Among other things.
Latent:	Not apparent at first sight.
Legislation:	Acts of Parliament and regulations made thereunder.
Liability:	Legal obligation or duty.
Litigant:	A person who takes legal action.

Litigation friend:	A person who brings a claim in his own name on behalf of another who cannot do so, eg a child (formerly next friend).
Mandatory:	A mandatory injunction (see above) directs a person to do a positive act.
Material:	Relevant.
Mens rea:	A guilty mind, ie a deliberate intention to do a wrongful act.
Negligence:	A technical legal concept, generally meaning careless conduct, but subject to strict and complex legal rules.
Obiter dictum:	A statement of law during the hearing of a case, not forming part of the decision in the case. See also "Precedent", below.
Onus:	Burden of proof.
Part 20 Claim:	A counter claim, or the joining of another person to the action.
Part 36 Offer:	An offer to settle the claim (generally without admission of legal liability).
Part 36 Payment:	A payment into court prior to the commencement of proceedings, generally without an admission of legal liability.
Particulars of claim:	Details of the claim.
Patent defect:	Arising at first sight, on the face of it.
Penal legislation:	Acts of Parliament creating criminal offences.
Per incuriam:	Without full legal argument.
Permission:	With the leave of the court.
Plaintiff:	A person who commences legal proceedings.
Precedent:	A judicial decision, creating a rule of law, which applies to later cases involving similar facts.
Prima facie:	On first impression; at first sight; on the face of it.
Procedure:	The normal method of conducting legal proceedings.
Res ipsa loquitur:	The facts speak for themselves.
Respondent:	A person who is defending or resisting an appeal.
Revocation:	Annulment.
Sanction:	A measure of punishment.
Sentence:	The penalty imposed upon a convicted person, normally subject to a statutory maximum.

Statement of case:	The document which sets out the issues between the parties in a civil action (previously known as pleadings).
Status quo (ante):	The same state as before.
Statute:	An Act of Parliament passed by the House of Commons and House of Lords and signed by the Sovereign.
Substantive:	Definite, complete.
Summary:	An offence which may only be dealt with in the magistrates' court.
Tort:	The branch of law dealing with liability for civil wrongs. The normal remedy for a tort is damages in compensation for the wrong done, or an injunction to prevent repetition of the wrong.
Tortfeasor:	A person alleged or proved to have committed a tort.
Uberrimae fidei:	Of the utmost good faith. A party to a contract *uberrimae fidei* must disclose all the material facts of which he is aware (for example, when seeking to take out a contract of insurance).
Vicarious liability:	Liability arising through one person's relationship with another. An employer may be liable for wrongful acts committed by an employee during the course of employment.
Volenti non fit injuria:	Consent to a risk of injury does not give rise to legal liability.
Without notice:	An application to a court made without notifying the other side, eg in an emergency (formerly *ex parte*).
Witness statements:	Sworn statements made by the witnesses (formerly affidavits).

Note: A number of changes to civil procedures have been made recently, known generally as the Woolf reforms. Legal terminology has been simplified. Latin phrases are explained here because, although no longer in use, they are found in older cases. Some examples of Woolf terminology are included in this glossary.

Subject Index

Introduction

The index covers Chapters 1 to 14 and the Appendices. Index entries are to paragraph numbers, but for the Appendices are in the form App.A. Alphabetical arrangement is word- by-word, where a group of letters followed by a space is filed before the same group of letters followed by a letter, eg "Gas installations" will appear before "Gasholders". In determining alphabetical arrangement, initial articles and prepositions are ignored.

551

A YOUNG RIDER'S GUIDE TO

HORSE
— and —
PONY CARE

A YOUNG RIDER'S GUIDE TO
HORSE
── and ──
PONY CARE

compiled by
Jane Kidd

a Salamander book

Published by Salamander Books Limited
LONDON

A Salamander Book

© 1988 Salamander Books Ltd
52 Bedford Row
London WC1R 4LR

ISBN 0 86101 386 7

Distributed in the UK by
Hodder and Stoughton Services,
PO Box 6, Mill Road, Dunton
Green, Sevenoaks, Kent TN13 2XX.

All correspondence concerning the
content of this volume should be
addressed to Salamander Books Ltd.

Publisher's note: This book is based
upon the material appearing in *The
Horse and Pony Manual.*

Contents

Credits

Jane Kidd is well versed in equestrian topics; having competed successfully in international show-jumping events, Jane now concentrates on dressage, organizing events, competing and judging. In addition to writing for books and magazines, Jane helps to run the family stud. She particularly enjoys helping other riders and training horses.

Editors: Geoff Rogers, Marita Westberg
Designer: Nick Buzzard
Copy-editor: Maureen Cartwright
Line drawings: Glenn Steward
(John Martin & Artists Ltd.)
© Salamander Books Ltd.
Photographs: A full list of credits is given on page 200.
Colour/monochrome reproductions: Metric Reproductions Ltd., Essex, UK. Bantam Litho Ltd., Essex, UK.
Filmset: Modern Text Typesetting Ltd., Essex, United Kingdom.

Printed in Belgium by Henri Proost et Cie, Turnhout.

Learning to Ride

In recent years 'horse-fever' has become almost an epidemic in the Western world. No one is exempt and few ever recover once the contact is made. Why this should be so is hard to say—perhaps because the horse can be all things to all men; because riding is a shared adventure; because the horse's speed and agility, which so exceeds that of man, can for a short while be his; and because horses have such courage and gentleness. Sadly the love and use of horses is not always to their benefit. Ignorance of the right way to care for horses can lead to unconscious cruelty.

HOW TO LEARN

The first stages

Much thoughtlessness can be avoided if newcomers are carefully instructed. The novice should start his riding career at a good riding school where he knows he will be safely mounted on horses suited to his ability. A few weeks' tuition at such an establishment, learning the basic seat and becoming familiar with the use of the aids, will pay dividends in the future.

Riding is rated a high-risk sport, and the figures for riders and animals killed—especially on the roads—grow yearly. For this reason alone, it is not enough to get a few lessons from 'that nice young girl down the road', who may know very little more than her pupil. Always seek expert tuition.

A good school will always be willing to advise beginners on what to wear and will insist that its pupils always ride in a hard hat. Strong shoes or boots with a full-

Below: This rider is badly dressed. The hat is too big and will come off in a fall. Wrinkled jeans will rub and bare legs may get pinched during riding. The shoes are too large and the rubber soles will easily catch in the stirrup.

length sole and a low heel are also essential, and for comfort and looks either jodhpurs or breeches and a hacking jacket or polo-neck sweater should be worn. Jeans or loose trousers tend to make the rider's seat unstable and provide less protection from saddle-sores than breeches.

Another good reason for starting a riding career at a school is that faults in the rider's position will be corrected before they become

Left top: Learning to ride on the lunge enables riders to forget about controlling the horse and concentrate on their position. Until confident and balanced it is wise to keep hold of the pommel. When the rider finds it natural to sit in the correct position and is relaxed enough to follow the pony's movement without bouncing around then she can take her hands off the pommel.
Left centre: In this exercise the rider swings the upper body and arms first to one side and then the other. This helps to make the hips and small of the back more supple.
Left bottom: Keeping the arms horizontal to the ground and swinging them backwards and forwards is good for the shoulders.
Below: The boy on the pony is too close to the horse in front; there should be at least one length between the horses.

established. It may also save the older rider from the painful back conditions that can spring from faulty posture. With a secure position in the saddle, a rider will gain confidence and will be able to use his reins to guide and control his horse rather than as a means of maintaining his own balance. He will learn to ride correctly over jumps instead of relying on the courage and speed of his horse to get him to the other side. For full advice on jumping see pages 24-25.

Owning a horse

Not until a rider is reasonably proficient should he think of acquiring his own horse. By then he should have ridden many different ones and will be able to assess which breed and size he prefers. He should have a much better idea of what is entailed in caring for horses, including the sort of saddle and bridle to buy. It is sometimes a good idea to keep the first horse at board (livery) for a while. Most riding schools welcome keen owners and encourage them to assist with the stable work, cleaning tack, etc. In this way, the rider will become more capable of caring for his horse at home, knowing when to get him re-shod or to call in a veterinarian, and understanding the feeding of horses in relation to their work and the tasks they perform.

MOUNTING AND DISMOUNTING

Above: When mounting face the hindquarters and take the reins in the left hand close to the withers and the stirrup in the right.

Above: Place the left foot in the stirrup, keeping the toe low to avoid encouraging the horse to move off; the horse should remain still.

The horse can be mounted in a number of ways. The athletic rider can vault on — spring up to lie across the horse and then swing one leg over. Those too short to reach the stirrup (eg jockeys) can be legged up quite easily, but the most practical and safest way is to mount using the stirrup on the nearside (left). It is a tradition in the horse world to use the nearside as opposed to the offside (right) of the horse, as much as possible. Buckles and girths are done up that side, saddlery is put on from the nearside and the rider mounts from there.

Accidents do happen when mounting, especially if the rider becomes careless. The three

important precautions to take are: choose a suitable site that is relatively peaceful and on firm ground; check the girths, as a saddle that slips around can frighten the horse and off-balance the rider; and if either horse or rider is inexperienced, get an assistant to hold the head, as the horse must stand still, both to avoid accidents and to establish discipline from the moment the rider gets on his back.

Below: When dismounting, remove the right foot from the stirrup to swing this leg over the saddle, taking the weight on the left leg. This rider has taken the left leg out of the stirrup to land on both.

Above: With the right hand on the offside back of the saddle pull on both arms at the same time as putting weight onto the left foot.

Above: Swing the right leg over the back of the saddle and hindquarters, lower into the saddle and put the feet into the stirrups.

The classical position of the rider on a horse is wholly practical and yet elegant. It places the rider over the horse's centre of gravity, which lies just behind the withers and roughly in line with the point of his shoulder.

To achieve the classical position

The rider must first take hold of the front of the saddle and pull himself forward until he is sitting in the deepest part, which should be just behind the arch of the saddle. Old-fashioned saddles with shallow seats will handicap the rider, and so will those that are very wide in the waist. Modern saddles, which should fit both the rider and the horse, are designed to help the rider to slide easily into the correct position.

Once the rider is sitting in the lowest part of the saddle he should make himself as tall and upright as possible. This is achieved by raising the upper body and by reaching down with the legs. Then, providing the waist and hips are not allowed to collapse backwards, his weight will come off the buttocks and on to the seat bones, the head will rise, the shoulders drop and the spine take up its natural line.

At the same time, the knee should be as low on the saddle as the rider's conformation permits, and the whole leg should lie close to the horse's side, with the toe higher than the heel. Once the rider has achieved this position it should be possible to draw an imaginary line from the lobe of his ear, through the point of his shoulder and his hip to the heel of the boot. He will then be in the basic position for all forms of riding on the flat, except racing.

If the imaginary line fails to touch the tip of the heel, the rider will be behind the balance and will probably have rounded his back and allowed his lower leg to swing forward. If the leg is behind the line, the rider is probably sitting on his fork. In other words, in the first instance he has transferred his weight back on to his buttocks,

and in the second he has gone forward off his seat bones and is balancing on his thighs. In neither position will his seat be stable and his weight related to that of the horse.

Even in the correct position the rider will not be able to maintain his seat once the horse is moving unless he is completely supple and relaxed. Any form of tension not only destroys his position but sets up a reciprocal stiffness in his horse, and this tends to make matters worse.

This particularly applies if he tries to grip with the knees or thighs. Contrary to what is sometimes believed this tends to weaken the rider's control by raising his seat out of the saddle. It defeats the whole object of the classical position, which depends on the united balance and harmony of horse and rider.

Thus, if the rider takes up the correct position and there is no tension in his body, he will be able to sink softly down into the horse's back on each stride (ie, as the hooves touch the ground). In this way the rider is carried up and gently forward by the horse's movement.

If, however, the rider is not seated over the horse's centre of gravity, the synchronization will be spoilt and the rider will have to maintain contact with the saddle by gripping and also to move his upper body to keep up with the horse's movement. Any displacement of the rider's weight that is out of harmony with the horse's natural balance is liable to set up mental and physical resistances, especially in the freedom of the horse's paces. Young animals in particular will be afraid of increasing their speed or lengthening their stride if they cannot rely on their burden to 'go with them'.

Provided his legs, and in particular the inner muscles of his thighs, are relaxed, the rider's knees will be deep on the saddle flap, and it is this depth that should help him to maintain his balance whatever the horse may do. At first, in his effort to lower the knee, the rider may find that his lower leg sticks out from the horse's side, but this tendency will correct itself once knee and leg are truly supple.

Then the rider will find that the inner side of his upper calf muscles automatically makes contact with the widest part of the horse's ribcage, enabling him to give light unobtrusive aids. At the same time, because his upper body is upright and his shoulders are relaxed, the upper arms will hang down quite naturally until the point of his elbow lightly touches the hip bone. The rider has only to bring his forearm up until, when seen from the side, there is a straight line from his elbow down the rein to his horse's mouth for his arms to be in the right position as well. The hands should be held as though he were reading a book, with the fingers closed on the reins, the thumbs on top and the back of the wrists facing outward. If the rider maintains his balance without tension he is then able to use his hands and reins independently of the rest of his body.

To remain in the classical position, no matter what saddle or horse the rider may sit on, takes years of practice and is best learned by riding without stirrups while on the lunge. But it is essential that the instructor should be very experienced.

A rider in the established position will find that, by closing the angles of his hips, knees and ankles, he will be in the right place for jumping and galloping. For these activities, the imaginary line becomes shorter and runs directly from the rider's shoulder to his heel with the knee in front and the hips slightly behind. The rider is still in harmony with the horse's centre of gravity, with the body adjusted to comply with the horse's speed.

The principal object of the classical position is to allow the rider to be motionless in relation to the movement of the horse and for the two to work as one.

Below: This rider is in good position as a vertical line can be drawn from the lobe of his ear through shoulder and hip to his heel. The rider must be over the horse's centre of gravity.

THE WESTERN SEAT

The purpose of the Western (also known as the stock) seat is to permit a rider to assume a comfortable and relaxed position, so that he can spend many hours in the saddle, while still being able to control and guide his horse according to the demands of ranch and trail riding.

The high pommel and cantle of the Western saddle helps to achieve this by giving the rider greater security. The seat slopes backwards to the cantle so that the rider sits further back than is customary in the English style.

Western riders sit almost straight-legged, using longer stirrup leathers than in any other style of horsemanship. The leather must not be so long, however, that it is difficult to keep the heel below the toe. A deep seat enables the rider to brace himself in the saddle while roping and to effect the quick starts and stops needed in ranch work. The lower leg is vital to control and must be able to swing freely. Knees and thighs rest, but do not press, against the saddle.

Both reins are held in one hand, because cowboys need a free hand for holding a rope or to flap a Stetson at a stray calf. The reins normally pass through the fist from over the index or under the little finger with the thumb up. However, when the ends of split reins fall on the nearside, then one finger can be placed between the reins. The free hand and arm should hang down in a relaxed manner.

Western horses are taught neck-reining, a term that describes changing direction through rein pressure on the animal's neck. To turn left, for example, the rider lays the reins across the neck to the left, and the horse will respond to the combination of direct and indirect reining. The reins can be held in either hand.

A good stock seat position is best learned on a responsive but gentle horse. Picking up the rhythm at all gaits is essential, because any stiffness or awkwardness on the rider's part will 'show daylight' between him and the saddle. Unlike English-style equitation, Westerners do not post while trotting, so that a supple lower back and shock-absorbent legs are needed to sit down to a jog (the Western word for trot) as well as lope (the word for canter).

The aids should be imperceptible, and the weight of the rider must stay in the centre of the saddle.

Below: Western riding with light rein contact for the extended walk.

The fundamental aim of the saddle seat position is to display a three- or five-gaited saddlebred or a Tennessee walking horse to the best advantage. A gaited horse or walker is characterized by a high degree of leg action that the rider wants to show off.

In the saddle seat position, the rider's legs are straighter than in the classic seat. Because gaited horses are trained to move forward with great energy, impulsion derived from leg pressure is less necessary in saddle seat equitation than in other disciplines. The rider is thus able to keep his legs ahead of the girth and slightly flared out at the knee, away from the horse.

To obtain the right position, the rider places himself comfortably in the saddle and finds his centre of gravity by sitting without irons and with slightly bent knees. The leathers can then be adjusted to the length needed to maintain the position. The iron is placed under the ball of the foot so that pressure on the centre of the iron is equal across the entire width of the foot. The feet point straight ahead.

The rider holds his body erect. Arms are held higher and elbows stick out further than in the classic position. The purpose of this is to influence the horse's head carriage directly through rein pressure, so that the height of the hands depends on where the horse is carrying his head. Hands do not have to be held thumbs-up.

Some people believe that the saddle seat position is easier to learn than other styles because the rider's legs can be used to brace him in the saddle, and also because gaited horses are comfortable to ride. The novice rider starts at the walk, when a slight motion in the saddle is permissible. Particular attention must be paid to the animal's head carriage, which is set by a combination of curb and snaffle bit pressure, but no sawing action should be used. The saddle seat rider posts during the trot, and must learn to do so rapidly, in time to the gaited horse's animated leg action. The hips are kept under the body, so that there is no mechanical up-and-down motion nor a forward-and-backward swing. In the canter, 'the saddle should be polished' with the rider going with the horse, and this is easier to achieve on a Tennessee walking horse, which has a rocking chair canter.

Below: Using the saddle seat position to show off the horse's gait.

'Aids' is the well-chosen word for the methods used by riders to communicate with the horse. They both control and direct the horse in his work for man.

Throughout the ages the great horseman has sought to improve and refine his use of the aids until the communication between himself and his mount is such that they almost think as one. Even to come anywhere near this standard requires years of dedication and practice, but the aids used do not vary from those taught in any good riding school, and a high degree of proficiency is within the reach of most riders.

Natural and artificial aids
Aids are usually divided into two groups: the 'natural aids' are those given by means of the rider's body or voice; 'artificial aids' are those requiring some form of strap or gadget to achieve the right effect.

In the second group, only the whip and spurs have any part to play in the training of horses, but for practical purposes other things (such as martingales) may be advisable if horse or rider lacks experience.

The success or otherwise of using 'natural aids' is directly related to the ability of the rider to sit in the correct position in the saddle and to maintain the position under all circumstances: in other words, to be 'still' in relation to the movement of his horse. This is possible only if the rider is supple, relaxed and in command of all his muscular reactions. Involuntary or unco-ordinated movement on the part of the rider will either confuse the horse or, if repeated too frequently, cause him to 'stop listening'. This can easily turn a free, intelligent horse into a dull automaton. It is therefore up to the rider to ensure that he knows and uses the correct aids if he does not want his horse to become indifferent to them.

The legs
A horse's first line of defence is flight, and his immediate reaction

Above: The leg is being applied on the girth when it is used to generate forward movement.

to the pressure of the rider's legs is to move forward in an effort to escape. All riding is based on this reaction, and the horse's desire to move forward must never at any time be lost. Even in the most advanced dressage movements, impulsion must still be in a forward direction, although — in the piaffe, for example — he may be actually trotting on the spot. Once a horse learns that he can evade the rider's aids by going backwards or by conserving his energy, man is no longer master. Then the horse may develop such vices as rearing, napping or bucking, which make him a danger to himself and to his rider, who may be thrown off.

If the rider wishes his horse to be 'light' to the aids he should use only enough pressure with his legs (in particular with the inside of the upper calves) to remind the horse to go forward. This pressure should never be a steady squeeze or a heavy thump with the leg and heel, but a quick vibrant action with both legs on or just behind the girth. If the rider is sitting correctly, his legs will automatically touch this spot. No leg aid should be prolonged; if it is ineffective, it should be repeated once more

Above: The leg is being applied behind the girth when it is used to ask for lateral movement.

with greater firmness. Should the horse still not react it is wiser to use the whip, not as a punishment but to supplement the rider's legs. This is done by giving one short tap on the horse's ribs just behind the rider's leg. In other words, the rider asks the horse once or twice to go forward to the leg, and then, if necessary, demands it. It should be remembered that frequent use of the whip can nullify its effect as an aid, so it should never be used unless the rider's natural aids have failed and then only as a

refinement of that aid. The same can be said of the use of spurs, which must never be used as a punishment and are in any case not suitable for use on young horses or by inexperienced riders.

The hands
Once the horse moves forward it is the rider's task to control and direct the energy created. This he does through the reins to the horse's mouth. Once again, unless his seat is secure and his hands and arms supple he will be unable to use his hands independently of the rest of his body.

Unless the horse feels that he can go forward and touch the bit without experiencing pain, he will try to withdraw from it by ceasing to go forward or (in an effort to escape) will pull against it. If, however, the rider's contact with the horse's mouth is both light and steady and if the flexion in his wrists follows the natural movement of the horse's head and neck, the animal will relax his mouth and accept the bit as an aid to control and understanding.

It should never be forgotten how easy it is to damage the sensitive bars in the horse's mouth and that

Below: The snaffle rein is held correctly in this picture with the thumbs pointing upwards and the hands close to, but not resting on, the neck of the horse.

this contact is the rider's closest link with the horse's brain.

Except in rare circumstances the reins should be held in both hands with the snaffle reins lying between the fourth and fifth finger of each hand or, in the case of a double bridle, outside the little finger while the bit (curb) rein takes the place of the snaffle rein. The slack can then be taken up through the palm of the hand and allowed to hang over the top of the first finger, with the thumb resting lightly on top of it. The reins should be held short enough to enable the rider to keep a steady but light contact with the horse's mouth. His fingers should be closed because an open hand leaves nothing to give to the horse when following the natural

Below: The reins of a double bridle held in acceptable fashion with the bit rein around the outside of the little finger. The bit rein can also be held between the little and the fourth finger.

movement in his head and neck. The movement is most noticeable at the walk and trot, and the rider must always allow his hand to follow this without losing contact or allowing the rein to 'flap'. In this way, the rider's hands will be 'still' in relation to the horse's movement.

The reins should be used only to tell the horse either the speed or the direction at which he should proceed. At all other times they merely retain a steady but light contact. If, like the legs, they are used without thought—for instance, when the rider is talking to friends and not attending to his horse—the animal will soon stop listening and will no longer respond to the slightest change in the contact on the rein.

Thus it can be seen that the legs help to create forward impulsion and the hands decide how it should be used. This is done by varying the position and the degree to which these aids are used.

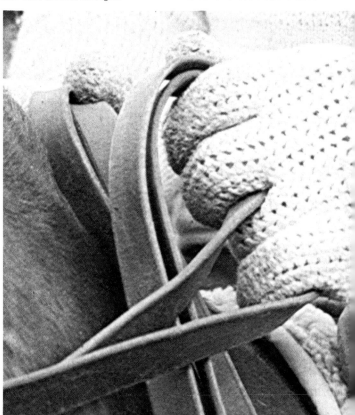

To turn a corner

The need to change the position of the leg and hand aids is partly to make a clear difference to the horse, who, having an amazing memory, will quickly associate the position with the required movements. The other reason is concerned with the way a horse actually moves. Once he knows that pressure of both the rider's legs is telling him to go forward, he will also move only one hind leg forward if he feels the increased pressure of that one of the rider's legs. On a circle the rider must apply his inside leg to ensure that the horse brings his inside hind leg not only well forward but also slightly under the weight of his body to maintain his balance while turning. Some of the impulsion created by this movement will then be carried diagonally forward towards the horse's outside shoulder. This impulsion is received and controlled by the outside rein: that is to say, the rider keeps a passive contact on this rein and, by closing his fingers, allows only sufficient of the impulsion to escape to maintain the required pace. At no time should this hand either lose contact or pull backwards. This is known as the passive outside rein controlling the pace while the rider's inside leg creates the impulsion.

At the same time the rider's outside leg should be very slightly behind the girth and ready to be applied if the horse tries to swing his quarters away from the pressure of the rider's inside leg. This is known as the outside leg holding or controlling the quarters. The role of the inside hand is to be very light and flexible and to ask for a slight bend in the direction of the circle.

When being ridden, a horse must be either going straight or turning, and these two basic positions and their appropriate aids apply from basic·to advanced stages of training. The one thing that alters is the degree to which the aids are applied, as we shall see in later sections of the book.

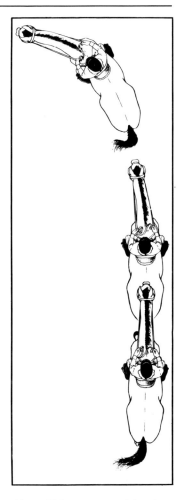

Above: This sequence of drawings illustrates the main points involved in turning a corner, a movement that needs careful control of the reins and use of the legs. The rider's head should be directed to look straight through the horse's ears. The outside leg is just behind the girth and stops the quarters from swinging out. The inside leg is on the girth; this is the most vital of all the aids when turning a corner. The inside rein asks for a slight bend, but the pressure should be less than on the outside rein. The outside rein controls the pace and should not be taken far from the neck.

To trot

This is a two-time gait with the horse's legs moving in diagonal pairs (see Gaits of the Horse). The rider has two alternatives: 'to sit', when his seat does not leave the saddle, or 'to post' (to rise), when he sits in the saddle as one pair of the horse's diagonals comes to the ground and rises out of it as this same pair of diagonals leaves the ground. It is important that the horse is not made one sided by the rider always sitting for the same pair of diagonals. This is very easy to develop as every rider finds it more comfortable to sit to one particular diagonal pair. The rider must learn to change diagonals by sitting down in the saddle for an extra beat before starting to rise again. He should do this frequently when hacking, and when schooling should learn to sit to the outside diagonals (ie rise when the inside hind leg and outside foreleg come off the ground, and sit when this pair returns to the ground).

Below: The rider is rising from the saddle when one diagonal pair of legs is off the ground, and sitting for the other pair. Here he sits as the inside diagonals reach the ground.

To canter

The only other position the rider needs is that which tells his horse to change pace into the canter. At the canter (a three-time pace) the foreleg and hind leg on one side will be slightly in advance of the pair on the other side. Consequently it will be easier for the horse to describe a circle if the inside legs are leading. When the horse has learned to bring forward a hind leg in answer to a touch from the rider's leg, he can be asked to strike off on the required lead.

To induce him to strike off into the canter on the correct lead he should go into a corner slightly bent towards his leading foreleg. The rider's outside leg should be drawn back to tell him to move his outside hind leg forward. Then, according to the sequence of the canter (see Gaits of the Horse page 176), the inside hind leg and outside foreleg will now move forward together and he will finally lead with the inside foreleg. Thus the rider's outside leg tells the horse to bring forward that hind leg. It should not be applied too strongly or it would then be asking the hindquarters to move sideways, thus causing confusion

in the future when lateral work is taught. It is the rider's inside leg that asks for the forward impulsion, so it must be applied on the girth at the same time as the outside leg. Any reluctance or laziness to go into the canter should be remedied by stronger use of this inside (not outside) leg and if necessary a few

taps with the stick on the inside.

Once the horse has struck off into the canter, both the rider's legs return to the correct position at the girth to keep up the impulsion. Should the rider wish to change the canter lead, he first brings the horse back to the walk or trot and then reverses his canter aids. Eventually, when both he and his horse are well-balanced and have sufficient collection, the change can be made during the short period of suspension in the canter pace that comes immediately after the leading foreleg hits the ground. The horse will then change the sequence of his stride while in the air. This, known as the flying change, is quite natural to the horse when unmounted, but it is very difficult to teach a horse to change both hind and fore leading legs (they usually just change in front) before he has mastered the medium standard movements of dressage: that is, the horse is straight, performs lateral movements happily and is collected.

These demands are made of dressage horses only, as show-jumpers and polo ponies have to do flying changes and few are trained to medium dressage, but change automatically.

The three photographs at left illustrate the technique of striking off into the canter.

Top left: The rider is drawing his outside leg back, to brush along the horse, but not to dig into him, in order to indicate to him to bring his outside (off hind) forward and so strike off with the near foreleg leading. Centre left: In response to this the horse has brought his off hind leg much further forward than he did when trotting, although in this case he is offering some resistance by opening his mouth. Bottom left: The horse has struck off into the canter to lead with his near foreleg, and the rider is returning his right leg to its position close to the girth. The rider will keep using his inside leg to generate impulsion.

USE OF AIDS

The seat

So far this chapter has dealt only with the use of the hand and leg aids, but a correct and supple seat can play an immense part in training a horse. If the rider is sitting in the right position and is supple and relaxed, he has only to sink softly down in the saddle as the horse's hooves touch the ground to ensure that he and his mount rebound together. In this way, the rider will be in harmony with his horse and able to absorb the strong upward thrust of the horse's back through his own supple loins and thighs instead of being thrown off the saddle and falling stiffly back. The latter type of riding invariably causes the rider to start gripping in an effort to maintain his position and the horse to tense the muscles of his back in anticipation of the jar when the rider's seat returns to the saddle.

If, on the other hand, both are relaxed and the impulsion is being maintained, the deeper the rider sinks down with his horse the greater will be their joint recoil, and the horse's steps will become lighter and the stride more rounded and therefore shorter. This is the true way to obtain collection and has nothing to do with the false collection created when the horse's head and neck are positioned by the use of the reins or when he is merely slowed down to take shorter but less elevated strides. Neither method will produce the soft muscular roundness of outline with slightly lowered quarters that is the aim of collection. Few riders have the ability or the time to train their horses to achieve great collection, but once a rider has learned to appreciate the power that lies in the correct use of a supple seat he will find that all horses work much more freely and willingly for him and that he can use almost invisible hand and leg aids. This applies whether he requires a collected or an extended pace. The latter is directly dependent on the first because unless there is spring and height in the collected paces there will be insufficient time in the air for each set of legs to lengthen the stride. A rider who tries to obtain extension from a pace that lacks impulsion or by the use of rough leg aids will achieve nothing but greater speed and hurried strides, whereas true extension should be performed in the same rhythm as the other working, medium or collected paces.

The lateral aids

Once a horse is going freely forward and is 'straight', with the hind feet following in the track made by the fore feet, and once the rider is truly in control of the quarters, it is possible to start riding lateral movements. These are any movements where the quarters do not follow the same line as the horse's forehand and are often referred to as work on two tracks, encompassing such exercises as leg yielding, shoulder-in, renvers, travers and half pass. All are used to increase the horse's balance and obedience, the suppleness of the quarters and the joints, and the freedom of the shoulders.

In all cases, the horse must be going forward well. Only leg yielding can be performed in a working trot; all other lateral movements require a degree of collection whether carried out at a trot or at a canter. They do not, however, require the rider to use the legs in a different position from those he adopted when riding a turn or circle. By varying the degree of pressure of the leg just behind the girth, yet still maintaining impulsion by his seat and other leg at the girth, he will be able to move the quarters to left or right.

By riding straight forward while holding this position the horse will perform renvers (quarters out) or travers (quarters in). If the pressure on the outside leg (ie the one behind the girth) is increased, the horse will go forward and slightly to the side in half pass. If, on the other hand, the horse is ridden forward as though to start a circle until the forehand has left the track and the pressure of the inside leg — which is at the girth — is increased while the rider's opposite hand prevents him from continuing in the circle, the movement will be shoulder-in. If this movement is correctly executed it should be possible at any time to return to the circle by slightly relaxing the pressure of the leg at the girth and the opposite hand, thus allowing the horse to move forward again on one track into the circle.

None of these lateral movements should be attempted until the rider is confident that he can produce enough forward impulsion and can ride a true circle at all paces. Then he will need only to vary the use of his individual leg and hand aids to master all lateral work. As there is so little natural impulsion in the walk, many advise against doing such exercises at this pace, because it can easily lose its regularity and sequence. It does, however, give the novice horse and/or rider a less hurried opportunity to understand the aids. Therefore as long as training at the walk is kept to a minimum and always followed immediately by some energetic movement straight forward, it can be beneficial. All lateral work can be done at the trot and eventually the canter.

Finally, whatever ambitions a rider may have, it cannot be stressed too strongly that if he and his horse are to reach their true potential every effort should be made to achieve the correct position in the saddle and to learn to use the aids effectively.

Below: The rider is performing the leg yield lateral movement.

Below: The shoulder-in, which is another lateral movement

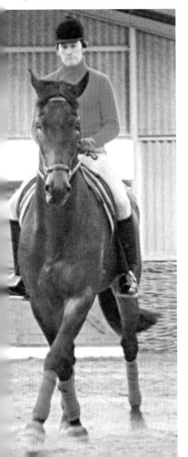

Many people believe that jumping requires a different seat and aids from those used for riding on the flat. This is not the case. A jump is only a very elevated canter stride and the position when jumping is the same seat. All that has changed is that the rider has closed the angles at his hips, knees and ankles, enabling him to ride with shorter stirrup leathers, to lift his seat just clear of the saddle and to lean slightly forward over his horse's withers. The imaginary line that was discussed under the classical position would now go directly from the point of the rider's shoulder to his heel. In other words, although his weight remains over the horse's centre of gravity, his whole body is compressed like a spring. It is also important that the rider should not collapse at the waist or curve his back, which should at all times remain as flat as the natural line of his spine allows. The elbows may go rather further forward and the reins will be shorter, but there should still be a straight line through the rider's forearm and hand to the horse's mouth. As in the more upright position, all the rider's weight should be going down through his supple seat, thighs and knees.

In the jumping position it is not essential for the actual seat to touch the saddle. Some show-jumpers believe it is advantageous to bring the upper body into an upright position and to lower the seat into the saddle three or four strides in front of a fence. They feel that they can then use their seat to exert a greater influence over the horse. Show-jumping, however, is a very specialized sport and it is wiser for the less experienced rider to perfect a correct jumping position and to concentrate on maintaining that position while coming into a fence, going over it and landing. In this way he will be less likely to be left behind the horse's movement and to pull his horse in the mouth, and will also be in the correct position to go straight into the next stride after landing. Once his position is truly established he will be able to influence the length of the horse's stride by using his legs and seat and by controlling with steady hands, which are independent of the rest of his body.

The position over the fence

Horses jump by dropping their weight on to their forelegs and bringing their hindquarters well under their centre of balance. As the forehand springs into the air the horse has time to tuck his forelegs under his chest before the hind legs hit the ground and propel his whole body over the fence. If the rider is sitting in a correct position and is supple and balanced, the less he moves or interferes with the horse the easier it will be for them both. As the horse's forehand rises, and the horse's hind legs come under the body, the withers will come closer to the rider's chest and the saddle will drop away from his seat. Relying on his balance and suppleness and, if necessary, gripping with his legs and particularly his knees against the saddle, the rider is ready to accept and go with the powerful forward thrust as the horse takes off. To make an efficient jump over the fence the horse has to round his back and to lower and stretch forward his neck and head. It is therefore necessary for the rider to give the horse sufficient length of rein to achieve this without actually losing contact. This he does by leaning forward, straightening his elbows and allowing his hands to go forward and down towards the horse's mouth. This must be done as the horse asks for the extra length of rein and not by throwing the rein forward and abandoning all contact, although this fault is better than causing the horse pain by getting left behind the movement and pulling on his mouth. This is serious because it soon causes a horse to lose confidence and to jump with a flat or hollow back. As the horse lands, the rider has only to rebend his elbows to maintain contact and to be in the correct position for the next stride.

Position on landing

If the rider has maintained the forward position while over the jump he will be able to absorb the jar of the horse's forelegs touching the ground through his supple loins and thighs. Because his seat is still just clear of the saddle it will be easier for the horse to bring his hind legs well forward and under his body on landing. Then both horse and rider will be in the correct position to go straight forward into the next stride.

The rider's task

The rider's task is principally to ensure that the horse is going forward to the fence in a calm balanced manner with sufficient impulsion in each stride to release power at the right moment and propel both of them over the fence. An experienced rider can also help the horse by controlling the length of the stride so that they are able to take off from the correct spot relative to the height and width of the fence. But it should never be forgotten that once this place has been reached it is the horse who has to jump, and the rider can best assist by staying still in relation to the horse's movements. Riders who throw themselves forward by straightening the knees or who practise other acrobatic feats are usually only compensating for the inadequacy of their own position or lack of suppleness, and rarely help the horse. All too often such riders rely on their horse's speed and courage and then have to use rough methods to control and/or go with him over a fence.

Top right: The rider is allowing with her reins so that the horse can lower his head to look at the fence and prepare himself.
Centre right: The rider has come forward too much, and she has lost contact with the reins.
Bottom right: The rider is returning to her normal position a little late.

Basic Schooling

The aim of schooling is to teach a horse to understand, respect and gain confidence in his rider and to make him more supple, balanced and relaxed. Schooling will help the horse to use his ability to the full. He might have been able to jump high fences before training, but he will be able to do so for many more years and more successfully if he can work in a relaxed, efficient way, accepting help from his rider rather than relying on his agility to get out of difficulties.

ON THE FLAT

Impatient riders may try to by-pass the flat work in their haste to get on with the action; but a little patience pays dividends, extending a horse's working life and making the animal more pleasurable and successful to ride whether in racing, jumping, hunting, eventing or merely hacking around.

For the best results, good basic training is needed. This involves getting the horse to go forward rhythmically, straight and relaxed, with the hindquarters engaged and the rider maintaining a light elastic contact with the bit. To achieve this, the programme must be varied according to the horse's temperament, conformation and natural ability.

A suitable programme for an average young horse would start with 20 minutes' work in an arena, ridden or lunged, before being taken for a hack, and on the sixth day having a longer hack. This would not suit all temperaments or types, however. Weak, lazy horses need hacking to give them some excitement, including if possible plenty of hill work to build up the muscles. On the other hand, a neurotic horse would be more relaxed with longer periods of steady work in the arena. A nappy one must not be given an opportunity to misbehave: he should always go hacking with another horse, and should never be worked until bored in an arena. The trainer can experiment and must be alert and flexible so as to work out a really constructive programme that will develop the horse's strong points and

overcome his weaknesses.

It is important to devise activities that are not too difficult for the stage of training and maturity that the horse has reached. Otherwise he may become crotchety, resisting if the work is beyond him. At the same time enough must be asked of the horse to keep him alert and attentive to the rider.

To go forward
This means first teaching the horse to respond to the rider's leg, making him want to go forward rather than slow up. This is best achieved by using the voice, and carrying a long schooling whip with which he can be tapped (not hit) just where the leg is applied.

To go on the bit
The horse must come to accept an elastic-like contact with the rider's hand, drawing toward the bit so that if the pressure is released he will try to find the contact again, rather than throw his head in the air with relief. He needs to have confidence in the gentleness of the rider's hands, so the rider must try to keep his hands steady but not stiff, maintaining a light contact with the mouth and not jerking or pulling. The bit should be a kind thick snaffle.

Engaging the hindquarters
This is necessary because they are the horse's source of impulsion and spring. The further they come under him the more power the horse will have (rather like compressing a spring). The rider asks the horse to place his

hindquarters further under him by using his legs and seat, while restraining him from going faster with a hand that resists but does not pull. It is very easy, however, for the impulsion created by these driving aids to escape if the horse is not accepting the bit. If the horse is above it (head too high), then he will tend to raise the head still higher when the legs are applied so that the effects of the driving action will disappear from the front.

The rider should aim at containing the driving action within the horse, ie, so that it goes 'through' from the horse's hindquarters to his body, then to the head and back along the reins to be felt by the rider's hands. If this is successful then the horse is under the rider's control, impulsion can be built up, and resistance, stiffness and loss of rhythm become much less likely to develop.

In most cases this is best achieved by getting the novice horse to go with a long low outline: ie, the top line of the back and neck is rounded and the head is stretched out and down. The horse might be a little on his forehand at first, but the rider should gradually ask more, using his legs and seat (never pulling on the reins). As the horse's hind legs come further underneath him, his body will be compressed and he will raise his head and neck. Taken very gradually, over months rather than weeks, the hollow outline can be avoided and the power of the horse should be controllable with the rider's driving aids being contained and not escaping.

Rhythm
As important in riding as in other sports. A horse that moves in rhythm is a balanced horse; with balance he is capable of jumping higher, galloping faster or performing dressage movements better. The horse must learn to walk (four hoofbeats), trot (two hoofbeats) and canter (three hoofbeats) rhythmically. Some horses have natural rhythm and

balance; others have to be taught. An excited horse will not learn easily, so the first aim must be to get him really calm and relaxed; conversely a lazy one will experience difficulty until he goes forward willingly, so he must be excited. After that it is up to the rider to remember the rhythm.

Straightness
This means the ability to turn in either direction without bias and to take contact with the bit evenly. All horses are born 'one-sided', finding it easier to turn one way than the other, and tending to take a stronger contact on one side of the bit than the other. They must therefore be 'suppled up', so that

crooked forward movement is avoided and the horse turns easily in both directions.

Suppling the stiff side is achieved by squeezing (not pulling) on the rein, and by applying pressure with the leg on the girth of the same side. The rein on the soft side should be held lightly. Eventually, though it may take a long time, the horse will relax his jaw on both sides and take an even contact.

Work to achieve these aims

Work can be done when riding across country, along paths and fields and up and down hills. It is usually easier to keep a horse wanting to go forward when out of doors, and changes of going and different surroundings help his balance and teach him to look after himself. Going up hills makes the animal use his hind legs and develop his loin muscles; going down hills forces him to extend his shoulders and forelegs.

When riding, always be on the alert. Young horses may misbehave out of genuine fear or in an attempt to try to master their rider. A young horse must never be allowed to get his own way, but he must learn to relax at the same time. The rider should therefore be firm but never violent. If possible, always go out with another horse and always carry a long schooling whip. New demands will keep the horse absorbed.

Left: The horse is not going straight. He is hollowing towards his left side and the rein contact will be lighter.
Right and below: Schooling figures for arena or field. Work in an arena becomes boring for the horse if the rider is too unimaginative to keep his pupil's concentration. When schooling a horse keep his interest by varying your directions as shown here.

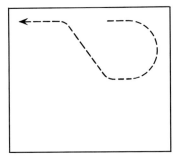

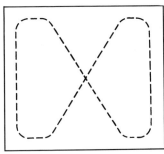

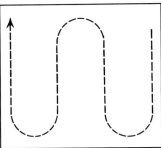

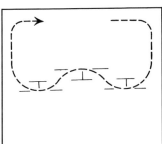

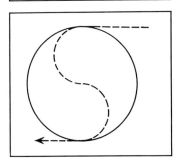

The movements

The walk can be easily ruined, because an untrained horse tends to tense up against the rider, losing the rhythm of the four hoofbeats. It is advisable to do no more than get the horse walking with a light contact on the bit until he is truly relaxed.

The trot

This requires a pronounced rhythm, and should be carried out at sufficient speed to make the strides both high and active. If too high, the trot may look pretty but the hock action will tend to be straight. If there is too much activity and speed, the trot will become rather flat and hurried.

At first the rider should post (rise) at the trot, only sitting for a few strides when the horse improves. If the horse does not lose his rhythm or go hollow in the back, and the rider is not thrown around, then he can sit for longer and longer periods. It is much

Below: Keeping a contact at the walk can cause resistance, and this horse is overbending.
Bottom: If a horse resists at the walk it is very easy for him to lose the rhythm of the four hoofbeats.

Below: A good trot. The diagonals are moving as pairs.
Centre: The outside diagonals are just coming off the ground.
Bottom: The outside diagonals have reached their highest level.

easier to control the horse from a sitting trot but if this is attempted too early the horse will become very stiff in the back.

The trot is usually the best pace at which to work a young horse, for the walk may make him tense and the canter is rarely sufficiently balanced. At the canter, it is more difficult to vary direction frequently because the leading leg has to be changed.

The canter
This should have a definite three-time hoofbeat and the danger is that it can easily turn into a four-time pace. It is important therefore that the horse must be kept going forward freely at all times.

Another danger is a disunited canter. The horse's inside foreleg

Below: The canter to the right in which the leading foreleg is about to come off the ground. This is followed by a short period of suspension when all the legs are off the ground. It is during this brief period of suspension that a flying change is made.

and hind leg should be in advance of the outside pair (leading with the inside legs). If he canters disunited (leading with the near foreleg and off hind leg or vice versa), the rider will feel uncomfortable and the horse will be unbalanced. He should be brought back to the trot immediately and the true canter re-established.

The most likely time for him to become disunited is if he strikes off into the canter on the wrong leg (with the outside legs leading, or counter canter). This will make it difficult to negotiate a corner and the horse will try to change. A young horse usually manages this only with the foreleg and thus becomes disunited. Always try to establish the correct lead from the start, by asking him to canter out of a circle. The animal should already be bending correctly, which will make it easier to strike off on the inside legs.

Turning a corner/circle
This may cause a young horse to want to change rhythm. This must not be allowed.

Aim to keep the head slightly bent to the inside, with fore and hind legs moving on the same track, so that the hind legs do not swing outward or come inward. To achieve this the rider has to co-ordinate his hands and legs (see page 18). It is also important to prevent the horse from falling in to the inside of the circle (a very common fault), achieved by using the inside leg on the girth (further behind would push the quarter out). Avoid neck reining with the

Below and below right: As the horse starts to turn the rider twists his shoulders to keep them parallel with those of his horse. His outside leg can be seen resting against the horse, to be brought into play if the hindquarters swing out. The other vital aid is the outside rein, which is used to regulate the pace.

inside rein (a natural reaction) because, although this might stop the horse falling in, it will give him the wrong bend and make him stiff through his back.

Remember that in changing direction the bend in the neck should be altered to the inside.

Transitions from a slower to a faster pace

The aim is to keep the rein contact and the outline of the horse the same, so the rider must not lean forward and let the horse go faster, but sit upright and urge him forward with his seat and legs. The first step of the new pace should be high and upward, ie, the horse should not be pushed forward on to his forehand. From the walk to the trot both legs of the rider should close on the horse. From the trot to the canter the inside leg

is applied with a series of nudges on the girth. This is better than one hard one, which might startle the horse and lead to a change of outline. The outside leg is applied behind the girth: gently, if the horse tends to swing his quarters in: strongly if they come outward.

Transitions from a faster to a slower pace

Here, the aim is not to pull the horse backwards (the horse usually resists this by going above the bit), but simply not to allow him to go on at a faster pace. The rider sits deep in the saddle and applies the legs, pushing the horse to a resistant hand. From the canter to the trot, the rider sits deep in the saddle, while his hands resist the forward draw instead of following the movement of the canter. At the first step of the trot the horse must

be ridden forward to ensure the hindquarters are engaged. The same principle is followed when moving from the trot to the walk, and into a halt.

As the horse learns to relax during the transitions, he can be asked to go directly from the canter to the walk. Do not attempt this too early, however, or he will be too stiff in the back, will be unable to lower his hindquarters and will either go heavy on the hands, falling onto his shoulder, or resist by going above the bit and becoming hollow in the back. With this more demanding transition, extra encouragement from the rider's seat and legs is needed to get the horse to place his hindquarters well underneath. Make the transition progressive and not too abrupt as this produces resistances.

Training should bring out the best in the horse, by building up his confidence and agility through progressive work. In jumping, this means starting with poles and cavaletti so that the period between not jumping and jumping is so short that the horse is not aware of it. Try to ensure that the progress is never forced so that the progress can remain relaxed.

The cavaletti

The cavaletti consists of a pole 3m (10ft) in length that is bolted to a cross piece at either end so that it can be used at three heights simply by turning it over on to different sides. The longer the sections of the cross piece, the higher these heights will be, but the normal measurements are a 92cm (3ft) cross piece so the bar can be 25cm (10in), 38cm (15in) or 48cm (19in) high.

No training stable should be without cavaletti, which are easy to make, carry and adjust in height. When walking or trotting over them, the horse has to lift his legs high, which flexes the joints and teaches him to concentrate and to co-ordinate his limbs. By placing the cavaletti at equal distances apart, you develop the horse's rhythm; and putting them at a set distance in front of a fence ensures that the horse will take the right length of stride before take-off, without learning to accelerate and flatten.

To start with, use poles on the ground. As with all other obstacles, the horse should be shown them first. As long as the horse has time to look at them and sniff them, he has no excuse for stopping in fright. The rider, too, knows that he must ride firmly.

Start with one pole and then add more progressively (up to eight) at 1.2m (4ft) to 1.5m (5ft) intervals depending upon the size of the horse's stride. During all jumping training, it helps to have an assistant who can give advice, move poles and adjust distances.

As soon as the pupil has learned first to walk and then to trot over the poles calmly and without losing rhythm, then cavaletti can be introduced. They should be at the lowest height at first and the rider should aim at developing a springy rhythmical trot over them.

By introducing variations, the rider can teach his mount to lengthen or shorten his stride. When he is taking one stride at the trot between each cavaletti the distance between them can be extended to 3m (10ft) or more or less, according to the pupil. The distances should be shortened or lengthened by a few inches at a time, eventually introducing two short distances followed by two long ones (but never vice versa).

Below: Jumping a series of cavaletti at the canter. They have been placed 3m (10ft) apart, which is an easy distance for the average horse. Right: Three trotting poles 1.2-1.5m (4-5ft) apart have been placed in front of a hog's back made out of cavaletti. The poles make the horse flex his hocks.

The horse can then be taught to canter over cavaletti, popping straight in and out (2-3m/6-10ft apart). At the end of the line a parallel or hog's back could be placed (see picture) at either 3m (10ft) or 6m (20ft) from the last single cavaletti.

Another excellent exercise is to put the cavaletti in a circle with a diameter of about 20m (65ft) placing them either 1.5m (5ft) apart for trotting or 2.5-3m (8-10ft) for cantering. Alternatively, cavaletti can be scattered around, so that the horse can be trotted over them out of turns, on angles or in succession.

At all times the horse should trot or canter over the cavaletti with rhythm, balance and calmness. The rider must approach them as if there were nothing there. Tensing up, which spoils the horse's rhythm, can be overcome by breathing deeply or by shutting the eyes when on a straight line for the cavaletti.

The exercises may be carried out at the sitting or posting (rising) trot. More control and greater activity of the hindquarters is achieved at the sitting trot and it is therefore preferable unless the horse is too weak and stiff in the back to accept the rider's continual weight, or unless the rider has an insecure or heavy seat and finds it difficult to sit softly.

The distances mentioned are not standard. Horses and ponies have different lengths of stride, and sloping ground or heavy going (such as sand) also affect the length of stride. Trainers must use their common sense, and if in doubt experiment with the cavaletti at their lowest. If the distance appears wrong, change it immediately and do not persevere under the illusion that it ought to be right—there are no hard-and-fast measurements.

If the horse gets in a muddle because either the exercise was too difficult for him or a mistake had been made in the distance, go back to a simpler exercise.

A horse's jumping is difficult to improve but easy to spoil. Consequently it is vital to have an ideal to aim for, to keep a check on progress and, if the horse is failing to keep up the standard, to seek advice from an expert. Ideally, the horse should approach the fence in a balanced, calm manner, listening to the rider and with a rhythmic stride. He should then jump the fence with a bascule (lowering his head and neck and rounding his back so that it forms an arc), because this is the most efficient way of clearing a fence. On landing, he should re-establish the balanced, calm, rhythmical pace of the approach. Jumping in this way calls for relatively little mental and physical effort.

It is easy to hinder or destroy a horse's natural ability by getting him over-excited or allowing him to jump very flat or to refuse to jump. With few exceptions, these problems arise because rider and horse are advancing too fast, so that the horse fails to understand what is expected of him, finds jumping difficult and loses confidence. If this happens, the horse must immediately be taken back to the early stages and given some more work — some on the flat to get him obedient, and some over poles and cavaletti to help restore his rhythm and agility. The rate of progress will depend not only on the horse's natural ability but also on that of the rider. If they are both learning together then great patience and thoughtful training are needed.

Jumping without a rider
Most trainers believe that a horse should be without a rider when he is introduced to fences. It is wise to extend this stage if the rider has had little experience of teaching horses to jump. Jumping loose forces the horse to think for himself and relieves him of the anxiety of carrying a rider. It can take place on the lunge, or in an indoor or fenced school, or down a chute (enclosed lane) of fences. Riders lacking the latter facilities will have to make do with lungeing, and this is just as effective if the lunger works carefully.

In lungeing it is important, as always ,to ask for only a little improvement at a time. Start with a pole on the ground before progressing to cavaletti and after a few days to a fence. Remember to show the horse each obstacle before asking him to go over it, and position the animal so that he arrives at the middle of the obstacle, and has two or three straight strides before having to take off. This

Above: On take-off the handler loosens contact on the lunge rein so the horse can lower his head. Red and white poles act as wings.

means that the lunger will have to be very active, moving quickly to get his pupil in the right place.

When the fence is introduced always place wings or sloping poles on either side to discourage the horse from running out, and ensure that the wings are low so that the lunge rein cannot get caught in them. When the horse is in the air, see that he has freedom to lower his head (the lunge rein must not be tight and the horse should not wear side reins). Finally, do not ask too much by starting jumping before he has warmed up with at least ten minutes at the trot and canter on the flat. Do not jump the horse for more than two or three consecutive circuits, but give him regular breaks of three or four circuits on the flat.

If the horse is to be jumped free in an enclosed school, start with a low fence, built with very large wings to prevent him from running out. Two or more assistants are needed to cover the school so that the pupil can be quietly but firmly encouraged (with the voice and cracking whips) to keep going around and

straight toward the fences.

Training a horse loose is invaluable as long as he is not excited through confused controls and does not discover, through incompetent or hesitant handling, that it is easier to go around the fence than over the top.

Jumping with the rider

When the horse has learned while free how to clear a fence in a relaxed manner, then the rider can take over. It is, however, an excellent idea to continue giving him occasional lessons free. The variety is good for him, and so is the opportunity to jump without relying on the rider.

The best way of introducing a fence is by extending the cavaletti lesson. For a 16hh horse, a 61cm (2ft) post and rails can be placed 6m (20ft) away from the last of three trotting poles or cavaletti at 1.5m (5ft) apart. In this way, as long as the rider helps the horse to keep up the rhythm and impulsion, he will arrive in a good place for take-off.

The rider is a vital aid in getting the horse to go calmly and confidently toward the fences. As he rides toward the fence he must reassure the animal that he is there to help, not to hinder. The reassurance comes largely from the rider's legs, which should feel as if they were enclosing the horse, and the tightening of the seat and legs on the approach encourages forward momentum. Some trainers like to give their horses a loose rein so that they learn to look after themselves and there is no risk of interference to the mouth from the rider. For competent riders, however, maintaining a light contact on the mouth (but not hooking or pulling) makes it easier to keep up the rhythm and to activate the hind legs. Choose one method or the other and stick to it. It is disturbing for the horse to expect a contact and lose it in the stride before take-off. Unfortunately, this is a common fault among riders, which makes it difficult for the animal to keep balanced, and can even ruin his confidence.

For the rider, the take-off can be tricky. At the trot it is difficult to judge the exact moment of take-off and the rider must be relaxed and have a good enough seat to be able to follow the horse's movements. If he anticipates the take-off he will unbalance his pupil; if he gets left behind, he may jab him in the mouth, which will make the horse fearful of using his head and neck. Unless the rider is confident of being able to follow the horse, it is best to jump on a loose rein and to put one hand on a neck strap.

Gridwork

Although most trainers prefer to introduce the early obstacles by setting them up after one or more cavaletti, opinions differ over the next stage of training. Some like to continue over single fences, others over grids (a line of fences with none, one or two strides between each). The danger of the grid is that unless distances are set correctly and measured frequently to ensure that fences have not been moved, they can create traps, perhaps causing a horse to crash into a fence. This could damage the horse's confidence, and it is best not to use grids unless there is an assistant to monitor their measurements.

A correctly measured grid builds up a horse's confidence, as the animal will always arrive at an easy take-off position. The rider can sit quietly without having to pull him back or push him forward, and this helps the animal to keep his balance and rhythm. Most important, however, the distances between the grid fences can be intentionally altered. A shorter distance teaches the horse to take shorter strides, to get close to the obstacles for take-off and to bascule to clear them. A greater distance encourages him to

Below: The two cavaletti help to engage the horse's hindquarters.

Below: The horse is in the middle of his non-jumping stride.

Below: The horse is about to take off, quite close to the fence.

extend his stride, to take off further back and to stretch himself in the air. The grids are thus excellent gymnastic exercises.

It is best always to start the grid line with one or two cavaletti or poles, as this helps to relax both horse and rider. The next fence can be 6m (20ft) away and the following 7.5m (23ft) apart for one stride or 10.5m (33ft) for two. The longer distance allows the horse to break into a canter. The fences can be between 61cm (2ft) and 1.07m (3ft 6in) high, and if a parallel is introduced the distance should be measured from the centre of the two poles.

Single fences

At first, single fences should be very low, between 61cm and 92cm (2-3ft), and it is best to jump them from the trot because the slower pace forces the horse to bascule in order to clear them. Here again, it is important to keep

up a rhythm, so if the animal darts toward a fence, act as if not intending to jump it, and circle the horse quietly to one side. Re-establish the rhythm and try again. Remember not to haul the horse out at the last moment, as this might get him into the habit of running out or stopping.

Try to build a variety of fences to jump. At first, they should not be too alarming or painful to the horse if he knocks them down. Later, however, the fences should be made more imposing to encourage a horse to put in a better jump. A fairly solid fence will teach an animal that it is wiser to try to clear them.

A horse that can approach a 92 cm (3ft) fence with a good outline at a rhythmical, balanced trot and jump it with a good bascule can be considered to have completed his basic schooling both on the flat and over fences. He should now be ready to specialize.

Below: The horse is rounding himself well; the rider sits quietly.

Below: The horse is sizing up the upright poles one stride ahead.

Below: The rider is in a very good position as the horse leaps well.

Below: On landing note how the horse's pasterns are bent.

For many centuries, Europeans have concentrated on the technique of riding, building up a large network of riding schools and developing a highly efficient system for producing trainers.

Riding schools and centres

Europeans are still the leaders in the world of equestrian education but other countries are following suit and today riding schools and centres are mushrooming all over the world. The facilities they offer range from a few ancient, work-worn ponies to the immaculate stables, indoor schools and extensive outdoor facilities of most up-to-date equestrian centres.

The United Kingdom

In the UK there are some 4,000 licensed riding schools, and it is illegal for anyone to accept payment for giving riding lessons on his own horse without first obtaining a license.

The classified pages of a telephone directory and advertisements in the local newspaper will yield the names of local riding schools; but such sources cannot tell an enquirer how good the schools may be. The British Horse Society and the Association of British Riding Schools both run approval schemes: any school approved by either body must conform to certain standards of stable management and instruction.

The BHS publishes an annual booklet, *Where to Ride,* which contains a list of riding schools in the UK. The riding schools are listed in three sections, 'approved' schools (in the BHS's opinion the best), 'recognized', or 'listed'.

The Association of British Riding Schools publishes its list of approved schools in a handbook, giving details of size, range of facilities and any specialities.

The UK's leading school is the National Equestrian Centre at Stoneleigh in Warwickshire. It was opened in 1967 with a view to making it a kind of university of the horse. A large number of different

courses are run there and include refresher courses for qualified instructors to bring them up-to-date with new techniques. There are also training courses for selected young showjumpers and advanced courses taken by specialist instructors in dressage, jumping and combined training.

The United States

The American Horse Shows Association (AHSA) has set up a Riding Establishment Committee, which lays down standards to be met before a riding school can become a member of the AHSA.

In addition, state and regional Professional Horsemen Associations have member-establishments, but membership does not necessarily indicate quality of horses or instruction.

The USA's most famous centre is at Gladstone, New Jersey, which is the home of the United States Equestrian Team's show-jumping and dressage squads. The three-day event squad opened its own Facility in Hamilton, Massachusetts.

The Potomac Horse Center in Maryland has been designed for men and women of any age with some riding experience. Potomac is well-known for dressage work.

The Bit o'Luck Stables are one of the newest large centres, specializing in dressage, cross-country and stadium jumping. They have three centres: at Alachua, Florida; Buck Hill Falls, Pa; and Middleburg, Va.

In October 1974, the Walnut stud farm at Lexington, Kentucky, became the Kentucky State Horse Park, the first state park devoted to horses and horsemastership.

Australia

Riding schools providing facilities from hack-hiring to instruction in advanced equitation exist in every state. There is no official control over riding schools, apart from local Board of Health regulations and zoning regulations. Surveys of riding schools and equestrian centres are published in *Australian Horse & Rider.*

Buying a Horse

Buying a horse is an absorbing, challenging and often hazardous business. The inexperienced can be taken in by wily sellers; even the experienced can misjudge a horse's quality. To make a successful purchase 'an eye for a horse' is needed—the ability to judge a horse's potential, to notice his good and weak points. The most important aspects to analyze are conformation and movement; soundness; suitability for proposed purpose; suitability for prospective rider; the personal preferences of the prospective owner; the future home; age; and value.

CONFORMATION

The first impression is important because it covers the overall proportions and appearance of the horse. All parts of the body should together form a harmonious whole. A head that looks too heavy for the neck to carry, for example, is not only ugly but weak and is likely to cause difficulty in establishing a good head carriage.

The head

The horse's character can be reasonably judged by studying the head. An eye that is bold, round and has a kind, generous expression is a generally reliable indication of good temperament. Any experienced buyer is suspicious of a horse that flashes his eyes nervously and looks backward frequently.

The position of the eyes is also important. Those placed wide apart usually belong to a horse or pony with a generous character. A fine, elegant head is usually a sign of a well-bred horse. More common features, however, usually indicate a more sensible temperament.

The neck

By its shape and length, the neck gives an indication of the natural head carriage, and only skilled riders can improve any defects. The neck should be in proportion. If it is too short, it makes a rider feel insecure, and the horse can balance himself only by holding it rather high; if too long, it is more difficult for the horse to support.

The most elegant and strongest shape for a neck is arched (convex top line). A straight line can normally be improved by corrective training, but a ewe neck (concave top line) is usually a permanent weakness.

The angle at which the neck joins the head is also important, as this affects respiration. If the depth from the poll to the jowl is particularly long then it will be difficult for the horse to flex without creasing the windpipe and restricting the flow of air along it.

The shoulders

The horse's movement and pulling strength can be judged by the shape of the shoulder. Thus a long, sloping shoulder, allowing more freedom of movement, is best for a riding horse. Long, sweeping strides rather than restricted ones can be taken. On the other hand, a straight shoulder provides more pulling power, and is favoured for carriage horses.

The back

This is the weight-bearing area, and indicates the strength and power of the horse. A short back makes a horse more stable and powerful, and gives him a greater weight-carrying capacity. An unduly short back, however, is not so supple, and can restrict the speed and action of the horse. Although a long back does make the horse more supple, it needs to be broad, muscular and supported by powerful loins to

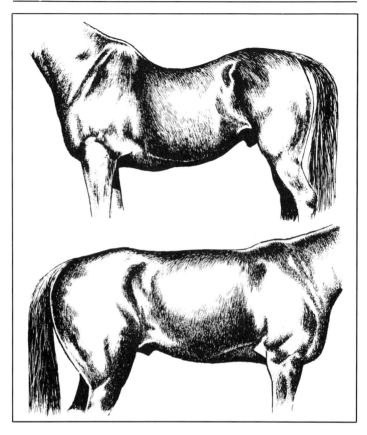

Top: This horse has a hollow back, indicating possible weakness.

Above: The back is too straight; it should be slightly concave.

offset the weakness due to its length. Check this carefully.

The shape of the back should be slightly concave, though not too much, as a hollow back is weak (but bear in mind that a horse's back becomes hollower as he grows older). Shapes to be avoided are a sway-back (lower part of back wrenched) and a roach-back (convex top line), as both normally indicate a horse that is too weak to carry heavy loads.

The quarters
The horse's propulsive power, the spring to jump and the ability to gallop, is given by the quarters; the upper line should be rounded, not falling away or flat. Large, wide quarters indicate well-developed muscles, although, if they are too wide, the horse may tend to have a rolling action of the hind legs.

The breast
This should be relatively wide, so that the forelegs can operate freely and there is plenty of room in the chest for the lungs to expand fully.

The chest
If the chest is rounded and deep, it has 'heart room', and the capacity for heavy breathing; this is a good indication of the stamina of the horse. Depth, taken to be the distance from withers to belly, just behind the elbow, is considered one of the most reliable signs of a good horse.

The forelegs

These have to take the strain of the horse's weight, and absorb the concussion that results from galloping and jumping. Consequently they are the commonest seat of lameness in the horse, and prospective buyers should be very wary of buying any animal with weaknesses in this area. The legs should be almost straight as far as the pastern, which should slope obliquely toward the foot. The knees should be neither 'in' nor bowed and the feet should face straight forward. If they are turned inward or outward, such a twist is a weakness.

The knees

These should be clean, flat and well-defined. A horse that is 'over at the knee (convex outline) puts much less strain on his tendons than one that is 'back at the knee' (concave outline). The former rarely suffers from strained tendons.

The bone

The larger the circumference (assessed by measuring the leg

Above: The croup of this horse is too straight and the tail too high.

Above: The hindquarters shown here slope too steeply in shape.

Below left: Too narrow a breast.
Below right: Too shallow a chest.

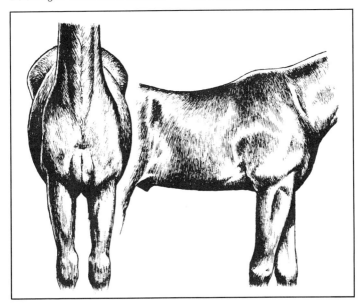

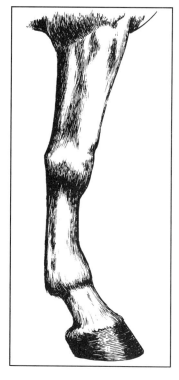

Above: Behind at the knee.

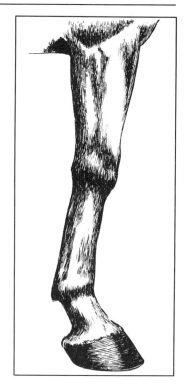

Above: Over at the knee.

below the knee), the greater the weight-carrying capacity of the horse. Also the flatter and more dense the bone, the greater the horse's chance of staying sound.

The fetlocks
These joints should be broad enough to provide a good area of articulation, and round joints must

be treated with suspicion; puffiness in the area of the fetlock joint is a sign of strain, and a warning that it cannot stand too much work. With a young horse, it suggests he has been brought on too quickly.

The pasterns
These should be neither too short

Below: A short and upright pastern.

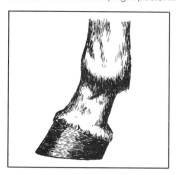

Below: A long and sloping pastern.

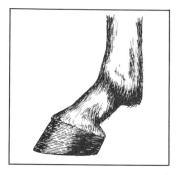

and upright, as this produces a bumpy ride; nor too long and sloping, as such pasterns are weak and place a greater strain on the tendons.

The tendons

Horses in demanding work (racing and eventing) are more liable to tendon trouble. The most reliable indications of weak tendons are:

1 Heat and soft swelling (puffiness) in the area of the tendon, which is usually evidence of a recent injury.
2 Hard swelling, in the form of either nodular lumps or overall filling, but without heat; this is evidence of a longstanding condition.
3 Heat and hard swelling.

In the case of the first, the horse may recover within a few days or it might be serious. It is better not to consider the immediate purchase of a horse in such a state but to ask to return when the heat and swelling have died down.

In the second instance, as long as the swelling is hard and cool, it is likely that the tissues have repaired. It is wise to find out, however, if the horse has been sound since the injury, and to get professional advice.

The third instance is the most serious, for it is likely to give continuous trouble.

The foot

As this is the base support for the horse it must be able to absorb jar, so a round and open-shaped hoof is best, providing a stronger and greater area to act as a shock absorber than one that is narrow, small or too upright. A large, flat foot, however, would be cumbersome. The feet should be symmetrical—matched in shape—so that the jar is shared evenly. The most important shock absorber, however, is the frog, which should be well-formed and in contact with the ground. A good blacksmith can do much to remedy defects of the frog.

Finally the material of the hoof should be strong and free from cracks, rings and any other signs of brittleness or crumbling.

The hind legs

These are a source of power and propulsion, most of which comes from the second thigh and the hock. Other points (joints, pasterns, etc) should be inspected for the same faults and good points as the front legs, paying good attention to the feet.

The second thigh

A broad, strong, muscular and relatively long second thigh is by far the most powerful.

The hock

This hardest-worked joint in the body is the source of much lameness, and weaknesses shown in it should, therefore, never be ignored. The shape should be wide from the front to the back; the quality should be

Below: A narrow foot; weak.

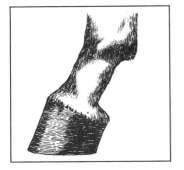

Below: A flat foot; cumbersome.

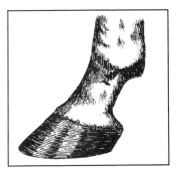

Above: A fine looking horse with good all round conformation.

high, with the bones neatly formed and well defined. Roundness and puffiness are warnings of possible

trouble developing in the hock.
 The most common defects of the hock are:

1 Cow hocks, when the points of the hocks are turned in. As long as there are no other weak-

Below: A very straight hind leg.

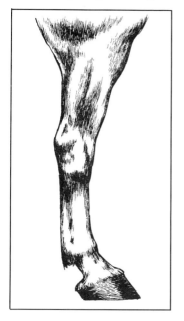

Below: A very bent hind leg.

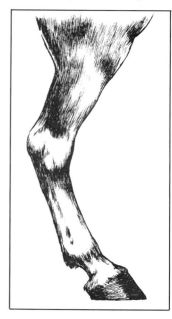

nesses of the hind legs, these are not a serious problem, although a horse with cow hocks does tend to take short, rolling steps.

2 Bowed hocks, which are the reverse of cow hocks. They usually result in the legs being set well apart and the toes turning inward. Bowed hocks usually lead to the hock twisting outward each time the leg is put to the ground, which places greater strain on this vital joint than can be easily borne.

3 Sickle hocks, in which the angle of the hocks is very acute and the hind legs are in the shape of a sickle. The more severe the angle, the greater the weakness.

4 Straight hocks, which are the opposite of sickle hocks, as the hock is structured so that there is a very large angle. Straight hocks result in rather stiff short strides and a lack of flexibility in the joints, which tends to put strain on the hind legs.

5 Curby hocks have a bony formation below the point of the hock, which can be seen when looked at from the side. Though an indication of weak hocks, this is not serious if there is no heat; and especially not if there are curbs on both hocks.

When considering the effect of any weakness of the limbs on the movement of the horse it is best to examine the shoes. Abnormal wear on the front or the side signifies that the movement is affected.

In the search for a horse it will be rare to find one without quite a number of the above defects, as the horse with perfect conformation does not exist. The main point to consider is how any defects will affect the work required of the horse. Few risks can be taken in the purchase of an eventer, but the buyer who wants a horse only for hacking need not worry too much about minor weaknesses. Remember that if a weakness does exist, but is supported by particularly sound and strong surrounding parts, there is much less cause for anxiety.

Below: Cow hocks; points turn in. *Below: Bowed hocks; toes turn in.*

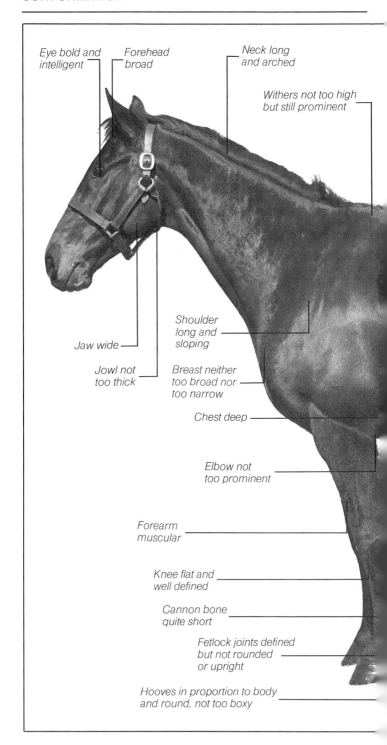

Eye bold and intelligent

Forehead broad

Neck long and arched

Withers not too high but still prominent

Shoulder long and sloping

Jaw wide

Jowl not too thick

Breast neither too broad nor too narrow

Chest deep

Elbow not too prominent

Forearm muscular

Knee flat and well defined

Cannon bone quite short

Fetlock joints defined but not rounded or upright

Hooves in proportion to body and round, not too boxy

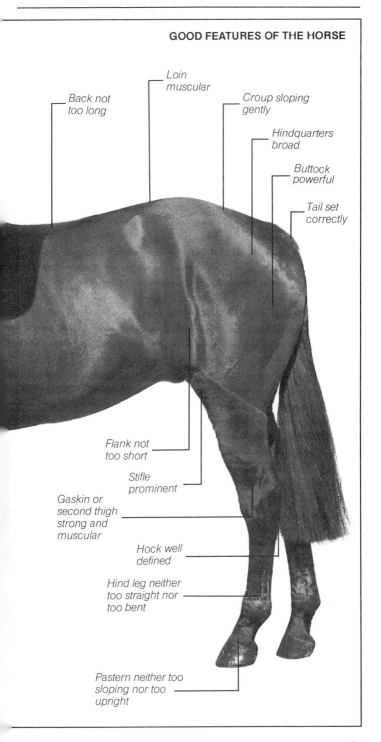

GOOD FEATURES OF THE HORSE

Loin muscular

Back not too long

Croup sloping gently

Hindquarters broad

Buttock powerful

Tail set correctly

Flank not too short

Stifle prominent

Gaskin or second thigh strong and muscular

Hock well defined

Hind leg neither too straight nor too bent

Pastern neither too sloping nor too upright

Movement

The horse should move with relatively straight strides. Swings and
twists in action often place undue
strain on one part of a limb. If the
legs move close to one another,
brushing can occur, although the
effects of this can be prevented to
some extent by the use of boots
and bandages.

The forelegs should not swing
inward and only a little outward
(too much and the horse is said to
'dish'). The hind legs, too, should
take relatively straight steps and
(most important) should come
well under the belly to provide
driving power. The joints
(especially the hocks) should
articulate freely. They must not
appear to restrict the action,
producing stiffness.

The paces should be true—ie
the walk four-time, the trot two-
time and the canter three-time.

Horses used for different purposes need different styles of
action. For those that pull
carriages, a high knee action is
acceptable; but if they are to
gallop or to perform dressage, a
freely moving shoulder and
sweeping action are better.
Generally, good jumpers do not
have too long a stride and take
athletic, springy steps, especially
at the trot. For the racehorse the
walk is the more important
indication of value, because
over-stepping by the hind foot of
the fore foot on the opposite side
and sweeping the ground is an
indication of the ability to gallop.

Soundness

A magnificent animal to whom the
proud new owner becomes nurse
and payer of veterinary bills, rather
than a rider, is of little use.
Although the experienced purchaser can spot many signs of
unsoundness, only a vet can
make a reliable diagnosis. It is
best, therefore, to arrange for a
veterinary examination before
paying for a horse. If the horse is
expensive, it is worthwhile having
X-rays taken of the feet, as these
can expose serious problems.

*When judging a horse for good
movement, always look at the
horse coming straight toward you
so that any crooked movement
becomes obvious. The bay shown
above is moving straight and well.
The grey shown below is not
moving straight but twisting his
foreleg, which puts great strain on
his joints.*

Suitability for proposed home

Buying a horse entails taking on an enormous responsibility. The amount of care and attention the animal needs, however, does vary from type to type. For example, if a purchaser has no stables and can only keep his animal at grass, then a hardy native breed (eg, Highland, Welsh Cob or Shetland) would be most suitable.

If the purchaser has a stable but is unable to provide constant supervision and daily exercise, then he can use the combined system of care when the horse is stabled by night in winter, and by day in summer, and turned out to grass for the other part of the 24 hours (in winter with a New Zealand rug). In this situation he

Below: A young rider well matched in size to a Welsh Mountain Pony. This native breed is sturdy and active — ideal as a child's pony. It can be kept at grass.

can think of buying a half-bred horse, which is more refined and usually has more performance ability than the native breed, but still has the toughness and good temperament to survive without constant attention.

If the purchaser wants an animal to carry him for long days of hunting or to do well in competitions, then he will need a horse with more class (closer to, if not wholly, Thoroughbred), and he must keep him fit. Such a horse needs constant attention in the stable and exercise every day; no purchaser should contemplate buying a high-grade refined animal unless he has the facilities and the time to cope with the enormous amount of work involved. There is, however, an option open to the ambitious rider with too little time to look after his horse, and that is to keep him at livery. As long as a reputable yard is chosen, then the professionals

can look after the animal and ride him when the owner is unable to do so.

Suitability for purpose
It is important to decide how much and what type of work will be demanded of the horse. Then the physical and temperamental assets needed to perform this work can be kept clearly in mind when examining possible animals.

Suitability for rider
It is vital that the horse is able to carry the weight of his owner, as an underhorsed rider not only looks unattractive but also puts great strain on the animal. The weight-carrying capacity of a horse is dependent on his height, depth, bone and chunkiness of body, although high-class animals—Thoroughbreds and Arabs—have denser bone and are able to carry comparatively more weight than a similarly shaped native breed.

It is important to make a fair assessment of the rider's ability, for it is no use buying a sensitive, athletic, class horse if the owner is not capable of controlling such a delicate creature. A novice rider needs a horse with a good temperament much more than one with ability. He must look for a co-operative partner, one that is not upset by confused aids and clumsy riding. There is little pleasure for the novice in riding a horse that can jump brilliantly but is highly excitable. There are exceptions, but inexperienced riders should not consider either horses with great ability (most have difficult temperaments) or Thoroughbreds (as riding these demands the greatest amount of horsemanship).

The character of the rider should be considered in relation to the type of horse to buy. The young, adventurous rider might enjoy and understand an excitable, forward-going horse. A more nervous, cautious rider will prefer a horse that needs urging on. This is one of the most important aspects of horse buying—choosing one that suits the buyer, and on whom he will produce good results. This is not necessarily the most brilliant horse that might be available.

Below: A handsome but unsuitable horse for this young rider. He will find it very difficult to control so large an animal.

Owning a horse is a pleasure, not a necessity, and the buyer who has personal preferences should, therefore, indulge them. 'If you like him, buy him' is, within reason, a good maxim.

Age

It is important to determine the age of the horse, and the prospective buyer's estimate can be confirmed by a veterinary examination. The main advantages of buying a younger horse are: he is less likely to have been spoiled or frightened; his potential has not been fully realized; and he can be trained in the buyer's

Below: Looking at a horse's teeth can give a fairly accurate idea of age. Up to the age of eight, the teeth undergo clear changes each year, after that age less so.

own way. A young horse's training, however, must be taken carefully, to avoid straining his immature limbs, although the pony, being smaller and tougher, can be brought on at a younger age than the horse. As he will have to be taught everything, he needs a patient, able rider. For the buyer who wants quick results, or who is not very capable, an older animal is advisable. This is especially the case with ponies. Wily horse-dealers break in ponies at two or three years, giving them little feed and much work. Prospective buyers are easily hoodwinked into believing the pony is older and has a good temperament. All too often, when the pony is taken to a new home and given more food and less work, his lack of training and youthful exuberance

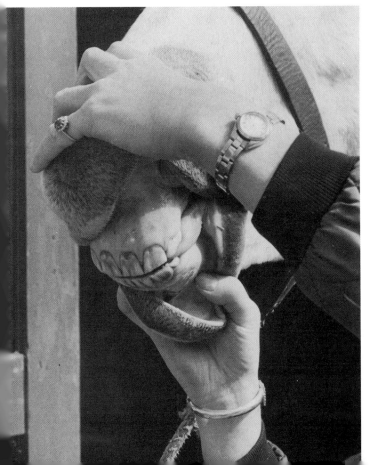

shine through, revealing him as a most unsuitable mount for a young and inexperienced rider.

Value

The price of a horse, unlike that of a car, is not necessarily an indication of quality; and certainly not of the horse's suitability for the rider. It is reasonable to ask: 'What is this horse worth to me?' It should be borne in mind, too, that upkeep is expensive. It is better for a buyer to pay a little more, if necessary, to acquire the horse he really wants; the costs of maintenance will then seem less of a burden.

Trying the horse

Start by inspecting the conformation of the animal, looking at him in and out of the stable and making note of his good points and weaknesses. Then feel for weaknesses by running the hands up the tendon, the cannon bone and over the joints, looking for splints (usually only on forelegs), heat, puffiness. Lift up the feet, to ensure they are healthy and that the frog can touch the ground. Follow this close examination by asking to see the horse led away at the walk and then trotted back. Look out for weaknesses (particularly if the animal moves straight) and consider if the movement is suitable for the purpose intended.

Finally ask for the animal to be tacked up and watch the horse's reactions (fear, anger, etc), as this gives an insight into his character and past handling. Ask the owner or groom to ride the horse and show him on the flat and over fences. (If he is too young to be ridden, ask to see him lunged or running loose.)

If you are still interested, ask for a ride. It is a good idea to take the animal to a different place — such as an open field (to ensure that he is controllable), past the stables (to ensure he is not nappy, and unwilling to obey) and, if appropriate, into traffic. Taking into account his age and training, ask him to do as much as possible before making any decisions.

If the animal is to be a hunter, then most sellers will allow prospective purchasers to try him for a few hours with the local pack. This is an opportunity that will expose most major weaknesses that the horse may have.

The purchase

If the horse is suitable, then call in the vet to make his professional examination. He can advise whether in his opinion the animal is sound, and also whether the conformation is apt for his proposed use.

Some sellers will issue a warranty (a guarantee that they will take back the horse within a certain period if the animal fails to meet any of the specifications of the warranty, such as soundness, safeness in traffic, good manners out hunting, etc). If the buyer can obtain one of these it is to his advantage.

The other arrangement of benefit to purchasers is a trial. The horse is allowed to go to the prospective owner's home for a specified period to ensure that he is suitable. Although most sellers of ponies will allow a trial period, sellers of horses are less inclined to agree to such an arrangement.

Below: When buying, it is a good idea to see the horse on a long rein to check its movement.

Horse-dealers

Buying a horse from a dealer has certain advantages. He probably has a large stock of horses, giving the customer a wider selection. If none is liked, he usually has enough contacts in the horse-bartering world to know where a suitable animal may be found. Furthermore, he may be willing to take back a horse that proves unsuitable and find another.

The dealer, however, does not sell bargains. He has his own profit to make, and the price of the horse will reflect this. Some dealers, too, become over-anxious to make a sale and are possibly not above deceiving or at least over-persuading the naive customer. Finally, the dealer is a master of the art of making a horse look good, jump well, etc, so try to look beyond the first impressions that you may have.

Private sales

As private sellers are rarely professionals, they tend to be more straightforward and less adept at covering up faults. To discover where a horse is being offered for sale privately, study newspapers and equestrian journals, which carry 'Horses for Sale' columns. For inexpensive horses, local papers are a good source. For competition horses, the specialist equestrian magazines should be scrutinized. Word-of-mouth and notices at tack shops and riding

Above: A pony sale in progress. The ponies for sale are paraded in the ring under the watchful eye of the auctioneer. Potential buyers look on and consult the catalogue.

schools are other fertile sources of information about impending sales.

Agencies

These are firms of specialists who, for a percentage of the final price, will relieve would-be buyers and sellers of the problems of searching for and finding out about a horse or locating a buyer.

Auctions

Auctions have long been the major market for Thoroughbreds, but have been less extensively used for the purchase and sale of other types of horse. With the growing interest in riding, however, many more horses for private use are changing hands by means of auction sales than in the past.

At an auction sale there is usually a good number of horses to consider. The auctioneer carries out much of the routine work, which is convenient, and the price paid is the market value. The horse can rarely be given more than an on-the-spot examination, however, which makes it difficult to form a fair picture of ability and temperament. As the buyer's inspection is so limited, weaknesses are more easily disguised and auctions have often been used as places to 'unload' bad horses. Also, bidding in itself needs experience. It is easy to be carried away by the atmosphere of the sale and to bid too highly and enthusiastically for the animal on offer in the ring.

When buying at an auction it is important to read the conditions of sale in the catalogue, particularly those covering the auctioneer's definition of a particular warranty, details of use of veterinary certificates and circumstances in which a horse is returnable. It is advisable to acquire the sale

Below: An auction held under cover. When bidding at auctions resist the temptation to offer too high a figure. Always try to examine the animals before the sale starts.

catalogue before the auction takes place so that it can be scrutinized in detail. It may be possible to inspect potential purchases at the sellers' homes.

On the day of the auction, carry out as extensive an examination as possible in the stable, have the horse led up and ask questions about it of all possible sources. If a horse is sold with a warranty, check *within the duration of the warranty* that the claims are true. If they are not, inform the auctioneers and arrange for the return of the horse. If a horse is bought with the right of re-examination by a veterinarian, arrange this for an early date. Remember that a veterinary certificate is only an expression of the opinion of a qualified practitioner; it is not a warranty with any legal weight.

TYPE OF HORSE

An event horse. He has good depth implying he has stamina. The bone is sufficient to carry his body. His limbs are strong, and his feet good, which make it more likely for him to stand up to the rigours of eventing. He has plenty of 'class' about him (not too coarse or common) which should give him the ability to gallop.

A child's pony. This is a purebred Welsh — a breed which has enormous ability but sometimes their characters are a little too wilful to be ideal for children. The conformation of this one is good — stocky, compact and with a strong front. The outlook too looks genuine and kind, which is the most vital factor in a pony to be ridden by a child.

A polo pony. Although only 15hh he is wiry and tough enough to carry a big man at a gallop. He gives the appearance of being very athletic, able to turn quickly, accelerate rapidly into a gallop and stop within a few strides. He also has to be brave enough to allow his rider to 'ride off' — ie push opponents' ponies out of the way at a gallop.

A dressage horse. Like the show jumper powerful hindquarters are needed, but not necessarily to the extent of a 'jumping bump'. These well-rounded quarters are good enough and the front is very high class — a good sloping shoulder and a long well-crested neck. With such a shoulder the movement is likely to be good. The outlook certainly is, for the eye is generous and the ears broad, which implies that the horse has that asset important in dressage — a good temperament.

A Western horse. *Although not very big he appears tough and stocky enabling him to turn quickly, accelerate and carry a heavy weight. He is similar to the polo pony but stockier in order to be able to carry his rider for long hours on the ranch. The pinto marking was thought good camouflage in times of fighting, and is today rather fashionable.*

A hunter. *He has good bone enabling him to carry a good deal of weight for the long hours of hunting. He has an intelligent, bold outlook, implying he will take care of his rider across country. He has strong hindquarters to give him the power to jump and a good sloping shoulder to help him in galloping.*

A show-jumper. *The most important part is the hindquarters, as these generate the power to spring. This horse has a distinct 'jumping bump', that is, the croup is well pointed. He has also a good hind leg and in particular a well-developed second thigh. Although the forehand is not so important this horse's strong deep sloping shoulder will help in the thrust off the ground.*

A driving horse. *This horse is out of an Irish Draught mare. There is plenty of bone, and good feet to stand the hammering on the roads. The shoulder is much straighter than that of the dressage horse, which restricts the movement but gives more pulling power. The height of about 15.1hh is good as this gives it enough strength yet makes it more manoeuvrable than a bigger horse.*

Breeding Horses

Horse-breeding is one of the most rewarding occupations
in the equestrian world. It provides the challenge of
gathering information about prospective parents' pedigrees,
performance records and conformation and using it to
try to achieve the most complementary matings. Also it gives
the great pleasure of seeing foals play, grow up and, with
luck, do well in the activity for which they were bred.

PRINCIPLES OF SELECTION

Responsibilities of the breeder

Though common sense is the
quality most essential to the aspir-
ing horse-breeder, a responsible
approach is also important. Mares
and foals need attention; only
horses used to the wild can be left
to fend for themselves. Breeding
is, moreover, a costly business;
adequate shelter and food must
be provided and veterinary assistance may sometimes be required.

Principles of selection

In view of the financial investment
and the long period before results
are achieved, considerable time
and thought should be spent in
preparation, particularly the
careful selection of parents. Selection is one of the most intriguing
aspects of breeding; in racing,
where it reaches its most
developed state, the question of
basis of selection has attracted
some of the best brains in the
equestrian world.

Establishment of clear aims is
the first stage. Two of the most
important aims are to breed a
sound animal and to establish the
type of horse required.

To increase the chances of
breeding a sound animal, parents
with hereditary defects must be
avoided. Defects include sickle
and cow hocks, feet that turn in or
out too much, very upright or
sloping pasterns, a ewe neck,
sway-back, parrot mouth, wind
that is not clear (roarers or
whistlers), eyes showing cataracts,
legs with sidebones or spavins.
The aim should be to use parents
with good conformation, as a well-

proportioned horse is not only
more pleasant to look at, but also
more likely to stay sound. Horses
that show weaknesses in conformation, however, need not be
disregarded (as must those with
hereditary defects) for breeding
purposes; they can simply be
mated with one whose shape
offsets the problem. A mare with
a short neck, for instance, can be
put to a stallion with a long neck.

It is advisable to decide what
work the offspring will be required
to carry out (showing, jumping,
farming, gymkhanas, etc), so that
the breeder can build up a clear
picture of the assets needed (ie,
size, shape, temperament, specific
ability).

After the objectives have been
decided, selection can begin, and
this is based on four sources of
information which are carefully
studied.

Appearance

Breeders can examine the
appearance, movement and
behaviour of prospective parents
knowing that many of their
features are likely to be passed on
to their progeny. The mare, in
addition, should have deep and
broad hindquarters with wide
hips, so that there is room for the
foal go grow and be born; her
genital organs and mammary
glands should also be examined
to make sure that they are normal.

Performance records

The performance records of
mares and stallions in the show-
ring, on the racecourse and

across country can be studied, as the progeny of successful parents is more likely to have ability than one from unsuccessful parents.

Pedigree

Appearance and performance records, though valuable, give an inadequate picture of genetic make-up; for instance, small mares can produce large stock. Examination of the conformation and performance of the grand-parents and great-grandparents, for example, helps to provide a more reliable basis of selection.

Produce

Studying the existing progeny of both mare and stallion is another valuable source of information on which to base selection. A stallion who 'stamps his stock' by trans-mitting definite characteristics is known as prepotent. Unfor-tunately, it takes time to prove a stallion's prepotency and the procedure for a mare is even slower. Most breeders have to rely on the previous three sources of information for their selection.

Choosing a stud

The other major consideration is to ensure that the mare will be well cared for if she is to be sent to a stud. Management of some studs is based on economy; feeding may be poor and mares with

foals, in particular, suffer from such treatment. Also, poor facilities are usually associated with low fertility in stallions. It is wise, therefore, to make a personal visit to the proposed stud, to find out as much as possible about it from other sources and, if the mare goes there, to make regular checks on her condition.

The stallion

Stallions (also known as studs or entires) vary in value from hundreds to millions of pounds or dollars, and the stud farms at which they stand range from ramshackle farm buildings to those where every possible equine luxury is provided.

A licence

In most countries, a licence must be obtained before a registered stallion can serve mares. The licence is issued after a veterinary examination has confirmed that the stallion will not pass on any hereditary disease, physical abnormality or infection.

Service fees

Fees are charged for mares visiting a stallion, and there are a number of ways this can be paid. For the services of the most valuable Thoroughbred stallions it is normal either to buy a share in

the stallion (up to 40 may be issued), or to buy a nomination that entitles the purchaser to send his mare for a service in that year. Nominations are usually bought at special auctions.

In general, however, a specified charge is made, either a straight fee demanded upon service or a fee payable only if a foal is born or the mare is certified in foal in the autumn. In the first case, the terms usually allow for a free return if the mare proves to be barren or the foal is born dead.

The stallions in the UK and USA are mainly privately owned, although some of those in England receive government subsidies. The UK scheme is operated through the Hunter Improvement Society, which receives a grant from the government to give selected stallions a premium. Consequently stallion owners can charge lower fees, and the services of the better horses are brought within the reach of most owners of mares.

The major contribution by governments towards breeding, however, is through their national studs. In the UK this is confined to Thoroughbred horses, but over most of Europe the national studs house stallions ranging from ponies to riding horses to work horses.

The success of a stallion
This is measured by both his ability to breed good progeny and his fertility rate.

His chances of breeding good produce are increased if good mares are sent to him. In the early years when he is unproven these are best attracted by having good stud facilities where owners of mares know their property will be well treated, by advertising, and by the stallion possessing assets required in progeny (conformation, temperament, performance record, good pedigree).

Although a high fertility rate is inherent it can be improved by ensuring that the stallion is kept fit and contented.

Care of the stallion
In the past, stallions have often been treated as dangerous animals; it is now established, however, that the more normal their handling, the more reasonably they behave.

Stabling
The stallion can be stabled near other horses, because he enjoys their company, but it is inadvisable

Below: The long-backed stallion at far left would be a bad partner for the mare on the right, but would be suitable for the shorter mare illustrated in the centre.

to have mares in season too close for both their sakes.

Handling

This requires a combination of firmness and sympathy. The stallion must grow to trust and respect his handler, who should never show fear. In the case of ponies, Arabs and similar types, confident handling is not too difficult; but with larger and more excitable entires (eg Thorough-breds), skill, courage and great understanding are required.

Below: A stallion being led by the stud groom to his mare. He is on a long lead line for the service. The stick is carried as stallions tend to bite, and is used to give him something to nibble. The halter is left on in case the bridle should break. He has no shoes behind to reduce the risk of damage.

Fitness

Some stallions serve more than 100 mares in a season, which is very strenuous work, so fitness is essential if high fertility is to be maintained.

The many tougher, less valuable stallions that live out and run with the mares require no special work to get fit. Most valuable stallions, however, are kept in. Some do have a small paddock or sand pit, with high, tough fencing, in which to run free; but they still need more work.

In the past, stallions were led out on regular walks lasting an hour or 90 minutes. This method of exercising is expensive and time-consuming, however, so lungeing or riding is more often used today. Both need skilful assistants; riding, in particular, calls for high-class horsemanship to ensure that these eruptive

creatures remain under control.

Feeding
During the stallion's rest time energy foods must be reduced, but as the working period approaches again they should be increased, together with proteins. Care must be taken not to give so much energy-producing food that the result is an unmanageable stallion. Skilful feeding is vital to health, well-being and fertility.

Worming, tooth filing and foot trimming
All these should be carried out at regular intervals. Any pain or indigestion will make a stallion reluctant to serve mares.

The mare
The heat, also called oestrum or season, lasts between five and seven days and normally occurs

every three weeks, from spring to early autumn. Mares with foals come into season for two to four days beginning seven to ten days after foaling. It is only when the mare is in season that insemination can take place.

Puberty
This usually occurs at 15-24 months, though it sometimes does not take place until four years of age. It is thought inadvisable to serve mares before three years (except for well-grown two-year-olds).

Covering
In most cases mares are covered in the spring, so that the foal can benefit from the spring grass a year later. The fourth time a mare comes into season is more likely to produce successful results. Thoroughbreds intended for racing need to be covered earlier, however, so that their progeny is as mature as possible for the two- and three-year-old races. In the UK, February 15th is the official start of the Thoroughbred stud season.

A mare to be covered should be neither too fat nor too fit, but she will accept the stallion only when she is in season. She indicates that she is in season by seeking the company of other mares, raising her tail, passing urine frequently, with 'vulval winking' and protruding clitoris (a rod-like organ at the lip of the vulva), discharging mucus, and showing willingness to accept the stallion in the process known as 'teasing' or 'trying'.

Aids to getting a mare in season
The presence of a stallion, frequent teasing, the presence of other mares in season, and veterinary assistance such as hormone injections will all help get a mare in season.

Teasing or trying means taking the mare to the stallion and observing her reactions. If she is not in season, she may attack the stallion with teeth and hooves, so

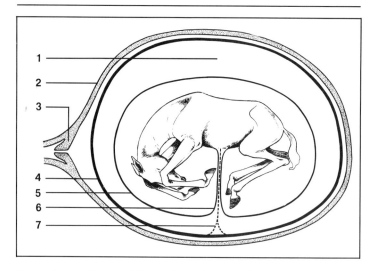

The embryo in the womb *(Above)*
1 *Allantoic fluid*
2 *Wall of the uterus*
3 *Cervix*
4 *Placenta*
5 *Amnion*
6 *Umbilical cord*
7 *Blood vessels running between the foetus and the placenta*

precautions are necessary. Such precautions include having a padded partition between the two horses, using a less valuable stallion called a teaser (if ready to be covered, the mare adopts a mating position, holding her tail to one side) and putting the mare in service hobbles and/or boots.

The service

This is usually carried out twice during the period a mare is in season. The fourth day is generally considered the best. It is advisable to have the mare swabbed before the service, which can be done only when she is in season, to ensure that she is clean.

A mare that has 'held' (is in foal) will refuse to accept a stallion when tried at her next scheduled heat periods (three weeks and six weeks). The cycle of sexual potency in a horse is, however, very irregular; up to eight weeks may pass between heats. Another danger is that pregnant mares can have 'false heats'; if served during these, they may 'slip' (give premature birth to) their foals. Consequently, the mare must be examined regularly to ensure that she does not come back into season.

Pregnancy

The mare's failure to come back into season and rejecting the stallion is a sign of pregnancy, a veterinarian can examine the uterus. To confirm, use a blood test 50 days after mating and/or a urine test after 110 days.

Duration of pregnancy

Average duration is 11 months (336 days). A variation of ten days either way is normal, however; and with maiden mares the variation might be as much as two weeks either way.

The foetus

This develops within an outer membrane (bag of waters, or allantois) and an inner envelope (foal kell, or amnion), both of which contain fluid that insulates the foetus against blows or shocks. Nourishment of the foetus is achieved by a flow of blood between mare and foetus. The umbilical (navel) vein, enclosed in the navel cord, is the other connection between the dam and the growing foetus.

Abortion (slipping the foal)
Kicks, blows, colic, chills, dusty poor food, over-exertion or infection can all cause abortion, and every precaution must be taken to prevent the mare from being subjected to these risks.

Work during pregnancy
The mare needs exercise right up to the time of foaling, but work should be graded; for the first five months, anything but exceptionally strenuous work is permissible. After this, the work should be gradually reduced; the mare should not be taken across rough terrain or over-exerted. During the last three and a half months, except for the very tough breeds, running free is the only advisable exercise.

Feeding
This will depend on the breed or type of mare. Ponies need only a few oats to supplement the grass in the winter time; Thoroughbreds will need much more supplementary food.

Points to remember
The foetus grows fastest in the second half of pregnancy, so the mare will need more food then. Too rich or dusty food can be harmful. Too little food will result in the mare's drawing on her own reserves, but too much bulk food will put pressure on the stomach.

During the last three weeks of pregnancy, reduce bulk food by half because there is less room in the mare's stomach.

Give her plenty of grass, and a bran mash once or twice a week, as there is a tendency for her to become constipated. Give supplements, available from most food manufacturers, and supplies of boiled linseed.

Below: A mare in foal. The pregnancy usually lasts about 336 days, during which time work loads should be gradually reduced but reasonable exercise maintained.

The foaling stall or box

This is needed for all but the tough breeds that foal outside, and should be at least 3·65m (12ft) square. It should be cleaned, disinfected and bedded down deeply; straw must be banked up the sides of the walls and door to help prevent draughts. The temperature should be kept at about 15°C (59°F). If possible, there should be a means of observing the mare without disturbing her.

The veterinarian

Especially in the case of Thoroughbred mares and/or if there are only inexperienced attendants available, a veterinarian may be needed during foaling. Consequently a veterinarian should be found who has stated willingness to attend and the telephone number must be placed in a prominent place.

Equipment

It is important that this should be readily available. Equipment includes two buckets that can be filled with warm water at the onset of labour; an old bucket for the afterbirth; cotton wool or gauze (gamgee); antiseptic powder or lotion for foal's navel stump; liquid paraffin, towels and soap.

Care of mare before foaling

Cut down the amount of hay, and correct, with a bran mash, any tendency for the droppings to harden. Gently handle the udder (mammary glands) to familiarize the mare (especially a maiden mare) with the sensation.

Indication of foaling

The udder starts to enlarge and is seen to be square when viewed from behind; this is known as 'bagging up' and can occur up to two weeks before foaling.

'Waxing up' takes place (drops of honey-like secretion form at the end of the teats), and although this usually happens in the last 24 hours before foaling it has been known to occur weeks before.

'Softening of the bones' occurs two weeks to a few hours before foaling, causing grooves to appear on either side of the root of the tail. The grooves are caused by the relaxation of muscles attached to the pelvis, to ease the passage of the foal. But it is possible for the mare to show none of these signs before foaling.

Signs of imminent foaling

The mare becomes restless, swishes her tail and starts to sweat as the time for foaling approaches. She may stale (pass urine) and get down and up again. The normal time for foaling to start is in the early hours of the morning.

Foaling down

The more natural the conditions and the less fussing done, the happier the mare will be, so stay out of the box as much as possible. Although most foalings are uneventful, it is advisable to have an experienced assistant available.

The normal contractions may not be seen. They start by being feeble and infrequent (one every five or ten minutes); but they should gradually become stronger and more frequent (one every half minute). Normally, within an hour from the start of contractions, the greyish water bag (the outer membrane of the foetus) appears between the lips of the vulva, then breaks to reveal the foal's forelegs wrapped in the yellowish membrane of the amnion.

When to seek veterinary advice

As long as the mare appears to be making reasonable progress, she is best left alone. However, if she is continually lying down and rising again without progress being made, and if the contractions become less frequent and/or more than an hour has passed since they started, then veterinary assistance should be sought in case serious difficulties arise.

Checking position of foal

When the foal appears under the tail, the position should be checked; the legs should be examined to see that knees, not hocks, are presenting. If the hocks are visible, then it is a breech presentation and a veterinarian or experienced helper is needed.

An experienced assistant can examine the mare to feel if the foal is in the correct 'diving' position (ie, both forefeet first and head straight and slightly behind).

Before checking the position, the assistant should clean his hands and wrists with disinfectant and lubricate them with liquid paraffin. After this a skilled person can slide a hand into the birth passage and, if any problems are felt, make gentle manipulative adjustment. In the case of the slightest doubt, the veterinarian should be called.

A breech presentation is when the hind legs appear first. As the

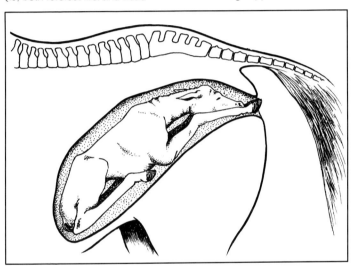

Above: A normal presentation.　　　*Below: A breech presentation.*

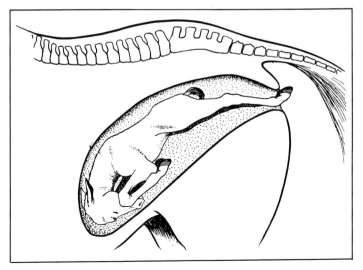

pelvis of the foal is broader than the skull, this angle of presentation makes foaling more difficult. The danger is that the umbilical cord is easily broken; if broken too soon, it can suffocate the foal. An experienced assistant may be able to pull the foal gently downwards and out (*never* straight) from the mare; but professional help is normally advisable.

Appearance of the foal

In a normal foaling, the chest and shoulders will follow after the forelegs appear, and the foal will then slide out, leaving only the last part of the hindquarters in the mare.

If the amnion does not burst after this process, the foal will suffocate; if necessary, the amnion should be broken by applying pressure between the foal's feet, while protecting his eyes from the straw.

At all times, care must be taken to disturb the mare as little as possible and not to try to hurry the process.

The umbilical cord should remain intact, because it supplies the foal with blood. Only when the foal starts to kick, freeing the hind legs, should the cord break. If this does not happen within a few minutes, the cord can be cut through with sterilized scissors at least four inches from the foal's belly. The stump should then be dressed with antiseptic powder or lotion. The cord should *not* be tied.

The amnion can be stripped from the foal and the mare encouraged to lick her offspring. This is the best means of stimulating the circulation and getting the foal dry. If the mare will not do it, the foal should be rubbed with a towel for about a quarter of an hour.

The afterbirth can then be tied up with twine so that it hangs at about the level of the hocks.

Care of the mare and foal

Healthy foals rise to their feet from 15 to 90 minutes after birth and start sucking milk. If the foal is weak, he may need assistance in standing up and finding his mother's udder. If the mare is a maiden or ticklish she may need to be held while the foal learns to suck. It is best to leave the mare alone until she has licked the foal; then she can be given a bran mash mixed with some linseed.

A stoppage
(no bowel movement)

This in the foal can be dangerous. Normally the foal should pass a small, hard piece of wax to free the anus within four to five hours of birth. If he does not and is standing with his tail up, then a mild enema, 1-2l (1¾-3½pt) of lukewarm soapy water, should be given. If there is no success after 18 hours, a veterinarian should be called.

If the mare does not cleanse (expel the afterbirth)

If this has not occurred four hours after foaling, a veterinarian should be called.

Aftercare of mare and foal

For the first few days, the mare and foal (except for hardy breeds) are best kept indoors. Then they can be let out to graze, and, depending on the weather and the type of horse, can soon be left out all the time or brought in only at night.

Feeding

In the first few days after foaling the food is intended to have a laxative effect. Bran mashes are best. Supplementary food is needed throughout the summer, according to the type of mare and the degree of nourishment to be gained from grass. Thoroughbreds need 5-7kg (12-15lb) oats, boiled linseed and 7-9kg (15-20lb) hay. Most ponies need about 450g (1lb) oats and no hay as long as the grass is good. The important point, however, is to use common sense and if the mare and/or foal start going back, to give them more hard and bulk feed. Foals will soon begin to eat oats and Thoroughbreds can be given up to 450g (1lb) for each month of their life.

Inadequate milk production
This may occasionally be a problem. If the mare is not producing enough milk the foal will be seen repeatedly trying to suck. In this case the mare should be given more protein (clover, lucerne, bran and linseed) and if this does not improve the milk supply, the veterinarian must be consulted.

Worming
This is extremely important; the mare should be wormed three weeks to a month before foaling, and then not again until after she

Below: A mare with her foal, just three weeks old. They should stay together for at least four months.

has been covered. The foal can be first wormed at eight weeks and then every month. The veterinarian will prescribe a dosage.

The feet
The foal's feet must be taken care of. They need regular trimming and picking out. If there are any deformities, corrections can often be made by the blacksmith; success is more likely when the bone is still relatively soft.

Weaning
The mare should not be separated from her progeny until the fourth month at the earliest. Thoroughbreds (except those that are weak and poorly formed) are usually weaned at five months, and other breeds at six months. If the mare is not in foal, weaning can be left until about eight months, as long as the mare is

keeping in good condition.

Preparation for weaning
The mare's concentrates should be cut down in order to reduce her milk production. Mares out at grass are brought in seven to ten days before weaning, and the foals encouraged to learn to eat grain and hay. These should be given to them in containers separate from the mother's.

A stable or stall should be thickly bedded and any projections likely to injure the foal removed. For the last few days, the stable need not be mucked out; the mare's smell will remain in the box. The mare is led out quickly and taken far enough away to ensure that neither mare nor foal will hear the other's whinnies.

The foal is happier if left with other youngsters and he can be

turned out to grass with them after two or three days. The mare's milk dries off better if the udder is left alone. Milk her only if she is very full, as milking encourages further milk production.

Care of weaners
Supplementary feeding is necessary in the autumn after weaning because the grass is not so rich. A balance must be struck between over-feeding, which causes limb troubles, and under-feeding, which restricts growth. Good hay should be basic, plus up to 2·3kg (5lb) crushed oats (depending on breed), 450g (1lb) bran, mineral supplements, and small doses of cod liver oil and linseed.

Below: Young foals, only a few days old, enjoy each other's company and the freedom to roam in a well managed and spacious paddock.

Shelter
This is necessary during the winter. If stabled at night, however, the youngsters should be allowed to run free for exercise during the daylight hours.

Worming
After weaning this is essential, preferably following a veterinary prescription.

Growth
This is at its fastest during the first year, when 80 percent of the growth in height occurs. In the second year, the bone strengthens and the body deepens. A lack of care at these stages cannot be compensated for later.

Colts and fillies
These must be separated not later than 18 months.

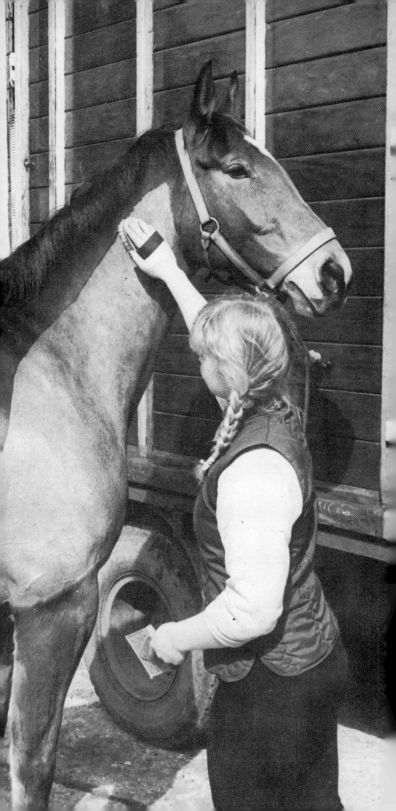

Care of the Horse

Horse riding has gained many new recruits. All over the world children and adults are taking up riding. This is a great development for the horse world, but only for the horses themselves if they are cared for with responsibility and knowledge. The following pages provide the vital information necessary for the horse's well-being, whether he is at grass, in the stable, ill or in the best of health. Everybody who looks after a horse or horses should be acquainted with this information.

AT GRASS

Supervision of horses at grass

Horses at grass have to be supervised. Otherwise they may damage themselves by kicking at one another or getting caught up in fences and gates. They can also very quickly lose condition through illness and bad weather. Daily checks are essential to ensure their well-being.

It is also important to handle livestock. Horses that are approached every day and patted, even when not being ridden, are unlikely to develop the infuriating habit of refusing to be caught.

The teeth of horses must be checked regularly. Rough edges on teeth make eating difficult and animals with this problem tend to lose condition. Feet, too, need constant attention. If the animal is not working, it is best to take the hind shoes off to reduce the risk of kicks damaging a field mate. Front shoes may be left on, but they must be removed regularly and hooves pared back. If the front shoes are taken off, the hooves must be trimmed at regular intervals and the feet examined for signs of cracking or crumbling. Many people recommend toe-clips as a good means of avoiding this.

The management of grassland

It is usually considered that about two to three acres per horse is sufficient. But it will be adequate only if the fields are looked after so that there is a good cover- ing of grass. They should not be allowed to become weed-ridden,

bare or poached so badly that there are potholes, ruts and mud. This means that looking after horses at grass also entails an elementary knowledge of grass management.

Horses are not good grazers. Unless it is a very large area, a field continuously grazed by them will become 'horse sick'. This means that the horses have cropped down the succulent grass and left the coarse and unpalatable remainder, so that the height of the grass is very uneven. In addition, their droppings further this unevenness by restricting growth where they fall and promoting tufts of weeds around them. Droppings are also a cause of red worm infestation of the field. It is important, therefore, to give the field a rest from horses (rotation) and to treat the grass.

Rotation

The best way of organizing rotation is to divide the land into small paddocks (if necessary, as small as half an acre) rather than have one large area. One area can then be grazed while the others are rested. A field should not be left full of horses until it is completely bare, for this makes it difficult for the grass to grow again. Ideally, when the horses are taken off they should be replaced by cattle, which are complementary grazers to them. Cattle like the long tufts, so they will level up the grass, and, as red worms do not survive when taken into their bodies, they also reduce

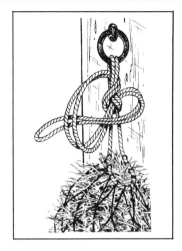

worm infestation. If there are no cattle to graze the land, the long tufts of grass should be cut down by hand or topped with a machine.

Harrowing and rolling

The second aspect of grass management is intelligent treatment of the grass. This entails chain harrowing and, if possible, rolling. Chain harrowing both aerates the soil by pulling out moss and matted growth and scatters harmful droppings. Many new horse owners will no doubt be horrified to read of the need to harrow horse-bound fields, envisaging expensive investments in a tractor and harrow. But frequently there is a friendly farmer nearby who will help by lending his machines, or harrows can be bought cheaply secondhand, and then towed by a truck, a Land Rover, or even a small car where the land is dry. Or, as happens in an increasing number of stables, a horse can be driven as well as ridden, and harrowing provides a very practical exercise for him. Finally, if all this fails, the fork and rake can be taken out for a few hours of good healthy work. If you find the effort tiring, remember that at most major studs the droppings are collected daily by hand.

The rolling of pastures is advisable, even if it is not as essential as harrowing. The treatment compacts the soil around the roots of the herbage after they have been pulled at and loosened by grazing horses. Heavy rains and frost disturb and loosen the topsoil, and compression by rolling will aid plant growth.

Fertilizing

Rotation, harrowing and rolling prevent pastures becoming horse sick and promote a good growth of grass. Growth can also be stimulated by fertilizing and the extra cost can be set against the fact that the additional grass will provide more feed. It is advisable to get a soil analysis made by an agricultural body, who can then suggest which materials are needed to counteract deficiencies. The most common recommendations are lime, basic slag (phosphatic fertilizer), potash salts (especially for sandy soils), nitrogen and simply manure, although the last should be applied only in the autumn and on fields destined for a hay crop in the spring, not for grazing.

Drainage

The final important improvement that can be made to keep grassland in good order is drainage. This is not so necessary for sandy and chalk land, which usually

drains adequately by itself, but in the case of clay it is often essential. Without drainage a clay soil is usually so boggy in winter that if the horses are turned out on it they will damage the grass by poaching it and probably get mud fever; in addition, there is unlikely to be much aeration in the subsoil, and this restricts plant growth. The digging of ditches around the field, and constant attention to keep them clear, helps drainage, but in the long run it is usually worth the expense of pipe drainage.

Feeding

Proper management of the grass will bring enormous gains in the feed value to grazing stock. However, no amount of care and attention will turn winter grass into nourishing foodstuff. Only in early spring to summer is the grass really rich, and by autumn it has lost nearly every beneficial quality except its value as bulk. This means that the majority of horses at grass will need supplementary feeding. No hard and fast rules can be made about this; the supervisor of the livestock must keep continual watch on their condition. As soon as an animal starts to lose weight, food must be provided — initially hay, and then, as condition deteriorates further, grain.

Native or wild breeds will need little, if any, supplementary feeding,

Above left to right: A round feed tin, a haynet tied up, a wooden feed box on a fence and a hay rack placed high up on a wall.

except in very bad weather. The more refined the breed, however, the greater the need to supplement the animal's natural diet. It should be added that even with supplementary feeding some horses, especially Thoroughbreds, suffer dreadfully from wintering out; so if stabling a horse is impossible it is more sensible to buy a hardy type that can withstand the rigours of winter.

There are times when the eating of grass must be restricted. In spring, when the grass is very rich, greedy horses often fill themselves to bursting point. This makes them too fat for their limbs, and can lead to the painful disease of laminitis. Consequently a horse that has such gluttonous habits should either be put on bare pasture, or be left free to eat the grass for only a few hours each day.

The other occasion when the eating of grass must be restricted is when the horse is being worked off grass. An animal will damage his limbs and his wind if asked to work hard when he is too fat. He will also need energy food, as grass only provides him with bulk.

The amount to feed at grass depends largely on common

sense, but the following points should be taken into account: the condition of the horse; the type of horse; the state of the grass; the season of the year; whether or not any work is being demanded of the grass-kept animal.

Utensils for feeding

Laying the hay out on the ground is very wasteful, as much of it will be trodden over and never eaten. It is better to use haynets, or even to buy one of the large hay racks built specifically for this purpose.

To feed grain, heavy round feeding bins are best, as light feeding bins get turned over easily.

Water

A constant supply of fresh, clean water is essential. A horse drinks about 35l (8gal) a day. An unpolluted stream is a suitable source of water, but stagnant ponds or pools must be fenced off. A large drinking trough is the easiest container; this can be in the form of an old enamel bath tub.

Shelter

The ideal field has some natural shelter, such as a stand of trees or a high hedge, which should provide the shade necessary in summer and the required protection from the wind and rain in winter. But such a natural shelter offers inadequate protection in snow and heavy rain, and actually attracts the flies that are such a menace to horses in the summertime. An artificial shelter can protect livestock against these hazards and, although horses will rarely use it except in extreme conditions, it is still worthwhile, especially as it can also provide a useful place for feeding.

An artificial field shelter need not be an elaborate structure provided it is sound enough to withstand winds. It should be at least the size of a loose box and be completely open on one side, but not into the sun; a narrow door might lead to quarrelling between animals, with the possibility of one horse being either permanently excluded or

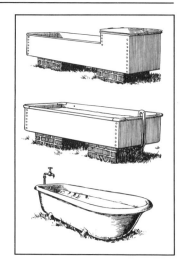

*Top: A self-filling water tank.
Centre: A tank which has to be filled by turning on a tap, but this is underneath so the horse cannot be hurt by it.
Bottom: A horse could be injured by the tap or the lip around the bath.*

trapped inside by the horses that are outside the shelter.

The safety of a field

A field is safe for horses only when there is a strong fence around its perimeter and when there are no objects in it that could cause damage, such as broken glass or pieces of wood etc.

The fence

It is worth spending money and time on a top-quality fence to avoid the inconvenience and danger of animals straying into the countryside and along the roads; poor fencing is one of the most common causes of horses being cut and damaged. Any fence must be high enough to stop horses jumping out—a minimum of about 1.13m (3ft 9in)—and strong enough to withstand being rubbed against, and it must have no pointed edges.

Of all forms of enclosure, stout post-and-rail (also called 'Man o'War') fencing, preferably three- or four-barred, is the best, both for appearance and for durability. A well-kept cut-and-laid hedge runs a close second. Hedges, unfortunately, are apt to develop weak spots and an inner rail may be necessary to prevent animals from pushing their way through. Stone walls are attractive and strong, but should be checked to see that they have not cracked and that the mortar is still intact. If they are drystone, make sure that none of the stones has shifted. Most people today, however, settle for wire, which is an excellent form of fencing if it has been properly erected. Plain, heavy-gauge, galvanized wire tightly strung between wooden creosoted posts is relatively cheap, and relatively safe provided that the lowest strand is no more than 30cm (1ft) from the ground and the wire does not sag. Electrified wire is becoming quite popular in the USA, and

Below: Two designs of field shelter with hay racks fixed inside.

appears to be surprisingly safe as the shock and jolt upon contact discourages the horse without injuring him.

There are types of fencing that can damage horses: these include barbed wire (especially if it is sagging), chicken mesh, spiked iron railings and sharp-pointed chestnut palings.

The gate

The gate needs to be easy for humans to open and close, but impossible for horses (it is surprising how ingenious a determined animal can be). Well-fitted five-bar gates are ideal; other means of closing and opening include slip rails secured by pins, or frame gates covered by galvanized steel mesh.

Poisonous plants and dangerous objects

The field should be checked, for glass bottles, cans, pieces of metal and plastic bags are often thrown

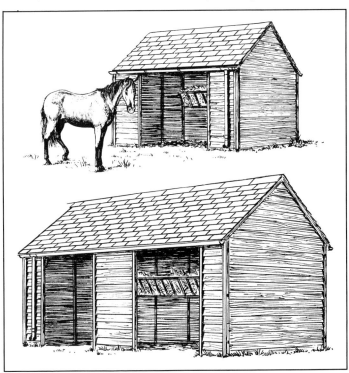

over the fence by passers-by, especially when a public footpath borders the field. Bottles and cans can lame a horse for life and it is not unknown for an animal to die after eating a plastic bag.

Any rabbit stops should be blocked up, as a horse can easily put his foot down one and this is especially dangerous to galloping animals.

Poisonous plants must be found and removed. Yew is particularly poisonous and dead clippings from this tree are fatal, as dead ragwort can be. Deadly nightshade

Below from top to bottom: Post and rail fence (safe but expensive), plain wire (safe if tight), broken barbed wire (very dangerous) and stone wall (safe if maintained).

is also toxic. Growing buttercups are poisonous, but the bitter taste of this plant makes most horses leave it alone. (In fact, once buttercups are cut and dried in hay, they completely lose their toxicity and are highly nutritious.) When ingested over a period of time, bracken may prove poisonous, although horses living in areas where bracken is common usually develop an immunity to it. Acorns, if eaten in large quantities, can have serious effects. Remember to check outside the fence as well as within, as horses will almost certainly stretch over to eat anything tempting that is within their reach.

Symptoms of poisoning
Purging, dryness of the mouth, dis-

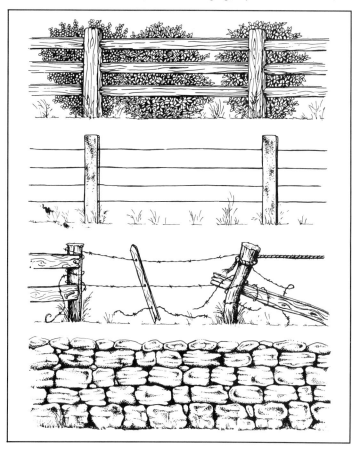

tension of the stomach, colic, excessive flow of saliva, giddiness, dilated pupils, convulsions or even paralysis are all indications of possible poisoning. If these develop in a horse at grass, it is important to act quickly. Take the victim into a stable and call the veterinarian.

Horses in work

Most horses, and all ponies, can be worked off grass. This has the advantage of avoiding the time-consuming routine of keeping them in a stable or stall. It also means that the animals need not be ridden every day, for they can exercise themselves. Care must be taken, however, to increase gradually the amount of work done off grass. Do not expect immediate fitness, and never demand fast work, or work of long duration, of grass-fed animals.

Grass provides bulk, but not energy food; so horses that are being hard ridden will need supplementary food (see pages 94-101). The most common subjects for working off grass are children's horses in the school vacations, and it is a good idea to start feeding them a few weeks before the vacation begins.

There are two other important points to bear in mind when grass-kept horses are in work. The first is that in cold weather the horse relies on the grease in his coat to keep him warm. In autumn and winter, therefore, grooming should be minimal, restricted merely to getting off the mud. The second point is that horses off grass, with shaggy coats, often sweat a great deal. If colds and colic are to be avoided, the animals must not be turned out until they are completely dry.

Keeping a horse at grass is less demanding than keeping him in the stable and, as long as he is cared for in a responsible fashion, can be very successful.

Right: Some common plants of the temperate regions known to poison horses (Latin names in brackets).

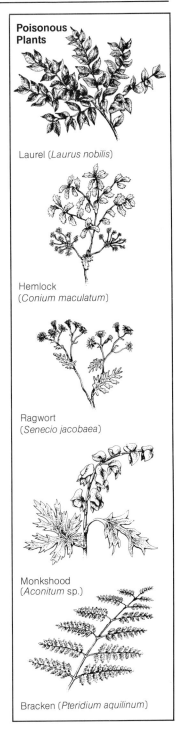

Poisonous Plants

Laurel (*Laurus nobilis*)

Hemlock
(*Conium maculatum*)

Ragwort
(*Senecio jacobaea*)

Monkshood
(*Aconitum* sp.)

Bracken (*Pteridium aquilinum*)

Reasons for stabling a horse

A horse may be stabled because the amount of work expected of him requires him to be in a fit condition, when he must carry no surplus flesh and his muscles must be firm, and this is impossible to achieve in a field. He has to become capable of arduous work without showing signs of distress, such as sweating or blowing, and to recover quickly from prolonged exertion. This hard condition takes time to achieve and is maintained only by giving enough of the correct type of food and the right amount of exercise. Such control is possible only in the stable.

Another reason for stabling a horse is that the animal may be too thin-skinned or constitutionally delicate to live out in all weathers. Some breeds have become so refined that they have lost the ability of native and wild breeds to bear bad weather. They cannot be left in the field throughout the winter months; if they were, they would lose condition even with special feeding supplements.

At board or livery

A delicate breed of horse, or one needed for hard work, has therefore to be stabled; but for owners who have neither the time nor the facilities to stable their horse there is an alternative — to keep him at board or livery. This is an expensive procedure. There are two ways of cutting costs, but both entail risks. The first is to choose a riding school and allow them to use the animal for others to ride. As long as he has a tolerant temperament and is used only by good riders, the system is satisfactory; but it is likely that at some time the horse will be treated carelessly, and possibly spoilt, by inexperienced or rough riders.

The second way of reducing costs is to choose a cut-rate stable. But, unless the lower price is due to the stable being run by a hard-working family business, the chances are that the costs are cut at the expense of your horse's food, exercise and general

attention. It is important to carry out extensive research into possible stables, to determine whether the stable management is good and the exercising of the horses safe and efficient. Most countries have an officially organized system, run by the National Federation, under which riding schools and stables are inspected and graded. You should examine this list, and ask the opinion of people who already have horses in the proposed stables.

If you can pay the cost of boarding or livery, it is generally worthwhile to spend a little extra money to ensure that the horse's treatment will be first class. You will also be able to enjoy better hacking, schooling, and jumping facilities when you go to ride him.

When the stables have been chosen, the best way of ensuring that the horse is properly cared for is to take a keen interest in his condition and to make a habit of

discussing (without cross-examining) what work he has done in your absence. This interest will help to keep the stable managers on their toes and will also enable you to recognize quickly any deterioration in the well-being of the horse.

The stable
Any stable must conform to basic standards in size, strength, safety, ventilation, insulation and drainage. If you take over an existing stable, you should check to ensure that it conforms to the standards discussed below. If it is necessary to build, whether by converting such buildings as barns, garages, or cattle sheds, or by starting from scratch, then make certain that the plans conform to these same standards.

New stables can be either custom built, or prefabricated versions erected on a concrete base. The second is probably the

Above: A good example of well-made custom-built stables. This is probably the easiest and safest type of stable to build, providing secure comfort for the horse.

simpler and there are a number of manufacturers, producing stalls and stables of varying quality and size, who will provide plans and estimates. Most of these manufacturers will also erect the stables, but it may be cheaper to have it done by a local builder or even to do it yourself, if you have the necessary skill.

If you are building a new stable it will probably be necessary to get planning permission, and to adhere to local regulations about drainage and so on. These restrictions vary, usually according to how built-up the area is. It is worth taking the trouble to find out about local regulations. By keeping within them you will avoid later trouble with the authorities.

Below: A horse in a well-equipped stall (stable) with the window protected by a grill and a fitted manger in the corner for feed.

Above left and above: Horses in straight stalls with ball and rope.

The site should preferably be close to existing electricity and water supplies, as the stable will require both these services. It is usually best for the stable to face into the midday sun, and care should be taken that the prevailing wind will not blow straight through the doors. When designing the layout it is worth thinking about the view. Some owners prefer to give their horses something interesting to look at so that they do not become bored; others advocate a peaceful prospect for their animals so that they can rest. The preference depends largely on the work of the horse: those wanting quiet for their horses generally work them hard so that they are less likely to have the energy to get bored. Race-horses are a good example.

The stable, if built from scratch, should be laid out on 'time and motion' principles: in other words, there should be the least possible distance to cover to the vital sectors—feed room, storage facilities, tack room and manure pile.

The stables can be either straight stalls or loose boxes. In a straight stall the horse is always tied up by a rope or chain attached to his headcollar and running through a ring or hole in the manger to a light weight that rests on the floor of the stable. This gives him freedom of movement and enables him to lie down easily. The advantages of these stalls are that they can be relatively small, cleaning them out is much simpler because all the droppings are in one place, they are cheaper and easier to construct, and the horse is under better control. On the other hand, there is not much freedom for the occupants, and they tend to get bored staring at a wall all the time. In the UK and USA, where most owners are unusually sympathetic towards their horses' feelings, these stalls are rarely seen; but all over Europe, where labour for stablework is hard to come by, they are very common.

A box stall or loose box does enable the horses to move around, and must be more comfortable for the animal. But make sure that it is large enough to minimize the risk of a horse getting hurt or cast. This is when a horse rolls over, and his legs are stopped in mid-air by the wall. Lying on his back, he is unable to roll to the original position, and so is trapped until humans can hold his legs and pull him over.

The size will depend on the height of its occupant but the table below gives an idea of the size to choose for a box stall or loose box. Anyone choosing a small size for a small pony should remember that smaller ponies are often succeeded by bigger ones.

The doorway must be wide enough to allow the horse to pass through without bumping against the frame. It should therefore be at least 1.5m (4½ft) wide, preferably more, and not less than 2.25m (7½ft) high. Most stables have Dutch doors (in halves), although internal boxes in a barn may have only the lower half, or a grille instead of a solid top portion. Both halves should open up a full 180°, so that they can be fastened back against the stable wall. Bolts should be carefully fitted to prevent the horse from opening the door. The lower half should be fitted with a foot-operated kick-bolt at the bottom, or a conventional bolt, as well as a bolt at the top.

Special bolts can be bought that the horse cannot open, for many mischievous horses find out how to nuzzle open a bolt, and owners may find them either trotting

around on investigatory tours or getting through dangerously large quantities of foodstuff in the feed room.

Ventilation should allow plenty of fresh air, but no draughts, as these at best make a horse uncomfortable, and at worst start chills and make the animal stiff. The wall should therefore be free of cracks and holes. Windows that open should be hinged at the base so that the wind blows in at the top. Whether or not to keep the top doors shut is a debatable point. It depends partly on whether the stable faces into the wind and partly on the work of the occupant. If a horse has to face cold winds and rain when being worked (hunting, for instance), then it is probably better not to coddle him too much in the stable, and to leave the top door open. If the animal leads a protected existence, however, and if a shiny coat would be of advantage, then he can be kept much warmer in the stable, although the atmosphere should never be allowed to become stuffy.

Insulation of stables is not essential, but is certainly of benefit. An extra layer on the wall will help to keep it cooler when the weather is hot, and warmer when the weather is cold. The second layer also makes it safer for a horse that tends to kick in the stable.

Roofs should be chosen for their insulation properties. Corrugated iron, although cheap, should not be used, because it is hot in summer and cold in winter. Wood or shingle covering is better.

STABLE CHART

Size of animal	Width	Length	Height
under 10hh	2¾m (9ft)	2¾m (9ft)	2½m (8½ft)
10-12hh	3m (10ft)	3m (10ft)	2¾m (9ft)
13-14.2hh	3¼m (11ft)	3¼m (11ft)	2¾m (9ft)
14.3-16.2hh	3½m (12ft)	3½m (12ft)	3m (10ft)
16.3-17hh	4m (13ft)	4m (13ft)	3m (10ft)
sick box foaling box	3½m (12ft)	4¾m (16ft)	3½-4¼m (12-14ft)

Above: A cast horse that cannot get his off foreleg and hind leg on the ground to give him the impetus to roll back. To help him up sit on his neck to keep his head on the ground, which will stop him struggling and hurting himself. Get an assistant to put a rope around both hind legs and a rope around both forelegs. Get off the neck and pull on the ropes to roll him back over so that he can get to his feet on his own.

Fittings are best kept to a minimum, to reduce the risk of a horse damaging himself on projections.

Windows provide the benefits of light and air, but can be dangerous if not protected. Horses can break them, and broken glass in the manger or on the floor may have serious consequences. It is therefore important to erect a grille on the inside of the window. If this is not possible, some wire mesh is usually sufficient protection.

Some horse-keepers do not have a manger fitted. Instead they give the feed in a container on the floor, which can be removed as soon as it has been cleared. This is satisfactory only if the feed tin is too heavy to be kicked or nuzzled over. For this reason plastic versions (except those specially designed not to be upset) should never be used. Iron feed tins or wooden feed boxes are thought to be the best types for general use.

The majority of stables, however, use fitted mangers, and these should be breast high. When choosing a type, ensure that it can be cleaned easily, and that it is broad enough to prevent the horse biting it and deep enough to stop the animal brushing the food out with his muzzle. Bars at the corners will also prevent food being brushed out.

Some stables use fitted hay racks, but there are disadvantages with these. The dust tends to fall into the eyes of the horse when he pulls out the hay, and also all over the person who fills it. It is better to use a haynet, which can be attached to a ring. The ring must be fitted firmly and at eye level. It is usual to fit a second similar ring to which the horse can be tied up.

It does save a great deal of time if automatically filling water bowls are fitted, but these should be sited away from the haynet and manger so that they do not become clogged with food. If using a bucket for water, a bucket container can be fitted breast high, but it is quite satisfactory to leave the bucket on the floor if it is heavy enough not to get upset.

All electric fittings must be out of the horse's reach. Switches should be of the outdoor variety and sited outside the stall or stable.

The floor of the stall or stable should be hard-wearing, non-porous and non-slip, and should slope slightly towards a drain or gully at one end. Concrete is the most popular form of flooring, but it must be dense and well compacted, and finished with a slip-proof treatment. A restless, stamping horse can quickly break up poor-quality concrete, so it is worth paying extra for the best. If a drain is fitted inside the box, it must be protected by a grille. Alternatively, a channel can carry urine through the wall to an outside drain.

The bedding, if abundant, reduces the risk of a horse injuring himself and encourages him to lie down. The bed should therefore be clean, dry, thickly laid and banked up around the walls. To keep it in good shape you will need a barrow, a shovel, one pitchfork with two prongs and one with four, a broom, a skep for droppings (this can be a plastic laundry basket) and a sheet of sackcloth or similar tough material for carrying straw.

Mucking out usually takes place first thing in the morning, when the manure and soiled bedding are separated from the clean bedding with the pitchfork, and taken away to the manure heap in the barrow. The dry bedding is forked into a heap so that the floor can be cleaned and aired before the bedding is relaid as a thinner day-bed. During the day, droppings should be picked up in the skep and removed to the manure heap. At night, the day-bed is tossed up and the new bedding laid on top, with the sides of the bed banked up higher against the walls. A good deep bed is not wasteful.

It saves both bedding and time to adopt a deep litter system, when only the droppings and wet patches are removed (but as frequently as possible) and small amounts of fresh bedding are added daily. The bed gradually builds up, and at some stage (every week, every month or every six months) must be removed in its entirety. The proud stable manager rarely favours this method but it does save labour.

Handling the stabled horse in the stable is important towards establishing the same respectful but trusting relationship with the horse as when riding him. The animal must learn to be obedient and well-mannered, and not frightened or spoilt into becoming a kicker, biter or spiteful animal. From the first moment the handler must be gentle in action so as not to startle him, firm in requirements so as not to confuse him, and quick to reward obedience or to reprimand the animal (with the voice or a slap on the neck) if he misbehaves. At all times he should be approached from the head so that he can see what is happening. He should be talked to before any action is taken and during any handling. He will quickly learn the difference in tone between being soothed and being scolded.

Tying up is often thought unnecessary by trustful owners who may like to leave their horses free, but this is a mistake. A horse never becomes as obedient as a dog, and most of them will seize an opportunity to escape through the door. And when a horse is free in the stable, accidents happen so easily — pitchforks are stepped on, people kicked, and the like — so it is much fairer on the horse, and on everyone, to tie him up when mucking out, feeding, grooming and saddling up.

To tie the horse up, approach with the halter (headcollar) from the front, talk to him and pat his neck. Pass the free end of the rope around the neck. Put the noseband over the muzzle and the headpiece over the ears. A rope halter is then knotted on the near side of the horse, and a leather halter (headcollar) is buckled up. Lead him then to the ring on the wall and use a quick release knot.

Right: To muck out, the girl is using a four pronged pitchfork to lift the soiled bedding into the wheelbarrow. The broom and spade are left outside the stable.

Blanketing (rugging up) is necessary in all but the hottest weather for the horse kept in a stall or stable. To put it on, tie the horse up, take the blanket (rug) at the front and gently swing it over the horse to lie centrally along the back but high up on the neck. Buckle up the front and then slide back into position, but not so far that it drags on the shoulders.

If there is no surcingle attached to the blanket (rug), use a roller pad under a roller. Position this pad behind the withers and put the roller over it, ensuring that there are no twists in it at all. Buckle up the roller so that it is firm, but not squeezing the horse. Run the fingers between the roller and the rug to ensure that there are no lumps. Check that the rug is not too small, and is not pulling on the shoulders and withers, as this can make the animal sore.

In cold weather a clipped horse may need an additional blanket for warmth. This is put on first, again well forward, and slid back so that it nearly touches the

Below: This horse has been tied up correctly with the free end put through the loop so that the horse cannot pull the knot out.

root of the tail at the back. The blanket (rug) is then added, the roller done up and the free portion of the under blanket, at the front, folded back over the rug, to make it neat and stop it slipping back.

To take the blanket (rug) off, remove the roller and unfasten the front buckle. With the left hand grasp the part of the rug that is over the withers, and with the right hand the part over the back. Slide it off in the direction of the hair and fold it up four-square.

Stable routine

A timetable for a normal day in the stable is given here:

7am	Tie up horse and inspect for injury. Refill water bucket unless the stall has an automatic water fountain. Refill haynet. Muck out stable. Brush over horse without completely removing blanket (night rug). Pick out feet. Lay day-bed.
7.45am	Give the horse his first feed.
9.30am	Remove droppings. Remove rug. Saddle up and exercise the horse. On return refill water bucket.

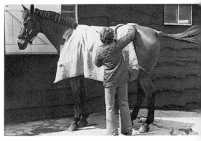

Right: The correct sequence for rugging up. From top to bottom: The blanket is thrown gently over to fall on the neck, and slid back into place. The front buckle is done up, the roller is lifted on and, unless well padded, a pad is placed underneath. It is done up and any wrinkles smoothed out. In cold weather a clipped horse may need an extra blanket for warmth.

Noon	Tie up horse. Groom thoroughly. Put on blanket (day rug). Refill water bucket. Untie horse.
12.30pm	Give second feed. Refill haynet.
4.00pm	Tie up horse and pick out feet. Remove droppings and shake up bedding. Remove blanket (day rug), brush over and put on blanket (night rug). Refill water bucket. Untie horse.
5.00pm	Give third feed.
7.30pm	Remove droppings. Lay night-bed; refill water bucket and haynet.
8.00pm	Give final feed.
Last thing at night	Visit stable to ensure all is well.

The combined system

From this timetable, it can be seen that caring for a stable horse is a full-time occupation, unless the duties can be shared. If there is no one to help during the day, or it is difficult to exercise the horse regularly, it is better to turn him out into a field in the daytime, and stable him only at night. When the weather is very hot and the flies are troublesome during the day, the procedure can be reversed so that the horse is at grass during the night.

In the winter a stabled horse, especially if he is clipped, will find the fields very cold. The New Zealand rug has been specially designed to be worn by horses at grass. It is waterproof and has special straps to keep it in place even when the wearer rolls.

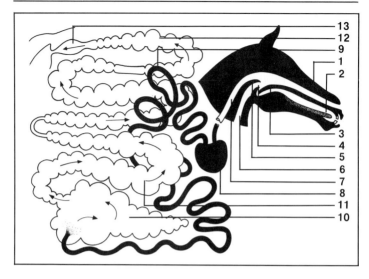

Horses have a very small stomach in relation to their size, and food passes through several digestive processes before waste matter is evacuated. The intestine narrows at various points, and bottle-necks can occur when food becomes impacted at these places; this leads to a build-up of doughy matter, the formation of gases, and ultimately an attack of colic.

It is essential, therefore, that horses should be fed small amounts several times a day and that their diet should contain plenty of fibrous foods to prevent impaction and fermentation. Grass, hay (dried grass) and, to a certain degree, bran (the outer husk of wheat grain) contain plenty of fibre. They also contain other nutrients, principally carbohydrates, some proteins, and minerals such as calcium, phosphorus and magnesium, as well as a number of essential trace elements. A horse that is required to do little work beyond gentle weekend hacking, and is living out with access to adequate grazing, needs no food other than grass in the summer and hay in the winter. Indeed, most native horses, with their powerful constitutions and extreme hardiness, fare better on a year-round diet composed entirely of grass or hay without any grain supplement.

The digestive system *(Above)*
1 *Nasal passages*
2 *Tongue*
3 *Soft palate*
4 *Larynx*
5 *Pharynx*
6 *Windpipe*
7 *Gullet*
8 *Stomach*
9 *Small intestine*
10 *Large caecum*
11 *Large colon*
12 *Small colon*
13 *Rectum*

But horses doing hard work, and refined breeds, require more proteins and carbohydrates than fields can provide. Proteins (nitrogenous substances) are needed to build and repair tissues (in particular, muscle tissue); and carbohydrates are needed for energy. Minerals and vitamins are also essential in small quantities; without them, health tends to decline, and such ailments as rickets develop in young stock.

Types of food
It is important to remember that concentrates rich in protein and carbohydrates are given in addition to grass and hay, never as substitutes. Bulk or roughage is essential to help the digestive process. Overfeeding of concen-

trates (especially protein) will upset the metabolism of the horse.

Hay

This is the staple diet of horses, however kept. The best hay for horses is seed hay, which contains a mixture of grasses especially sown for a hay crop (in other words, the hay comes from arable land where it is one of a rotation of crops). Clover hay, which is highly nutritious, should be mixed with another type of hay before feeding; on its own, it is too rich and heating for horses. Meadow hay comes from permanent grassland and may be good or bad, depending on its source. In many countries lucerne hay (alfalfa) is in common use. It is very rich in protein and a horse not used to eating it should be given only very small quantities at first.

Good-quality hay is greenish in colour, sweet smelling, free of dust, not too coarse, and between six and 18 months old. Yellow, blackish, damp or mouldy hay must be rejected, and every effort should be made to get good hay (the best if a horse is in fast work). Hay forms between one half and two thirds of the diet of a stabled horse and its quality will have a major effect on the animal's condition. During the winter months a horse may get through two tons of hay or more as part of its normal daily diet.

Bran

This is a by-product of the milling process of wheat. Although it is bulky and rich in proteins, bran contains relatively few energy-giving carbohydrates. The best bran is broad in flake, dry and not musty. It has a tendency to absorb moisture and become sour, so unless dry storage facilities are available it should be bought in small quantities.

Bran is used as a normal nutrient in daily feeds and in addition it can have a laxative effect if fed wet (dampened). Dampened bran mashes are usually given to mares in foal. In a normal feed it is

Above: Filling a haynet. The girl is taking small handfuls of hay from an opened bale, shaking them and pushing them into the net.

dampened, and is usually mixed with oats, in the ratio of three units of oats to one unit of bran.

Oats

This is the most effective energizing food for horses and must be used cautiously with spirited animals or children's mounts. Oats can be used whole but it is more usual to crush, roll or bruise them, so that the kernel is exposed to the digestive juices. This helps the process of digestion. Oats should not be crushed flat, which makes them lose their floury content, nor should they be kept for more than a few weeks after crushing, as they begin to lose their food value. The best oats are dry, without must, plump and short, more or less uniform in size and pale gold, light grey, dark chocolate brown or black in colour.

Barley

This is an excellent grain for improving condition. When used for this purpose, it should be boiled before being given to a horse. Raw barley should always be crushed and introduced to the diet very gradually. It is not a good substitute for oats if the horse is used for very demanding or fast work.

Wheat
Except in very small quantities, this is not a suitable grain for horses. It should be crushed or boiled, then fed with other concentrates.

Corn (maize)
High in energy value but poor in proteins and minerals, it has good fattening effects but should not be fed in large quantities. It should never make up more than a quarter of the grain ration. As it is rather indigestible, it is best fed flaked.

Peas and beans
These are rich in protein and they should therefore be used sparingly, and only for a horse in hard work, one whose condition has deteriorated badly, or one that is wintering

Below: Samples of the main foods normally given to horses. **1** *Barley* **2** *Oats* **3** *Compound food cubes* **4** *Carrots* **5** *Cod liver oil* **6** *Bran* **7** *Chaff* **8** *Sugar beet pulp cubes.*

out at grass. Peas and beans should be split or crushed with a hammer before being mixed with the feed.

Sugar beet
Usually available dried and pulped, this must be soaked in water overnight before being mixed with the feed. If fed dry it would swell in the stomach, and could cause colic. It is a good conditioner.

Horse cubes
Known in the USA as pellets, these contain most of the required nutrients in well-balanced proportions. According to the market for grain, they are made up of varying quantities of oats, bran, maize, barley, locust bean, linseed cake, groundnut meal, grass meal, molasses, vitamins and minerals. They have great advantages as a foodstuff. They are convenient to store, and as they provide a balanced diet they can be used on their own, making it unnecessary to mix the feed. Because they create less energy, they are an especially beneficial substitute for oats when feeding spirited horses

and children's mounts. Their only drawback is that they are relatively expensive.

Chaff
This is chopped hay or oat straw. About 450g (1lb) of chaff should be added to all feeds, as it ensures proper chewing of concentrates and acts as an abrasive on teeth. The chaff sold by feed merchants tends to be of very poor quality and is therefore of little use. The only sure way of getting good chaff is to use a chaff cutter; these can be bought secondhand, or perhaps a neighbour will lend one at regular intervals.

If neither of these alternatives is possible, chaff may be left out of the diet; although advisable, it is not essential. Bran and horse cubes both to some extent stop the horse bolting its food.

Root vegetables
These help to provide variety and a different taste for horses that are stabled. Roots are of special value to poor feeders and to horses in bad condition. Carrots are probably the best, but turnips,

mangels, swedes and parsnips are thoroughly appreciated by most horses. Roots should be sliced into finger-shaped pieces and mixed with the regular food.

Molasses
This may be sprinkled on a feed, to encourage a finicky eater or to promote a shiny coat. It should never be used to disguise mouldy, dusty or poor-quality hay. Hay in bad condition will not become more nutritious as a result of being made more palatable, and it may even be harmful.

Cod liver oil
This helps to build up condition and improve the horse's coat. As it has an unpleasant taste, manufacturers make it more attractive to shy feeders by mixing it with more tasty materials. It is then sold under a brand name as either cake or in a liquid form.

Mineral salt licks
There are a number of mineral salt licks available, which can be fixed into special containers and attached to the wall, or simply left in the manger. Some horse-keepers, however, prefer to use lumps of rock salt rather than these prepared licks.

Linseed
This is rich in oil, which makes it an excellent means of improving condition and giving gloss to a coat. It must be well cooked to destroy the poisonous enzyme that is present in raw linseed. The linseed can be made into a jelly or tea, according to the amount of water used. To make jelly, soak the linseed in water for 24 hours, then add more water and bring to the boil. After being allowed to cool, the jelly is tipped out and mixed with the feed. Linseed tea is prepared in the same way as jelly but more water is added; the resulting liquid can be used to make linseed mash. Linseed can also be bought as cubes and fed directly, which relieves the feeder of this preparation process.

A bran mash

Usually fed the night before a rest day, or after a great exertion, such as a day's hunting, it is an excellent laxative. To make it, pour boiling water over half a bucket of bran, stir it well, cover with a sack, and leave it to steam until it is cool enough to be eaten. The mash should be 'crumbled dry', neither stiff nor watery. About a quarter of an ounce (7g) of salt may be added to half a bucket of bran.

Basics of good feeding in the stable

1 Feed little and often. Times of feed will vary according to stable routine, but an acceptable time-table would be feeds at 7.45 am, 12.30 pm, 5.00 pm and 8.00 pm.

2 Feed plenty of bulk food (hay or grass). Using a haynet prevents hay from being wasted, but it should be tied securely and high enough to prevent the horse getting his feet tangled in it. A haynet should be given about three times a day, and the total quantity divided unevenly, with the smallest amount in the morning and the largest amount in the evening.

3 The amount of the feed should be adjusted according to the work being done by the horse and the size and temperament of the animal. A horse that becomes excitable and difficult to manage should have his oat ration decreased; cubes should be given instead.

4 Any change in types of food or times of feed should be gradual and spread over several days.

5 Avoid using musty, dusty food-stuffs and always dampen (but do not soak) the feed.

6 Do not work a horse hard immediately after feeding, or when the stomach is full of grass. Quiet work is possible

FEEDING CHART

TYPE OF HORSE	7.45am	12.30pm
Hunter, working or event horse more than 16hh	2lb oats, 1lb bran plus chaff, 2lb hay	3lb oats, 1lb bran plus chaff, 5lb hay
Hunter, working or event horse less than 16hh	2lb oats, 1lb bran plus chaff, 2lb hay	3lb oats, 1lb bran plus chaff, 4lb hay
14.2hh pony, working, hunting or eventing (turned out for a few hours)	2lb cubes, 1lb bran, chaff, 2lb hay	turned out
Show-jumper over 16hh	2lb oats, 1lb bran, chaff, 2lb hay	2lb oats, 1lb cubes, 1lb bran, chaff, 5lb hay
Riding horse of about 15hh (turned out by night in summer, or for a few hours during the day)	1lb oats, 2lb cubes, 1lb bran, 2lb hay	1lb oats, 2lb cubes, 1lb flaked maize, 1lb bran, chaff 3lb hay
Child's pony of about 13.2hh being worked daily (but turned out for a few hours)	1lb cubes, 1lb bran, 1lb hay	2lb cubes, 1lb bran, 2lb hay

after a small feed of 1-1.5kg (2-3lb), but after a full feed no strenuous work should be done for 1½ hours.

7 Water before feeding.

8 Always use clean feeding utensils. The trough or manger, bucket, pan or feeding bowl must be kept clean; any remains of the previous feed must be removed before a fresh feed is given.

Good feeding is an acquired skill; it demands experience and a close interest in the animals, as each individual will have varying requirements. Some animals look well on very little feed and become too excitable if fed any more; others need as much feed as they will take, to maintain their energy and condition. Although there can be no absolute rules about quantities to feed, the following table does provide a rough guide, but it must

5.00pm	8.00pm
3lb oats, 1lb bran, linseed jelly, roots, chaff	4lb oats, 1lb bran, chaff, 7lb hay
2lb oats, 1lb bran, linseed jelly, roots, chaff	3lb oats, 1lb bran, chaff, 6lb hay
2lb oats, 1lb bran, chaff	2lb oats, 1lb cubes, 1lb bran, 6lb hay
3lb oats, 1lb cubes, 1lb bran, chaff	3lb oats, 1lb cubes, 1lb bran, chaff 7lb hay
2lb oats, 1lb cubes, 1lb bran, roots, 6lb hay	
1lb oats, 2lb bran, chaff, 1lb carrots, 5lb hay	

be used in conjunction with continual observation so that any changes in condition or performance can be noted at an early stage, and the feed adjusted accordingly.

Specimen diets

NB These are for horses with a sensible temperament. If the animal becomes unmanageable, substitute cubes for oats, or turn him out to grass for a few hours each day, or do both.

In the field

For owners of horses turned out in pastures, the usual problem is when to start feeding hay in the autumn and when to stop in the spring. But so much depends on the extent and quality of the available grazing; there can be no hard and fast rules. Weather is also a factor. During a mild winter, the grass will continue to grow and will contain some nutritive value, right up to the end of the year. The wisest plan is to start offering hay in late autumn but discontinue for a while if the hay is ignored. By mid winter, however, a daily haynet will be necessary. Once the grass starts to grow again in spring, the horse should be encouraged to eat some hay; you may have to tie the animal up and give him a haynet for two or three hours each day. Too much rich grass eaten too quickly may cause colic or laminitis. By spring, it should be possible to stop giving hay.

Concentrates may be given at any time, if the horse is in work or losing condition. Ponies, however, are usually best kept on cubes. Oats often go to their heads, turning them into unruly beasts.

The feed should be taken to the field at the same time each day to avoid any impatient fretting, which can impair the digestion.

Watering

This is as important as feed to a horse. Although the animal could stay alive for about a month without food, it would die in about a week if deprived of water. As a general rule, water should be offered to horses before a meal and after exercise; watering on a full stomach, or immediately before energetic work, may cause pain and distress. Some horses, however, seem to like the opportunity of taking a light drink after a feed, and as long as they have been able to drink deeply beforehand, this should do no harm.

Watering in the stable
In the stable, water is usually contained in a bucket, which can be emptied and refilled four or five times a day. It should be placed in a corner away from the manger and haynet, so that it cannot become contaminated by loose hay or spilt feed. A bucket-holder will prevent it from being knocked over. Alternatively, an automatic

drinking bowl may be fitted in the box; the bowl should be checked regularly, however, to ensure that the mechanism is working and has not become clogged. Problems are especially likely to arise in cold weather when the supply pipes may freeze solid.

Watering in the field
Far less control over a horse's

drinking habits is possible in a field, but here the animal will most probably conform to the routine followed by horses in the wild, drinking at morning and evening but rarely in between.

A pastured (grass-kept) horse is visited less often than a stabled one, however, and it is easy to forget to check the water container at every visit. If the field possesses a running stream or an automatic water trough, fresh water will always be available. A running stream is the best watering system, provided that the ground bordering it is sound and that neither the ground nor the bed of the stream is composed of boulders or thick mud. A stagnant pond is better fenced off.

Automatic troughs draw water from pipes, with the supply being controlled by a ballcock and valve mechanism or a stop cock. The troughs should be situated in the open, away from hedges or over-hanging trees, so that several horses can drink at the same time and falling leaves will not pollute the water. If no other source is available, water must be supplied manually, by means of a hose or buckets. An old bath makes an adequate container, but it should be cleaned regularly and should be boxed in to prevent any sharp rim from injuring the horse. Buckets by themselves are unsatisfactory as they hold little water and are easily knocked over. A horse may drink as much as eight gallons during a day, so capacity is an important factor to consider.

In freezing weather, ice on the surface of the water must be frequently broken and removed. During a prolonged frost, water in the trough may freeze solid; in these circumstances, carrying water in buckets will be the only means of ensuring that your horse has enough to drink.

Left: A horse and foal enjoying excellent conditions: a large paddock with a stout post and rail fence and a sensible water trough supplied from a piped water system.

The purpose of grooming

First and foremost, grooming keeps a horse clean. It also massages, stimulates circulation of the blood and lymph, and tones up the muscles. Thus, grooming is a means of preventing disease (especially of the skin), of maintaining condition, and of improving appearance. For the horse in the stable, deprived of a natural life, daily grooming is essential to his well-being.

The grooming routine

Brief grooming, or quartering, is a five- or ten-minute grooming before a stable horse is worked. The feet are picked out and stable marks removed with a dandy brush or, if necessary, a damp sponge. The mane and tail are brushed with a body brush and put in place with a water brush. The eyes, muzzle and dock are sponged.

Grooming after exercise

When the horse returns to the stable after exercise the feet, if muddy, should be washed and then picked out. Any dry sweat marks may be removed with a dandy or body brush, but not until the coat is completely dry. If the horse is hot or wet, he may need to be sponged down before being dried off.

Thorough grooming (strapping)

Thorough grooming is the hardest part of the horse's routine; the best effects will be achieved only by 'elbow grease'.

Start with the dandy brush, to remove mud and sweat marks. This can be done only if the dirt has dried. Although it is possible to sponge marks off, it can lead to chapping and sores unless the area is dried adequately afterwards.

The field-kept horse stimulates his circulation by moving around, and the grease in his coat acts as a natural waterproofing agent. Because a horse kept in the stable has lost both these safeguards, it is best to avoid wetting the coat.

Brush off dirt wherever possible.

The real hard work starts with application of the body brush. The bristles must be driven through the horse's coat, beginning at the neck on the near side, to remove all the dirt and dried sweat. Stand far enough away from the horse to get your weight behind the brush. More force can be put into the task if the brush is held in the left hand on the nearside and the right hand on the offside. With a strong, circular motion, work the brush from the neck along the body, occasionally cleaning the brush with the curry comb. The belly, the flanks and the area between the forelegs should be covered. When grooming the hind legs, it is best to stand as close as possible at the side (not behind), so as to feel and see more easily if the horse is about to kick or move.

The head, especially around the eyes and ears, is a very sensitive area; use the brush gently but firmly. A dandy brush must never be used on the head. The mane and tail should be groomed into place and the hairs separated with the body brush. A dampened water brush can then be applied to keep the mane lying over. The tail can be bandaged to keep it in the correct shape.

The dock, eyes and nostrils should then be cleaned with the sponge, and the finishing touch is to wipe the horse over with a damp stable rubber.

A good grooming, however, should include some wisping, which both develops and hardens the muscles and stimulates the circulation. To be effective the dampened wisp must be brought down with some force on the horse to follow the lie of the hair. Aim for a rhythmical pattern of lift, down, thump and along. This wisping should be done in the regions of the muscles, ie, the shoulders and neck; the head, loins, belly and legs should not be wisped.

Setting fair (touch-ups)

Most horses have an additional

blanket or thicker rug put on them at the end of the day. This is a good opportunity to give them a quick brush-over and wisping.

The standard grooming kit *(Below)*
1 *Stable rubber (for polishing)*
2 *Sponge*
3 *Large mane comb*
4 *Sweat scraper*
5 *Hoof pick*
6 *Small mane comb*
7 *Curry comb*
8 *Grooming kit bag*
9 *Water brush*
10 *Dandy brush*
11 *Body brush*

To make a wisp
Twist some dampened hay into a rope of about 2m (7ft). At one end, arrange the rope into two loops, one slightly longer than the other. Twist each loop in turn under the rest of the rope, until there is none left. To finish, twist the end of the rope through the end of each loop and tuck in (see diagram on page 104).

To pick out the feet
Stand beside the horse's shoulder or hindquarters. Run the hand down the back of the leg towards the hoof, which the average animal

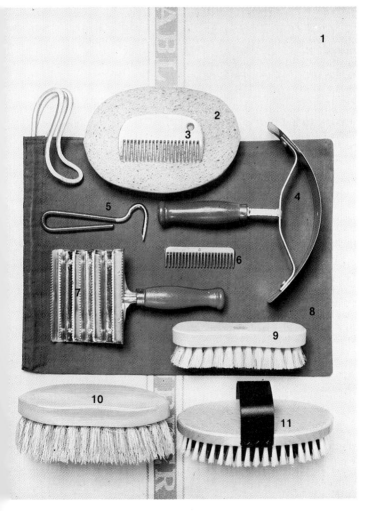

Above: Make a wisp from twisted hay by forming two loops and pulling tight as shown here.
Right: Picking out the hoof. With short strokes work towards the toe, removing all mud, dirt and stones.

will then pick up. If he does not, push on the shoulder or hind-quarters to make him transfer his weight to the other leg and pinch the back of the leg with the hand. When the leg is lifted, hold it firmly around the coronet and pick out the hoof with a blunt-ended hoof pick, starting from the heel.

The grass-kept horse
Only limited grooming is needed for animals living outside. The grease and dandruff in the coat help to waterproof the hair and keep the animal warm; it is inadvisable, therefore, to clean a grass-kept horse too vigorously, in case his natural means of protection is removed.

Grooming should be limited to picking out his feet, removing mud with a dandy brush or rubber curry comb, brushing mane and tail with a body brush, laying the mane with a water brush, and finally sponging the muzzle, eyes and dock.

The grooming machine
Grooming machines (vacuum cleaners) are a great help in busy stables. They must, however, be operated intelligently; it is easy to frighten a horse and to damage the machine. It is inadvisable to groom with them every day—normal practice is to use them once or twice a week. On the other days, the horse can be groomed by hand, a process that usually takes much less time than a normal grooming because so much of the grease and dirt has been removed from the horse's coat by the machine on the preceding day.

Removal of all or part of a thick coat is needed for horses in hard, regular work. Clipping both prevents excessive sweating and enables the horse to dry quickly afterwards. It also makes him look trim and neat, although this is not the main reason for clipping.

The first clip of the season is carried out as soon as the new winter coat is well established, usually in the autumn. The first sign that the winter coat is on the way is the disappearance of the high gloss of summer. Suddenly, the coat feels more woolly beneath the fingers as the short hairs thicken, the top hairs grow longer and the finer summer hairs begin to fall out. At work the horse sweats more easily.

Electrically operated clippers are the most efficient means of removing the coat. They are quick, easy to use after some practice and, when oiled during the cut and sharpened at intervals, give a satisfactory clip. Hand-operated clippers are good, but rather tiring to use.

Types of clip
The extent of the clipping should depend on the work the horse will be expected to do, and on how much he sweats.

A full clip
This clip is one in which all the hair is removed from the head (except muzzle and ears), neck, body and legs of the horse. This is used on heavily coated animals, on whom the hair on the legs is ugly and so thick that it becomes difficult to dry.

The hunter clip
This leaves hair on the legs as far as the elbow and top of the thighs. This protects the horse against gorse, thorns and other matter encountered in cross-country riding, and reduces the risk of heels cracking. Sometimes, a patch of hair is left on the back under the saddle to help stop rubbing, but if the hair is excessively thick it is best removed to prevent excessive sweating.

The blanket clip
This leaves most of the body hair (in the shape of a blanket) and all the leg hair. The head, neck, belly, part of the thighs and a thin strip up the back of the quarters are clipped. It is used in particular for Thoroughbreds who, because of their fine coats, do not need to have so much removed to reduce the sweating.

The trace-high clip
The briefest clip of all, this removes hair only from the belly, chest, and part of the thighs and up the back of the quarters. A strip on the underside of the neck is also sometimes removed. The trace-

Below: Clipping styles. The hunter clip (left) and blanket clip (right).

high clip is popular for horses that are to be kept out during the winter but will be hunted during winter holidays; it prevents excessive sweating without removing any of the animal's protection against the weather.

How to clip

Clipping takes time and patience. An assistant should be available to help if required.

The horse's coat should be as dry and well-groomed as possible. The most important factor is not to upset the animal. Before the clip is started, the assistant should hold the horse, talk to him, pat him, and be reassuring. If the horse becomes restless when the ticklish areas (for instance, the belly) are being clipped, the assistant can lift one of the horse's legs to prevent him from moving around.

Start clipping in the areas that are least ticklish and sensitive, such as the shoulder — not the head, groin or belly.

Ensure that the clippers do not overheat, and that the blades are sharp and do not pull the hairs; clippers must be run flat along the skin and not dug into the horse, and they should be guided, not pushed, against the lie of the coat.

Do not clip into the sides of the mane or the root of the tail, or inside the ears. The backs of the tendon and fetlock are usually better dealt with by scissors and comb. The comb and scissors should be moved upward against the hair, in the same way as a professional hairdresser trims human hair.

Care of a clipped horse

The clipped horse needs a blanket to compensate for the loss of his thick coat. A blanket made of jute or hemp and lined with wool is used in most cases, with or without an additional blanket underneath. A recent innovation in the UK is a quilted rug, which is warm and light and can be used in place of the night rug and blanket.

Right: How to braid the mane.

Mane- and tail-pulling

These tasks are forgotten by many horse owners, who perhaps worry that they may do a poor job and produce more problems than they solve. But a well-pulled mane and tail give a good appearance and, in the case of the mane, make it easier to plait for hunting or showing.

Pulling thin hair from the mane makes the ends even (scissors should never be used) and helps it to lie flat. The task is best carried out when the horse is warm and the pores of the skin are open so that hairs will come out easily and without discomfort. Always remove the hairs from the underside of the mane, and never take out more than a few hairs with each pull. It is best to do a little each day rather than keep going for a long time, which could make the animal sore.

Tail-pulling means removing (never with scissors) the short, bushy hairs from the top of the tail. It is done solely to give a neat appearance. It should not be carried out on grass-kept animals, who need the short hairs at the top of the tail to protect the region around the dock.

Mane- and tail-braiding (plaiting)

These give the final touch to the overall show-ring appearance of a horse, and show off his neck and quarters to best advantage. Braiding is also a useful means of making an unruly mane lie flat on the correct side.

Braiding the mane

The mane should be braided on the morning of the show, and the braids must be taken out at the end of the show to avoid damaging the hair by splitting or tearing.

Braids are made from withers to forelock, usually about a mane-comb's length apart. There should be an uneven number of braids up the length of the neck.

The hair is first damped with a water brush and divided into sections. Each section in turn is then braided so that the top of the braid is tight against the roots of the hair. The end is then secured, by means of a needle and thread passed through the plait and wound tightly around it, before being folded under and stitched to the braid about half way up. The resulting loop is then rolled up tightly until it forms a knob close to the poll, where it is stitched firmly in place. Sharp-pointed embroidery scissors are needed to remove the stitches at the end of the day.

Braiding with rubber bands is a quicker method, but it is difficult to achieve such a smart result as that given by needle and thread. The hair is braided in the same manner and a rubber band is looped around the long braid several times. The end is then turned up into the desired position and the band looped around the entire braid to make it secure.

Tail braiding

Tail braiding is carried out in a similar manner, starting at the top of the tail, braiding down the centre and drawing in the side hairs on the way. When the braid is two thirds of the way down the tail bone, start leaving out the side hairs. Continue the braid, using only the centre hairs. The end of the braid should be stitched and bound securely with needle and thread, doubled under and attached to the point where the braiding of the side hairs ends.

Below: How to braid the tail.

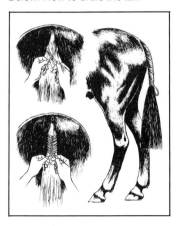

A stabled horse must be regularly exercised. Otherwise he runs the risk of swollen legs, azoturia and colic, and is also likely to show spirited behaviour when ridden. One rest day a week is acceptable, but on the evening before this it is advisable to give a laxative bran mash.

The amount of exercise given to the horse will depend on his type (Thoroughbreds need more than ponies), the type of work being prepared for (three-day eventers need more than hacks), the amount of energy food the animal is receiving (horses being given large quantities of oats need more than those on pellets [cubes]), and his fitness (a horse that has been in work for only a week requires less than one that is ready to go hunting).

Preparation for exercise

Exercise should not take place until at least one and a half hours after a large feed, or one hour after a small one. It is also advisable to take the hay away one hour before exercise, as a horse or pony stuffed full of hay will find breathing more difficult. In the case of a horse about to be put to fast work, this precaution is essential, and must be observed.

Below: Almost ready for exercise. The horse is tacked up, the Yorkshire boots are in place on the hind legs and the girl is just buckling up the brushing boots, with the straps pointing towards the hind legs.

When ready to exercise the horse, he should be tied up and quartered (see Grooming above) before tacking up. If boots or bandages are worn, these should be put on first. Yorkshire boots are used if the horse brushes his hind fetlocks; they are attached firmly just above the fetlock so that they cannot slip down. Brushing boots are used on the forelegs, and are advisable on all valuable horses as they reduce the likelihood of injuries or splints being caused by blows or brushing. The brushing boots should be put on with the ends of the straps pointing towards the hind legs. The bottom strap should be done up first, to stop the boot slipping down, and the straps should be tight enough to stop the boot passing over the fetlock joint.

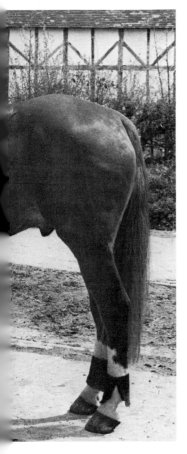

Some horse owners use exercise bandages, either because they like the additional protection these provide, or because the horse has weak tendons that need support. Others argue that this regular support to the leg prevents it hardening up to withstand the strain. Bandages need to be put on very carefully, because if they are too tight they can cause damage and if too loose they will slip. They should be applied over a layer of tissue or gamgee and should be neither so high nor so low as to interfere with the action of the joints. They should be applied firmly in the manner shown (see diagram). The tapes should be knotted in a bow at the side of the leg; not at the front or at the back, where they might interfere with the bone or the tendon. Ends of tapes should be tucked in.

If the exercise includes jumping, all but small ponies should wear over-reach boots, which are worn just above the hoof. Some varieties of these boots can be buckled into position, but many have no buckles and have to be pulled on. It is best to start by turning them inside out. The foot is then picked up and rested on the attendant's knees while the over-reach boot is held by the broader rim and pulled over the hoof. When the narrower rim is over the hoof, the boot can be turned the right way out, to hang in the correct place.

After all the necessary clothing protecting the legs is in position, the saddle and martingales, and finally the bridle, can be put on.

The horse is then ready, but in stables where turnout is considered important, hoof oil is put on the feet to add a finishing touch to his appearance.

Care after exercise

Ideally the horse's exercise should end with a walk so that he returns to the stable cool and relaxed. The bridle can then be taken off, and the horse can be tied up before the saddle and leg clothing are removed. The animal should then be inspected for any injuries and feet picked out to clear them of mud and to ensure that no stones or foreign bodies are lodged in them. The feet may be washed if muddy, but try not to get the heels wet; if this is unavoidable, take care to dry them out, or cracked heels may develop.

Depending on the stable routine, the exercised horse may be strapped immediately or merely have the saddle and bridle sweat marks brushed or sponged off before being rugged up. In the latter case the strapping can be done at a more convenient time. This is more usual, because the horse is so often warm after exercise, and a sticky sweaty coat cannot be groomed properly.

Occasionally the horse cannot be returned to the stable dry and relaxed — for instance, if his coat has been soaked by rain. In this case it is better to trot the animal back to the stable so that he is warm on arrival. Untack the horse as before and rub him down with straw, a stable rubber or an old towel. When he is reasonably dry put a cooler (sweat sheet) on or cover his back with straw. A blanket (night rug) can then be put on top, but it is advisable to turn it inside out so that the lining does not get damp. It is also best to fold the blanket back over the horse's shoulders so that the air can get to, and dry, the neck and shoulders. The vital area to keep warm is the back.

There are occasions, such as during strenuous work, or in a summer heatwave, when the horse gets very hot. Then he will need to be sponged down, preferably with buckets of lukewarm water. Some people advocate bathing him all over, whereas others just sponge the sweaty areas, fearing that too much water will take the grease out of the horse's coat and make him susceptible to chills. These objections are valid, but there is little danger if proper precautions are taken. The horse should not be bathed every day, and should be thoroughly dried before being returned to the stall or box.

The drying process starts (in the case of both a sponge and a washdown) with the sweat scraper. This is run firmly along the coat in the direction of the lay of the hair to squeeze out the water. In order to be effective the edge of the sweat scraper should be relatively sharp, and therefore should not be used on sensitive areas such as the head.

After being scraped the horse may be rubbed down. Ideally a cooler or sweat sheet should be put on, and the horse led around until dry. On returning to the stable it is a wise precaution to leave the cooler or sweat sheet on, and to put the blanket (night rug) over it, folded back and upside down.

A horse that has been hunted or worked in competitions will need special attention when he returns to his stable. Colic or chills may develop unless this treatment is

thorough. Firstly the horse should be given a drink of warm water. Then, if he likes to roll, turn him loose in a thickly bedded stable for a few minutes. Do not leave the horse, however, if he stands still and does not roll, for he must be kept warm.

Tie the horse and remove sweat and wet mud with a damp sponge. Rug him up with a cooler or sweat sheet or straw under a folded-back blanket (rug) and inspect him for any injuries. If there is dry mud on the legs, brush this off; any that remains can be washed off as long as the legs are dried immediately afterwards. The feet can then be picked out and if necessary washed, but the heels must be dried.

If his coat is not sticky with sweat, the horse can be unrugged for a few minutes and given a quick going-over with the body brush. Finally, he should be given a good warm bran mash and left to rest. Check later to ensure that the horse has eaten up and is warm enough, but has not started to sweat. If he has started to sweat he should be rubbed down and walked around. To find out if he is cold, feel his ears. If they are not warm at the base, remedies are needed. The ears themselves should be rubbed and more blankets should be put on the horse.

Some horse-keepers think they can keep their horse warmer and happier by using stable bandages.

Below: Washing down after hard exercise. The horse has been sponged down all over and the girl is using the seat scraper to remove as much of the water and sweat as possible. After a sponge down and scrape the horse should be rubbed down and led around until he is dry. Put on a cooler to prevent chills.

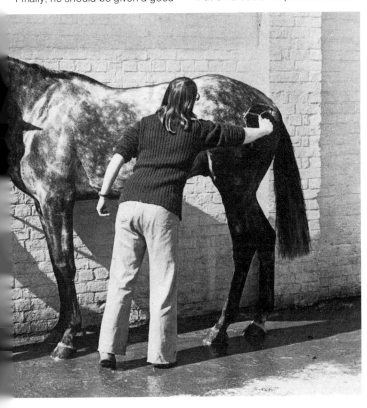

In order to make the most of a rally, competition or hunt, it is vital to plan the preparations. If this is not done, everything may be ruined by arriving too late, getting into a panic or forgetting some vital piece of equipment. But these preparations are fun, for almost everyone enjoys the excitement of anticipating the sport ahead, whether that sport is to be in the hunting field, in the competition arena or with the Pony Club. It is no hardship, therefore, to put aside time on the preceding days to organize a timetable, and to prepare the equipment, the horse and the rider.

The arrangements for transportation

The method of travel should be planned well in advance. If the event is to take place up to 16km (10 miles) away, it should be possible to hack, and an average fit horse should walk and trot the distance at 10kph (6mph). An animal that is off grass, however, should be kept to the walk as much as possible, which will reduce the average speed by about 3kph (2mph).

If the distance is too far to be hacked, those without transport will have to hire a trailer or lorry and driver, hire a trailer that they can tow behind their own car, or persuade friends to collect the horse. Whichever method is decided upon, it must be arranged well ahead of the event.

Those with their own transportation may enjoy the independence, but it does entail more work. The fuel tank, tyre pressures, and condition of the vehicle all need to be checked, in addition to preparing accommodation for the horse. The travelling compartment must be clean, and a haynet hung up to keep the animal happy on the journey. If he is expected to work hard soon after arrival, though, the filled haynet should be put out of reach until the work has been done. The vehicle should then be loaded with all the equipment needed at the rally, show or meet.

Preparation of tack and clothing

Those who travel to many events find it best to list all the necessary equipment and to keep the list in the tack room, where each item can be checked off as it is loaded into the transport. This list will vary according to the type of activity, and those who are hacking to a rally or meet do not need one at all, for nothing is needed other than the tack the horse wears. The only important thing is that the tack is cleaned the day before and inspected to make sure that it is in good order.

For those going by trailer or lorry the list expands to include a fork, shovel and brush to keep the transport clean; a haynet for the journey; a feed if the horse is to be away for a long time; a blanket (day rug) or sheet and bandages, for travelling; a cooler or sweat sheet to place under the rugs to help the horse cool down if he gets hot; a spare halter or headcollar in case one gets broken; water in a container, and a bucket from which to drink it.

If going hunting, and if the journey is not too long, it is probably easiest to transport the horse or pony tacked up, with a rug over the top of the saddle and a tail bandage to prevent any rubbing. If going to a competition, as the animal is usually more valuable and the journey longer, special clothing for travelling may be used to give the best possible protection (see Transportation below). The competition horse will also need additional equipment when he arrives, and most seasoned travellers to competitions have trunks in which to keep it. A full grooming kit will be needed; studs if the going is likely to be slippery; brushing, Yorkshire and over-reach boots, and exercise bandages, as necessary. Then there is the saddlery, which can include a line and cavesson for lungeing to get some of the spirits out of over-fresh or excitable horses. A first-aid box should be part of the kit (see page 171), and when the going is very hard this can include a cooling wash to be applied to the legs after work. A useful luxury is a mackintosh sheet to keep the horse dry in heavy rain.

Preparation of the rider
It is a tradition in the horse world to pay great attention to the turnout of the rider. A handsome effect, it is thought, gives horse and rider a feeling of pride that makes them perform just a little bit better. Although expensive and beautifully fitting clothes can be an advantage, the most valued factor is cleanliness. Gleaming boots, brushed jackets and hats and clean breeches make rack or 'off the peg' equipment look just as good as the custom-made or tailored items, and so, before any event, time must be set aside for polishing boots and washing and brushing clothes.

Clothes are not the only key to smartness; hair is often overlooked. Girls should experiment to find out how their hair can be arranged for the most becoming and tidy effect. The coiffure should be fastened securely, for overhanging branches and hedges can play havoc with any tresses that are precariously arranged. Men should consider a short hair style.

The dress for children under about 16 years can be the same for all activities. It consists of:
A riding crop.
Jodhpur boots (brown with a tweed jacket, or black with a black or blue jacket).
Spurs—but only for lazy ponies with good riders.
Jodhpurs, although children sometimes prefer breeches and top boots.
A white shirt.
A tie—if the child is a member, the Pony Club tie may be worn.
A tie pin to keep the tie from blowing around.
A waistcoat or V-necked sweater in cold weather.
A tweed jacket (although a black or blue coat may be used for smart occasions).
A riding cap (or a derby [bowler]) for hunting.
Gloves.

The riding attire for older riders should vary according to the activity, with well-kept clothes presenting a smart, neat turnout. **Hunting** has the strongest traditions with regard to dress, but

Below: Members of the hunt in traditional dress, a style known throughout the world.

certain modernizations are becoming acceptable. For instance, although a hunting whip is correct, more and more people carry a crop in the hunting field. Top boots are more normal than jodhpur boots, but modern manufacturers make such good rubber versions (which can be polished) that there is no need to buy expensive leather ones. Spurs should be worn, but a rider with a skittish animal would probably be forgiven for leaving them off. Jodhpurs may be worn, but breeches are more acceptable and are usually cheaper. It is best to buy thick ones; skimpy nylon breeches will not be warm enough. The hunting shirt is made of wool or silk, and is thus warmer than a normal shirt; it has no collar, which makes it easier to wear the hunting tie (stock). The stock can be bought ready tied but it takes only a little study and practice to tie one's own. An ordinary shirt and tie may be worn with a tweed jacket. The coat can be tweed, but it is smarter to wear black or blue. Traditionally, only the hunt servants and farmers had the right to wear a derby (bowler) or top hat: fewer and fewer hunts, however, are enforcing this rule. Gloves are essential for all but the very tough in winter time. When in doubt what to wear, ask the Master or Honorary Secretary's advice.

In competitions the dress was originally based on what was acceptable in the hunting field, but practical variations have crept in. Breeches, coats and shirts are now more lightweight, as competitors do not have to wait about for long periods in the cold and rain. The tie worn with a blue, black or red coat is rarely a stock, simply a white or blue tie. Most types of spurs and crops are accepted and the hat is normally a hunting cap.

In dressage those in the higher echelons (Prix St Georges and above) are expected to wear top hats and tail coats.

In the cross-country phase of eventing the emphasis is on protection, so crash helmets are worn. Coats are replaced by high-necked sweaters or shirts.

Riders competing in Saddle-horse classes wear saddle suits consisting of a long-skirted jacket and bell-bottomed (Kentucky) jodhpurs of the same material and colour, and occasionally a matching vest (waistcoat). Other items are a derby (bowler) or soft hat, shirt and tie, and jodhpur boots. More conservative colours are preferred for eventing classes.

Western Division riders must wear a Western-style hat, a long-sleeved shirt, and cowboy boots. The choice of trousers is left to the competitor, although most people wear either slim-cut frontier pants or jeans. Chaps should be worn.

Hunting dress *(Below)*
1 *Hunt cap*
2 *Stock (tie)*
3 *Hunt coat*
4 *Gloves*
5 *Breeches*
6 *Whip (or crop)*
7 *Garter straps*
8 *Top boots*

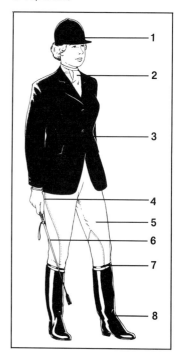

Preparation of the horse

Little can be done to prepare the horse the day before an event other than giving him an extra good grooming, and washing his mane and tail, and even this might have to be done again if they are of a light colour and get stained during the night.

If the horse is normally kept at grass, bring him in the night before if possible. This will help to keep him cleaner and save time in the morning. It is on the day of the show that so much of the work has to be done, and the vital factor is that it starts early enough to avoid panic and rush.

The initial work should consist of the normal stable routine: watering, feeding and mucking out. After this the horse can be groomed, and (if there is time) given as good a strapping as possible. For most events the mane must be braided (plaited) and the tail bandaged.

The final preparations will depend on the intended programme. Horses for rallies, and hunters, can be saddled up. Competition horses can have their legs bandaged (see page 146), and a blanket (day rug) or sheet put on for travelling.

After all this, it is to be hoped that there will be time to set things right for the return, ensuring that the mash can be prepared easily, that the horse's bed is clean and that water and hay are ready.

The preparations over, it is at last time for the start of the action.

Saddle-horse dress *(Below)*
1 *Derby*
2 *Tie*
3 *Saddle coat*
4 *Gloves*
5 *Whip*
6 *Kentucky jodhpurs*
7 *Jodhpur boots*

Western riding dress *(Below)*
1 *Western hat*
2 *Western style shirt*
3 *Gloves*
4 *Lasso*
5 *Chaps (Worn over jeans or slim-cut frontier pants)*
6 *Cowboy boots*

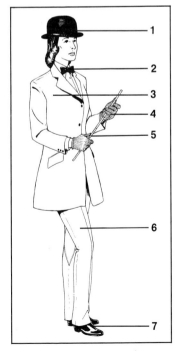

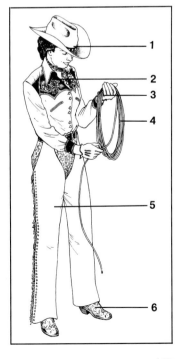

Barely 150 years ago, the only means of travelling any distance by land was on horseback. Now ironically, except on long-distance rides, mounted expeditions or pony treks, the last method to be considered for getting a horse from A to B is on his own legs. Today, horses travel by trailer, horse-box, plane, or even occasionally by ship. A few years ago trains could have been added to the list, but in most countries it is becoming less and less popular as a means of transporting horses, and in the UK the rolling stock of British Rail no longer includes a horse-wagon.

The journey

Fortunately, most horses travel well, and appear to suffer no ill effects from a long journey. The interior of a trailer or horse-box is well padded and designed to give the animal support against jolting and swaying when the vehicle is under way. A haynet should be all that is necessary to keep the horse occupied while on the move but, if desired, a light feed may be given in a nosebag.

If the journey is to take several hours, arrangements should be made for occasional stops so that

Below: This horse has been dressed for travelling. He is wearing a halter (headcollar), day rug, roller with felt pad attached, knee caps, travelling bandages, hock boots and a tail bandage.

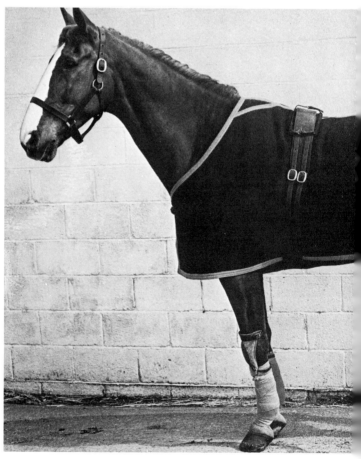

the horse can be watered. He can also be unloaded and walked around to ease any stiffness. The horse will appreciate the chance to graze quietly for 20 minutes or so. If the journey is to last more than about four hours, the diet should be fairly light during the 24 hours before departure, with the oat ration reduced by half.

Clothing
Valuable animals should be equipped with protective clothing. Flannel or wool travelling bandages should always be worn, as should a tail guard or tail bandage to stop the top of the tail being rubbed. On long journeys or for bad travellers, knee caps and hock boots are advisable to protect

these highly susceptible joints. On an air journey, when the horse may have to pass under a low beam or doorway, a poll pad is desirable to guard against injury to the top of the head. If no poll pad is available, cotton wool or foam rubber, wrapped around the headpiece of the halter or head-collar and held in place by a stable bandage, will serve instead.

All horses should wear a well-fitting halter. Blankets or rugs are necessary only if the horse is accustomed to wearing one in the stable. On a hot day, a cooler (sweat sheet) or a summer sheet is advisable.

Loading
Loading should present no problems as long as the horse has been carefully loaded and driven in the past. But it is very easy to frighten an animal by not being patient and thoughtful when first getting him accustomed to being loaded, and by driving too fast, especially before he has learned to balance himself with the strange movement. Horses must be driven smoothly and steadily, so that they are not swung off their feet when the vehicle goes around corners, or jolted backwards and forwards by heavy braking and acceleration.

If there is any possibility of a horse being a 'shy loader', or if he is travelling for the first time, the timetable should allow for delays.

The person leading a horse into the transport should walk confidently ahead, and should not look behind and pull. Staring at the horse tends to put him off going forward. Any helpers should be behind the horse.

Apart from thoughtless driving and handling, one of the main reasons for reluctance to load is fear of the ramp, which reverberates when struck by the horse's hoof. Straw may be liberally spread on it to deaden the sound, and a non-slip mat is an advantage. A reluctant traveller will sometimes enter the trailer or horse-box quite readily if he can follow a stable companion, or a feed bucket containing a few oats may tempt a greedy one. If all else fails, you may have to resort to ropes attached to the rails of the ramp and crossed behind the horse just above his hocks. Two assistants are needed to hold the loose ends of the ropes, and to tighten them as the horse and his handler approach the ramp. If ropes are not available, the linked arms of the two assistants can be used to push against the horse's rump to help loading.

Forms of road transport

Those who do not transport their horses very often may prefer to hire the services of professional transporters. Although this is relatively expensive, there are enormous benefits. The drivers are experienced in loading and driving, and the horse owner avoids the expense and worry of maintaining personal transport.

But as journeys become more frequent, it becomes inconvenient to have to rely on others. Most horse owners start by buying a trailer. These come in various sizes and can be towed behind any powerful car or jeep, which means that no special lorry license is needed. In the USA these trailers have been developed into a very sophisticated method of horse transportation, but the versions in the UK are more primitive and have disadvantages. They must be driven slowly or the trailer starts to sway, and even the largest is not suitable to carry more than two medium-sized horses.

So, particularly in the UK, horse-boxes are more popular than trailers with people who have to transport their horses for long distances. In them the horses enjoy a smoother ride, but the driver does need to be experienced to manage such a large vehicle. Today most governments require drivers to take special heavy goods vehicle tests before a license is granted to drive these vehicles.

Air travel

Though more expensive than sea travel, air travel is becoming a much more usual means of taking horses abroad. Racehorses going abroad to race are carried in freight planes. These are especially chartered by blood-stock agencies, who normally make all arrangements, including the supply of trained grooms to attend the horses on their journey. It is also possible to make private arrangements with air-ferry companies.

Travelling abroad

All over the world there are strict controls regarding the import and export of horses, and this includes temporary visits to a foreign country for races or competitions. Anyone contemplating taking a horse abroad should contact the appropriate government department, and an agent who specializes in the transport of horses, for accurate and up-to-date advice about documents required (ie, import/export license and veterinary certificates).

The major purpose of these restrictions is to prevent the spread of contagious diseases. South Africa is one country that has these precautions. Europeans, fearful that African horse-sickness could be introduced into their territory, have banned the import of horses from South Africa.

Insurance when travelling

Special insurance policies are available to cover animals against transportation risks, either during a specific journey or for a period of time, for instance during the show season. Most professional transporters, however, are covered against the risk of damaging horses that are travelling in their vehicles.

To what extent you insure a horse against accidental injury may depend on the value of the animal. More details of insurance policies are given on page 180.

Above: A horse being unloaded in the correct way—at a steady pace.
Left: A horse loading willingly. The assistant walks confidently by his side without pulling him or looking back at him.

The blacksmith is a very important person in a horse's life, for a good smith can correct certain faults of conformation, improve the condition of the feet and prevent weaknesses from developing. A bad one can ruin a horse for life.

The choice of blacksmith must, therefore, be made with care. Few places these days have a forge, and more often the blacksmith has to come to the horse, rather than wait for his clients to visit him. Conversely, the necessity of going outside the immediate locality in search of a smith may offer a choice of two or three of them. The best method of selection is to find out which blacksmith visits neighbouring horses and arrange for your own horse to be shod at the same time.

Hot and cold shoeing

The lack of forges has led to an increase in cold shoeing. This is the system whereby a smith measures a horse's feet, and makes a set of shoes at his forge, then fits them cold. At this stage, he cannot make any further adjustment to the shoes; so they are unlikely to be as good a fit as with hot shoeing. In hot shoeing, the shoe is heated on the spot. It is then hammered into shape and placed on the foot for a few seconds to char a brown rim on the hoof. The shoe can then be altered if necessary, and so can the hoof; for an incomplete brown rim indicates that there is some space between the shoe and the hoof. The bearing surface of the hoof should be made level by rasping it before attaching the shoe.

The shoe

The horseshoe has changed little in style since the first iron shoe was nailed by a Celtic horseman to his horse's hoof nearly 2,000 years ago, but it has undergone certain refinements. Most shoes are now fullered (that is, they have a groove on the underside to improve grip with the ground). Most, too, are concave, so that they are narrower on the ground surface than above. This makes the shoe lighter and less likely to be pulled off in sticky ground.

Clips help to keep the shoe in place. These are small triangular extensions of the outer edge of the shoe that fit into the wall of the hoof. It is usual to have one clip on each fore shoe, and two clips on each hind shoe (one on each side). Central clips are rare on hind shoes, for without them there is less risk of the metal causing an over-reach.

Grip is an important requirement of a shoe. A fullered surface helps, and there are other possible modifications. Calks or calkins can be forged on the heels of hind shoes by turning the ends of the shoe downward to provide a small projection. Even more grip can be

Below: A blacksmith checks a shoe against the hoof for a good fit.

obtained with the small mordax studs that the blacksmith can attach to the hind shoes. They are especially beneficial for horses that do a lot of roadwork (for instance, hunters and driving horses). The greatest grip of all is provided, however, by studs larger than the mordax versions. They are too large to leave in permanently, as they would make walking on hard road surfaces very awkward. Consequently, the smith prepares screw holes on the outer edge of the hind shoes, and sometimes on the fore shoes too. Studs can then be screwed into the holes as required for such activities as show-jumping.

A horseshoe should be held securely by nails that are hammered through the horny part of the foot until they emerge higher up, when their points are twisted off and the ends, known as clenches, are hammered down. A properly fitting shoe should not interfere in any way with the functions of the various parts of the foot.

The foot

It is important for keepers of horses to have at least an elementary understanding of the structure of the foot so that they can recognize if the work of the blacksmith is good or bad.

The inner core of the foot consists of three major bones: the lower section of the corner bone (short pastern); the coffin, or pedal, bone; and, situated between the wings of the pedal bone; the navicular bone. These bones are surrounded by very sensitive fleshy parts that, if pricked or damaged, will make a horse lame. These sensitive parts produce corresponding horny and insensitive structures that form the protective outer casing of the foot.

The wall

This is the horny insensitive structure seen when the foot is on the ground. It is comparable to our finger nails and, like them, is always growing. This growth is downward, originating from the area of the coronary band. Some water is present in the horn, adding flexibility to this casing of the foot, and its evaporation is reduced by a thin layer of hard 'varnish' outside.

The wall is divided into three areas: the toe, which is at the front and is the highest section; the quarters, which are at the sides; and the heels, which are at the back where the wall curves inward to form the bars.

The horn of the wall is continuously growing. When the foot is unshod, the horn will wear down with friction, but when shoes are attached, it will start to spread after a few weeks and can eventually overlap the shoe, break away from the nail holes and possibly make the horse lame. The shoes must therefore be removed at regular intervals and the hoof pared into shape.

The sole

This protects the foot from injury from below. Although horny and insensitive, its outer layer grows from the sensitive area of the sole, which covers the under part of the

Underside of the foot *(Below)*
1 *Cleft of frog*
2 *Bar*
3 *Heel*
4 *White line*
5 *Wall*
6 *Point of the frog*
7 *Sole*
8 *Toe*

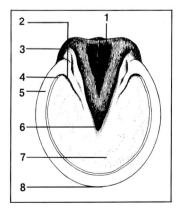

121

pedal bone. The outer layer is thin; it can very easily be pierced or damaged and the sensitive area made vulnerable.

The healthy sole is slightly concave to the ground. Dividing it and the wall is a white line, visible from below, which is a layer of soft horn. Its position is important, for it indicates to the smith the thickness of the wall and consequently how much room there is for the nails, which must never be allowed to penetrate the sole.

The frog

This is visible from below as a triangular area of horn at a lower level than the sole. The sensitive or fleshy frog is above it, inside the hoof, and like the sensitive sole, produces the horn of its insensitive area. The sections of the frog are made of relatively elastic material, providing the foot with both a shock absorber and a non-slip device. The heel meets the ground before the toe, so that it is this area that bears the brunt of the shock. For the frog to carry out this vital function it must be in contact with the ground. The smith, therefore, must never pare it back, but only remove any ragged ends. It is important, though, that the frog, like the sole, does not get any sharp objects lodged in it. It should therefore be picked out regularly with a hoof pick.

Reasons for shoeing

People sometimes wonder whether shoeing is strictly necessary, because a horse in the wild wears no shoes at all. As with additional feeding, the answer to this depends on the sort of work the animal has to do.

Plenty of work, part of it on solid surfaces such as roads, will wear the hoof down faster than it grows and lead to friction, soreness and finally lameness, as the softer parts of the foot have to take the weight. Another factor is climate; in the temperate zones of the Northern Hemisphere, the hard part of the foot tends to be comparatively soft. In Mediterranean countries, the

Arab has traditionally gone unshod for centuries; but the atmosphere is drier there and hooves harder, so that the hoof wears more slowly and evenly.

Shoeing is not necessary on hardy animals doing light work on grass or in sandy areas, provided their feet are in good shape and regularly inspected and trimmed by the smith. If their hooves are brittle, however, with a tendency to crack or split, shoeing is essential and may be the only means of preventing lameness. For example, a horse with severe sandcrack (in which a crack in the hoof extends upward into the coronary and downward towards the bottom of the hoof) may be helped by the trimming of the foot and the use of a special corrective shoe to prevent pressure on the wall.

Checks to be made on a newly shod foot

1 The type of shoe should be suitable for the work required of the horse, and the weight of iron proportional to the size of the animal. Normally a horse's set weighs in the region of 2kg (4½lb), whereas a pony of about 12hh needs a set weighing just over 1kg (2¼lb).

2 The shoe should be made to fit the foot, not the foot made to fit the shoe (so not too much rasping and severe paring back of the hoof).

3 The length of the foot should have been reduced evenly at toe and heel.

4 The frog should be in contact with the ground.

5 An adequate number of nails should have been used, but not too many. The usual number is three on the inside and four on the outside.

6 The clenches should be neat, in line and the right distance up the wall.

7 There should be no space between shoe and foot.

8 The heels of the shoe should be neither too long nor too short.

9 It is important that the clip should fit well on each shoe.

Special types of shoe

Horses with conformation faults
(such as a tendency to brush and
injure the opposite leg) can be
fitted with feather-edged shoes.
The inner side of such a shoe is
very much thinner than that of a
normal shoe, so that it fits close in
under the inside wall. Nails are
used only around the toe and outer
arm of the shoe.

Hunters out at pasture during
the summer usually have their
shoes removed and replaced by
toe-clips. These small, half-size
shoes, fitted only to the toe, prevent
the hoof from cracking and
encourage the frog to come into
full contact with the ground.

Racehorses use two types of
shoes: a light fullered concave
shoe of mild steel for training, and
a fullered, concave 'plate', usually
of aluminium, for racing. A set of
racehorse plates weighs only 250-
500g (½-1lb) a set.

Great improvements have been
made in recent years to the
materials used for hoof pads.
Various forms and shapes of
plastics have been developed
which, when placed between the
shoe and the hoof, help to
reduce jar. They are being used
more and more for horses with
foot or tendon problems and for
horses that are required to jump
on hard ground or to do much
road work.

Indications that re-shoeing is necessary

1 Loose shoe.
2 'Cast' shoe (one that has been
   lost).
3 Shoe wearing thin.
4 Clenches rising and standing
   out from the wall.
5 Long foot and/or one that has
   lost its shape.

Depending on the amount of
work a horse does, re-shoeing is
usually necessary about once a
month; either new shoes or
'removes' can be fitted. Removes
are old shoes that, if not worn too
thin, can be replaced after the foot
has been trimmed.

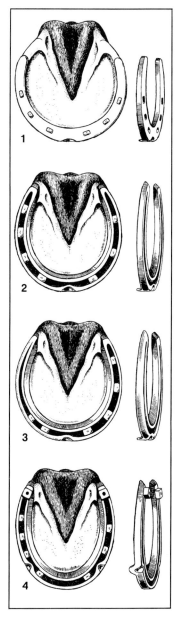

Types of horseshoe [Above]
1 *A half shoe fitted onto a
   fore foot.*
2 *A fullered fore shoe with
   toe clip.*
3 *A fore shoe with a feathered
   edge.*
4 *A hind shoe with studs.*

Saddlery

Saddlery is an important aspect of horsemastership. In the interests of safety, appearance, durability and comfort it is important to be able to recognize and buy good quality tack and to look after it correctly.

THE SADDLE

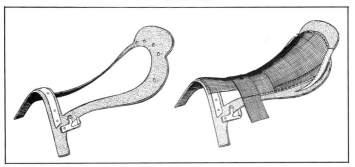

Above: A saddle tree before (left) and after (right) being strained.

The saddle tree
The framework is known as the 'tree', and was traditionally made of beech wood, but laminated wood or metal is more usual today. A 'spring tree' is used in most modern saddles. This has two pieces of tempered steel running lengthwise along the tree from the front arch to the cantle. This makes the seat more resilient and so more comfortable for the rider, who can feel and follow the horse's movements more closely.

The seat
Built on to the tree, this is usually made of pigskin.

The flaps
These are attached to the seat.

The panels
These are stuffed with wool or shaped felt, and act as a cushion between the tree and the horse. There is a channel (gullet) running through the centre, which ensures that weight is not placed on the horse's spine. The panels may be full (reaching almost to the bottom of the saddle flap) or half (reaching only halfway down).

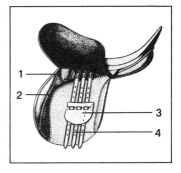

Above: Side view of a saddle.
1 Pocket for point of tree 2 Panel
3 Buckle guard 4 Girth straps.
Below: Underside of a saddle.
1 Cantle 2 Gullet 3 Lining
4 Saddle flap 5 Panel.

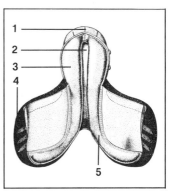

The types of saddle
Variation in the design of the tree, panels, etc, are made because the

Parts of a saddle *(Below)*
1 *Pommel*
2 *Skirt*
3 *Twist or waist*
4 *Seat*
5 *Cantle*
6 *Panel*
7 *Girth*
8 *Stirrup leather*
9 *Saddle flap*
10 *'D'*
11 *Skirt*
12 *Stirrup bar closed*
13 *Stirrup leather*

best place for the rider's weight is as near as possible to the centre of gravity of the horse. This varies with changes in the posture and speed of the horse: for example, in racing, the horse is extended and the rider's weight needs to be well forward. In dressage, the horse is collected and the weight needs to be further back.

The jumping saddle
This has to bring the rider's weight well forward. To do this the bars for the stirrup irons are placed forward, the panel is extended and forward cut with rolls to support knee and thigh; the tree is deep.

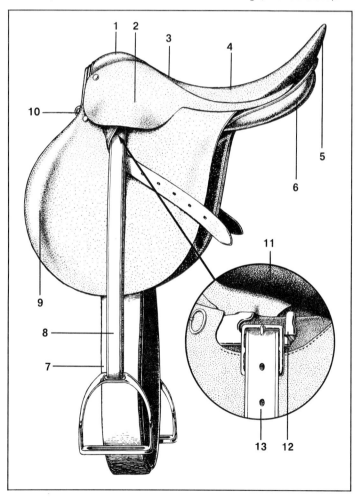

The all-purpose saddle

This saddle is a modification of the above, with panel and flap less forward cut, thus making it possible to ride with longer stirrups.

The dressage saddle

As the rider has to use very long stirrups and to have a deep seat, the dressage saddle is straighter cut, the roll for lower thigh is on the forward edge of the panel, and the dip in the tree is deep, positioning the rider well back.

The show or saddle seat saddle

This is designed to show the front of the horse to its best advantage. It is therefore excessively straight cut and it fits as closely as possible to the horse's back with normally a half panel used, having little padding and no knee rolls.

The racing saddle

The seat is unimportant because the rider rarely sits. Its outstanding feature is that it is very light, weighing about 0.5-1kg (1-2lb). Light materials are used, such as kangaroo-skin and aluminium, the panels are cut to a minimum and the stirrup bars are usually omitted, leathers passing over side bars of the tree.

The stock saddle

This is used for the Western style of riding and has a high pommel with horn in front for securing a lasso when roping. The cantle is also high. Fenders (like long narrow saddle flaps) on each side protect the rider's legs from sweat. There are leather thongs along the back on to which to tie lassos, saddlebags and other gear, and the cinch (girth) is secured by two thongs in cloverleaf knots. The stirrups are wide and of solid wood. Saddle may weigh 13½kg (30lb).

Different types of saddle *(right)*
1 *Jumping saddle*
2 *All purpose saddle*
3 *Dressage saddle*
4 *Showing saddle*
5 *Racing saddle*
6 *Stock saddle*

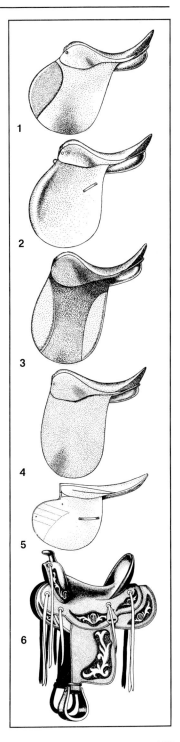

THE SADDLE AND THE BRIDLE

To fit a saddle
An ill-fitting saddle can make both horse and rider sore, and make it difficult for the rider to get into the correct position. It is important to check the saddle carefully, bearing the following points in mind.

The weight must not be concentrated on a particular point but distributed evenly over the back muscles. None must fall on the loin muscles or on the spine. The withers must not be restricted: the front arch of the saddle should be high and wide enough to prevent them from being pinched or pressed upon. The horse's shoulder blades must be able to move freely. Panels must be stuffed so that the rider sits in the correct position. Too much or too little stuffing, or wrong tilting, can result in the rider's seat not being in contact with the horse and/or sliding backwards. It is possible for a tree to break in a fall, or if the saddle itself is dropped. The saddle with a broken tree must not be used, because it would hurt the horse.

To ensure that the saddle fits correctly, it is advisable for the saddler to carry out an annual check-up.

Care of the saddle
When placing the saddle on the ground, rest it on the front arch (not flat), taking care that the leather is not scratched. When carrying, place the front arch in the crook of the elbow. Clean regularly in accordance with general instructions (see below).

Cleaning the lining
Take care to use the appropriate materials. A leather lining should be sponged off, ensuring that water does not run under the lining to dampen the stuffing. Dry with chamois leather, and finally soap. If it is made of linen, sponge or scrub it first, and dry away from direct heat with the saddle standing on its arch. A serge or wool lining should be dried and brushed. It is not advisable to scrub the lining unless it is extremely dirty.

Washing leather
Make sure that the small black spots of grease found under the flap are removed: a small pad of horsehair is the best means of doing this.

The pad or numnah
Worn underneath the saddle, the numnah helps to protect the horse's back. It is made in many types of material, the most common being leather, felt, sponge rubber, synthetic fibres and sheepskin.

It is usually held in place by straps attached to the girth straps. Correctly fitted, it should be large enough to project about 2cm (1in) all round the saddle. Before the girths are tightened, the forward part of the numnah should be pulled up in order not to put pressure on the withers or spine.

Cleaning a numnah depends on the material from which it is made. Leather should be washed with pure soap; felt and sheepskin should be dried and brushed (scrub only when necessary). A synthetic fibre pad may be washed in a machine.

The girth
The girth secures the saddle and there are a number of types.

Web girths
These wear out more quickly than other types and can snap. Always use two.

Leather girths
Excellent as long as they are kept supple and used with caution on soft, unfit horses, when the leather can cause girth galls. They may be shaped, straight, cross-over or three-fold. The last-mentioned should have an oiled flannel inside the fold to keep it soft.

Balding girths
These are narrow in the centre and reduce the chance of rubbing. They allow air to circulate. They are easy to clean with a brush, although an occasional wash is advisable for general cleanliness.

Stirrup irons

The best are made of hand-forged stainless steel. Rubber treads are a useful addition as they help to prevent the rider's foot from slipping. Safety irons are used by many children and these have a rubber band on one side of the stirrup, allowing the foot to come free in a fall. (The rubber is worn on the outside.) This iron does have disadvantages, as it does not hang straight and the rubber often breaks.

A well-fitting stirrup iron should leave the rider's foot with 13mm (½in) on either side, between it and the iron. Less space means the foot might be wedged in a fall, and more can cause the entire foot to slip through.

The bridle

The major purpose of the bridle is to hold the bit in the mouth. The snaffle bridle provides attachments for one bit and the double bridle for two bits.

The snaffle bridle

This, the simpler of the two bridles,

consists of the following:

1   The headpiece and throat latch (lash) are in one piece, with the throat lash preventing the bridle from slipping forwards.
2   The brow band prevents the bridle from slipping backwards.
3   The two cheek pieces are attached at one end to the head-piece and at the other to the bit.
4   The noseband is on its own headpiece.

There are three basic nosebands:

1   The cavesson fastens below the projecting cheekbone and normally serves no purpose other than providing an attachment for the standing martingale.
2   A dropped noseband is fastened under the bit and prevents the horse from evading the bit by opening his mouth.

Parts of the snaffle bridle (Below)

1   *Head piece*
2   *Brow band*
3   *Cheek piece*
4   *Cavesson noseband*
5   *Throat latch (lash)*
6   *Snaffle bit*

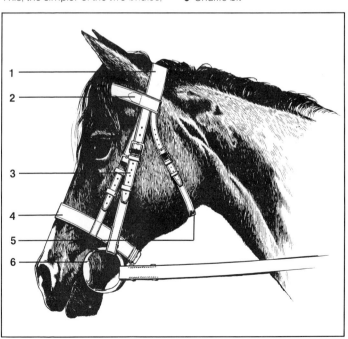

3 The crossed or grackle noseband has two crossed straps fastening above and below the bit. The pressure preventing the mouth from opening and the jaws from crossing is higher with the grackle than with the dropped noseband.

The bit is attached to the cheek pieces and rein by either stitches (neater), studs (convenient for bit changes) or buckles (convenient, but clumsy in appearance).

The reins have a central buckle. They can be plain, plaited or laced leather (the last two are less likely to slip), covered in a rubber grip (which is the best means of preventing slipping), or plaited or plain linen or nylon.

The double bridle
The double bridle has the same constituents as the snaffle bridle, plus the following:
1 The bridoon headpiece and one cheek piece.
2 Two bits, comprising a bridoon (thin snaffle) and a curb bit (usually called 'the bit').
3 An additional pair of reins of which both are of plain leather, but the bridoon rein is wider than the curb bit rein.
4 The curb chain, which is attached to hooks on either side of the curb bit.
5 The lip strap, which is attached to the small 'D's on the curb bit and runs through the fly link of the curb chain.

To fit the bridle
The throat lash should be loose enough to allow an adult's fist to be placed between it and the jawbone. (If too tight, it restricts the breathing and flexion; if too loose, it will not serve its purpose of preventing the bridle coming over the head, which could lead to a serious accident.)

Different types of bridle (Right)
1 *Bosal bridle*
2 *Western bridle with roping bit*
3 *Cutting horse bit/split ear bridle*
4 *Double bridle*
5 *Hackamore bridle*
6 *Snaffle bridle with drop noseband*

The brow band prevents the bridle from slipping back too far, but must not be so tight that it touches the ears or pulls on the headpiece. The fit of the noseband varies a great deal according to the type.

A cavesson should lie halfway between the projecting cheekbone and the corners of the mouth. Normally, it should be loose enough to

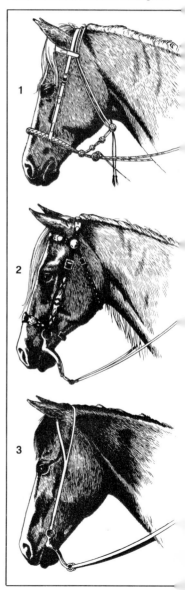

allow two fingers between it and the horse's nose but if done up tightly it can help to prevent the mouth from opening.

A dropped noseband is the normal way of preventing the mouth from opening, but it can be used only with a snaffle bridle and it must be very carefully fitted if it is not to pinch or restrict breathing.

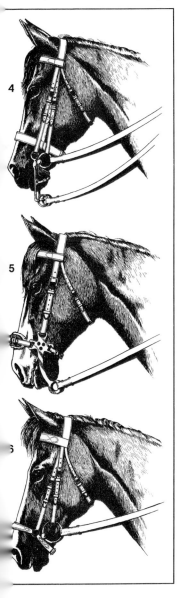

The front piece must be well above the nostrils and the back strap should lie in the chin groove, firmly but not tightly fastened.

The bit must be of the right width and attached so that it hangs in the correct position. If it is too narrow or too high, it will wrinkle or pinch the horse's lips. Too wide or low, it will fall on the teeth. In a double bridle, the bridoon should be higher than the curb bit.

The curb chain is attached to the hook on the offside of the bit, twisted until flat and then attached to the nearside. The length should be such that it comes into play when the bit is drawn back to an angle of 45°.

The lip strap is attached to one side of the curb bit, passed through the fly link of the curb chain and buckled to the other side of the curb bit.

The bit

Bits can be made of various materials. Nickel has a yellow appearance. It is relatively cheap but tends to wear badly, resulting in rough edges, and it may bend or break. Plated steel is stronger than nickel but tends to chip. Hand-forged steel is the strongest but also the most expensive material. Mouthpieces of rubber, rubber-coated metal or vulcanite are comparatively soft, producing a very mild bit.

The purpose of the bit

The bit is used in conjunction with the rider's seat and legs to control the horse. The pressure of the bit on the mouth conveys a message to the horse. With good training, the horse will react by relaxing his jaw and will not resist. He will obey not out of fear or pain but because he has learned to understand and trust his rider. Consequently the key to any horse's mouth does not lie among the numerous types of bits that apply varying degrees of pressure to different parts of the mouth and chin, but in good training, and reliance on a rider with a firm seat and good hands. Mechanical contrivances should be resorted to only if the horse has already been spoilt.

The snaffle

This has a single mouthpiece, which acts upwards against the corners of the lips, particularly when the horse's head is low, on the bars of the lower jaw, particularly when the horse's head is high, and on the tongue. There are many different types and shapes of snaffle.

The snaffle is a very mild bit, especially if made of rubber, and can be used on young, sensitive horses or those with injured mouths.

The single-jointed snaffle has a joint in the centre of the mouthpiece. This creates a 'nutcracker' action causing more pressure to be applied than with the half-moon. It is the most common type of snaffle and has a number of variations.

The thickness of the mouthpiece alters the severity of the bit. The thinner the mouthpiece, the more severe the bit becomes, because the pressure is more concentrated. The thin version is known as a racing snaffle, and the thick one as a German snaffle. The latter is a gentle bit and most riders use it on their young horses.

The rings can be large, small, fixed to the mouthpiece or loose (traversing rings). The two most common types are the egg-butt snaffle (in which the rings are fixed to the mouthpiece and are straight where attached, so that they are less likely to pinch the lips) and the Fulmer snaffle (which has metal cheek pieces to prevent the bit from rubbing the mouth and to ensure the bit is not pulled through from one side to the other). The rings are the loose (traversing) type.

The texture of the mouthpiece also varies. A rough texture helps to prevent the horse or pony from leaning on the bit. The most common variation is the twisted snaffle, in which the mouthpiece is twisted, sharpening the pressure on the horse's mouth. It is a severe

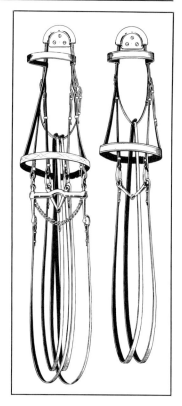

Above: A double bridle (left) and snaffle bridle (right) hung up correctly on wide supports so that the leather keeps its shape and does not crack. The snaffle bridle, the simpler type, is often used with a mild bit on young horses.

bit and should be used only on hard-mouthed horses. Other variations are ridged or square mouthpieces and those with chains and rollers. These are all hard on a mouth and should be used only with caution.

The method of attaching the bit to the leather cheek piece can affect the severity of the bit. The cheek pieces are normally looped on to the rings of the bit, but in the gag-bit they are rounded and pass through holes at the top and bottom of the ring so that the rein is attached directly to the cheek piece. A pull on the rein results in the bit rising against the corners of the horse's mouth. It has a very severe action and the gag-bit should be used only in the last resort.

A double-jointed snaffle has two joints, thus reducing the 'nutcracker' action. Furthermore, the bit will not rest so low and gives the horse more freedom to move his tongue. Sensitive horses and those that put their tongue over the bit are often more relaxed in this snaffle.

The bits of the double bridle

These give a more precise control, and a double bridle, therefore, should not be used until the horse accepts a snaffle bit. To use it before a horse or pony has learned to relax will tend to frighten him, and get him to stiffen against it, so he will obey only because of its severity. The result of this is that he develops resistances in order to try to avoid the action of the bits. The double bridle has two bits.

The bridoon is a snaffle that is usually thinner than the simple snaffle. The curb bit provides additional control and makes possible more refined aids. It acts partly on the tongue, and the pressure is greatest when the mouthpiece is straight. If there is a port in the centre of the curb bit, then there is more room for the tongue to move.

Pressure is also felt on the bars of the mouth (area of gum between the incisor and molar teeth) through the action of the metal cheek piece, which may be fixed (action more direct) or movable; in either case, it has a lever effect.

The third area of pressure is on the curb groove, for as the metal cheek pieces are pulled back, they cause the curb chain to apply pressure on the curb groove. The greater the length of the cheek piece, the greater the leverage and the severity of it and the curb chain.

The fourth area of pressure is on the poll; when the metal cheeks are pulled back, the eye (the ring of the bit to which the leather cheek pieces are attached) goes forward

and, as it is connected to the bridle, exerts down pressure on the poll.

The Pelham

This aims to combine the effect of a snaffle and a curb bit in one. Two reins are normally used. The bridoon rein is attached to rings level with the mouthpiece, and the curb rein to the bottom of the metal cheek piece, thus obtaining the lever and curb chain effect. The mouthpiece may be vulcanite and straight or half-moon, with a port or even jointed.

A 'Pelham converter' or leather roundings are curved couplings that join the bridoon and curb rings on a Pelham bit, so that only one rein need be used. Having only one rein reduces the variation in pressure that can be applied, but it is simpler for the rider to handle.

The Kimblewick

Using the same principle of round-ings, it consists of a single, large metal 'D' running from the mouth-piece to the bottom of the cheek piece. It is a severe bit, and must be used with caution.

Parts on which bit works *(Below)*
1 *Nasal cartilage*
2 *Nasal bone*
3 *Roof of mouth*
4 *Tongue*
5 *Corner of lip*
6 *Bars of mouth*
7 *Chin groove*

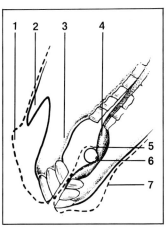

The bitless bridle

This bridle has no mouthpiece; pressure is placed on the nose and chin. The hackamore is the best-known type; it has two long metal cheeks that are curved so that their leather attachments act across the nose and behind the chin when the rider pulls on the reins. The same principle is used on a similar type, the bosal bridle.

The principles of bitting

Whenever possible, use the mildest bit. A severe bit can often worry a horse so much that he becomes more excitable and more difficult to control. If the horse resists the bit or is too strong, always consider other possible causes before selecting another bit. These could include bad riding, rough teeth, too much energy-giving food, an injured mouth, a badly fitting bit or bridle, or simply that the horse is too inexperienced to respond.

Different types of bit *(Below)*

1 *Egg-butt snaffle*
2 *Rubber snaffle*
3 *Double-jointed snaffle*
4 *Gag-bit*
5 *Pelham*
6 *Kimblewick*
7 *Bridoon & curb bit/double bridle*
8 *Fulmer snaffle*
9 *German snaffle*
10 *Twisted snaffle*

If none of these applies, the next step is to analyze the form of resistance before making a selection. If the horse or pony is too strong and has the experience and temperament to accept a stronger bit then try one, but with caution and good hands. If the resistance takes the form of crossing his jaw and opening his mouth, a dropped or crossed noseband should be used. If the tongue is brought over the bit, then the bit is acting only on the bars of the mouth and not on the tongue. To prevent this from occurring make sure the bit is high in the mouth, use a dropped or crossed noseband (as the horse needs to open his mouth to get his tongue over) or try a mouthpiece that has a port or is double-jointed (as these give more freedom for the tongue to lie beneath the bit). If all else fails then a device to prevent the tongue getting over the bit can be used.

The most common forms of resistance are going behind the bit when the head is tucked in, or going above the bit when the head is raised. In the former case a less severe bit is needed, so that the horse will not be frightened to take hold of it. The latter might be due to a lack of training or fear of a severe bit (shown by nervous jerks of the head), and only if the mouth is hard can a curb bit help.

The halter
There are two types of halter, both used to tie up or lead a horse. One is made of hemp or cotton and usually has no throat lash or buckles. The more expensive variety is made of leather or nylon and fitted with buckles and a throat lash. In the USA the term halter still applies, but in the UK this type is known as a headcollar or headstall.

Martingales
These are used to control the position of the horse's head. There are various types.

The standing martingale
This consists of a strap running from the girth to a cavesson noseband (never to a dropped noseband, as this can restrict breathing); it prevents a horse from throwing his head in the air.

The running martingale
This is a strap that runs from the girth, divides in two and ends in rings running along the reins. The effect of this martingale is thus felt on the bit, and a very short running martingale has a severe lever action on the mouth. It should be fitted so that the rings are in line with the withers, thus discouraging the horse from raising his head above this level. The neck strap must not be too tight, as this would rub the animal. Leather or rubber stoppers should be used on the reins to prevent the rings from getting caught on the buckles of the reins.

The Irish martingale
This is used to stop the reins from going over the head.

The Chambon
A strap which runs from the girth through the bit to rings on an attachment over the poll. It is advisable to use the Chambon only on the lunge. It is harmful if used too tightly; ideal only for experts.

The draw rein
This runs from the girth through the rings of the bit to the rider's hands, giving him greater control over the horse's head position. It is frequently used by top show-jumpers but can do much damage in the hands of a rider with limited experience or rough hands.

The breastplate
This is a neck strap with attachments to two 'D's of the saddle and to the girth, which prevents the saddle from slipping back. To fit the breastplate ensure the neck strap is not too tight and that the attachments are not strained.

Below: The draw rein can be seen running from the girth strap.

Putting on the saddle and bridle

Tie up the horse on the halter or headcollar before collecting the saddlery from the tack room. The saddle should be carried with the front arch in the crook of the elbow, with the irons run up, the girth attached on the offside lying over the seat and the pad/numnah (if being used) underneath them all. The bridle and martingale can be hung over the shoulder.

The martingale and the saddle are put on first, so the bridle can be hung up nearby. Check that there is no mud or dirt on the horse where the saddle will lie. Put the neck strap of the martingale over the head so that the buckle is on the nearside.

Putting on the saddle

With the left hand on the front arch and the right hand on the cantle, approach the nearside and place the saddle well forward of the withers. Slide it back so that it sits in the deep part of the back. Check to see that the flaps are straight, and if a numnah is used that it too is flat, pulled well up into the arch of the saddle and protruding evenly around the entire rim of the saddle.

Go to the offside, let down the girth and check that it is straight. Return to the nearside, take the girth, put it through the martingale, if using one, and buckle up. Ensure that the girth is not pinching the skin and that there are enough holes left to be able to tighten it later. Where two webbing girths are used the two should overlap, with the underneath one attached to the forward buckles on either side. Make sure it is done up tightly before mounting.

Above: The boy is carrying the bridle over his left shoulder and the saddle on his lower right arm.
Above right: The saddle with girth on top and stirrups run up is placed well forward of the withers.
Above extreme right: The saddle is then slid back to the low part of the back, the girth slipped over and fastened loosely on near side.
Right: Before tightening the girth, the fingers are run between it and pony to check for wrinkles.
Below: Side and back views show a saddle placed too far forward and resting on the withers. The inset shows the correct position.

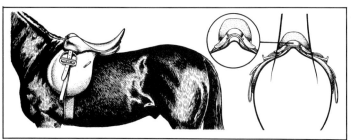

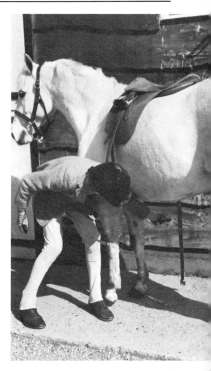

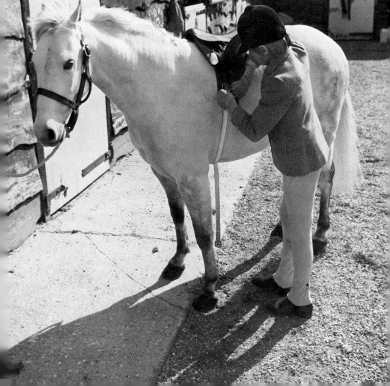

Putting on the bridle

Untie the horse and put the reins over his head. Still holding the bridle, remove the halter and hang it up. With the right hand take the headpiece of the bridle and let the bit rest against the left hand, which is then positioned under the muzzle. Insert the thumb or first finger where there is a gap between the horse's teeth and gently prise the mouth open. The bridle can then be lifted with the right hand while the left hand guides the bit into the horse's mouth. Use both hands to ease the headpiece over the ears, ensuring that no skin or hair is pinched and that the leather is not twisted.

The buckles can then be done up, starting with the throat lash and followed by the noseband, which must lie inside the cheek pieces. All the keepers have to be checked to ensure that the flaps are held in place. With a curb bit, the curb chain must be fastened, twisting it until straight, followed by the lip strap (if there is one).

Check that the bridle is on straight and that the bit is level (ie, that the buckles on both cheek pieces are in matching holes).

With a running martingale the reins should then be undone and put through its rings. With a standing martingale, the loop should be hooked to the noseband before the latter is buckled up.

Right (L to R): Putting on the bridle.
1 *With the pony tied up, the bridle is held in the left hand and the reins taken over the head.*
2 *The halter can be undone and dropped as soon as the reins are securely around the pony's neck.*
3 *With bit held close, the mouth is opened by pushing the thumb between the molars and the incisors.*
4 *When the bit goes into the mouth the bridle headpiece is lifted carefully over the ears.*
5 *The throat latch (lash) is done up first. There should be a fist's space between latch and pony jowl.*
6 *The noseband buckle is fastened next. The drop noseband shown here must not be too low or tight.*

THE DRIVING HARNESS

The collar
The collar is a pad that encircles the horse's neck. It can be straight or bent back and is lined with leather, wool or serge, with the outside of brown leather or black patent leather.

It is vital that the collar fits, or the rubbing will cause sores. It should be possible to put the flat of the hand between the top of the collar and the neck; the flat of the fingers at the sides; and the hand and wrist at the bottom.

The breast collar
This serves the same purpose as the collar and is a broad padded strap fitting around the chest and held up by a strap passing over the neck in front of the withers. Although simpler to fit than the collar, it is not considered so smart, nor can such heavy loads be pulled by it.

The hames
These are metal arms that fit around the collar and to which the

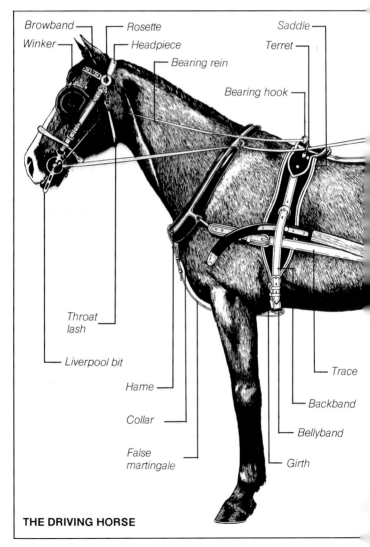

Browband — Rosette — Saddle

Winker — Headpiece — Terret

Bearing rein

Bearing hook

Throat lash

Liverpool bit

Hame

Collar

False martingale

Trace

Backband

Bellyband

Girth

THE DRIVING HORSE

traces are attached. The hames must fit into the groove of the collar behind the rim. At the top are driving rings, through which the reins pass. These can be seen clearly in the drawing below.

The hame strap
This fastens the hames at the top and bears a great deal of strain so it must be regularly examined to ensure that it has not stretched or weakened. It is vital to check all parts of the harness regularly.

The driving bridle (*Below*)
1 *Headpiece*
2 *Browband*
3 *Face drop*
4 *Blinker or winker*
5 *Cheek piece*
6 *Noseband*

The army bridle (*Bottom*)
1 *Headpiece*
2 *Browband*
3 *Cheek piece*
4 *Jowl piece*
5 *Bridlehead*
6 *Noseband*

Backstrap
Loin strap
Crupper
Rein
Breeching
Shaft
Breeching strap

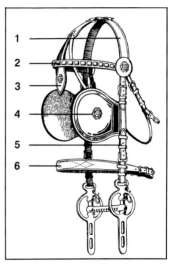

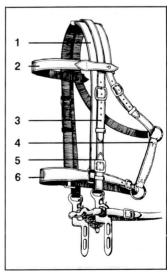

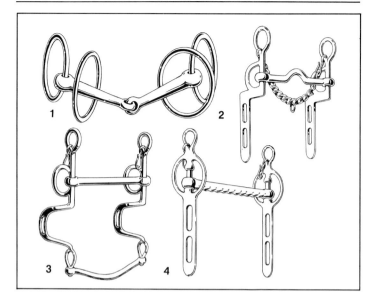

The pad or saddle
The saddle should be used if the horse or pony has to take any of the weight of the vehicle on his back. The pad is a lighter version of the saddle. Like a riding saddle, neither should bear down upon the back and both should be held securely by the girth.

The crupper
The crupper prevents the pad or saddle from slipping forward. It is a back strap connecting the pad or saddle to a crupper dock, which goes under the tail.

The breeching
This enables the horse or pony to stop the vehicle without the assistance of brakes. It hangs horizontally just above the level of the shafts so that when the horse is pulling down hills the strap goes against the animal's quarters, enabling him to hold the vehicle back.

The traces
These connect the collar to the vehicle and bear the strain of pulling the vehicle. They are usually made of leather.

The bridle
There is basically no difference

Types of driving bit (*Above*)
1 *Wilson snaffle*
2 *Elbow*
3 *Buxton*
4 *Liverpool*

between this and the bridle on a riding horse, but blinkers are usually attached to the cheek pieces. The lower parts of the cheek pieces pass through loops on the inside of the noseband, around the rings of the bit and up to loops on the outside of the noseband, before being buckled.

The bits
These are again basically the same as for riding. The snaffle, however, has two rings on either side. One is fixed on the mouthpiece and the other, which floats along the mouthpiece, is used for the attachment of the bridle's cheek pieces. For more severe action the reins are attached to the floating rings but for gentler control they are buckled to the fixed rings.

The most common curb bits are the Liverpool and the Buxton, the severity of each depending on where the reins are attached to the metal cheeks of the bit; if low down there is a strong leverage but if level with the mouthpiece none.

Regular inspections are essential, because it is safer and cheaper to replace rotting stitches or repair cracked leather in the early stages of deterioration. Tack should always be hung up or stored carefully so that air can circulate around it and prevent mildew. It must be kept clean and the leather in a pliant condition.

Equipment for cleaning tack

In order to clean tack efficiently, the following equipment is needed: a towel for washing; sponge for saddle soap; chamois leather for drying; saddle soap; metal polish and several soft cloths; rubber for drying metal work; dandy brush for removing mud from girths, lining, etc; nail for cleaning out curb hooks, etc; glycerine for covering tack to be stored; a bucket; a hook on which to hang bridles; and a saddle horse.

The dos of tack cleaning

Hang bridle and leather accessories on tack-cleaning hook, and place the saddle on a saddle horse. Undo all buckles and remove fittings (bit, stirrup leathers, irons, etc). Wash leather and metal with lukewarm water and dry with chamois leather. Apply saddle soap to leather with a sponge, using as little water as possible. If using bar soap, it is best to dampen the soap and not the sponge. Apply metal polish to metal and then thoroughly clean off. On any parts of the tack that need washing (eg, girths, pads) use pure soap, not detergent. When cleaning is finished put all the parts together again.

The don'ts of tack cleaning

Never wash leather with washing soda or hot water, or saturate it with water. Never let it dry too close to a strong heat. Never use linseed, neatsfoot oil or mineral oils; use saddle soap, glycerine, olive oil or castor oil to keep leather soft.

Storing the tack

The bridle should be hung up by placing the rein or reins through the throat lash and the noseband outside cheek pieces. There is no need to buckle, but the end of the strap should be put through the keepers. Put the bridle on a wide bridle rack so that the leather keeps its shape and does not crack. Do not use a nail or coat hook. If there is no special hanger, an empty round saddle soap or coffee can, nailed to the wall, makes a good substitute.

The saddle

Place the saddle on a bracket about 45cm (18in) long attached to the wall. The accessories can be hung beside the saddle.

Below: Cleaning tack in a well-equipped and tidy tack room.

BOOTS

Brushing boots
These can be made of many types of material (felt, leather, etc). They are worn around the cannon bone and the upper half of the fetlock joint.

Over-reach boots
These are bell-shaped and fit over the hoof to protect the heels of the forelegs.

Knee caps
Horses' knees can be protected when travelling by the use of knee caps. It is also advisable to use them when exercising on hard roads, in case of a fall.

Hock boots
Worn over the hock, they are made of heavy wool and protect the horse when travelling or, in the stable, if he is a kicker.

Yorkshire boots
These are worn to protect the hind fetlocks and/or coronet.

Below: Brushing boots, showing the leather protection pads inside.

Above: Protective over-reach boots.
Below: A heavy woollen hock boot.

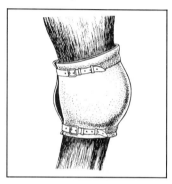

Below: Knee caps in place, with travelling bandages also fitted.

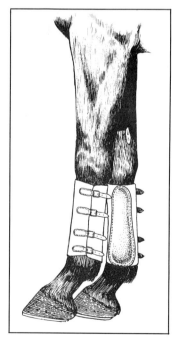

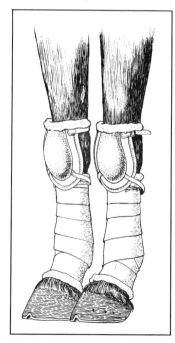

Above: Wrapping a Yorkshire boot around the fetlock before tying.

Below: A Yorkshire boot tied above the fetlock (left); fitted (right).

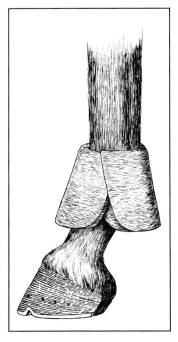

Exercise bandages
Made of stockinette or crepe, 65-75mm (2½-3in) wide, they are used for support and protection. They cover the legs below the knee or hock and above the fetlock joint.

Stable or travelling bandages
These are made of flannel or wool and are about 10cm × 2.5m (4in × 7-8ft). They are used to keep the horse warm, and for protection when travelling. They should cover as much of the leg as possible, from the knee or hock down to the coronet. They should be firmly, but not too tightly, applied over gamgee or cotton wool. Start at the top and wind it around the leg until the fetlock is covered, then work upward until the starting point is reached.

Tail bandage
Made of stockinette or crepe, 6.5-7.5cm (2½-3in) wide, this is used to protect the tail when travelling and/or to improve its appearance by getting the hairs to lie flat. To apply, dampen the tail. Unroll 15cm (6in) of the bandage and hold the end under the tail. Make two turns, to secure the bandage, and then two above, to cover the highest part of the tail; then wind downward around the tail to the end of the tail-bone, where the tapes should be tied. To remove, slide off, grasping bandage at the top of the tail.

To roll up bandages
Tuck tapes in on the side where they are sewn in; then roll up with the sewn side facing inward.

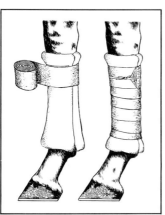

Left: The exercise bandage. This is wound firmly around the leg, starting just below the knee or hock, continuing down to the fetlock joint and then back to the starting point for tying.
Below: The stable or travelling bandage. This is started at the centre of the cannon bone, taken up to below the knee, down to cover the pastern and then back to the knee for tying.
Right: The tail bandage. This is started from the top of the dampened tail and taken down to the end of the tail bone, where it is tied firmly as shown.

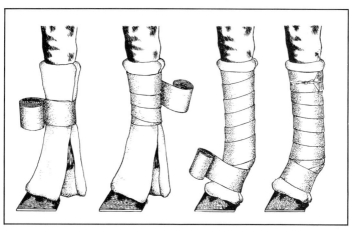

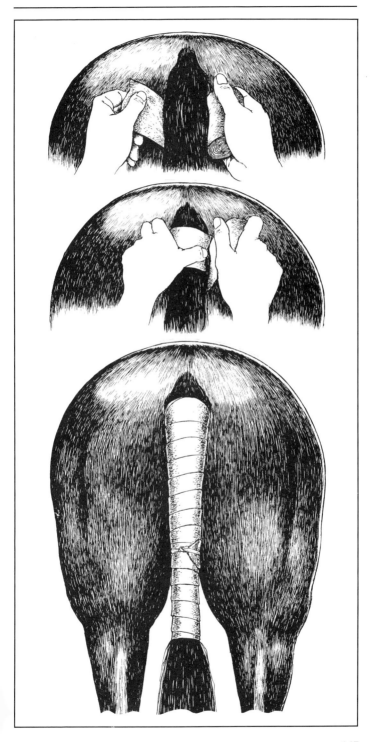

BLANKETS AND RUGS

The stable blanket or rug
This is made of heavy jute, hemp or sail canvas and is lined with wool blanketing. It is used in the stable to keep the horse warm.

The day blanket or rug
A wool rug, often decorated with braid, it is used to keep the horse warm when travelling, and on any occasion when he needs to look smart.

The woollen blankets
These are worn under rugs to give extra warmth when it is cold. They are oblong or square.

The roller
This is used to keep rugs in place and is made of leather, web or jute, padded on either side where it passes over the backbone so that presure does not fall on the spine (a pad is often used in addition to give further protection against pressure on the spine). Surcingles, which have no padding, should be used with caution; they often cause sore backs.

The anti-cast roller
Two pads are joined by a metal

Below: A day blanket (rug), used for travelling and for when the horse should look smart.
Bottom: A cooler (sweat sheet). The open mesh of the material allows ventilation for cooling.

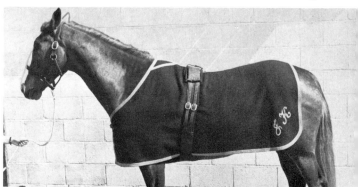

hoop which prevents the horse from rolling over and getting cast.

The summer sheet
Made of cotton, this is used instead of a rug in hot weather. It provides some warmth and is a protection against flies and dust in the summer months.

The cooler or sweat sheet
The holes in this sheet made of open cotton mesh allow ventilation;

Below: A summer sheet, worn when the weather is too hot for a blanket (rug) to be used.
Bottom: A stable blanket (rug) for general use. It provides warmth for the horse in his stall (stable).

it is therefore used for cooling off horses that have sweated. If worn under a rug, it provides a layer of insulation against heat and cold and helps to prevent a horse from 'breaking out' (sweating) after heavy work or other strain.

The New Zealand rug
This is made of waterproof canvas, partly lined with wool, and has special straps to stop it from slipping. It is used to keep horses warm when turned out to grass. For a horse with a full coat, this is unnecessary, but for stabled horses, who may be turned out for a few hours during the day, New Zealand rugs are advisable for extra warmth during cold weather.

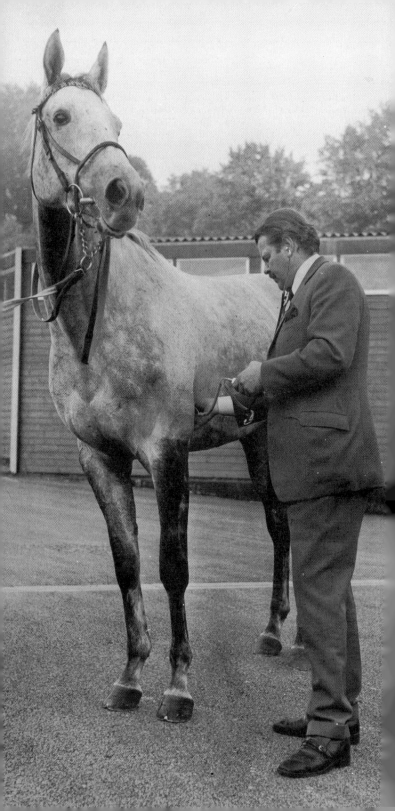

The Health of the Horse

Horses are remarkably tough creatures. In spite of the hazards they have to face—including ignorant owners—the occasions on which they require the attentions of the veterinary profession are usually few. These occasions would be even fewer if horse owners knew the causes of illness and lameness and were careful to avoid them. The advice in this section will help owners to treat simple disorders and to recognize symptoms that require veterinary attention.

THE VETERINARY PROFESSION

Like a doctor, a veterinarian has to undergo a long training; in the UK the course is within a university and takes five years. In addition to the basic sciences the subjects covered are veterinary hygiene and dietetics, pharmacology, bacteriology, pathology, parasitology, medicine and surgery. Those who succeed in their final examinations are awarded a Bachelor of Veterinary Science degree and Membership of the Royal College of Veterinary Surgeons (MRCVS). In the USA the title is Doctor of Veterinary Medicine (DVM), which university graduates can earn after three years.

During veterinary training, there is no special course in equine medicine. Horses are studied as part of the general curriculum and any specialist study must be undertaken as post-graduate work.

Duties of a veterinarian
A very large part of the work entails personal visits to the stables and farms in the area where the veterinarian examines, diagnoses and prescribes treatment for horses.

This veterinary work in the field involves not only treating illness and lameness but also issuing certificates of soundness. These consist of a full description of the animal, the results of a thorough examination, and the final conclusion as to whether in the opinion of the veterinarian the animal is sound or unsound in wind, eye, heart and limb. If requested, the veterinarian will usually also give his opinion as to the suitability of the horse for the proposed work and its chances of remaining sound in the future. In issuing these certificates the veterinarian plays a major part in the buying and selling of horses, and in their insurance (a company will not insure an animal without such a certificate).

Veterinarians are also trained as surgeons, and in this field there have been great advances due to improvements in anaesthesia. Major operations are usually performed in special operating theatres. Minor operations, though, can still be performed at the patient's stable.

X-rays play a large part in equine diagnosis and, although there are some mobile units that can be brought to the stables, the best results are gained from bringing patients to a practice where there is a permanent machine.

Professional etiquette
Veterinarians are governed by rules of professional conduct, and owners are most affected by the one forbidding a veterinarian to take over a case from another veterinarian without agreement. If a horse owner is dissatisfied with the treatment his animal is receiving, he should inform the veterinarian that he no longer wishes him to attend the case, ask for him to bring a 'second opinion', or if it is a serious case request a consultant specialist in the particular field. If an owner fails to follow this procedure, he may find it difficult in the future to get the co-operation of a veterinarian.

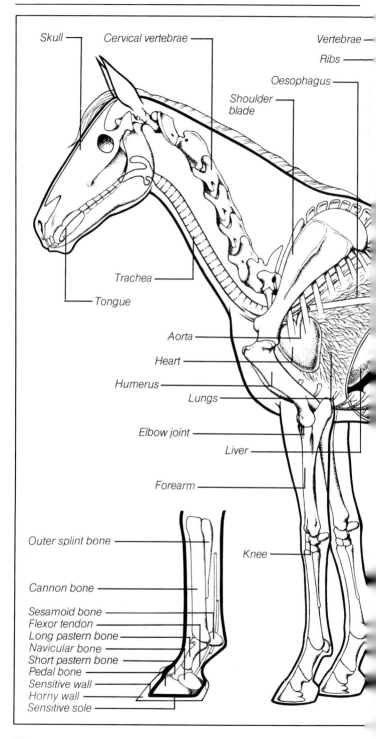

Skull
Cervical vertebrae
Vertebrae
Ribs
Oesophagus
Shoulder blade
Trachea
Tongue
Aorta
Heart
Humerus
Lungs
Elbow joint
Liver
Forearm
Outer splint bone
Knee
Cannon bone
Sesamoid bone
Flexor tendon
Long pastern bone
Navicular bone
Short pastern bone
Pedal bone
Sensitive wall
Horny wall
Sensitive sole

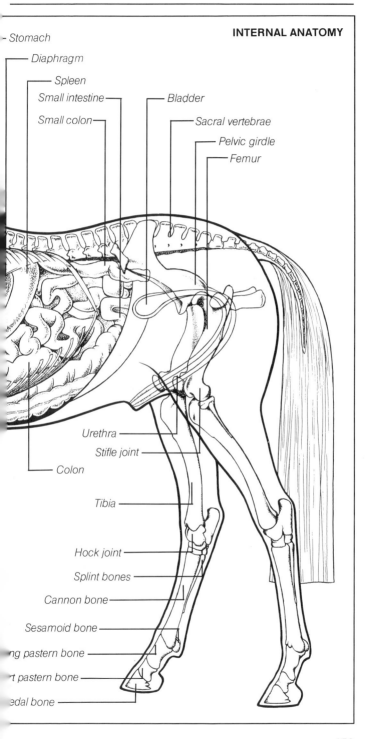

INTERNAL ANATOMY

- Stomach
- Diaphragm
- Spleen
- Small intestine
- Small colon
- Bladder
- Sacral vertebrae
- Pelvic girdle
- Femur
- Urethra
- Stifle joint
- Colon
- Tibia
- Hock joint
- Splint bones
- Cannon bone
- Sesamoid bone
- ng pastern bone
- rt pastern bone
- edal bone

1 Lacks interest in feed, loses weight, becomes 'tucked up' (hind part of abdomen gets smaller).
2 Droppings— no longer round balls that break on hitting the ground; bad smell; shape and/or consistency changes; mucus or parasites visible in them; may not be passed regularly.
3 Coat becomes dull and/or tight. Horse starts sweating.
4 Eyes become dull and unalert.
5 Discharge from the eyes and the nostrils.
6 Legs become puffy.
7 Temperature above or below the normal 37.7-38.3°C (100-101°F) Temperature should be taken with clinical thermometer that has been lubricated with oil or soap. The tail is raised and the

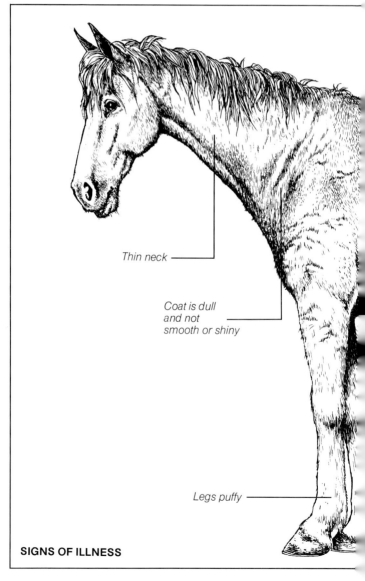

Thin neck

Coat is dull and not smooth or shiny

Legs puffy

SIGNS OF ILLNESS

thermometer inserted into the rectum. Thermometer must touch one side and not stay in the middle, where it would measure only the temperature of the faeces.

8 Breathing looks restricted and respiratory rate rises (normal rate is 10-15 a minute; can be counted by watching flank rise and fall).

Any of these signs of illness should lead to a careful examination to ascertain whether a simple explanation (eg, sweats due to hot weather) can be found. If not, and especially if condition is deteriorating, a veterinarian should be called. It is helpful to the veterinarian if careful note of all signs of illness has been taken and an account of the horse's recent activities made.

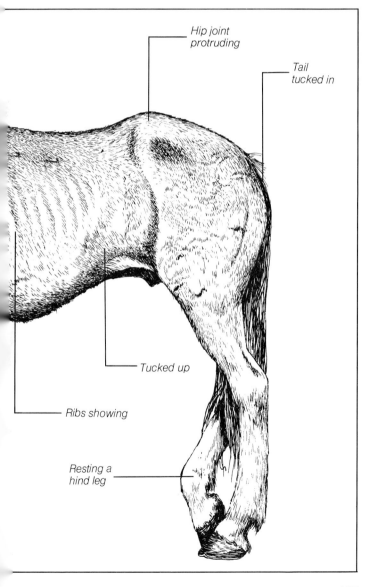

Hip joint protruding

Tail tucked in

Tucked up

Ribs showing

Resting a hind leg

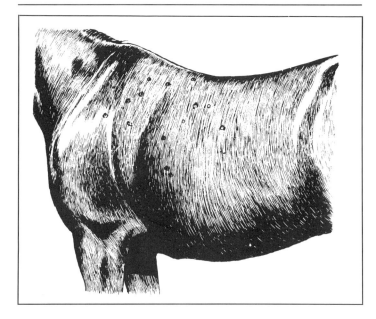

Ringworm
Circular patches caused by fungus.

Symptoms: Small, round, hairless patches develop, exposing greyish, scaly skin. The horse tends to lose condition.

Treatment: Paint iodine on to every single patch daily. It is essential that not one is missed and it is often a help to clip the horse. Ringworm is exceptionally contagious, so the victim should be isolated. Tack and groom kit should be kept separate. Attendant should change clothes before approaching another horse. Any item that comes into contact with the victim should be disinfected. (Humans can be infected by some forms of ringworm.)

A veterinarian should usually be consulted; he can often recommend a more effective form of treatment than the traditional iodine.

Prevention: This fungus is best prevented by thorough disinfecting of any strange tack, stable/ stall or transportation, especially if there is a possibility that a horse with ringworm might have used them.

Above: The circular patches on the skin typical of ringworm infection.

Lice
Lice-infested skin.

Symptoms: Itchiness; small patches, which the horse tries to rub. Careful examination reveals slate-grey lice, up to 1.5mm ($\frac{1}{16}$in) long, or nits (eggs) on the skin.

Treatment: It is advisable to clip the horse, then apply lice-powder or -wash; repeat every few days. The horse is likely to lose condition, so he must be fed well and given mineral additives.

Prevention: Cleanliness of horse and stable.

Sweet itch
An irritation of the skin, usually confined to the crest, withers and croup. It tends to occur annually in the late spring and summer.

Symptoms: Horse rubs affected areas, eventually removing the hair and exposing a wrinkled inflamed skin.

Treatment: Sunshine appears to agitate irritation, so keep horse stabled by day. Lotions (zinc and sulphur ointment, sulphur and tar, or calamine) applied to the area usually ease the irritation.

Nettlerash
Round swellings on the skin's surface.
Symptoms: Squeezy bumps that do not cause irritation.
Treatment: Laxative diet. Administration of anti-histamine.
Prevention: Attention to diet; avoid sudden changes in types of food. Too much high-energy food (especially accompanied by too little exercise) and lush spring grass can bring on nettle-rash.

Mud fever
An inflammation of the skin occurring on the inside of limbs and/or on the belly.
Symptoms: Puffiness and heat in legs. Skin gets rough, scabby and sore. Occasionally horse becomes lame.
Treatment: Essential to keep legs dry. If they get muddy, dry and brush off; or, if necessary to wash, dry thoroughly with chamois leather or dry cloth.
  Apply soothing lotion or cream (zinc ointment, lanolin—or other treatment, prescribed by veterinarian).
Prevention: Avoiding riding in the muds that are known to cause it. After work, ensure legs are thoroughly dry and avoid excessive washing. Horses with

white hair on legs tend to be more liable, so special care must be taken with them.

Warbles
Warble-fly maggots hatch from eggs laid on the horse. The maggots get into the horse's system and appear as small lumps under the skin.
Symptoms: Small lumps, usually in the saddle region.
Treatment: Attempts to remove maggot might cause an infection. If left, the maggot bores its way out of the skin, after which iodine or antibiotic powder should be applied to the hole. A saddle should not be placed on top of a bump containing the warble maggot, as it will cause soreness.

Cracked heels
Cracks in the hollow at the back of the pastern.
Symptoms: Skin becomes sore, red and scabby.
Treatment: As for mud fever.
Prevention: As for mud fever. Horses that tend to develop cracked heels can have their heels coated with petroleum jelly or lanolin before work.

Below: Clear signs of cracked heels at the back of the pasterns.

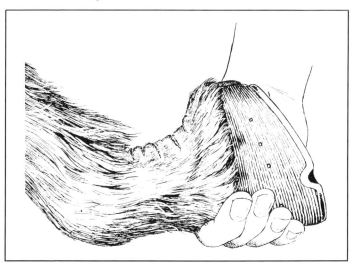

Colds

Symptoms: Thin nasal discharge, becoming thicker.

Treatment: Isolate, keep warm, consult a veterinarian, who may decide to administer antibiotics if the cold is severe.

Prevention: As for humans: avoid subjection to extremes of temperature.

Coughs

Treatment: This varies according to cause of cough. A horse brought up from grass may develop a cough, so try to keep conditions as constant as possible (food, temperature, etc). If a sore throat or laryngitis causes cough, keep horse warm and give small doses of a good cough syrup on tongue and back of teeth, two or three times a day.

If poor condition might be cause of cough, it is wise to test for worms. In all cases, dampen food, put on laxative diet and do not over-exert. Exercise is advisable only if the cough is very mild; even then, no hard work must be undertaken.

Broken wind

Respiratory distress due to the breakdown of air vesicles or vessels (alveolar walls) of the lung.

Symptoms: A deep, persistent cough. Expiratory movements of chest are exaggerated and horse's flank can be clearly seen to heave twice during each exhalation.

Treatment: Incurable unless caused by an allergy but effects can be alleviated by avoiding dust and an excess of bulk food. Linseed oil about three times a week is a help; food should be dampened and stable bedding should be of shavings or peat so that horse cannot eat straw or inhale dust.

Prevention: Do not give dusty food, especially prior to work. Care must be taken with sufferers of a respiratory complaint; asking a horse to work with a cough can lead to broken wind.

Whistling

Caused by rupture of one of the nerves of the larynx resulting in paralysis of the vocal cord. Whistlers make a high-pitched noise when breathing in.

Symptoms: Whistling rarely heard until the horse is asked to work. More pronounced at the faster paces.

Treatment: *Tubing:* The veterinarian inserts into the windpipe a tube though which the horse can breathe freely.

Hobdaying: An operation to remove the membrane from the pouch behind the vocal cord. In a successful operation, the cord sticks to the wall of the larynx so that there is no obstruction to the progress of wind through the passage.

Prevention: Can be hereditary; occurs only in larger horses.

Roaring

Due to partial paralysis of the soft palate.

Symptoms: Horse makes a deep, rumbling noise during exhalation at exercise.

Treatment: Difficult to treat. Line firing of the soft palate has been recommended.

Prevention: Avoid working too soon after an attack of strangles.

High-blowing

An abnormality of the false nostril resulting in noisy exhalation. High-blowing is not an unsoundness and does not restrict breathing.

Influenza

Contagious virus infection.

Symptoms: These vary according to the strain of the virus; usually temperature rises, horse goes off his food, becomes lethargic and often starts to cough.

Treatment: Isolation. Warmth, tempting food, and the attention of a veterinarian. Rest; any exertion can lead to pneumonia and permanent damage to the respiratory passages if the cough has not gone.

Prevention: Immunize with injections, followed by an annual

booster. In the case of an out-
break, take the temperature of all
horses before work (a rise in
temperature is normally the first
indication of influenza).

Strangles

A disease affecting the lymph
glands, usually only those of
horses under six years old are
affected.

Symptoms: Lethargy, temperature
rises as high as 40°C (105°F),
nasal discharge, glands under
jaw swell and eventually form an
abscess, which usually bursts.

Treatment: As the disease is highly
contagious, isolate horse and dis-
infect all items that come in contact with the victim. Convalescence
must be taken slowly. The
disease lasts about six weeks;
this period must be followed by
two or three months of gentle
work or some time in the field.

*Below: Swollen lymph glands under
the jaw may indicate strangles.*

NON-RESPIRATORY
Azoturia

Usually occurs after hard exercise
that has been preceded by a
period of rest during which the
horse remained on full rations.

Symptoms: Stiffness of the
muscles of the loins and quarters may cause staggering; eventually, the horse can collapse.
The horse sweats, his breathing
speeds up and his temperature
rises. If any urine is passed, it is
brownish.

Treatment: If azoturia starts when
riding, dismount and allow horse
to rest. Arrange for his transportation back to stables so he
does not have to walk. Keep
warm, massage tight muscles,
give plenty of water and feed a
laxative diet. Call a veterinarian.

Prevention: Always reduce diet
when horse is to be rested
(hence tradition of giving a mash
on Saturday night, Sunday being
a rest day). Azoturia is likely to
recur; diet must, therefore,
always be adjusted according to
work, and plenty of exercise
should be given daily, by riding
or turning out to grass.

Tetanus (lockjaw)

An infection caused by bacteria
that live in the soil and penetrate
the horse's skin through an open
wound. Tetanus is fatal unless
treated quickly.

Symptoms: Symptoms are never
noticed until well after the bacteria have entered through the
wound. The horse starts to move
stiffly and the third eyelid flickers
across the eye. Co-ordination
becomes increasingly restricted.
Jaws eventually lock.

Treatment: The veterinarian must
be called, to give doses of
serum. Stable must be kept
darkened and absolutely quiet;
diet should be laxative and plenty
of water should be available.

Prevention: Two injections followed
by an annual booster, then 3- to
5-yearly boosters, provides
immunity from this dreadful
disease.

  If any horse that has not
undergone this permanent
immunization is wounded
(particularly a puncture wound),
or if there is any doubt as to
whether such a horse has been
immunized, then a veterinarian
should be called to give an
injection of anti-tetanus serum.

DIGESTIVE PROBLEMS

Sharp teeth

If upper jaw grows down and out-ward while lower jaw groups up and inward, uneven wear of teeth and formation of sharp edges that cut tongue and cheeks can result.

Symptoms: Chewing becomes painful so horse may not masticate food (whole oats seen in droppings) and/or not eat up and so lose condition. Sharp teeth can be felt if mouth is opened, the tongue held and finger run over teeth.

Treatment: Floating (rasping) teeth by a veterinarian or specialist.

Prevention: Regular inspection and floating (rasping) of teeth.

Colic

Abdominal pain; equine 'tummy ache'.

Symptoms: *Spasmodic colic* pain fluctuates; horse may be free from pain for up to an hour before next attack. When in spasm, horse appears unsettled, paws ground, lies down and gets up, tries to roll, may look at belly and start to sweat. Temperature may rise and breathing become hurried.

Flatulent colic, or wind colic, is due to partial or temporary obstruction in the bowels, leading to a build-up of gas. Pain tends to be continuous and not so severe. The horse rarely tries to lie down but otherwise symptoms are the same as for spasmodic colic.

Twisted gut occurs when the membrane suspending the bowel becomes twisted or when the bowel becomes twisted on itself, so cutting off the blood supply. The pain is more severe and the temperature higher.

Treatment: As long as the horse is not exhausted, it is best to lead him for quiet walks. He should be kept warm, the stable well bedded and he should be constantly watched to ensure no injury occurs if he should get down and roll. For wind colic, give a laxative; 0.25-0.51 (½-1pt) linseed oil depending on the size. For spasms give a colic drink, which you should have from the veterinarian and keep with the first-aid equipment. If no improvement occurs after an hour, or if pain is severe, call for professional help, and you should stay with the horse until the veterinarian arrives.

Constipation

Symptoms: Droppings not passed regularly and consistency becomes hard.

Treatment: Bran mashes, green food, 0.25-0.51 (½ to 1pt) linseed oil or 14-85g (½-3oz) Epsom salts in water or food.

Worms

Intestinal parasites found in all horses; when present in large numbers worms may cause severe problems.

The most common types are:

Small strongyles, which do not usually cause problems unless another infection impairs the horse's overall health.

Large strongyles (red worms), reddish in colour and up to 5cm (2in) long, which spend their adult life in the bowel; earlier in their life cycle they pass through the abdomen, where they often damage blood vessels. Because they suck blood, they can cause anaemia. These are sometimes called blood worms. The eggs are passed out in the faeces.

Symptoms: Horse loses condition, bowel movement tends to be irregular. Eggs are passed out in the droppings; a fresh dung sample can be examined under the microscope for a worm egg count.

Treatment: The veterinarian will recommend the best remedy.

Large roundworms (ascarids), white or yellow and up to 7mm (¼in) in diameter and 30cm (12in) in length. They are a problem only with young horses.

Treatment: The veterinarian can dose through a stomach tube

Whipworms, thin parasites about 25-45mm (1-1¾in) long that live in the rectum. The female lays eggs around the anal region, where they can be seen as a waxy mass. They cause irritation so horse rubs tail.

Treatment: The veterinarian will recommend the best modern dosage.

Prevention: Regular doses of a wormer is the best method. Precautions must be taken against paddocks becoming 'horse sick': ie having grass on which there are many worm larvae. (Worm eggs pass out in droppings, and hatch out; hatched larvae attach themselves to grass stems; horses that eat the grass become infected.)

This state is prevented by: regular worming, which will reduce the production of worm eggs; changing the stock on particular fields on an annual basis (horse worms will not generally infect sheep and cattle, and vice versa); removing droppings from the pasture; reducing overall horse-stocking density; ploughing and re-seeding.

Diarrhoea

Symptoms: Droppings loose.

Treatment: Kaolin can be given with food, but best to ask for veterinary medicine. Feed hay and not fresh grass.

Prevention: Spring grass is a common cause, and hay should therefore be substituted as soon as possible.

WOUNDS AND INJURIES

Treatment of wounds: If bleeding does not stop of its own accord, apply a pressure bandage over wound. Call the veterinarian immediately, if stitching is required. Clean wound; clip away surrounding hair if it is in the way. Trickle cold water from a hose pipe over wound, or use salt and water. If the wound is a puncture, leave any probing to the veterinarian. Harsh antiseptics and disinfectants are no longer recommended as they kill healing cells as well as harmful organisms. Dress the wound with antibiotic powder. Protect, if necessary and possible,

by applying a bandage lightly over a layer of cotton wool, with lint next to the wound. Give anti-tetanus injection, if not already immunized. Ensure maximum cleanliness of surroundings. If swelling is excessive, use fomentations.

Antibiotics are advisable for punctures, especially if wound is near joint, tendon sheath or foot.

Constant attention to potential signs of infection: refusing food, extension of swelling, sweating.

Mouth injuries

Use salt-and-water washes. Avoid use of bit until healed. Change bit, if injury was due to it.

Girth gall

Occurs on soft skin behind the elbow, due to the girth's rubbing. Treat injury with fomentations; when healed, use salt and water or methylated spirit to harden. Avoid using saddle for a few days and then use a more comfortable girth.

Saddle-soreness

Due to the saddle's rubbing, so do not ride in a saddle until soreness heals. Ensure cause of problem (eg badly fitting saddle) is removed. Use a thick numnah with a hole cut over the sore. Treat as for girth galls.

Broken or cut knees

Usually caused by a fall on to knees. If injury is more than skin deep, call a veterinarian. Otherwise, treat with slow trickle of cold water from a hose pipe. Apply kaolin poultice but no bandage.

Capped knee

A swelling resulting from a blow to the knee. Treat with rest, massage, pressure bandage and, if swelling persists, a mild blister.

Capped hock

A swelling around the point of the hock, due to a blow or kick.

Treatment: Prevent aggravation of injury by providing thick bedding and the use of hock boots when travelling. Cold treatment followed by a poultice. If swelling persists, apply a mild blister.

If lameness renders a horse unfit to work, he must be fed a laxative diet.

Finding the seat or place of the lameness

1 Decide which leg is causing the pain by watching horse being led at the trot (it shows best if trotted downhill).
2 Search with eyes and hands for heat, pain and swellilng. Start with the feet, as they are the most common source of lameness.
3 Call in a veterinarian, if there is danger of infection or any doubt as to reason for lameness.

Pricks and punctures

Symptoms: Localized tenderness, heat swelling of pastern.

Treatment: Remove nail or other cause of puncture/prick. Scrape hole to release pus. Poultice, or submerge foot in bucket of warm salty water for 20 minutes several times a day and clean out hole. After a few days, apply liquid antiseptic to a puncture. Rest patient until sound. Call the veterinarian if in doubt.

Prevention: Errors when shoeing are a common cause, so care should be taken to choose a blacksmith of good repute.

Corns

Bruises to the sole in heel region.

Below: Corns can develop on the sole either side of the frog.

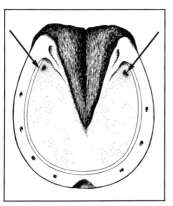

Symptoms: Lameness increases with work. Sensitivity to sharp blows over heels. To confirm, professional must remove shoe and pare horn away, to search for corn (red spot).

Treatment: Remove shoe. Poultice, if severe. Re-shoe with ¾-length shoes. Rest.

Prevention: Avoid pressure on seat of corn by: (a) careful shoe-ing, (b) frequent shoeing, to prevent hooves growing long.

Founder (laminitis)

'Fever in the feet', due to inflamma-tion of the sensitive tissue lining the inside wall of the foot.

Symptoms: Acute pain shown by reluctance to move; flinching observed when sole of affected foot tapped. Horse stands with weight on heels. In chronic cases of laminitis, ridges (due to horn being produced irregularly) form on the hoof.

Treatment: Relieve inflammation and pain. Ask the veterinarian to give an injection of cortisone or anti-histamine. Give cold treatment (stand horse in, or hose feet with, cold water). Remove his shoes, get feet cut down and exercise him on soft going.

Prevention: Avoid feeding too much, especially rich food (barley, wheat, etc), and take care when he is first put out on

Below: A laminitic foot, with ridges developing on the hoof.

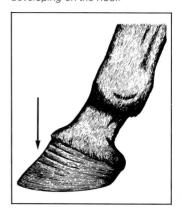

spring grass. Frequent and regular exercise. Do not go at a fast trot on hard roads. Take special care of horses with flat feet and weak horn. If disease is diagnosed, prompt treatment is essential to prevent a permanent disability due to a change in structure of the foot.

Pedal Ostitis

Bruising of the pedal bone (usually in forelegs).

Symptoms: 'Going short' (trotting with short strides). Heat in foot. Lameness, wearing off with exercise. X-ray to confirm.

Treatment: Turn out to grass where land is soft, for six or more months. Introduction to work should be gradual and start with walking.

Prevention: Avoid riding horse hard on firm or stony ground.

Bruised sole

Symptoms: Sole tender under pressure.

Treatment: Rest.

Prevention: Thin-soled horses are especially susceptible; they are less vulnerable if shod with a leather sole or pads.

Canker

A disease of the horn; tissue is secreted in and spreads from the frog.

Symptoms: Grey-white discharge; spongy swellings on frog. Pain is not severe.

Treatment: As for thrush, but canker is more serious. It calls for immediate treatment and the attention of the veterinarian.

Prevention: As the cause has not been confirmed, there is no specific preventative measure, but cleanliness helps.

Thrush

A disease of the cleft of the foot, in which the glands of the region excrete excessively.

Symptoms: Nasty odour from discharge.

Treatment: With brush, soap and water, clean frog and cleft. If severe, apply poultice; if mild, apply boracic powder, sulphanilamide or Stockholm tar to dried cleft. Shoe so that heels are lowered, bringing frog into contact with the ground. Keep in gentle exercise, unless lameness is severe.

Prevention: Attention to cleanliness. Feet must be picked out regularly and bedding not allowed to get dirty or damp. Care that horse is shod so that frog touches the ground and is thus able to function.

Sandcrack

Symptoms: The wall of the hoof cracks and splits.

Treatment: Grooves can be burned into wall with a hot iron, to cross the crack at the top and bottom. Encourage new horn to grow with applications of a mild blister to coronet band or of cornucrescine to hoof, and good food. Crack can be stopped from opening by professional insertion of a nail across the crack and clenching at both ends.

Prevention: Weak, brittle feet especially liable. Regular applications of cornucrescine and attention to diet encourage a better growth of horn.

Navicular disease

The navicular bone changes in shape and texture, making it

Below: An example of a severe sand crack in the wall of the hoof.

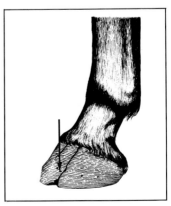

painful for the flexor tendon to run over the surface. It is suspected that the disease is hereditary and may be induced by trotting fast on roads.

Symptoms: Initially intermittent lameness. Usually points the affected foot in the stable. X-ray needed to confirm diagnosis.

Treatment: No satisfactory treatment has yet been discovered. With early diagnosis, steps can be taken to relieve the pressure of the tendon's passing over the navicular bone. Shoes with thin rolled toes and thick heels will help in this.

Neurectomy/denerving is the only means of keeping developed cases in work. In this operation, the affected sensory nerves are cut so that the horse will not feel the pain.

Splint

Bony enlargement of splint bones or cannon bone, or between any of these three bones. Usually found on inside of forelegs.

Symptoms: Pressure from fingers on area results in the horse's flinching. Splint can usually be seen.

Treatment: It is usually only during the formation of the splint that pain occurs, unless near the knee joint or by the suspensory ligament. Normally, six weeks is enough time for recovery but if lameness persists, the splint can be blistered or pin-fired. During time of pain, cold treatment, a working blister or an injection of cortisone can help to speed recovery. The horse should only be walked.

Prevention: Splints can be caused by blows; brushing boots or bandages worn during work reduce this risk. Excessive work on immature legs should be avoided. NB Splints are rarely thrown by horses over six years.

Bone spavin

Enlargement of the bone on the lower and inner side of the hock.

Symptoms: Lameness usually wears off with exercise. The hock moves stiffly, which usually results in the hind toe being dragged.

Treatment: A long rest is advisable. Hot fomentations, alternated with cold-water treatment, helps to reduce the initial inflammation. Blistering or pin-firing can be of use; but surgical treatment may be necessary.

Prevention: Bone spavin is thought to be hereditary, but excessive work or exertion, especially with young horses, may bring it on. Horses with cow, sickle or weak hocks tend to be more vulnerable to spavins because of the abnormal stress.

Bog spavin

Fluid distension of the hock joint capsule; shows as a soft swelling on the front inner side of the hock.

Symptoms: Bulges can be seen. Heat is rarely present, except in

Signs of a splint (*Below*)
1 *Splint on inside of off foreleg*
2 *Splint bones*
3 *Splints*
4 *Cannon bone*

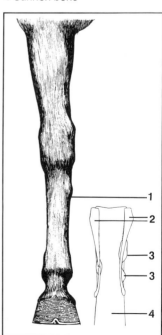

acute cases. Lameness occurs only if swelling interferes with action.

Treatment: None necessary for horse that is not lame. If needed, cold treatment, astringents and massage help. Rest and pressure bandaging may be necessary. Firing is advisable for bad cases, or injections into the area of the sprain.

Prevention: Where there are signs of a bog spavin, shoeing with high heels and rolled toes helps to relieve the strain. As in the case of the bone spavin, horses with straight, cow or sickle hocks are more vulnerable and should not be subjected to excessive work or exertion, especially when young.

Thoroughpin

A small swelling above and in front of the point of the hock.

Symptoms: Rarely leads to lameness, except if caused by recent injury. The swelling can be seen;

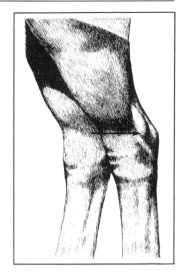

Above: A thoroughpin on the hock.

larger ones go through from one side of the hock to the other.

Treatment: Thoroughpins are no problem unless very large, when

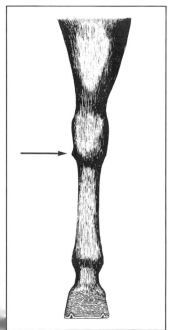

Below: A bone spavin on the inner side of the near hock.

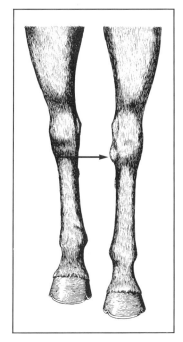

Below: A bog spavin on the inner side of the near hock.

the horse should be rested and blistered, or the vet can give an injection of hydrocortisone. In normal cases, massage helps to get rid of them.

Prevention: Avoidance of exercise that might put an exceptional strain on the hocks, especially in the case of a young horse or one with weak hocks.

Curb

Enlargement, visible below the point of the hock, due to enlargement of the ligament that attaches the bones of the hock to the cannon bone.

Symptoms: The enlargement can be seen when looking at the hock from the side. Lameness is rare.

Treatment: If causing lameness, inflammation should be removed with kaolin poultice or cold-water treatment. The horse should rest.

Prevention: Excessive strain should not be inflicted on the hocks of young horses, especially those with weak hocks, by too much galloping and jumping. When early signs of a curb appear, the horse should be given a period of rest.

Sprained tendon

Symptoms: Heat and swelling always present. In bad cases, there is a bow when leg looked at from the side (in the UK referred to as 'broken down'). As foot problems often cause swelling to rise up the tendon, it is wise to remove shoe and ensure that lameness does not come from the foot, before attempting to treat the tendon.

Treatment: Rest is most important. If swelling is slight, use cold treatment. If more severe, alternate hot poultice (animalintex, antiphlogistine or kaolin) with cold treatment. It may be advisable to follow this with blistering or firing and a long rest. The re-introduction to work should be graduated, starting with long walks on the roads to toughen up the tendons without jarring or straining. Call a veterinarian for severe cases.

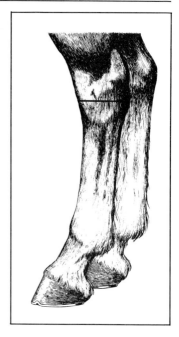

Above: A curb below the hock.

Sprained fetlock joint

Symptoms: Heat and swelling around the joint.

Treatment: Rest. Kaolin poultice, which can also be alternated with cold treatment. As for

Below: Wind galls, small swellings that appear above the fetlocks.

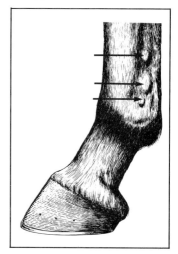

sprained tendons; the re-introduction to work must be gradual.

Prevention: Horses with upright joints, which are not so elastic, are more liable to this injury and care must be taken to avoid jarring them on hard ground or twisting legs in rough going.

Wind galls

Usually small swellings found above the fetlocks, arising from strain in the fetlock joint itself, which causes excess joint fluid to be secreted.

Symptoms: The swelling can be seen and felt.

Treatment: Can be reduced with cold treatment or by using pressure bandages when at rest.

Prevention: Avoid strain, toes growing long and heels too low.

Ring-bone

Bony enlargement of the pastern bone. A 'low' ring-bone is in the coronet region, a 'high' above the coronet.

Symptoms: Lameness usually occurs only if enlargement interferes with the movement of the pastern joint. Tendency for heat and pain to develop on hard ground. Eventually 'high' ring-bone can be felt but a 'low' ring-

Below: A 'low' ring-bone (left) and a 'high' ring-bone (right).

bone is more difficult and usually needs an X-ray for accurate detection.

Treatment: Rest. Cold treatment can be used to reduce inflammation. Cortisone can be injected. If lameness persists, blistering or pin-firing may be necessary.

Prevention: Care should be taken lest feet grow too long, which would prevent the frog from doing its work of absorbing jar. Horses with upright or very long pasterns are more susceptible; care should be taken not to work them on hard ground. Sharp blows and pulled ligaments will induce a ring-bone, so a clumsy horse should undergo corrective shoeing. It is thought to be hereditary in some cases.

Side-bone

Ossification of the lateral cartilages of the foot.

Symptoms: Can be felt. Lameness unusual, unless foot starts to contract leading to pressure on sensitive areas.

Treatment: No need for any unless horse starts to go lame; then rest and apply cold treatment. Blacksmith can shoe so as to encourage expansion of hoof. Blistering or firing can be used.

Prevention: Side-bone is thought to be hereditary; but concussion or a blow may bring it on.

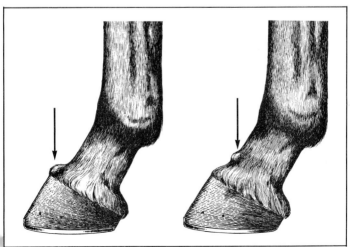

Biting

Causes: Ticklishness. Bad treatment. The giving of snacks. Playful nibbling not corrected.

Remedies:

1 Handle kindly but firmly; reprimand with voice or slap on muzzle.
2 Take care not to irritate, especially when grooming.
3 Incurable biters can be tied up for grooming. Muzzles can be worn.

Kicking

Causes: Boredom as a result of too little work. A spirited nature. Fear, especially in a strange stable or when travelling. Ticklishness. Rats, mice or other animals in the stable.

Remedies:

1 Increase exercise to prevent boredom.
2 Turn out to grass.
3 Handle kindly but firmly; reprimand with voice and slap when horse raises leg.
4 Intruding animals should be eliminated.

5 For incurables, use a box padded with bales of straw or matting or prickly bushes (gorses). In the last resort, attach hobbles to headcollar.

Weaving

When a horse swings head, neck and sometimes forehand from side to side, usually over the stable door, it wastes energy and often loses condition. Weaving is considered an unsoundness.

Causes: Nervousness. Imitation.

Remedies:

1 Exercise and turn out to grass.
2 Attach by length of string two bricks or tyres to top of door-frame so that swaying horse hits one then the other.
3 Various grates can be bought that prevent horse from moving when looking over the top half of the door.

Below: Weaving, a stable vice in which the horse swings from side to side. It can be caused by nervousness and may result in the horse losing healthy condition.

Tearing rugs and bandages
Remedies:
1 Treat cause of itch, if any
2 Put bad-tasting substance on clothing.
3 Hang bib below back of head-collar or muzzle.

Eating bed and droppings
Causes: Boredom. Lack of bulk food. Lack of mineral salts. Worms.
Remedies:
1 Remove cause.
2 Bed on shavings or peat moss.
3 Sprinkle bed with disinfectant.
4 Use a muzzle.
5 Tie horse up before work.

Halter-pulling
Causes: Fear as tightening over the poll felt when pulling back. Realization that he can escape.
Remedies: If frightened either
1 Attach rope to ring of string that breaks when he pulls back, or
2 Stay with tied-up horse to ensure he is not frightened.
3 If he wants to get free, use unbreakable (nylon) halter (headcollar) and rope and tie up tightly

Brushing
When two forelegs or two hind legs brush one another, marks or damage to the fetlock joints or coronet may result.
Causes: Conformation or action. Clenches risen on shoe. Bad shoeing.
Remedies:
1 Correct shoeing and/or use of feather-edged shoes (inner side is built up and has no holes).
2 Use brushing boots and/or Yorkshire boots. Bandages can also be used but they need to be put on by an expert.

Over-reaching
Hind toe/toes hit forelegs, usually on the heel.
Causes: Horse's action results in forelegs not extending enough, or hind legs too much. Galloping and jumping.
Remedies:
1 Treat wound or bruise.

2 Shoe so that hind hoof is wide, square and even concave in front. Clips must be level with hoof.
3 Use over-reach boots.

Crib-biting and windsucking
Crib-biters or cribbers, by gripping objects with their teeth and gulping in air, can damage teeth, making it difficult to eat. Windsuckers suck in air without gripping anything; but sucking air into stomach can cause indigestion and colic. Both habits are considered an unsoundness.
Causes: Lack of exercise and boredom. Imitation. Irritation of stomach. Lack of bulk food.
Remedies:
1 Plenty of exercise.
2 Constant supply of hay, or a salt lick to keep horse entertained in stable.

Below: Brushing, when the inside of a hoof interferes with the opposite leg, causing cuts and abrasions. It can occur on both hind and forelegs.

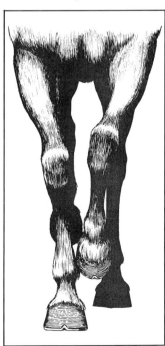

3 Removal of projections that can be gripped with teeth.

4 Muzzle can be worn, except when feeding.

5 Cribbing strap (available from saddlers) can be used.

6 Fluted bit with perforated hollow mouthpiece can be worn; prevents air being sucked in.

7 Paint woodwork with anti-chew mixture (available at saddlers). NB Keep horse away from others, who may copy habits.

Forging

When toe of the hind shoe strikes underneath of the fore shoe.

Causes: Weak young horse. Bad conformation. Feet too long in toe.

Remedies:

1 None necessary for the weak or young horse who will normally just grow out of the habit.

2 Front shoes can be made concave; hind shoes should be set well back under the wall at toe and be squared off. Hind shoe can have thin heels so that the forward action of the hind hooves is restricted.

Above: Crib-biting or cribbing, when a horse grips a surface or object and gulps in air.
Below: Forging, when a rear hoof strikes the toe of a front hoof, making a clicking noise. Young horses affected with this problem usually grow out of the habit.

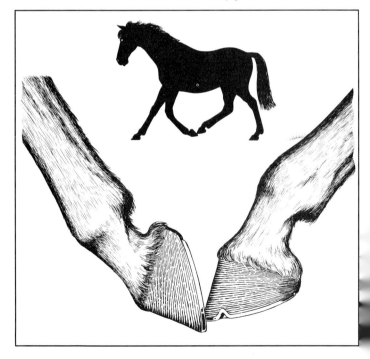

General treatments

Poulticing: Used for bruises, abscesses, swelling and pain. Animalintex or kaolin can be applied in accordance with maker's instructions.

Fomentation: Used for relief of pain and swellings. Cut a piece, approximately 60 × 75cm (24 × 30in) out of towelling or blanket. Fold into four and hold by two corners. Dip into a bucket of warm, salty water (handful of salt to half a bucket of water). Remove, wring and wrap around the injury. Repeat frequently, maintaining temperature by adding hot water to bucket. To test the temperature: before applying to injury, hold back of hand against soaked material and it should be just bearable to keep it there.

Cold treatment: Used for relief of pain and swelling, except in cracked heels and mud fever. Hold a hose pipe over affected area and allow a trickle of water to drop on to the injury.

Cotton wool or gamgee soaked in cold water or lead lotion can then be lightly bandaged on to the injury; renew dressing at regular intervals.

FIRST-AID EQUIPMENT

Items	Use
Veterinary clinical thermometer	
Pair of blunt surgical scissors	
Calico bandages five 5cm (2in) and five 7cm (3in)	
Cotton wool (in small rolls)	
25g (1oz) packets of lint	
Roll of gamgee tissue (gauze bandage)	
Cough expectorant	coughs
Colic drink (from vet)	colic
Lanolin or glycerine	sores (eg, cracked heels)
Antibiotic powder	wounds
Iodine	wounds and fungi
Boracic lotion or ointment	eyes
Animalintex or kaolin	poulticing and reducing inflammation
Lead lotion	sore back
Worming powder	worms
Epsom salts (Magnesium sulphate)	14-85gm (½-3oz) in food or water as a laxative
Methylated spirt	girth galls, etc
Anti-parasitic dressing	ringworm
Cornucrescine	growth of hoof
Dermoline shampoo	skin disorders

Note: Store the above items in a cupboard, box or trunk.

Nature has provided the horse with a tangible calendar—its teeth. Up to the age of eight, the teeth undergo recognizable changes each year, and it is perfectly possible, if you know the signs, to make an accurate assessment of the animal's age. From nine to 18 or so, age is less easy to pinpoint but, allowing for approximately one year's error on either side, it can still be done. Over 20, other indications of age must be sought; and the margin of error is considerable. Because of the difficulty in making a really accurate judgment, horses over the age of eight are often described as 'aged'.

Methods of ageing

The guidelines to age are the six incisors—the tearing teeth—in each jaw at the front of the mouth. In both the lower and the upper jaw they are divided into two centrals, two laterals on either side of the centrals, and two corners on either side of these. The molars —the grinding teeth—at the back may be ignored.

The sets of teeth

The horse has two sets of teeth, deciduous (milk) and permanent. By examining the types of teeth in the mouth, the age of horses up to four and a half years (the age at which the last permanent teeth erupt) can be ascertained. The teeth erupt in order; first the centrals, then the laterals, and finally the corners.

Wear of teeth

The other aid to ageing is the wear of the teeth. Horses' teeth are not enclosed in enamel, and therefore wear down. By examining the wearing surface, known as the table, age can be judged.

The table changes in shape as the tooth—which tapers towards its roots—is worn down. On a new tooth the shape of the table is oval, but with wear it becomes circular and eventually triangular.

The nature of the surface of the table changes too, as continuing wear exposes parts of the tooth closer and closer to its roots. The new tooth has a cavity in its centre called the infundibulum. As the tooth wears, this cavity is flattened and becomes dark as it is filled up with food. A tooth that has a flat table and a dark ring in the centre is said to be 'in wear'. Eventually the tooth is worn down so much that the infundibulum disappears altogether and its dark ring can no longer be seen on the table. Before this occurs, a brown line in front of the infundibulum appears, on the table of the central incisors at first, then on the table of the laterals and corners. It is called the dental star and is part of the substance of the tooth (dentine) that comes to the surface as the tooth wears down.

The profile

When the set of teeth is viewed from the side, in the case of a young horse, the profile is vertical, but as the teeth wear more behind than in front, their profile becomes increasingly horizontal with age.

Stages in the ageing process

At birth, a foal may already possess the two central incisors at top and bottom, or they may appear at any time within the first four weeks. The teeth on either side of the central incisors (the laterals) erupt within two months, and are followed during the next six months by the outside (corner) incisors. Milk teeth are white, fairly small and shell-shaped—that is, they narrow toward the base. Wear is quite noticeable on these teeth by the time the horse is two years old.

Two and a half to six years

At the age of two and a half years, the central incisors drop out and the first permanent teeth appear. These are larger than the milk teeth, have straighter sides and are brownish-yellow in colour. At three and a half to four years the teeth on either side of the central incisors (the laterals) are replaced by second teeth. At about the same time tushes, or canine teeth, will appear in stallions and geldings, although they are usually absent in mares. Between four and a half and five years the last of the milk teeth are lost and new corner incisors grow.

At first the permanent teeth are quite small, with cavities, but they gradually come into wear, and about 18 months after eruption the tables become flattened so that the dark ring of the infundibulum becomes obvious. By the time the horse is six years old, the tables of all the incisors will meet evenly, and show signs of wear. At this stage a horse is said to have a full mouth.

Seven to 15 years

At seven years old, the upper corner incisors sometimes develop a hook, called the 'seven year hook'. It disappears by the time the horse is eight years old. At seven years the dental star, a brownish line, appears on the tables of the teeth, between the infundibulum and the other edge. It will first be seen on the central incisors, and by the time the horse is nine will be present on the corners.

The next noticeable change in the teeth occurs at about ten years. A slight depression will become apparent near the gum on the outer surface of the upper corner incisors. This feature is known as Galvayne's groove. Over the next few years, it will

The horse jaw (*Below*)
1 *Incisors—tearing teeth*
2 *Molars—grinding teeth*

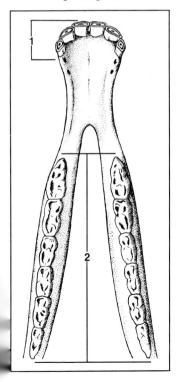

Longitudinal section through an incisor (*Below*)
1 *Infundibulum*
2 *Central enamel*
3 *Peripheral enamel*
4 *Cement*
5 *Dentine*
6 *Pulp cavity*
7 *Root*

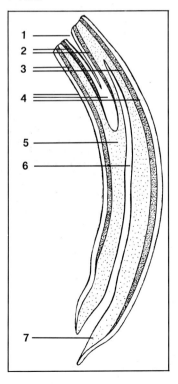

gradually extend down the tooth, reaching a third of the way down when the horse is 13.

During these years the blackish mark, or infundibulum, becomes lighter. It disappears from the central incisors at 12 and from all teeth by 15; the dental star will now be in the centre of each tooth. At the same time the wearing away of the teeth gives them a more triangular shape.

Fifteen to 30 years
From 15 onwards, age assessment is very uncertain. It is based mainly on the length of Galvayne's groove, which should be halfway down the tooth by the time the horse is 15. As Galvayne's groove lengthens, so, too, do the teeth. A 20-year-old horse will have rather long, sloping teeth and quite a pronounced Galvayne's groove. From 25 onwards Galvayne's groove starts to disappear, and by 30 it has gone completely, leaving only dental stars (brown lines).

A horse's life span can be anything from 20 to 40 years, and an aged appearance is not necessarily an indication of the animal's real age. In fact, as with humans, a full and interesting life may well delay the onset of old age. Provided he receives proper care, a horse can continue to lead a useful working existence well into the late 20s or 30s.

Care of teeth
Proper care includes regular

AGEING

Age	Teeth	Table	
Birth—2 years			
1-4 weeks	central incisors erupt	gradually teeth lose cavity and come into wear,	
4-8 weeks	lateral incisors erupt	assuming uniform size and appearance	
6-9 months	corner incisors erupt		
2 years	full mouth of deciduous teeth of uniform size		
2-6 years			
2½ years	central incisors erupt		
3½ years	lateral incisors erupt		
4 years		central incisors in wear	oval
4½ years	corner incisors erupt		
5 years		lateral incisors in wear	
6 years		corner incisors in wear	
7-15 years			becoming mor
7 years	7-year hook in upper corner incisor	dental star in centrals	circular
8 years		dental star in laterals	
9 years		dental star in corners	
10 years	Galvayne's groove appears		
12 years		infundibulum goes from centrals	becoming mor
13 years		infundibulum goes from laterals	triangular
14 years		infundibulum goes from corners	
15 years	Galvayne's groove half way down	infundibulum all gone	
15-30 years			completely
20 years	Galvayne's groove complete	infundibulum all gone and only dental stars (brown line) visible	triangular
25 years	Galvayne's groove half way out		
30 years	Galvayne's groove gone completely		

attention to the teeth. Filing will be necessary from time to time, especially as the horse grows older. An old horse with overlong teeth will have difficulty in eating, and so will be unable to take in sufficient food to cope with the work he has to do. Sharp edges on the teeth can make it painful for a horse to accept the bit when ridden, so check the teeth if any mouthing problems arise.

Signs of old age
An extremely old horse will suffer from a general slowing down of his metabolism. Hollows appear above the eyes, joints may become swollen and rheumatic, and the coat will lose the shine of youth. Dark-coloured horses will show an ever-increasing number of white hairs, particularly in the winter coat and on the face and head.

It is tempting to keep an old favourite until he dies from natural causes, and modern veterinary treatment is so efficient that many an old horse can survive conditions that would have killed him in the past. But though a long and peaceful retirement may seem a fair reward for years of loyal service, old horses may suffer acutely from boredom and loneliness even if they are not in pain. Generally speaking, it is better to have a horse humanely put down rather than allow him to pine away through lack of work and attention and a feeling of uselessness.

e		Diagram	
cal profile			*At 2 years* teeth uniform and almost all in wear
al profile			*At 4 years* temporary teeth lost cavity-in wear permanents (still have cavity) not in wear permanents-in wear
e starts to change from al to horizontal yne's groove ay down			*At 10 years* infundibulum present in all teeth corners still oval dental stars in all teeth centrals becoming more triangular
singly horizontal			*At 15 years* all infundibulum gone dental stars visible

THE GAITS OF THE HORSE

The walk
A four-beat gait.
The horse moves one leg after another so that four hoof beats can be heard.

Sequence
1 Left foreleg.
2 Right hind leg.
3 Right foreleg.
4 Left hind leg.

Two or three legs are always on the ground, so there is no moment of suspension. It is a comfortable pace for the rider.

Faults
1 Hoof beats not rhythmical.
2 The four hoof beats not distinct: two-time walk is possible and is a bad fault which needs correcting.
3 Hooves dragged.
4 Horse does not 'track up'; ie, hind legs do not overlap the fores. In a good walk, the hind should be placed further forward than the lateral foreleg just raised.

The gaits of the horse (Below)
1 *Walk—a four-beat gait*
2 *Trot—a two-beat diagonal gait*
3 *Canter—a three-beat gait*

The trot
A two-beat gait known as the jog by Western-style riders.
The horse moves the diagonal hind and forelegs together.

Sequence
1 Left foreleg and right hind leg leave ground.
2 Right foreleg and left hind leg leave ground *before* left fore and right hind touch the ground; therefore, there is a brief moment of suspension.

At the moment when all four legs are suspended in the air, the rider finds it difficult to sit in the saddle. This has led to the development of posting (rising trot), in which the rider puts weight in the stirrups and rises, to sit again when the horse's legs are on the ground.

Faults
1 If trot becomes hurried and forelegs reach the ground before the hinds, four instead of two hoof-beats are heard.
2 Hind legs may be dragged so they reach the ground before forelegs. (Again, this means a four-time pace.)
3 One hind leg moves further under the body than another.

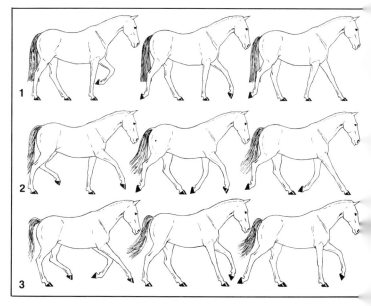

The canter

A three-beat gait known as the lope by Western-style riders.
The horse moves in bounds with either the right foreleg or the left foreleg leading.

Sequence of canter to the right

1 Left hind leg on the ground.
2 Right hind leg and left foreleg placed on ground at the same time.
3 Right foreleg placed on ground after left hind leg has risen.
4 All four legs in the air.

Faults

1 Four hoof beats are heard. This occurs when hind leg is put to the ground before corresponding foreleg (2 above); it usually happens when the horse loses impulsion (forward-driving force).
2 A disunited canter. Left leg leads in front, right leg behind, or vice versa.

The gallop

A four-beat gait.
The gallop is an unrestrained canter. The strides are longer and the moment of suspension (stage 4 in sequence) is much longer.

The pace

A two-beat gait.

Sequence

1 Left hind and left foreleg strike ground together.
2 Right hind leg and right foreleg strike the ground. This is not a comfortable pace for the rider.
In America, where the saddle-horse uses five gaits, adaptations of the pace are taught. Particular attention is paid to the animal's head carriage in this riding style.
NB Although these additional gaits come naturally to this breed of horse, training is needed to produce them correctly.

The stepping pace or slow gait

A four-beat gait sequence as for the pace, except that the left foreleg strikes the ground just before the left hind; similarly, right fore before right hind.

The rack

A four-beat gait.
Sequence the same as for the stepping pace but there is a longer interval between the foreleg striking the ground and the hind leg on the same side striking the ground.

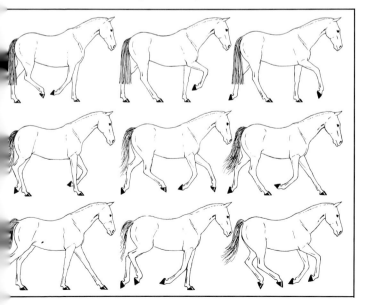

THE HORSE IN LAW AND INSURANCE

Basic law
The law relating to horses is basically simple, although it can be complicated by such factors as the duty of care and contributory negligence. There is a saying that every dog is allowed one bite, which means that, the first time a dog bites anyone, its owner can plead ignorance of the vice. The same applies to horses: the first kick does not constitute breach of the duty to take care on the part of the person in charge of the horse. The second kick does, provided it can be proved that the owner was aware of the previous incident or of the horse's general temperament.

Previous knowledge
There are subtle interpretations to be put on incidents in which previous knowledge is claimed by the injured party. Every horseman knows that a red ribbon tied to a horse's tail indicates that the horse is a kicker—that is to say, a kicker of horses—and injury to any horse it kicked would be the responsibility of its owner. But if, while wearing the red ribbon, it kicked a person or a car, which it had never done before, legal liability would not rest with the owner, although the onus of proving ignorance would fall on him.

Similarly, liability in damages lies with the owner only where a vice, such as kicking or biting, is concerned. Playfulness, at least in law, is not deemed a vice and the owner is not necessarily liable if his horse knocks someone over in play. This is important in relation to a public footpath passing through a field in which horses are kept.

Reason and the law
The law seeks at all times to be reasonable. It would not be reasonable for someone to claim damages if he was bitten by a horse while feeding it with tit-bits over a fence, even if the owner was aware of its tendency to bite. If, however, the land close to the outside of the fence was a public footpath and people passing along the footpath were within reach of the biter, it would be the responsibility of the horse either to see that the horse could not reach the passers-by, or to erect a warning sign that is clearly visible from the footpath.

Straying animals
In the UK the Animals Act of 1971 laid down for the first time that damage caused by straying livestock is the responsibility of the person having possession of the stock. There are a few exceptions, such as straying from a highway that the animal is using lawfully, or from unfenced common land; but, generally speaking, it is up to the owner to see that fences enclosing his horses are strongly built and adequate for their purpose.

In the USA the law is similar and the touchstone in torts (the lawyer's word for civil liability) is 'reasonable standard of care'. That is to say, liability occurs when someone's behaviour falls below what a reasonable and prudent person would or should have done under similar circumstances. Consequently, an owner who leaves a paddock gate unlocked, enabling a horse to break out and cause damage, is liable.

Nevertheless, accidents do happen. Gates are left open or unlatched, and animals have an annoying habit of finding weak spots in hedges before the owner does. This seems invariably to happen at dusk; often the first the owner knows about it is a telephone call or visit from a neighbour. Almost always the horse can be retrieved and the gap closed at a cost of nothing more than a few wasted hours. Perhaps once in 100 such incidents, however, horse and owner find themselves in trouble; there may be damage to a person or car, or a loved horse may be killed or injured; and later, litigation may add further worry and distress.

Contributory negligence
If an incident results in an action being brought, there may be grounds for the defendant to claim contributory negligence on

Below: This spectacular fall under-lines the hazards of eventing.

the part of the plaintiff. Patting a confirmed biter when asked not to do so might constitute contributory negligence, as would taunting a horse until it became savage. Sounding a car horn right beside a known kicker of cars could also be held in law to have contributed to the resulting damage.

The acceptance of risk
Knowledge and acceptance of the risks involved could absolve the owner from any liability. Injuries from a fall, in circumstances where falls are possible, would not form the basis of a claim — for example, on a racecourse, or hunting, or in a cross-country event. Similarly, a groom who is kicked and injured, after willingly entering the stable of a horse that is known to kick, cannot claim damages from his employer.

Riding schools and public stables
Anyone who runs a riding school or public stable is deemed to owe a higher standard of care (because of the profit motive) than a person who merely lends a horse without compensation. Although posted notices may disclaim liability for accidents, an establishment cannot contract away gross negligence, such as renting a horse known to be difficult to an obviously inexperienced rider, or failing to inform about dangerous conditions along trails where accidents have previously happened. As a practical matter, insurance will cover most liability, but no school or stable wants to be known as a place where accidents are a frequent occurrence.

A sales contract
In the USA it is becoming more common to use a written sales contract when purchasing a horse. A written agreement is better than a handshake to hold both buyer and seller to all terms and conditions. The method of payment should be spelled out; for example, one half now, and the balance as soon as a chosen veterinarian has certified that the horse is sound and in good health. It is advisable to include any claims made by the seller, as well as the duration of any trial period during which the purchaser may assess the suitability of the horse.

Insurance against liability for damages
The only essential insurance for any horse owner is personal liability coverage. This protects the policy-holder, or anyone riding or driving the animal with the policy-holder's permission, against legal liability for personal injury to, or damage to the property of, third parties, caused by the horse.

The insurance of a horse
The problem of what insurance to take out may be difficult to settle. The owner of a valuable animal does not hesitate: his horse is insured as a matter of course to protect his investment. However much the owner may wince at the premiums, they constitute part of the expected annual cost of maintaining his property, an entry on the expenditure side of his balance sheet as necessary as the price of a ton of hay.

A decision is difficult to reach if the horse concerned has a comparatively low market value. Though a family horse's sentimental worth may be high, the premium for insuring him may represent the cost of several weeks of winter forage, a new bridle or a visit to the farrier. For this reason, many animals live out their lives without ever appearing on an insurance company's books.

The size of the premium depends on:
1 The age of the horse (those over 12 years are more expensive to insure).
2 The use of the horse. A low rate is quoted for hacking, gymkhanas, driving and dressage; a slightly higher rate for show-jumping; still more for eventing, point-to-pointing and hunting; and the highest rate of all for steeplechasing.

The type of cover
1 Death from accident.
2 Death from accident, illness or disease.
3 Death from accident, illness or disease, or loss of use of the horse.

A combination policy
It is possible, however, to take out a combination policy, which covers a number of risks connected with horses and riding. These include: death or humane slaughter resulting from accidental injury or illness (foaling [except in the case of mares over 12 years old having their first foal], fire, lightning and travelling are covered); permanent loss of use; veterinary fees and expenses incurred in foaling and protective inoculations; loss by theft or straying. Riders are insured against death or injury, and the personal liability of the policy-

Above: Eventing is rated as a high risk for insurance purposes. Falls such as this may injure both horse and rider quite badly.

holder is covered. Saddles, bridles and other tack are covered against any accidental loss, damage or theft, provided that they are kept in a private house or in locked premises.

The average premium in the UK for such a policy is about six percent of the sum insured for horses kept for private hacking, showing, gymkhana events, driving, Pony Club events, jumping, polo, hunting, hunter trials and one-day events, or five percent if the last five are excluded. Cover is further limited when horses reach 15 years of age, and are more likely to become unsound. A horse may live anything from 20 to 40 years.

If there is any doubt as to the colour of the coat, then the colour of the points (muzzle, tips of ears, mane and tail and extremities of the four legs) is the deciding factor.

Bay
Brownish colour (shades vary from reddish and yellowish to approaching brown). The points are black.

Black
Coat, limbs, mane and tail are black. Any markings are white.

Brown
Dark brown or nearly black, with brown to black points.

Sorrel (Chestnut)
Ginger, yellow or reddish colour, with similarly coloured mane and tail. The three shades of chestnut are dark, liver and light chestnut.

Dun
Blue dun is a diluted black, with black points, and may or may not have a dorsal band and a withers stripe.
Yellow dun is yellowish on a black skin. Points are normally black and there is often a dorsal band and stripes on withers and limbs.

Cream
Cream-coloured on an unpigmented skin. The eye often has a pinkish appearance.

Grey
Hairs are white and black, on a black skin. There are many shades, including flea-bitten grey (dark hairs occurring in tufts) and iron grey (black hairs more numerous).

Roan
A blue roan has a basic colour of black or brown and a sprinkling of white.
A strawberry or chestnut roan has a basic colour of chestnut with a sprinkling of white.

Palomino
Golden colour with flaxen mane and tail.

Pinto or calico
A blotched or spotted pattern.
A piebald has large, irregular patches of black and white.
A skewbald's coat has large patches of white and any colour but black.
An odd coloured horse has a blotched coat which consists of more than two colours.

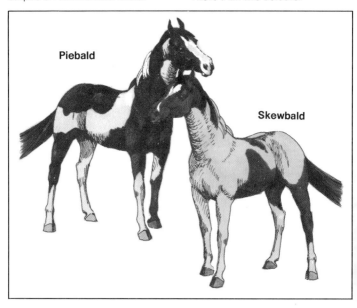

Piebald

Skewbald

Markings are areas of white on the head, body and limbs.

Head
Star is a white mark on the forehead.

Stripe is a narrow white mark down the face.

Blaze is a broad white mark down the face, usually extending from eyes to muzzle.

White face is white forehead, eyes, nose and parts of muzzle.

Snip is a small area of white in the region of the nostrils.

Wall eye is white or blue-white colouring in the eye, due to lack of pigment in the iris.

Legs
Stocking is white on the leg, from coronet to knee or hock.

Sock is white covering the fetlock and part of the cannon region.

Body
Zebra marks are stripes on the limbs, neck, withers or quarters.

Whorls are patterns formed by hairs around a small central spot.

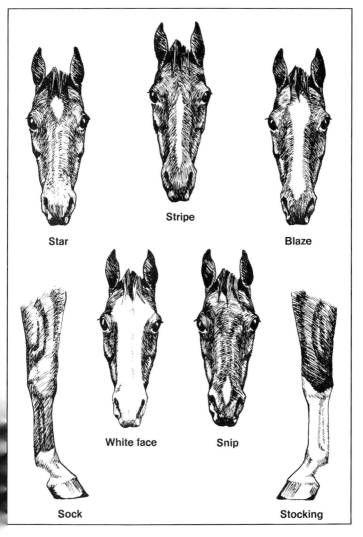

Star

Stripe

Blaze

White face

Snip

Sock

Stocking

BREEDS OF THE WORLD

	Breed	Usual colour	Average height
Western Europe			
Austria			
Riding horses	Lipizzaner	Grey or bay	15.1hh
Ponies	Haflinger	Chestnut Palomino with flaxen mane and tail	13.3hh
Belgium			
Work horses	Belgian Ardennes	Any	15.3hh
	Brabant or Belgian	Red roan, chestnut	16.2hh
British Isles			
Riding horses	Cleveland Bay	Bay with black points	16hh
	Hackney	Dark brown, black, bay and chestnut	Horse 14.3hh-15.3hh Pony 14.2hh and under
	Welsh Cob	Any except piebald or skewbald	14.3hh
	Thoroughbred	Any whole colour	15.3hh
Work horses	Clydesdale	Bay, brown, white on face and legs	16.hh-17hh
	Shire	Bay and brown. A few are black and grey	16.2hh-17.3hh Can be over 1 tor
	Suffolk Punch	Chestnut	16hh About 1 ton
	Irish Draught	Grey, bay, brown, chestnut	Mare 15.1hh Stallion 16.2hh
Ponies	Exmoor	Bay, brown or dun with black points, light mealy muzzle, no white	Stallion 12.3hh Mare 12.2hh
	Dartmoor	Bay, black or brown	Maximum 12.2hh
	New Forest	Any except piebald or skewbald	13.1hh
	Welsh Section A	Any except piebald or skewbald	Maximum 12hh
	Section B	Any except piebald or skewbald	Maximum 13.2hh
	Section C	Any except piebald or skewbald	Maximum 13.2hh
	Section D	Any except piebald or skewbald	14.2hh
	Fell	Black, brown, bay, grey	13.2hh
	Dale	Jet black and dark colours	Up to 14.2hh
	Connemara	Usually grey, but also black, brown, bay	13hh-14hh

Ability and purpose	Features
Intelligent and athletic. Used for High School work, in particular the Spanish Riding School	Originated from Spanish breeds in seventeeth century. Compact body. Largish head
Sure footed. Tough and hardy. General riding, transport, agricultural work	Tyrolese breed produced for mountain work
Lighter type of work horse. Similar to French namesake	Early origins but recently been crossed with other breeds to increase size. Used as a cavalry horse in seventeenth century
Heavy draught work	Originally known as the Flanders Horse. Thick set, stocky, heavily feathered legs. Convex head
Hardy, riding and driving	Short legs, minimum of 9in bone, relatively long back, quarters level
Lively, harness work	Compact body, tail set high, upright feet
Strong, free, forceful action, great presence and zest. Riding and driving	Strong shoulders, silky feathers on legs
Fast, athletic. Racing and competition riding	Developed in seventeenth century from imported Oriental stock. Now the most valuable breed in the world
Lively, active, free elastic action	Long pasterns, long arched neck, great quality, feather on legs
Docile, can be worked at 3 years	Wide chest, white markings, heavy feathers
Long life span, economical feeder, stamina	Square body, massive neck, no feathers, except tuft on fetlock
Good jumpers	No feathers, good shoulders
Very strong. Riding	Prominent 'toad' eyes, deep wide chest, clean legs. Winter coat thick with no bloom
Long life. Riding. Draught work	Head small and fine, strong shoulders, back and loins, full mane and tail
Riding	Short coupled
Riding	
Excellent riding pony	Head tapering to muzzle, long neck, sloping shoulder, great quality
Sturdy, active and strong. Driving	Great substance. Silk feather on legs. Cob type
Sturdy, active and strong. Driving and riding	Great substance. Silk feather on legs
Strength, stamina. Riding, light draught work	Great substance, minimum of 8in bone, fine hair on heels and long curly mane and tail
Strength, docility. Riding and transport	Fine hair on heels, shoulders relatively straight, powerful hinds
Riding	Compact, short-legged

BREEDS OF THE WORLD

	Breed	Usual colour	Average height
British Isles continued			
	Highland a) mainland	Black, brown, varying to dun and grey	14.2hh
	b) islands	Has dark eel stripe along back	As small as 12.2hh
	Shetland	Foundation colour black but now found in all colours	10.2hh
Denmark Riding horses	Danish sports-horse	Any	16hh
	Fredericksborg	Chestnut	16hh
	Knabstrup	Spotted horse	15.3hh
Work horses	Jutland	Black, brown, chestnut	15.3hh
Finland Work horses	Finnish	Chestnut, bay	15.2hh
France Riding horses	Anglo Arab	Any	16hh
	French Trotter	Any	16hh
	Selle Français	Any	16hh
Work horses	Ardennes	Roan, iron grey, bay	16hh
	Boulonnais	Grey	16.2hh
	Breton	Chestnut, grey, roan	16hh
	Percheron	Grey, black	16.1hh
Ponies	Basque	Most	13hh
	Camargue	Grey	14.0hh
	Landais	Most	13.2hh
Germany Riding horses	Bavarian	Any	16hh

Ability and purpose	Features
Riding and light draught work	Broad, short coupled, straight, silky feather on legs, much bone
Independent and headstrong, so needs firm handling. Riding	Double coat in winter, smooth in summer, short back, deep girth, sloping shoulders
General riding and competitions	New breed formed by crossing imported riding horses (Hanoverian etc) with own stock
Driving	Breed nearly died out and outcrosses made with Oldenburgs and East Friesians
Circus work and driving	Lighter but similar to Fredericksborg
Agricultural work	Compact, short legs with feather
General purpose. Transport, military and trotting. Draught work, forestry	Created by crossing Finnish Universal with Finnish Draught stock
Free paces. Racing, jumping, dressage and general riding	Based on crosses between Oriental breeds in South West France and Thoroughbred, or pure Arab and Thoroughbred
High action. Used for riding and competitions but main purpose is trotting races	Crosses between British Trotter and Thoroughbred, and Anglo Normans led to production of the breed in the early nineteenth century
Athletic. All forms of equitation	Regional breeds (notably Anglo Norman), all of which were based on crosses between local work mares and purebreds, were amalgamated under one stud book — Selle Français — in 1964
Sober temperament. Draught work	Originating from the same mountains as their Belgian namesakes, they have very early origins. Flat rectangular head with short light feathered legs
Draught work	Arab ancestors. Elegant for their size. Clean legs
Adaptive and energetic. Draught work	Compact bodies. Short legs, which are almost clean
Stamina. Active. Draught work	Bred by farmers in Le Perche last century. Now one of the most popular work horses in the world. Relatively small fine head. Well proportioned. Clean legs
Quick to mature. Used in mines and for riding	Still roams wild in Pyrenees and Atlantic cantons. Origins unknown but thought to be very ancient as it resembles primitive ponies
Most run wild. Some tamed for herding bulls	Barb origins. Large head
Riding and driving	Elegant, strong. Arab-like head
Riding and agricultural work	Similar development to that of the Württemburg

BREEDS OF THE WORLD

	Breed	Usual colour	Average height
Germany continued			
	Hanoverian	Any	16.1hh
	Hessian Rheinlander Pfalz	Any	16hh
	Holstein	Any	16.1hh
	Oldenburg	Brown, bay, black	16.2hh
	Trakehner	Any	16.1hh
	Westphalian	Any	16.1hh
	Württemburg	Brown, bay, chestnut, black	16hh
Work horses	Noriker/South German Cold-Blood	Bay, brown, chestnut, spotted	16.1hh
	Rhineland Heavy Draught	Sorrel, chestnut, roan	16.2hh
	Schleswig	Chestnut	15.3hh
The Netherlands			
Riding horses	Gelderland	Chestnut, grey	16hh
Work horses	Dutch Draught	Dun, grey, sorrel	16.1hh
	Friesian	Black	15hh
	Groningen	Black, brown	15.3hh
Norway			
Riding horses	Döle Trotter	Black, brown	15hh
Work horses	Döle Horse	Black, brown	15hh
Ponies	Fjord	Dun with dorsal stripe	14hh
Portugal			
Riding horses	Alter-Real	Chestnut, bay, piebald	15.1hh
	Lusitano	Any	15hh
Ponies	Garrano/Minho	Chestnut	11hh
Spain			
Riding horses	Andalusian	Grey, black	15.3hh

Ability and purpose	Features
Very powerful with extravagant action. Riding and driving	Originally a famous carriage horse but crossed with Arab and Thoroughbred to refine. It is the most successful and numerous breed of riding horse in Germany
General riding	Similar types of horses all bred around the Rhine; but each has own stud book
Strong horses. General riding and competitions	Breeding dates from 1300 when used as war horse. Oriental then Cleveland Bay and today the Thoroughbred used to upgrade
Driving and riding	This is the heaviest of the German riding horses
Good action. Competition work and general riding	Refugees in West Germany, originally bred at stud at Trakehnen in East Prussia, which was founded by Frederick William I of Prussia in 1732. Elegant horses
General riding, competitions and driving	Developed largely from Hanoverian strains and is very similar to them
Riding and agricultural work	The central stud is at Marbach where they have been developed by crossing many German breeds
Agricultural work. Transport especially in mountains	Originally bred in Noricum by Romans. Heavy head on short neck
Powerful. Heavy draught work	Heavily crested neck. Low to ground. Feathered legs
Driving and agricultural work	Similar to Jutland Cob type
Active type. General riding and competitions. Driving	Originated by crossing native stock in Gelderland with Trotters, Thoroughbreds and Anglo Normans
Docile. One of the most massive of the draught horses	Breed started mid-way through last century
Very active	This breed is old and was popular in medieval times. Particularly compact
Docile. Heavyweight saddle horse. Driving	Strong back and stylish action
Trotting	Lighter version of Döle Horse
Riding and agricultural work	Short feathered legs with very thick mane and tail
Agricultural work and riding	Resembles horses of Ice Age. Upright mane
Extravagant action. Energetic. Famous as High School horses	Originated from Andalusians in eighteenth century. Bred in Alentejo Province
Riding and light agricultural	Fine head with full low-set tail
Hardy light build. Pack ponies, trotting races	Arab ancestry
Intelligent. Attractive action made them popular High School horses in Europe	Barb origins. Still has this breed's flat, almost convex head

BREEDS OF THE WORLD

	Breed	Usual colour	Average height
Sweden			
Riding horses	Swedish warm-blood	Any	15.3hh
Switzerland			
Riding horses	Einseidler	Any	15.3hh
	Swiss warm-blood	Any	16hh
Work horses	Freiberger	Blue roan, grey	15.3hh
Eastern Europe			
Czechoslovakia			
Riding horses	Kladruber	Originally black or grey	16.2hh
Hungary			
Riding horses	Furioso	Black, brown	16hh
	Nonius	Black, brown	Large over 15.3hh. Small under 15.3hh
Work horses	Murakosi	Chestnut, bay, black	16hh
Poland			
Riding horses	Malopolski	Any	15.3hh
	Wielkopolski	Any	16hh
Ponies	Konik	Yellow, grey, blue, dun	13hh
	Tarpan	Brown, dun with dorsal stripe	12.1hh
USSR More than 40 recognized breeds but following most well known.			
Riding horses	Akhal-Teke	Any but with characteristic golden sheen	15.1hh
	Budjonny	Chestnut, bay	15.3hh
	Don	Chestnut, grey	15.3hh
	Kabardin	Bay, black	15hh
	Karabair	Bay, grey, chestnut	15.1hh
	Lokai	Any	14.3hh

Ability and purpose	Features
Intelligent. Free paces. General riding. Good competition results	Originated from systematic crossing of native stock with Thoroughbred and German riding horses
Used by military, for riding and transport	Bred for centuries at Einseidler
Good action and temperament. General riding and competitions	New breed created by crossing imported French, Swedish, German and home bred riding horses, and Thoroughbreds
Stamina. Light agricultural work. Transport	Compact strong horse
Riding, driving and light agricultural work	Originated from Spanish breeds. Typically has a long straight back
General riding and driving	Originated in nineteenth century from crosses between Thoroughbred Trotters and native mares
Reliable, active with long stride. General riding and agricultural work	The Anglo Norman was influential in development of the breed. Has an impressive head with long neck
High quality draught horse	Developed this century from crossing Ardennes, Oriental and local breeds
Lighter than Wielkopolski and used mainly for riding	Originated from crosses between local mares, Arabs and Anglo Arabs
Dual purpose, used for general riding and driving	Breed formed by merging older breeds of Masuren and Poznan
Hardy with great vitality. Valuable work ponies	Konik — meaning small horse — is used to cover other types with own names ie Zmudzin, Hucul and Bilgoraj
	Primitive wild horse of northern Europe that vanished. By selective crossing of Przewalski stallions and Konik mares the breed is said to have been re-established
Desert horse, able to withstand great heat and lack of water. Racing, competitions and general riding	Elegant, refined horse bred in Turkemenia. Skeletons of similar fine boned horses found dating back 2,500 years
Good temperament with substance. Riding, competitions and racing	Created this century by crossing Thoroughbreds with Dons
Great stamina. Harness work, general riding, long distance racing	Used by Don cossacks in eighteenth century
Sure footed, good pack horse, especially able in mountains. General riding	Developed by crossing mountain breeds with southern breeds
Great stamina. Dual purpose, used for riding and driving	Bred in Uzbekistan for about 2,400 years
Powerful. Used as pack horse or for general riding, especially in highlands	Originated in seventeenth century in Tadjikistan and have Arab and Karabair ancestors

BREEDS OF THE WORLD

	Breed	Usual colour	Average height
USSR continued			
	Novokirghiz	Dark colours	15hh
	Orlov Trotter	Grey, black	15.3hh but up to 17hh
	Russian Trotter (Metis)	Any	15.3hh
	Tersk	Grey	15.1hh
Ponies	Karabakh	Chestnut, bay, dun with metallic sheen	14.1hh
	Kazakh	Bay and most others	14hh
	Yakut	Greyish, mousy	13hh
Work horses	Latvian	Bay, black, chestnut	16hh
	Russian Heavy	Chestnut	14.3hh
	Soviet Heavy Draught	Any	15.3hh
	Toric	Any	15.1hh
	Vladimir Heavy Draught	Chestnut, bay, roan	15.3hh
Turkey			
Riding horses	Karacabey	Solid colours	15.3hh
Iran			
Riding horses	PlateauPersian	Solid colours	15.0hh
	Turkoman	Any	15.2hh
Yemen			
Riding horses	Arab	Originally bay and chestnut, grey is now common	15hh
Morocco & Algeria			
Riding horses	Barb	Bay, brown, chestnut, grey	14.3hh
South Africa			
Ponies	Basuto	Chestnut, bay	14.2hh

Ability and purpose	Features
General riding—especially good in high altitudes and for herding stock	Improved by crossing Kirghiz, which was smaller, with Don and Thoroughbred
Harness work and trotting races	Developed in 1770s by Count Orlov who crossed Arab, Thoroughbred, Dutch, Mecklenburg and Danish horses
Trotting races	Developed by crossing American Standardbred and Orlov when former became faster than latter. Faster but not so handsome as Orlov
Good temperament. Used for general riding, circus and dressage work	Originated from Strelets breed—Arabians that nearly died out after World War I. Outside Arabians and their cross breeds used. Larger than pure bred Arabs
Lively mountain horse used for riding and racing	Originated in Karabakh in Trans-Caucasian uplands and has Arab ancestors
Tough, able to withstand steppe life. Herding cattle, long distance riding, especially in highlands	Originated as horses of nomads in Kazakhstan. Today are being crossed with Don to produce larger version— the Kustanair
Used for riding, pack work, transport, harness	Long hairy coats. Survive in Yakut territory (beyond Polar circle)
Great pulling strength—draught horses	These extremely powerful work horses are bred in Baltic states by crossing local Zhmuds with larger imports—Finnish Draught and Swedish Ardennes
Lively, fast gaits	Founded in Ukraine where local breeds were crossed with Ardennes, Percherons and Orlov Trotters
Active and relatively fast. The most popular heavy horse in USSR	Developed by crossing local breeds with Belgians, Ardennes, and Percherons. Not so massive as European heavy horses
Agricultural work and in harness	Originated by crossing Hackney and East Friesian with local Estonian breeds
Strong puller, energetic. Agricultural work	Created in nineteenth century by crossing local horses with Clydesdale and Shire
Riding and harness work	Developed from native horses crossed with Nonius from Hungary
Strong, sure footed. Riding	Amalgamation of plateau breeds
Floating action. Long-distance racing, endurance rides, and general riding	Originated, like the Akhal-Teké, from the Turkemene horse
Light, graceful action; fast, with great stamina. General riding and racing	Origins vague but thought to have roamed wild in Yemen until tamed c. 3000BC. Oldest pure breed and has had great influence on all other breeds. Typically has a concave head; croup level with the back
Fast. Used for general riding	An old breed with Arab blood. Typically has the tail set lower than Arab. Convex ram-shaped head
Riding and general transport	Thick set and long in the back. Originated from Arab and Barb stock

BREEDS OF THE WORLD

	Breed	Usual colour	Average height
Australia			
Riding horses	Australian Stock Horse	Any	16hh
Ponies	Australian pony	Any	13hh
South America			
Argentina			
Riding horses	Criollo	Dun, sorrel, palomino	14.3hh
Brazil			
Riding horses	Crioulo	Dun, sorrel, palomino	14.2hh
	Mangalarga	Grey, sorrel, roan	15.3hh
Peru			
Riding horses	Peruvian Stepping Horse	Dun, sorrel, palomino	14hh
Venezuela			
Riding horses	Llanero	Light colours, pinto, with dark mane and tail	14hh
North America			
Riding horses	Appaloosa	White coat with black or brown spots	15.1hh
	Mustang	Any	14.2hh
	Morgan	Any	15hh
	Quarter-horse	Any	15hh
	Palomino	Golden with light mane and tail	Any
	Pinto	White splashes on black (piebald) or on other colours (skewbald)	Various
	Saddle-bred	Any	15.2hh
	Standard-bred	Any	15.3hh
	Tennessee Walking Horse	Any	15.2hh
Ponies	Pony of Americas	Any	13hh

Ability and purpose	Features
Riding, herding	Originated by crossing Arab, Anglo Arab and Thoroughbred with local stock in last century. Became known as the Waler
General riding	Foundation stock was Welsh
Great stamina. Used for endurance work and for general riding	Short head, stocky. Originated from Andalusians, imported in sixteenth century, which ran wild on the pampas
General riding and herding	Similar background to Criollo but original stock mainly Alters from Portugal
General and long-distance riding and harness work	Originated from Crioulo crossed with imports from Spain and Portugal. Also selective breeding of Mangalarga has produced a heavier breed — the Campolino
Especially smooth gaits; the amble (a pace) enables the rider to cover great distances at speed and in comfort	Developed, like Criollos, from Spanish and Portuguese horses that ran wild
Great stamina; used for endurance riding	Smaller and finer than other Criollos but from similar origins
Used by Indians who took advantage of camouflage colouring. Now popular for Western riding	Developed by Nez Percé Indians in Palouse, Idaho
Sturdy. Riding, showing, stock	Spanish origins. Ran wild
Short active stride; great stamina. Very versatile, used for riding and harness work	Originated in New England from the Justin Morgan Horse (1789). Particularly short in the back and legs
Sure footed with great acceleration; excellent ranch horses. Racing, rodeo work, polo and general riding	Developed as quarter-mile sprinters. Foundation sire was the Thorough-bred 'Janus'. Largest stud book in the world. Stocky with powerful hindquarters
All types of use	Not yet an established breed as not yet breeding true to type but stud book now exists for which horses qualify through colour
Tough. Used by Indians. General riding horse	Not a true breed. Defined by colour like palominos
High action; either 3-gaited, when mane is roached, or 5-gaited. Riding and driving	Short back, long tapering neck. Foundation stock was Thoroughbred and Arab
Tough. Can trot nearly as fast as Thoroughbred can gallop. Some pace rather than trot when they move lateral rather than diagonal pairs	Foundation sire was the Thoroughbred 'Messenger' imported from UK in 1795. Strong hindquarters and long back
Comfortable paces. High-stepping gaits with fast running walk. General riding and driving	Developed as hacks for plantation owners in nineteenth century from a mixture of US breeds
Riding	New breed developed by crossing Quarter-horse, Arab and Appaloosa

INDEX

Page numbers in **bold type** refer to main text entries, including any illustration captions on that page; numbers in Roman type to other text entries; *italic* numbers to captions.

INDEX

Picture Credits

The Publishers wish to thank the following photographers and agencies who have supplied photographs for this book. Photographs have been credited by page number and position on the page: (B) Bottom, (T) Top, etc.

Animal Photography Ltd: Half title page, 41, 48, 53, 62
Eric Crichton: 6
Anne Cumbers: 56-7, 58, 59, 113
Findlay Davidson: 73
Marc Henrie: 69, 150
Roger Hyde (©Salamander Books

Ltd.): 42, 55, 76, 143, 145(T)
Jane Kidd: 60-61, 74-5, 148-49
E.D. Lacey: 26, 52, 66, 84-5, 91, 95, 96-7, 134, 179, 181
Picturepoint: Contents page
W. Rentsch: 14, 15
Mike Roberts: Endpapers, 100-101
Bruce Scott (© Salamander Books Ltd.): 7-11, 13, 16-18, 20, 21, 23, 25, 28, 30-36, 38, 39, 54, 92, 93, 108-9, 110-111, 116-120, 124, 135, 136-37, 138-39
M. Stannard: 103
Tony Stone: Title page

PRINTED IN BELGIUM BY

proost
INTERNATIONAL BOOK PRODUCTION